Millwright

Level Four

Trainee Guide
Fourth Edition

 Pearson

NCCER

President and Chief Executive Officer: Boyd Worsham
Vice President of Innovation and Advancement: Jennifer Wilkerson
Chief Learning Officer: Lisa Strite
Senior Manager of Projects: Chris Wilson
Senior Manager of Production: Erin DuRant
Millwright Project Manager: Dario VanHorne
Technical Writing Manager: Gary Ferguson
Technical Writers: Don Congdon, Troy Staton
Art Manager: Carrie Pelzer
Production Artists: Judd Ivines, Chris Kersten
Digital Content and Licensing Coordinator: Amanda Smith

Permissions Specialists: Rachel Roque, Adam Black
Managing Editor: Graham Hack
Lead Editors: Karina Kuchta, Hannah Murray
Editors: Zi Meng, Alexandria Willbond
Desktop Publishing Manager: Denise Baco
Desktop Publishing Coordinator: Eric Caraballoso
Production Specialists: Daphney Milian, Olga Trofymenko
Digital Content Manager: Kelly Beck
Digital Content Coordinator: Yesenia Tejas
Testing/Assessment Project Manager: Elizabeth Schlaupitz
Testing and Assessment Project Coordinator: Chelsi Santana

Pearson

Manager of Project Management: Vanessa Price
Associate Project Manager: Monica Perez
Senior Digital Content Producers: Shannon Stanton, Alma Dabral

Composition: NCCER
Printer/Binder: Lakeside Book Company
Cover Printer: Lakeside Book Company
Text Fonts: Palatino and Univers
Content Technologies: Gnostyx

Cover Image
Prüftechnik, a Fluke Reliability Brand

Credits and acknowledgments for content borrowed from other sources and reproduced, with permission, in this textbook appear at the end of each module.

ISBN-13:   978-0-13-817567-2

Preface

To the Trainee

In choosing to continue millwright training, you are seizing the opportunity to enjoy a career that demands complex mechanical knowledge and sharp analytical ability in a variety of industrial work environments. Since its humble beginnings in the construction of wood mills, the millwright trade has expanded to include work in metal and machinery of ever-increasing technology and precision. Millwrights install, align, and troubleshoot machinery in factories, power plants (particularly the precision machinery required in nuclear power plants), and other industrial sites. They install conveyor systems, connect machinery to power supplies and piping, direct hoisting and setting of machines, and adjust the moving and stationary parts of machines to certain specifications. Millwrights are extremely skilled at mathematics and interpreting blueprints and specs to set machines at perfect measurements, sometimes working with clearances no bigger than thousandths of an inch.

Millwrights are a specialized and elite group, as there are only a little more than 40,000 millwrights employed in the United States today. However, over the next decade, there will be a demand for a third more of that number (US Bureau of Labor Statistics). As the population grows, especially in developing countries, increased demands for energy and travel in particular will require more millwrights working in power plants, refineries, and factories. A trained and experienced millwright enjoys a comfortable salary and the chance for different avenues of professional development. A millwright can progress upwards in the trade, undergoing full apprenticeship, becoming a supervisor, and/or obtaining higher education. Millwrights may also opt for careers in related professions, such as machinist, equipment engineering, or aircraft assembly.

This is the fourth and last installment of a four-level curriculum that meets the requirements of a standard millwright apprenticeship program (5 years and 10,000 hours of on-the-job training). If you employ discipline in working with detail, problem-solving, and if you enjoy working independently in a variety of work environments, you will excel in this training program. NCCER wishes you luck as you embark on your chosen career path. With solid millwright training, you are opening the doors to a field scheduled for growth in the next decade.

We invite you to visit the NCCER website at **www.nccer.org** for information on the latest product releases and training.

Your feedback is welcome. You may email your comments to **curriculum@nccer.org** or send general comments and inquiries to **info@nccer.org**.

New with *Millwright Level Four*

Millwright Level Four will help you finalize this fraction of your journey to master the essential millwrighting skills. This book is written for students, apprentices, journeymen, and professionals who wish to sharpen their skills in the millwright craft.

The text is organized into fourteen modules. A group of modules provides information on individual components of systems a millwright interacts with and provides guidance on how to install, remove, troubleshoot and maintain these components. Two modules explain the usage of optical and laser tools in the placement and alignment of equipment. Last you will be instructed in safe and effective verbal and nonverbal communication with crane operators in varying field conditions. The doors for success in this field are now open to you.

NCCER Standardized Curricula

NCCER is a not-for-profit 501(c)(3) education foundation established in 1996 by the world's largest and most progressive construction companies and national construction associations. It was founded to address the severe workforce shortage facing the industry and to develop a standardized training process and curricula. Today, NCCER is supported by hundreds of leading construction and maintenance companies, manufacturers, and national associations. The NCCER Standardized Curricula was developed by NCCER in partnership with Pearson, the world's largest educational publisher.

Some features of the NCCER Standardized Curricula are as follows:

- An industry-proven record of success
- Curricula developed by the industry, for the industry
- National standardization providing portability of learned job skills and educational credits
- Compliance with the Office of Apprenticeship requirements for related classroom training (*CFR 29:29*)
- Well-illustrated, up-to-date, and practical information

NCCER also maintains the NCCER Registry, which provides transcripts, certificates, and wallet cards to individuals who have successfully completed a level of training within a craft in NCCER's Curricula. *Training programs must be delivered by an NCCER Accredited Training Sponsor in order to receive these credentials.*

For information on NCCER's credentials and the NCCER Registry, contact NCCER Customer Service at 1-888-622-3720 or visit **https://www.nccer.org**.

Special Features

In an effort to provide a comprehensive and user-friendly training resource, this curriculum showcases several informative features. Whether you are a visual or hands-on learner, these features are intended to enhance your knowledge of the construction industry as you progress in your training. Some of the features you may find in the curriculum are explained below.

Introduction

This introductory page, found at the beginning of each module, lists the module Objectives, Performance Tasks, and Trade Terms. The Objectives list the knowledge you will acquire after successfully completing the module. The Performance Tasks give you an opportunity to apply your knowledge to real-world tasks. The Trade Terms are industry-specific vocabulary that you will learn as you study the module.

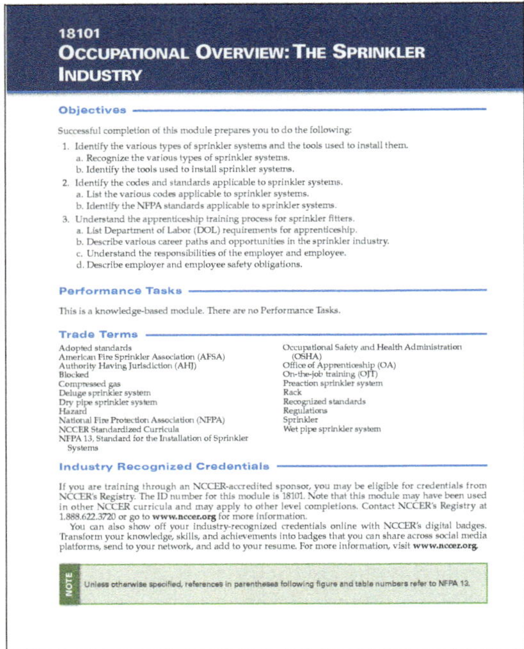

Trade Features

Trade features present technical tips and professional practices based on real-life scenarios similar to those you might encounter on the jobsite.

Figures and Tables

Photographs, drawings, diagrams, and tables are used throughout each module to illustrate important concepts and provide clarity for complex instructions. Text references to figures and tables are emphasized with *italic* type.

Figure 31   Marking a cutting line.

Notes, Cautions, and Warnings

Safety features are set off from the main text in highlighted boxes and categorized according to the potential danger involved. Notes simply provide additional information. Cautions flag a hazardous issue that could cause damage to materials or equipment. Warnings stress a potentially dangerous situation that could result in injury or death to workers.

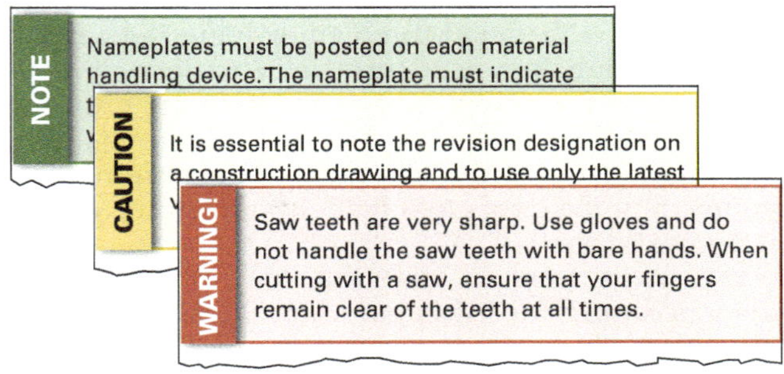

Going Green

Going Green looks at ways to preserve the environment, save energy, and make good choices regarding the health of the planet. Through the introduction of new construction practices and products, you will see how the greening of America has already taken root.

Did You Know?

The *Did You Know?* features offer hints, tips, and other helpful bits of information.

Step-by-Step Instructions

Step-by-step instructions are used throughout to guide you through technical procedures and tasks from start to finish. These steps show you not only how to perform a task but also how to do it safely and efficiently.

Perform the following steps to erect this system area scaffold:

Step 1 Gather and inspect all scaffold equipment for the scaffold arrangement.

Step 2 Place appropriate mudsills in their approximate locations.

Step 3 Attach the screw jacks to the mudsills.

Step 4 Adjust the screw jacks to near their lowest position.

Step 5 Determine the location of the highest base.

Trade Terms

Each module presents a list of Trade Terms that are discussed within the text and defined in the Glossary at the end of the module. These terms are denoted in the text with **bold, blue type** upon their first occurance. To make searches for key information easier, a comprehensive Glossary of Trade Terms from all modules is located at the back of this book.

During a rigging operation, the **load** being lifted or moved must be connected to the apparatus, such as a crane, that will provide the power for movement. The connector—the link between the load and the apparatus—is often a sling made of synthetic, chain, or **wire rope** materials. This section focuses on three types of slings:

- Synthetic slings
- Alloy steel chain slings
- Wire rope slings

Section Review

Section Review questions can be found at the end of each section to test your knowledge of the content.

1.0.0 Section Review

1. The type of sprinkler system that might be found in an aircraft hangar is a _____.
   a. dry pipe sprinkler system
   b. wet pipe sprinkler system
   c. preaction sprinkler system
   d. deluge sprinkler system

2. A type of ladder that provides a platform for standing is a(n) _____.
   a. A-frame
   b. extension trestle ladder
   c. podium ladder
   d. movable leg ladder

Review Questions

Review Questions are provided to reinforce the knowledge you have gained. This makes them a useful tool for measuring what you have learned.

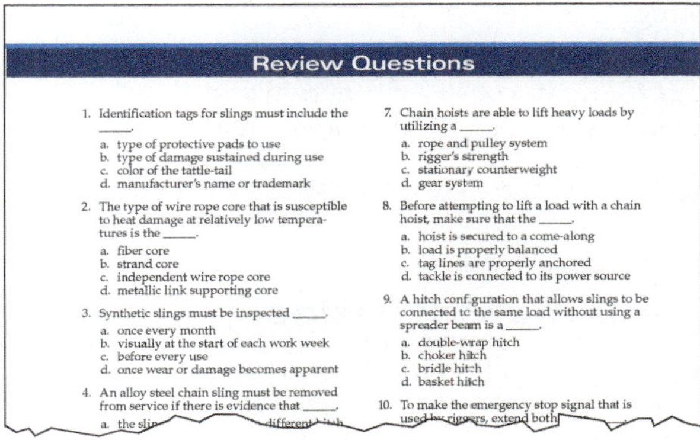

Review Questions

1. Identification tags for slings must include the _____.
   a. type of protective pads to use
   b. type of damage sustained during use
   c. color of the tattle-tail
   d. manufacturer's name or trademark

2. The type of wire rope core that is susceptible to heat damage at relatively low temperatures is the _____.
   a. fiber core
   b. strand core
   c. independent wire rope core
   d. metallic link supporting core

3. Synthetic slings must be inspected _____.
   a. once every month
   b. visually at the start of each work week
   c. before every use
   d. once wear or damage becomes apparent

4. An alloy steel chain sling must be removed from service if there is evidence that _____.
   a. the sling

7. Chain hoists are able to lift heavy loads by utilizing a _____.
   a. rope and pulley system
   b. rigger's strength
   c. stationary counterweight
   d. gear system

8. Before attempting to lift a load with a chain hoist, make sure that the _____.
   a. hoist is secured to a come-along
   b. load is properly balanced
   c. tag lines are properly anchored
   d. tackle is connected to its power source

9. A hitch configuration that allows slings to be connected to the same load without using a spreader beam is a _____.
   a. double-wrap hitch
   b. choker hitch
   c. bridle hitch
   d. basket hitch

10. To make the emergency stop signal that is used by riggers, extend both

NCCER Standardized Curricula

NCCER's training programs comprise more than 80 construction, maintenance, pipeline, and utility areas and include skills assessments, safety training, and management education.

Construction and Maintenance

Boilermaking
Cabinetmaking
Carpentry
Concrete Construction
Construction Craft Laborer
Construction Technology
Core: Introduction to Basic
  Construction Skills
Drywall
Electrical
Electronic Systems Technician
Heating, Ventilating, and Air
  Conditioning
Heavy Equipment Operations
Heavy Highway Construction
Hydroblasting
Industrial Coating and Lining
  Application Specialist
Industrial Maintenance Electrical
  and Instrumentation Technician
Industrial Maintenance Mechanic
Instrumentation
Ironworking
Manufactured Construction
  Technology
Masonry
Mechanical Insulating
Millwright
Mobile Crane Operations
Painting
Painting, Industrial
Pipefitting
Pipelayer
Plumbing
Reinforcing Ironwork
Rigging
Roofing
Scaffolding
Sheet Metal
Signal Person
Site Layout
Sprinkler Fitting
Tower Crane Operator
Welding

Supplemental Titles

Applied Construction Math
Tools for Success

Maritime

Maritime Industry Fundamentals
Maritime Electrical
Maritime Pipefitting
Maritime Structural Fitter
Maritime Welding
Maritime Aluminum Welding

Green/Sustainable Construction

Building Auditor
Fundamentals of Weatherization
Introduction to Weatherization
Sustainable Construction
  Supervisor
Weatherization Crew Chief
Weatherization Technician
Your Role in the Green
  Environment

Energy

Alternative Energy
Introduction to the Power Industry
Introduction to Solar Photovoltaics
Power Generation Maintenance
  Electrician
Power Generation I&C
  Maintenance Technician
Power Generation Maintenance
  Mechanic
Power Line Worker
Power Line Worker: Distribution
Power Line Worker: Substation
Power Line Worker: Transmission
Solar Photovoltaic Systems Installer
Wind Energy
Wind Turbine Maintenance
  Technician

Pipeline

Abnormal Operating Conditions,
  Control Center
Abnormal Operating Conditions,
  Field and Gas
Corrosion Control
Electrical and Instrumentation
Field and Control Center
  Operations
Introduction to the Pipeline
  Industry
Maintenance
Mechanical

Safety

Fall Protection Orientation
Field Safety
Safety Orientation
Safety Technology

Management

Construction Workforce
  Development Professional
Fundamentals of Crew Leadership
Mentoring for Craft Professionals
Project Management
Project Supervision

Spanish Titles

Acabado de concreto: nivel uno,
  nivel dos
  (*Concrete Finishing Levels One and Two*)
Aislamiento: nivel uno
  (*Insulating Level One*)
Albañilería: nivel uno
  (*Masonry Level One*)
Andamios (*Scaffolding*)
Carpintería: Formas para
  carpintería, nivel tres
  (*Carpentry: Carpentry Forms, Level Three*)
Currículo básico: habilidades
  introductorias del oficio
  (*Core Curriculum: Introductory Craft Skills*)
Electricidad: nivel uno
  (*Electrical Level One*)
Herrería: nivel uno
  (*Ironworking Level One*)
Herrería de refuerzo: nivel uno
  (*Reinforcing Ironwork Level One*)
Instalación de rociadores: nivel uno
  (*Sprinkler Fitting Level One*)
Instalación de tuberías: nivel uno
  (*Pipefitting Level One*)
Instrumentación: nivel uno, nivel
  dos, nivel tres, nivel cuatro
  (*Instrumentation Levels One through Four*)
Orientación de seguridad
  (*Safety Orientation*)
Paneles de yeso: nivel uno,
  nivel dos
  (*Drywall Levels One and Two*)
Seguridad de campo
  (*Field Safety*)
Construcción de techos: nivel uno,
  nivel dos
  (*Roofing Levels One and Two*)

Acknowledgments

This curriculum was revised as a result of the vision and leadership of the following sponsors:

Air Liquide Large Industries U.S. LP
Cianbro Corporation
FLSmidth USA Inc. - Sioux City Operations

Great Basin College
Turner Industries

This curriculum would not exist were it not for the dedication and unselfish energy of those volunteers who served on the Authoring Team. A sincere thanks is extended to the following:

Dave Roberts
James Maloney

Maurice Gould
Michael Stirrat

Neil Steagall
Thomas Bruns

NCCER Partners

NCCER partnering organizations are national associations and organizations that share a common interest in the goals and objectives of NCCER. To learn more about NCCER business partners, go to **https://www.nccer.org/about-us/partners**.

You can also scan this code using the camera on your phone or mobile device to view these partnering organizations.

Contents

Module Eleven

Preventive and Predictive Maintenance

Explains preventive and predictive maintenance programs. Provides information on nondestructive testing, and introduces the basic techniques for nondestructive evaluation. Discusses lubricant analysis, and acoustic, infrared, and vibration testing. (Module ID 15508; 10 Hours)

Module Twelve

Maintaining and Repairing Turbine Components

Describes the process of inspecting and repairing key components of turbines. Explains the guidelines for maintaining large steam turbines. (Module ID 15506; 12.5 Hours)

Module Thirteen

Crane Communications

Describes the communication process between the signal person and the crane operator. Covers electronic communications as well as the standard hand signals in *29 CFR 1926*. (Module ID 53101; 10 Hours)

Module Fourteen

Crane Safety and Emergency Procedures

Covers safety standards and best safety practices relevant to the operation of cranes. Describes safety considerations related to power lines, weather conditions, and specific crane functions. (Module ID 21106; 25 Hours)

Glossary

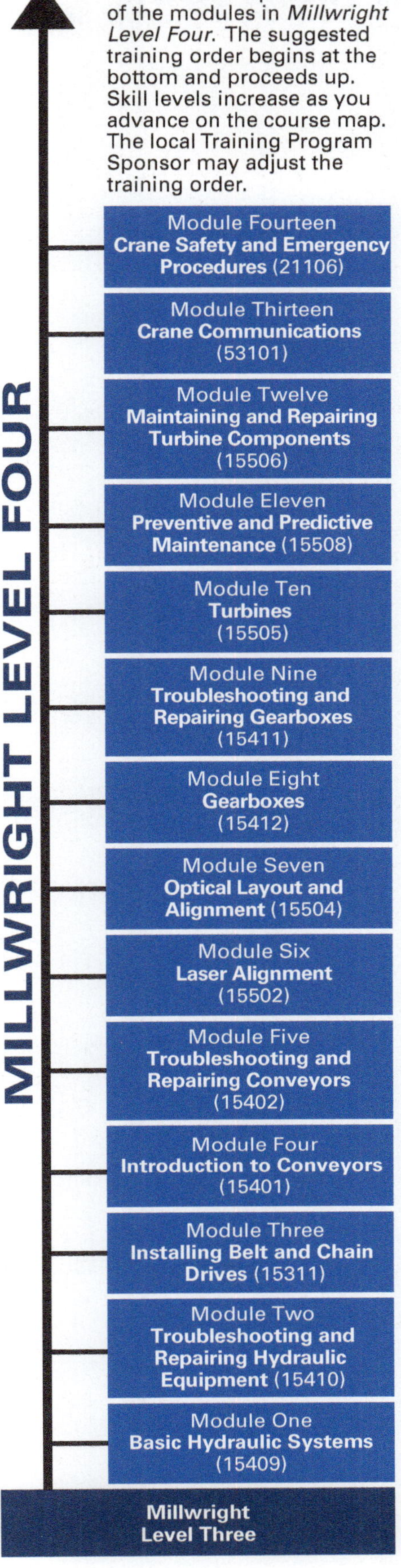

Basic Hydraulic Systems

OVERVIEW

If someone asked you to name the most important kind of energy in today's industrial world, you'd probably reply, "Electricity!" Of course, you'd be correct. Electrical energy is the most versatile way to power equipment. Sometimes, however, electricity isn't the right tool for the job. Instead, industry turns to an older technology that's been around for a very long time—hydraulics.

Module 15409

15409
BASIC HYDRAULIC SYSTEMS

Objective

Successful completion of this module prepares you to do the following:

1. Recognize hydraulic principles and components.
   a. Outline basic hydraulic science.
   b. Summarize hydraulic system safety practices.
   c. Describe hydraulic fluid's role and define its qualities.
   d. List and describe hydraulic power unit components.
   e. List and describe hydraulic pumps.
   f. List and describe hydraulic system components.

Performance Task

Under supervision, you should be able to do the following:

1. Identify specific components in a working hydraulic system, describing their purposes and associating the correct schematic symbols.

Trade Terms

Accumulator
Actuators
Cam
Cavitation
Cylinder

Emulsion
Hydraulic
Laminar flow
Lockout/tagout (LOTO)
Oxidation

Pressure
Strainer
Turbulent flow
Viscosity
Working fluid

Industry Recognized Credentials

If you are training through an NCCER-accredited sponsor, you may be eligible for credentials from NCCER's Registry. The ID number for this module is 15409. Note that this module may have been used in other NCCER curricula and may apply to other level completions. Contact NCCER's Registry at 1.888.622.3720 or go to **www.nccer.org** for more information.

You can also show off your industry-recognized credentials online with NCCER's digital badges. Transform your knowledge, skills, and achievements into badges that you can share across social media platforms, send to your network, and add to your resume. For more information, visit **www.nccer.org**.

This module uses US standard and metric units in up to three different ways. This note explains how to interpret them.

Exact Conversions

Exact metric equivalents of US standard units appear in parentheses after the US standard unit. For example: "Measure 18" (45.7 cm) from the end and make a mark."

Approximate Conversions

In some cases, exact metric conversions would be inappropriate or even absurd. In these situations, an approximate metric value appears in parentheses with the ~ symbol in front of the number. For example: "Grip the tool about 3" (~8 cm) from the end."

Parallel but not Equal Values

Certain scenarios include US standard and metric values that are parallel but not equal. In these situations, a slash (/) surrounded by spaces separates the US standard and metric values. For example: "Place the point on the steel rule's 1" / 1 cm mark."

How to Access Resources

This craft has additional videos and resources to enhance your learning experience. To view these resources, scan the QR below. The videos and resources are separated by module.

You can scan this code using the camera on your phone or mobile device to view these videos and resources.

Contents

1.0.0 BASIC HYDRAULIC TECHNOLOGY

Objective

Recognize hydraulic principles and components.

  a. Outline basic hydraulic science.
  b. Summarize hydraulic system safety practices.
  c. Describe hydraulic fluid's role and define its qualities.
  d. List and describe hydraulic power unit components.
  e. List and describe hydraulic pumps.
  f. List and describe hydraulic system components.

Performance Task

1. Identify specific components in a working hydraulic system, describing their purposes and associating the correct schematic symbols.

Trade Terms

Accumulator: A device that smooths out hydraulic fluid flow by delivering extra pressurized fluid when required.

Actuators: Devices that change electrical, pneumatic, or hydraulic energy into mechanical motion.

Cam: A rotating component whose shape causes another component to move back and forth as it rests against the cam's surface.

Cavitation: A condition in which bubbles form in a fluid and then collapse violently, creating shock waves that cause vibration and possibly damage.

Cylinder: A pneumatic or hydraulic actuator that produces linear motion from a piston sliding inside a hollow tube.

Emulsion: A mixture formed by two liquids that don't combine, with droplets of one dispersed throughout the other.

Hydraulic: Any technology that transfers energy and does mechanical work with a pressurized liquid.

Laminar flow: Fluid flow in which the fluid travels smoothly in layers that don't interfere with each other.

Lockout/tagout (LOTO): A safety process that secures an activated isolation device and identifies the person responsible for activating it.

Oxidation: The process of chemically combining with oxygen.

Pressure: The force that a fluid develops against a specific area of a container's walls or a surface.

Strainer: A filter that removes large particles from a fluid.

Turbulent flow: Fluid flow in which the fluid swirls, changes direction, and interferes with its own motion.

Viscosity: A liquid's thickness, which determines how it flows, pours, and behaves when stirred.

Working fluid: A liquid or gas used by an industrial system to carry energy and do work.

Humans have used waterpower throughout their history. Watermills ground grain, sawed lumber, and powered all kinds of machines. Starting in the 1650s, however, scientists began to explore water's other capabilities. They discovered that under the right conditions, water could do some impressive things. By the late 1800s, **hydraulic** technology was powering industrial machinery and carrying energy over long distances through pipes.

Electricity eventually replaced hydraulic power in many settings. Nevertheless, industry still relies on hydraulics to operate some of its largest machines. It's also extremely useful in flammable or explosive environments since it's safer. Along with *pneumatics*, hydraulics plays an important role in today's industry.

NCCER Module 15407, *Basic Pneumatic Systems*, introduces pneumatic technology. As you'll discover in this module, pneumatics and hydraulics share many qualities. Both are *fluid power* technologies. This means that they deliver energy and do work with a pressurized fluid—a gas or liquid. Pneumatic systems use compressed air, while hydraulic systems use a pressurized liquid.

A *hydraulic power unit (HPU)* pumps *hydraulic fluid* through pipes and hoses to machinery. Valves regulate and direct the flow. **Actuators** in the machines turn the fluid power into mechanical motion. Finally, the hydraulic fluid returns to the pump to begin the cycle again. *Figure 1* shows a simple hydraulic system.

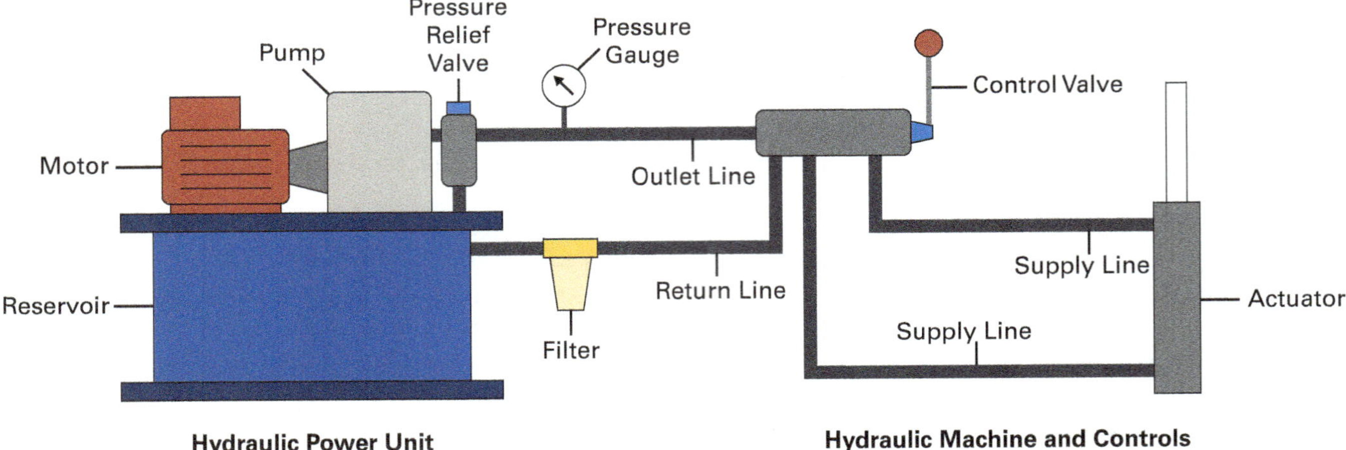

Figure 1 Basic hydraulic system.

Pneumatic and hydraulic equipment use similar components. Schematic symbols representing pneumatic and hydraulic components are almost identical. Understanding one technology makes understanding the other relatively easy.

Pneumatics and hydraulics differ in a few crucial areas. Pneumatic systems store energy in the **working fluid** (air) by compressing it. Gases can be packed tightly into a pneumatic receiver because their molecules can move closer together. Compressed gas is like a squeezed spring, holding energy that it can release by expanding.

Liquids, on the other hand, are essentially *incompressible*. Their molecules won't move closer together, so you can't store energy in the liquid. A hydraulic reservoir will hold a quantity of hydraulic fluid equal to the container's volume and no more. The hydraulic pump forces the fluid through the system. The liquid doesn't store energy. It just transfers the energy from the pump to the actuators.

A second major difference between pneumatic and hydraulic technology is that hydraulic systems are *loops*. After powering the equipment, the hydraulic fluid returns to the pump. However, pneumatic systems aren't loops. They release the used air to the atmosphere. Air is free and doesn't pollute the environment. Hydraulic fluid is costly and polluting. Recirculating it over and over makes sense.

If you're already familiar with pneumatics, you'll find the following material familiar. Pneumatic and hydraulic science share many qualities. There are a few differences, however, so pay careful attention as you learn about this useful industrial technology.

1.1.0 Pressurized Fluid Science

As you know, all matter is made from particles—atoms and molecules. Particle behavior and the distances between them determine the form that the matter takes. Gases have particles that are far apart. They zoom around, occasionally bouncing off each other and their container walls. Liquids have particles that are much closer together. They bounce off each other and their container walls constantly. These differences cause gases and liquids—both fluids—to behave quite differently.

1.1.1 Pressure

In liquid systems, the liquid exerts a force on its container's walls. In an open container, the liquid's weight alone creates this force. *Depth* determines the force that the liquid exerts at a particular location. *Figure 2* shows two containers filled with water. If you measure the force at the bottom of each container, the force will be twice as great in the taller container since the water is twice as deep.

On the other hand, the *quantity* of liquid has nothing to do with the force. The containers in *Figure 3* hold different amounts of water. All have the same depth, however, so the force at the bottom is the same.

Hydraulics engineers call the liquid's force **pressure**. Identifying the force that presses on a specific area is a good way to express pressure. In the United States, pounds (lb) and square inches (in^2) are common force and area units. Pounds per square inch (psi) is therefore a convenient pressure unit. A force of 1 lb pressing down on a 1 in^2 surface produces a pressure of 1 psi (*Figure 4*).

Adding an external force to a liquid in a closed container increases the liquid's pressure. The liquid in *Figure 5* exerts a pressure proportional to its depth. Pressing the plunger adds an external force, so the pressure increases. A hydraulic power unit's pump pressurizes the hydraulic fluid in the same way.

> Notice that the liquid in *Figure 5* doesn't compress (get smaller). Liquids are essentially incompressible, so the pressure increases but the volume stays the same. This is an important difference between gases and liquids.

A crucial truth about liquids in closed containers is that they exert pressure equally in all directions. The liquid in *Figure 5* presses on the syringe walls in all directions with equal force. Hydraulics engineers call this behavior *Pascal's principle*, after Blaise Pascal, who discovered it in 1652.

Hydraulic technology couldn't work without it. It's the reason that hydraulic fluids transfer energy from the pump to the actuators. Pressure makes the hydraulic fluid flow through the system. The moving fluid operates the actuators, which do useful work.

1.1.2 Pressure Units

To operate correctly, hydraulic machines require the fluid to be properly pressurized. Low pressure won't operate the equipment correctly. High pressure can damage it. *Pressure gauges* monitor and report the pressure at key points within the system (*Figure 6*).

The hydraulic world uses three pressure units. In the United States, pounds per square inch (psi) is the most popular. The metric-speaking world uses two other units. You should be familiar with these too.

Pascals (Pa)

In the metric system, newtons (N) and square meters (m^2) are common force and area units. Instead of psi, metric-speaking countries use newtons per square meter (N/m^2). For convenience, this unit combination goes by the name *pascal* (Pa). A pressure of 1 psi equals 6,895 Pa.

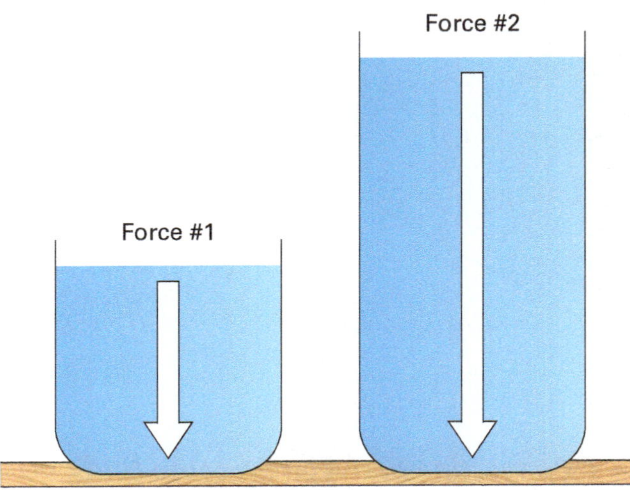

Figure 2 Depth determines force.

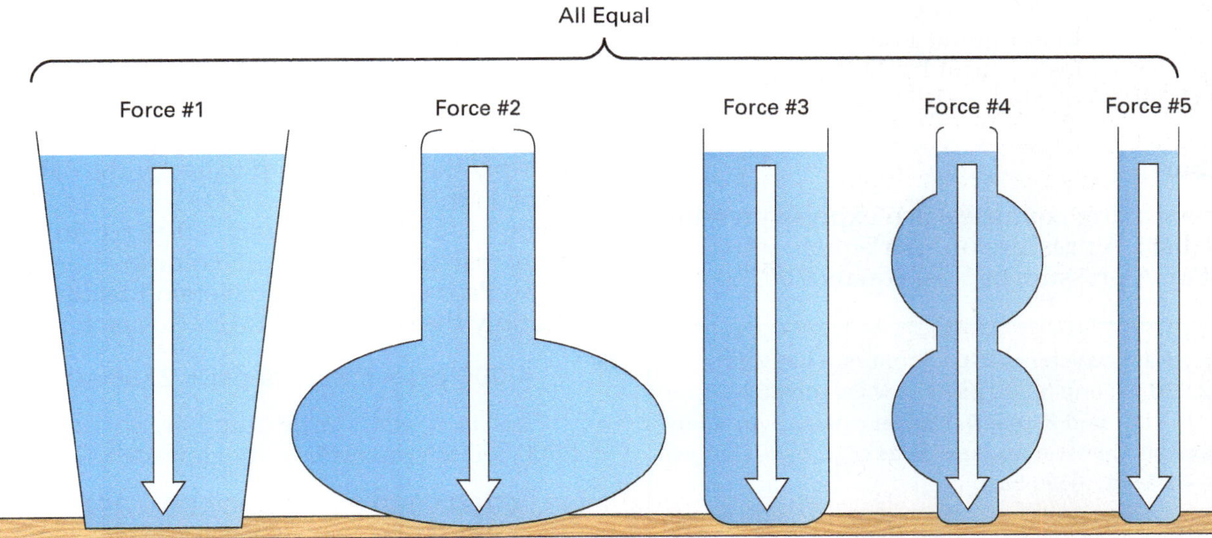

Figure 3 Equal force in liquids.

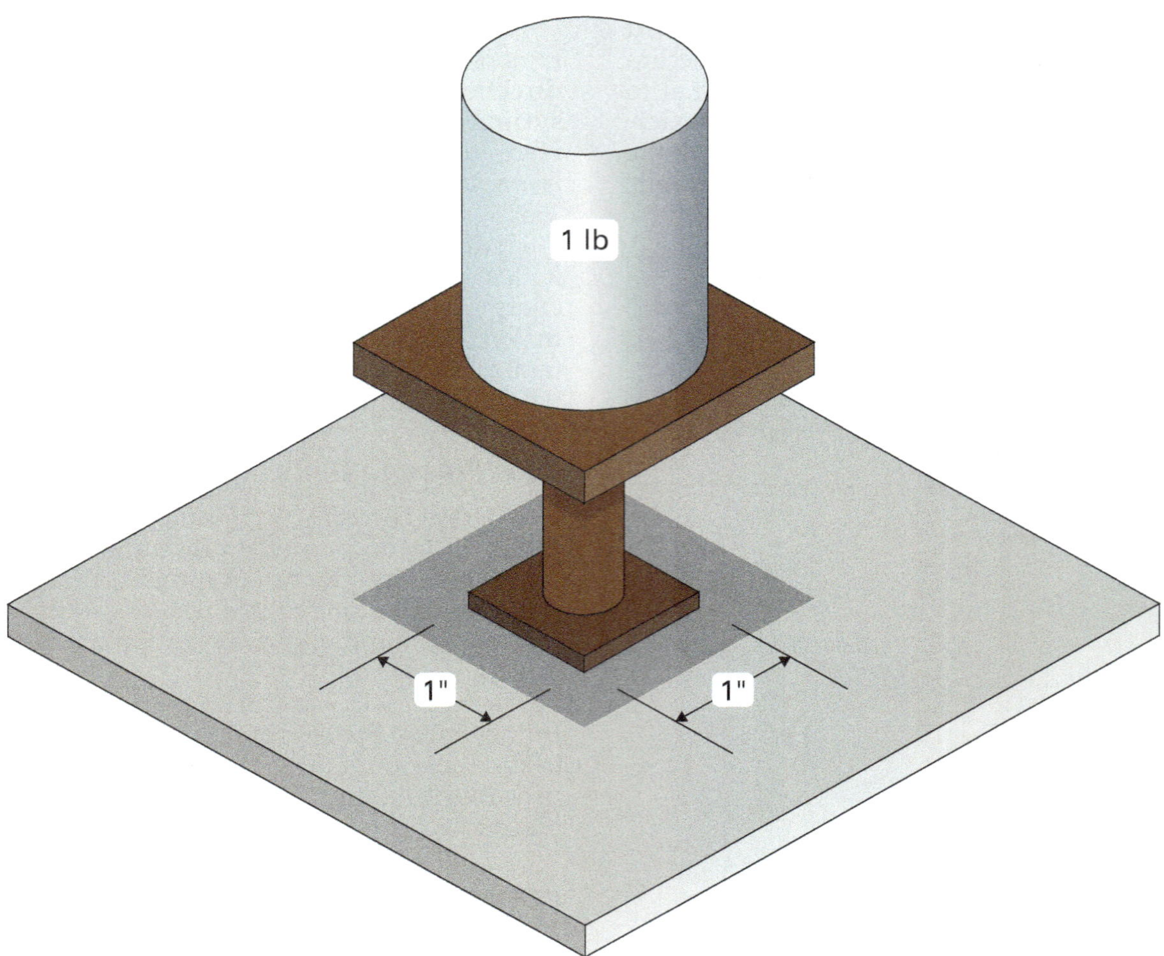

Figure 4 A pressure of 1 psi.

The pascal is a very small unit. Expressing everyday hydraulic pressures in pascals gives very large numbers. To keep values manageable, scale the unit with a prefix. For example, adding the *kilo-* prefix scales the unit by 1,000. A kilopascal (1 kPa) equals 1,000 Pa. Adding the *mega-* prefix scales the unit by 1,000,000. A megapascal (1 MPa) equals 1,000,000 Pa.

Bars (bar)

Metric-speaking countries also express pressures in *bars* (bar). A pressure of 1 bar equals 100,000 Pa (100 kPa). A pressure of 1 psi equals 0.069 bar.

> **NOTE**
>
> Hydraulic systems usually operate between 2,000 psi and 5,000 psi (~14 MPa and 35 MPa / ~140 bar and 350 bar). High-pressure hydraulic systems, however, may go as high as 10,000 psi (~69 MPa / ~690 bar).

1.1.3 Converting between Pressure Units

Hydraulic systems usually contain several pressure gauges. These may be scaled in any common pressure unit. At times, you may need to convert between units. *Table 1* provides conversion factors for hydraulic pressure units.

To convert from one unit to another, find the original unit in the leftmost column. Read across until you come to the desired unit's column. Multiply the original unit value by the conversion factor in that location.

For example, to convert 4,000 psi to pascals, locate **psi** in the leftmost column. Read across to the **Pa** column. The conversion factor is **6,895**. Multiply the original value by this factor:

$$4,000 \text{ psi} \times 6,895 \text{ Pa/psi} = 27,580,000 \text{ Pa}$$

This is a very large number, so divide it by 1,000,000 to convert it to megapascals (MPa).

$$27,580,000 \text{ Pa} \div 1,000,000 = 27.6 \text{ MPa}$$
$$(\text{rounded})$$

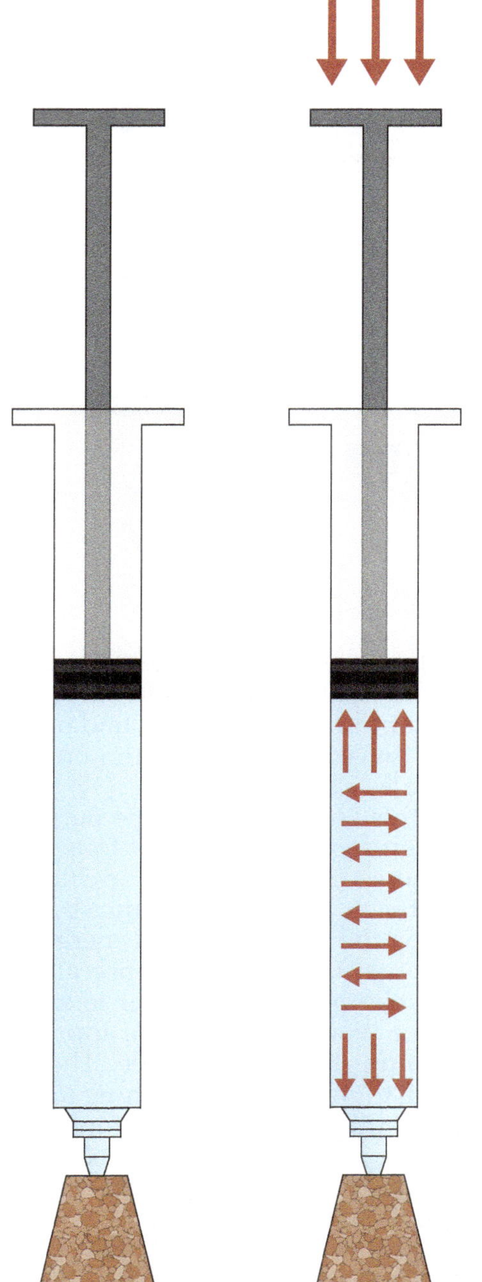

Figure 5 Increasing liquid pressure with an external force.

Table 1 Pressure Unit Conversion Factors

Unit	psi	Pa	bar
psi	1.000	6,895	0.069
Pa	0.000145	1.000	0.00001
Bar	14.504	100,000	1.000

Figure 6 Pressure gauge.

1.1.4 *Work and Hydraulic Machines*

All hydraulic machines do *work*. They apply a force to make something move. In fact, that's work's formal definition—a force multiplied by a distance (Work = Force × Distance). *Energy* does work by being transferred from point to point. A hydraulic power unit transfers energy through the fluid to the actuator, where it does mechanical work.

Both work and energy share a common unit—the foot-pound (ft-lb). If you apply a force of 1 lb to move an object 1', you've done 1 ft-lb of work. That work required 1 ft-lb of energy.

Hydraulic machines take advantage of work's two components (force and distance) to do their job. Let's examine a simple hydraulic lift that changes a small input force into a larger output force (*Figure 7*). The lift is made of two water-filled syringes connected by a tube. Notice that they have different diameters.

Syringe A's piston has a surface area of 1 in^2. Syringe B's piston has a surface area of 5 in^2. If you apply a 1 lb force to syringe A's plunger, you will generate a pressure of 1 psi in the hydraulic machine (1 lb ÷ 1 in^2 = 1 psi). Pascal's principle says that this pressure affects the *entire* system equally. This means that the plunger in syringe B will also experience a 1 psi pressure on its surface.

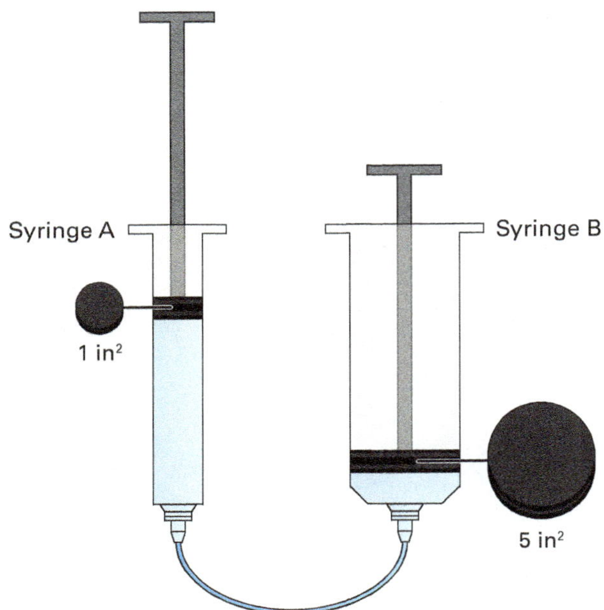

Figure 7 Hydraulic lift.

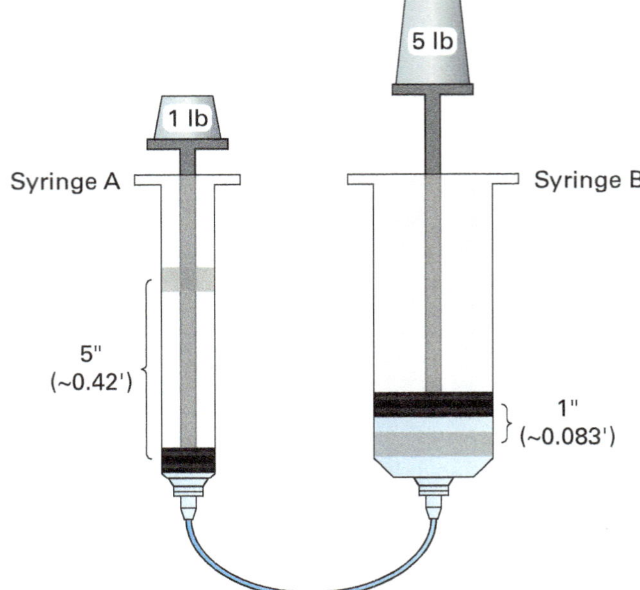

Figure 8 Hydraulic force multiplier.

Since syringe B's piston has a surface area of 5 in², however, that 1 psi generates 5 lb of force (1 psi × 5 in² = 5 lb). In other words, syringe B's plunger can lift a 5 lb weight (*Figure 8*). The hydraulic machine is a *force multiplier*. It turns a small force into a larger one. Automobile lifts work this way.

Examine *Figure 8* and notice an important truth. Syringe A's plunger went down 5", but syringe B's plunger rose only 1". The output force was five times greater than the input force. The output motion, however, was only one-fifth the input motion. Let's calculate the work for each syringe.

Syringe A (input work)
Force = 1 lb
Distance = 5" (~0.42')
Work = 1 lb × 0.42'
Work = 0.42 ft-lb

Syringe B (output work)
Force = 5 lb
Distance = 1" (~0.083')
Work = 5 lb × 0.083'
Work = 0.42 ft-lb (rounded)

Notice that even though the input and output *forces* are different, the input and output *work* values are identical. Since the input and output work values are the same, the input and output *energy* values are also identical.

Why is this so? It's simple. The output force is five times greater than the input force. The input distance, however, is five times greater than the output distance. Force and distance balance each other, giving the same work and energy values.

Never forget this principle since all hydraulic machines rely on it. If you want to increase the output force, you must increase input distance. You're trading distance for force. The hydraulic machine isn't "giving you something for nothing."

The hydraulic excavating machine in *Figure 9* delivers huge forces. To do this, the pump in its hydraulic power unit moves large amounts of fluid. Work in equals work out.

1.1.5 Hydraulic Flow

Hydraulic equipment requires more than just fluid at the right pressure. It also requires sufficient *flow*. Some devices, like hydraulic motors, require continuous flow. Other devices, like hydraulic lifts, require flow for short periods only.

In large systems, multiple actuators draw hydraulic fluid from the system. The hydraulic power unit must meet the system's demand to keep everything working smoothly. To size a hydraulic power unit, engineers must know each actuator's flow and pressure requirements.

NCCER – *Millwright*

Figure 9 Hydraulic excavator.

In the United States, actuator manufacturers specify flow rates in *gallons per minute* (gpm). Machines made in metric-speaking countries have flow rates specified in *liters per minute* (lpm or L/min). Specifications will include the pressure associated with the flow. Similarly, hydraulic power supplies will have a rated pressure, flow, and reservoir capacity (in gallons or liters). Properly sized systems will work reliably under all operating conditions.

To improve reliability, many hydraulic systems contain an **accumulator**. It connects to the hydraulic power unit's outlet (*Figure 10*). The accumulator holds extra hydraulic fluid under pressure. If several actuators demand fluid at the same time, the accumulator smooths the flow and keeps the pressure from dropping. The accumulator serves the same purpose as the receiver in pneumatic systems.

Ideally, hydraulic fluid flows smoothly through pipes, hoses, and hydraulic devices. *Figure 11* shows fluid flowing through a straight pipe. It flows in layers that move at different speeds. Those near the walls move more slowly since friction slows them down. Those near the center move faster. This **laminar flow** is ideal. It wastes very little energy and powers the system smoothly.

Laminar flow can quickly change to **turbulent flow**. Instead of flowing in layers, the fluid swirls, changes directions, and interferes with its own motion (*Figure 11*). Turbulent flow wastes energy and makes the system run less smoothly. If it's too severe, it can damage components.

Many factors can change a laminar flow into a turbulent one. High flow rates are more likely to be turbulent. Obstacles in the flow path can cause turbulence, as can sharp bends in hoses. Sudden changes in a pipe's diameter can produce turbulence too. Well-designed hydraulic systems minimize turbulence-causing factors.

Figure 10 Hydraulic accumulator.

Other factors can affect a hydraulic system's flow as well. *Figure 12* shows a pipe that transitions to a larger diameter. Later, it transitions back to a smaller one. Interestingly, both pressure and flow change with diameter. When the smoothly flowing fluid enters the larger pipe, its flow speed *decreases*, and its pressure *increases*. When it enters the smaller pipe, the reverse happens. This behavior is called *Bernoulli's principle* after Daniel Bernoulli, who discovered it in 1738.

Sometimes, bubbles will form in the hydraulic fluid and then violently collapse. These generate tiny shock waves that combine, becoming large forces. Turbulent flow can cause the bubbles, as can air getting sucked in by the pump. Sometimes, the hydraulic fluid boils, creating tiny vapor bubbles. Whatever the cause, this problem, called **cavitation**, can damage hydraulic components. It also reduces the system's efficiency.

Cavitating equipment may vibrate badly or make strange noises. Since cavitation damages components, they'll often look eroded or chipped. If the problem becomes too severe, the system may shut down to protect itself. Debris from cavitation damage can travel through the system, causing damage to valves, cylinders, and pistons.

Basic Hydraulic Systems   7

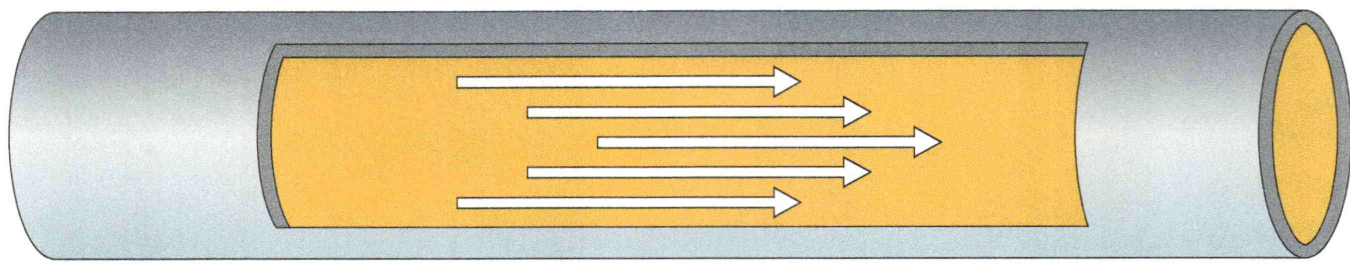

Figure 11 Laminar and turbulent flows.

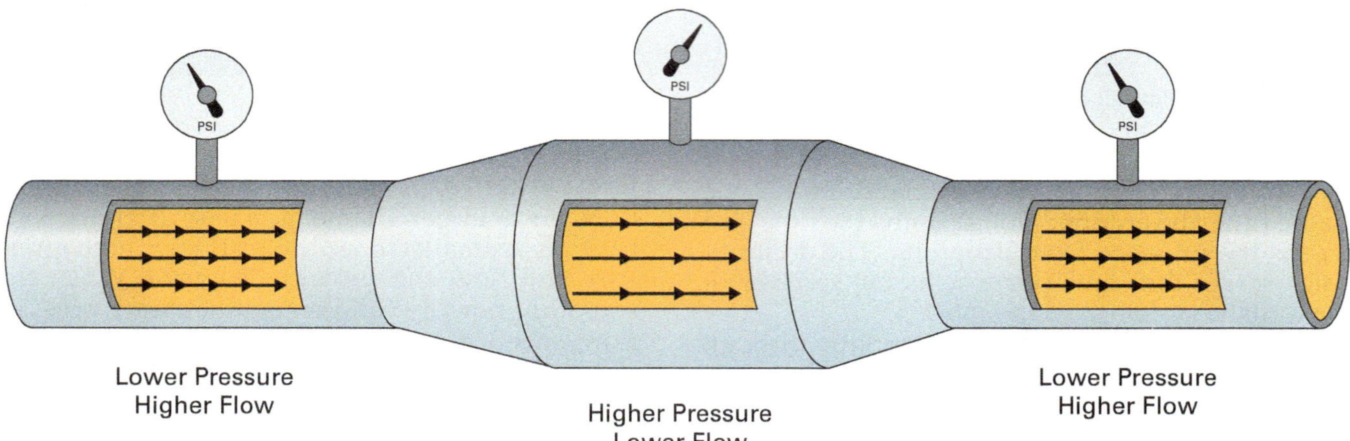

Figure 12 Bernoulli's principle in a pipe.

1.1.6 Temperature Issues

All hydraulic systems get hot as they operate. Motors and pumps generate heat. Friction between other moving parts also generates heat. Even friction between the hydraulic fluid and the pipes contributes to the total heat.

Heat affects the hydraulic fluid in two ways. First, some hydraulic fluids become thinner and work less effectively when they're hot. They leak through seals and don't lubricate as well. Overheated fluid has a shorter lifespan than fluid used at its rated temperature. Second, heat causes the fluid to expand, which raises the system pressure. Higher pressures damage components and shorten their lifespan. If the pressure rises too high, it will activate safety devices.

Well-designed hydraulic systems cool the fluid as it circulates. Small systems with low flow rates rely on natural airflow around the pipes, hoses, and reservoir to remove heat. Larger systems or those with high flows use fans, radiators, and other devices to manage temperature.

Cold also affects hydraulic fluid. When cold, it can become thicker and harder to pump. Systems that operate in cold environments may have heaters in their hydraulic power units. Some specialized hydraulic fluids are designed to handle cold conditions.

1.2.0 Hydraulic Safety

Hydraulic systems can be very dangerous because they contain a lot of energy. Pneumatic systems usually operate at pressures below 150 psi. Hydraulic systems, on the other hand, may contain pressures as high as 10,000 psi. Hydraulic fluid escaping from a tiny leak at this pressure behaves like a needle. It can penetrate skin, injecting itself into the body and causing serious tissue damage.

Loosening a pneumatic fitting to release trapped air is usually safe. The air escapes harmlessly into the atmosphere. This practice *isn't* acceptable with hydraulic systems. Hydraulic fluid can be dangerously hot. Some types are flammable or toxic. All are messy and create slip hazards. Many hydraulic safety principles parallel pneumatic ones. Implementing them, however, often requires different methods.

Besides their obvious hazards, hydraulic systems include other dangers too. They may power industrial processes involving heat, toxic chemicals, or flammable substances. Nearby equipment could contain electrical or pneumatic hazards.

Whenever you work with a hydraulic system, think ahead. What else could endanger you or nearby workers? Ask yourself the question, "If I work on this system, could I affect anything else?" Remember, shutting down one system could alter another one. It could even cause a cascade of undesirable events. Never do anything without considering the downstream consequences!

Every workplace has its own unique hazards. Each one also has its own safety guidelines and protocols. Always follow these. If your workplace standards don't provide specific guidance, follow general safety principles. Don't forget OSHA standards and guidelines.

Be sure you have the right PPE for the tasks you're planning to do. Usually, this includes eye and hearing protection, as well as gloves. Check the PPE, confirming that it's in good condition. If you aren't sure about something, ask your supervisor before starting work. Never guess. Hydraulic systems can be very unforgiving.

The following guidelines offer useful general safety principles for working with hydraulics:

- Before beginning work, be sure that you understand the system's overall layout. Confirm that you know what each major component does.
- Consult appropriate manuals, documentation, and company maintenance handbooks.
- Before opening or closing any valve, consider possible hazardous consequences.
- Before de-energizing anything, confirm that machines are safe. Block or secure loads and moving parts so that they can't fall or move when de-energized.
- When possible, de-energize and isolate the system. Then, lock out and tag it. Follow relevant industry standards and workplace protocols. If troubleshooting requires an active system, be especially vigilant and careful. You may require additional PPE.
- Remember that hydraulic systems don't depressurize when you de-energize them. They can hold their pressure for a long time. Individual sections may remain pressurized even when the main system has been depressurized.
- After isolating the system, release pressure through appropriate bleed valves. Never loosen a fitting to release pressure. Check gauges or use instruments to confirm zero pressure before disassembling anything. Be alert for unexpected pressure releases. Stand out of the path of possible fluid releases.
- Remember that hydraulic isolation valves can leak. A poorly designed system could repressurize, causing actuators to move. Well-designed safety systems can deal with a leaking isolation valve. They route pressure safely away from the isolated section.
- Never run your hands over pressurized hydraulic hoses to check for leaks. Pinholes can cause dangerous injection injuries. Instead, hold a piece of cardboard near suspected leaks and look for oily spots to appear.
- Wear gloves when handling hoses with an outer metallic braid. Broken strands can pierce your hands.
- Hydraulic fluid and equipment are often very hot. Beware of getting burned.

- Never operate machines without their guards or safety features in place.
- Think about nearby workers' safety. Don't perform tasks or operate equipment that could put them at risk. Don't restart machines without alerting those affected or those working nearby.
- Always use appropriate replacement parts. Confirm correct sizes and ratings. Never substitute parts without engineering authorization.

1.2.1 Hydraulic Lockout/Tagout

Whenever possible, work on de-energized and de-pressurized equipment. Code-compliant systems include *isolation devices*. When activated, these devices disconnect hydraulic equipment from any potential pressure source either upstream or downstream. They also release pressure from the isolated section and return hydraulic fluid to the reservoir. Isolation devices incorporate gauges or indicators to confirm zero pressure.

Completely de-energizing a hydraulic system may also require isolating non-hydraulic energy sources. Many systems include electrical and/or pneumatic equipment. These must have suitable isolation devices of their own. As with any powered system, lockout/tagout (LOTO) procedures protect you and others from accidents.

Lockout/tagout prevents the wrong people from deactivating an isolation device. A padlock with a single key secures the mechanism. The tag identifies the person who activated the isolation device. With the lock in place, only the keyholder can re-energize the system.

Some tags have holes for multiple locks (*Figure 13*). Everyone working on the system must add a lock to the tag. Only when the last worker removes the final lock can the isolation device be deactivated.

Hydraulic lockout/tagout protocols follow the same basic steps as those used in other crafts:

- De-energize the system or appropriate subsection.
- Activate the isolation devices.
- Fill out the tags.
- Lock and tag the isolation devices.
- Confirm that the isolation devices cannot be deactivated.
- Always keep the keys in your possession.

Figure 13 Tag with multiple lock holes.

1.2.2 Hydraulic Isolation Valves

Isolating a hydraulic system is trickier than isolating a pneumatic one. Since hydraulic systems are loops, devices must be isolated at both ends. Closing a single valve between the hydraulic power unit and the device isn't enough. A pair of valves on each side of the device isn't much safer. Either could leak and re-pressurize the device.

The best and safest isolation solution is a *double block and bleed* valve system. It has three valves (*Figure 14*). Two valves block the section's ends. The bleed valve in the middle releases pressure back to the reservoir. If either blocking valve leaks, the open bleed valve prevents pressure from building up.

Hydraulic isolation valves must be lockable in the isolating position only. With a double block and bleed system, the block valves must be lockable only in the closed position. The bleed valve must be lockable only in the open position. A valve that can be locked in either position isn't a true isolation valve. When activating a hydraulic isolation device, be sure to lock and tag each valve.

1.3.0 Hydraulic Fluid

Early hydraulic systems used water as the working fluid. Some modern systems still do. Most, however, use an oil instead. Oil transfers energy as effectively as water. It lubricates and seals equipment, while also protecting it from corrosion. Most oils can handle a wider temperature range than water.

Mineral (petroleum-based) oils are the most popular hydraulic fluids. Synthetic oils with optimized properties may be better for some applications. Specialized situations require other synthetic liquids or even natural (vegetable-based) oils. Always use the right hydraulic fluid for the application. The wrong fluid can damage equipment, shorten its lifespan, or affect the system's performance. Follow the equipment manufacturer's guidelines. Never mix different hydraulic fluid types.

1.3.1 Hydraulic Fluid Properties

Manufacturers classify hydraulic fluids by their physical properties and ability to resist undesirable changes. These affect how the fluid behaves under different conditions. To find this information, consult the product's *technical data sheet*. It's available on the manufacturer's website. The following categories summarize essential hydraulic fluid qualities.

Flowing and Pouring

Some liquids flow like water. Others behave more like syrup. What causes the difference? Internal friction between a liquid's layers determines its viscosity, the way it flows and pours. Low-viscosity liquids are thin, while high-viscosity liquids are thick. Oils have higher viscosities than water, so they flow and pour more slowly.

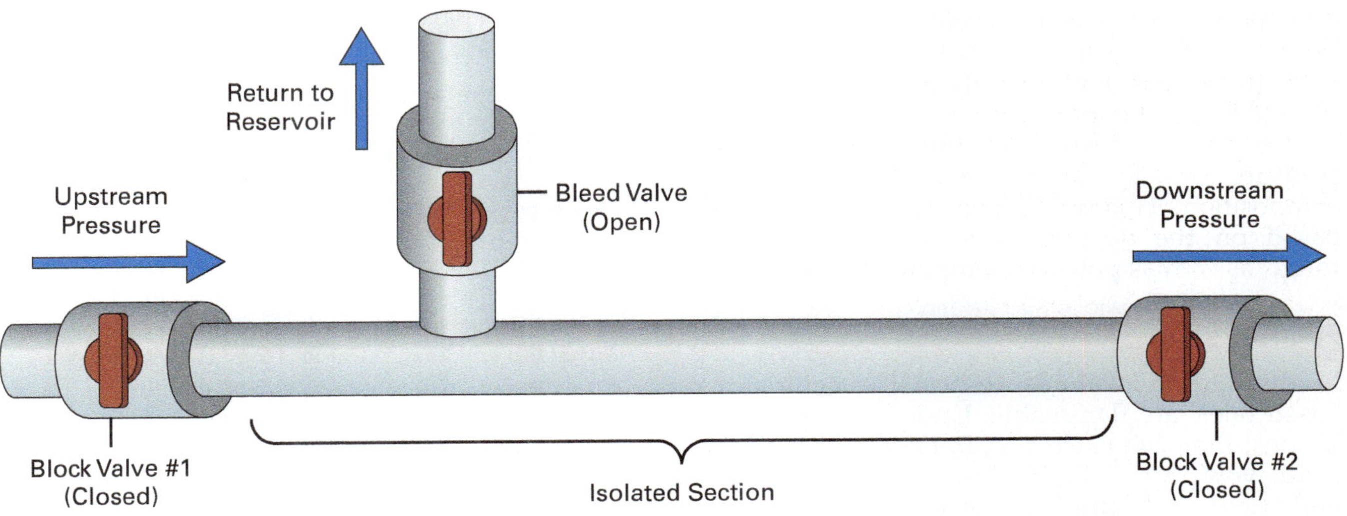

Figure 14 Double block and bleed valves.

A hydraulic fluid's viscosity determines how freely it flows through the system. Thick fluids require more energy to move them around. They get hotter and waste energy because of their greater friction. On the other hand, thick fluids stick to surfaces better. This makes them better lubricants and corrosion inhibitors. Thick fluids don't leak through seals as easily. Hydraulics engineers must balance these contradictory qualities when they select hydraulic fluids.

Temperature affects viscosity. A cold liquid is more viscous than a hot one. How much the viscosity changes depends on the liquid. For example, water's viscosity changes far less than an oil's. Engineers rate oils by assigning them a *viscosity index (VI)*. This is a number between 0 and about 400. Oils with low VIs (<35) experience large viscosity shifts when the temperature changes. Oils with high VIs (>80) don't change nearly as much.

If large temperatures swings are likely, comparing VIs is a simple way to decide if one hydraulic fluid is better than another. In situations where temperatures are stable, VI is less important.

A hydraulic fluid's *pour point* is closely related to viscosity and VI. It's the lowest temperature at which the fluid will pour freely. At low temperatures, using a fluid with a high pour point is a bad idea. The fluid will become so thick when the machine is idle that the pump won't be able to move it at startup.

A hydraulic fluid's high-temperature behavior is important too. If its VI is too low, the fluid's viscosity will drop excessively as the temperature rises. Thin hydraulic fluid doesn't lubricate properly and may leak through seals. Some hydraulic fluids rapidly break down at high temperatures. Even those that don't usually have shorter lifespans at higher temperatures.

How well a hydraulic fluid handles temperature changes or extremes depends on its composition. Hydraulics engineers select fluids based on the expected operating temperature range, as well as potential temperature extremes.

Fire Risks

Many hydraulic fluids, especially petroleum-based ones, are flammable. Under the right conditions, they can catch fire. In general, hydraulic fluid won't ignite in the reservoir. Spills, leaks, and accidental sprays, however, can catch fire more easily.

To know the risks associated with a particular hydraulic fluid, look up its *flash point*. The manufacturer provides this information in the fluid's technical data sheet or Safety Data Sheet (SDS). The flash point is the temperature at which the fluid's vapors will catch fire if they contact a spark or flame. They won't keep burning at this temperature, but there will be a flash.

Resisting Undesirable Changes

To achieve maximum lifespan, hydraulic fluids must resist undesirable changes. All hydraulic fluids combine with oxygen from the air. It happens faster when the fluid is hot. Oxidation changes the fluid, so it doesn't function as well. Many hydraulic fluids contain additives to help them resist oxidation.

As they age and oxidize, petroleum products can start depositing a sticky, waxy coating called *varnish* on surfaces. This usually happens as the fluid cools down. Varnish can clog or damage hydraulic equipment. Some hydraulic fluids contain additives to inhibit varnish.

As you know, oil and water don't combine. If added to water, oil rises to the top and forms a layer. Sometimes, however, the water and oil form an emulsion. When this happens, the water mingles with the oil as tiny droplets (*Figure 15*). These droplets can trap dirt and reduce the oil's lubricating ability. Demulsifying additives prevent emulsions from forming.

Additives can help hydraulic fluids handle higher operating temperatures. Others enhance the oil's natural corrosion-inhibiting qualities. Detergent additives keep equipment cleaner inside. A typical hydraulic fluid contains much more than oil.

Did You Know?

Flammability Confusion

Besides the flash point, flammable fluids also have a *fire point* and an *autoignition point*. The fire point is the temperature at which the fluid's vapors will catch fire and keep burning if they contact a spark or flame. At the autoignition point, the fluid will start burning on its own. The flash point is the lowest temperature, and the autoignition point is the highest. The fire point's temperature lies somewhere in between. Data sheets may not list all three temperatures.

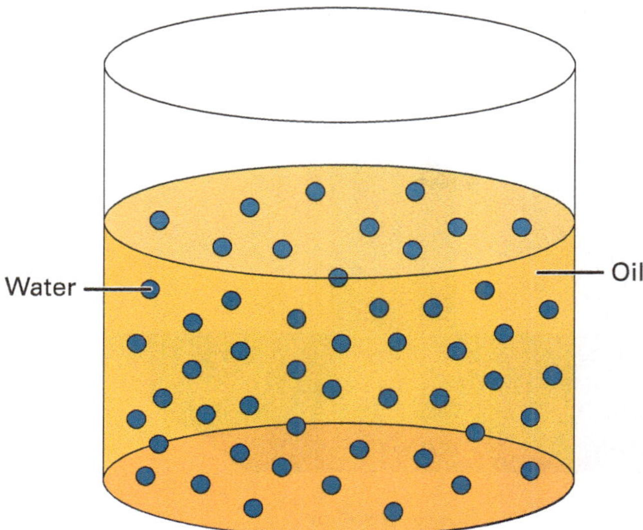

Figure 15 A water-in-oil emulsion.

1.3.2 Hydraulic Fluid Contamination

Ideally, hydraulic fluid should be totally pure, but this is rarely true. Usually, it contains air, water, corrosion products, and dirt. Some contaminants reduce the fluid's performance. Others damage hydraulic components. Contaminants usually change the hydraulic fluid's appearance. Uncontaminated oil-based hydraulic fluids are clear yellow- or amber-colored (*Figure 16*).

Air gets in through leaking seals. It also enters from the reservoir if the fluid level is too low. Air accelerates oxidation and makes hydraulic fluid foamy. Foam interferes with lubrication and can cause erratic operation. Air dissolved in the hydraulic fluid may cause cavitation. Degraded or oxidized fluid is dark and opaque.

Moisture from the air and condensation inside the reservoir adds water to the fluid. Eventually, the two liquids will form an emulsion. The emulsion encourages oxidation and doesn't lubricate as well. Water-contaminated hydraulic fluid is milky and opaque.

Rust and other corrosion products form when oxygen, water, and certain chemicals react with metals. Corrosion particles circulate in the system, reducing its efficiency and damaging components. Dirt causes similar problems if it gets in the fluid. Rust and dirt make the hydraulic fluid dark and opaque.

Many hydraulic fluids contain additives to control oxidation, foaming, and corrosion. Keeping the reservoir properly filled reduces air and moisture in the system. Moisture absorbents in the vent keep the air inside the reservoir drier. Special filters in the hydraulic lines can remove water from the fluid. Regular particle filters trap rust and dirt. Clean work habits during maintenance also help keep dirt out. Of course, regularly changing the hydraulic fluid solves many problems.

1.3.3 Hydraulic Fluid Types

Hydraulic fluids come in many varieties, each suitable for certain applications. Normally, millwrights and industrial mechanics don't choose hydraulic fluids. Instead, they follow the equipment manufacturer's recommendations. Occasionally, they'll have to identify a compatible substitute. Understanding hydraulic fluids helps them do this task.

Most hydraulic fluids contain additives. These enhance desirable properties and reduce undesirable ones. Consult the manufacturer's technical data sheet to learn more. Also consult the hydraulic fluid's SDS to learn about proper handling and safety.

Hydraulic fluids fall into the following three major categories.

Petroleum-Based

The most common and popular hydraulic fluids have a petroleum base. They're inexpensive and have relatively few health risks. On the other hand, petroleum products are flammable. The oil isn't likely to catch fire in the reservoir. A leaking connection, however, can spray an oil mist, which catches fire easily. Petroleum-based hydraulic fluids divide into two types.

Mineral oils are distilled from crude oil, just like many other petroleum products. They have a moderate lifespan and work well at normal temperatures. Chemical engineers create *synthetic oils* from the same substances as mineral oils. They behave similarly but have a longer lifespan. Many synthetic oils can operate over a wider temperature range. They often tolerate high temperatures better than regular mineral oils. Unfortunately, they're also more expensive.

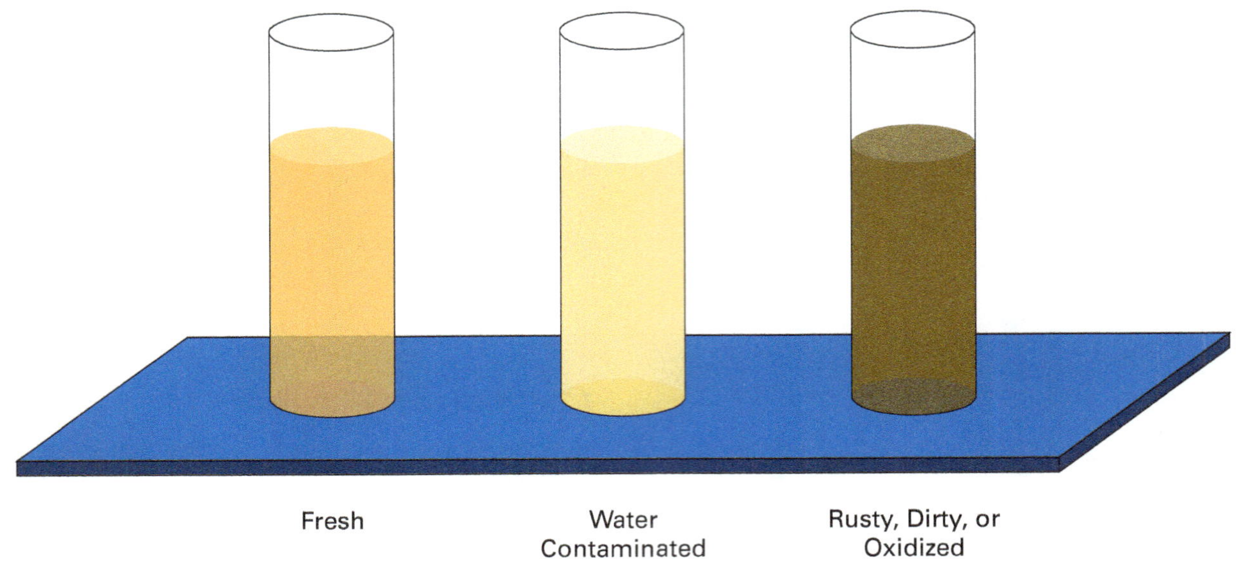

Figure 16 Uncontaminated and contaminated hydraulic fluid.

Fire-Resistant

Some applications have significant fire risks. To stay safe, these require hydraulic fluids that don't catch fire easily. Fire-resistant hydraulic fluids divide into two types.

Water-based hydraulic fluids combine water with other liquids. Water alone isn't an ideal hydraulic fluid since it encourages rusting and doesn't lubricate. On the other hand, water turns into steam during a fire, which slows or stops the flames.

Mixing water with oil usually is undesirable. Some applications, however, deliberately use oil/water emulsions as hydraulic fluids. An *oil-in-water emulsion* is mostly water. It has a low viscosity and some lubricating qualities. A *water-in-oil emulsion* is mostly oil. It's a better lubricant but still contains enough water to resist fire. These mixtures require additives to keep the liquids from separating. They also require corrosion inhibitors.

Water-glycol hydraulic fluids are a mix of water and glycol, a common antifreeze. Together, they make a fire-resistant hydraulic fluid with good low-temperature properties. Many contain additives to increase the mixture's naturally low viscosity.

Nonaqueous hydraulic fluids contain no water, so they don't cause rusting. They're synthetic chemicals engineered to have the required properties. *Phosphate ester* hydraulic fluids are popular in the aviation industry. They resist fire and lubricate well. They're toxic and irritating, so they require careful handling. Since phosphate esters attack some plastics and rubbers, seals must be compatible, or they'll fail.

Silicone oil is a synthetic hydraulic fluid that's nonflammable. It works well over a broad temperature range and has relatively few health risks. Unlike many hydraulic fluids, it's electrically nonconductive.

Specialized

Some applications have unique or demanding hydraulic fluid requirements. The fluid may have to be safe around food or pharmaceutical products (*food safe*). Other applications require environmentally friendly (*biodegradable*) fluids. These can't linger in the soil or water.

Natural oil hydraulic fluids are made from plants. They're usually both food safe and biodegradable. Agricultural and marine hydraulic systems sometimes use them since accidental spills won't be as harmful.

> **NOTE**
>
> Never assume that a food-safe hydraulic fluid is completely harmless. Food-safe products are nontoxic at low concentrations. Some can make people sick at higher concentrations or cause allergic reactions. Read the fluid's SDS to understand its risks.

1.4.0 The Hydraulic Power Unit

Since a hydraulic system runs on pressurized hydraulic fluid, its power unit is critical. It must deliver clean fluid to the actuators at the right pressure and flow rate. The flow can't falter, or the pressure drop, even if several actuators require fluid at the same time.

As you know, the reservoir and hydraulic pump are the heart of the power unit. Several surrounding components condition the hydraulic fluid. Others ensure that the system operates safely and keeps up with demand. *Figure 17* shows a hydraulic power unit. Not all systems contain every component, although many do.

As you learn about hydraulic components, never forget that hydraulic systems are loops. The hydraulic fluid endlessly circulates. Sometimes, however, not all hydraulic fluid makes it to the actuators. Safety devices may have to release excess pressure. A pneumatic safety device vents to the atmosphere. In contrast, hydraulic safety devices can't just spray fluid all over the floor. Instead, they must return the released fluid to the loop. Normally, they drain into the reservoir. This basic truth is a key difference between pneumatic and hydraulic systems.

More Than Just Fried Foods

Canola oil is a popular and healthy food oil. Produced from the seeds of the canola plant, it tolerates high temperatures, so it's good for frying. It makes an excellent hydraulic fluid for specialized applications since it's sustainable, food safe, and biodegradable. Canola oil also works as a biodiesel fuel and as a lubricant.

Figure Credit: iStock@Geo-grafika

1.4.1 Reservoirs, Coolers, and Heaters

Hydraulic power units store their fluid in the reservoir. These are plate steel boxes. Most have a drain and an access cover for maintenance. A sight glass or level indicator lets craftworkers monitor the fluid. Reservoirs hold three to five times as much fluid as the pump can deliver per minute. For example, if the pump has a maximum flow rate of 10 gpm, the reservoir will probably hold 30–50 gallons.

Besides storing the fluid, the reservoir gives it a place to cool. Suspended particles will settle out as well. An internal baffle plate divides the interior space to reduce turbulence. It also slows the returning fluid, keeping it in the reservoir long enough to settle and cool.

The reservoir's interior stays at normal atmospheric pressure. Every reservoir includes a *breather* (vent) to let air enter and exit. Breathers may have an air filter if the environment is dirty. The filter helps keep the hydraulic fluid clean. Some reservoir filler caps have a built-in breather.

Hydraulic systems may need extra help to stay cool. These use a *cooler* to remove heat from the fluid. *Air-cooled* units work like a car radiator, circulating the hot fluid through a finned tube. Many have a fan to improve heat transfer (*Figure 18*). *Water-cooled* units circulate the hot fluid through a heat exchanger. Cold water flows through the heat exchanger's outer jacket, removing heat. Water-cooled units are more efficient than air-cooled ones but require a water supply and extra plumbing.

An *inline cooler* connects between the return line and the reservoir. It cools the hydraulic fluid as it returns from the actuators. An *offline cooler* isn't part of the main hydraulic loop. Instead, it independently circulates and cools the reservoir's fluid with its own pump. The cooler in *Figure 17* is an offline model.

Hydraulic fluid can become too thick to pump when it's cold. If the hydraulic power unit operates in a cold environment, the reservoir may include a heater. This keeps the fluid warm when the equipment is idle. Most reservoirs have a thermometer or an electronic sensor to monitor the fluid's temperature.

1.4.2 Motors and Hydraulic Pumps

The hydraulic pump draws fluid from the reservoir and delivers it to the system. Usually, an electric motor drives the pump. Mobile power units may use a combustion engine instead. A flexible coupling or belt links the driver to the pump. Millwrights and industrial mechanics regularly remove and install drivers, couplings, and belts. They're also responsible for keeping everything properly aligned or tensioned.

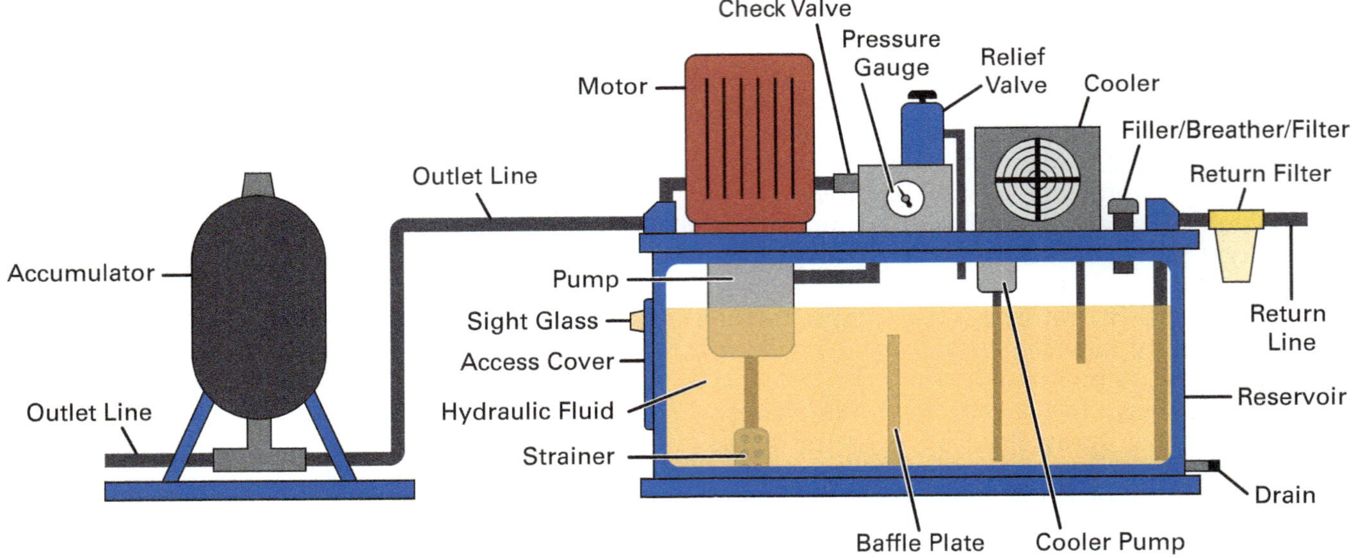

Figure 17 Hydraulic power unit.

Manufacturers mount the driver/pump combination in one of several positions. Many power units have the driver/pump on top. Some mount them beside the reservoir. Larger hydraulic systems may have several driver/pump units side by side.

Sophisticated hydraulic power units may have two driver/pump combinations. One generates a high flow rate at a low pressure. The other generates a low flow rate at a high pressure. An electronic control system switches between them, depending on the actuators' demands.

Millwrights don't size pumps or drivers. Equipment manufacturers make those decisions. Since millwrights do maintain them, they need to understand their construction and operating principles. Hydraulic pumps are a complex topic, so this module explores them in greater detail later.

1.4.3 Suction Strainers and Inline Filters

Even fresh hydraulic fluid contains suspended particles. As it runs through the system, it becomes progressively dirtier. Particles reduce performance and can damage components, especially valves and actuators. For this reason, hydraulic systems include several *filter stages* to clean the fluid.

The first stage is a suction **strainer** attached to the pump's intake (*Figure 19*). Strainers trap larger particles in a metal mesh. Maintenance workers must clean strainers regularly. Power units may also run the fluid through an *inline filter* before delivering it to the system. These trap smaller particles in a replaceable filter element made from paper or soft fibers. Finally, most systems run the returning hydraulic fluid through an inline filter before it drains into the reservoir. Maintenance workers must check and replace filter elements regularly.

Some filters include a *bypass valve* that diverts the flow around a clogged filter. This feature prevents an unexpected system shutdown. Bypass valves always have an indicator to show when they're working. Never operate the system in bypass mode for too long since the hydraulic fluid will quickly become contaminated.

1.4.4 Pressure Relief Valves and Check Valves

For the system to run safely and correctly, the power unit must deliver the hydraulic fluid at the correct pressure. It must always stay within an acceptable range regardless of the system's demands. If multiple actuators are operating, the pressure shouldn't drop. If everything is idle, it can't rise to dangerous levels. Hydraulic power units manage pressure with several strategies.

NCCER – *Millwright*

Figure 18 Fan-type cooler.

(A) Pump Suction Strainer   (B) Return Line Filter

Figure 19 Hydraulic fluid filters.

Some units have *pressure-compensated, variable-displacement pumps*. These can adjust their output to manage demand. They'll even spin without delivering fluid when the actuators are idle. Other units switch the driver on and off as required. Units with multiple driver/pump combinations can switch between them to match the current operating conditions. Regardless of their specific features, all power units include a *pressure relief valve* to keep everything safe.

Pressure relief valves have a fixed or adjustable *setpoint*. If the pressure rises above the setpoint, the valve opens and releases hydraulic fluid back to the reservoir. Once the pressure drops below the setpoint, the valve closes (*Figure 20*). Larger hydraulic systems have multiple pressure relief valves at key locations. Every hydraulic power unit has a pressure relief valve mounted near the pump. It drains directly into the reservoir.

Simpler hydraulic power units use the pressure relief valve to keep the system pressure from rising too high when the actuators are idle. It opens and continuously drains fluid into the reservoir until the actuators start operating. While this strategy effectively protects the system, it has a major disadvantage. If the system idles for too long, the fluid gets hot. This degrades the fluid and wastes energy. For these reasons, most hydraulic power units use better methods to manage pressure. For them, the pressure relief valve is just a safety device.

The hydraulic power unit's pressure relief valve sets the system's *maximum* pressure.

Hydraulic fluid must never flow backwards. This could happen if several driver/pump combinations supply the system. It's also possible if local pressures within a large system vary. *Check valves*, which are simple one-way devices, keep the fluid flowing correctly.

A check valve has a ball or plunger inside the valve body. A weak spring holds it in place against the valve seat (*Figure 21*). Hydraulic fluid flowing in the correct direction easily overcomes the spring force and opens the valve. Fluid flowing backwards pushes the valve closed.

1.4.5 Accumulators

Pressure relief valves protect the system from excess pressure. Keeping the pressure and flow from dropping during periods of high demand requires different strategies. Some hydraulic systems simply use a power unit large enough to handle the worst-case scenario. This is costly and wasteful, especially if the system rarely needs the maximum capacity. A better tactic is to add an energy storage device to the system.

Pneumatic systems hold their energy reserves and extra air in the receiver. Remember, compressed gases store energy like springs. During high-demand periods, the compressed gas expands, releasing extra energy and volume. Hydraulic fluids, however, are incompressible, so they can't store energy.

Instead, hydraulic systems hold extra energy in accumulators. These play the same role in hydraulic systems as receivers do in pneumatic ones. Accumulators usually attach to the hydraulic power unit's outlet. Some actuators have their own accumulators.

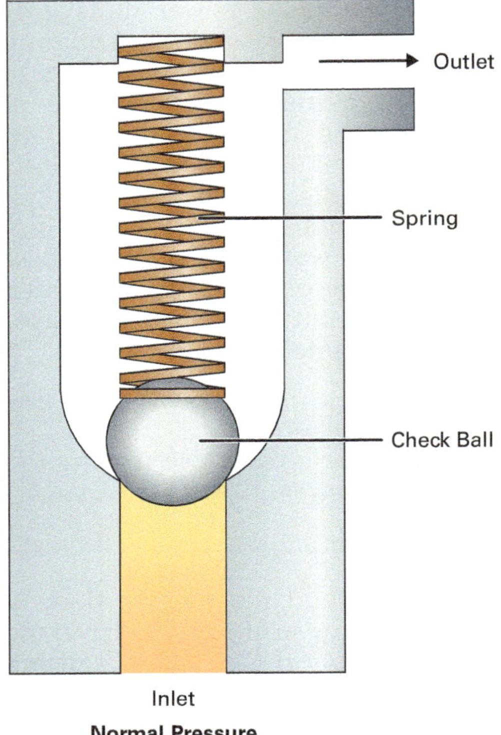

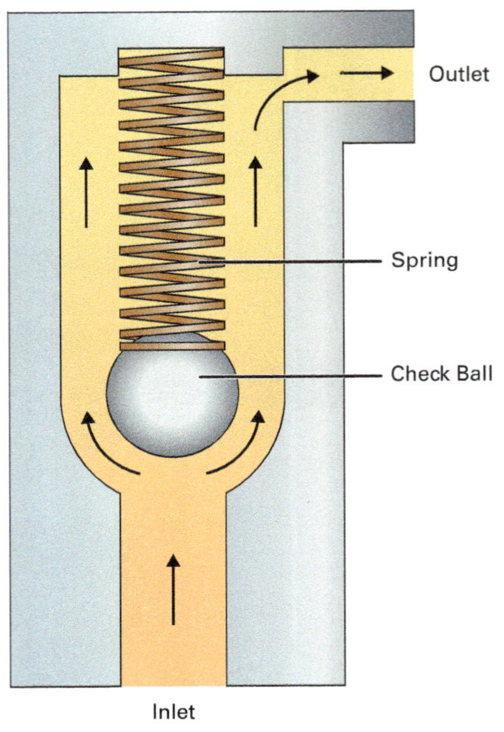

Figure 20 Pressure relief valve.

An accumulator is a tank that holds extra hydraulic fluid. It also contains an energy storage device that keeps the fluid pressurized. When demand is low, the accumulator fills with fluid and stores energy. When demand is high, it releases energy and fluid. Accumulators allow hydraulics engineers to use smaller power units. They also absorb shocks, making the system run smoothly.

Millwrights don't select accumulators. Equipment manufacturers or hydraulics engineers make those decisions. Since millwrights maintain accumulators, they need to understand their construction and operating principles. Accumulators are simple devices that come in many styles.

Gas-Charged Accumulators

These devices, also called *hydropneumatic accumulators*, keep the hydraulic fluid pressurized with a compressed gas. Most use nitrogen since it doesn't support combustion as air does. The gas interacts with the hydraulic fluid from behind a flexible or movable barrier. Gas-charged accumulators are flexible and function across a wide pressure range. Before installation, a craftworker *precharges* the accumulator with gas at a lower pressure than the system's normal operating pressure.

WARNING!

Before working on a system containing a gas-charged accumulator, release the compressed gas stored inside. Don't forget that some actuators have their own accumulators. Confirm that machines can't move or fall when you release the stored energy.

When the hydraulic power unit starts operating, fluid enters the accumulator and pushes against the barrier. This compresses the gas to a smaller volume and raises its pressure to the system's operating pressure. Hydraulic fluid fills the space created by compressing the gas.

During demanding times, the compressed gas in the accumulator expands. This expels the stored hydraulic fluid. When demand returns to normal, the accumulator refills and recompresses the gas.

A *bladder accumulator* stores the compressed gas inside a balloon-like rubber bladder. When precharged, the bladder fills the entire accumulator. A valve keeps the bladder from expanding into the inlet. Pressurized hydraulic fluid enters the accumulator, opening the valve and compressing the bladder to make room for itself (*Figure 22*). During normal operation, the bladder expands and contracts as required to keep the system operating smoothly.

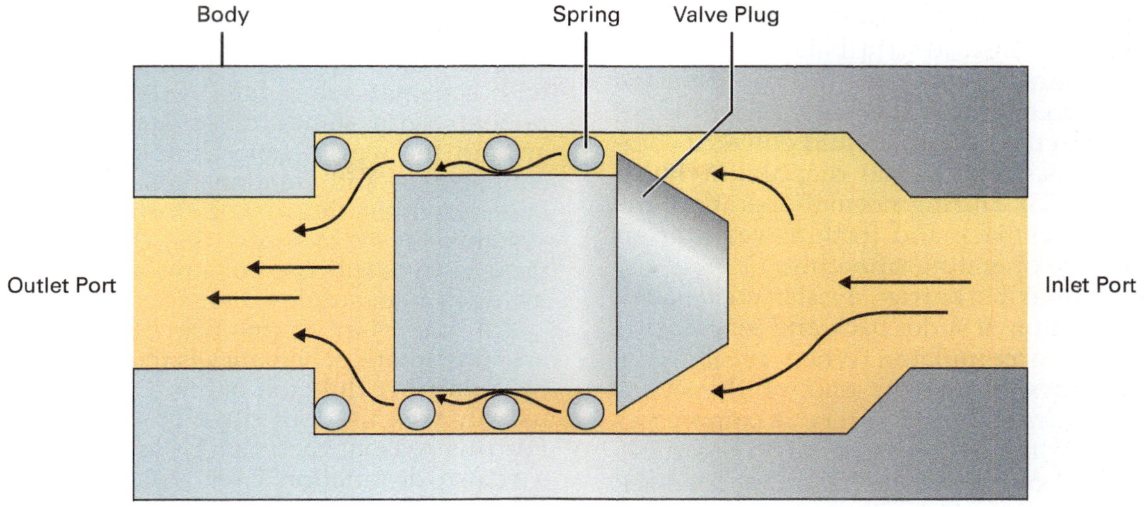

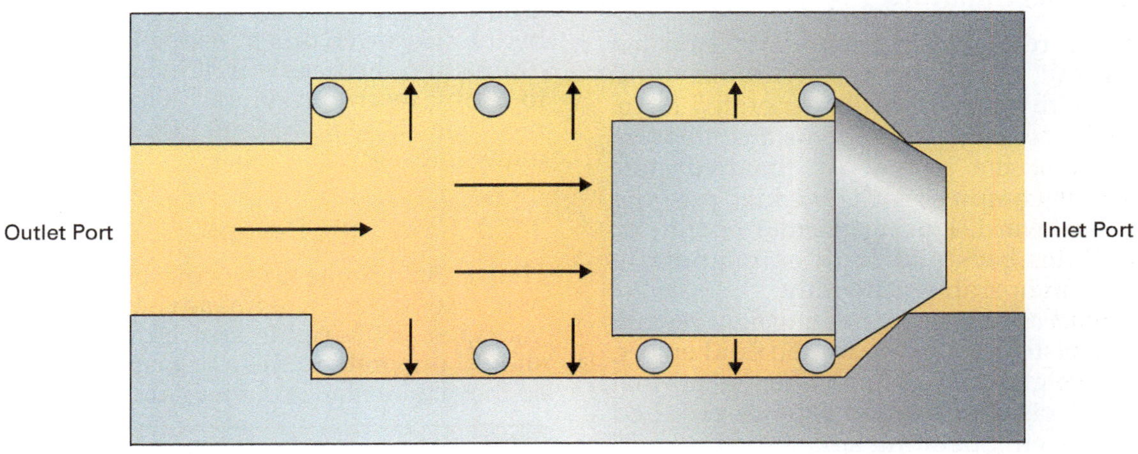

Figure 21 A check valve.

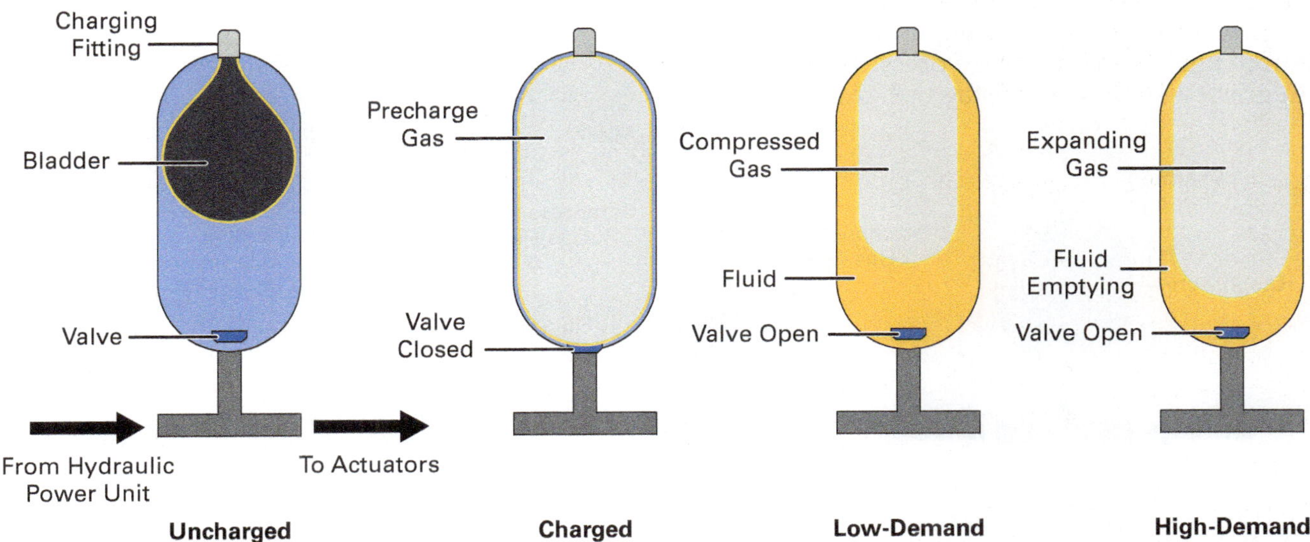

Figure 22 Bladder accumulator.

A *diaphragm accumulator* works like the bladder accumulator. Instead of a balloon, however, a flexible diaphragm separates the gas from the fluid. When precharged, the diaphragm bulges outward. When the hydraulic fluid enters, it compresses the gas, making the diaphragm bulge inward (*Figure 23*). During normal operation, the diaphragm flexes back and forth as required to keep the system operating smoothly.

Instead of a flexible barrier, a *piston accumulator* uses a metal piston. It slides back and forth inside the cylindrical accumulator. When precharged, the piston slides to the far end of the cylinder. As the hydraulic fluid enters, it compresses the gas, sliding the piston backward (*Figure 24*). During normal operation, the piston slides back and forth as required to keep the system operating smoothly.

Mechanical Accumulators

These devices resemble gas-charged piston accumulators, but they keep the hydraulic fluid pressurized with a mechanically generated force. A *spring-loaded accumulator* contains a coil spring pressing against the piston. As the hydraulic fluid enters, it compresses the spring, pushing the piston backward. During normal operation, the piston slides back and forth as required to keep the system operating smoothly.

A *weight-loaded accumulator* has a weight resting on top of the piston. As the hydraulic fluid enters, it lifts the weight and piston. During normal operation, the piston rises and falls as required to keep the system operating smoothly. *Figure 25* shows both accumulator styles.

Spring-loaded and weight-loaded accumulators aren't as flexible as gas-charged models. Adjusting the pressure that they produce requires changing the spring or weight. Weight-loaded accumulators generate the pressurizing force with gravity, so they must stay upright.

1.4.6 Common Schematic Symbols

Most facilities document their hydraulic systems with schematic drawings. These represent components with standardized symbols recognized around the world. Lines link symbols, showing connections and relationships. Hydraulic symbols resemble those that document pneumatic systems. *Figure 26* shows the symbols commonly used in hydraulic power unit schematics. It also includes an example schematic.

An important difference between hydraulic and pneumatic schematics is the way they handle the returning fluid (oil or air). Pneumatic systems usually vent used air directly to the atmosphere. For this reason, they don't show return lines or a return destination. Hydraulic systems, on the other hand, constantly recirculate the hydraulic fluid. Usually, it returns to the reservoir.

As you examine hydraulic system schematics, you'll notice multiple reservoir symbols scattered around (*Figure 26* has three). All represent the hydraulic power unit's reservoir. If a component drains into the reservoir, it includes a connection to a tiny reservoir symbol. This method is simpler than showing a single reservoir symbol with many lines returning to it.

1.5.0 Hydraulic Pumps

Hydraulic pumps are complex. They come in many styles, each with advantages and disadvantages. Millwrights and industrial mechanics should understand their principles and qualities, so they can install and maintain them.

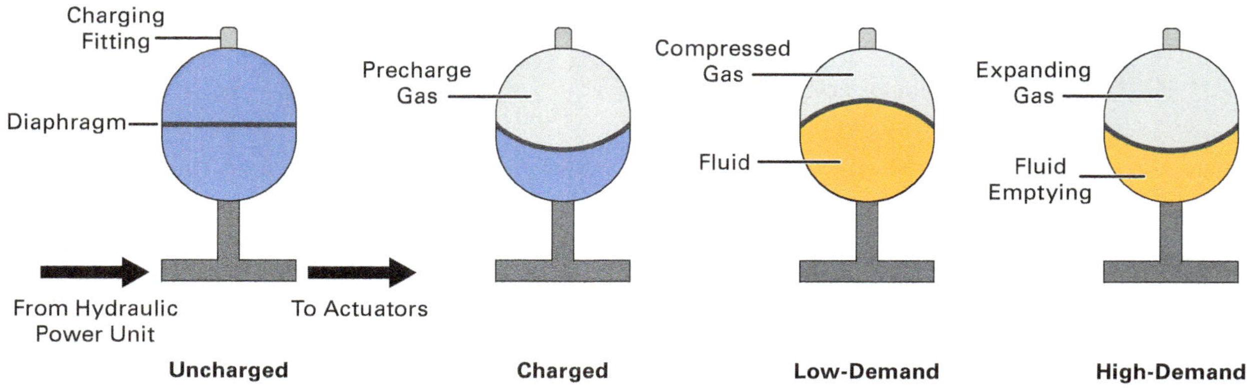

Figure 23 Diaphragm accumulator.

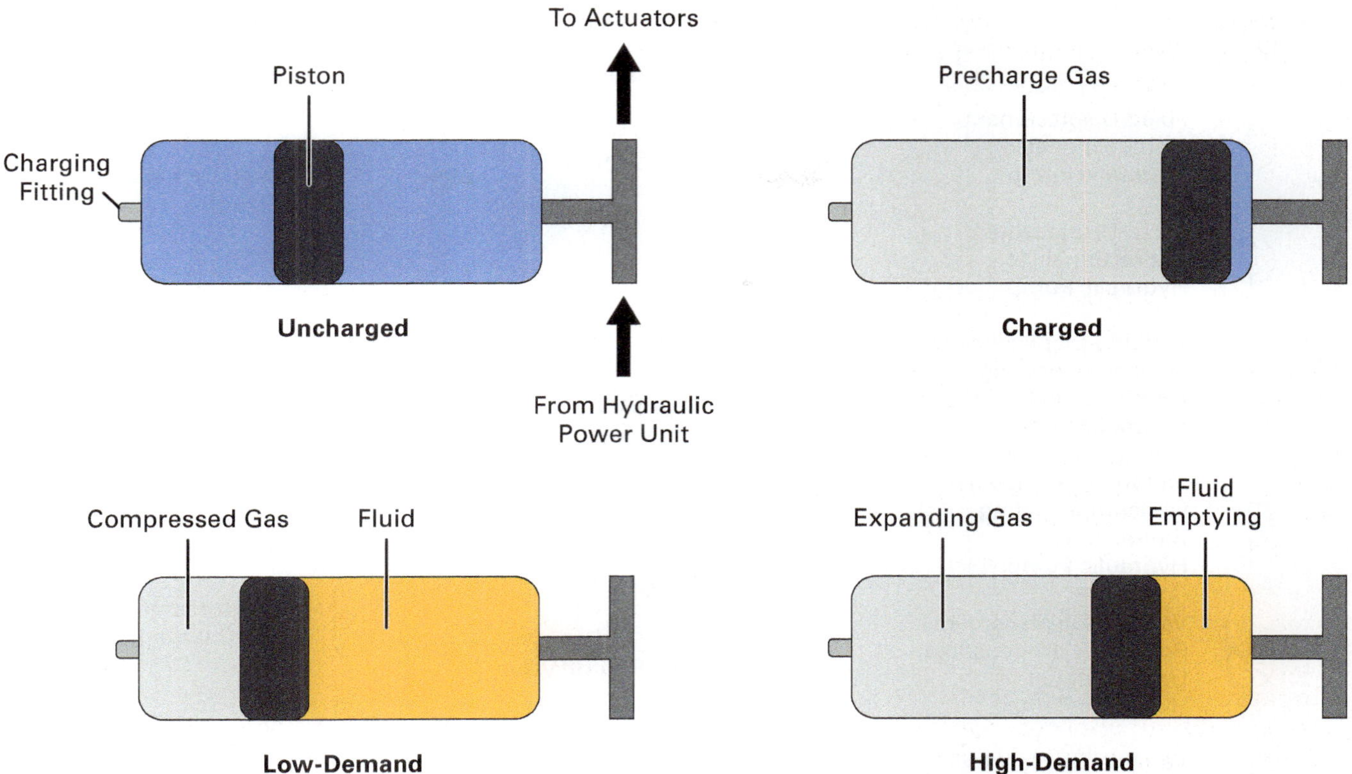

Figure 24 Piston accumulator.

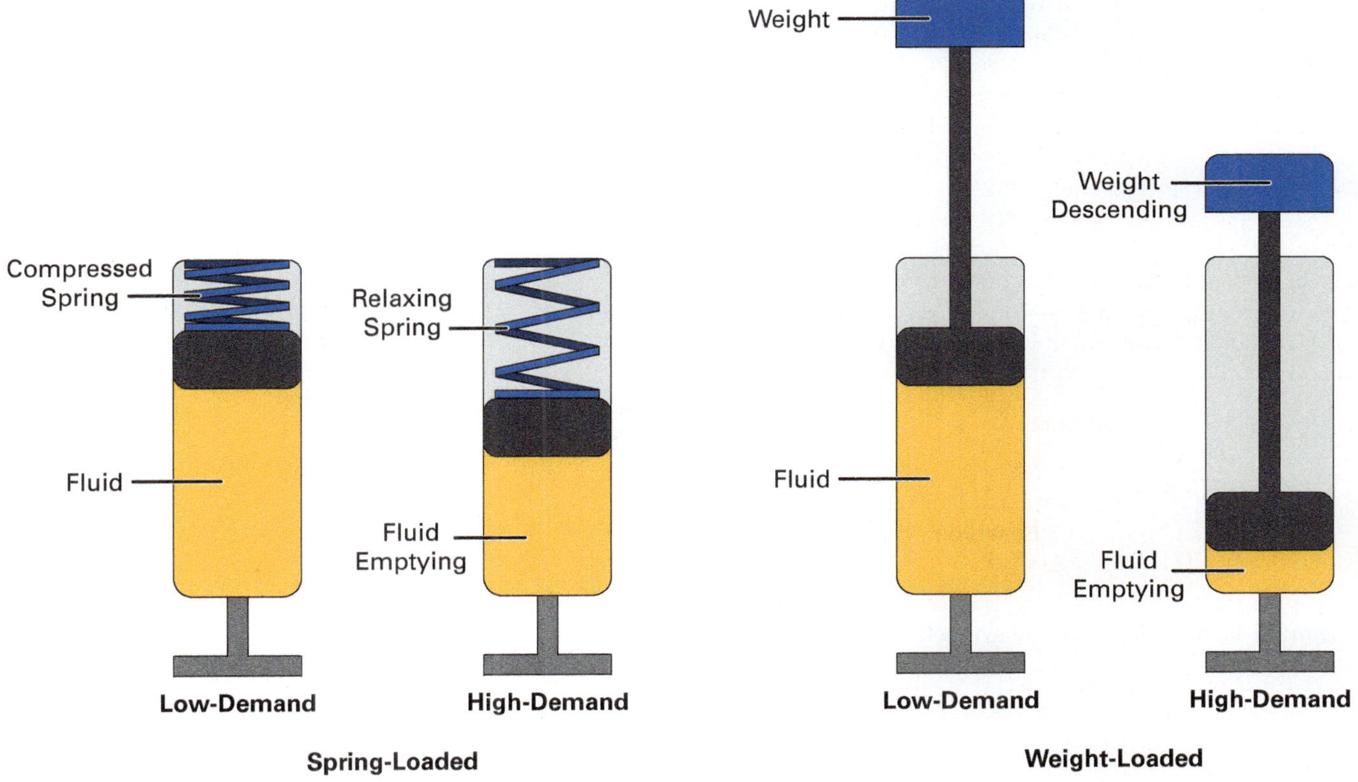

Figure 25 Mechanical accumulators.

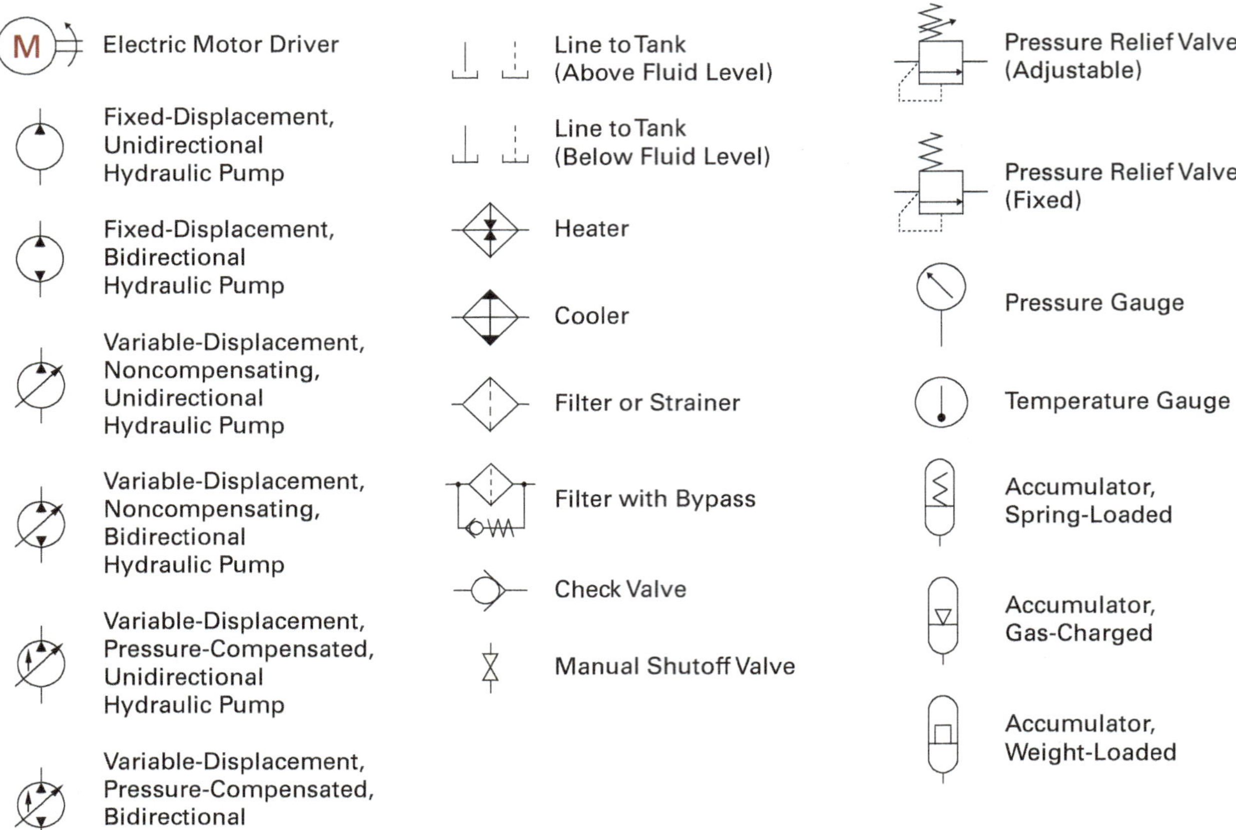

(A) Power Unit Symbols

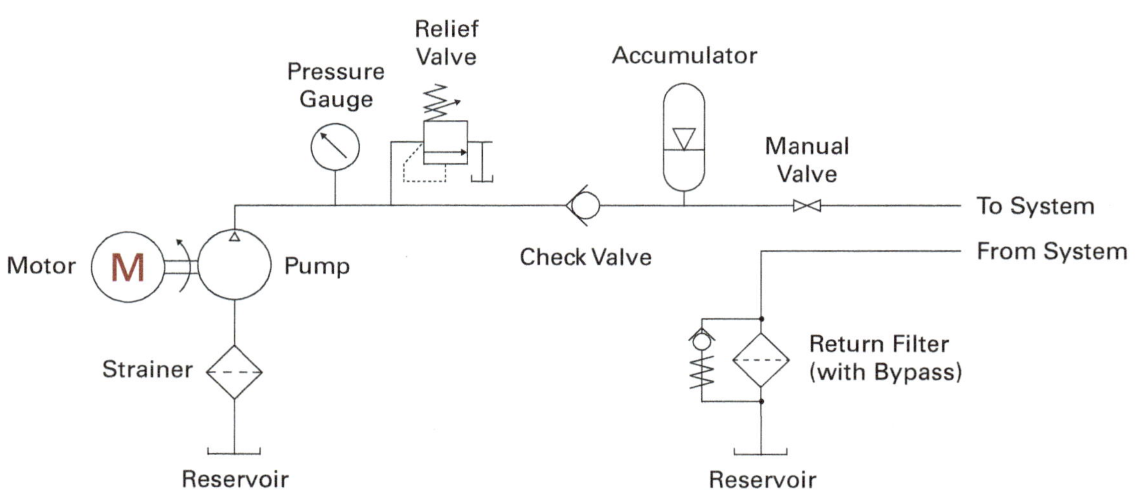

(B) Power Unit Schematic

Figure 26 Hydraulic power unit symbols and example schematic.

1.5.1 Hydraulic Pump Properties

Regardless of the type, all hydraulic pumps do one important thing—deliver hydraulic fluid at a specific flow rate and pressure. Hydraulics engineers consider many properties when they select pumps. Millwrights and industrial mechanics concern themselves with just a few.

Displacement and Capacity

A pump's *displacement* is the amount of fluid that it ejects per shaft rotation. The internal design determines displacement (*Figure 27*). Displacement is measured in cubic inches per revolution (in^3/rev) or cubic centimeters per revolution (cm^3/rev). For example, if a pump has a displacement of 10 in^3/rev, every time the shaft turns, the pump moves 10 cubic inches of hydraulic fluid.

Displacement directly affects the pump's *capacity*, the amount of fluid that it pumps per minute. Capacity is measured in gallons per minute (gpm) or liters per minute (lpm or L/min). For example, if a motor running at 1,760 rpm drives a pump with a displacement of 3 in^3/rev, the following calculations give the capacity:

$$\text{Capacity} = (\text{Displacement} \times \text{Speed}) \div 231\ in^3/gal$$
$$\text{Capacity} = (3\ in^3/rev \times 1{,}760\ rpm) \div 231\ in^3/gal$$
$$\text{Capacity} = 23\ gpm\ \text{(rounded)}$$

A pump's capacity determines whether it can maintain the flow that the system requires. Of course, other factors, such accumulators, affect the total picture, but pump capacity remains a key property.

> **NOTE**
>
> Manufacturers base a pump's rated capacity on its nominal rotational speed. Operating the pump at a lower speed reduces its capacity. Some equipment manufacturers use electronic motor speed controllers to manage the hydraulic pump's output.

Pressure

Hydraulic pumps generate pressure when they force fluid through the system against the load's resistance. The system's components also contribute resistance. The pump's maximum pressure depends on its driver's maximum torque and its parts' physical limits. Manufacturers specify a pump's maximum pressure at its rated flow. For example, a pump might have a flow rate of 2 gpm at a maximum pressure of 2,000 psi.

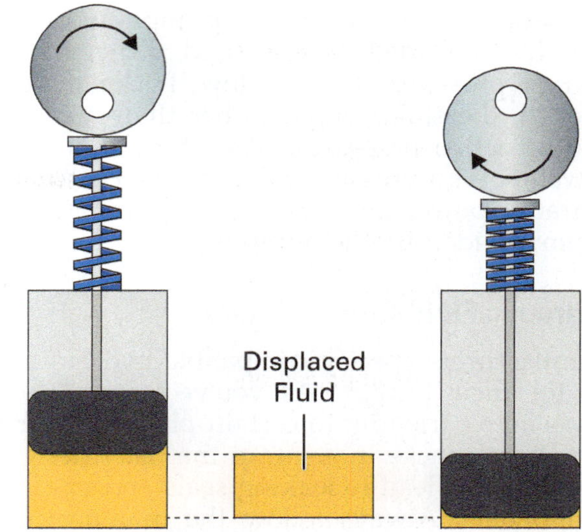

Figure 27 Displacement.

Displacement Type

Pumps divide into two main categories: *positive displacement* and *nonpositive displacement*. Most hydraulic pumps are positive displacement. These pumps deliver a constant amount of fluid per revolution. It doesn't matter if they must deliver it at a low or high pressure. This quality gives them consistent performance, but it's also a weakness. The pump can destroy itself if the outlet is blocked or restricted since pressure will build up.

> **NOTE**
>
> A positive-displacement pump's driver usually has safety features to halt it if the output pressure rises too high. All hydraulic power units also have a pressure relief valve that opens to release pressure.

Positive-displacement pumps further divide into two more categories: *variable displacement* and *fixed displacement*. A variable-displacement pump's output per revolution is adjustable. However, variable-displacement pumps still deliver a consistent amount of fluid regardless of the output pressure. A fixed-displacement pump's displacement isn't adjustable, so it outputs a fixed amount of fluid every revolution.

> **NOTE**
>
> Sophisticated hydraulic power units contain a *pressure-compensated, variable-displacement pump*. It can vary its output from zero up to a maximum value. During idle times, it will spin but not pump fluid. This prevents pressure from building up and opening the pressure relief valve.

Nonpositive-displacement pumps work differently. They deliver less fluid per revolution at high pressures than at low. If the outlet is blocked, the fluid "slips" rather than builds up to destructive pressures. Since they don't work as well at high pressures, they're less common in hydraulic power units. Hydraulic pump symbols (*Figure 26*) identify the pump type.

Hydraulic Fluid Compatibility

Manufacturers specify compatible hydraulic fluids for their pumps. As you've learned, some fluids aren't friendly to certain plastics and rubbers. Using these in a pump that isn't designed for them will lead to leaking seals and damaged components. Always follow the manufacturer's guidelines. Check the hydraulic fluid's technical data sheet if you're uncertain.

1.5.2 Gear Pumps

Gear pumps move hydraulic fluid from the inlet to the outlet with two gears. The driver rotates one gear, which drives the other. The gears trap the fluid between their teeth and the pump housing, pushing it through the pump. Gear pumps come in two styles.

External gear pumps have two identical gears turning side by side (*Figure 28*). As they rotate, their teeth come together (mesh) on one side and move apart (unmesh) on the opposite side. The pump's inlet is on the side where the teeth unmesh. The outlet is on the side where they mesh.

When the teeth unmesh, they create a bigger space, so the pressure within it drops. Hydraulic fluid rushes through the inlet to fill the space. The gears continue rotating, pushing the fluid towards the outlet. As the fluid approaches the outlet, the gears mesh, pressurizing the fluid and squirting it through the outlet.

Internal gear pumps have one gear rotating inside another one (*Figure 29*). The driver turns the inner gear, which drives the outer one. Like the external gear pump, the gear teeth mesh and unmesh at opposite sides. When they unmesh, fluid rushes through the inlet and travels to the opposite side. As they mesh, the increasing pressure ejects the fluid through the outlet. Internal gear pumps have a special arc-shaped seal along one side to keep the fluid moving in the right direction.

1.5.3 Lobe and Screw Pumps

Lobe pumps work like external gear pumps. They move hydraulic fluid with a pair of lobed rotors (*Figure 30*). The rotors don't touch, although they come very close together. Gears turn them in opposite directions and keep them synchronized. As the rotors turn, the lobes move apart on the inlet side. Fluid rushes into the space. The lobes carry it to the outlet side. When the lobes come together, they reduce the available space, forcing the fluid through the outlet.

Screw pumps move hydraulic fluid with three screw-shaped rotors (*Figure 31*). The driver turns the central screw, which drives the outer screws. Fluid enters at one end, where the rotating screw threads move apart to create a low-pressure space. The threads carry the fluid to the other end. Here, the threads move together, creating a high-pressure space that ejects the fluid through the outlet.

Gear and lobe pumps produce a pulsating flow that can churn the hydraulic fluid. Screw pumps, by contrast, produce a very smooth flow with little turbulence.

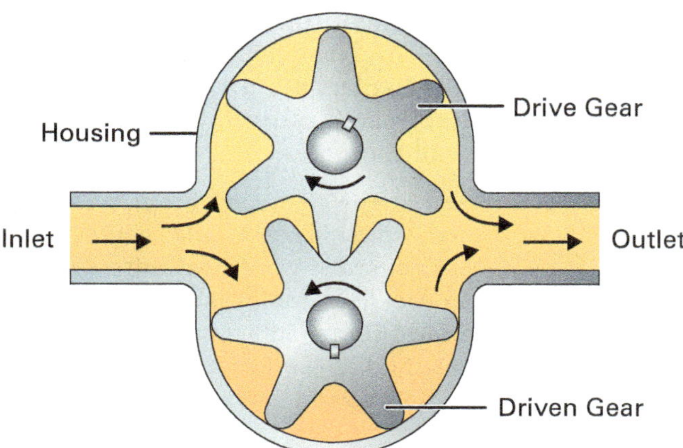

Figure 28 External gear pump.

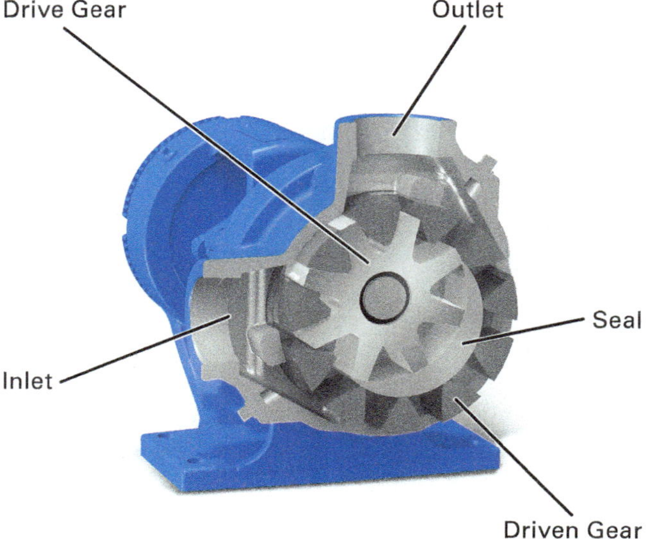

Figure 29 Internal gear pump.

Figure 30 Lobe pump.

Figure 31 Screw pump.

1.5.4 Vane Pumps

The *unbalanced vane pump* has an off-center rotor that spins inside the pump housing (*Figure 32*). Vanes slide in and out of the rotor slots, staying in contact with the housing. This action maintains a seal. The inlet and outlet openings are on opposite sides. The gaps between the rotor and the housing are very narrow at these locations.

As the vanes rotate past the inlet, they extend, opening the space and reducing the pressure. Fluid rushes into the space. The vanes sweep the fluid towards the outlet side. As they approach the outlet, they retract, making the space smaller. The increased pressure ejects the fluid through the outlet.

A *balanced vane pump* works the same way but has a few differences. The rotor is centered within an elliptical housing. The pump has two inlets and two outlets (*Figure 33*). Since the housing is elliptical, the pump creates two low-pressure zones at opposite corners as it rotates. Similarly, it creates two high-pressure zones at the other corners. This design balances the forces on the pump shaft and its bearings. It also gives a smoother fluid flow.

1.5.5 Piston Pumps

Piston pumps move hydraulic fluid with pistons that slide back and forth in cylinders. As the piston retracts, it creates a low-pressure space in the cylinder. Fluid rushes in through the inlet. The piston then reverses direction, forcing the fluid through the outlet.

Hydraulic pumps usually have several pistons driven by a common shaft. *Radial piston pumps* arrange the piston/cylinder pairs perpendicularly around the shaft. *Axial piston pumps* arrange the piston/cylinder pairs around the shaft and parallel to it.

A *rotating shaft radial piston pump* has its cylinders in the pump housing. The piston rods protrude into the open center. Rod springs extend the pistons, causing fluid to enter the cylinders. As the shaft turns, it rotates an off-center circular cam. The cam sequentially pushes the piston rods down into their cylinders, ejecting the fluid. As the cam rotates away, the rod springs retract the pistons, refilling the cylinders (*Figure 34*). Valves in each cylinder keep the fluid flowing in the correct direction.

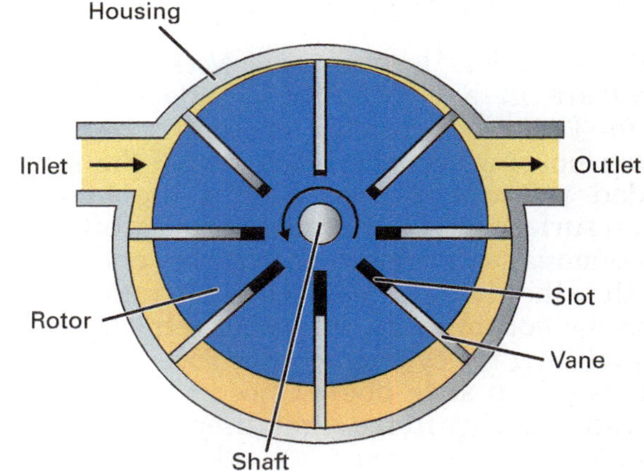

Figure 32 Unbalanced vane pump.

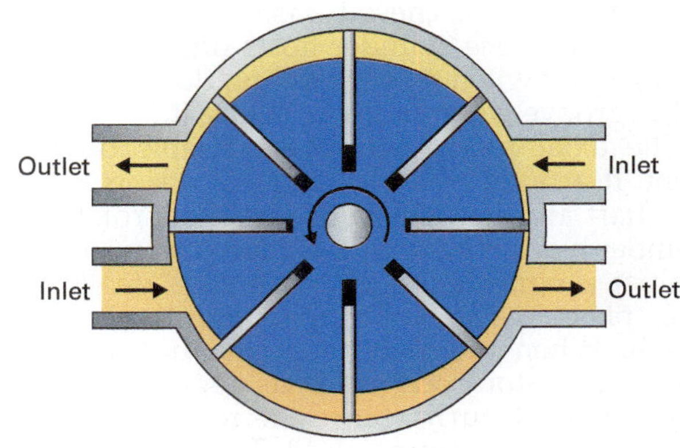

Figure 33 Balanced vane pump.

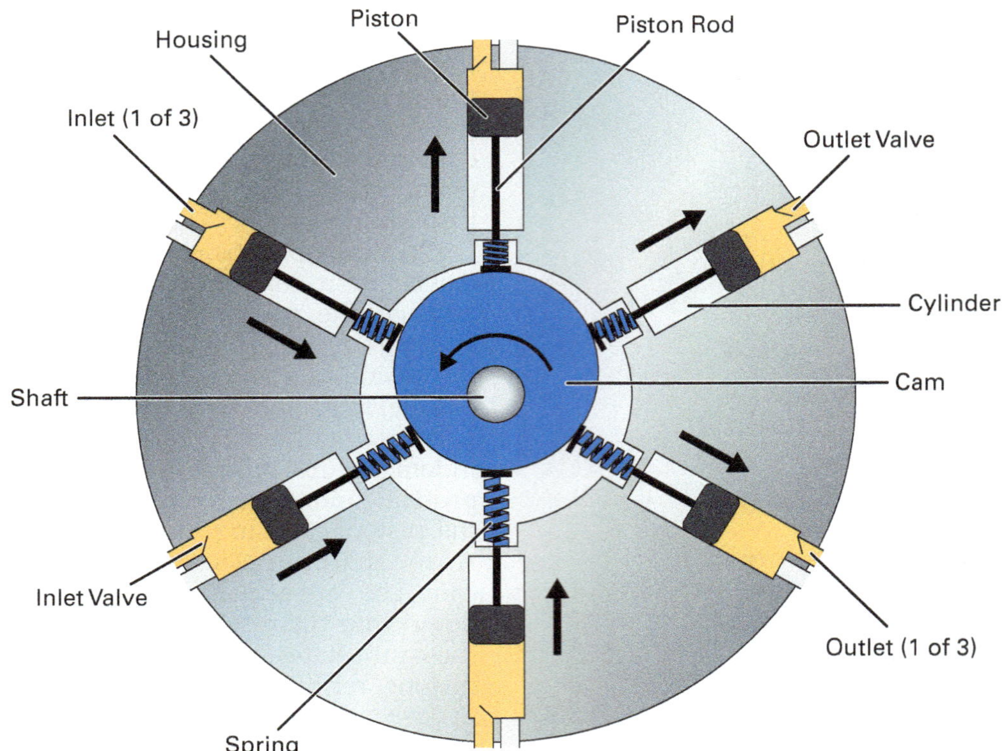

Figure 34 Rotating shaft radial piston pump.

The cylinders in a *rotating block radial piston pump* are in a circular block attached to the shaft. The block rotates off-center inside the pump housing. As the block turns, the spring-loaded piston rods rest against the housing's inner surface. Since the block rotates off-center, it sequentially depresses the pistons one by one, ejecting the fluid. As each cylinder rotates away from the housing wall, its spring retracts the piston, refilling the cylinder (*Figure 35*).

This pump style doesn't need valves to keep the fluid flowing in the right direction. Instead, a *port plate* presses against one side of the rotating block. It has two arc-shaped grooves that connect to the pump's inlet and outlet. As the block rotates, holes connected to the cylinders align with the grooves. These transfer fluid to or from the cylinder. The cylinder holes line up with the inlet groove when they're pulling fluid in and the outlet groove when they're ejecting it.

The axial piston pump is variable displacement. It arranges the cylinders in a ring around the shaft and parallel to it. The shaft rotates the cylinder block. The spring-loaded piston rods rest against a nonrotating plate called a *swash plate*. This plate has an adjustment mechanism that tilts it. When the plate is perpendicular to the shaft, the piston rods just brush against it as the cylinder block turns. Since the rods don't move, the pistons don't pump fluid. This is the pump's "idle" position.

Tilting the swash plate causes the pump to start operating. As the cylinder block turns, the piston rods sequentially push against the plate as they approach it. As they move away from it, they extend. This motion pumps fluid (*Figure 36*). Axial piston pumps link the cylinders to the pump's inlet and outlet with a port plate. It works like the ones in rotating block radial pumps.

Tilting the swash plate to a sharper angle causes the pistons to have longer strokes. Longer strokes give greater displacement, so the pump moves more fluid per minute. This quality gives these pumps their variable-displacement capabilities.

> **NOTE**
>
> Sophisticated hydraulic power units may include an electronic or hydraulic control system that automatically adjusts the swash plate's angle to maintain optimal output.

1.6.0 Hydraulic System Components

When the hydraulic fluid leaves the power unit, it moves into the hydraulic system. Pipes, tubes, and hoses carry it to different devices. Broadly, these devices fall into two categories: *control* and *actuator*. Control devices manage the fluid flow. They start, stop, adjust, or route it. Actuator devices convert the fluid's energy into mechanical motion.

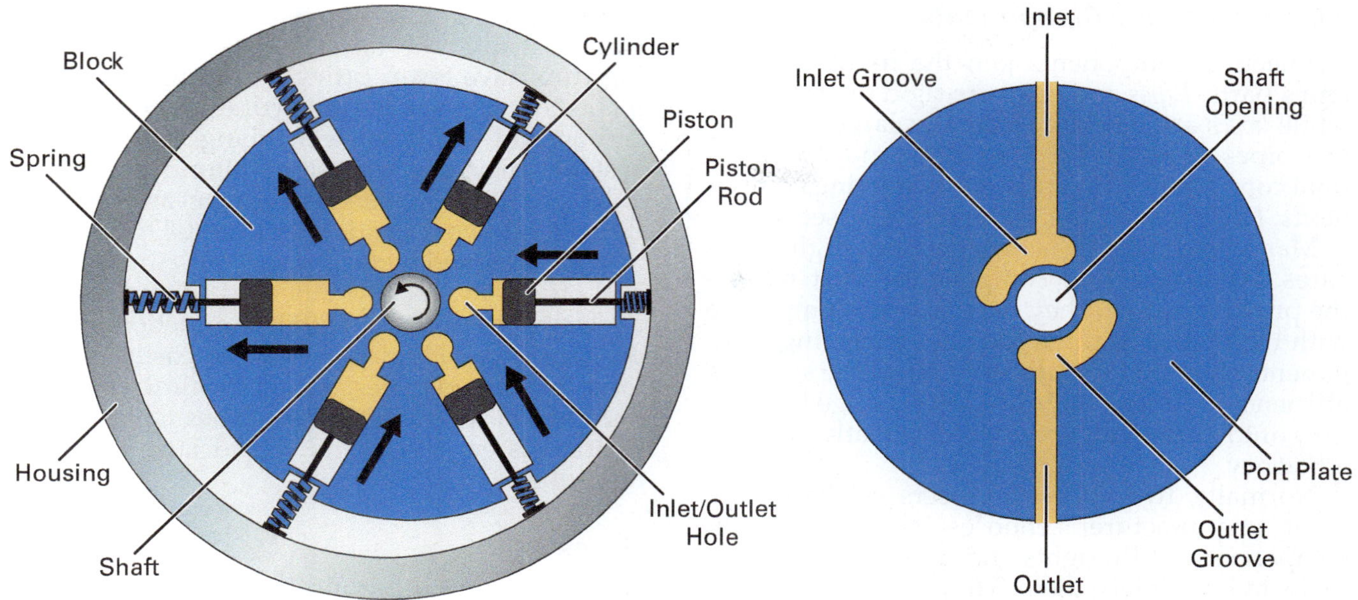

Figure 35 Rotating block radial piston pump.

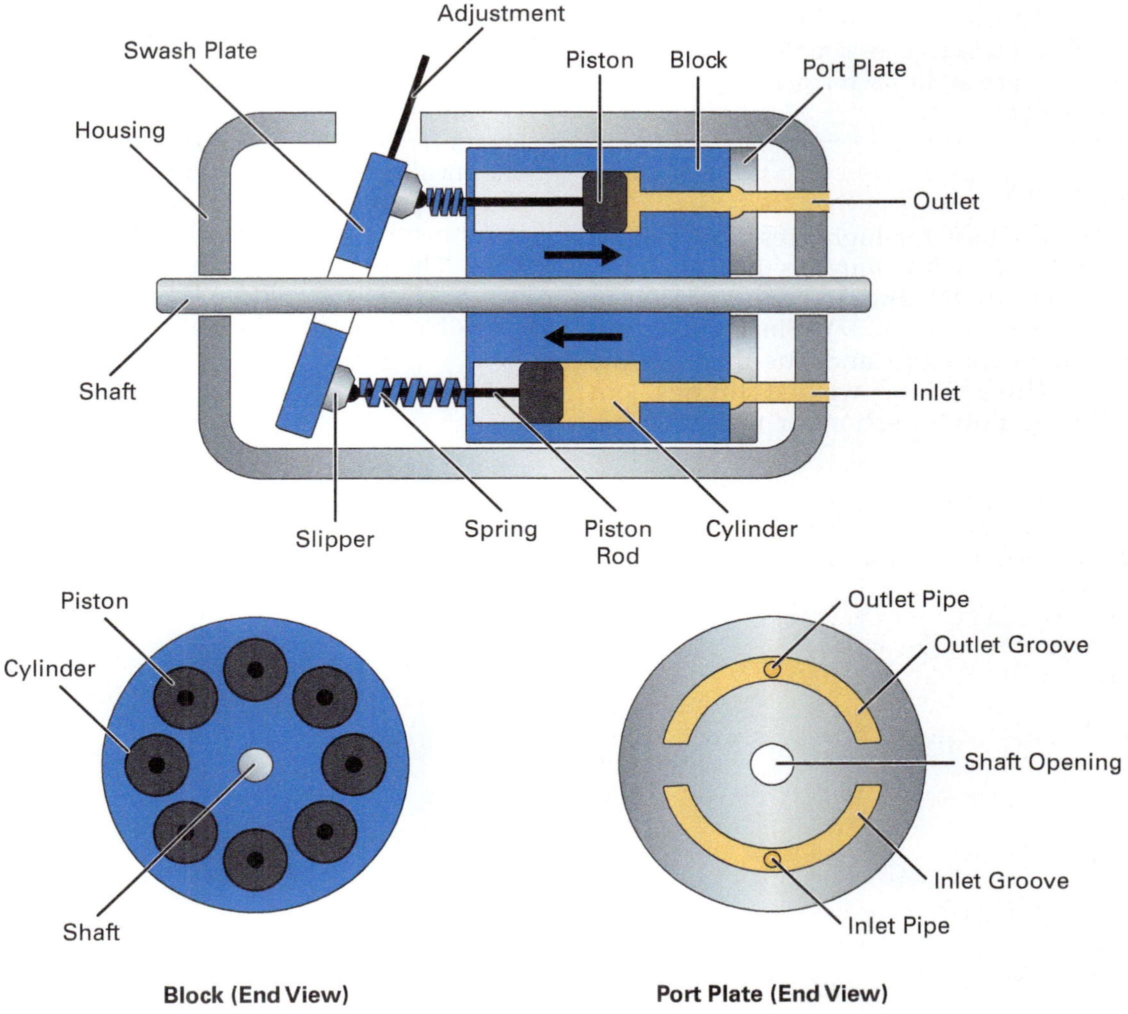

Figure 36 Axial piston pump.

1.6.1 Connecting Components

Connecting components join the hydraulic system's parts. *Pipes* and *tubes* are rigid or semirigid, while *hoses* are flexible. Generally, larger systems use pipes or tubes for long runs and hoses for final connections. Hoses also link moving components. *Fittings* join pipe, tube, and hose sections.

Many hydraulic systems contain high pressures. All connecting components must handle the pressure safely. They must also be compatible with the hydraulic fluid. Ideally, connecting components shouldn't significantly affect the system's efficiency. Sudden bends or kinks change laminar flow into turbulent flow, which greatly reduces efficiency.

Normally, hydraulics engineers or the equipment manufacturer chooses the connecting components. Millwrights and industrial mechanics install or replace them. They must understand these components and be able to select appropriate replacements.

> **NOTE**
>
> In many facilities, pipefitters rather than millwrights manage pipes and tubes. Millwrights and industrial mechanics install and maintain hoses.

Pipes and Tubes

Steel pipe works best for high-pressure systems with long runs. *Schedule numbers* identify pipe sizes. Schedules 40, 80, and 160 are common in hydraulic systems (*Figure 37*). Since pipes are rigid, pipefitters measure and cut them to the correct size. Threaded or welded fittings join sections, change flow direction, or transition between pipe sizes.

Tubing is semirigid, so pipefitters bend it to the correct shape with special tools. Generally, tubing runs have fewer fittings, making them easier to install. High-pressure hydraulic systems use carbon and stainless steel tubing. Low-pressure systems may use copper or aluminum tubing. Tubing is sized by thickness (gauge) and its inside diameter (ID) or outside diameter (OD).

Well-designed hydraulic systems run smoothly and efficiently. Ideally, pipe and tubing runs are as straight as possible, with few direction changes or transitions. Fluid moves more easily through large pipes and tubes, which minimizes energy loss. ASTM International publishes tables to help hydraulics engineers and technicians size pipes and tubes.

Hoses

Hoses provide flexibility where it's required. They're useful for attaching components that are connected and disconnected frequently. Hoses also absorb vibration and shocks. For safety reasons, most companies buy prefabricated hoses rather than making their own. These have the right connectors installed at each end (*Figure 38*).

Manufacturers construct hoses from multiple layers (*Figure 39*). The inner layer is smooth and chemically compatible with the hydraulic fluid. The middle layers add strength and pressure resistance. They're usually woven from wire or fiber. The outer layer, made from a durable rubber, protects the middle layers. Some hoses have a flexible outer metal sheath for extra protection.

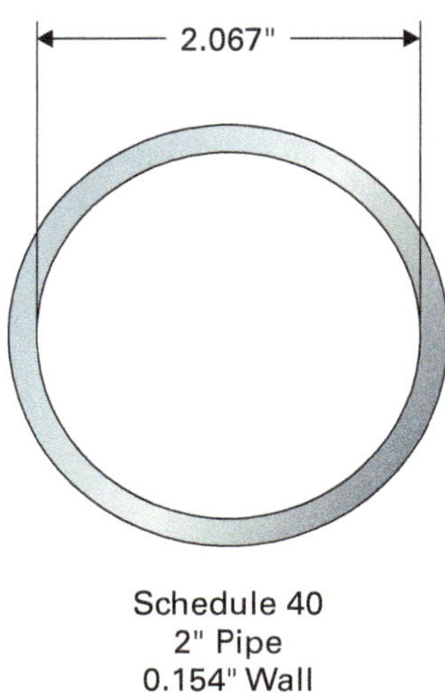

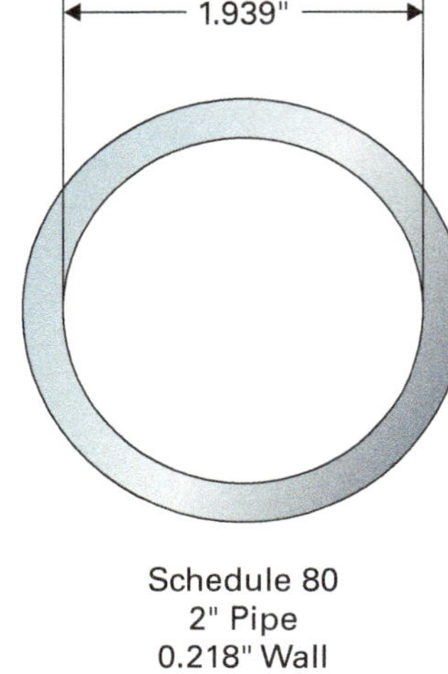

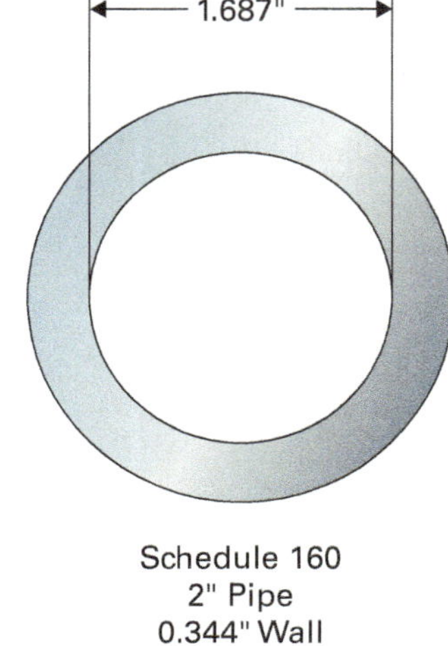

Figure 37 Steel pipe schedules.

Hoses are common failure points since they move. If they rub against other components, the hoses can wear and fail. Millwrights and industrial mechanics regularly inspect hoses and replace them if they look questionable. When replacing a hose, select one with the right pressure rating. Confirm that it's compatible with the hydraulic fluid. Also confirm that its fittings match the existing ones in type and material.

Hose manufacturers and distributors provide tables to help select and compare hoses. These include the hose's OD and ID. They also list the hose's intended working pressure and the pressure at which it will burst. Finally, most identify the smallest radius at which the hose can safely bend. *Table 2* shows a small section of a hose distributor's comparison table.

Fittings

Fittings (couplings) join pipes, tubes, hoses, and hydraulic components. They can change direction, transition to another size, or provide extra flexibility. Most fittings have male or female threads. *Figure 40* shows several common fittings.

Figure 38 Prefabricated hose.

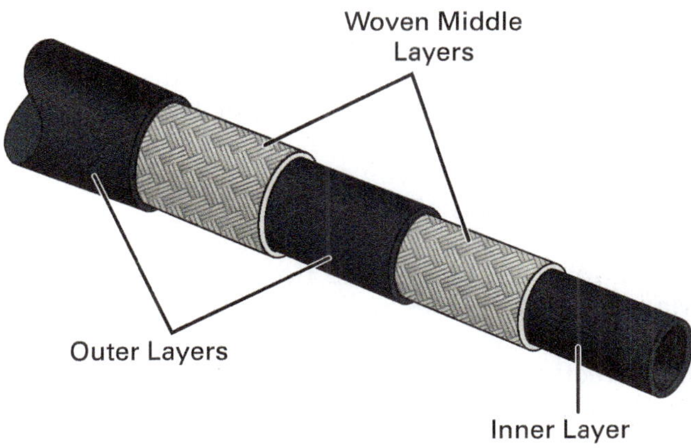

Figure 39 Hydraulic hose construction.

Hydraulic components like filters, valves, and actuators come with fittings installed. Pipes, tubes, and hoses require matching fittings. *JIC flare fittings* have cone-shaped sealing surfaces. They're very common in hydraulic systems because they seal well. They also handle high pressure and tolerate repeated connect/disconnect cycles. *Swivel fittings* provide extra flexibility for hoses. *Quick disconnect fittings* support rapid connecting and disconnecting without tools.

> **CAUTION**
>
> JIC flare fittings have sealing surfaces that form a 37-degree angle. Don't mix these with other flare fitting types. The angles won't match, so the fittings won't seal properly.

Since hydraulic systems are under significant pressure, fittings are common leak points. Properly installing and tightening them reduces this problem. Replace damaged fittings since they won't seal properly. Quick disconnects start to leak as they age, so plan to replace them periodically.

> **CAUTION**
>
> Never use pipe tape or pipe dope on fitting threads unless the manufacturer specifically recommends it. Only use products rated for hydraulic applications.

1.6.2 Valves

As control devices, valves manage the hydraulic fluid. Workers operate *manual valves* with a handle or wheel. *Automatic valves* use electrical, pneumatic, or hydraulic mechanisms to open and close. Hydraulic valves fall into the following major categories.

Flow Control Valves

These valves start, stop, and adjust the fluid flow. Some valves offer little or no control between the fully open and fully closed positions. Essentially, they're On/Off control devices. *Ball valves* fit this description (*Figure 41*). The rotating ball either opens or blocks the flow path completely. For this reason, ball valves make good shutoff valves.

Table 2 Hose Specifications

OD (in)	Nom. ID (in)	Working (psi)	Bursting (psi)	Min. Bend Radius (in)
0.57	¼	5,800	23,200	2
0.74	⅜	4,780	19,120	2.5
0.86	½	3,980	15,920	3.5

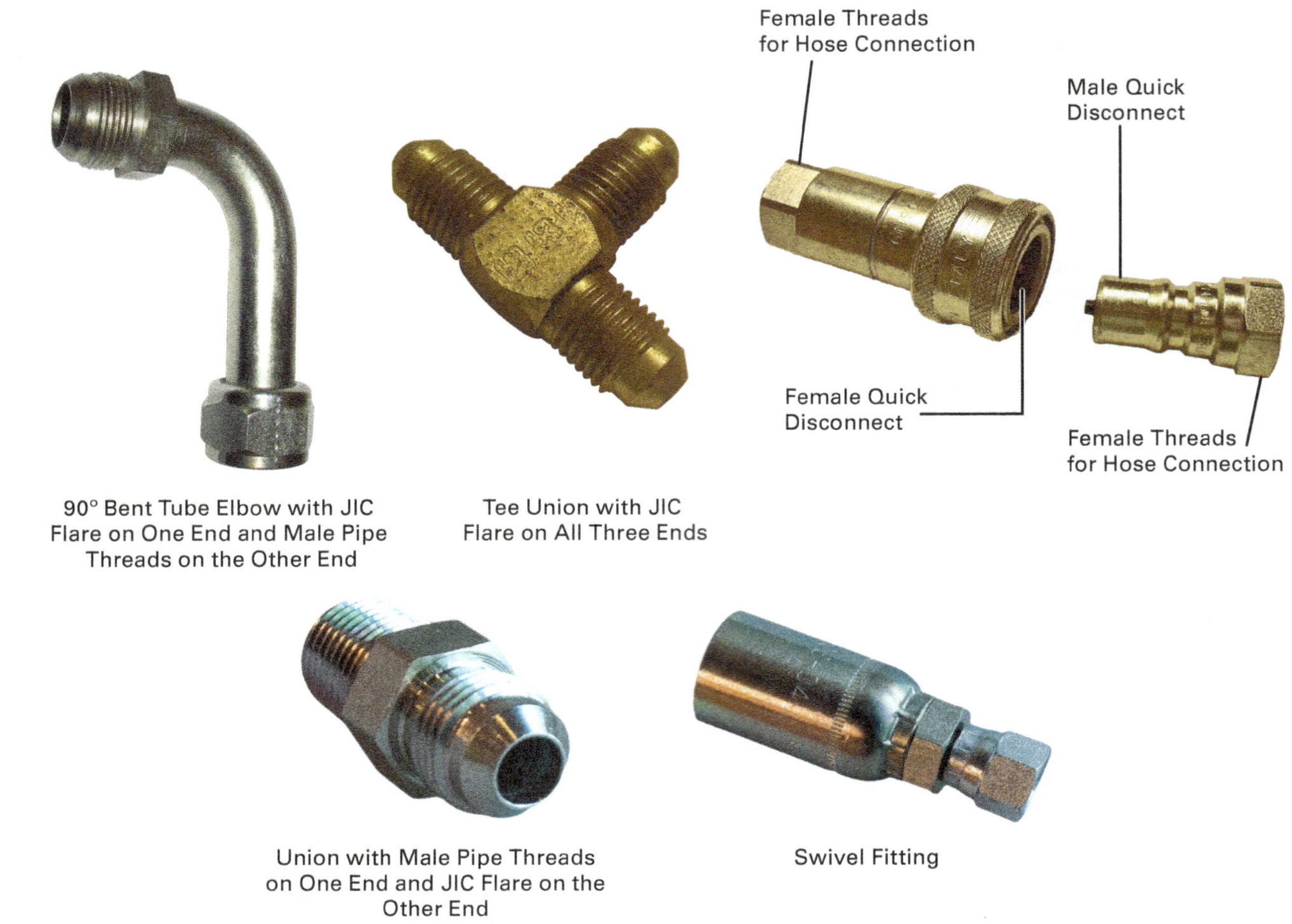

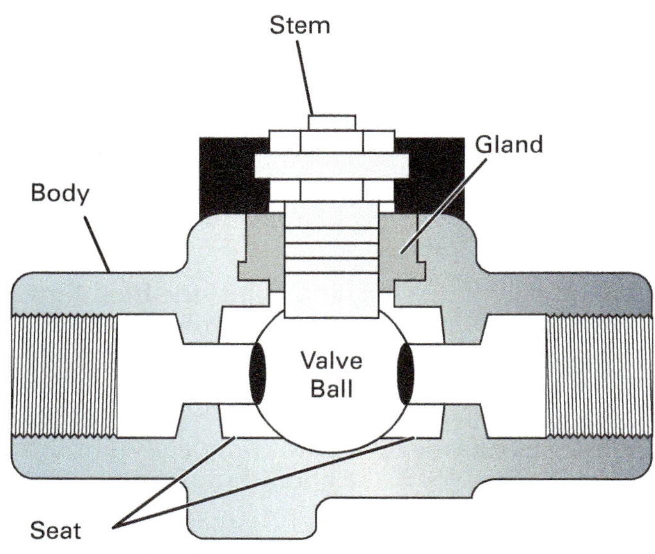

Figure 40 Hydraulic fittings.

Figure 41 Ball valve.

Some applications need to control how fast an actuator operates. These use *throttle valves* to restrict the fluid flow. A *meter-in* throttle valve regulates how fast the fluid enters the actuator. A *meter-out* throttle valve regulates how fast the fluid exits the actuator.

Simple throttle valves have an adjustable restriction that blocks the flow path (*Figure 42*). Many throttle valves include an internal bypass valve that allows unrestricted flow in the opposite direction. Sophisticated throttle valves have a mechanism that automatically tweaks the restriction to maintain consistent flow even when the load changes. These are *pressure-compensated flow valves*.

Check Valves

As you learned earlier in this module, check valves are one-way devices. They prevent fluid from flowing in the wrong direction. Most hydraulic systems have check valves at locations where *backflow* could cause problems. Check valves can also function as *bypass valves*.

NCCER – *Millwright*

Pressure Control Valves

These valves open or close based on the pressure level from a particular part of the system. Pressure relief valves are a simple example. As you learned, they protect the system from excessive pressure by opening and releasing fluid.

Closely related to pressure relief valves are *pressure reducing valves*. These lower the hydraulic system pressure to the value required by a component or machine. Many are adjustable. They operate like pressure relief valves, draining back to the reservoir to reduce pressure.

More complex pressure control valves help hydraulic systems perform sophisticated tasks. A *counterbalance valve* provides a precisely controlled pressure release from an actuator's outlet. Counterbalance valves are common on hydraulic lifts and hoists. They keep the load from falling or gradually sinking. They also help lower the load smoothly and safely when it's time to release the pressure.

Hydraulic fluid can flow through the valve in either direction. In one direction, it flows freely and without restriction (bypass mode). The valve blocks the flow in the other direction unless it senses a pressure above its setpoint (pressure control mode). When this happens, the valve opens and allows fluid to pass through. If the sensed pressure drops below the setpoint, the valve closes, stopping the flow.

A *sequence valve* works like a counterbalance valve, but it's used differently. It prevents fluid from entering an actuator's inlet until the sensed pressure rises above the setpoint. The valve then opens and allows the fluid to pass through.

Applications with multiple actuators use sequence valves to ensure that the actuators operate in the correct order. Adjusting the valves' setpoints to different pressures causes the actuators to activate sequentially. Actuators whose valves have low pressure setpoints activate first. Those with higher setpoints activate later.

Directional Control Valves

These valves, commonly called DCVs, control the system's behavior by routing the fluid flow through one of several possible paths. For example, a hydraulic actuator might spin clockwise or counterclockwise depending on the fluid flow. A DCV routes the hydraulic fluid correctly.

DCVs come in many styles and configurations. Some have manual controls, such as buttons or levers (*Figure 43*). Others respond to electrical, pneumatic, or hydraulic control signals.

> **NOTE**
>
> Counterbalance valves, sequence valves, and DCVs are complex devices. NCCER Module 15410, *Troubleshooting and Repairing Hydraulic Equipment*, discusses their internal operation and applications in more detail.

1.6.3 Hydraulic Cylinders

A hydraulic **cylinder** is a linear actuator. It produces straight-line motion. Hydraulic fluid pushes a piston that slides inside the cylinder. The piston rod transfers the motion to the application. Hydraulic cylinders drive lifts, hoists, presses, and mobile construction equipment like excavators.

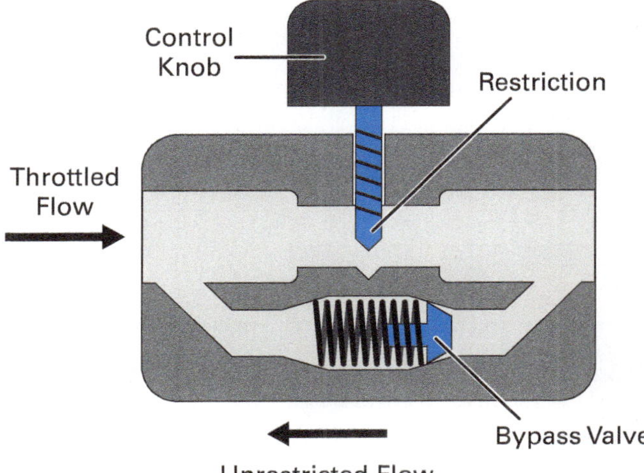

Figure 42 Simple throttle valve.

Figure 43 Directional control valves.

Hydraulics craftworkers refer to the cylinder's closed side as the *cap end*. The side through which the rod protrudes is the *rod end*. Both the piston and the rod end have seals to prevent hydraulic fluid from escaping. Fluid enters and exits the cylinder through *ports*. The number of ports and their locations depend on the cylinder type. Some cylinders also have an air vent. *Figure 44* shows an example hydraulic cylinder.

Hydraulic cylinders are either *single-acting* or *double-acting*. Single-acting cylinders have one combined inlet/outlet port. Fluid entering the port pushes the piston, generating the power stroke. The return stroke isn't hydraulically powered. A spring or gravity returns the piston to the original position. During the return stroke, the hydraulic fluid drains through the inlet/outlet port. The cylinder's unpressurized side has a vent, so air can enter and exit freely. *Figure 44* is a single-acting cylinder that uses gravity for its return stroke. Hydraulic presses often contain single-acting cylinders.

Double-acting cylinders have two inlet/outlet ports. Fluid can push the piston in either direction, so each stroke is hydraulically powered. One port receives pressurized fluid, while the other drains fluid. The role each port plays determines the direction that the piston moves. *Figure 45* shows a double-acting cylinder.

DCVs manage hydraulic cylinders (*Figure 46*). With single-acting cylinders, they route fluid to the single port for the power stroke. For the return stroke, they route fluid back to the reservoir. As the fluid drains, the spring or gravity moves the piston to the rest position. With double-acting cylinders, the valve applies fluid to one port and drains the other to the reservoir. It reverses the connections to move the piston in the other direction.

Some cylinders have two pistons that can move together or separately (*Figure 47*). These cylinders, called *dual-piston cylinders*, have three inlet/outlet ports. Controlling the fluid flow through each determines which pistons move. The fluid enters the middle of the cylinder and pushes on both pistons. If the end inlet/outlet ports are open, both pistons move. If either inlet/outlet is closed, the piston at that end doesn't move.

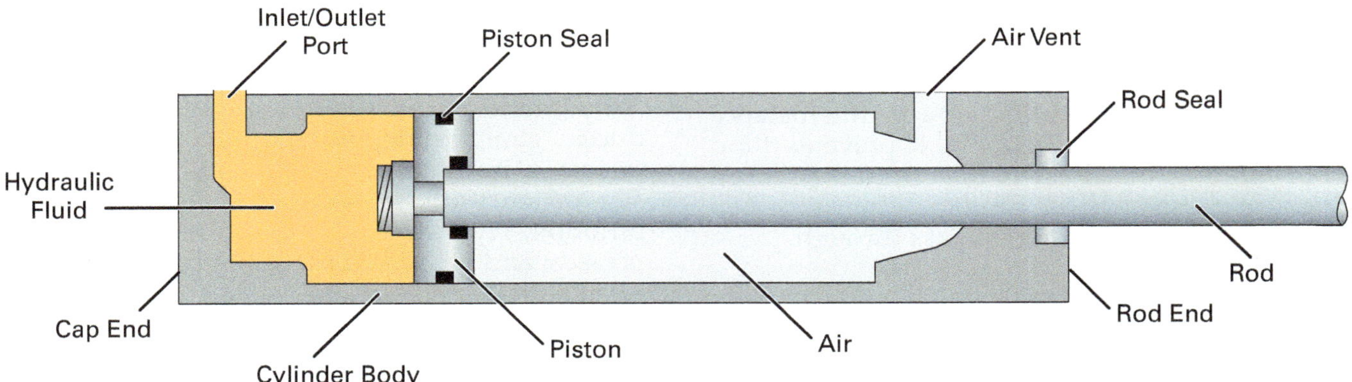

Figure 44 Hydraulic cylinder (single-acting).

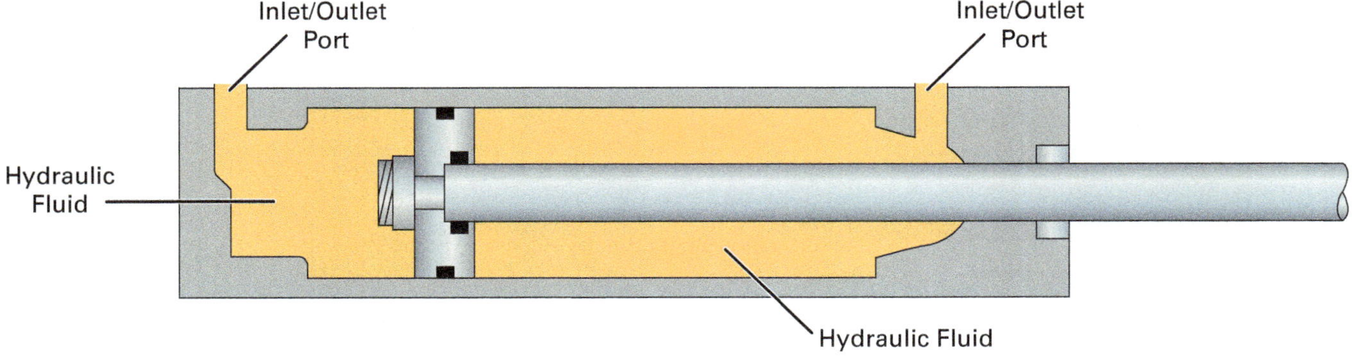

Figure 45 Hydraulic cylinder (double-acting).

NCCER – *Millwright*

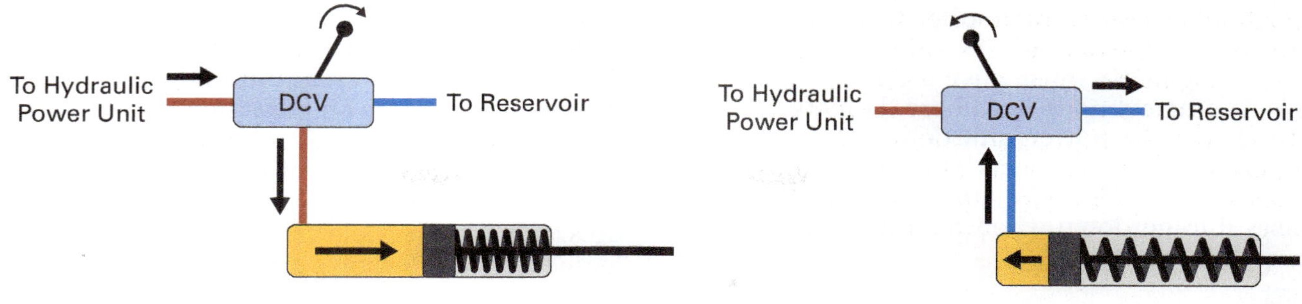

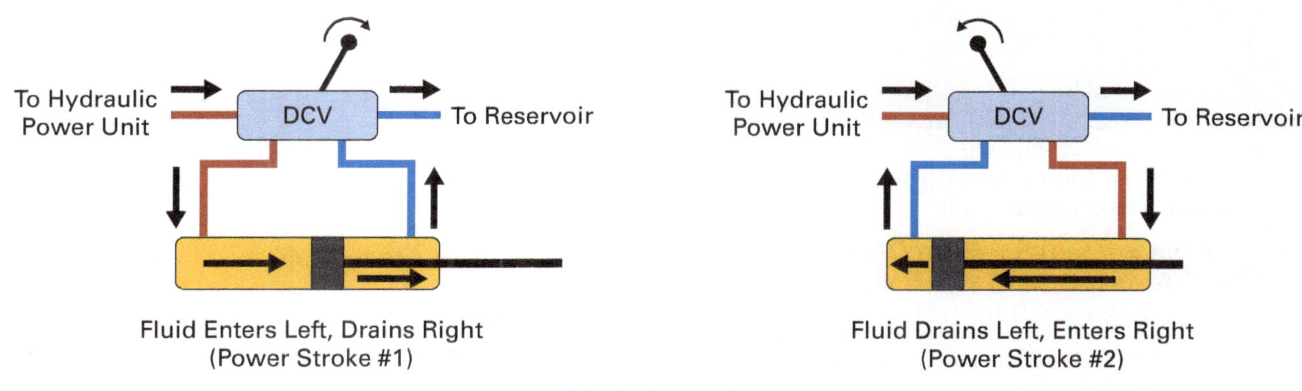

Figure 46 Controlling hydraulic cylinders.

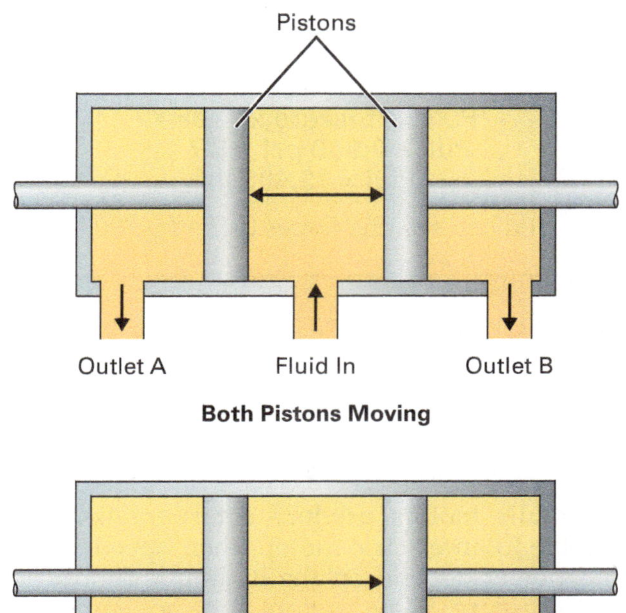

Figure 47 Dual-piston cylinder.

1.6.4 Hydraulic Cylinder Specifications and Calculations

Manufacturers rate hydraulic cylinders by their maximum force and stroke distance. In the United States, the most common force unit is the pound-force (lbf). Stroke distance is usually specified in inches. A cylinder with an 8" stroke at 9,400 lbf moves 8" when fluid enters the cylinder. It can exert up to 9,400 lbf on the load. Metric-speaking manufacturers rate their cylinders in newtons (N) and millimeters. A force of 1 N is about 0.225 lbf.

A cylinder's specifications also include the bore diameter, the rod diameter, and the hydraulic fluid volume. In the United States, diameters are specified in inches. Fluid volume may be in cubic inches (in^3), quarts, or gallons. Metric-speaking manufacturers use millimeters for diameters. Fluid volume may be in cubic centimeters (cm^3) or liters. Hydraulics engineers and craftworkers use these specifications to calculate basic facts about a hydraulic system.

The force that a hydraulic cylinder delivers depends on the load. For example, the hydraulic hoist in *Figure 48* must raise a 3,250 lb load. Its single-acting cylinder has a bore diameter of 2.5". If the hydraulic power unit delivers fluid at the proper pressure, the load will rise when fluid enters the cylinder. Gravity acting on the load causes it to go down when the fluid drains from the cylinder.

To determine the required pressure, first calculate the piston's surface area:

$$\text{Area} = \pi \times (0.5 \times \text{Bore Diameter})^2$$
$$\text{Area} = 3.1416 \times (0.5 \times 2.5")^2$$
$$\text{Area} = 4.9 \text{ in}^2 \text{ (rounded)}$$

The fluid pressure acting over this area must generate 3,250 lbf to raise the load. The following calculation determines the necessary pressure:

$$\text{Pressure} = \text{Weight} \div \text{Area}$$
$$\text{Pressure} = 3,250 \text{ lbf} \div 4.9 \text{ in}^2$$
$$\text{Pressure} = 664 \text{ psi (rounded up)}$$

Provided the hydraulic power unit can develop at least 664 psi, it will raise the load. How fast the load moves depends on the cylinder's volume and the power unit's flow rate. If the cylinder has a volume of 3 quarts (0.75 gallons) and the power unit has a flow rate of 2 gpm, it's simple to calculate the rise time:

$$\text{Time} = (\text{Volume} \div \text{Flow Rate}) \times 60 \text{ sec/min}$$
$$\text{Time} = (0.75 \text{ gal} \div 2 \text{ gpm}) \times 60 \text{ sec/min}$$
$$\text{Time} = 23 \text{ sec (rounded)}$$

Double-acting cylinder specifications always have *two* maximum force values. One will be significantly smaller than the other. They're sometimes called the *push force* and the *pull force*. Why are they different? It has to do with the piston rod.

The force that the piston exerts on the load depends on the hydraulic fluid's pressure and the piston's surface area. With single-acting cylinders, the fluid acts on the piston's entire surface area. With double-acting cylinders, however, the fluid acts on two different surfaces. The rod side has a smaller surface area because the rod takes up space. Some simple calculations show the difference. *Figure 49* shows a double-acting cylinder. It has a 3" bore and a 0.75" rod diameter. The hydraulic power unit delivers fluid at 2,000 psi.

Calculate the piston's surface area on the non-rod end:

$$\text{Area \#1} = \pi \times (0.5 \times \text{Bore Diameter})^2$$
$$\text{Area \#1} = 3.1416 \times (0.5 \times 3")^2$$
$$\text{Area \#1} = 7.1 \text{ in}^2 \text{ (rounded)}$$

Calculate the rod's area:

$$\text{Rod Area} = \pi \times (0.5 \times \text{Rod Diameter})^2$$
$$\text{Rod Area} = 3.1416 \times (0.5 \times 0.75")^2$$
$$\text{Rod Area} = 0.44 \text{ in}^2 \text{ (rounded)}$$

Calculate the piston's surface area on the rod end:

$$\text{Area \#2} = \text{Area \#1} - \text{Rod Area}$$
$$\text{Area \#2} = 7.1 \text{ in}^2 - 0.44 \text{ in}^2$$
$$\text{Area \#2} = 6.7 \text{ in}^2 \text{ (rounded)}$$

Calculate the push and pull forces:

$$\text{Push} = \text{Pressure} \times \text{Area \#1}$$
$$\text{Push} = 2,000 \text{ psi} \times 7.1 \text{ in}^2$$
$$\text{Push} = 14,200 \text{ lbf}$$
$$\text{Pull} = \text{Pressure} \times \text{Area \#2}$$
$$\text{Pull} = 2,000 \text{ psi} \times 6.7 \text{ in}^2$$
$$\text{Pull} = 13,400 \text{ lbf}$$

As you can see, the forces differ by 800 lbf.

1.6.5 Hydraulic Motors

Hydraulic motors produce rotary motion comparable to an electric motor. Their speed, torque, and power depend on the hydraulic fluid's flow and pressure. Some motors have adjustments to control their behavior. Others use valves to modify the fluid's flow and pressure. The hydraulic power unit's output affects the motor too, so adjusting the pump can control the motor.

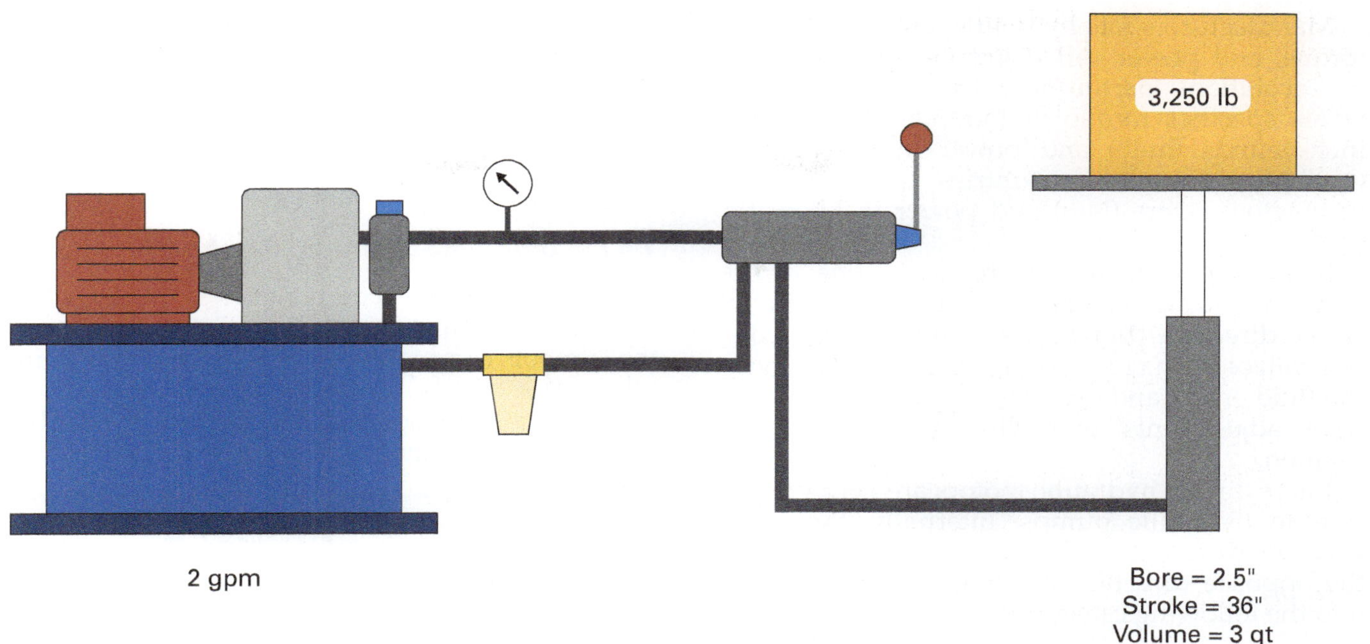

Figure 48 Hydraulic hoist.

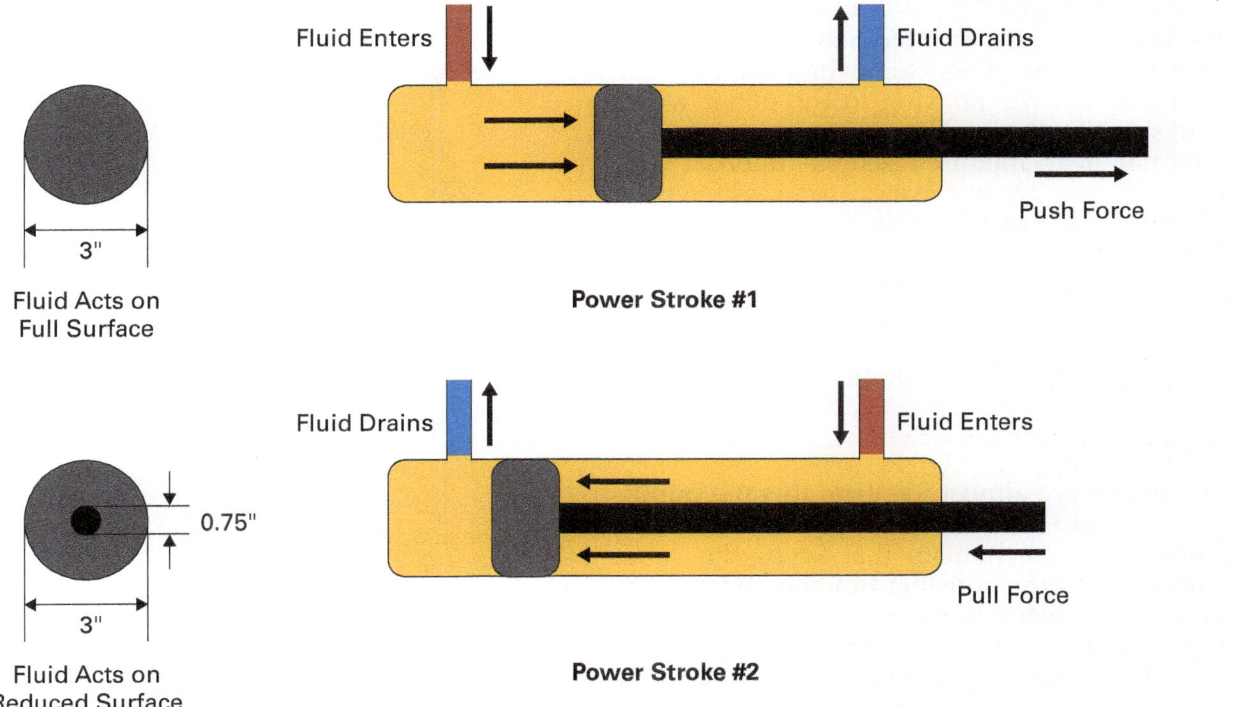

Figure 49 Push vs. pull forces.

Manufacturers rate hydraulic motors by speed, torque, and power. All countries specify speed in revolutions per minute (rpm). The United States specifies torque in foot-pounds (ft-lb) or inch-pounds (in-lb) and power in horsepower (hp). Metric-speaking countries specify torque in newton-meters (Nm) and power in kilowatts (kW).

Some hydraulic motors rotate in one direction only (unidirectional). Others can spin in either direction (bidirectional). Directional control valves manage rotation by controlling how the fluid enters and exits the motor. Some motors have adjustments that directly control their rotation.

Interestingly, hydraulic motors are nearly identical to hydraulic pumps. Internally, there are very few differences. The fluid, however, flows in the opposite direction. Hydraulic motors divide into the following categories.

Gear Motors

External gear motors are identical to external gear pumps (*Figure 28*). Hydraulic fluid entering at the inlet forces the gear teeth to unmesh, which rotates them. The gears carry the fluid between their teeth and the housing to the outlet where the meshing teeth expel it.

Internal gear motors resemble internal gear pumps (*Figure 29*) but have a few differences. The inner gear has one tooth less than the outer (*Figure 50*). Fluid enters where the teeth are close together. The pressure forces them apart, turning the gears and the shaft. The teeth carry the fluid to the opposite side. As they move closer together, they expel the fluid through the motor outlet.

Vane Motors

Vane motors are almost identical to vane pumps (*Figure 32* and *Figure 33*). The only important difference is the mechanism that keeps the vanes in contact with the housing. In vane pumps, centrifugal force extends them as the driver spins the pump shaft. In many vane motors, springs behind the vanes extend them. The spring force keeps them in contact with the housing. Some vane motors use hydraulic fluid pressure to extend the vanes.

Piston Motors

Hydraulic piston motors are internally identical to their piston pump counterparts. They come in both radial and axial versions (*Figure 34*, *Figure 35*, and *Figure 36*). The axial version is especially useful since the tilting swash plate directly controls the motor's behavior. When the swash plate is perpendicular to the shaft, the motor doesn't spin. Tilting the swash plate causes the shaft to turn. Tilting it in the opposite direction reverses the motor's direction (*Figure 51*).

1.6.6 Common Schematic Symbols

Hydraulic system component symbols also resemble pneumatic symbols. *Figure 52* shows the symbols commonly used in hydraulic system schematics. It also includes an example schematic. Since the schematic also contains hydraulic power unit components, refer to *Figure 26* as well.

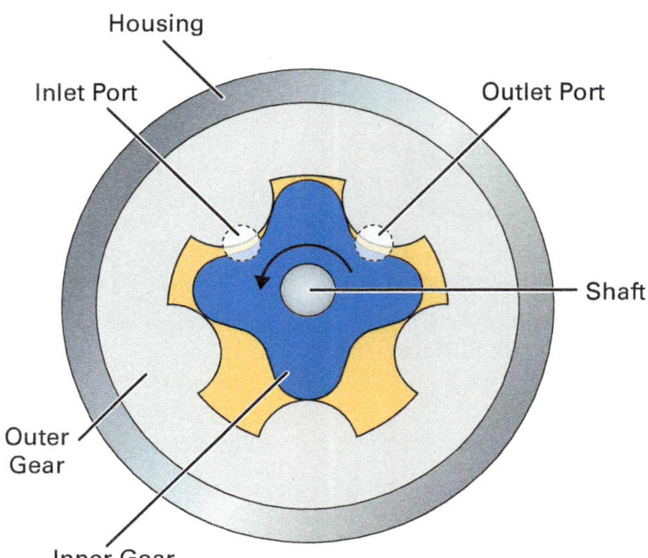

Figure 50 Internal gear motor.

Figure 51 Axial piston motor.

(A) System Symbols

(B) System Schematic

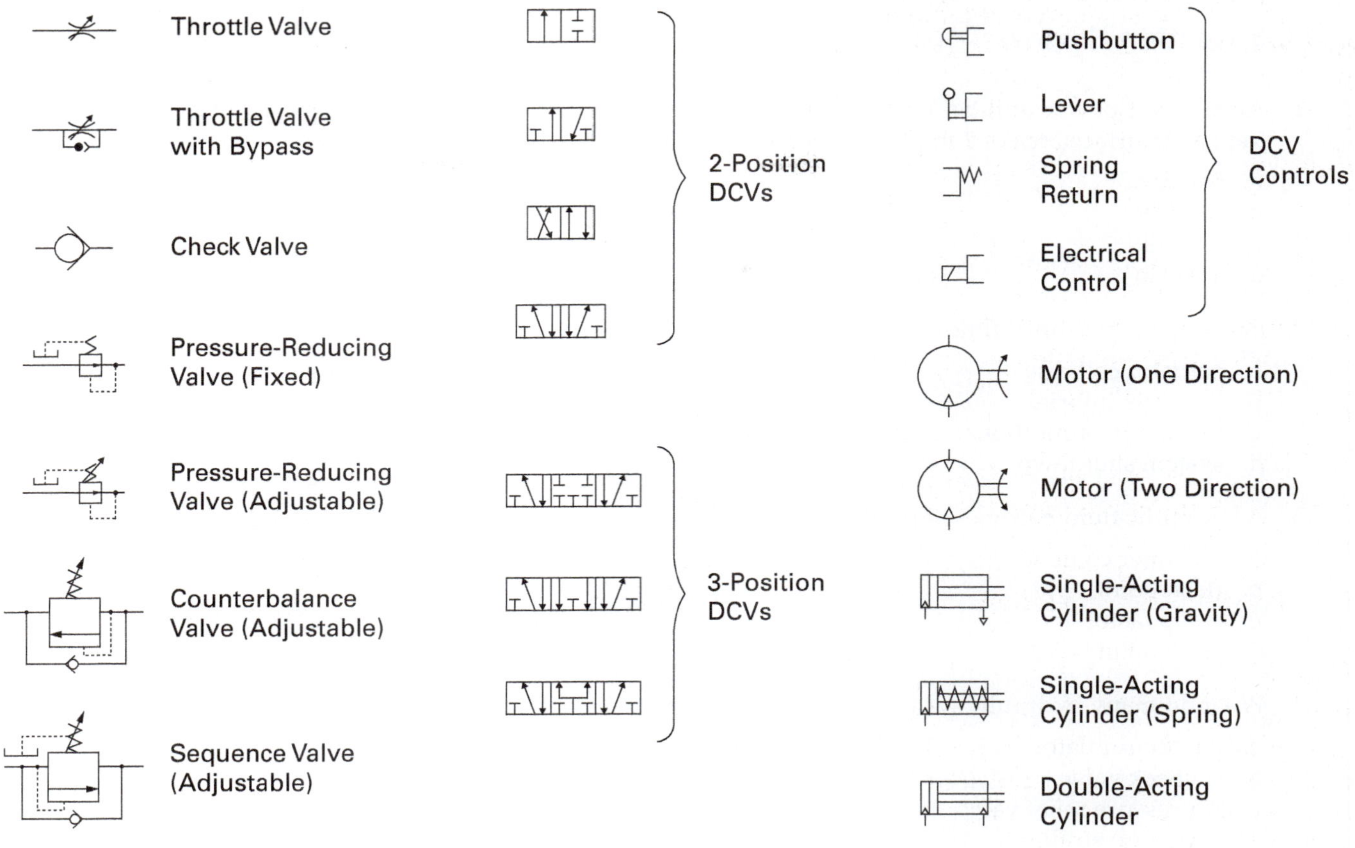

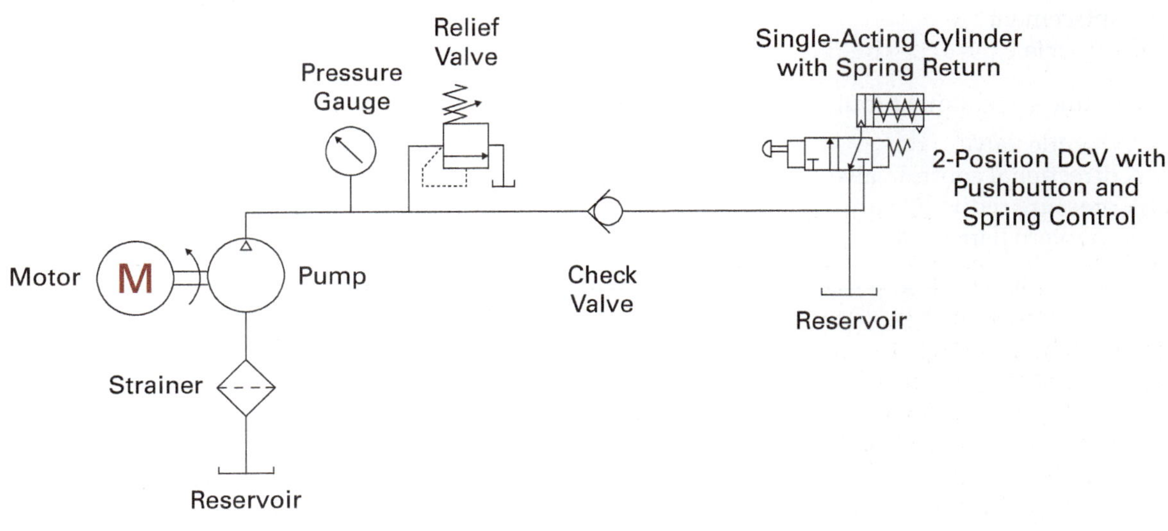

Figure 52 Hydraulic symbols and example schematic.

1. A hydraulic power unit delivers fluid to a hoist's cylinder at a pressure of 1,000 psi. If the cylinder's piston has a surface area of 2 in^2, how much weight can the hoist lift?

    a. 500 lb
    b. 1,000 lb
    c. 2,000 lb
    d. 4,000 lb

2. Pressurized hydraulic fluid escaping from a pinhole leak can cause _____.

    a. actuator collapse
    b. injection injuries
    c. tension pneumothorax
    d. system shutdown

3. A hydraulic fluid becomes very thick on an ordinary winter day. It probably has a high _____.

    a. oil-water content
    b. flash point
    c. creep factor
    d. pour point

4. What do many hydraulic systems include to smooth the fluid flow and prevent sudden pressure drops?

    a. An accumulator
    b. A check valve
    c. A pressure relief valve
    d. A suction strainer

5. A hydraulic pump ejects 3 in^3 of fluid for every shaft rotation. This value is its _____.

    a. capacity
    b. ejection fraction
    c. displacement
    d. duty cycle

6. A hydraulic system must route fluid to one of three actuators. Which valve could accomplish this task?

    a. A throttle valve
    b. A directional control valve
    c. A pressure reducing valve
    d. A counterbalance valve

1. Which hydraulic device converts fluid power into mechanical motion?

   a. An accumulator
   b. An actuator
   c. A hydraulic power unit
   d. A directional control valve

2. What is the *most* common hydraulic pressure unit in the United States?

   a. Pa
   b. psi
   c. bar
   d. torr

3. It's acceptable to release pressure from a hydraulic system by loosening a fitting.

   a. True
   b. False

4. A hydraulic fluid whose viscosity changes significantly as the temperature changes will have ______.

   a. a significant flammability index
   b. a high VI
   c. a low VI
   d. a minimal oxidation potential

5. A petroleum-based hydraulic fluid with a long lifespan and a wide operating temperature range is probably ______.

   a. synthetic oil
   b. mineral oil
   c. silicone oil
   d. phosphate ester

6. Many hydraulic power units run the returning hydraulic fluid through a(n) ______.

   a. sight glass
   b. pressure relief valve
   c. suction strainer
   d. inline filter

7. Which hydraulic component contains a rubber balloon pressurized with nitrogen gas?

   a. A diaphragm accumulator
   b. A piston accumulator
   c. A bladder accumulator
   d. A spring accumulator

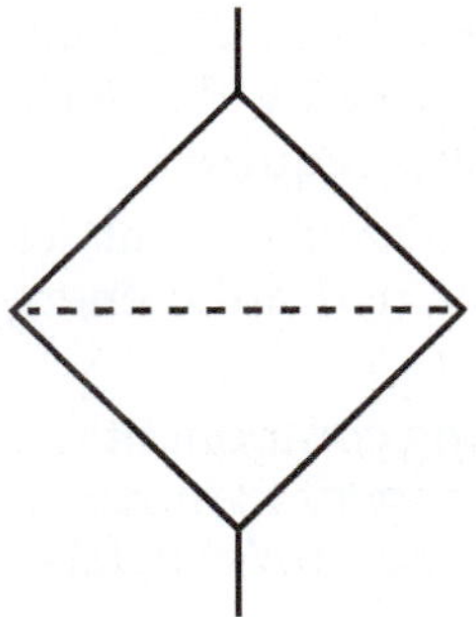

Figure RQ01

8. Which hydraulic device does the symbol shown in *Figure RQ01* represent?

   a. A gas-charged accumulator
   b. A filter or strainer
   c. A bidirectional pump
   d. A pressure relief valve

9. Which of the following hydraulic pumps contains a swash plate?

   a. A balanced vane pump
   b. A lobe pump
   c. A screw pump
   d. An axial piston pump

10. A single-acting hydraulic cylinder has a bore diameter of 1". If the cylinder must move a 1,200 lb load, what hydraulic fluid pressure will the cylinder require? Round your answer to the nearest 10 psi.

    a. 380 psi
    b. 1,200 psi
    c. 1,520 psi
    d. 2,400 psi

Trade Terms Introduced in This Module

Accumulator: A device that smooths out hydraulic fluid flow by delivering extra pressurized fluid when required.

Actuators: Devices that change electrical, pneumatic, or hydraulic energy into mechanical motion.

Cam: A rotating component whose shape causes another component to move back and forth as it rests against the cam's surface.

Cavitation: A condition in which bubbles form in a fluid and then collapse violently, creating shock waves that cause vibration and possibly damage.

Cylinder: A pneumatic or hydraulic actuator that produces linear motion from a piston sliding inside a hollow tube.

Emulsion: A mixture formed by two liquids that don't combine, with droplets of one dispersed throughout the other.

Hydraulic: Any technology that transfers energy and does mechanical work with a pressurized liquid.

Laminar flow: Fluid flow in which the fluid travels smoothly in layers that don't interfere with each other.

Lockout/tagout (LOTO): A safety process that secures an activated isolation device and identifies the person responsible for activating it.

Oxidation: The process of chemically combining with oxygen.

Pressure: The force that a fluid develops against a specific area of a container's walls or a surface.

Strainer: A filter that removes large particles from a fluid.

Turbulent flow: Fluid flow in which the fluid swirls, changes direction, and interferes with its own motion.

Viscosity: A liquid's thickness, which determines how it flows, pours, and behaves when stirred.

Working fluid: A liquid or gas used by an industrial system to carry energy and do work.

Additional Resources

This module presents thorough resources for task training. The following reference material is suggested for further study.

Danfoss Power Solutions (Eaton Hydraulics). **eaton.com**.

Essential Hydraulics: *Fluid Power. M. Winston*. Latest Edition. CreateSpace Independent Publishing Platform.

Hosecraft USA. **hosecraftusa.com**.

Hydraulics and Pneumatics: *A Technician's and Engineer's Guide*. Andrew Parr. Latest Edition. Amsterdam: Elsevier.

Parker Hannefin. **parker.com**.

Figure Credits

iStock@Nordroden, Module Opener, Figure 31

iStock@Spitfire1973, Figure 6

iStock@oman023, Figure 9

Shutterstock.com/sujit kantakat, Figure 10

Panduit Corporation, Figure 13

Shutterstock.com/Dovzhykov Andriy, Figure 18

iStock@orcearo, Figure 19 (A)

Courtesy of Viking Pump®, Figure 29

iStock@sorapol1150, Figure 30

iStock@K-Paul, Figure 43

iStock@NosUA, Figure 51

Section Review Answer Key

SECTION 1.0.0

Answer	Section Reference	Objective
1. c	1.1.4	1a
2. b	1.2.0	1b
3. d	1.3.1	1c
4. a	1.4.5	1d
5. c	1.5.1	1e
6. b	1.6.2	1f

Section Review Calculations

SECTION 1.0.0

QUESTION 1

$1{,}000 \text{ psi} \times 2 \text{ in}^2 = \mathbf{2{,}000 \text{ lb}}$

User Update

NCCER makes every effort to keep its textbooks up-to-date and free of technical errors. We appreciate your help in this process. If you find an error, a typographical mistake, or an inaccuracy in NCCER's curricula, please submit a User Update form by visiting **https://www.nccer.org/olf**. You can also scan the QR code using the camera on your phone or mobile device to access the form.

Troubleshooting and Repairing Hydraulic Equipment

OVERVIEW

Hydraulic equipment varies widely in its complexity. Lifts and hoists have just a few components that produce simple up/down motion. Mobile hydraulic machines, like excavators, are more complex. They have multiple actuators and several power units. Heavy industrial product-handling machines produce sophisticated motion with numerous actuators. All hydraulic systems, however, break down into the same major sections. These are like the links in a chain. Break one and the chain falls apart. Millwrights and industrial mechanics inspect, maintain, troubleshoot, and repair the hydraulic chain to keep equipment running.

Module 15410

15410
TROUBLESHOOTING AND REPAIRING HYDRAULIC EQUIPMENT

Objective

Successful completion of this module prepares you to do the following:

1. Summarize troubleshooting, repairing, and maintaining hydraulic systems.
   a. Read and interpret hydraulic schematics.
   b. Describe typical hydraulic maintenance tasks and procedures.
   c. Outline inspecting hydraulic system components.
   d. Outline troubleshooting hydraulic machines.
   e. Outline repairing hydraulic systems.

Performance Tasks

Under supervision, you should be able to do the following:

1. Inspect hydraulic system components.
2. Disassemble and reassemble one or more hydraulic system components.

Trade Terms

Directional control valves (DCVs)
Just-in-time (JIT)
Solenoid

Industry Recognized Credentials

If you are training through an NCCER-accredited sponsor, you may be eligible for credentials from NCCER's Registry. The ID number for this module is 15410. Note that this module may have been used in other NCCER curricula and may apply to other level completions. Contact NCCER's Registry at 1.888.622.3720 or go to **www.nccer.org** for more information.

You can also show off your industry-recognized credentials online with NCCER's digital badges. Transform your knowledge, skills, and achievements into badges that you can share across social media platforms, send to your network, and add to your resume. For more information, visit **www.nccer.org**.

How to Access Resources

This craft has additional videos and resources to enhance your learning experience. To view these resources, scan the QR below. The videos and resources are separated by module.

You can scan this code using the camera on your phone or mobile device to view these videos and resources.

Contents

1.0.0 WORKING WITH HYDRAULIC SYSTEMS

Objective

Summarize troubleshooting, repairing, and maintaining hydraulic systems.

a. Read and interpret hydraulic schematics.
b. Describe typical hydraulic maintenance tasks and procedures.
c. Outline inspecting hydraulic system components.
d. Outline troubleshooting hydraulic machines.
e. Outline repairing hydraulic systems.

Performance Tasks

1. Inspect hydraulic system components.
2. Disassemble and reassemble one or more hydraulic system components.

Trade Terms

Directional control valves (DCVs): Devices that route a working fluid down one of several paths based on the device actuator's position.

Just-in-time (JIT): A strategy that keeps on-site inventory low by ordering required materials just before they're needed for a job.

Solenoid: An electrical control device that pushes or pulls when energized.

When working with hydraulic systems, millwrights and industrial mechanics exercise several important skills. They read schematics to understand the equipment they're servicing. As they move around a facility, they inspect machines, identifying problems and noting what requires attention. When a critical link breaks, they troubleshoot the equipment and repair it. Between repairs, they maintain equipment to help avoid breakdowns.

1.1.0 Hydraulic Schematics

Hydraulics engineers, technicians, and craftworkers use a universal language—schematics. Created from standardized symbols, schematics communicate a system's essential details. Millwrights who can read schematics use them to understand how the system works. Lines linking symbols show relationships. By examining upstream and downstream components, the millwright can determine why something isn't operating correctly.

Suppose a hydraulic system like *Figure 1* stops working. Consulting the system schematic is a good idea. It shows the hydraulic power unit, a directional control valve, and a hydraulic motor. The schematic not only identifies the system's devices, but it also shows how they affect each other. Working systematically through the device chain, the millwright can find the critical break that stopped the system. After localizing the problem, troubleshooting and repair can begin.

Sometimes, it isn't necessary to work through the entire device chain. A little observation and a few good questions can help you identify the most likely problem spots. Reading the schematic to understand relationships guides and streamlines this process.

1.1.1 Common Symbols

As a millwright or industrial mechanic, you should recognize common hydraulic symbols. Understanding these will help you interpret schematics. You don't need to know every symbol. Learn the common ones and look up those that you don't recognize. *Figure 2* shows typical examples that appear frequently in schematics.

> **NOTE**
>
> Hydraulic and pneumatic schematic symbols are almost identical. Once you've learned the common symbols, plus a few unique ones, you'll be able to read both hydraulic and pneumatic schematics.

Most symbols are obvious and easy to understand. Pressure control valves and **directional control valves (DCVs)**, however, require additional explanation. Pressure control valves have simple symbols, but their internal operation can be confusing. You need to understand each type, so you'll know how they affect the system.

DCVs have multiple connections and positions. Hydraulic fluid can take several paths through them. They're extremely useful for controlling a hydraulic machine's behavior. For this reason, you need to understand how they work and how to interpret their schematic symbols.

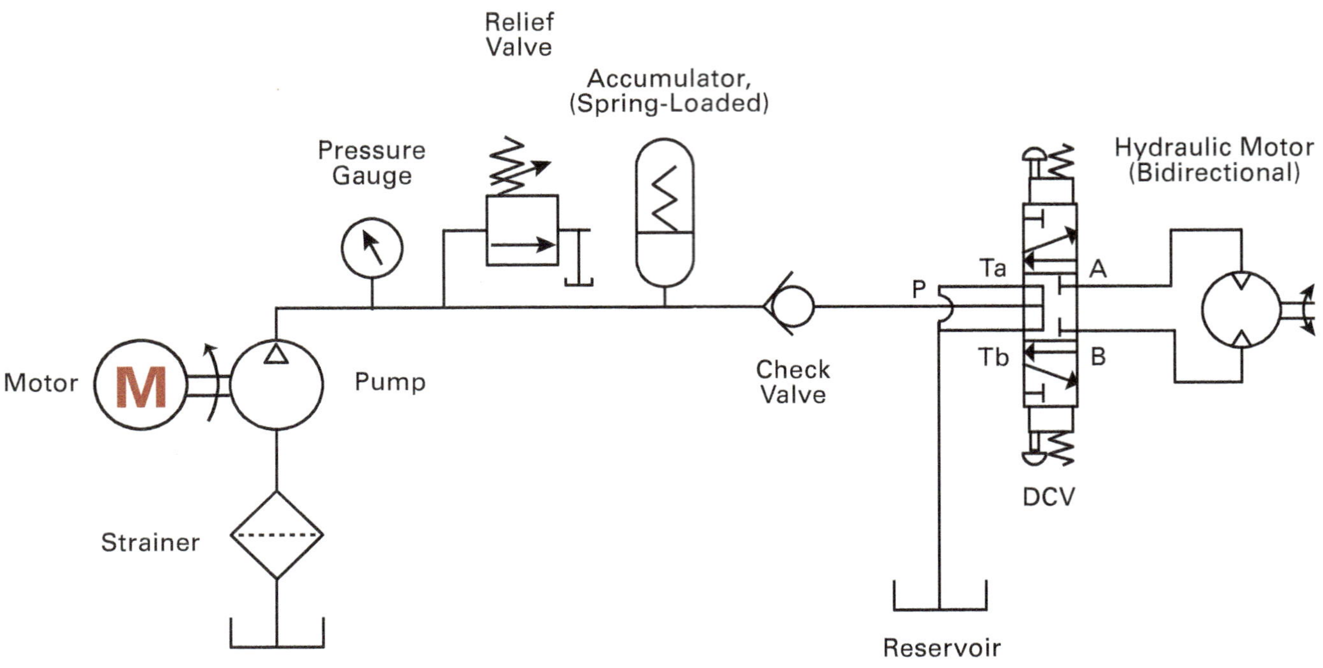

Figure 1 Hydraulic system schematic.

1.1.2 Understanding DCVs

Figure 3 shows a typical DCV, which also goes by the name *spool valve*. A control rod slides four *valve spools* back and forth. These open or close passages, controlling where fluid can and can't go. This DCV has a single *input port* through which fluid enters. Two *tank ports* return fluid to the reservoir. Two *output ports* route fluid to or from the controlled hydraulic device.

> **NOTE**
>
> In hydraulic systems, the terms "input" and "output" are often relative. For example, hydraulic fluid can flow either into or out of a DCV's output ports. Similarly, many hydraulic actuators have combined input/output ports through which fluid can flow in either direction. Whether a port is an input or an output depends on what the device is doing at the moment.

Manufacturers label ports with numbers or letters. The letter "P" (pressure) identifies an input port. The letter "T" identifies a tank port. Letters like "A" and "B" identify output ports.

> **NOTE**
>
> The tank ports (T) on a hydraulic DCV correspond to the exhaust ports (E) on a pneumatic DCV. Tank ports must return to the reservoir, while exhaust ports just vent to the atmosphere.

Rotary DCVs manage fluid flow differently. They have a cylindrical outer shell and a rotating inner core (*Figure 4*). The port connections open into the shell. The core has holes, called *passages*, drilled through it. Rotating the core creates different flow paths by aligning the passages with specific ports. Some rotational positions block ports.

DCVs have a specific number of *positions* (or *states*). Each selects a unique fluid path through the valve. The valve in *Figure 5* has three positions. In position #1, fluid flows from input port P to output port A. Fluid from the device returns through output port B and drains from tank port Tb. Position #3 is reversed. Fluid flows from input port P to output port B. Fluid returns through output port A and drains from tank port Ta. Position #2 is a neutral position that blocks all ports, so no fluid flows.

> **NOTE**
>
> Some DCVs link all tank paths internally, so they can drain from a single T port. Other DCVs have multiple tank ports. All must return to the reservoir.

The machine operator selects position with the *valve actuator*. This can be a lever, button, or pedal. A lever controls the DCV in *Figure 6*. Moving it to the left selects position #3. Moving it to the right selects position #1. Many actuators include a spring that returns the valve to a "rest" position.

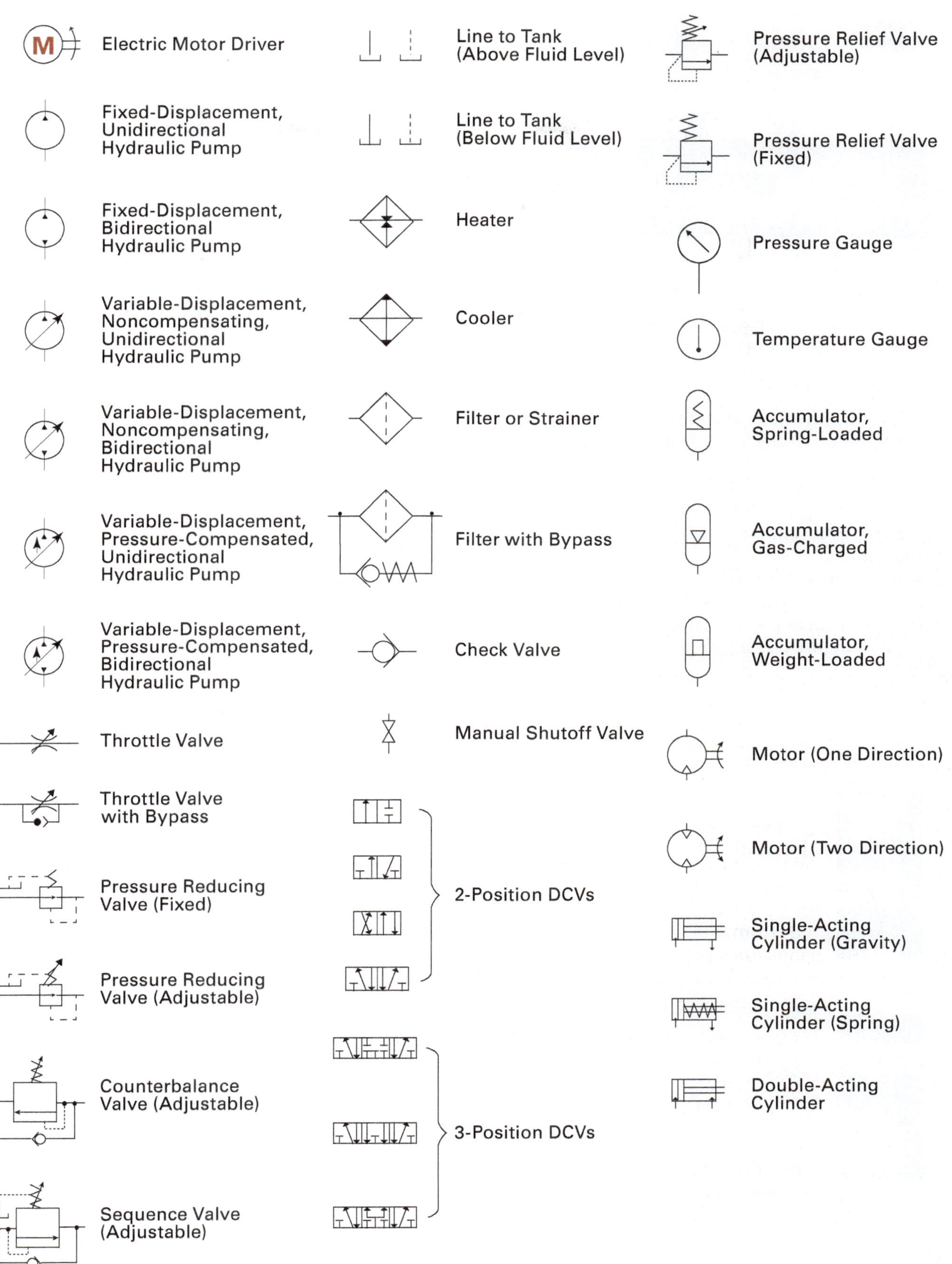

Figure 2 Common hydraulic symbols.

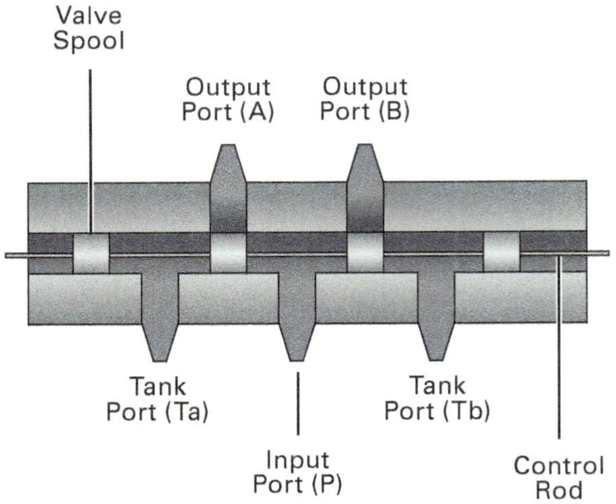

Figure 3 Spool-type DCV.

The DCV in *Figure 6* has two springs. These return the lever to the center and select position #2 (no flow).

Some DCVs have a solenoid actuator. An electrical signal energizes the solenoid and moves the valve. Electronic control systems often manage solenoid valves.

Manufacturers identify their DCVs by two numbers. The first indicates the number of ports. The second indicates the number of positions. The DCV in *Figure 6* is a 5/3 valve—5 ports and 3 positions.

1.1.3 DCV Schematic Symbols

DCV schematic symbols can look complicated and confusing. Once you understand them, however, they're simple and logical. Interpreting them requires breaking the symbol into its key parts. *Figure 7* shows the symbol for the valve in *Figure 6*.

The left and right sections identify the valve actuators. The middle sections, called *flow boxes*, show the fluid's path for each valve position. Since this valve has three positions, there are three flow boxes. One flow box includes port labels (either numbers or letters). Assume the same labeling for the other flow boxes.

Actuators

Figure 8 shows common actuator symbols. Use this information to determine how a DCV operates. For example, the DCV that *Figure 7* represents has a lever and spring as its left actuator. It has a spring as its right actuator. The springs cause the valve to default to position #2 (no flow). Pulling the lever to the left selects position #3. Pulling it to the right selects position #1.

Flow Boxes

A flow box shows the valve's ports and the fluid's path between them. Arrows identify the flow direction. A port marked with a T-shaped symbol is "blocked" and has no flow through it. Remember that DCV symbols have one flow

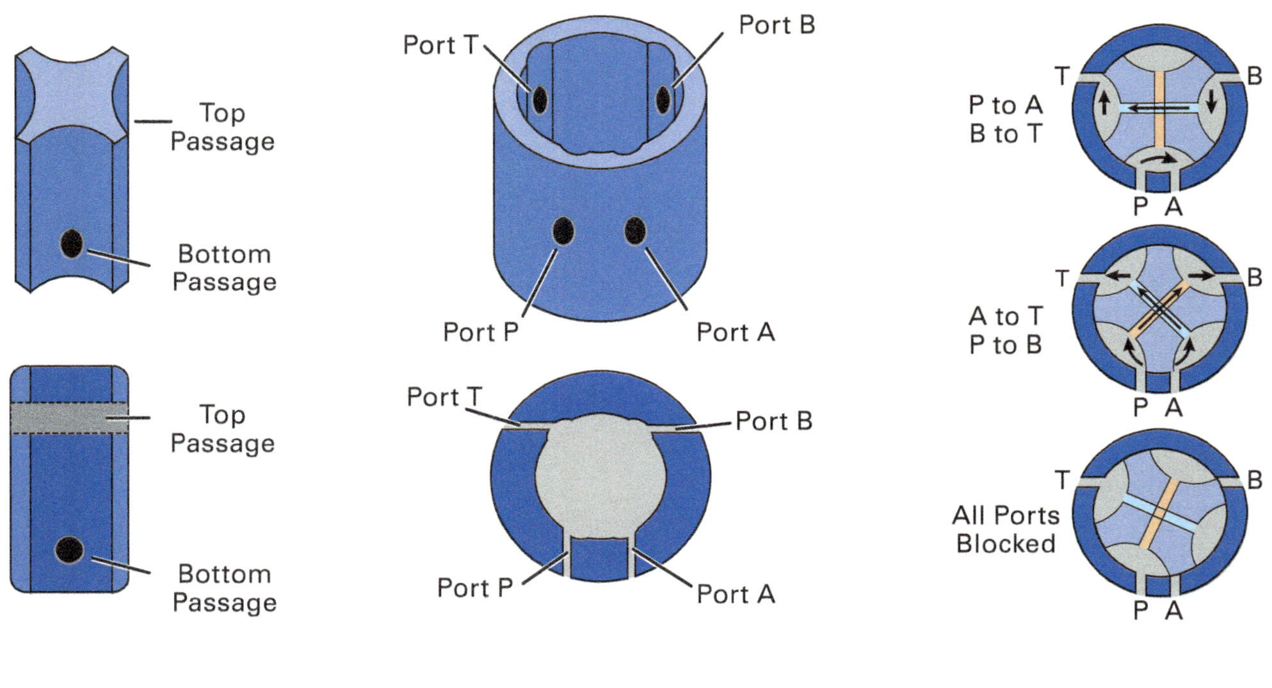

Figure 4 Rotary DCV.

box for each valve position. Since the symbol in *Figure 7* has three flow boxes, the DCV has three positions.

To understand the valve's behavior, examine the flow boxes one at a time. *Figure 9* shows them individually. The left flow box corresponds to position #1. Fluid enters port P and exits port A. Returning fluid enters port B and exits port Tb. The right flow box corresponds to position #3. Fluid enters port P and exits port B. Returning fluid enters port A and exits port Ta. The middle flow box corresponds to position #2. All ports are blocked, so no fluid flows.

Example

Examine *Figure 10*. See if you can figure out what kind of DCV it represents. Refer to *Figure 8* and *Figure 9* for assistance.

Ports vs. Ways

Hydraulics engineers and equipment manufacturers sometimes use the term *ways* in place of *ports*. Depending on the valve, these terms may or may not mean the same thing. Ports are the valve's physical connections to the outside world. Counting the valve's openings or fittings gives the port count.

Ways are unique places that the fluid can enter or exit the valve. Even though a valve may have several tank ports, they're considered a single way since they all go to the same place (the reservoir). The DCV in *Figure 6* has five ports but only four ways since two ports—Ta and Tb—go to the same place. On the other hand, the valve that *Figure 10* represents has four ports and four ways since all ports go to unique places.

To avoid confusion, this module classifies valves by port count only.

Begin by identifying the valve's ports and positions. The right flow box includes four port labels (P, T, A, and B). These indicate that the valve has one input port, one tank port, and two output ports. The symbol has two flow boxes, so the valve must have two positions. You identify it as a 4/2 DCV.

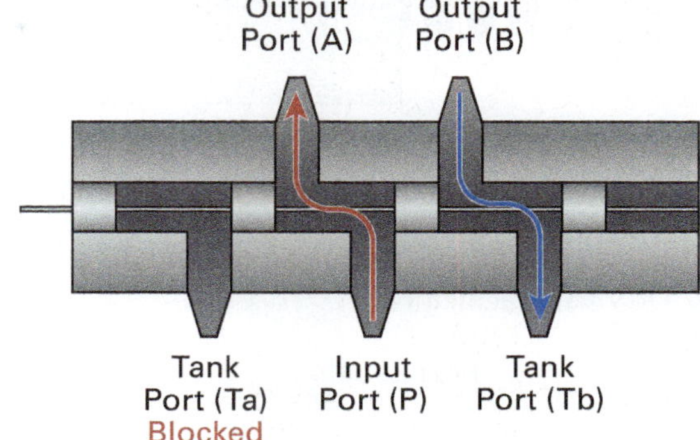

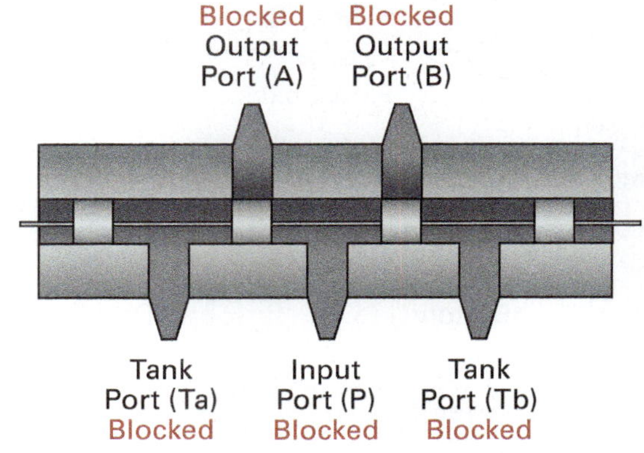

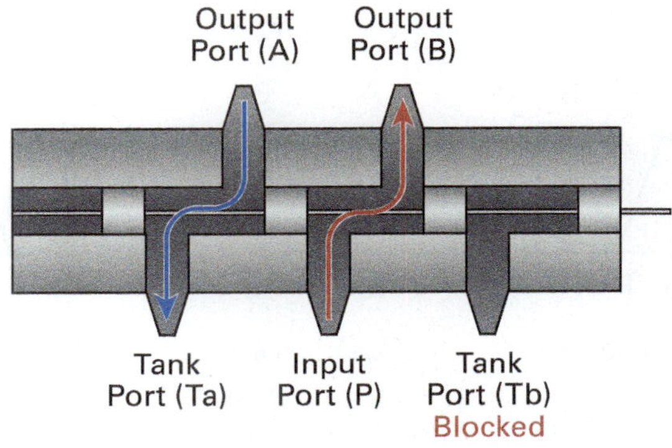

Figure 5 DCV valve positions.

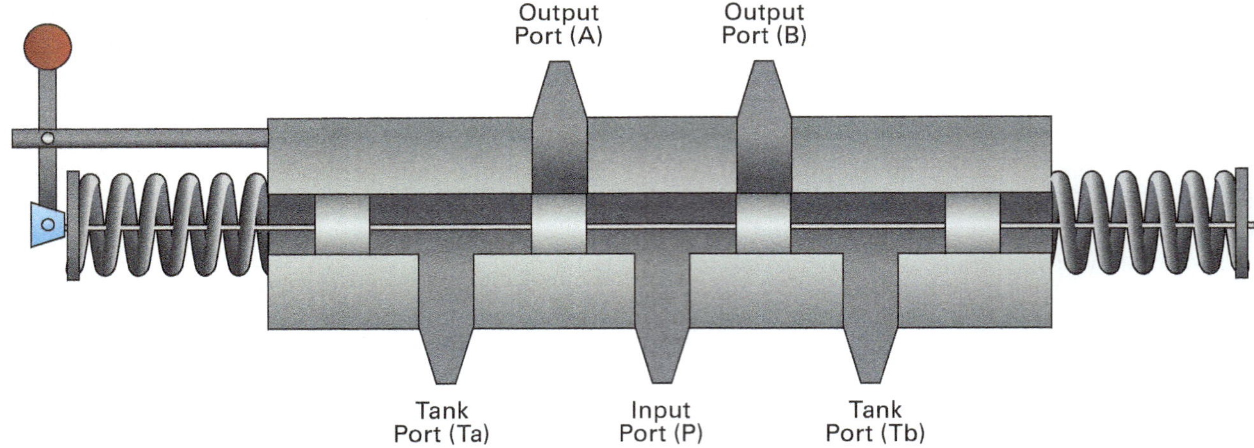

Figure 6 DCV valve actuators.

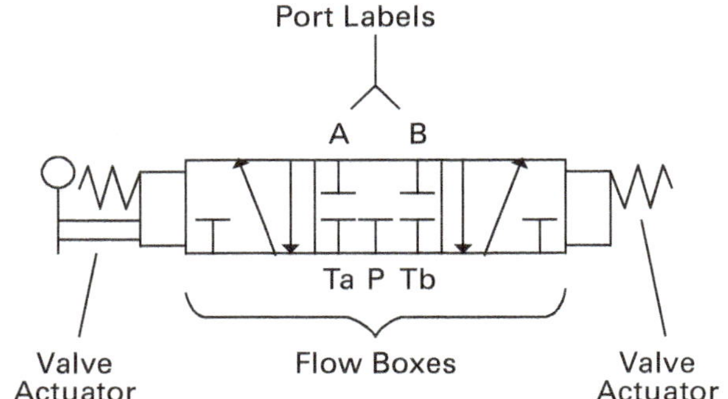

Figure 7 DCV schematic symbol.

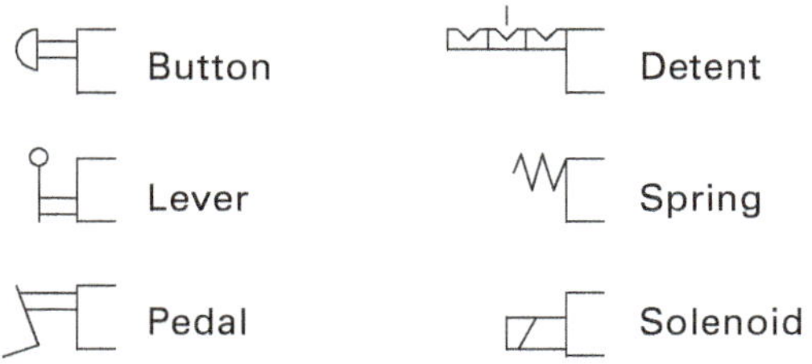

Figure 8 Common DCV actuator symbols.

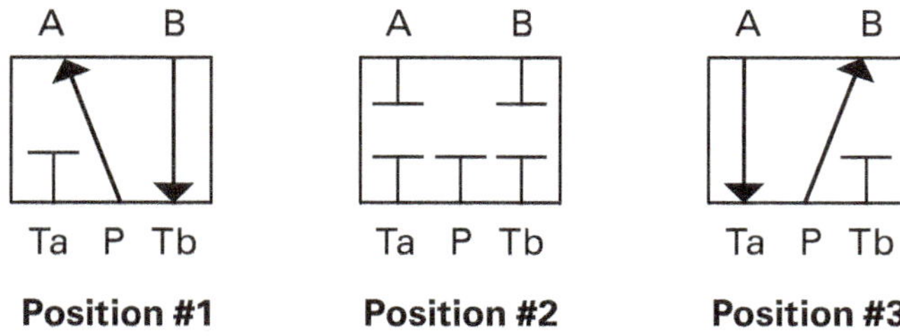

Figure 9 Individual flow boxes.

Next, identify the actuators. The left is a solenoid, and the right is a spring. The right flow box is the valve's default position since it has port labels. You conclude that the spring returns the valve to position #2 when the solenoid is de-energized. Energizing the solenoid selects position #1.

Finally, identify the fluid flow paths for each position. In position #1, fluid enters port P and exits port A. Returning fluid enters port B and exits port T. In position #2, fluid enters port P and exits port B. Returning fluid enters port A and exits port T.

1.1.4 DCV Center Positions

Hydraulic systems differ from pneumatic systems in two crucial ways. First, the hydraulic fluid circulates in a loop. Once the fluid has done its work, it returns to the reservoir. Pneumatic systems just release the used air to the atmosphere. Second, hydraulic fluid, unlike air, is incompressible.

Examine *Figure 11*. It shows a hydraulic pump connected to a 5/3 DCV. The DCV has a lever actuator and two springs. The springs keep the DCV in the center (all ports blocked) position by default. Blocking all ports is acceptable for most pneumatic systems. Unfortunately, this strategy can be dangerous for some hydraulic systems.

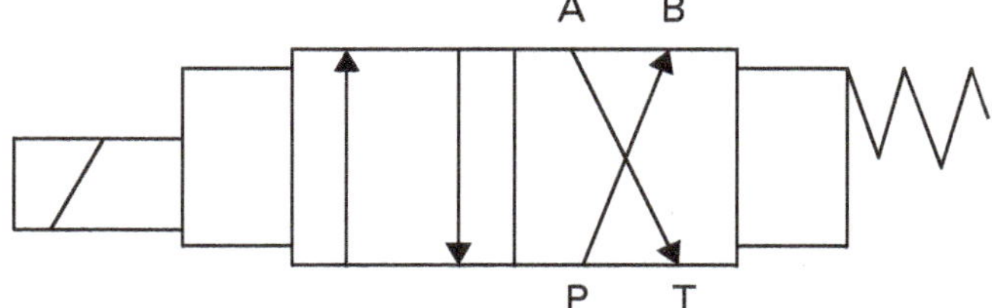

Figure 10 Example DCV symbol.

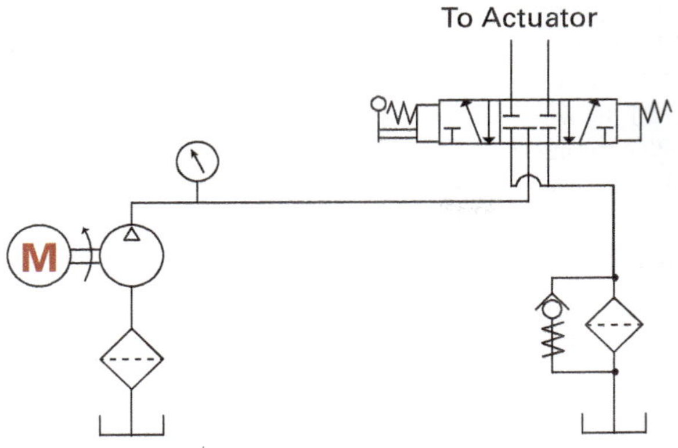

Figure 11 A potential problem.

The hydraulic power unit in *Figure 11* has a fixed-displacement pump. This pump type tries to move a constant fluid volume each time it rotates. When the DCV is in the center position, however, the pump is pushing against a blocked port. Since hydraulic fluid doesn't compress, the blocked port creates a powerful back pressure. This pressure will damage the pump.

To prevent damage from back pressure, all hydraulic power units contain a pressure relief valve (*Figure 12*). It drains directly into the reservoir. When a blocked port creates back pressure, the valve opens and relieves the pressure. This method isn't perfect. Constantly pumping fluid through the relief valve heats the fluid, wasting energy.

A *pressure-compensated, variable-displacement pump* manages back pressure differently (*Figure 13*). If a blocked valve causes back pressure, the pump keeps spinning but reduces displacement to zero. Later, when the valve opens, the pump ramps up displacement to deliver fluid. Unfortunately, variable-displacement pumps are more complicated and expensive. Manufacturers may avoid using them in simple hydraulic power units.

Some DCVs automatically prevent back pressure. The hydraulic system in *Figure 11* uses a *blocked center* DCV (also called *closed center*). It creates back pressure in its default position, causing the power unit's pressure relief valve to operate continuously. Using a DCV with a different center position style can avoid this problem.

Valve manufacturers offer three additional center styles besides the blocked center (*Figure 14*). Two of these prevent back pressure. The third solves another unrelated application challenge.

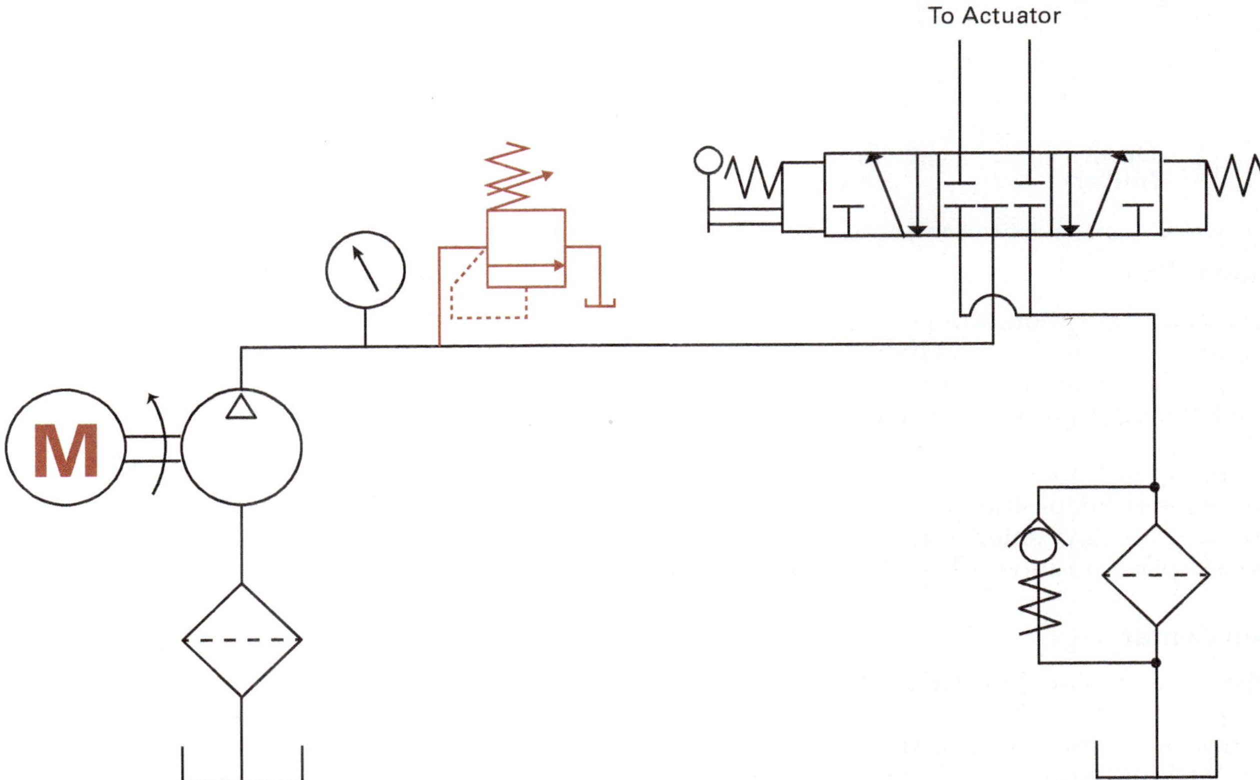

Figure 12 Solving the problem with a pressure relief valve.

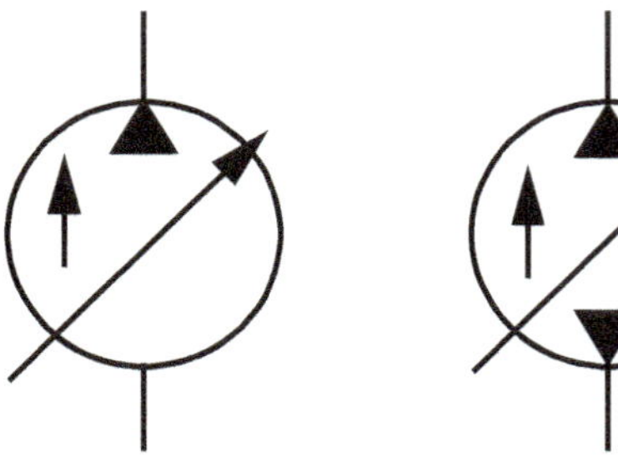

Figure 13 Pressure-compensated, variable-displacement pump symbols.

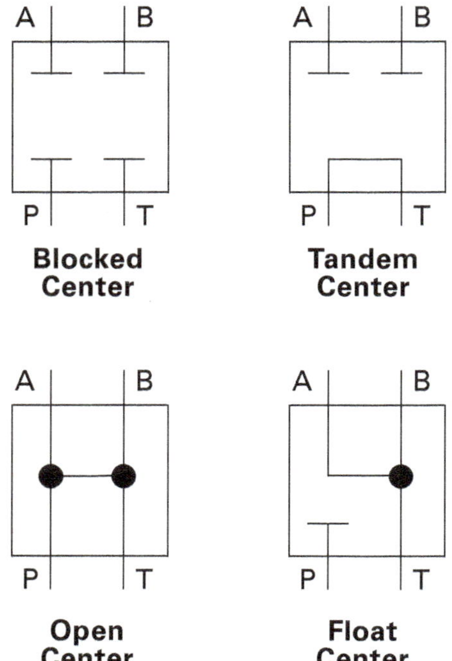

Figure 14 DCV center position flow boxes.

Tandem Center

In the center position, the DCV connects the P port directly to the T port. Hydraulic fluid loops through the valve and returns to the reservoir. Since back pressure doesn't develop, the power unit's pressure relief valve never opens. The DCV does block the output ports (A and B). This arrangement keeps the actuator from moving because fluid can't enter or exit. When the DCV moves to other positions, fluid flows normally.

Open Center

In the center position, the DCV connects all ports together. Fluid from the power unit and the actuator returns to the reservoir through the T port. Since back pressure doesn't develop, the power unit's pressure relief valve never opens. The actuator can move freely since it isn't pressurized. When the DCV moves to other positions, fluid flows normally.

> Tandem and open center DCVs don't develop back pressure in their center position. The flowing fluid does generate heat, however, which wastes energy.

Float Center

In the center position, the DCV blocks the P port and connects both outputs (A and B) to the T port. Back pressure develops, opening the power unit's pressure relief valve. The actuator can move freely since it isn't pressurized. When the DCV moves to other positions, fluid flows normally.

1.1.5 Understanding Pressure Control Valves

As explained in NCCER Module 15409, *Basic Hydraulic Systems*, most pressure control valves block flow until the fluid's pressure rises to a specific value. Once the pressure reaches the valve's *setpoint*, the valve opens. When the pressure drops sufficiently below the setpoint, the valve closes. Pressure relief valves are the simplest pressure control valves. When they open, they return fluid to the reservoir, relieving the pressure.

More complex pressure control valves help hydraulic systems perform sophisticated tasks. *Counterbalance valves* and *sequence valves* coordinate fluid flow by selectively blocking it or letting it through. The following examples show common applications.

Counterbalance Valves

Examine the hydraulic lift in *Figure 15*. Also examine the DCV's schematic symbol. When the machine operator isn't touching the actuator's lever, it stays in the center (position #2). This DCV has a tandem center, so hydraulic fluid just loops through the valve from P to T.

When the operator moves the DCV's lever to position #3, fluid enters the actuator's cap end. Pressure rises to 1,600 psi, which is what the actuator requires to lift a 5,000 lb load. The piston moves upwards, raising the load. During the lift, the DCV blocks the T port. When the actuator reaches the top, the operator releases the lever, which returns to the center position.

In the center position, the DCV loops fluid from P to T. It also blocks the A port. Since fluid can't escape the actuator, the load remains raised. If the DCV should leak, however, the load will gradually sink. This is undesirable.

When the operator moves the DCV's lever to position #1, fluid drains from the actuator's cap end. The 5,000 lb load pressurizes the fluid to

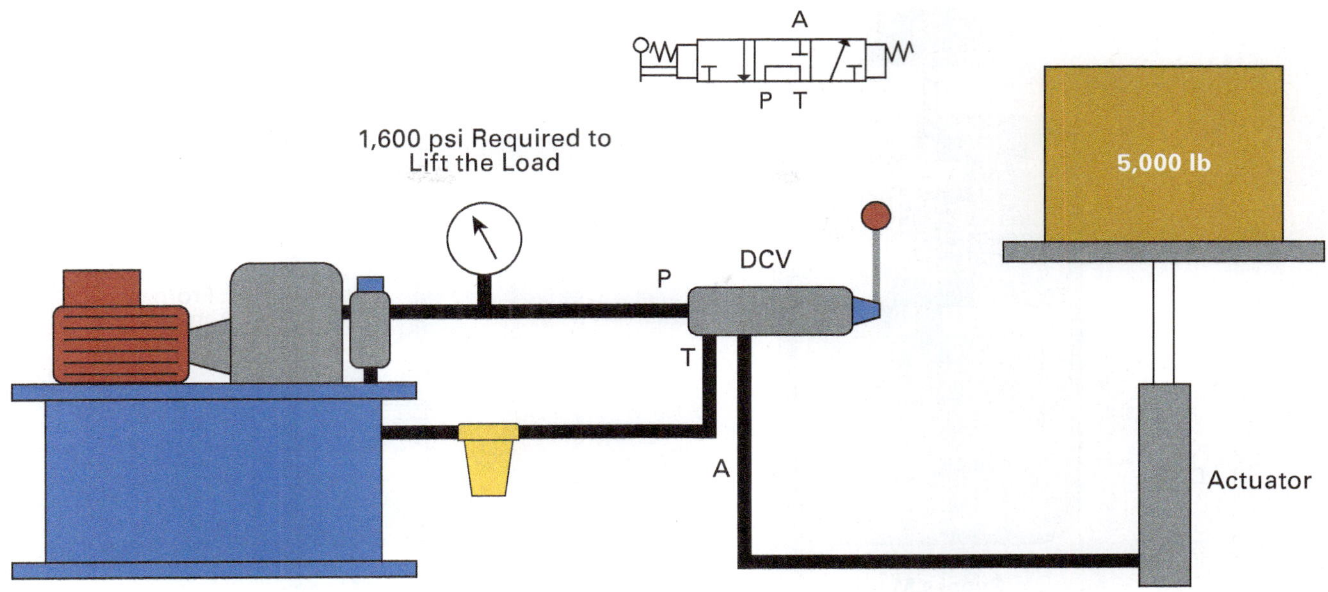

Figure 15 Hydraulic lift.

1,600 psi, so it rushes through the DCV back to the reservoir. The load crashes down. This too is undesirable.

A *counterbalance valve* solves both problems. It's a two-way valve. Fluid flows freely through it in one direction. Fluid won't flow through it in the other direction until the fluid's pressure rises above the valve's setpoint. *Figure 16* shows a counterbalance valve's internal design.

If fluid enters from the port on the left, the bypass valve opens. The fluid flows freely through the valve to the port on the right. If fluid enters from the port on the right, however, the bypass valve closes. The spring-retained valve spool also blocks the flow.

The pressurized fluid travels through the small *pilot passage* and presses on the *pilot piston* attached to the valve spool. If the fluid's pressure is weaker than the spring force, the spool stays down and blocks the passage. If the fluid's pressure is stronger than the spring force, however, the spool rises and open the passage. The fluid flows through the valve to the port on the left. *Figure 17* shows the counterbalance valve's behavior in each direction.

Adding a counterbalance valve to the hydraulic lift in *Figure 15* solves its problems. *Figure 18* shows the modified design. Notice that the counterbalance valve fits between the DCV's port A and the actuator's cap end. Also notice that the DCV is different. It can direct hydraulic fluid to or from both ends of the actuator. Finally, notice that the counterbalance valve's setpoint is 1,800 psi. That's 200 psi higher than pressure required to lift the load.

When the machine operator isn't touching the actuator's lever, it stays in the center (position #2). This DCV has a tandem center, so hydraulic fluid just loops through the valve from P to Ta and Tb.

When the operator moves the DCV's lever to position #3, fluid enters the counterbalance valve from the left. The internal bypass valve opens, allowing fluid to flow to the actuator's cap end. Pressure rises to 1,600 psi, which is what the actuator requires to lift the 5,000 lb load. The piston moves upwards, raising the load.

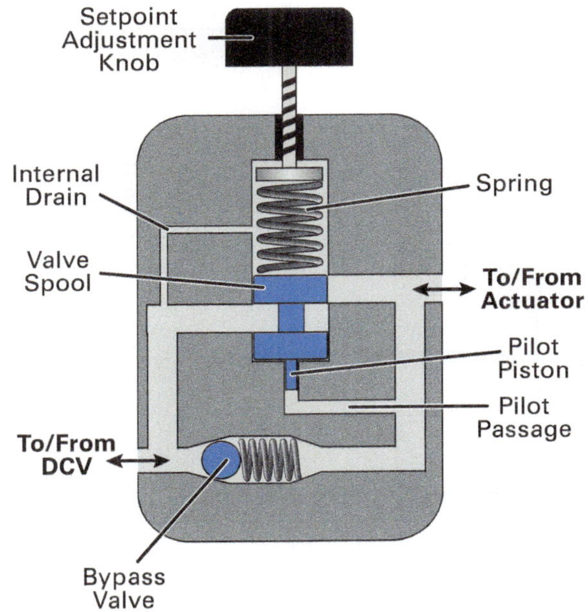

Figure 16 Counterbalance valve design.

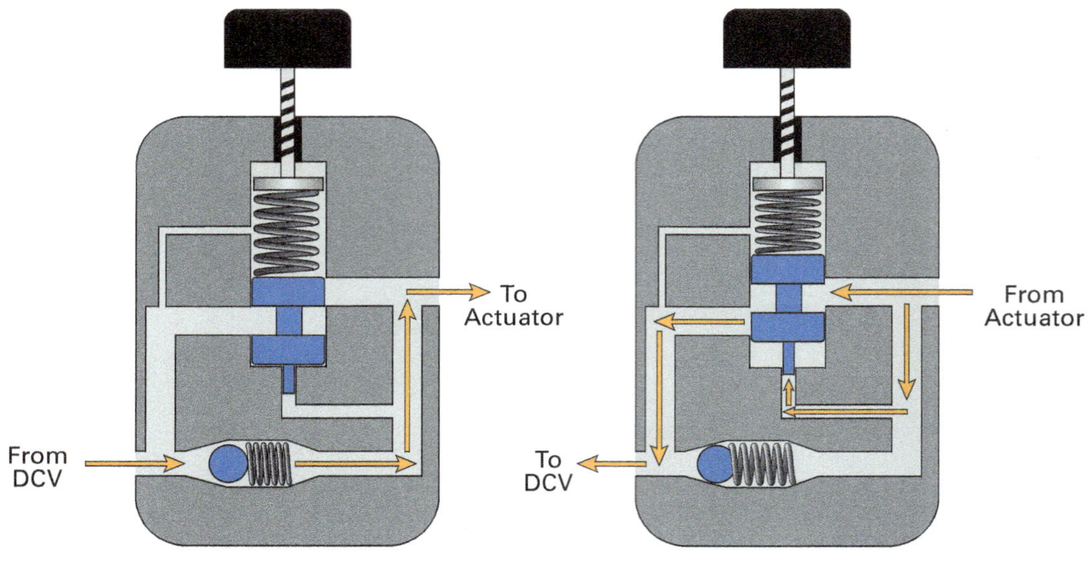

Figure 17 Counterbalance valve operation.

Fluid from the actuator's rod end drains and enters the DCV's port B. It returns to the reservoir by port Tb. The DCV blocks Ta. When the actuator reaches the top, the operator releases the lever, which returns to the center position.

In the center position, the DCV loops fluid from P to Ta and Tb. It also blocks the A and B ports. Notice that the counterbalance valve, not the DCV, keeps the fluid at the actuator's cap end from escaping. The 5,000 lb load generates a 1,600 psi back pressure on the counterbalance valve. Since that valve's setpoint is 1,800 psi, it stays closed, keeping the load raised.

> **NOTE**
>
> Counterbalance valves are less likely to leak than DCVs. Using a counterbalance valve to keep the load raised reduces the possibility that the load could gradually sink. The counterbalance valve also reduces wear on the DCV.

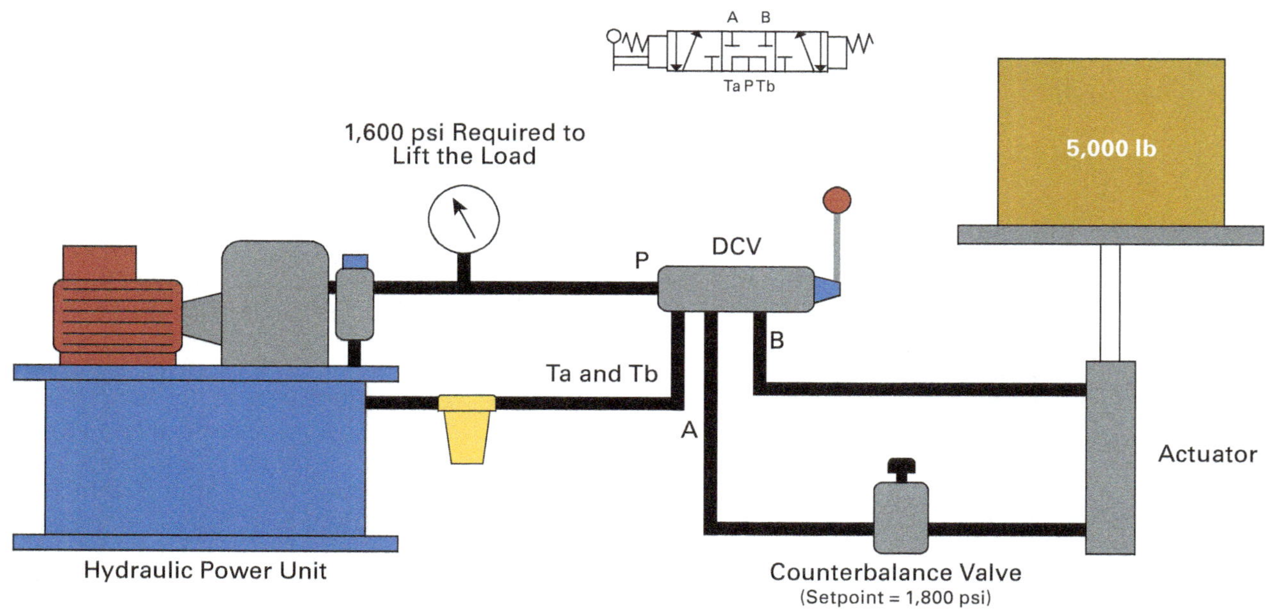

Figure 18 Hydraulic lift with counterbalance valve.

NCCER – *Millwright*

Lowering the load looks problematic. Positioning the DCV to drain the actuator's cap end back to the reservoir isn't going to work. With only 1,600 psi on its right side, the counterbalance valve won't open to release the fluid. What's the solution?

To make the counterbalance valve open, the pressure on its right side must rise to 1,800 psi. That's the reason this design uses a different DCV than the lift in *Figure 15*. When the operator moves the DCV's lever to position #1, fluid enters the actuator's rod end. The pressure at the top of the actuator rises to 200 psi. This pressure adds to the 1,600 psi generated by the load. Since the total pressure is 1,800 psi, the counterbalance valve opens.

The fluid from the actuator's cap end drains through the counterbalance valve and the DCV. The load goes down slowly, however, rather than crashing. The counterbalance valve's spring maintains a 1,600 psi back pressure on the escaping fluid. Since it drains under a pressure of only 200 psi, it flows more slowly.

Sequence Valves

A sequence valve is nearly identical to a counterbalance valve. There's just one small difference. Examine the counterbalance valve in *Figure 16*. Notice the tiny drain passage connected to the left port. It empties the space above the valve spool if fluid enters it when the spool moves. Sequence valves have this drain too, but it connects to the reservoir through a separate port. Since sequence valves have pressure on both sides at once, an internal drain wouldn't operate correctly.

Figure 19 shows a hydraulic punch with two actuators. The first clamps the workpiece in place. The second punches a hole through it. The clamp must come down before the punch. Two DCVs could produce this sequence. The machine operator would bring down the clamp, followed by the punch. A sequence valve can do this operation automatically, however, which is much better.

Notice that the clamp actuator connects directly to the DCV's port A. The sequence valve fits between port A and the punch actuator. The valve's setpoint is 2,200 psi. Until the pressure on its left side reaches this value, the sequence valve won't open.

When the machine operator moves the DCV's lever to position #3, fluid enters the clamp actuator. The piston moves down. When the clamp contacts the workpiece, pressure rises to 2,000 psi, the required clamping pressure. The pressure continues rising until it reaches 2,200 psi. The sequence valve now opens, and fluid enters the punch actuator. The piston descends and punches the hole.

The machine operator retracts the punch and clamp by moving the DCV's lever to position #1. Fluid flows from port B into both actuators' rod ends. The pistons rise. Fluid exits the clamp actuator's cap end and returns to the reservoir through the DCV. The sequence valve's internal

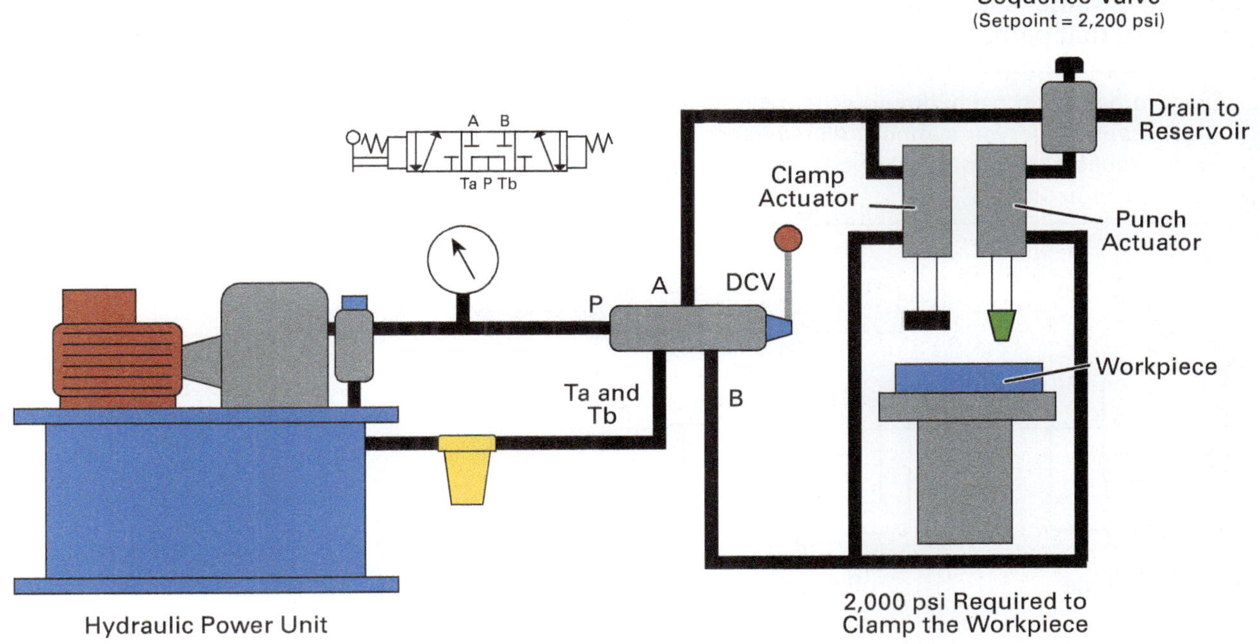

Figure 19 Hydraulic punch with sequence valve.

bypass valve opens so fluid can exit from the punch actuator's cap end. The fluid returns to the reservoir through the DCV.

Pressure Control Valve Symbols

Counterbalance valves and sequence valves have nearly identical schematic symbols (*Figure 20*). The arrow shows the pressure-controlled flow direction. Notice the dashed lines between the inlet side and the bottom of the valves. They represent the pilot passages that control the valve spools.

Notice also that the sequence valve has a second dashed line going to a reservoir symbol. This indicates that the sequence valve has an external drain port. Since counterbalance valves have internal drains, their symbols don't include this line.

1.1.6 Interpreting Schematics

To interpret a hydraulic schematic, identify each symbol. Look up any that you don't recognize. Reference handbooks, online resources, and quick-reference cards are all useful. Be sure that you understand complex devices, like pressure control valves and DCVs. Examine the lines linking the symbols. These show the fluid's path through the system. Ask yourself what happens at each step in that path.

Figure 21 shows a typical hydraulic schematic. See if you can identify each symbol. Then try to visualize the complete system. Refer to *Figure 2*, *Figure 7*, *Figure 8*, *Figure 9*, and *Figure 14* for assistance.

The first symbol is the reservoir. An offline cooler removes excess heat from the hydraulic fluid. You can tell that it's an offline cooler since its inlet and outlet go directly to the reservoir. An inline cooler's inlet would connect to the return line.

A motor-driven hydraulic pump pulls fluid from the reservoir through a suction strainer. A temperature gauge monitors the fluid's temperature as it leaves the reservoir. Notice that the pump is a variable-displacement pump that's pressure compensated. Those qualities affect how the system behaves when closed valves block fluid flow.

Next comes a gas-charged accumulator and a fixed pressure relief valve. The valve returns fluid to the reservoir if it opens. A gauge reports the outlet pressure. Finally, a check valve prevents fluid from moving backwards. Together, all these devices make up the hydraulic power unit (*Figure 22*).

After leaving the power unit, the fluid enters a DCV by its P port. The DCV has three ports and two states, so it's a 3/2 valve. A foot pedal and a spring select its position. By default, the spring holds the DCV in position #2 (right flow box).

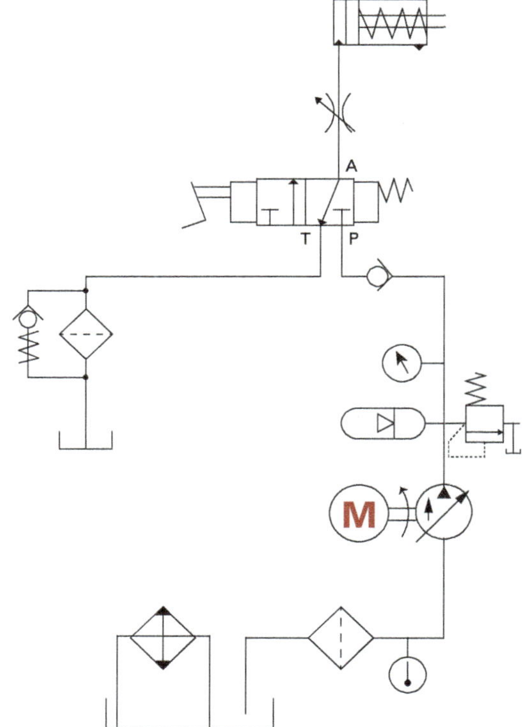

Figure 21 Practice hydraulic schematic.

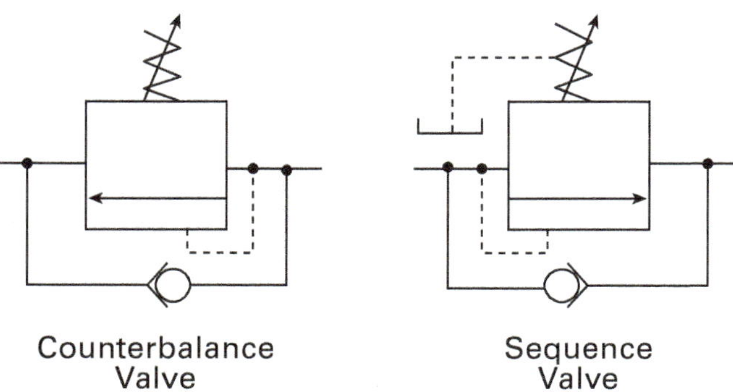

Counterbalance Valve   Sequence Valve

Figure 20 Pressure control valve symbols.

NCCER – *Millwright*

Pressing the pedal moves the DCV to position #1. Pressurized fluid exits the valve through port A. It passes through an adjustable throttle valve, which regulates the flow. The fluid passes into a single-acting hydraulic cylinder actuator. The pressure extends the actuator, compressing its internal spring. The throttle valve controls how fast the actuator extends.

When the operator releases the pedal, the spring returns the DCV to position #2. The actuator's spring ejects the fluid from the cylinder. The fluid passes through the throttle valve, which controls the actuator's retraction speed. It enters the DCV through port A and exits from the T port. The T port returns fluid to the reservoir through a filter. The filter has a bypass valve that opens if the filter becomes clogged. Together, all these devices make up the hydraulic control system and actuator (*Figure 23*).

1.2.0 Hydraulic System Maintenance

Preventive maintenance (PM) helps machinery work more reliably and have a longer life. Its main goal is preventing problems from becoming failures. Successful PM depends on good analysis, careful scheduling, and setting priorities. It also requires knowing which tasks to perform and how often to do them. Finally, PM includes documenting all work.

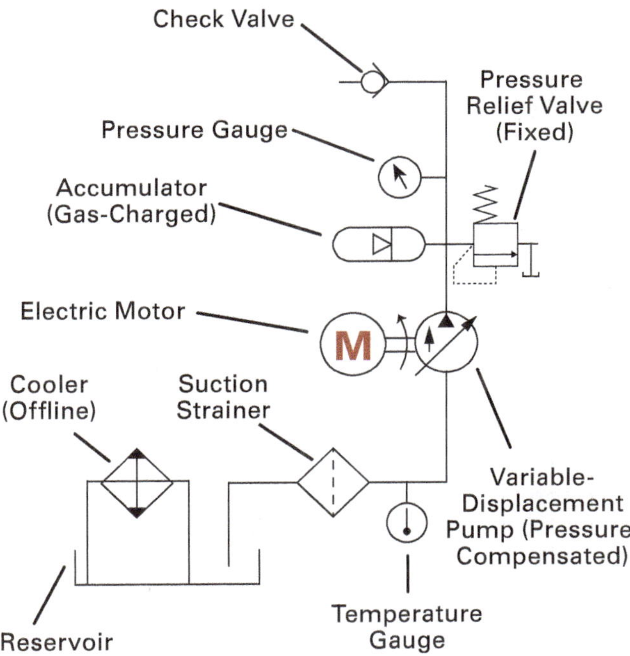

Figure 22 Hydraulic power unit.

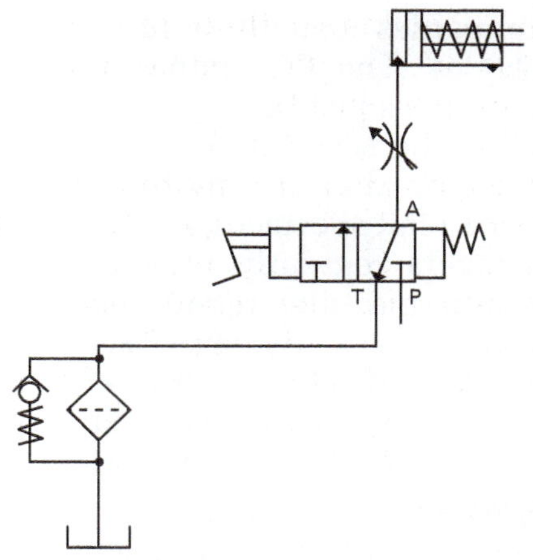

Figure 23 Hydraulic control system and actuator.

1.2.1 Analyzing, Scheduling, and Prioritizing

A successful PM program requires a well-planned schedule. The PM manager begins by analyzing a machine's history. Timing is crucial since maintenance tasks must prevent failures. Studying past failures, as well as their causes, frequency, and costs, helps shape the schedule. The PM manager also examines the machine's history to identify parts requiring regular replacement.

Equipment manufacturers provide maintenance and repair manuals to guide these processes. PM managers consult them to identify standard maintenance tasks. They use them to develop the company's maintenance and repair procedures. Equipment manuals include parts lists to make ordering spare parts simple and accurate.

PM schedules must fit into the facility's production schedule. Minimizing downtime reduces PM's financial impact. Scheduling also ensures that qualified craftworkers are available at the right time. Coordinating these factors can be very challenging!

Good PM schedules prioritize tasks. If they conflict, more essential tasks override less important ones. For example, a hydraulic power unit might affect many machines and tools. Keeping it running has a higher priority than maintaining a single tool.

> **WARNING!**
>
> Always prioritize human safety over economic impact. If you must choose between PM that affects safety and PM that affects costs, handle safety-related matters first.

Besides scheduling tasks, PM managers monitor spare parts and supplies. In the past, most companies stocked many different spare parts.

Today, companies usually follow just-in-time (JIT) strategies. The PM manager orders most parts and supplies just before they're needed. JIT works well if the schedule is accurate and suppliers deliver on time. If anything goes wrong, however, it can fail spectacularly.

PM managers regularly review maintenance schedules and machine repair logs. Too much maintenance wastes money. Excessive breakdowns usually indicate too little PM. Managers tweak schedules to balance reliability and costs.

1.2.2 Inspecting

Some problems turn into failures without warning, but most develop over time. Inspections identify these future failures. For example, parts like belts wear out. If an inspection reveals a worn belt, a craftworker can replace it before it breaks. Scheduling these tasks reduces or eliminates inconvenient downtime.

> **NOTE**
>
> Machines that run continually, like hydraulic power units, often have *hour meters*. These indicate how many hours the machine has run since it was new. During inspection, read and record hour meters. Some maintenance tasks must happen at specific intervals. The hour meter helps you know when it's time to do these.

Most maintenance workers use checklists to reduce mistakes and omissions. A completed checklist confirms that the worker performed all tasks. Checklists may be paper or electronic. Sophisticated plant management software can automatically schedule maintenance tasks based on inspection checklists.

1.2.3 Cleaning, Lubricating, and Adjusting

All machines require basic maintenance to keep them running smoothly. Machines work better and run cooler when they're clean. Lubricants dry up or become clogged with dust. Parts move with more friction and start to wear out faster. Grimy surfaces trap heat and contaminate other parts. Maintenance workers regularly clean parts and surfaces, removing dirt, grime, and old lubricants.

> **WARNING!**
>
> Cleaning equipment usually involves solvents. Many are flammable and/or toxic. Take appropriate precautions against fire. Ensure sufficient airflow and wear all required PPE. Place rags and waste in approved containers.

Once clean, moving parts require fresh lubricant, usually grease or oil. Good maintenance procedures specify lubricant types and indicate where to apply them. Never guess about lubrication. If your company's procedures don't guide you, consult the manufacturer's maintenance manual. Don't over-lubricate!

Before completing routine maintenance, good millwrights and industrial mechanics confirm that equipment is running properly and smoothly. Machines often drift out of adjustment, causing greater wear and vibration. Belts lose their tension and fasteners loosen over time. Hydraulic fluid may leak from fittings. Checking and readjusting eliminates future problems. Good maintenance procedures identify components that commonly need adjustment.

1.2.4 Replacing Worn Parts

Worn or borderline parts usually turn up during inspections or routine maintenance. Whenever possible, replace these parts immediately. If they can't be replaced at once, put the machine on the repair schedule so it gets attention soon. Be sure to check the spare parts inventory and order anything that isn't in stock.

> **NOTE**
>
> Mission-critical systems often have redundant machinery that takes over after failures. You can use this backup equipment to keep the system running while you do PM tasks. Be sure to maintain the redundant equipment as well. If it's in bad condition, it won't do its job during an emergency!

1.2.5 Documenting Your Work

Plants require maintenance workers to document their activities. These records help other workers when they maintain or repair the same machine. PM managers use records to build schedules and plan budgets.

Accidents turn records into legal evidence. Records help establish an accident's cause or determine liability. They can exonerate a company by proving that it properly maintained equipment.

Records are also important to employees when their companies *don't* maintain equipment properly. Good documentation legally protects an employee who conscientiously reports and documents problems. While documenting your work isn't particularly enjoyable, it's an essential task. Perform it conscientiously.

Some smaller facilities keep records on pre-printed paper forms. Many companies, however, use plant management software to keep records and manage schedules. Millwrights document their work through the plant management system. Advanced systems communicate with tablet devices that plant personnel carry around as they work (*Figure 24*).

Typical maintenance records capture the following information:

- Equipment identifier (name or number) and/or location
- Date and time (start/finish)
- Task(s) performed
- Parts replaced and spare parts used
- Worker notes

1.3.0 Inspecting Hydraulic Systems

Preventive maintenance depends on regular inspections. These reveal problems that could turn into failures. Inspections also identify parts nearing end-of-life. As they inspect, millwrights and industrial mechanics confirm that machines are operating properly. When they discover problems, millwrights usually schedule repairs rather than dealing with them immediately. Sometimes, however, they perform minor service tasks during inspection.

Specialists like maintenance millwrights handle scheduled inspections. In contrast, machine operators check their equipment daily. If they spot a problem, they submit a maintenance

Figure 24 Plant worker using a tablet device.

request. When possible, talk to machine operators. Since they know their equipment well, they are more aware of its problems than other personnel. Asking a few thoughtful questions before starting work can save a lot of time later.

Whenever you inspect a hydraulic system, stay alert for leaks at all locations. Sometimes, you can see fluid escaping. Oily spots or puddles near connections may indicate leaks. Repair leaks promptly since they reduce system efficiency. Clean up oil since it creates a slip hazard.

The following sections summarize typical inspection points for each link in the hydraulic chain. If you can't remember a component's function, review NCCER Module 15409, *Basic Hydraulic Systems*.

1.3.1 Inspecting Reservoirs

The reservoir stores the hydraulic fluid, giving it a place to cool (*Figure 25*). Suspended particles settle and air escapes while the fluid waits to return to the system. If the fluid level is too low or the fluid doesn't cool well, the system won't operate correctly.

Check the fluid level by examining the sight glass or level indicator. Be sure that you're looking at the actual fluid level and not a stain. If the fluid is low, add extra fluid of the correct type. Also note the fluid's color. If it's milky, discolored, or very dark, it's contaminated or degraded. Schedule a fluid change. Look for leaks around the drain and access cover.

Predictive Maintenance

It's always better to prevent a problem from turning into a failure. *Predictive maintenance* goes beyond normal PM by spotting problems in their earliest stages. Increased vibration or an elevated temperature often suggests an emerging problem. Predictive maintenance techniques use technology to spot these early warning signs and alert craftworkers.

Smart machines include built-in sensors that report vibration and temperature to a maintenance computer. The computer identifies worrisome patterns and alerts the maintenance team. They can investigate and prevent the problem from becoming a failure.

With older machines, maintenance workers take measurements with a handheld sensor. It collects vibration and temperature data, passing it to a smartphone app. The app analyzes the information and consults a database containing thousands of failure patterns. From these, it diagnoses the machine's condition and reports it to the craftworker.

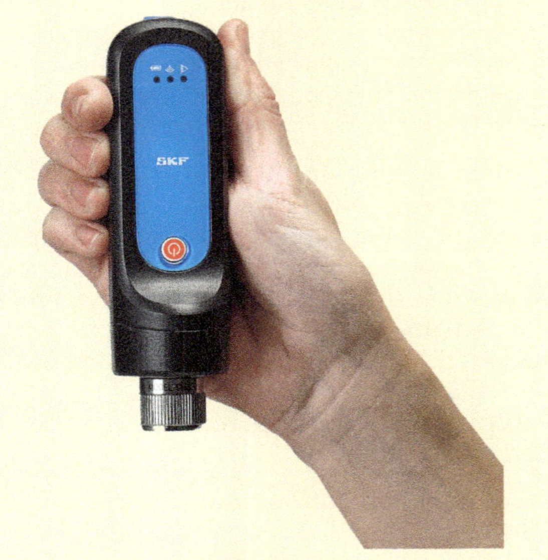

Figure Credit: Courtesy of SKF, Lincoln Industrial Products, Alemite LLC

Examine the filler cap and breather. If they're dirty, clean them so dirt doesn't get into the reservoir. Check the reservoir's surface. If it's oily and dusty, the fluid inside won't cool efficiently. Clean off the grime.

If the reservoir has an external cooler, check its radiator for dust and bent fins. Correct any problems that you discover. Confirm that coolers with pumps or fans operate correctly. If the reservoir has a temperature gauge, verify that the fluid isn't too hot.

Examine pipes, hoses, valves, gauges, and other accessories mounted on the reservoir. Look for damage, leaks, or oily grime. Clean dirty surfaces and correct simple problems. Put more complex problems on the repair schedule.

1.3.2 Inspecting Strainers and Filters

Strainers and filters help keep the hydraulic fluid clean (*Figure 26*). Dirty fluid reduces the system's efficiency and damages components. Good PM programs schedule cleaning strainer screens and replacing filter elements. This practice reduces clogging and poor fluid flow.

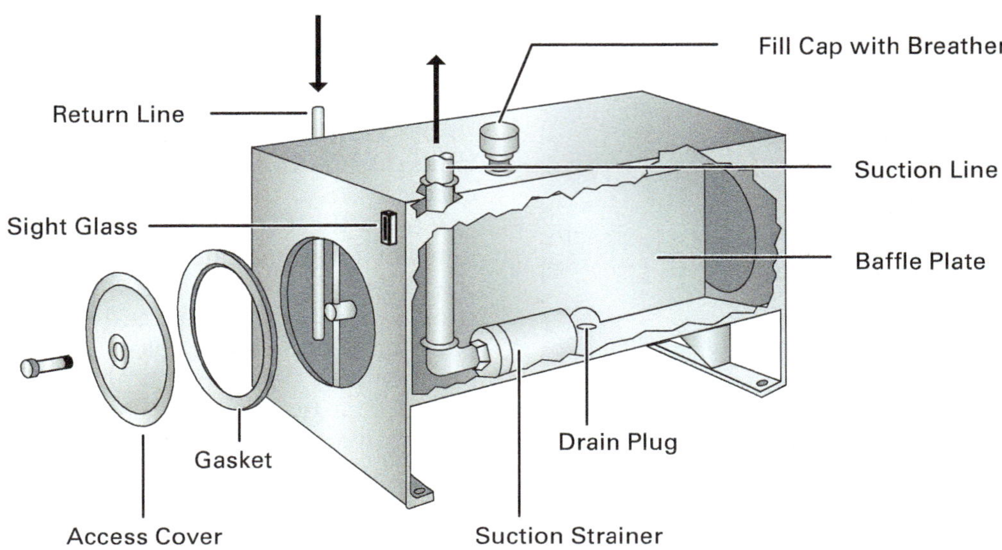

Figure 25 Hydraulic reservoir.

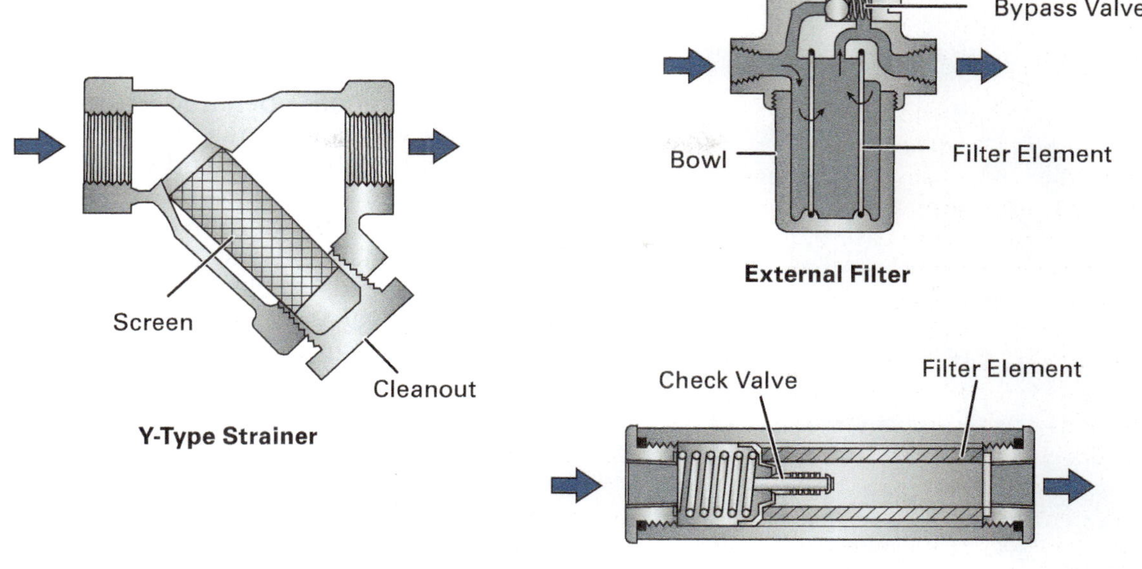

Figure 26 Strainers and filters.

Strainers may or may not be easily removable since they're usually inside the reservoir. Some have an external cleanout plug for accessing the screen. Most external filters open easily for replacing the element.

Check external filters for leaks and cleanliness. Correct any problems that you discover. Examine filters equipped with a bypass valve. If a filter is in bypass mode, schedule replacing the element as quickly as possible.

> **NOTE**
>
> If you discover problems that require repair, check the strainer/filter PM schedule. If the next cleaning/replacement cycle is imminent, schedule the repair and PM at the same time.

1.3.3 Inspecting Hydraulic Pumps and Motors

The pump and its drive motor are the heart of the hydraulic power unit. Inspect them carefully since a failure can be costly in time and money. Wear and misalignment cause most problems. Fortunately, these usually create symptoms that show up during inspection.

Observe the pump and motor when they're running. Listen for unusual sounds or excessive vibration. An erratic, noisy pump may be cavitating due to low fluid or air in the system. If the pump has a flowmeter, monitor it while the pump is running. Confirm that the flow is within the normal operating range.

Measure the pump and motor's temperatures with an infrared temperature probe (*Figure 27*). High temperatures can indicate worn parts or bearings. Misalignment in direct-drive machines also causes high temperatures.

> **WARNING!**
>
> Never check temperatures by touching components with your bare hands. You could burn yourself.

If possible, shut down the hydraulic power unit and then restart it. Listen to the pump and motor as they come up to speed. Hesitation or struggling could indicate binding, misalignment, or an electrical problem.

Have a qualified electrician check for electrical problems by measuring the motor current (amperage) with an ammeter (*Figure 28*). Three-phase motors have three legs (phases), each carrying its own current. The electrician should measure the current in each phase. High motor current indicates either mechanical or electrical problems. With three-phase motors, significantly different phase currents may indicate a damaged motor. They can also suggest a wiring problem.

> **WARNING!**
>
> Unless you are a qualified electrician, do not perform electrical diagnostics yourself.

Figure 27 Infrared temperature probe.

Check the pump for leaks. If it has external accessories, inspect them as well. Note anything that's behaving abnormally. Wipe off dirty or oily surfaces. Confirm that mounting bolts are torqued to the correct values.

Shut down the hydraulic power unit. Lock out and tag it. Remove the guards from around the coupling on a direct-drive machine. Remove the belt guards from a belt-driven machine. If the machine has a flexible coupling, inspect the element for wear. If it has a belt, check it for wear and confirm the proper tension. Replace the guards and restart the machine.

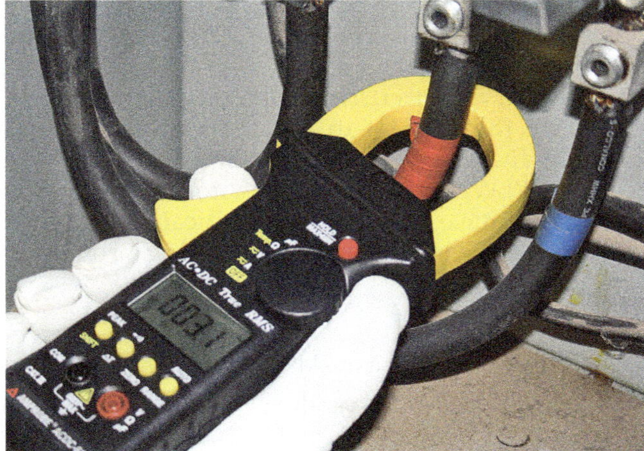

Figure 28 An electrician measuring current.

1.3.4 Inspecting Valves

Valves perform many tasks in a hydraulic system. A misbehaving valve can halt the system or hinder its smooth operation. During inspection, check all valves for leaks and obvious problems. Document malfunctions and valve behavior carefully to make later troubleshooting easier.

Low or high pressure in an operating hydraulic system may indicate a pressure relief valve problem. An adjustable valve may be improperly set. A fixed valve may be broken. Sluggish actuator response suggests a partial blockage or an improperly set throttle valve.

Hydraulic fluid returning to the reservoir when valves are supposedly closed can indicate a partially blocked valve. Malfunctioning counterbalance or sequence valves can cause abnormal actuator behavior. A stuck check valve that allows fluid to flow backwards can produce many strange behaviors.

If possible, operate DCVs to confirm normal machine operation. For electrically controlled DCVs, you may need to involve an automation specialist. Note sluggish or incorrect actuator response.

> **WARNING!**
>
> Before testing a machine, warn those working nearby. Unexpectedly operating a machine can cause accidents, injuries, or even a fatality.

1.3.5 Inspecting Hoses, Lines, and Gauges

Hoses and lines carry hydraulic fluid between components. They're common failure points, particularly hoses that constantly move (*Figure 29*). Gauges report the pressure at different points within the system. Since they're fragile, they can break easily.

> **WARNING!**
>
> Leaks in pressurized lines can cause injection injuries. Always wear gloves and eye protection. Get prompt medical attention for all injection injuries.

Inspect hoses, lines, and fittings carefully. Look for leaks, oily patches, and damaged connectors. Tighten loose fittings with the proper tools. Clean up oily patches. Note damaged or worn hoses. Schedule replacing any hoses with abrasions, kinks, rot, or burned spots. Examine hose hangers and supports, correcting any problems that you discover.

NCCER – *Millwright*

Figure 29 Moving hoses commonly fail.

Examine gauges for obvious damage or leaks. Any gauge reporting an unrealistic pressure value may be broken. Note the reading and schedule further troubleshooting. For electronic gauges or sensors, inspect the instrumentation wiring for damage.

1.3.6 Inspecting Actuators

Hydraulic actuators—cylinders and motors—convert fluid power into mechanical motion. Machine operators usually notice and report major actuator problems. Inspections identify the more subtle ones.

When inspecting a cylinder actuator, look for obvious leaks or oily spots near the connections or seals. Leaks around the piston rod indicate failing seals. Check mounting bolts and hardware for damage and proper tightness. Examine the piston rod for damage or burrs. Bent rods can't move smoothly and may damage seals.

If possible, operate the machine and watch the cylinder in action. It should move smoothly and quietly. Sluggish movement could indicate leaking piston seals or a partially clogged line. Noisy or jerky movement indicates damaged components.

> **WARNING!**
> Before testing a machine, warn those working nearby. Unexpectedly operating a machine can cause accidents, injuries, or even a fatality.

If an actuator can't move the load, check the input pressure first. If the pressure is correct, suspect internal leaks. An actuator that can't hold its position may also be leaking internally. Alternatively, a leaking DCV or counterbalance valve may prevent an actuator from holding its position.

When inspecting a hydraulic motor actuator, look for obvious leaks or oily spots near the connections or seals. Leaks around the shaft indicate failing seals. Check mounting bolts for proper tightness. Examine the shaft for damage.

If possible, operate the machine and watch the motor in action. Confirm that the control lever on axial piston motors operates freely. Motors should speed up and slow down smoothly. Bidirectional motors should run equally well in both directions.

Sluggish movement could indicate leaks or a partially clogged line. Noisy or jerky movement may indicate damaged components. Excessive vibration suggests an alignment problem between the motor and the load. Motors that can't move the load may have low input pressure. Alternatively, they could be leaking internally.

All hydraulic actuators will run hot if their parts are worn or operating under abnormal stress. Use an infrared temperature probe to measure a noisy or misbehaving actuator's temperature. Check the temperature where a hydraulic motor's shaft enters the housing. High temperatures here often indicate misalignment or a bearing problem.

1.4.0 Troubleshooting Hydraulic Machines

When hydraulic equipment stops unexpectedly, a company starts losing money. Getting the broken machine running again becomes a top priority. Companies rely on troubleshooters to identify problems quickly.

Randomly searching for the problem wastes time. Good troubleshooters deploy their efforts systematically. Understanding how equipment works helps them understand how it can fail. They examine the system schematic, identifying the failure points. Working through these usually leads to the problem.

> **WARNING!**
> Before troubleshooting a machine, warn those working nearby. Unexpectedly operating a machine can cause accidents, injuries, or even a fatality.

1.4.1 Remembering Key Principles

Before troubleshooting a problem, mentally review key hydraulic principles. These explain most hydraulic system failures. Looking for compromised principles often leads to the failure's cause. The following five principles underlie all hydraulic machines:

1. Movement depends on fluid flow. If the fluid isn't moving, nothing moves.

2. Flow rate determines actuator speed. Insufficient flow produces sluggish behavior.

3. Pressure causes flow. If there's no pressure, there won't be flow.

4. Pressure depends on the load. The larger the load, the higher the pressure will be.

5. The hydraulic power unit has a maximum pressure limit.

It's also helpful to review the key parts of all hydraulic systems. Remind yourself what those parts do. Ask yourself which hydraulic principles they affect. The following components underlie all hydraulic machines:

Hydraulic power unit — Moves the fluid and develops pressure against the load's resistance.

Valves — Start, stop, and modify the fluid's flow.

Actuators — Turn fluid power into mechanical motion.

Hoses, lines, and fittings — Tie everything together.

1.4.2 The Troubleshooting Process

Think of a hydraulic system as a long chain with many links (*Figure 30*). When one breaks, everything after it stops. The easiest way to find the broken link is to start at one end and work to the other. For example, if a machine powered by a hydraulic motor stops running, you could start at the motor and work back to the hydraulic power unit. Alternatively, you could start at the hydraulic power unit and work towards the motor.

> **NOTE**
>
> Expert troubleshooters may start somewhere in the middle and work towards one end. They use their experience to identify the most likely fault location and start troubleshooting near it. This strategy often saves time. Unfortunately, it can waste time if the troubleshooter starts at the wrong place.

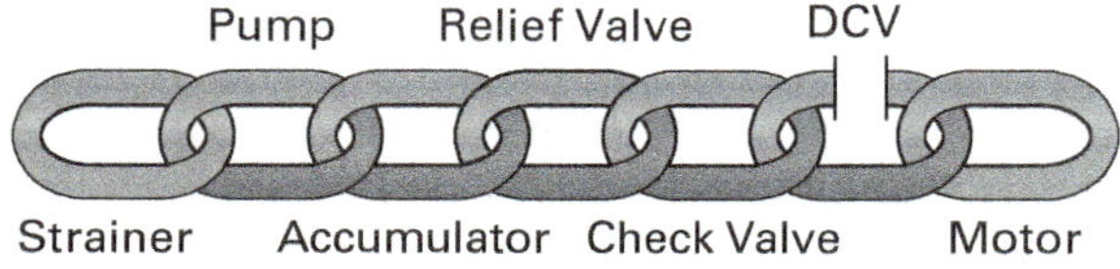

Figure 30 The hydraulic chain.

Sometimes, a little common sense eliminates unnecessary work. For example, if only one machine in a large system stops, the power unit's components can't be the problem. Starting at the hydraulic pump would be foolish. Instead, it's better to begin where the faulty machine connects to the fluid supply.

Many companies develop their own troubleshooting charts. *Table 1A* and *Table 1B* show a generic example. For actual troubleshooting, however, always follow your company's procedures. If it doesn't have one, consult the equipment manufacturer's troubleshooting guide. To use a troubleshooting chart, first find the problem's description. Then examine the suggested causes and solutions.

When troubleshooting, always examine gauges and other status indicators. Pressure gauges report the hydraulic fluid's pressure at key locations. Flowmeters show the fluid's flow rate through the system. Temperature gauges let you know if the fluid is too hot. Advanced hydraulic power units may have electronic control systems with graphical status panels. These provide very detailed and helpful information.

1.4.3 Checking the Hydraulic Power Unit

Without fluid flow, nothing happens. Check the power unit or accumulator's pressure gauge. If you don't know the machine's correct operating pressure, look it up in the manual. If the pressure is low, confirm that the motor and pump operate. Check the pressure relief valve to verify that it's set correctly and isn't stuck open.

If there's adequate pressure but no flow, look for blockages. Examine any filters between the power unit and the rest of the system. A clogged filter can reduce or block flow. Check for crimped or kinked lines and hoses. Sometimes, a line will have an internal blockage.

1.4.4 Checking the Valves

Usually, several valves lie between the power unit and the actuator. Any of these can interrupt the flow or divert it elsewhere. Confirm that shutoff valves are open. Pressure relief valves must be closed. Verify that check valves aren't stuck shut. Be alert for leaks, either from connections or around valve stems.

DCVs often malfunction since they're complex valves that cycle frequently. Mechanically controlled DCVs are easier to test than solenoid units. You may need an automation specialist's help to test solenoid-controlled DCVs. Check each valve position, confirming that the fluid flows through the correct paths.

Problem	Possible Causes	Possible Solutions
The actuator isn't moving.	• The pump isn't running.	• Repair or replace the motor.
	• The pump/drive motor coupling or belt is loose or broken.	• Tighten or replace the coupling or belt.
	• The fluid level is low.	• Add extra fluid.
	• The relief valve is stuck open.	• Repair or replace the relief valve.
	• A valve is stuck or clogged.	• Correct or clear the valve.
	• The DCV isn't shifting.	• Repair or replace the DCV.
	• The actuator is binding.	• Adjust the actuator.
The actuator is moving too slowly.	• The pump speed is too low.	• Increase the motor speed or adjust the pump.
	• The line is restricted.	• Locate and clear the blockage.
	• The throttle valve is set too low.	• Adjust the throttle valve.
	• A valve is stuck or clogged.	• Correct or clear the valve.
	• The DCV isn't shifting completely.	• Repair or replace the DCV.
The actuator is slowing or stalling under load.	• The pump is leaking.	• Repair or replace the pump.
	• The relief valve is set too low.	• Adjust the relief valve.
	• The actuator is leaking.	• Repair or replace the actuator.
	• The actuator is binding.	• Adjust the actuator.
The actuator is moving too fast.	• The pump speed is too high.	• Reduce the motor speed or adjust the pump.
	• The throttle valve is set too high.	• Adjust the throttle valve.
The actuator is moving in a jerky or erratic manner.	• The accumulator is defective.	• Recharge, adjust, or replace the accumulator.
	• The DCV solenoid is defective.	• Replace the solenoid.
	• The actuator is damaged or leaking internally.	• Repair or replace the actuator.
	• The fluid is contaminated.	• Change the fluid.
The actuator is creeping.	• The pump speed is too low.	• Increase the motor speed or adjust the pump.
	• The line is restricted.	• Locate and clear the blockage.
	• The throttle valve is set too low.	• Adjust the throttle valve.
	• A valve is stuck or clogged.	• Correct or clear the valve.
	• The DCV isn't shifting completely.	• Repair or replace the DCV.
	• The DCV is leaking.	• Repair or replace the DCV.
The load is sinking.	• The counterbalance valve is set too low or is leaking.	• Adjust or replace the counterbalance valve.
	• The actuator is leaking.	• Repair or replace the actuator.
The hydraulic pump is noisy.	• The pump is worn.	• Repair or replace the pump.
	• The pump speed is too high.	• Decrease the motor speed or adjust the pump.
	• The pump and motor are misaligned.	• Align the pump and motor.
	• The fluid level is too low.	• Add extra fluid.
	• The suction strainer is plugged.	• Clean the suction strainer.
	• The suction line is restricted.	• Locate and clear the blockage.
	• The suction line is leaking.	• Replace the suction line.
	• The relief valve is set too high.	• Adjust the relief valve.

Problem	Possible Causes	Possible Solutions
The pump is too hot.	• The pump is worn.	• Repair or replace the pump.
	• The pump and motor are misaligned.	• Align the pump and motor.
	• The relief valve is set too high.	• Adjust the relief valve.
The relief valve is too hot.	• The relief valve is leaking.	• Replace the relief valve.
	• The relief valve is set too low.	• Adjust the relief valve.
The pump is not delivering sufficient flow.	• The pump is worn.	• Repair or replace the pump.
	• The fluid level is low.	• Add extra fluid.
	• The suction strainer is clogged.	• Clean the suction strainer.
	• The suction line is restricted.	• Locate and clear the blockage.
	• Air is entering the suction line.	• Replace the suction line.
The system pressure is low.	• The pump is worn.	• Repair or replace the pump.
	• The relief valve is set too low.	• Adjust the relief valve.
	• There are leaks in the system.	• Locate and repair the leaks.

Throttle valves regulate variable-speed actuators. If a hydraulic motor or cylinder operates too slowly, check for an improperly set or clogged throttle valve. Counterbalance and sequence valves manage part of an actuator's cycle. If the actuator moves but behaves incorrectly, check these valves. A setpoint may be incorrect or the valve may be malfunctioning.

1.4.5 Checking Control Logic

Some hydraulic machines have devices that decide how and when DCVs may operate. These components, called *control logic*, manage timing and ensure that the system behaves correctly. Control logic coordinates safety features, prevents inappropriate actions from happening, and generates event sequences. Ultimately, it controls DCVs and other valves.

Testing complex control logic can be difficult. If an industrial computer or electronic controller implements it, you'll need an automation specialist's help. Simple mechanical logic with manual controls is easier to test. Always study the hydraulic schematics before testing. Be sure you understand how the system should behave.

1.4.6 Checking Interlocks

Interlocks prevent machines from doing something inappropriate. For example, a saw can't begin cutting until the material moves into place. Similarly, cut material can't exit until the saw finishes. Interlocks prevent incompatible actions from happening at the same time.

They also make machines safer. For example, some machines shouldn't operate if a person moves too close to certain parts. A safety sensor detects the person and prevents the machine from running.

Malfunctioning interlocks can prevent equipment from operating. Confirm that they're working correctly. Verify that mechanical interlocks move freely. Involve an automation specialist if you suspect that an electronic interlock is misbehaving.

> **WARNING!**
>
> Never disable interlocks. You could damage the machine or cause an injury.

1.4.7 Checking the Actuator

Actuators convert fluid flow into motion. Machines use them to move loads, operate tools, and create complex motion. Hydraulic motors rotate, while hydraulic cylinders move back and forth in a straight line.

If fluid reaches the actuator at the correct pressure and flow rate, it should move. If it doesn't, it requires troubleshooting. Read the pressure gauge closest to the actuator. If the pressure isn't correct, work backwards to find the problem.

If the actuator is getting fluid at the correct pressure, determine why it isn't moving. Disconnect the actuator from the mechanism that it drives. If the actuator operates correctly, check the driven mechanism. It could be jammed, damaged, or overloaded. Dried lubricant can prevent free movement. If the mechanism moves freely, the actuator may be leaking or have bad seals. Sometimes, a malfunctioning actuator will move normally when unloaded but can't handle a load.

An actuator receiving fluid but not moving could be jammed or have a serious leak. It may require cleaning and lubrication. Check its seals, supply lines, and connectors. Any of these could be the problem.

1.5.0 Repairing Hydraulic Systems

Repairs usually follow troubleshooting. Inspections also trigger repairs. Some repairs are minor, such as tightening a leaky connector or replacing a filter element. Many, however, require shutting down all or part of the system. Usually, this requires approval. Some plants may allow repairs only at certain times. Normal PM repairs happen during scheduled downtime.

Companies vary in what they choose to repair. In the past, many organizations repaired almost everything. Today, labor costs often exceed component costs, so repairs are less popular. Most organizations simply replace cheaper components. Similarly, they usually send complex machines to specialist repair companies rather than servicing them in house.

Repair procedures depend on the machine and its complexity. When possible, follow the manufacturer's guidelines. Get the service manual or download an electronic copy. If your company has its own repair procedures, follow those. Before starting work, confirm that the required spare parts and supplies are available.

1.5.1 Preparation

Prepare for all repair tasks, even emergency ones. Thinking ahead avoids unnecessary delays and problems. It also reduces accidents. The following steps outline preparation:

Step 1 Get the proper PPE and check its condition.

Step 2 Gather the required tools, parts, and supplies. Read the manufacturer's service manual and/or your company's repair procedures.

Step 3 Lower all loads and return moving parts to safe positions. Block anything that could move unexpectedly.

Step 4 Shut down the machine. Isolate it and release the pressure by activating the double block and bleed valves. If present, shut down other power sources (electrical or pneumatic).

Step 5 Lock out and tag *all* energy sources (hydraulic, electrical, and pneumatic). Confirm that you can't restore power with the locks in place.

Step 6 Bleed off pressure within the system by activating the correct release valves. Confirm zero pressure on all pressure gauges. Verify that no machine parts move unexpectedly.

1.5.2 General Disassembly Procedures

Once the equipment is shut down and safe, you're ready to start repairs. All but the simplest will require disassembly. The following steps outline common tasks:

Step 1 Remove any guards or panels covering the equipment.

Step 2 Before removing a component, clean around its connections. This step prevents grime from getting into equipment and contaminating threads.

Step 3 Disconnect any control piping or wiring.

Step 4 Disconnect the hoses, tubes, or pipes. Cap or seal the ends. Collect small fittings and hardware in a container.

Step 5 Before removing components, note their positions and attachment methods. If necessary, take photos to help you during reassembly.

Step 6 Remove the component. Capture any hydraulic fluid in a container. If you're replacing the component, set it aside so you won't reinstall it accidentally. If you're repairing it, set it aside in a clean place.

Step 7 If a component requires further disassembly, clean it first. Follow the manufacturer's instructions to disassemble it. Keep all parts in order. Collect small parts in a container.

Step 8 Clean and inspect each component or component part. Remove old gaskets and seals. Identify damaged or worn parts.

Step 9 Arrange good parts and new spares in assembly order. Keep spare parts in their packages until you're ready to use them.

1.5.3 General Reassembly Procedure

Reassembly is the reverse of disassembly. Consult the manufacturer's guidelines and procedures. The following general steps apply to reassembling components before reinstalling them:

- Inspect parts before assembling them. Confirm the correct spare parts and check their fit.
- Apply any manufacturer-specified lubricants or treatments.
- Install seals, gaskets, and O-rings. Handle them carefully to avoid nicks and cuts.
- Tighten all fasteners to the manufacturer-specified values using an appropriate torque tool. Follow the correct tightening sequence.
- Check clearances or tolerances with appropriate measuring tools.
- Confirm that moving parts operate freely and smoothly.

Once the components are ready, reassemble the equipment. The following steps outline the process:

Step 1 Install the component. Confirm the correct position. Tighten all fasteners to the correct values using an appropriate torque tool.

Step 2 Uncap and clean hose, tube, or pipe ends.

Step 3 Reconnect the supply and return lines. Tighten all fittings.

Step 4 Reconnect control piping or wiring.

Step 5 Complete any final installation steps. Replace panels and guards.

Step 6 Confirm that it's safe to restart the equipment. Remove your locks and tags. When other craftworkers have removed theirs, remove isolation and re-energize the equipment.

Step 7 Cautiously start the machine. Unblock loads and moving parts. Test each machine function.

Step 8 Check for leaks.

Step 9 Return the machine to service. Notify the machine operator and other relevant personnel.

1.5.4 General Cleanup Procedure

Never skip final cleanup! Craft professionals always leave a workplace better than they found it. The following steps summarize common wrap-up tasks:

Step 1 Clean the area around the machine. Remove tools, packaging, trash, and old parts.

Step 2 Check for spilled hydraulic fluid and lubricants. Make sure everything is clean and safe.

Step 3 Discard packaging, old gaskets, and rags in the proper containers.

Step 4 Discard hydraulic fluid and old lubricants in the proper containers.

Step 5 Recycle old parts or send them out for rebuilding.

Step 6 Complete all documentation. Record detailed information in the log to help others who will work on the machine in the future.

1.5.5 Repairing a Hydraulic Pump

Repairing a hydraulic pump is a complex task requiring great care and attention. Each model has its own unique requirements. Obtain and read the manufacturer's service manual. The following steps outline the general procedure for removing a hydraulic pump:

Step 1 Prepare the system for repair by following the procedures outlined in this module.

Step 2 Clean the pump, especially around the connections.

Step 3 Disconnect the piping from the pump. Cap or seal the pipe ends.

Step 4 Disconnect the coupling from a direct-drive pump. Remove the belt from a belt-driven unit.

Step 5 Remove the pump's mounting bolts.

Step 6 Remove any shim packs under the feet. Document the number of shims under each foot. Note each shim's thickness.

Step 7 Remove the pump and take it to a clean work area.

Follow the manufacturer's guidelines for disassembling, repairing, and reassembling the pump. The process should resemble the general procedures outlined in this module. Work carefully and keep everything clean. Replace all questionable parts with suitable spares. Replace all gaskets, seals, and O-rings. Follow the manufacturer's guidelines for lubricating moving parts. Confirm that parts fit properly and move freely.

The following steps outline the general procedure for reinstalling a hydraulic pump:

Step 1 Clean the baseplate.

Step 2 Place the pump on the baseplate.

Step 3 Loosely install the pump's mounting bolts.

Step 4 Replace the shim packs under each foot in the original positions. If any shims are damaged or wrinkled, replace them with new shims of the same thickness.

Step 5 Verify that the piping connections are clean.

Step 6 Install any required gaskets or seals.

Step 7 Loosely connect the piping.

Step 8 For a direct-drive pump, install the coupling. Prealign the pump and motor. Check for soft foot and pipe strain.

> **NOTE**
>
> NCCER Module 15307, *Couplings and Alignment Fundamentals*, and NCCER Module 15313, *Prealignment and Shim Fabrication*, outline these procedures in detail.

Step 9 Tighten all piping connections to the proper values with suitable tools.

Step 10 Perform a precision alignment. Skip to *Step 13*.

> **NOTE**
>
> NCCER Module 15314, *Dial Indicator Alignment*, and NCCER Module 15502, *Laser Alignment*, outline precision alignment in detail.

> **CAUTION**
>
> A misaligned pump and motor could bind, run hot, or wear out rapidly. Always align direct-drive equipment.

Step 11 For a belt-driven pump, install the sheave and belt. Align everything correctly. Check for soft foot and pipe strain.

Step 12 Properly tension the belt.

NCCER Module 15311, *Installing Belt and Chain Drives*, outlines these procedures in detail.

Step 13 Confirm that the pump's mounting bolts are tightened to the correct torque. Confirm that the piping is properly tightened.

Step 14 Return the pump to service by following the procedures outlined in this module.

Step 15 Check for leaks and proper operation. Correct any problems.

Step 16 Clean up and document your work by following the procedures outlined in this module.

1.5.6 Repairing Valves

Hydraulic valves come in many styles, so no one repair procedure applies to all. Most companies replace rather than repair smaller valves. Many companies send larger or more complex valves to a valve rebuilding service. If you do have to rebuild a valve, obtain and read the manufacturer's service manual. The following steps outline the general procedure for removing a valve from the system:

Step 1 Prepare the system for repair by following the procedures outlined in this module.

Step 2 Examine the valve's position and all connections before disconnecting anything. If necessary, take photos or make notes. This will help you later when you reinstall the valve.

Not all facilities allow workers to take photos during service tasks. Ask first!

Step 3 Clean the valve's connections.

Step 4 If the valve has electrical supply or control wiring, disconnect it. If present, disconnect pneumatic control lines. Label all connections.

Some valves have power or control connectors that non-electricians may safely disconnect. Otherwise, you must involve a qualified electrician. Never disconnect live circuits of any type. You could be injured or damage the equipment. When in doubt, ask before disconnecting anything.

Step 5 Disconnect the piping. How you do this depends on the fitting types. For larger valves, you may have to set up rigging to support the valve before disconnecting it.

Step 6 Remove the valve and take it to a clean work area.

Follow the manufacturer's guidelines for disassembling, repairing, and reassembling the valve. The process should resemble the general procedures outlined in this module. Work carefully and keep everything clean. Contaminants getting inside a valve can ruin it.

Replace all questionable parts with suitable spares. Replace all gaskets, seals, and O-rings. Sealing surfaces are especially crucial in valves. Follow the manufacturer's guidelines for lubricating moving parts. Confirm that parts fit properly and move freely.

The following steps outline the general procedure for reinstalling a valve:

Step 1 Verify that the piping connections are clean.

Step 2 Install any required gaskets or seals.

Step 3 Install the valve in the correct orientation. Connect the piping. Tighten connectors or flange bolts. Don't overtighten.

Step 4 Reconnect power and control leads. If present, reconnect pneumatic lines.

Some valves have power or control connectors that non-electricians may safely connect. Otherwise, you must involve a qualified electrician. Never connect live circuits of any type. You could be injured or damage the equipment. When in doubt, ask before connecting anything.

Step 5 Return the system to service by following the procedures outlined in this module.

Step 6 Check for leaks and proper operation. For DCVs and complex valves, operate them in all positions. You may need an automation specialist's help to test solenoid-controlled DCVs. Correct any problems.

Step 7 Clean up and document your work by following the procedures outlined in this module.

1.5.7 Repairing Actuators

Repairing a hydraulic cylinder actuator is relatively straightforward. Hydraulic motor actuators are more complex. They require greater skill and experience. Every actuator has its own unique requirements. Obtain and read the manufacturer's service manual. The following steps outline the general procedure for removing an actuator:

Step 1 Prepare the system for repair by following the procedures outlined in this module.

Step 2 Clean the actuator, especially around the connections.

Step 3 Disconnect the piping or hoses from the actuator. Cap or seal the ends.

Step 4 Disconnect a cylinder actuator from the mechanism that it drives. For a motor actuator, remove the coupling, belt, or chain.

Step 5 Remove mounting bolts or other hardware securing the actuator.

Step 6 If present, remove any shim packs under a motor actuator's feet. Document the number of shims under each foot. Note each shim's thickness.

Step 7 Remove the actuator and take it to a clean work area.

Follow the manufacturer's guidelines for disassembling, repairing, and reassembling the actuator. The process should resemble the general procedures outlined in this module. Work carefully and keep everything clean. Be especially careful around cylinder bores and pistons. Contaminants can badly damage these precision surfaces. Replace all questionable parts with suitable spares. Replace all gaskets, seals, and O-rings. Follow the manufacturer's guidelines for lubricating moving parts. Confirm that parts fit properly and move freely.

The following steps outline the general procedure for reinstalling a hydraulic cylinder actuator:

Step 1 Clean the actuator mounting area.

Step 2 Position the actuator and install any mounting hardware. Loosely install the bolts.

Step 3 If required, lubricate the linkage between the actuator and the driven mechanism.

Step 4 Connect the driven mechanism.

Step 5 Adjust the actuator so it can operate the driven mechanism without binding. Tighten the bolts to the correct value with a suitable torque tool.

Step 6 Verify that the piping connections are clean.

Step 7 Install any required gaskets or seals.

Step 8 Reattach the piping and tighten all connections.

Step 9 Return the actuator to service by following the procedures outlined in this module.

Step 10 Check for leaks and proper operation. Confirm that the actuator and driven mechanism move smoothly without binding. Correct any problems.

Step 11 Clean up and document your work by following the procedures outlined in this module.

The following steps outline the general procedure for reinstalling a hydraulic motor actuator:

Step 1 Clean the baseplate.

Step 2 Place the actuator on the baseplate.

Step 3 Loosely install the actuator's mounting bolts.

Step 4 Replace the shim packs under each motor foot in the original positions. If any shims are damaged or wrinkled, replace them with new shims of the same thickness.

Step 5 Verify that the piping connections are clean.

Step 6 Install any required gaskets or seals.

Step 7 Loosely connect the piping.

Step 8 For a direct-drive application, install the coupling. Prealign the actuator and the driven machine. Check for soft foot and pipe strain.

NCCER Module 15307, *Couplings and Alignment Fundamentals*, and NCCER Module 15313, *Prealignment and Shim Fabrication*, outline these procedures in detail.

Step 9 Tighten all piping connections to the proper values with suitable tools.

Step 10 Perform a precision alignment. Skip to *Step 13*.

NCCER Module 15314, *Dial Indicator Alignment*, and NCCER Module 15502, *Laser Alignment*, outline precision alignment in detail.

A misaligned actuator and driven machine could bind, run hot, or wear out rapidly. Always align direct-drive equipment

Step 11 For a belt- or chain-driven application, install the sheave/sprocket and belt/chain. Align everything correctly. Check for soft foot and pipe strain.

Step 12 Properly tension the belt/chain.

NCCER Module 15311, *Installing Belt and Chain Drives*, outlines these procedures in detail.

Figure 31 Local hose fabrication shop.

Step 13 Confirm that the actuator's mounting bolts are tightened to the correct torque. Confirm that the piping is properly tightened.

Step 14 Return the actuator to service by following the procedures outlined in this module.

Step 15 Check for leaks and proper operation. Confirm that the actuator and driven mechanism move smoothly. Correct any problems.

Step 16 Clean up and document your work by following the procedures outlined in this module.

1.5.8 Replacing Hoses

In the past, millwrights and industrial mechanics fabricated their own hydraulic hoses. After cutting suitable hose stock to the right length, they installed the correct fittings. Today, most companies no longer allow maintenance personnel to make their own hoses. Labor costs are higher and hose failures can be extremely dangerous.

Instead, companies purchase prefabricated hoses from a supplier. These have the correct fittings installed and come in many lengths. Some companies work with a local hose fabrication shop that creates custom hoses very quickly (*Figure 31*). Online hose fabrication services offer an alternative when a local business isn't available.

To replace a hose, measure its length. Identify the hose material, diameter, and pressure rating. Examine the fittings and identify their type, material, and size. It's crucial that the replacement hose be functionally identical to the original. Once you've properly identified the hose, obtain a replacement. Install it using the proper tools and check for leaks.

Never use a replacement hose with a pressure rating lower than the original. Similarly, the replacement hose's fittings must never have pressure ratings lower than the original fittings. The hose itself must be compatible with the hydraulic fluid. Using the wrong pressure ratings or hose type could cause a catastrophic failure.

Managing a Hard Life

Hydraulic pressure gauges have a rough life. Every time an actuator operates, the pressure changes, usually abruptly. This constant hammering eventually takes its toll, and the gauge fails or becomes inaccurate. To improve gauge lifespan, some systems include a *snubber* between the gauge and the system. As you can see from the picture, a snubber is just a short pipe with a narrow bore. It dampens the hammering action from pressure changes.

A better solution is a *gauge isolator*. This is a valve that disconnects the gauge from the system. Craftworkers briefly open it when they need to check the pressure. The most convenient gauge isolator has a push-to-read control that briefly connects the gauge to the system when the worker presses the button.

1.5.9 Replacing Gauges

Not all repairs require shutting down and isolating the whole system. Isolating a single component may be appropriate. Replacing a pressure gauge is a good example. The following steps outline the process:

Step 1 Get the proper PPE and check its condition.

Step 2 Get a suitable replacement gauge. It must have the same operating range and fittings as the old unit. You'll also need an appropriate wrench.

Step 3 Close the gauge's isolation valves and release pressure through the bleed valve (*Figure 32*).

> **NOTE**
>
> Pressure gauges should have an isolation valve assembly since it makes replacing them easier. If the gauge doesn't have an isolation valve assembly, you'll need to shut down and isolate the entire system. Install an isolation valve assembly while replacing the gauge to avoid future inconvenience.

Step 4 Carefully loosen the gauge with the appropriate wrench. Unscrew the gauge by hand.

Step 5 Install the new gauge by hand. Tighten it with the wrench.

Step 6 Close the bleed valve. Slowly open the isolation valves until the gauge reacts. Open the valves the rest of the way.

> **CAUTION**
>
> A sudden pressure burst can damage the gauge. Slowly opening the isolation valves prevents this problem.

Step 7 Check for leaks.

Step 8 Confirm that the new gauge operates correctly.

Step 9 Clean up and document your work by following the procedures outlined in this module.

Figure 32 Pressure gauge isolation valve assembly.

1.0.0 Section Review

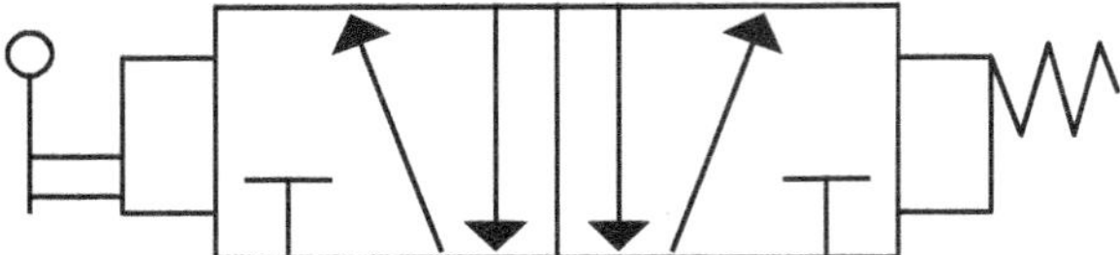

Figure SR01

1. What kind of DCV arrangement does the symbol shown in *Figure SR01* represent?

    a. 3/2
    b. 3/3
    c. 5/2
    d. 5/3

2. Basic maintenance tasks include cleaning, lubricating, and _____.

    a. purging
    b. adjusting
    c. bleeding
    d. cycling

3. If you discover a filter operating in bypass mode, you should _____.

    a. remove the strainer screen
    b. shut down the system
    c. override the bypass valve
    d. schedule replacing the element

4. What explains almost all hydraulic system failures?

    a. A clogged strainer
    b. Hydraulic fluid contamination
    c. Compromised key hydraulic principles
    d. Leaks in the system

5. What is the *first* thing you should do before starting a hydraulic system repair?

    a. Get the correct PPE and check its condition.
    b. Lock out and tag the system.
    c. Isolate the affected section.
    d. Bleed off the system pressure.

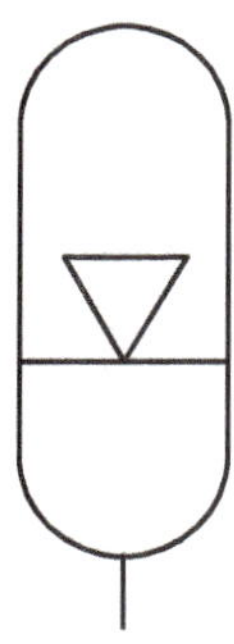

Figure RQ01

1. Which hydraulic device does the symbol in *Figure RQ01* represent?

   a. A counterbalance valve
   b. A DCV
   c. A pump
   d. An accumulator

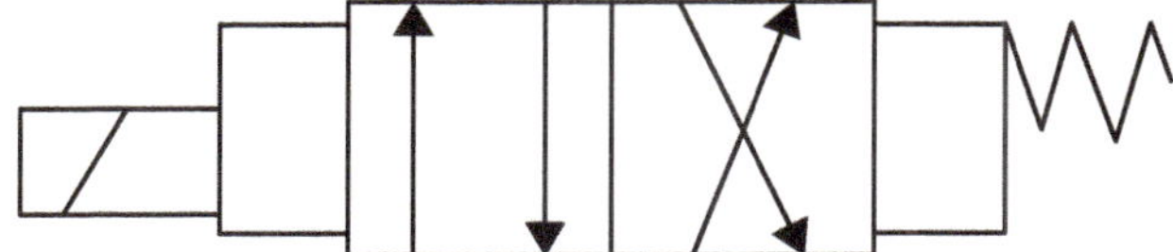

Figure RQ02

2. What kind of actuators does the DCV represented by the symbol in *Figure RQ02* have?

   a. A lever and a spring
   b. A solenoid and a spring
   c. Two springs
   d. A pedal and a spring

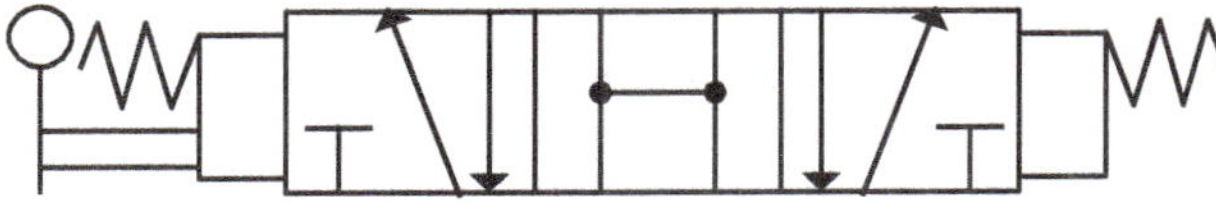

Figure RQ03

3. Which center position type does the DCV represented by the symbol in *Figure RQ03* have?

   a. Tandem
   b. Blocked
   c. Float
   d. Open

4. How can preventive maintenance minimize the financial impact of downtime?

   a. By repairing problems only as they occur
   b. By keeping the spare parts inventory small
   c. By developing carefully planned schedules
   d. By using on-the-fly (OTF) decision making

5. Which task helps to spot emerging problems before they become failures?

   a. Inspection
   b. JIT strategies
   c. Lubrication
   d. Reactive management

6. When you're inspecting a hydraulic system, what is the *best* way to spot leaks?

   a. Listen for a hissing sound.
   b. Look for oily spots or puddles.
   c. Look for erratic pressure gauge behavior.
   d. Be alert for a smell like rotten eggs.

7. If a hydraulic pump is behaving erratically and making a lot of noise, what should you suspect?

   a. A DCV may be sticking.
   b. A counterbalance valve may be open.
   c. The pump may be cavitating.
   d. The motor may have an electrical problem.

8. A cylinder actuator is behaving erratically. You notice that the piston rod is very oily. What could be wrong?

   a. The cylinder may have a bad seal.
   b. The hydraulic fluid may be contaminated.
   c. The cylinder bore may be scratched.
   d. The hydraulic fluid may be too thick.

9. You're troubleshooting a new machine that has failed. Your company hasn't yet developed a troubleshooting procedure. The machine is vital, so downtime is very costly. What is the *best* strategy to follow?

   a. Try to troubleshoot the machine as best you can.
   b. Use the closest company procedure that you can find.
   c. Get a copy of the manufacturer's troubleshooting chart.
   d. Wait for a more experienced millwright to become available.

10. You're repairing a DCV managed by an electronic controller. Who else should you involve?

    a. Your supervisor
    b. A senior millwright
    c. The valve manufacturer
    d. An automatic specialist

Trade Terms Introduced in This Module

Directional control valves (DCVs): Devices that route a working fluid down one of several paths based on the device actuator's position.

Just-in-time (JIT): A strategy that keeps on-site inventory low by ordering required materials just before they're needed for a job.

Solenoid: An electrical control device that pushes or pulls when energized.

Additional Resources

This module presents thorough resources for task training. The following reference material is suggested for further study.

Danfoss Power Solutions (Eaton Hydraulics). **www.eaton.com**.

Essential Hydraulics: Fluid Power. M. Winston. Latest Edition. CreateSpace Independent Publishing Platform.

Hosecraft USA. **www.hosecraftusa.com**.

Hydraulics and Pneumatics: A Technician's and Engineer's Guide. Andrew Parr. Latest Edition. Amsterdam: Elsevier.

Parker Hannefin. **www.parker.com**.

Figure Credits

iStock@Nordroden, Module Opener
iStock@arrowsmith2, Figure 24
Reproduced with Permission, Fluke Corporation, Figure 27
iStock@SINGTO2, Figure 29
Shutterstock.com/Rawi Rochanavipart, Figure 32

Section Review Answer Key

SECTION 1.0.0

Answer	Section Reference	Objective
1. c	1.1.3	1a
2. b	1.2.3	1b
3. d	1.3.2	1c
4. c	1.4.1	1d
5. a	1.5.1	1e

User Update

NCCER makes every effort to keep its textbooks up-to-date and free of technical errors. We appreciate your help in this process. If you find an error, a typographical mistake, or an inaccuracy in NCCER's curricula, please submit a User Update form by visiting **https://www.nccer.org/olf**. You can also scan the QR code using the camera on your phone or mobile device to access the form.

Installing Belt and Chain Drives

OVERVIEW

Previous modules have introduced direct-drive arrangements and the alignment of shafts to produce a smooth, dependable connection between the driver and the connected load. But drive applications often place the drive and driven shafts parallel to each other. In this module, you will learn how belts and chains are used to connect parallel shafts and how the various components are related. It also provides information on the various chain and belt products and how each is best applied.

Module 15311

INSTALLING BELT AND CHAIN DRIVES

Objectives

Successful completion of this module prepares you to do the following:

1. Identify and explain how to install common belt drives.
   a. Describe basic belt drives and how power is transmitted.
   b. Identify and describe various types of drive belts.
   c. Identify and describe various types of sheaves.
   d. Explain how to install and maintain belt drives.
2. Identify and explain how to install various types of chain drives.
   a. Describe common drive chains.
   b. Identify and describe the characteristics of chain drive sprockets.
   c. Explain how to install and maintain chain drives.

Performance Tasks

Under supervision, you should be able to do the following:

1. Properly install, align, and tension a V-belt drive.
2. Properly install, align, and tension a roller chain drive.

Trade Terms

Belt whip
Cut-tooth sprockets
Idler pulley
Master link

Offset link
Sprocket
Synchronous belts

Industry Recognized Credentials

If you are training through an NCCER-accredited sponsor, you may be eligible for credentials from NCCER's Registry. The ID number for this module is 15311. Note that this module may have been used in other NCCER curricula and may apply to other level completions. Contact NCCER's Registry at 1.888.622.3720 or go to **www.nccer.org** for more information.

You can also show off your industry-recognized credentials online with NCCER's digital badges. Transform your knowledge, skills, and achievements into badges that you can share across social media platforms, send to your network, and add to your resume. For more information, visit **www.nccer.org**.

This module uses US standard and metric units in up to three different ways. This note explains how to interpret them.

Exact Conversions

Exact metric equivalents of US standard units appear in parentheses after the US standard unit. For example: "Measure 18" (45.7 cm) from the end and make a mark."

Approximate Conversions

In some cases, exact metric conversions would be inappropriate or even absurd. In these situations, an approximate metric value appears in parentheses with the ~ symbol in front of the number. For example: "Grip the tool about 3" (~8 cm) from the end."

Parallel but not Equal Values

Certain scenarios include US standard and metric values that are parallel but not equal. In these situations, a slash (/) surrounded by spaces separates the US standard and metric values. For example: "Place the point on the steel rule's 1" / 1 cm mark."

How to Access Resources

This craft has additional videos and resources to enhance your learning experience. To view these resources, scan the QR below. The videos and resources are separated by module.

You can scan this code using the camera on your phone or mobile device to view these videos and resources.

Contents

1.0.0 BELT DRIVES AND COMPONENTS

Objective

Identify and explain how to install common belt drives.

  a. Describe basic belt drives and how power is transmitted.
  b. Identify and describe various types of drive belts.
  c. Identify and describe various types of sheaves.
  d. Explain how to install and maintain belt drives.

Performance Task

  1. Properly install, align, and tension a V-belt drive.

Trade Terms

Belt whip: A condition where excess slack in a drive belt causes it to begin riding up and out of the sheave grooves, primarily on the slack side. The slack side is the side exiting the drive pulley as it rotates.

Idler pulley: A pulley or sheave with no attached load, used to help maintain drive belt tension or alignment.

Synchronous belts: Belts with teeth that correspond to grooves in matching sheaves, eliminating slippage, and maintaining synchronized rotation of the shafts; also referred to as *timing belts*.

Previous modules have presented a great deal of information about direct-drive applications relying on shafts that share a centerline. Belt and chain drives are used to transfer power between a driver and a load(s) that have parallel shafts.

Installing, adjusting, and maintaining belt and chain drives are common tasks for millwrights and industrial mechanics. The service life of these drives largely depends on proper installation and timely maintenance. This section will introduce the many types of drive belts and related components.

Rotating belt and chain drives represent significant physical hazards. Always lock out and tag equipment according to local policy before any guards are removed and work is performed on any drive system.

1.1.0 Belt Drives

Belt drives are a quiet, smooth, and economical form of power transmission. They are available in many forms and styles and are widely applied. Drive belts are typically made from a combination of fabric, cord, and/or metal reinforcement joined with natural rubber compounds.

A basic belt drive consists of a driver with a shaft-mounted sheave, a driven load with a sheave, and a belt(s) to match the sheave grooves (*Figure 1*). Multiple belts are used on a drive when the power to be transferred is not within the capacity of a single belt (*Figure 2*).

Drive belts can be divided into two basic types: V-belts and synchronous belts. Synchronous belts are sometimes referred to as *timing belts*. Synchronous belts are formed with angled or rounded teeth. Corresponding grooves or notches in the matching sheaves eliminate belt slippage, keeping the driver and driven sheaves synchronized.

V-belts rely on friction to maintain grip and transfer power. *Figure 3* shows the cross section of a belt where it meets the sheave. The bottom of the belt, at the base of the V, doesn't normally contact the base of the sheave groove. The all-important friction develops only on the tapered, V-shaped sides of the belt. With the belt(s) properly tensioned, friction and grip increase due to a wedging action. When the sides of the belt do not make firm contact with the sheave, excessive slippage results.

Belts are fabricated with strong cords that run the length of the belt. Their position in the belt structure represents the *pitch line* of the belt (*Figure 4*). In recent years, the terminology has changed, and it is now often referred to as the *datum line*.

Belt manufacturers generally consider the datum line to be the effective part of the belt since the cords are the foundation of belt construction. Without the cords, drive belts would be relatively weak. Therefore, the length of the belt measured along the datum line (*datum length*) represents the *effective length* of the belt. The outer circumference of the belt, also provided in many belt specifications, is always slightly longer.

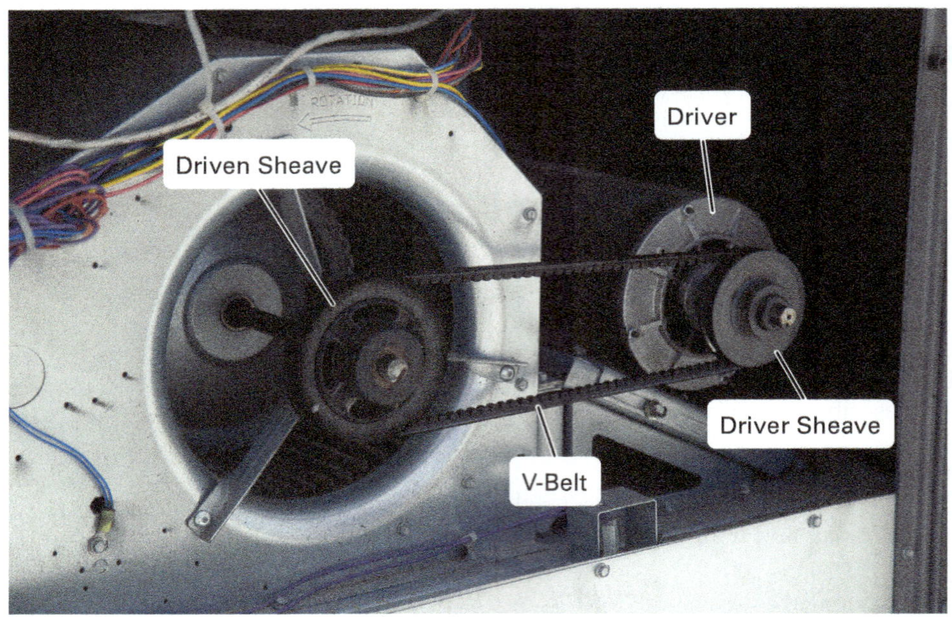

Figure 1 Basic belt drive.

Figure 2 Belt drive with five drive belts.

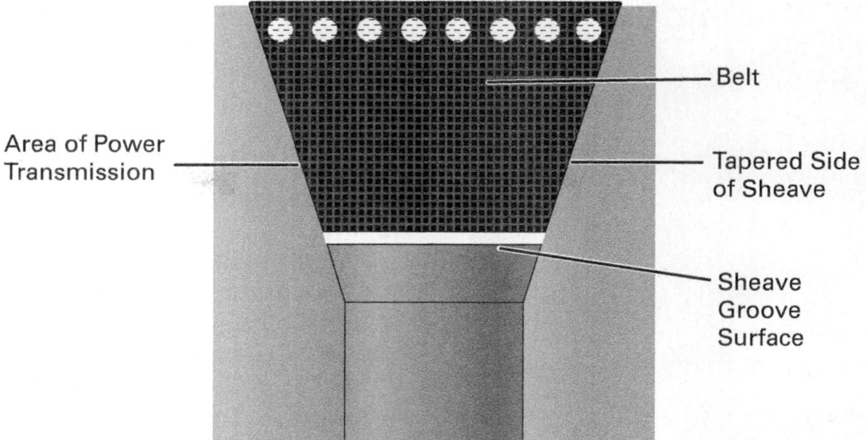

Figure 3 V-belt area of power transmission.

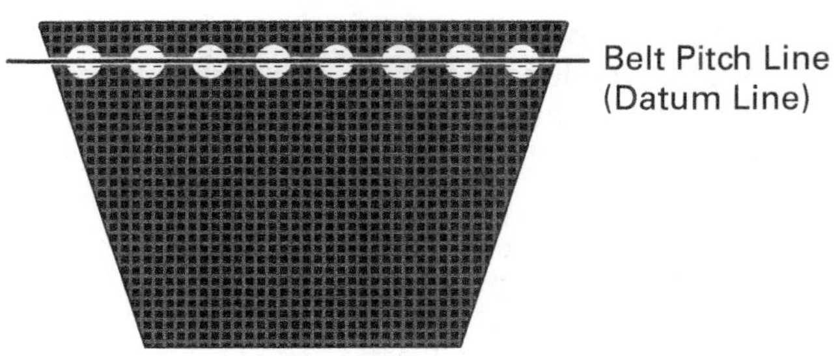

Figure 4 Belt pitch line (datum line).

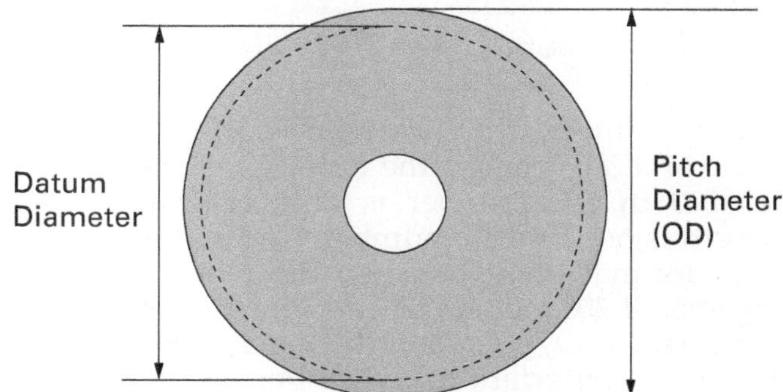

Figure 5 Sheave datum and pitch diameters.

For sheaves, the pitch diameter is simply another term for the outside diameter (OD), which is understandably confusing. The *datum diameter* represents the diameter of the circle where the belt's datum line is expected to ride (*Figure 5*).

Understanding these dimensions allows a craftworker to better understand drive belt and sheave specifications. Sheaves and belts must be properly matched for the drive to perform as expected.

1.2.0 Drive Belts

Drive belts include V-belts and synchronous belts. V-belts have a tapered shape that causes them to wedge firmly into the grooves of the sheave when they are properly tensioned. The types of V-belts that will be introduced in this section include the following:

- Fractional horsepower (FHP)
- Classic
- Wedge
- Banded
- Double-angled

Notched belts will also be discussed, although they aren't considered a separate category. Notching is an optional feature found in more than one type of belt.

Note that FHP and classic belts can often be mounted on the same sheaves, but not all sheaves are designed to accommodate both types of belts. However, wedge belts require unique sheaves designed to fit their profile. FHP and classic belts should never be mounted on sheaves designed for wedge belts, and vice versa.

1.2.1 Fractional Horsepower Belts

Fractional horsepower (FHP) belts are considered light-duty belts, with only one belt on a drive. As the name implies, this type of belt is usually found on small exhaust hoods, centrifugal fans, and similar applications that are driven by a fractional horsepower motor (<1 horsepower). FHP belts may occasionally be found in multiples to accommodate more horsepower and load, but those arrangements are rare.

The size of an FHP belt (*Figure 6*) is indicated by a code marked on the outside of the belt. The first number and letter in the code tell the width of the belt in eighths of an inch. The next three numbers in the code identify the outside length (outer circumference) of the belt, in inches.

Figure 6 FHP V-belts.

For example, a belt marked 4L300 is $\frac{4}{8}$" ($\frac{1}{2}$") wide and 30" long on the outside perimeter. The final 0 in the number is only relevant if the length is not a whole number. Imagine that there is a decimal point between the two zeros. The number 4L305 would indicate that the belt is 30.5" long. However, such lengths are extremely rare. It is very important to remember that FHP belts are measured on the outside circumference of the belt, not along the inside or datum line.

The depth of an FHP belt depends on the width. The depth is standard for each given width. FHP belts come in standard widths and depths as shown in *Figure 7*. The sides form an angle of 40 degrees.

1.2.2 Classic Belts

Classic belts (*Figure 8*) may also be referred to as *conventional belts*. They are more common than FHP belts in the industrial environment. They are also commonly used in multiples to increase strength and grip. However, single belt applications are also very common.

Classic belts are used for continuous service and generally outlast FHP belts. The size of classic belts is also indicated by a code marked on the belt, with a letter (A through E) indicating the width and a number to indicate the length. However, this number should be considered a nominal length only.

For example, a belt marked A42 is nominally 42" long. However, the 42" length of a classic belt refers to its length along the *inside* of the belt. The outside length is usually 2" to 3" longer. An A42 belt, for example, measures about $44\frac{1}{4}$" on the outside. The effective length of the belt (measured along the datum line) falls somewhere between 42" and $44\frac{1}{4}$".

Classic belts are available in various lengths and in standard widths and depths, as shown in *Figure 9*. The sides form an angle of 40 degrees, matching the angle of FHP belts. Since they have the same angle as FHP belts, they can often be mounted on the same sheaves.

1.2.3 Notched Belts

Notched belts (*Figure 10*) don't represent a separate class of belts. Both classic and wedge belts are available in notched forms. It is important to recognize that notched belts are not designed for use with sheaves that have matching grooves, like synchronous belts. They are used with standard sheaves only.

Notched belts have several advantages. They are generally more efficient at transmitting power and have a higher load capacity. This is due to the increased edge contact against the sheave along the sides of the belt. The notched design also makes the belt more flexible. This makes it a good choice for small-diameter sheaves, as it can wrap around a tighter circle than plain belts. The notches also serve to encourage air movement around the belt as it moves, allowing it to run cooler.

Notched belts are a bit more sensitive to proper sheave alignment. Slight misalignment may have little effect on a plain belt, where a notched belt may tend to turn or roll over on the sheave. This is due to their increased flexibility.

Notched belts are identified with the letter X placed after the letter in the original belt number. For example, an AX42 belt has the same basic dimensions as an A42 belt but has a notched design.

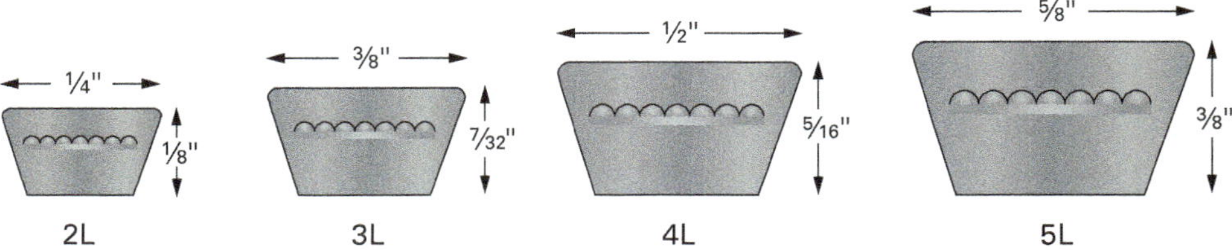

Figure 7 FHP belt standard widths and depths.

Figure 8 Classic V-belts.

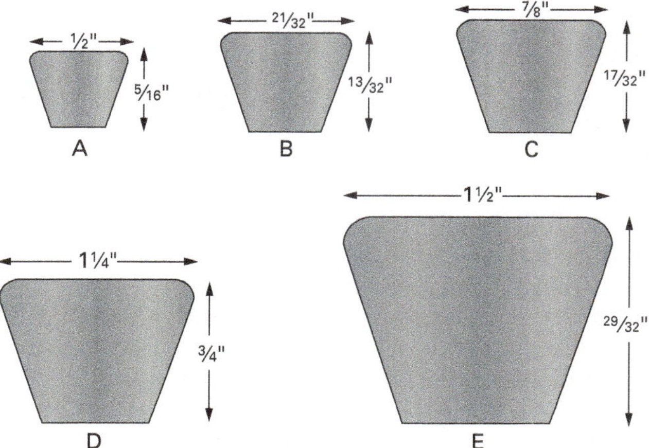

Figure 9 Classic belt standard widths and depths.

Figure 10 Notched V-belt.

Flat Belts and Belt Conditioners

Flat drive belts are used in some drive applications. A flat belt drive works well in applications where the sheaves are far apart, and when small sheaves are needed. However, they certainly have other applications as well.

Flat belts can also be crossed on a drive when enough room is available. This reverses the load's direction of rotation. Since there are no grooves in the sheaves to help keep the belt engaged, flat belts tend to creep to one side or another. To avoid this, sheave alignment must be very precise. Sheaves for flat belts also have a slight crown at the center which helps keep the belt from creeping off.

There are products called *belt dressings* or *belt conditioners* on the market. These products are sold as an answer to squealing belts, primarily to auto owners or service centers. However, craft professionals largely agree that the only type of belt that a dressing should be applied to today is the flat belt. Dressings were helpful on older belts that were made of neoprene, but they should not be used on today's belts made from ethylene propylene diene terpolymer, commonly known as *EPDM*.

Figure Credit: File "Overhead lineshaft" by Les Chatfield is licensed under CC BY 2.0.

1.2.4 Wedge Belts

Wedge belts (*Figure 11*), or *narrow-edge belts*, are typically used in multiples. Multiple wedge belts can be used on drives up to roughly 1,000 horsepower. Due to their construction, wedge belts can transmit up to three times the horsepower of a classic belt when all other factors are equal. They are often found on applications using smaller-diameter sheaves with shorter center-to-center distances. Wedge belts are not interchangeable with standard multiple belts and should not be run on sheaves made for classic or FHP belts.

Like the other types, the size of wedge belts is indicated by a code marked on the outside of the belt. The first number in the code identifies the width and cross-section of the belt in eighths of an inch. The V following this number identifies it as a wedge belt. An X inserted in the third position indicates it is a notched belt. For example, a 5VX belt is a notched wedge belt.

The next three numbers in the code identify the length of the belt, in inches. For example, a belt marked 3V500 is 50" long. Like FHP belts, the final 0 in the number is only relevant if the length is not a whole number.

The length of a wedge belt is measured along the outside perimeter, like FHP belts. Therefore, their datum length will be slightly shorter, but not significantly. The cords are placed very close to the top surface of the belt.

Wedge belts are available in various lengths and in standard widths and depths, as shown in *Figure 12*. The sides form an angle of 40 degrees, but a few variations exist. Always make sure the sheaves and belts match each other. When changing belts and using another brand, for example, be sure that the belt angle is compatible with the current sheave. When the sheave and belt angles do not match, a significant amount of grip is lost, and the belts wear quickly. The difference in the angle between two belts may be difficult to determine visually.

1.2.5 Banded Belts

Banded belts, also known as *joined belts* and *polyband belts*, combine multiple drive belts into a single piece (*Figure 13*). Banded belts are often chosen where belt vibration or belt whip is a problem. A set of long, individual belts may tend to whip as they rotate. This is especially true if the belts are not perfectly matched, leaving one or more belts slightly longer than the others in a set. These situations are relatively common. Unusual and sudden changes in the driven load while the belt is in motion may also cause belt whip. Belt whip can cause singular belts to roll over in the sheave grooves or fly off completely. Banded belts solve this problem.

Figure 11 Notched wedge belt.

Multiple banded belts can also be used together when necessary. For example, two banded belts, each with three belts attached to a single top, can be used together to create a six-band drive.

Both classic and wedge belts can be found in a banded configuration. Some manufacturers use a numeral and a slash in front of the belt code to identify it as banded, and to identify the number of belts in the band. For example, a belt code of 6/B80 generally identifies a banded belt comprised of six ribs and otherwise built to classic B standards. However, the means of identifying these belts varies by manufacturer.

1.2.6 Double-Angle Belts

Double-angle belts (*Figure 14*) are also known as *double-sided belts* and *double-V belts*. They are used on multiple-sheave, V-belt drives with reverse bends, as shown in *Figure 15*. Double-angle belts are V-shaped on both sides.

Some double-angle belts have recesses on the top and bottom like the profile shown in *Figure 16*. This improves flexibility and helps the belt maintain good contact against the walls of the sheaves.

Double-angle belts typically follow the same basic numbering pattern as classic belts. For example, an A60 belt represents a standard classic belt, while an AA60 would be a double-angled version. The 60 represents the measure of the inside perimeter, in inches, like a classic belt. The outer perimeter will always be longer than the stated length.

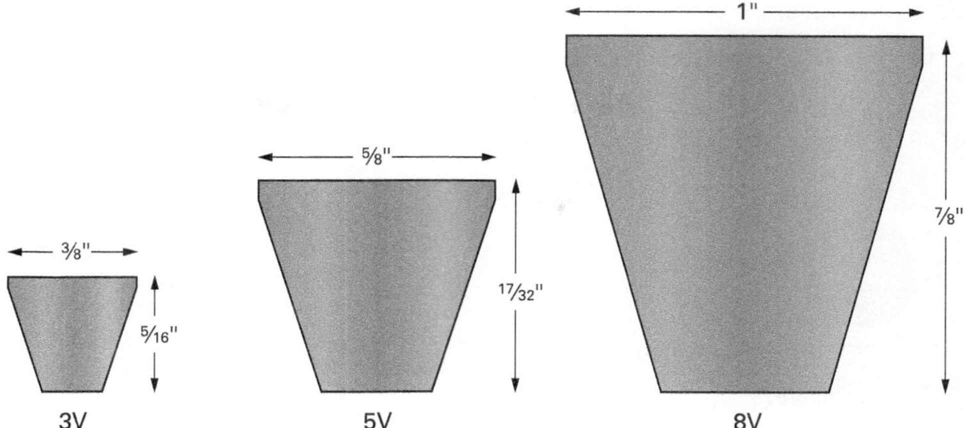

Figure 12 Wedge belt standard widths and depths.

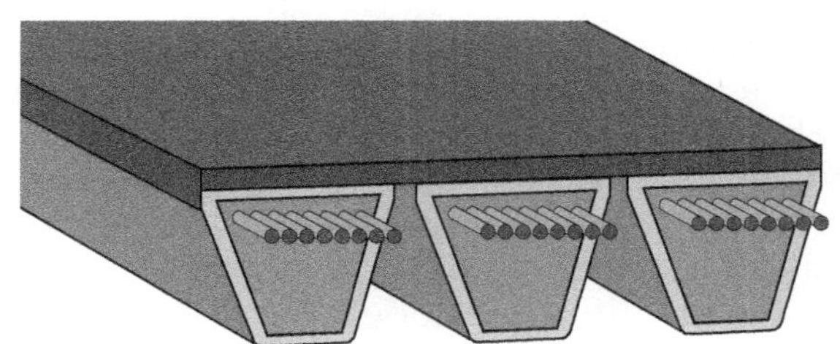

Figure 13 Banded belt.

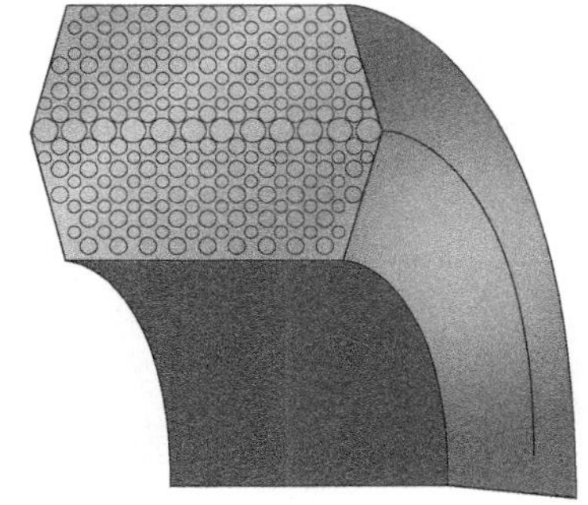

Figure 14 Double-angle V-belt.

1.2.7 Metric Belts

The term *metric belt* refers to belts that are exclusively constructed to metric dimensions and standards. Many belts constructed to US standards of measurement comply with standards from the Rubber Manufacturers Association (RMA). However, some of the belts constructed to metric standards have the same dimensions as belts constructed to RMA standards. As you review manufacturers' specifications for many of the belts introduced, you will find that they have both metric and US standard dimensions listed.

Metric belts may be manufactured to Germany's DIN standard, which is an abbreviation of the German words for German Institute for Standards. Another common source of metric belt standards is the International Organization for Standardization (ISO). Metric belts may also be constructed to meet both standards, as well as others.

One popular series of metric belts is the SP/XP series. They are comparable to the US standard classic belt series. *Figure 17* shows the common dimensions of these metric belts. The XP series is notched, while the SP series is not. The length may be specified along the datum line, along the outside, and/or along the inside, in metric units.

There are conversion charts available for metric and US standard belts, but most craft professionals agree that it is best not to interchange them. While small differences in length can be dealt with through drive adjustment, the cross sections may vary. For example, some metric belt manufacturers list the belt angle as 40 degrees (like classic belts), while others show it to be 38 degrees. To avoid mismatches, use the belt recommended by the manufacturer for a particular machine. Alternatively, both the belts and the sheaves can be changed to ensure a match.

1.2.8 Synchronous Belts

Synchronous belts have teeth, or *cogs*, molded into them. The matching sheaves look somewhat like gears, with teeth that conform to the teeth in the belt (*Figure 18*). This eliminates slippage. Think of synchronous belts as a more flexible and quieter alternative to chain drives. In fact, synchronous belt drives have replaced chain drives in many applications. In automobiles, for example, timing belts have replaced the timing chains used in older models.

Synchronous drives are used to maintain synchronization between multiple rotating shafts. Both the shape and size of the teeth can vary substantially. While some teeth are angular, others are rounded or have another unique profile.

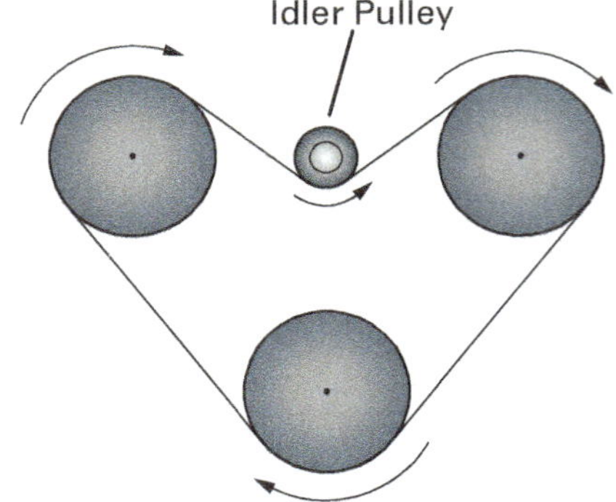

(A) Four-Point Drive

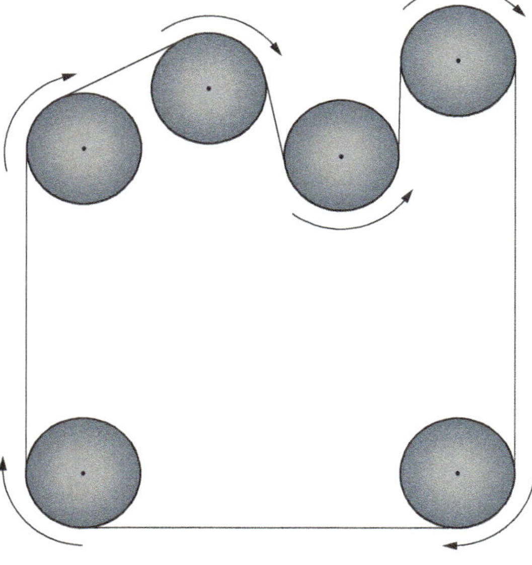

(B) Serpentine Drive

Figure 15 Multi-sheave drive arrangements.

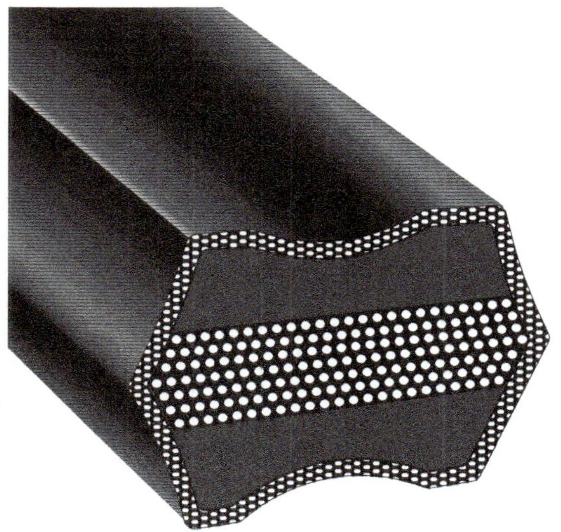

Figure 16 Double-angle belt with recessed top and bottom.

Synchronous belts are available as single-sided or dual-sided. Single-sided synchronous belts have teeth on only one side, while the double-sided version has teeth on both the inside and outside. The double-sided version can be used on multi-sheave drives like those shown in *Figure 15*.

Since the back of a single-sided synchronous belt is very flat and smooth, a small idler pulley can be used to maintain belt tension. An idler pulley is shown in the four-point drive in *Figure 15*. Idler pulleys are often perfectly smooth, with no angled groove or teeth. Idler pulleys are never attached to a driven load nor used to transfer power. They are simply used to help guide the belt and/or maintain tension.

Due to the unique nature of synchronous belts and the importance of using fully compatible drive components, belt numbering codes differ among manufacturers. If components from more than one manufacturer are used in a drive, care must be taken to ensure they are compatible.

Synchronous belts and sheaves are often specified in metric units. Rather than try to translate information from a synchronous belt or sheave identification code, it is best to acquire the information directly from the manufacturer's catalog. Critical characteristics to consider include the tooth profile (shape) and the pitch of the teeth. In this case, *pitch* refers to the distance between the centers of adjacent teeth. Mismatches of any kind must be avoided.

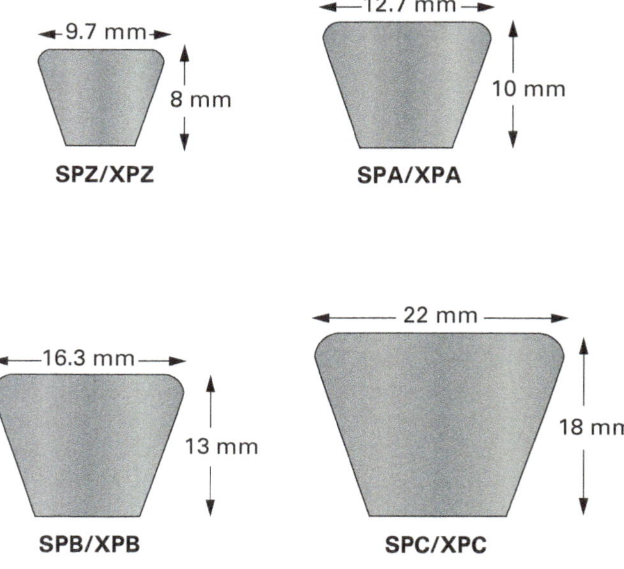

Figure 17 Metric SP/XP belt dimensions.

NCCER – *Millwright*

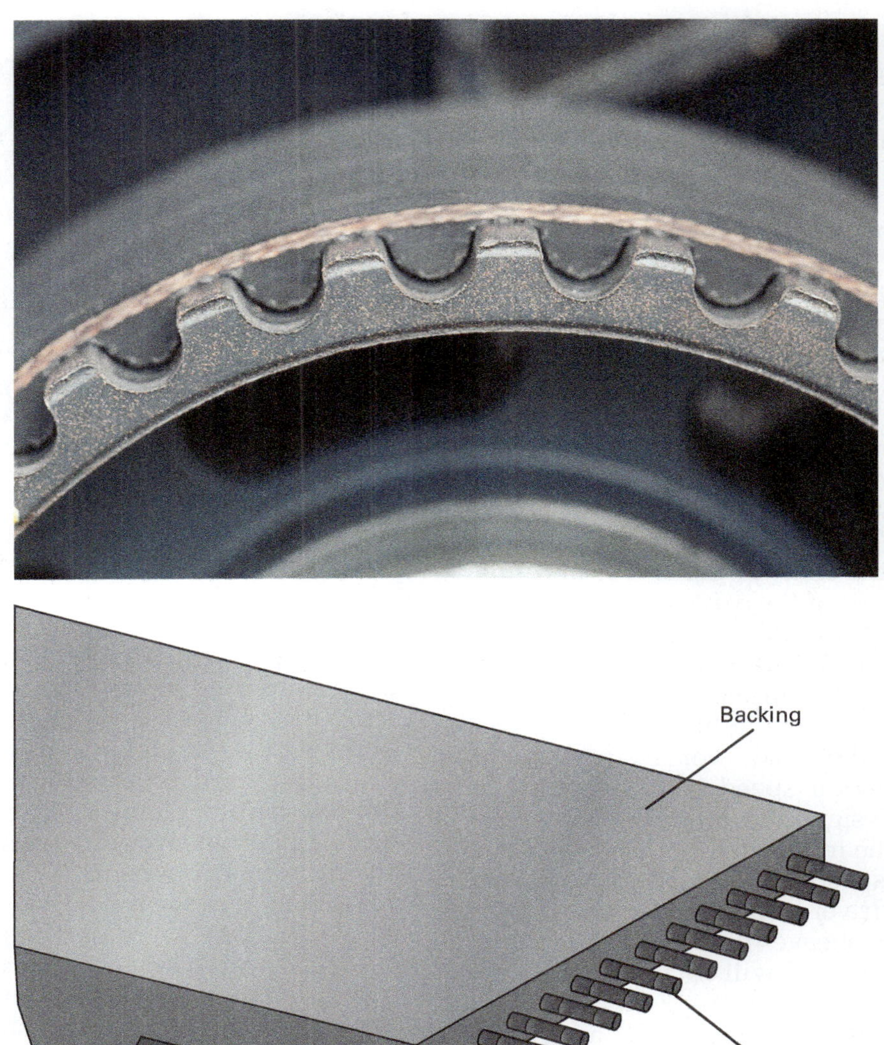

Figure 18 Synchronous belt and matching sheave.

Temporary Belts

There are times when a piece of equipment goes offline due to a damaged or broken drive belt. Although replacement belts are generally stocked at most facilities, perhaps the one you need isn't readily available. Millwrights, HVACR technicians, and industrial maintenance craftworkers can sometimes turn to temporary belts. This type of belting is easily adjusted for length and can often be installed on the sheaves without moving the driver. They are commonly available to fit FHP and classic belt sheaves.

1.3.0 Sheaves

Sheaves (*Figure 19*) are the other major components in a belt drive. The terms *sheave* and *pulley* are often used interchangeably, so don't be surprised when you hear both terms. Technically, a pulley represents an assembly of sheaves, ropes or cables, and other components often used for lifting, managing boat sails, and similar applications. The wheels on which the rope rides through the pulleys are called sheaves. *Sheave* is therefore the correct term for belt drive components, but again, you will quite often hear the term *pulley* used instead.

Sheaves come in many sizes and designs. They are often made from cast iron, but they can also be made from cast aluminum or machined from steel. A typical V-belt drive has two sheaves—one mounted on the shaft of the driver and one mounted on the shaft of the driven load.

As shown in *Figure 20,* the drive sheave is usually smaller than the driven sheave. This is because the motor speed, measured in revolutions per minute (rpm), is generally faster than the design speed of the load. For example, one common electric motor speed is 1,750 rpm, but the load may be designed to rotate at 875 rpm—half the speed of the motor shaft.

The rotational speed of the load depends on the speed of the driver and the ratio of the two sheaves. When two sheaves of the same diameter are used, the driven load will rotate at the same speed as the driver.

Multiple-groove sheaves (*Figure 21*) are made for equipment that requires two or more belts on the drive. Multiple belts offer far more grip, which is needed to drive substantial loads. Multi-groove sheaves are also used with banded belts.

Variable-pitch sheaves (*Figure 22*) are very common. The term *pitch*, in this case, refers to the position of the belt in the groove. The specifications for a variable-pitch sheave show a range of datum diameters within which they can be adjusted.

Variable-pitch sheaves are made with parts of the assembly threaded onto a hub. By turning the movable portion in or out, the groove width is adjusted. This causes the belt to ride higher or lower in the sheave groove and changes the speed of the driven load. A setscrew(s) locks the movable portions in place once they are positioned. Variable-pitch sheaves for multiple belts are also available and commonly used.

Figure 19 Examples of sheaves.

Variable-pitch sheaves are placed only on the drive shaft, while a standard fixed-pitch sheave is installed on the driven shaft. They allow a limited range of speed adjustment. Ideally, variable-pitch sheaves are used temporarily to adjust the speed of the driven sheave. Once the correct speed is obtained, the variable-pitch sheave is replaced with a standard fixed sheave that matches the adjusted datum diameter. However, in practice, variable-pitch sheaves often remain in service for the life of the equipment.

The *bore* of a sheave refers to the shaft size it will fit. A *fixed-bore sheave* fits only one size of shaft. The variable-pitch sheave shown in *Figure 22* is an example of a fixed-bore sheave. To allow a single sheave to fit various shaft sizes, the bore can be cast very large, and the sheave is installed using a *bushing* (*Figure 23*). These are referred to as *bushed-bore sheaves.*

Bushings are designed to fit different sheaves and accommodate different shaft sizes. Most bushings are tapered and are split along their length, as shown in *Figure 24*. They are often keyed to both the sheave and the shaft. The key for the sheave is visible in *Figure 24*, and the keyway for the shaft can be seen in the bore of the bushing.

Note that the bushing has several bolts inserted through the flange. The bolts are used to pull the bushing into the bore of the sheave. The holes in the bushing flange are not threaded. As they are tightened, the taper of the bushing causes it to clamp down tightly on the shaft. For this reason, when installing a bushed-bore sheave on a shaft, the bushing must be inserted into the sheave and tightened while it is on the shaft. You cannot fully install the bushing into the sheave and then slide the assembly over the shaft.

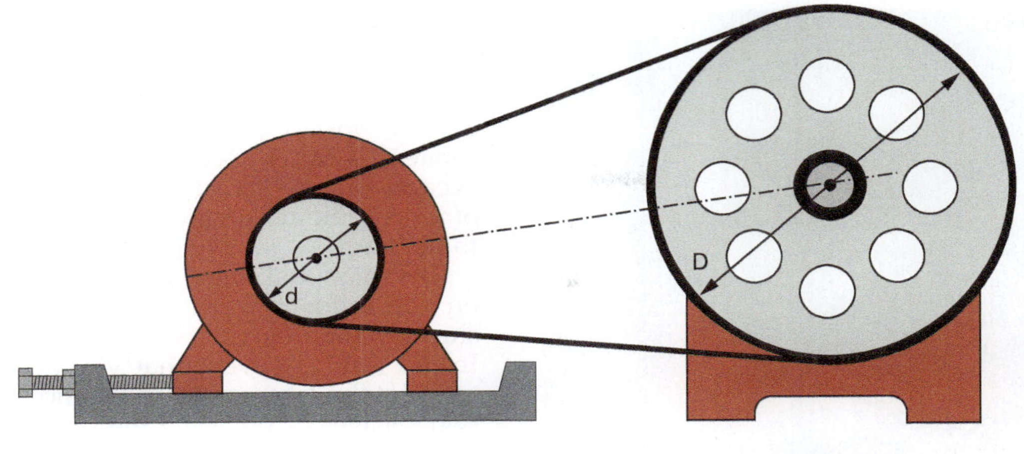

Figure 20 Typical V-belt drive arrangement.

Figure 21 Multiple-groove sheave.

Figure 22 Variable-pitch sheave.

Figure 23 Bushed-bore sheaves.

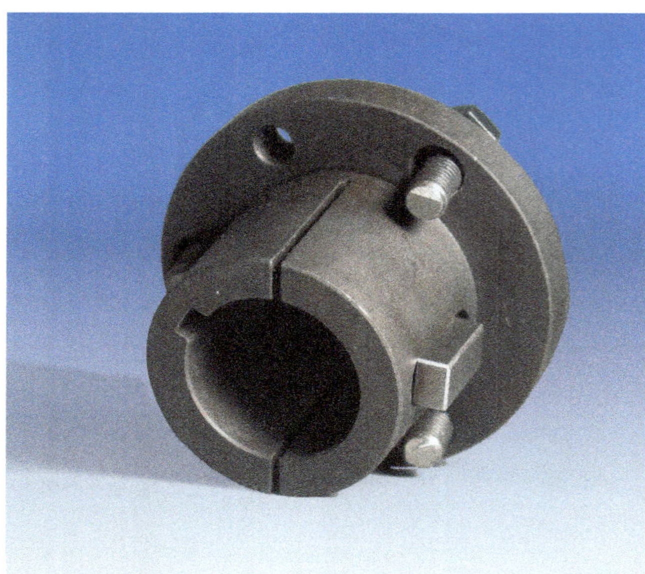

Figure 24 Typical tapered sheave bushing.

In *Figure 24*, also note the extra hole in the bushing flange with no bolt inserted. There is a second hole on the opposite side that is not visible in the figure. These holes are threaded and are used to remove a bushing from a sheave. Once the bolts securing the bushing to the sheave are removed, they are threaded into the other holes and used as jackbolts to push against the sheave, forcing the bushing out of the sheave bore.

It is important to note that, although this style of bushing is very common, there are many other styles. Always consult the manufacturer's literature to determine the correct bushing for a given sheave and avoid mixing components from different manufacturers.

Many sheaves are designed to accommodate both FHP and classic belts. However, due to small dimensional differences between the two types, they often ride in a slightly different position in the groove. Again, always consult the manufacturer's literature to determine what belt types can be used with a given sheave. Some manufacturers use a sheave numbering system that makes it easier to select belt and sheave combinations. For example, the product number for a sheave designed for 5V wedge belts may also begin with 5V. But it is always best to review the specifications carefully to ensure a match unless you are intimately familiar with a manufacturer's product line.

1.3.1 Speed Calculations

As mentioned previously, the required speed of the driven load is rarely the same as that of the driver. Most of the time, the driven load must rotate at a lower speed than the driver. You will occasionally be called upon to change the speed of a drive. Some simple calculations are required to do that.

The rotational speed of the driven load is based on the ratio between the diameter of the two sheaves and the rotational speed of the driver. In the unlikely event that you need the load to rotate at the same speed as the motor, you can use two sheaves of precisely the same diameter. The diameter chosen for the two sheaves won't matter as far as speed is concerned, as long as they are the same.

Some speed ratios are very easy to understand. If, for example, you need the load to rotate at exactly half the speed of the driver, then make the driven sheave twice as big. A 3" drive sheave matched with a 6" driven sheave will produce the desired result. Again, the chosen size doesn't matter if the driven sheave is exactly twice the diameter of the drive sheave.

Unfortunately, the situation is rarely that simple and some calculations are required. There is one equation that forms the basis of the equations you'll work with to find the information you need:

$$\frac{\text{Driver rotational speed}}{\text{Driven rotational speed}} = \frac{\text{Driven pitch diameter}}{\text{Drive pitch diameter}}$$

You'll recall that the pitch diameter of a sheave typically represents its outside diameter. For very precise work, you will need to determine the exact datum diameter for the sheaves. However, when working with fixed-pitch sheaves, using the pitch diameters will provide good results. The datum diameter of a variable-pitch sheave can change, though, so working with the datum diameter is necessary for accuracy when using a variable-pitch sheave.

The four equations used to determine sheave sizes and resulting speeds are as follows:

$$\text{Driven rotational speed} = \frac{P_{driver} \times S_{driver}}{P_{driven}}$$

$$\text{Driven pitch diameter} = \frac{S_{driver} \times P_{driver}}{S_{driven}}$$

$$\text{Driver rotational speed} = \frac{P_{driven} \times S_{driven}}{P_{driver}}$$

$$\text{Driver pitch diameter} = \frac{S_{driven} \times P_{driven}}{S_{driver}}$$

Where:

$$P_{driver} = \text{Driver pitch diameter}$$
$$P_{driven} = \text{Driven pitch diameter}$$
$$S_{driver} = \text{Driver rotational speed}$$
$$S_{driven} = \text{Driven rotational speed}$$

This example problem demonstrates the use of these equations. A drive motor is rotating at 1,800 rpm and the drive sheave has a pitch diameter of 4". The driven sheave has a pitch diameter of 12". How fast will the driven load rotate?

$$\text{Driven rotational speed} = \frac{P_{driver} \times S_{driver}}{P_{driven}}$$

$$\text{Driven rotational speed} = \frac{4" \times 1,800 \text{ rpm}}{12"}$$

$$\text{Driven rotational speed} = \frac{7,200}{12"}$$

$$\text{Driven rotational speed} = 600 \text{ rpm}$$

That result makes sense, because the driven pitch diameter happens to be three times that of the drive sheave. Therefore, the speed will be one-third of the driver.

Now the plant engineer asks you to change the rotational speed of the load to 750 rpm—an increase of 150 rpm. You can do this in one of two ways. The drive sheave can be replaced with a larger sheave, or the driven sheave can be replaced with a smaller one. In this example, we will choose to replace the driven sheave.

Use this equation to determine the size of the new driven sheave:

$$\text{Driven pitch diameter} = \frac{S_{driver} \times P_{driver}}{S_{driven}}$$

$$\text{Driven pitch diameter} = \frac{1,800 \text{ rpm} \times 4"}{750 \text{ rpm}}$$

$$\text{Driven pitch diameter} = \frac{7,200}{750}$$

$$\text{Driven pitch diameter} = 9.6"$$

In summary, replacing the 12" driven sheave with a 9.6" sheave will increase the speed of the driven load from 600 rpm to 750 rpm.

1.4.0 Belt Drive Installation and Maintenance

Belt drives are designed to provide many hours of reliable service. Belt failures can often be traced to improper belt tension or sheave misalignment, although normal wear takes its toll. Excessive belt tension stretches the belt, and more importantly, places excessive stress on the shaft and bearings. When there is too little tension, the belt will slip and wear quickly. This will usually affect the driven equipment as well. A blower, for example, won't deliver the desired airflow if it isn't turning at the correct speed.

Installing a belt drive can be broken down into the following tasks. Each of these tasks will be discussed in the sections that follow:

- Installing and aligning the sheaves
- Determining the required belt length
- Installing the belts
- Adjusting the tension
- Maintaining the drive components

1.4.1 Installing and Aligning Sheaves

There are three types of misalignment to consider when working with sheaves. They are illustrated in *Figure 25*:

- Parallel misalignment
- Angular misalignment
- Sheave groove (axial) misalignment

In some cases, it may be helpful to determine if the driver and driven shafts are parallel before installing the sheaves. The assumption is that, if the two shafts are parallel to each other, the sheaves will also be parallel to each other. However, this step is of little value if one or both shafts are short. For example, if one or both shafts are only a few inches long, the measurements used to check for parallelism won't be far enough apart to be useful.

In this case, you can install the sheaves and use them to check the alignment. Checking the sheaves for parallel alignment is usually more accurate, and it is a step that shouldn't be omitted. Even when you check the shafts first, parallel alignment of the sheaves should still be checked after their installation.

You can determine if the shafts are parallel before the sheaves are installed by making two measurements between the shafts as shown in *Figure 26*. Take one measurement near the end of the shortest shaft (assuming they are different lengths) and one near the equipment housing. If the shafts are parallel, the measurements will be the same. If they are not the same, the position of either the driver or the driven equipment must be adjusted. The driver is typically moved to accommodate the driven equipment; the driven load remains stationary.

Angular misalignment can be addressed before the sheaves are installed. The best way to eliminate angular misalignment is to accurately level both shafts. If the shafts are not in a horizontal plane by design, then you must ensure that both shafts have the same inclination angle.

Sheave groove (axial) alignment must be checked as the sheaves are installed. The grooves are brought into alignment by moving one of the sheaves along the shaft. This also raises the question of where along the shafts the sheaves should be positioned. Sheaves should generally be placed close to the driver and driven equipment bearings, but with enough clearance to avoid any interference. The farther out on the shafts the sheaves are placed, the more leverage applied to both bearings when the belt is under tension. This condition is referred to as an *overhung load* (*Figure 27*).

Installing the sheaves requires the following basic steps. However, it is always important to review and follow the manufacturer's installation instructions:

Step 1 Inspect the shafts and address any burrs or nicks, using a fine file.

Step 2 Clean both shafts thoroughly, using a solvent and a rag.

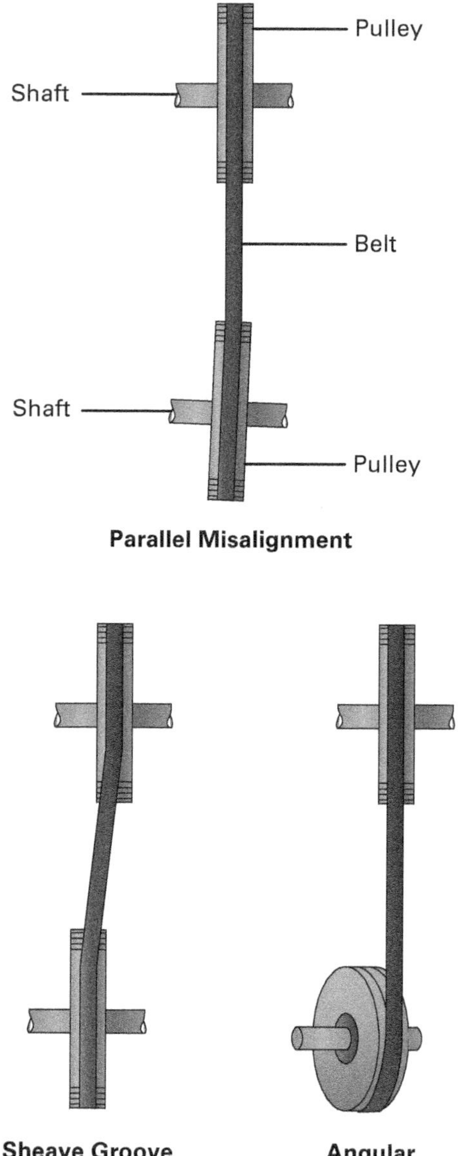

Figure 25 Examples of misalignment.

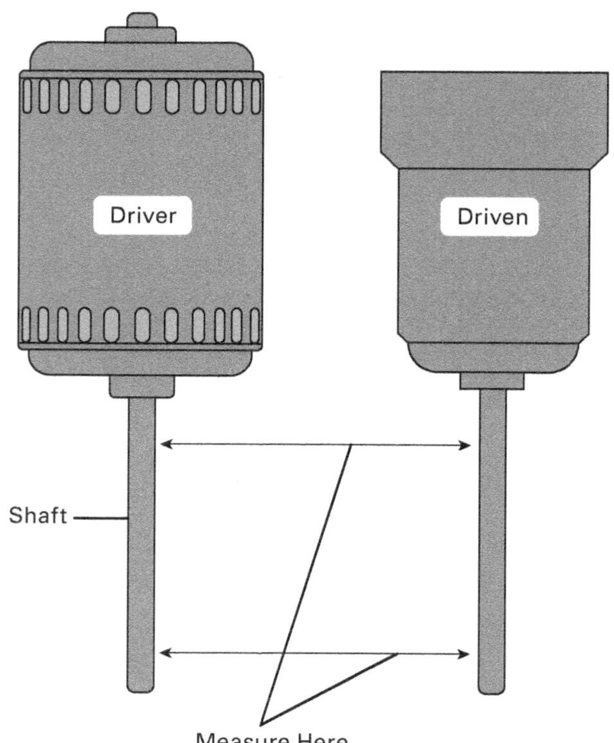

Figure 26 Checking shafts for parallelism.

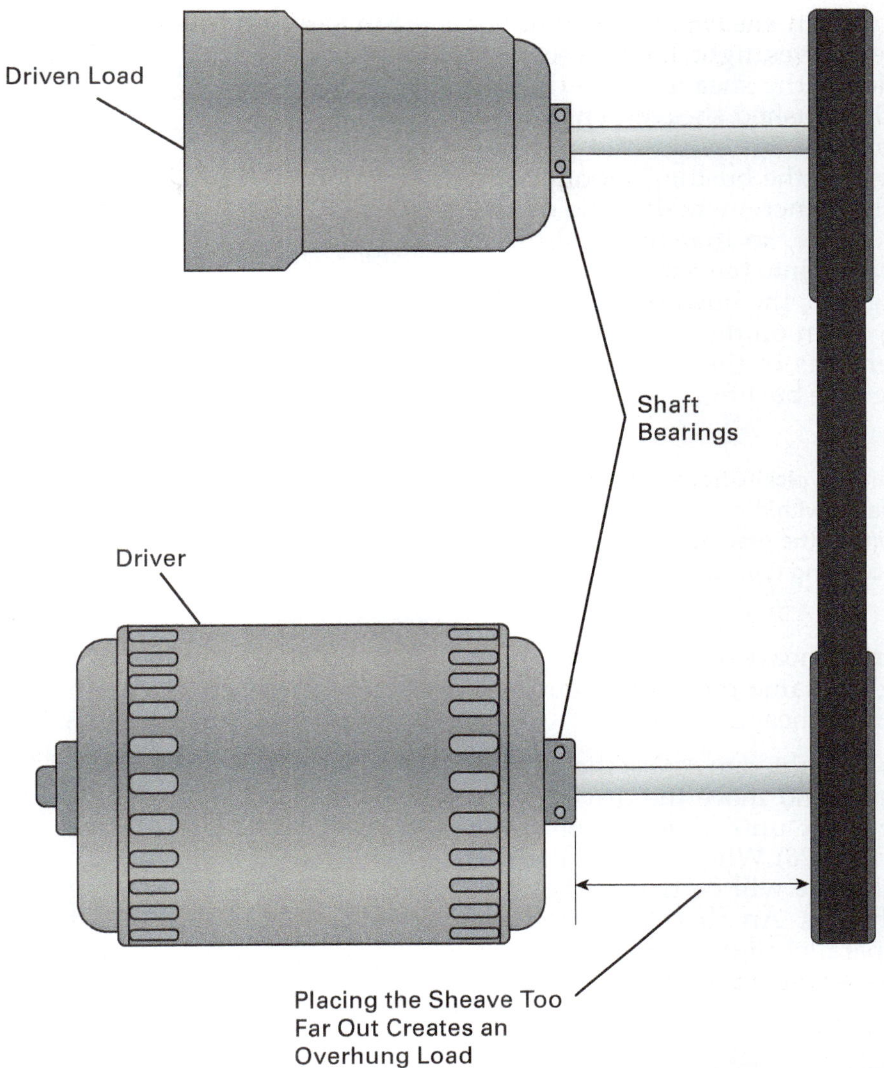

Figure 27 Sheaves placed too far out on the shaft create an overhung load.

Many solvents are toxic and/or flammable. Wear appropriate respiratory protection and gloves when handling these products. Ensure there is sufficient ventilation in the work area. All rags should be disposed of in approved containers.

Step 3 Ensure you have the proper size and length of keystock. When using a bushed sheave, you will often need two keys and perhaps different sizes. Check and clean the keys and address any burrs that may be present.

Step 4 Inspect the bore of the sheaves, address any visible flaws, and clean them as necessary. Ensure any setscrews are backed out.

Step 5 Slip the driven sheave onto the equipment shaft. If the sheave requires a bushing, loosely mount it to the sheave with the bolts provided. Make sure that any keys are properly positioned in the keyways. The sheave is usually positioned close to the motor housing, but it must be far enough away to avoid any possibility of interference with the motor as well as any guards.

Do not lubricate the bore of the sheave nor the exterior of the tapered bushing before inserting it into the sheave. In some cases, the shaft itself might be lubricated or coated with an anti-seize compound, but never the area where the bushing and sheave bore are in contact.

Step 6 Lock the driven sheave in position. For fixed-bore sheaves, tighten the setscrew(s) while holding the sheave at the desired location. For bushed sheaves, ensure the sheave remains in the desired position as you tighten the bushing mount bolts. Tighten them incrementally, one or two turns at a time, so that the bushing is pulled straight into the bore of the sheave. As you tighten, the bushing will also be clamping down on the shaft. Ensure the sheave remains in the right position as you engage the bushing.

Sheave bushings typically have specific torque values associated with the mount bolts. Torque the mount bolts to the manufacturer-specified value for the bushing type being installed.

Step 7 Slip the drive sheave onto the motor shaft, following the same procedures outlined for the driven sheave.

Step 8 Position a straightedge across the faces of both sheaves and move the drive sheave along the shaft until they are perfectly aligned (*Figure 28*). When they are aligned, the straightedge will be flat on the faces of both sheaves. An alternate method of checking parallel alignment is to pull a piano wire or string tightly across the faces.

Remember that one important goal is to align the sheave grooves. Due to differences in construction between the two sheaves, aligning the sides may not result in aligned grooves. If there is a difference in the width of the sheaves, for example, you must factor that in as you position the second sheave. However, aligning the sides will reveal whether the two shafts are parallel. Once parallel alignment is confirmed, you must focus on sheave groove alignment as the second sheave is installed, before it is secured in place.

Step 9 With the sheave grooves aligned, lock the drive sheave to the motor shaft by tightening the setscrew(s) or drawing the bushing into the sheave bore.

Sheave Alignment with Instruments

Sheave alignment with a straightedge, wire, or string may be sufficient for small drives. Larger drives and those where the sheaves are a significant distance apart require a more precise method.

Laser-based alignment tools, also called *sheave lasers*, use laser technology to align sheaves with great precision (*Figure 29*). The alignment components shown in the figure are equipped with powerful magnets, making them easy to attach to the sheave. These tools can detect all three types of misalignment by aligning a laser beam with one or more targets.

Note that the tool in *Figure 29* attaches to and aligns the sides of the sheaves. The type shown in *Figure 30* mounts against the grooves, making groove alignment easier. This tool is useful when the driving and driven sheaves have different widths. It is also capable of detecting all three forms of misalignment.

Sheave lasers are accurate across a significant distance (typically 20' to 30') and can be operated by one person. Adjustments can be made while using the laser as a guide.

Using these tools for sheave alignment is highly recommended. Although belt drives can be forgiving, properly aligned sheaves reduce belt wear and power consumption. This also reduces maintenance costs and can save a great deal of money in a large plant. Review the instructions for the chosen tool and follow the manufacturer's guidance carefully.

1.4.2 Determining the Belt Length

After the sheaves are mounted and aligned, the belts can be installed. The first step is to ensure the belts and sheaves match. The catalog data for a sheave will indicate the belt types it will accommodate. The identifying information is usually stamped into the hub of a sheave.

Note that the procedures presented here are related to V-belts. There are two important things to remember as you select and acquire the belts:

- If there are multiple belts on the drive, never mix old and new belts.
- Avoid mixing belts from different manufacturers, even if they have the same identifying markings.

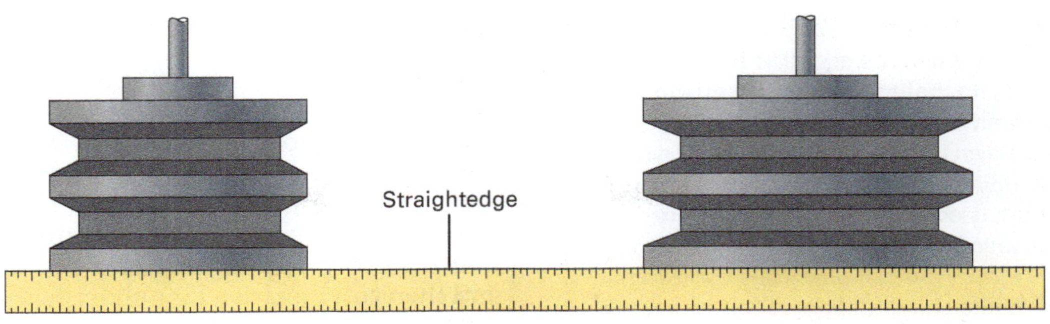

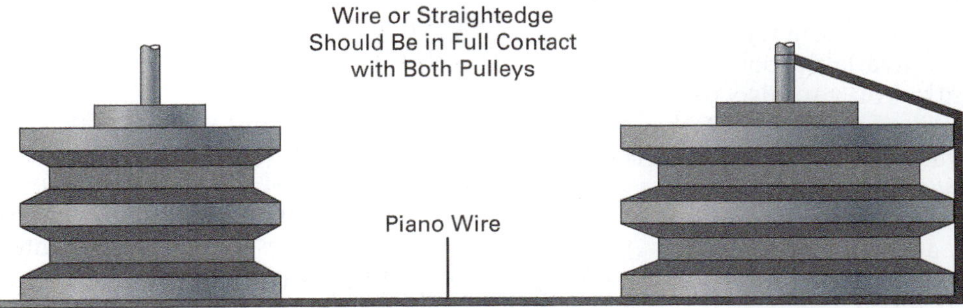

Figure 28 Checking sheave alignment.

Figure 29 Laser-based sheave alignment tool, or sheave laser.

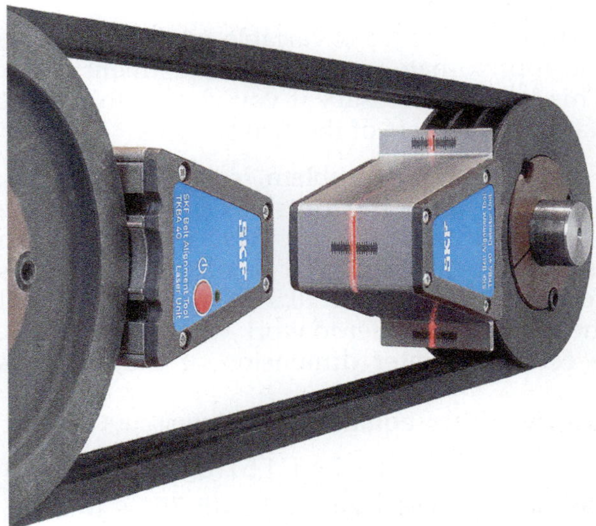

Figure 30 Laser-based groove alignment tool.

Next, you'll need to determine how long the belt(s) need to be, unless you are simply replacing it for maintenance purposes. In that case, you can use the same length, but examine the tension adjustment mechanism first. If it appears to be very close to the end of its travel in either direction, you may wish to adjust the belt length accordingly.

The adjusting mechanism on drives allows for some leeway in selecting the belt length. If the calculations are made correctly, you should be within the range of adjustment. Precision is not usually necessary.

Use the following equation to determine the belt length:

$$\text{Belt length} = 2c + 1.57(d_L + d_S)$$

Where:
c = center-to-center distance between the two shafts
d_L = diameter of the larger sheave
d_S = diameter of the smaller sheave

You can use the outer diameter of the sheaves, and then select the available belt length based on its outside length. You can also use the listed pitch diameter (datum diameter) of the sheave. If so, choose an available belt length based on its datum length. Either way, the calculations should place you very close to the proper length.

Before taking any measurements, do the following:

- Set the motor tensioning mechanism (usually one or more jackbolts) to the approximate center of its range.
- If the drive sheave is variable pitch, adjust it to the approximate center of its adjustment range. This is only necessary if you choose to use the datum diameters of the two sheaves.

For an example problem, refer to *Figure 31*. We'll work with the outside diameter of the sheaves in this case. The drive sheave has an outside diameter of 5.75". The driven sheave has an outside diameter of 10.5". Note that decimal inches are much easier to work with in equations. The center-to-center dimension of the shafts is 24".

Now work the equation as follows:

$$\text{Belt length} = 2c + 1.57(d_\text{L} + d_\text{S})$$
$$\text{Belt length} = (2 \times 24") + 1.57(5.75" + 10.5")$$
$$\text{Belt length} = 48" + 1.57(16.25")$$
$$\text{Belt length} = 48" + 25.5"$$
$$\text{Belt length} = 73.5"$$

In this case, select the proper type of belt with an outside diameter of 74", or the next available size. Since this example was based on the outside diameter of the sheaves, moving to the next smaller size might provide a better fit.

1.4.3 Belt Installation

To install the belt(s), adjust the drive motor to close the gap between the two pieces of equipment using the jackbolt on the driver. This will allow you to slip the belts over the sheaves and drape them over the grooves. Do not "roll" belts over the edge of the sheaves under significant tension.

It is best to approximate the required tension and then run the drive for a short period, allowing the belt to seat in the sheave groove. If a rotational speed for the driven load has been specified, this also provides an opportunity to measure its speed with a tachometer.

If the speed is too low, you can adjust the variable-pitch sheave by bringing the halves closer together, forcing the belt to ride higher in the groove. If the speed is too fast, open the sheave to adjust. Then adjust the belt tension. If the sheave isn't adjusted before tensioning the belts, the process must be repeated afterwards. Adjusting a variable-pitch sheave changes where the belt rides in the groove, affecting the tension. If a variable-pitch sheave is not used, speed changes are made by replacing the sheave with a different size.

1.4.4 Belt Tensioning

Belt drive reliability and efficiency rely heavily on the proper belt tension. Loose belts slip, wasting energy and causing excessive wear on the belt and sheave. Belts that are too tight place excessive stress on the shafts and bearings, and the belt itself can be damaged as well.

A popular belt-tensioning tool is shown in *Figure 32*. Its use is based on the premise that the force required to deflect a drive belt crossing a given span is directly related to the belt's tension. This particular tool is also made in assemblies of two and three devices bound together. They are used to measure tension on banded and very large belts, beyond the range of the spring in a single device.

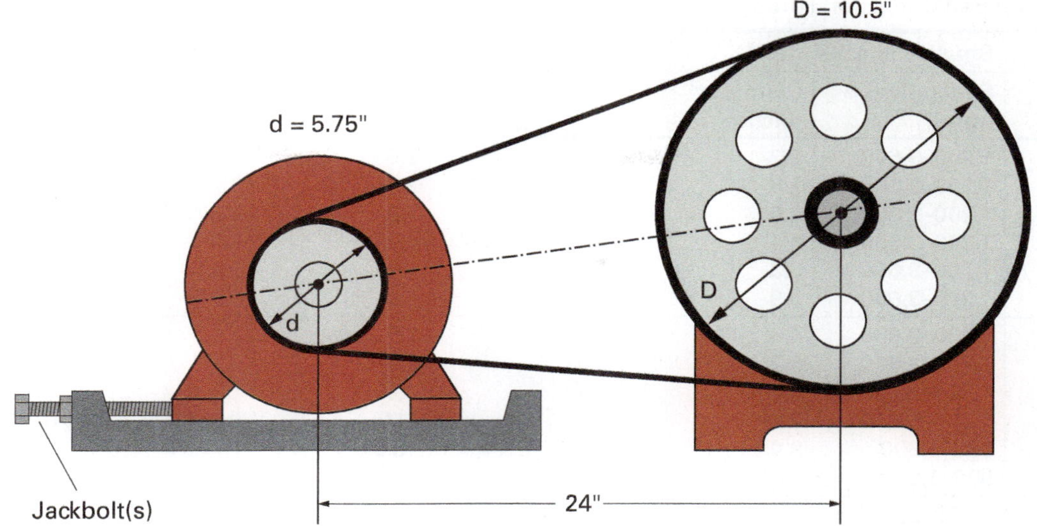

Figure 31 Drive-belt length calculation example.

Figure 32 Mechanical belt tension gauge.

The first step is to determine the required tension for the belt(s). This information can come from a variety of sources. The equipment manufacturer is likely the best source if it provides that information in the manuals. Belt manufacturers are also a reliable source. Perhaps the most accessible source of information is the manufacturer of the tension measurement tool. Most provide tables based on factors such as drive speed and sheave diameter that show the required deflection force. *Table 1* is an example.

> **CAUTION**
>
> *Table 1* provides an example only and should not be used for field work. Use the table(s) provided by the equipment, belt, or tensioning tool manufacturer.

Tables and charts may also have footnotes, some of which indicate that new belts should be tensioned to a higher value than the value shown on the chart, perhaps twice as much. This accommodates expected stretching that will occur early in the life of the belt. However, there are belt products on the market today that do not stretch significantly. It is very important to be familiar with the specific belt product in use.

Installing Belt and Chain Drives

Table 1 Minimum Belt Deflection Force

Belt Section	Smaller Sheave		Deflection Force[1] (lbf) for a Drive Speed Ratio of:			
	Speed Range (rpm)	Diameter[2] (inches)	1.0	1.5	2.0	4.0+
3VX	1,200–3,600	2.2	2.2	2.5	2.7	3.0
	1,200–3,600	2.5	2.6	2.9	3.1	3.6
	1,200–3,600	3.0	3.1	3.5	3.7	4.2
	1,200–3,600	4.1	3.9	4.3	4.5	5.1
	1,200–3,600	5.3	4.6	4.9	5.1	5.7
	1,200–3,600	6.9	5.0	5.4	5.6	6.2
5VX	1,200–3,600	4.4	6.5	7.5	8.0	9.0
	1,200–3,600	5.2	8.0	9.0	9.5	10.0
	1,200–3,600	6.3	9.5	10.0	11.0	12.0
	1,200–3,600	7.1	10.0	11.0	12.0	13.0
	900–1,800	9.0	12.0	13.0	14.0	15.0
	900–1,800	14.0	14.0	15.0	16.0	17.0
A or AP	1,800–3,600	3.0	2.0	2.3	2.4	2.6
	1,800–3,600	4.0	2.6	2.8	3.0	3.3
	1,800–3,600	5.0	3.0	3.3	3.4	3.7
	1,800–3,600	7.0	3.5	3.7	3.8	4.3
B or BP	1,200–1,800	4.6	3.7	4.3	4.5	5.0
	1,200–1,800	5.0	4.1	4.6	4.8	5.6
	1,200–1,800	6.0	4.8	5.3	5.5	6.3
	1,200–1,800	8.0	5.7	6.2	6.4	7.2
AX	1,800–3,600	3.0	2.5	2.8	3.0	3.3
	1,800–3,600	4.0	3.3	3.6	3.8	4.2
	1,800–3,600	5.0	3.7	4.1	4.3	4.6
	1,800–3,600	7.0	4.3	4.6	4.8	5.3

Notes:
[1] Double the values to tension a new set of belts.
[2] Use closest sheave diameter for sizes not shown.

To use the tension gauge shown in *Figure 32*, follow these basic instructions. However, always refer to the instructions for the specific type and brand of tool in use:

Step 1 De-energize the system and lock out the power source.

Step 2 Measure the distance between the centers of the two sheaves.

Step 3 Refer to *Figure 33*. Set the *large* O-ring to a value that represents the number of inches between sheave centers, multiplied by $\frac{1}{64}$". For example, if the distance is 68", set the large O-ring to $1\frac{4}{64}$", as shown in *Figure 33*.

Step 4 Set the *small* O-ring at zero on the upper scale. Note that it will move when a reading is taken.

Step 5 If there is only one belt on the drive, set a straightedge across the top of the belt between the two sheaves, as shown in *Figure 34*. A string can also be pulled taut between the sheaves if the span is too long for an available straightedge. Note that this step is unnecessary if there is more than one belt.

Step 6 Carefully push the base of the tension gauge down on the belt in the center of the span, with attention to one of these two scenarios (*Figure 35*):

- If there is only one belt, push down until the large O-ring is even with the bottom of the straightedge.

- If there are multiple belts, push down until the large O-ring is even with the top of the adjacent belt. In this case, take a reading from each belt. Remember to reset the small O-ring to zero before taking each measurement.

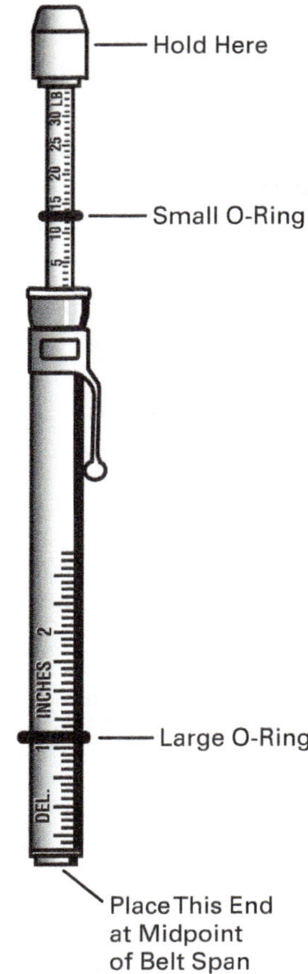

Figure 33 Belt tension gauge settings and use.

Step 7 Examine the tension gauge and note the new position of the small O-ring. It now indicates the force required to deflect the belt, in pounds. If there are multiple belts on the drive, take a reading on each belt and average the readings.

Step 8 Compare this value to the chart in use. If the force is lower than prescribed, add more tension using the jackbolt and measure the force again. If it is higher than prescribed, reduce the tension and measure the force again.

Step 9 With the proper tension established, reinstall any belt guards, remove the locks, and restore power to the driver. Observe the drive as it operates for a short time to ensure that it is operating as expected.

> **WARNING!**
>
> Do not operate the equipment without the belt guards. Serious injury can result if your hand or clothing is caught in the drive.

Electronic tension gauges, or *tensiometers*, are become increasingly popular. Most of the electronic models, also referred to as *trummeters*, base the force value on the frequency of belt vibration.

The model shown in *Figure 36* uses a pulsed beam of light to measure the frequency of a vibrating belt. With the instrument ready and the beam pointed at the belt surface in the correct location, the user merely strums the belt to initiate vibration. Algorithms determine the tension based on the vibration frequency. The digital display can provide readings in units of newtons (N) or pounds force (lbf).

After installing a new drive or changing the speed of a driven load, the operating current of the drive motor should always be checked to ensure it remains at or below its ratings. This may be a task for other crafts. Before checking the current, ensure that the equipment is fully assembled and under a normal operating load. An open access door on a blower assembly, for example, can significantly change the load and, in turn, the current readings.

1.4.5 Belt Drive Maintenance

Belt drives are simple to maintain. The primary task is checking the condition of the belts and replacing them when the wear is excessive. Inspect belts regularly and look for the following:

- Cracks developing along the inside or outside. Belts tend to crack due to excess tension, excess heat, and oxidation. Once significant cracks develop, the next step is usually chunking, which simply means that chunks of the belt have separated from the cords and spun away.
- A shiny or deeply glazed surface where the belt contacts the sheave. Some gloss is normal, but when it becomes too deeply glazed, slippage and squealing generally result.

Belts that squeal, especially when the driver starts, may be worn and need to be replaced. However, it might also indicate a different problem. Drive motors that come up to speed quickly and are connected to a load that is difficult to move often cause belts to squeal. If the belt tension is correct, and both old and new belts tend to squeal when the motor starts, then other changes may be in order. For example, an electronic variable-speed drive could possibly be installed, allowing the motor to slowly build speed at startup. When you suspect that a squealing problem is not related to the condition of the belts, report the problem to your supervisor for further evaluation.

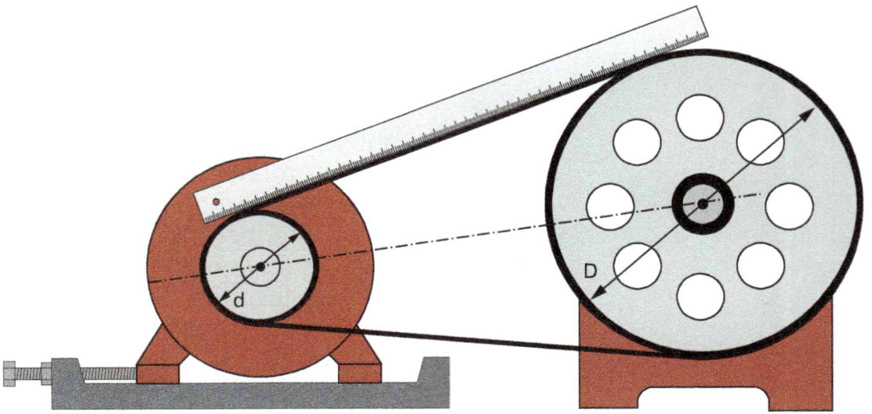

Figure 34 Straightedge placed across the top of the belt.

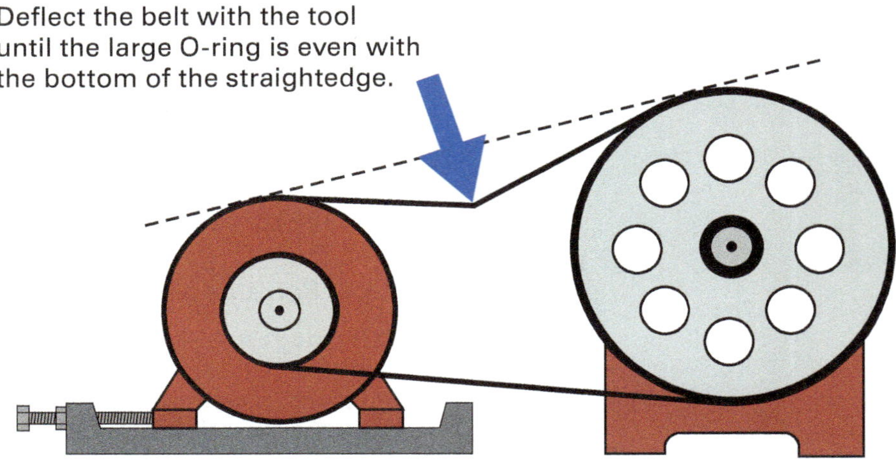

Figure 35 Taking a force reading.

Sheaves are also subject to wear. They will last much longer than a set of belts, but they do experience wear. Sheaves wear more quickly when the belts are slipping.

Belts should not ride along the bottom of the sheave groove. Only the sides of the belt should be in contact with the sheave. A small amount of clearance should remain between the belt and the bottom of the sheave groove. If it is apparent that the belt is riding on the bottom of the groove (the paint is worn away, for example), replace the sheave and the belt(s).

Sheave gauges (*Figure 37*) are used to measure sheave wear. Excess wear compromises belt grip. When the wear is excessive, the sheave is replaced.

Before using a sheave gauge, ensure that it is correct for the type of belt and sheave in use. In addition to having gauges that fit a wide variety of sheaves, many sheave gauge sets also include a gauge(s) that helps identify the belt type. Most belts clearly indicate their type and size, but there may be cases where the information is unreadable and confirmation is needed.

Refer to *Figure 37*. Follow these steps to use a sheave gauge:

Step 1 Acquire the technical data for the sheave from the manufacturer. The information needed to determine which gauge to use includes the groove angle, groove dimensions, and diameter of the sheave.

Step 2 Select a gauge that is correct for the sheave groove and type of drive belt in use. For example, if the belt is a classic B belt, use a sheave gauge with markings for B belts.

Step 3 Insert the gauge into the groove of the sheave and observe the fit. Note the flashlight behind the gauge in *Figure 37*. Backlighting helps to see the fit in detail. Also note the visible gap between the gauge and the bottom of the sheave groove. If the wear is significant, replace the sheave.

Step 4 Clean the gauge, ensure that it is dry, and store it with similar precision tools.

Figure 36 Electronic tension gauge.

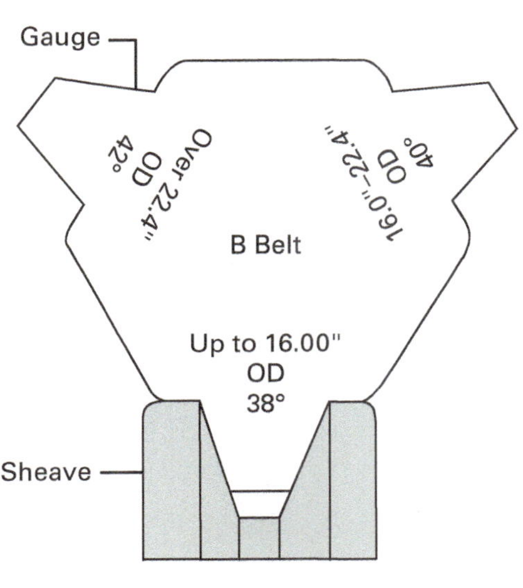

Figure 37 Sheave gauges.

1. The *pitch diameter* and *datum diameter* of a sheave represent the same measurement.

    a. True
    b. False

2. The type of belt typically used in multiples and sometimes referred to as a *narrow-edge belt* is the _______.

    a. wedge belt
    b. classic belt
    c. notched belt
    d. synchronous belt

3. A new drive motor rotates at 1,200 rpm. The driven load already has a 14" diameter sheave installed, and it must rotate at 500 rpm. What should the diameter of the drive sheave be? Round your answer to two decimal places.

    a. 3.66"
    b. 5.83"
    c. 7.66"
    d. 8.33"

4. You are installing a new belt drive. The drive sheave provided has an outside diameter of 6.25", while the driven sheave has an outside diameter of 14". The center-to-center distance between the two shafts is 26". What length of drive belt do you need for the installation? Round your answer to the nearest inch.

    a. 59"
    b. 67"
    c. 74"
    d. 84"

2.0.0 CHAIN DRIVES

Objective

Identify and explain how to install various types of chain drives.

   a. Describe common drive chains.
   b. Identify and describe the characteristics of chain drive sprockets.
   c. Explain how to install and maintain chain drives.

Performance Task

  2. Properly install, align, and tension a roller chain drive.

Trade Terms

Cut-tooth sprockets: Chain sprockets made by machining the teeth for greater precision.

Master link: A chain-connecting link that is easily assembled and disassembled for repair or changes in the chain length.

Offset link: A specific type of connecting link that is used to connect chain with an odd number of links, designed to connect a roller link to a pin link.

Sprocket: A toothed wheel or disk designed to engage in the gaps between drive or conveyor chain links, typically for power transmission.

Chain drives are also widely used for power transmission. A chain drive consists of a driving sprocket, one or more driven sprockets, and an endless chain that travels around and meshes with the sprocket teeth (*Figure 38*).

Chain drives maintain a consistent speed ratio between the driving and driven sprockets because they do not slip or creep. They are the metal equivalent of synchronous belts. Chain drives typically operate at lower speeds than belt drives. Since metal can't absorb impact and sudden stress like a belt, chain drives may tend to jump or jerk at startup or when the load suddenly changes.

2.1.0 Drive Chains

There are many different types of chain available today. Some are designed primarily for lifting, while others are used extensively for conveying materials. You'll learn more about those in NCCER Module 15401, *Introduction to Conveyors*, and NCCER Module 15402, *Troubleshooting and Repairing Conveyors*. The two most common types of chain used for power transmission are *roller chain* and *silent chain*.

2.1.1 Roller Chain

Roller chain (*Figure 39*) is the most common type of power transmission chain. A roller chain consists of a series of connected links that are an assembly of pins, bushings, rollers, and side plates, as shown in *Figure 40*. A roller chain is made by alternately connecting roller links and pin links and can be made to virtually any length. A final master link (*Figure 41*) is used to connect the two ends, creating an endless loop. The master link can be secured by cotter pins, spring clips, or similar hardware. An offset link, also shown in *Figure 41*, is used to connect a roller link to a pin link when there are an odd number of links in the chain.

Roller chain can be assembled in single strands or in multiple strands (*Figure 42*). Like banded belts, multiple chain strands increase the amount of power that can be transferred.

Common roller chain is manufactured to meet one of several possible standards, regardless of the manufacturer. If they are constructed to the same standard, common roller chain and matching sprockets from different manufacturers are interchangeable. Identification is also standardized, so replacements can easily be selected from a different manufacturer's stock. Typical standards are provided by the American National Standards Institute (ANSI), the International Organization for Standardization (ISO), and the American Petroleum Institute (API). API standards are relevant to oil fields and refineries.

Roller Chain Dimensions

Standardized roller chain products have consistent dimensions, allowing them to be interchangeable. The three principal dimensions used to size roller chains are the pitch, chain width, and roller diameter. In this case, *pitch* refers to the center-to-center distance between the pins (*Figure 43*).

Figure 38 Typical chain drive.

Figure 39 Roller chain.

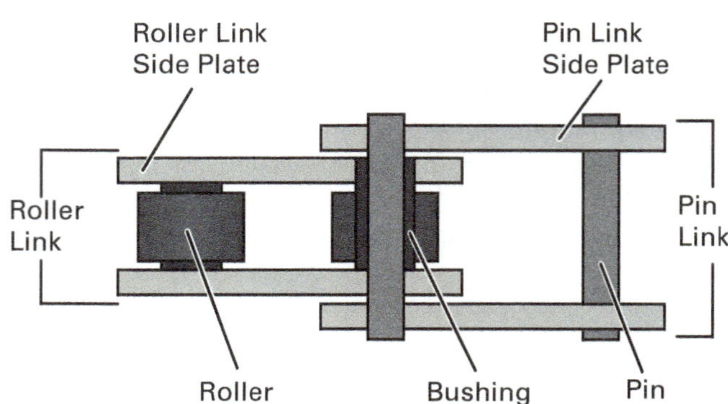

Figure 40 Basic roller chain components.

Figure 41 Roller chain connecting links.

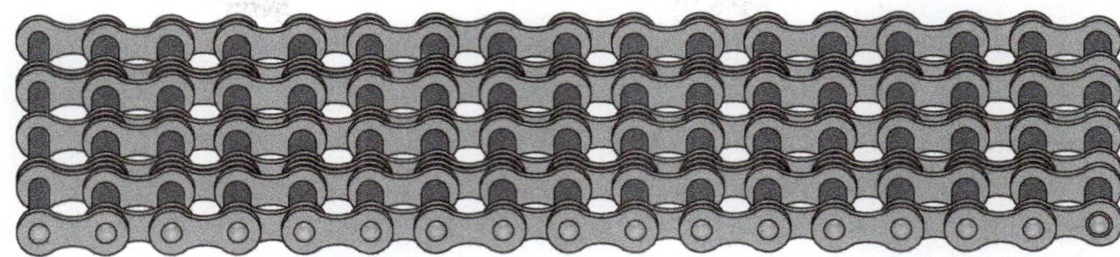

Figure 42 Single-strand and multistrand roller chain.

Chain width is the minimum distance measured between the side plates of a roller link (as opposed to the pin link). This dimension determines the width of the compatible sprocket teeth.

The *roller diameter* is the outside diameter (OD) of the individual chain rollers. The form of the sprocket teeth is determined by this dimension.

Other dimensions related to chain construction include the following:

- Side plate height
- Side plate thickness
- Pin diameter
- Roller diameter
- Roller width

Roller Chain Identification

The basic numbering system for roller chain is also standardized, which helps to quickly identify compatible products. The first one or two digits in the number denote the pitch in $\frac{1}{8}$" increments. For example, #40 chain has a $\frac{4}{8}$" ($\frac{1}{2}$") pitch, while a #120 chain has a $\frac{12}{8}$" ($1\frac{1}{2}$") pitch.

The right-hand digit of the number identifies a specific characteristic. For instance, a zero in the right-hand position indicates that the roller chain is constructed to standard proportions and characteristics. A 1 in the last position, such as #41 chain, identifies it as lightweight chain. The lightweight version is smaller than #40 chain, apart from its pitch, and is selected for less demanding applications than #40 chain. A 5 in the last position, such as #45 or #125 chain, indicates that it is *bushing chain*—chain constructed without rollers.

When the identifying number is hyphenated, e.g., #40-3 chain, the number to the right of the hyphen indicates the number of strands. To summarize, a #40-3 chain is built to standardized proportions with a pitch of $\frac{1}{2}$" and three strands.

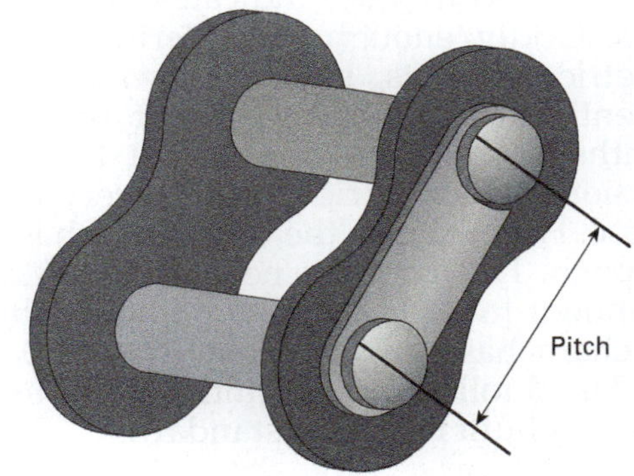

Figure 43 Roller chain pitch.

Double-Pitch Roller Chain

Double-pitch (or *extended-pitch*) chain is also made to ANSI standards. The pitch is twice that of standard chain. Double-pitch chain is less costly and used in lightly loaded drive applications and some conveyor systems.

For power transmission chain, the number 20 is placed in front of the standard numbers to designate double-pitch chain. For example, a #2050 chain has similar dimensions to #50 chain, but the normal pitch of 0.625" is doubled to 1.25".

Figure Credit: Courtesy USA Roller Chain & Sprockets

Table 2 shows the 14 ANSI-standard sizes of roller chain. Of course, there are many custom chain types as well, engineered for specific applications. But the products listed in *Table 2* represent the most widely used roller chain products.

Metric Roller Chain

Metric chains are constructed to British and/or ISO standards. These products are occasionally encountered in the United States as well.

Metric chain pitch varies from 5 mm to 88.9 mm. *Table 3* shows the specifications for standardized metric chain. Like ANSI chain, the hyphenated number indicates the number of strands. Oddly enough, considering that these are metric products, the first two numbers of the identifying number represent the pitch in sixteenths of an inch. It may not be an exact conversion to the metric pitch in every case, but it is close. For example, the #20B chain has a $^{20}/_{16}"$ ($1^1/_4"$) pitch. This converts neatly to the 31.75 mm pitch shown in *Table 3* for #20B chain. Thus, #10 ANSI chain has the same pitch as #20B metric chain. The B following the initial digits indicates the chain is built to British standards.

2.1.2 Silent Chain

Silent chain, also called *inverted-tooth chain* (*Figure 44*), is constructed with inverted teeth that are designed to engage **cut-tooth sprockets**. Cut-tooth sprockets have machined teeth, while many roller chain sprockets are either cast or flame-cut steel plates. Silent chain drives efficiently transfer power with less noise and vibration than standard roller chain. Silent chains can take a lot of abuse and can operate at higher speeds than roller chain.

Silent chain is comprised of stacks of flat, tooth-shaped links. The links engage sprockets with compatible teeth. Silent chains usually contain guide plates that help keep the chain properly engaged with the sprockets. Washers or spacers may also be present in a silent chain assembly. The components are held together by long pins at each joint.

There are several different approaches to the guide plates. *Figure 45* shows two basic types of guide plates. *Center-guide chain* has a single plate in the center of alternating links. When there are two plates inset from the sides, it is referred to as *two-center-guide chain*. A third type is called *side-plate guide chain*. An example of this type is shown in *Figure 44*. Silent chain with less than a $^1/_2"$ pitch typically has side plates. Chain with a larger pitch typically has center or two-center-guide plates.

The pitch of silent chain is measured as shown in *Figure 46*. It is interesting to note that pitch is generally measured in inches, even when the other dimensions are metric.

Figure 44 Silent drive chain.

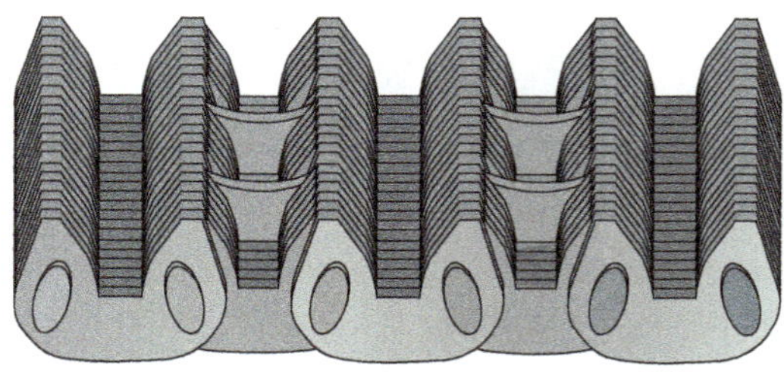

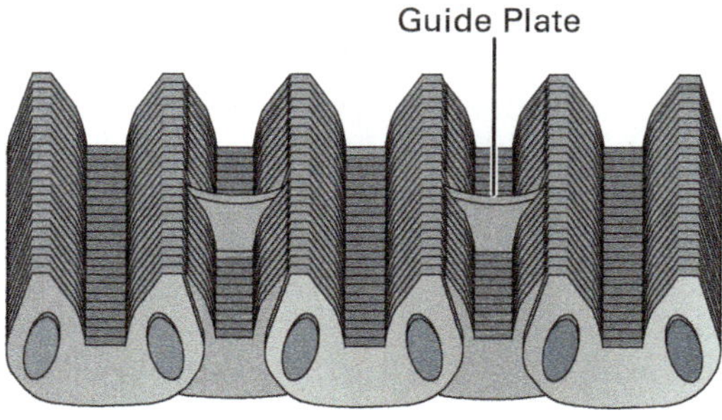

Figure 45 Center-guide and two-center-guide chain designs.

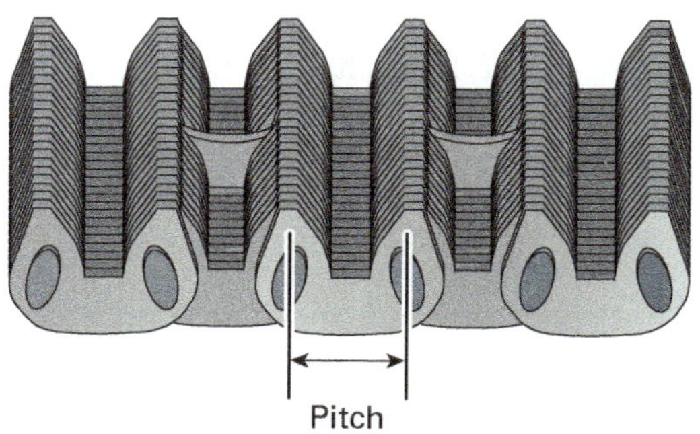

Figure 46 Silent chain pitch measurement.

Table 2 Standardized ANSI Roller Chain Sizes

ANSI Chain Size	Pitch	Roller Width	Roller Diameter	Overall Width	Plate Height	Plate Thickness	Pin Diameter	Average Ultimate Strength (lb)	Weight (lb/ft)
25-1	0.250"	0.125"	0.130"	0.306"	0.228"	0.029"	0.091"	930	0.09
35-1	0.375"	0.188"	0.200"	0.456"	0.356"	0.050"	0.141"	2,320	0.22
40-1	0.500"	0.312"	0.312"	0.642"	0.475"	0.058"	0.156"	3,970	0.42
41-1	0.500"	0.250"	0.306"	0.522"	0.390"	0.050"	0.141"	2,760	0.28
50-1	0.625"	0.375"	0.400"	0.794"	0.594"	0.079"	0.200"	6,620	0.68
60-1	0.750"	0.500"	0.469"	0.994"	0.712"	0.093"	0.234"	9,270	0.97
80-1	1.000"	0.625"	0.625"	1.290"	0.950"	0.125"	0.312"	16,540	1.71
100-1	1.250"	0.750"	0.750"	1.578"	1.188"	0.157"	0.375"	25,360	2.65
120-1	1.500"	1.000"	0.875"	1.966"	1.425"	0.189"	0.437"	32,640	3.79
140-1	1.750"	1.000"	1.000"	2.132"	1.663"	0.219"	0.500"	45,210	4.96
160-1	2.000"	1.250"	1.125"	2.564"	1.901"	0.255"	0.563"	57,780	6.32
180-1	2.250"	1.406"	1.406"	2.808"	2.130"	0.283"	0.687"	80,480	9.04
200-1	2.500"	1.500"	1.562"	3.160"	2.376"	0.312"	0.782"	109,150	10.31
240-1	3.000"	1.875"	1.875"	3.772"	2.850"	0.375"	0.937"	152,140	16.40

Table 3 Standardized Metric Roller Chain Sizes

Metric Chain Size	Pitch	Roller Width	Roller Diameter	Pin Diameter	Plate Height	Overall Width	Breaking Load (kN)	Weight (kg/m)
03B-1	5.0 mm	2.5 mm	3.2 mm	1.49 mm	4.1 mm	7.4 mm	2.4	0.08
04B-1	6.0 mm	2.8 mm	4.0 mm	1.85 mm	5.0 mm	7.8 mm	3.2	0.12
05B-1	8.0 mm	3.0 mm	5.0 mm	2.31 mm	7.1 mm	8.9 mm	5.9	0.18
06B-1	9.525 mm	5.72 mm	6.35 mm	3.28 mm	8.2 mm	14.1 mm	10.4	0.41
081B-1	12.7 mm	3.3 mm	7.75 mm	3.66 mm	9.9 mm	10.2 mm	9.97	0.28
083B-1	12.7 mm	4.88 mm	7.75 mm	4.09 mm	10.3 mm	12.9 mm	12.7	0.42
085B-1	12.7 mm	6.38 mm	7.77 mm	3.58 mm	9.9 mm	14.0 mm	12.26	0.4
08B-1	12.7 mm	7.75 mm	8.51 mm	4.45 mm	11.8 mm	18.2 mm	19.4	0.7
10B-1	15.875 mm	9.65 mm	10.16 mm	5.08 mm	14.7 mm	20.9 mm	27.5	0.9
12B-1	19.05 mm	11.68 mm	12.07 mm	5.72 mm	16.0 mm	24.2 mm	32.2	1.3
12BH-1	19.05 mm	11.68 mm	12.07 mm	5.94 mm	16.0 mm	26.8 mm	40.0	2.0
16B-1	25.4 mm	17.02 mm	15.88 mm	8.28 mm	21.0 mm	37.4 mm	72.8	2.7
20B-1	31.75 mm	19.56 mm	19.05 mm	10.19 mm	26.4 mm	45.0 mm	106.7	3.6
24B-1	38.1 mm	25.4 mm	25.4 mm	14.63 mm	33.4 mm	57.8 mm	178.0	6.7
28B-1	44.45 mm	30.99 mm	27.94 mm	15.90 mm	37.0 mm	29.5 mm	222.0	8.3
32B-1	50.8 mm	30.99 mm	29.21 mm	17.81 mm	42.2 mm	71.0 mm	277.5	10.5
40B-1	63.5 mm	38.1 mm	39.37 mm	22.89 mm	52.9 mm	89.2 mm	394.0	16.0
48B-1	76.2 mm	45.72 mm	48.26 mm	29.24 mm	63.8 mm	107.0 mm	621.6	25.0
56B-1	88.9 mm	53.34 mm	53.98 mm	34.32 mm	77.8 mm	123.0 mm	940.0	35.0

Silent chain is manufactured to ANSI standards, which does result in interchangeability between products of different manufacturers. However, the standards don't provide standardization of all joint components and guide plate shape. These characteristics can differ as a result. All silent chain meeting the ANSI standards is made to fit ANSI-standardized sprockets. However, the silent chain products from two manufacturers should not be connected to lengthen or repair a chain.

As you might expect, there are also many engineered and customized silent chain products and matching sprockets that are not interchangeable. Careful research is required when you wish to switch a product from one manufacturer to another.

Silent Chain Identification

ANSI-standard silent chain has a sizing code that begins with a two-letter symbol (SC) indicating that it is a silent chain product. The next digit (or two digits for larger sizes) indicates the pitch in eighths of an inch. The next two digits indicate the nominal width of the chain in quarter-inch increments.

For example, chain coded as SC408 has a pitch of $^4/_8$" ($^1/_2$") and a nominal width of $^8/_4$" (2"). The actual overall width, a measurement that includes the pins that protrude on both sides, is usually wider than the nominal width by ~$^1/_8$" to $^1/_4$".

2.2.0 Sprockets

Drive chains ride on sprockets that are attached to the shafts, as shown in *Figure 38*. They must match the characteristics of the chain to prevent damage to both the sprockets and the chain. Since chain drives represent metal-to-metal power transmission, damage occurs quickly when incompatible components are installed.

There are sprockets for every type of drive chain. ANSI-standard sprockets use the same numbering system as the chain, making it easier to match the components. A #40 sprocket, for example, has the proper pitch and other characteristics needed to match #40 chain. The number of strands follows the ANSI identification number. A #40-3 sprocket, for example, accommodates three strands of chain.

Duplex Silent Chain

Duplex drive belts are used in applications where both sides of the belt must ride in a sheave groove, usually due to changes in direction when using more than two sheaves. However, common roller chain is symmetrical, allowing it to easily ride along a sprocket on either side. Silent chain, though, has unique construction features. But duplex silent chain, although rare, is available for those unique applications that require a change of direction in the drive.

Sprockets have a few more mounting options than sheaves. There are four basic styles to choose from, as follows:

- *Type A* — A flat plate style, with no hubs. They are also referred to as *plate sprockets*.
- *Type B* — A sprocket with a mounting hub found on one side. It is generally keyed and locked in place with a setscrew.
- *Type C* — A sprocket with mounting hubs on both sides of the plate.
- *Type D* — A style that requires a detachable hub matching the shaft size needed.

A fixed-bore sprocket fits only one size of shaft. But there are also sprockets with large bores designed to accommodate detachable hubs (*Figure 47*). Idler sprockets (*Figure 48*), like idler pulleys, are used to maintain proper tension and/or help guide the chain between sprockets.

Sprocket specifications typically include the dimensions shown in *Figure 49*, in addition to the thickness of the plate and hubs (if present). You will also see references to *caliper diameter*. The caliper diameter is identical to the bottom diameter on a sprocket with an even number of teeth. When the sprocket has an odd number of teeth, it is measured from the bottom of one tooth gap to the bottom of the nearest opposing tooth gap. The difference in the measurement is very small but may be important to an engineer.

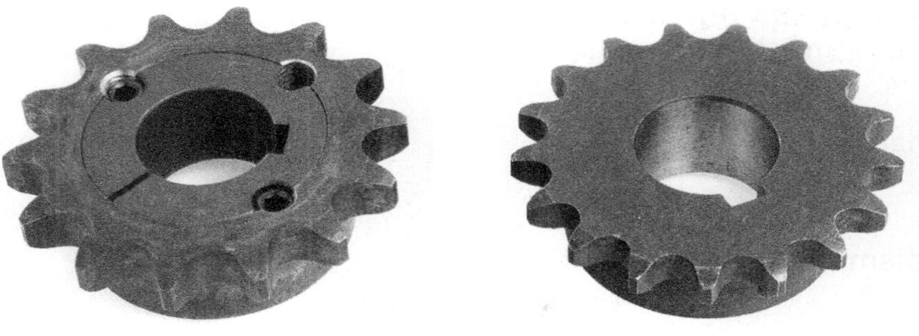

Figure 47 Type D detachable-hub and Type B fixed-bore sprockets.

Figure 48 Idler sprockets.

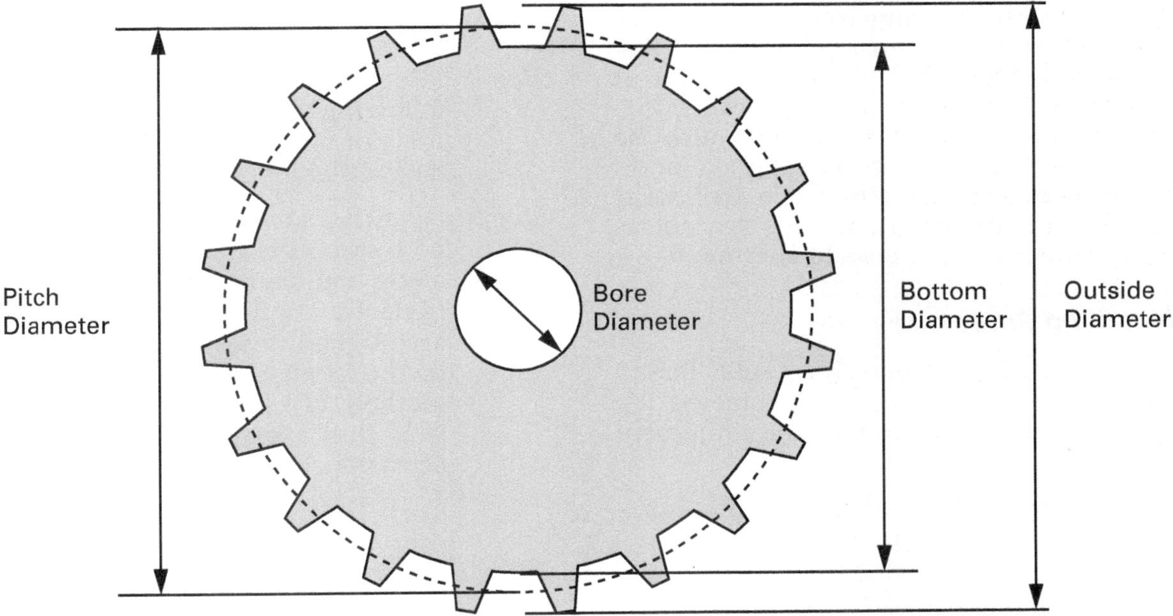

Figure 49 Sprocket diameters.

Speed calculations for chain drives are made using the pitch diameter and the same equations used for belt drives:

$$\text{Driven rotational speed} = \frac{P_{driver} \times S_{driver}}{P_{driven}}$$

$$\text{Driven pitch diameter} = \frac{S_{driver} \times P_{driver}}{S_{driven}}$$

$$\text{Driver rotational speed} = \frac{P_{driven} \times S_{driven}}{P_{driver}}$$

$$\text{Driver pitch diameter} = \frac{S_{driven} \times P_{driven}}{S_{driver}}$$

2.2.1 Silent Chain Sprockets

Silent chain sprockets are thicker than roller chain sprockets since the chain itself is wider. The sprockets are very similar in appearance to gears. Remember that silent chain also has guide links, so the sprocket design must match the chain guide plate pattern. *Figure 50* shows an example of center-guide silent chain on its matching sprocket.

ANSI-standard silent chain sprockets are designed to match the standardized chain products. The identification numbers for sprockets also begin with SC, making it easier to ensure a match.

2.3.0 Installing Chain Drives

The proper installation of chain drives requires that the shafts and the sprockets be accurately aligned. You can use the same tools and methods to align sprockets that you use to align sheaves. Magnetic sheave lasers that mount on the side of a sheave work just as well to align sprockets.

The chain, like a drive belt, must also be set to the proper tension. A misaligned and/or improperly tensioned chain drive will wear rapidly and fail prematurely. Chains are not as forgiving as belts when it comes to alignment.

2.3.1 Installing Sprockets

Follow these steps to install sprockets. Before beginning, ensure that you have completed the necessary steps to lock out and tag the equipment energy source(s):

Step 1   Inspect the shafts and address any burrs or nicks, using a fine file.

Step 2   Clean both shafts thoroughly, using a solvent and a rag.

Many solvents are toxic and/or flammable. Wear appropriate respiratory protection and gloves when handling these products. Ensure there is sufficient ventilation in the work area. All rags should be disposed of in approved containers.

Step 3   Ensure you have the proper size and length of keystock, if required. Clean the keys and address any burrs that may be present.

Step 4   Inspect the bore of the sprocket, address any visible flaws, and clean it as necessary. Ensure any setscrews are backed out so they won't interfere as you slide the sprocket onto the shaft.

Step 5   If the shafts are long enough, you can check to ensure they are parallel as shown in *Figure 26*. Alternatively, you can check for parallelism after the sprockets are installed. This step is required either way to ensure proper alignment of the sprockets.

Step 6   Slip the driven sprocket onto its shaft and position the sprocket along the shaft as needed.

Step 7   Lock the driven sprocket to the shaft. Sprockets are usually locked to the shaft with a setscrew(s) and a key. However, since there are several mounting styles, be sure to follow the manufacturer's installation instructions.

Step 8   Slip the drive sprocket onto its shaft, following the manufacturer's instructions. It is not unusual for the two sprockets to have different mounting characteristics.

Step 9   Position a straightedge across the face of both sprockets and move the drive sheave along the shaft until the sprockets are perfectly aligned (*Figure 51*). When they are aligned, the straightedge will be flat on the faces of both sheaves. An alternate method of checking sheave alignment is to pull a piano wire or string tightly across the faces.

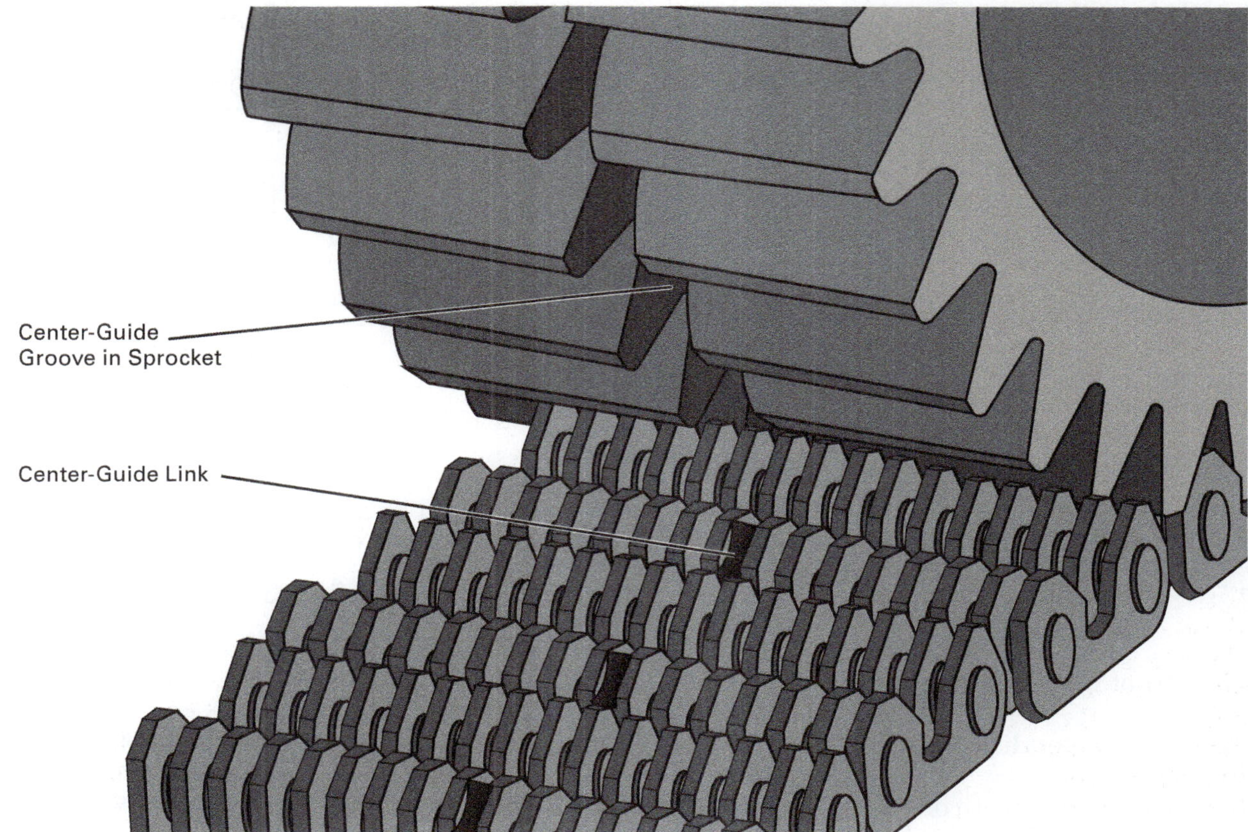

Figure 50 Center-guide chain and matching sprocket.

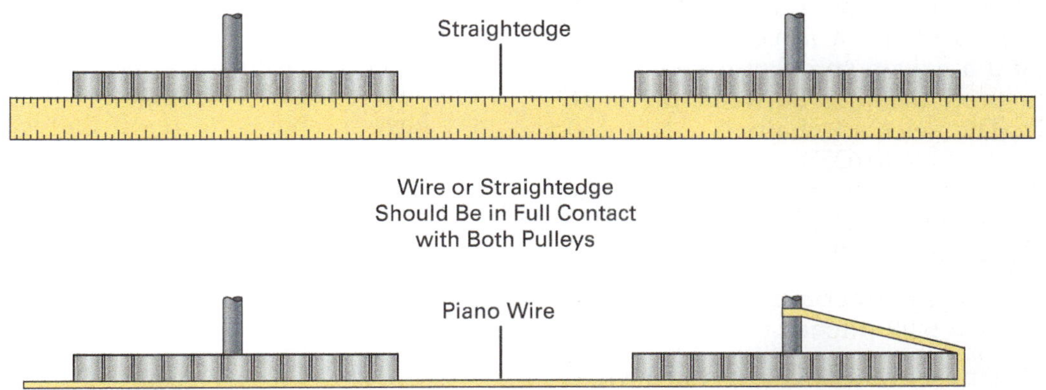

Figure 51 Checking sprocket alignment.

> **NOTE**
>
> Remember that a very important goal is to align the sprocket teeth. Due to differences in construction between the two sprockets, aligning the sides of the sprockets may not result in aligned teeth. If there is a difference in the thickness of the sprockets, for example, you must factor that in as you position the drive sprocket. However, aligning the sides will reveal whether the two shafts are parallel.

Step 10 Lock the drive sprocket into position on the motor shaft.

2.3.2 Determining Chain Length

Before you can install the drive chain, the proper length must be determined. In many cases, this will be determined beforehand. The chain length can be determined once the engineer has selected the chain pitch and sprockets if the shaft center-to-center distance is known. However, an accurate center-to-center measurement may not be available until the equipment has been set and/or assembled.

The equation used determines the length of the chain in pitches (links). This is very important to remember! The chain length needed will be counted off in pitches, rather than measured in inches or another unit of measure. The following equation is used to determine the length of the drive chain in pitches:

$$L = 2c + \frac{n_L + n_S}{2} + \frac{0.1013(n_L - n_S)^2}{4c}$$

Where:
L = length of the chain in pitches (the number of links)
c = center-to-center distance between the shafts (also in pitches)
n_L = total number of teeth on the larger sprocket
n_S = total number of teeth on the smaller sprocket
For an example problem, refer to *Figure 52*. Assume a chain drive has a drive sprocket with 20 teeth (n_S) and a driven sprocket with 45 teeth (n_L). The measured distance between the shaft centers is 32". The selected chain is ANSI #50, which has a pitch of $\frac{5}{8}$" (0.625").
Begin by determining c, which is the shaft center-to-center distance in pitches. Divide the measured distance by the pitch as shown here:

$$c = 32" \div 0.625" \text{ chain pitch}$$
$$c = 51.2 \text{ pitches}$$

Although you must eventually arrive at a whole number of pitches, it is best to use the decimal value as is for now since you cannot join a chain with two-tenths of a link. With c now determined, we can populate the equation with the known information:

$$L = 2(51.2) + \frac{45 + 20}{2} + \frac{0.1013(45 - 20)^2}{4(51.2)}$$

Solve the equation as shown below:

$$L = 102.4 + \frac{45 + 20}{2} + \frac{0.1013(45 - 20)^2}{4(51.2)}$$

$$L = 102.4 + \frac{45 + 20}{2} + \frac{0.1013(25)^2}{204.8}$$

$$L = 102.4 + \frac{45 + 20}{2} + \frac{0.1013(625)}{204.8}$$

$$L = 102.4 + \frac{45 + 20}{2} + \frac{63.3}{204.8}$$

$$L = 102.4 + \frac{65}{2} + \frac{63.3}{204.8}$$

$$L = 102.4 + 32.5 + 0.31$$

$$L = 135.21 \text{ pitches}$$

If the resulting pitch is fractional (as is the case here), rounding up to the nearest whole number is generally preferred. Having an even number of pitches is also preferred. When there is an odd number of pitches, an offset link is required rather than a master link (*Figure 41*). Installing an offset link reduces the tensile strength of the chain. In other words, it is weaker than the other links. As a result, the width of the drive chain may have to change to reach the necessary load capacity, and that leads to different sprockets.
In the example, rounding up to 136 pitches results in an even number of links, and an offset link is not required. To prepare the chain, count off 135 links and remove the section from the roll. The 136th link is the master link needed to assemble the chain.

2.3.3 Breaking the Chain

Disassembling a roller chain link is also referred to as *breaking* the chain. A common style of chain breaker is shown in *Figure 53*.

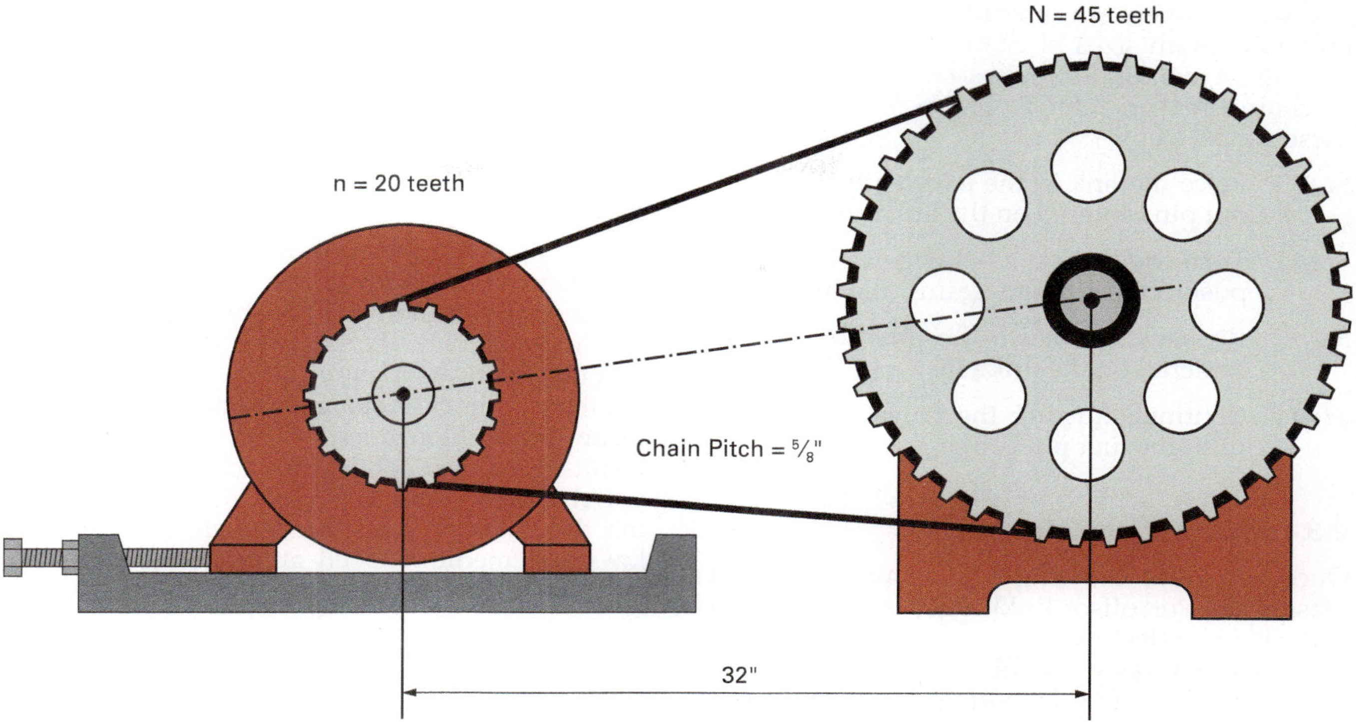

Figure 52 Chain drive example for length calculations.

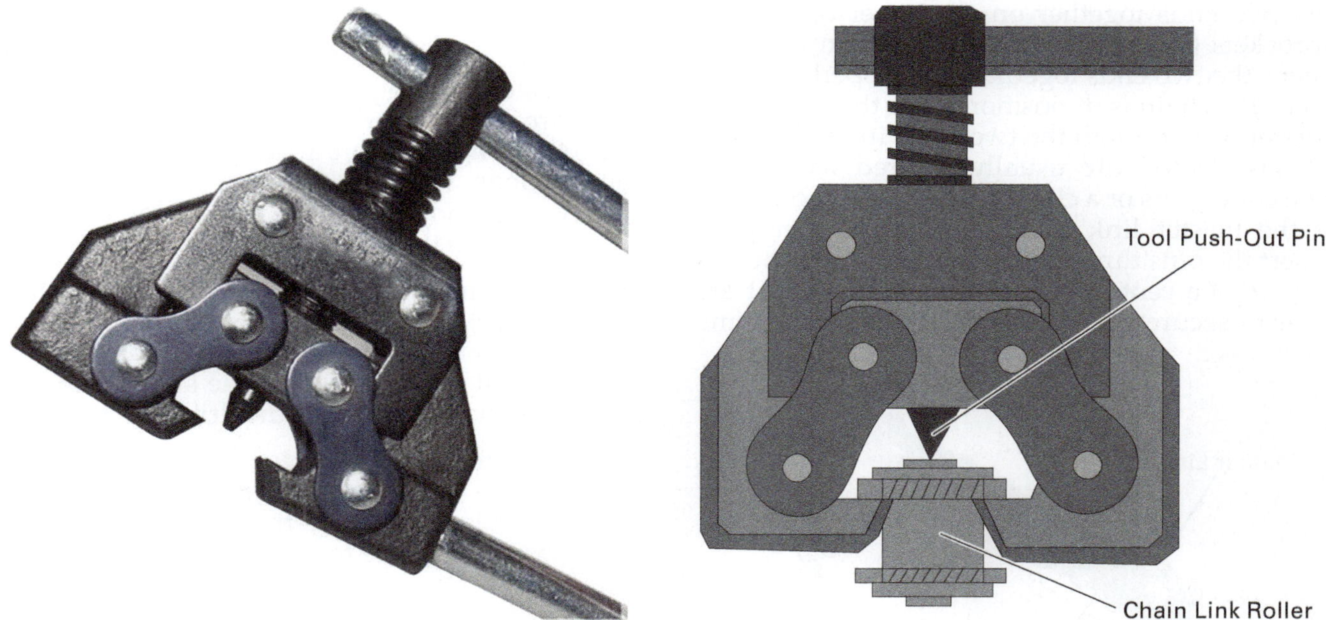

Figure 53 Chain breaker for smaller chain sizes.

Figure 54 Removing a roller chain link pin.

Chain breakers are typically designed to work only on certain sizes of chain. Ensure you have the correct tool for the chain size. To use this type of chain breaker, refer to *Figure 54* and follow these simple steps:

Step 1 Place the link in the jaws with the push-out pin centered on the link pin.

Step 2 Turn the handle clockwise to bring the push-out pin down against the link pin.

Step 3 Recheck to ensure the push-out pin is centered on the link pin.

Step 4 Continue turning the handle clockwise until the link pin is free.

2.3.4 Installing the Master Link

Once you have the length of chain needed, a master link (or offset link) must be installed to make it an endless loop.

The easiest way to do this is with the chain on the sprockets. Before installing the chain, make sure both the chain and sprockets are clean and free of grit, weld spatter, and other contaminants. Place the chain on the sprockets and bring the two ends together on the larger of the two sprockets (*Figure 55*). Placing the chain this way keeps the two ends together and properly spaced. Once the chain is in position, slide the pins of the master link through the two holes in the chain.

Master links are usually secured with either two cotter pins or a clip that slides over both pins. If the master link is secured with cotter pins, insert the pins through the openings with the tips toward the center of the link. The tips that are bent to secure the pin in place should be facing each other.

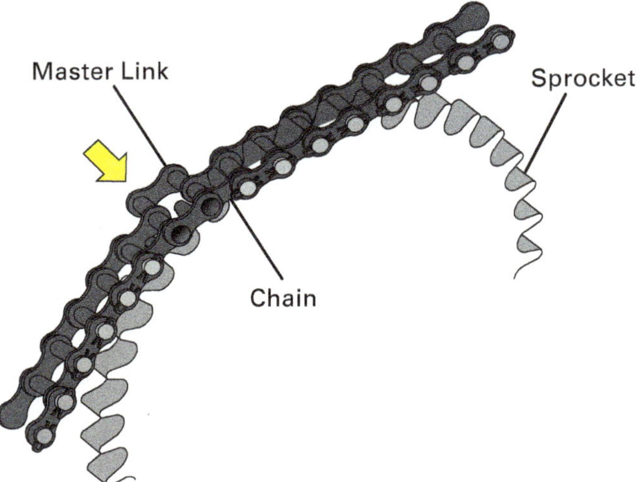

Figure 55 Preparing the chain for master link installation.

If the master link is secured with a clip, it slides into place over both pins. However, pay attention to the direction. The closed end of the clip should be facing the direction of travel.

2.3.5 Adjusting Chain Tension

A drive chain must be properly tensioned before use. If it is too loose, it will sag between the sprockets. This usually causes excessive noise and vibration. If it is too tight, the chain and sprockets will wear quickly, the bearings will be stressed, and the chain will *elongate* quickly. It's worth noting that, in this case, elongation doesn't necessarily mean stretch. Elongation in drive chains generally results from wear at the pins and bushings.

Drive chain tension is determined by measuring the amount of slack in the chain. For many low- and medium-speed applications, adjusting to a sag of 3 to 4 percent of the shaft center-to-center measurement is typical. In the example used to determine chain length, the center-to-center measurement was 32". Multiply 32" by 4 percent (0.04) to determine that the sag should be 1.28"—just slightly more than $1\frac{1}{4}$" (1.25"). This is measured at the midpoint of the chain between the two sprockets. Note that extreme precision in the measurement isn't necessary.

For drives that run at higher speeds, experience inconsistent loading, or operate in both directions, a 2 percent sag is preferred. The sag then would be 0.64"—slightly more than $\frac{5}{8}$" (0.625"). Vertical applications, with one sprocket above the other, are typically adjusted to a 2 percent sag as well.

To measure the sag, follow these steps:

Step 1 Adjust the sprockets so that all the chain slack is on the top of the drive. For a vertical drive, adjust the sprockets so that all the sag is on the side leaving the driver sprocket as the driver rotates.

Step 2 Place a straightedge on the chain from one sprocket to the other and use a scale to measure from the bottom of the straightedge to the chain (*Figure 56*). The sag must be measured at the midpoint between the sprockets. If the sprockets are too far apart to use a straightedge, piano wire or a taut string can be used as a measuring guide instead.

Step 3 Adjust the chain tension by moving the driver until the required sag measurement is achieved.

Step 4 Once the sag is correct, lock the driver in place. Ensure that all sprocket setscrews and other hardware are also secured.

Also ensure that sprocket alignment is maintained.

Step 5 Lubricate the chain according to the manufacturer's recommendations and the application. Lubrication requirements vary widely, as discussed in the next section.

Step 6 Ensure that all tools and equipment are removed from the work area, then reinstall all safety guards.

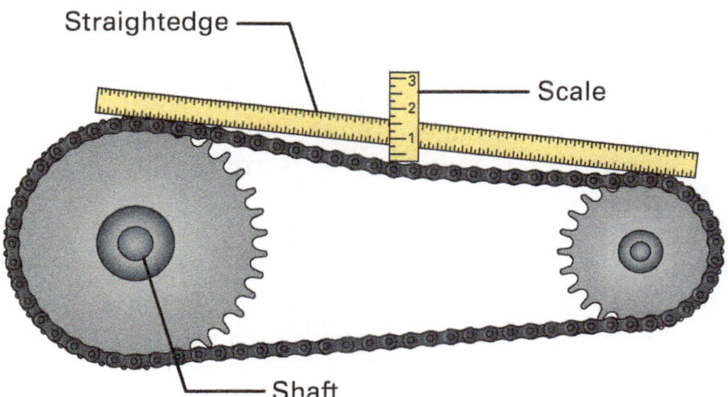

Figure 56 Measuring chain sag.

2.3.6 Chain Drive Lubrication and Maintenance

Like belt drives, chain drives require periodic maintenance and inspection to sustain reliability. Unlike belt drives, however, lubrication is a very important consideration for chain drives. The life of the drive components is significantly extended when proper lubrication is provided.

Lubrication

Lubrication is needed to reduce wear of the moving parts of a chain and reduce friction between the chain and the sprockets. Proper lubrication also flushes away foreign materials, prevents corrosion, and cools the chain.

Although manufacturers often apply a type of grease or even petroleum jelly to chain products to prevent corrosion in storage, grease products are not used to lubricate chain. Thick, heavy lubricants tend to pick up and hold grit and debris. Chain lubricants need to be light enough in viscosity to access the areas that need lubrication most—the voids between the pins and bushings. Basic oils without significant additives are usually chosen.

The ambient temperature helps determine the correct oil viscosity. While SAE 10 oil is recommended for temperatures of -20°F to 80°F (-29°C to 27°C), SAE 50 oils are best applied at temperatures of 40°F to 150°F (4°C to 66°C).

In most cases, the equipment manufacturer or plant engineers select the chain lubricant. But when the conditions do not seem to match the viscosity of the lubricant provided, you may wish to discuss it with your supervisor. Once a lubricant is specified for maintenance processes, you are expected to look for and report deficiencies. Otherwise, those that specify the lubricants will never know there is a problem until a failure occurs.

> **WARNING!**
>
> Remember to conduct the locally required energy lockout and tagout process before inspecting or servicing any type of drive system.

Chain drives are typically lubricated in one of the following ways:

- *Manual lubrication* — The lubricant is applied by hand with an oil can or brush. This type of lubrication may be required several times daily.
- *Oil bath* — An enclosed chain drive passes through a sump of oil where it picks up a small amount of oil and carries it around the chain path (*Figure 57*). Maintaining the correct oil level is important. The oil level is generally maintained so that it is even with the pitch line of the chain as it travels around the lower sprocket. If there is too much oil in the sump, the chain passing through introduces too much air into the oil, causing it to foam.
- *Oil slinger* — This approach is similar to the oil bath. Instead of the chain passing through the oil, a *slinger* (scoop) mounted on the lower shaft picks up oil and deposits it on the chain. The oil level in the sump should remain just below the chain.
- *Drip lubrication* — The lubricant is contained in a reservoir above the drive and oil simply drips onto the chain at a steady rate. The rate can vary from just a drop or two per minute to 25 drops per minute.
- *Forced oil stream* — An oil pump is placed in the sump and lubricant is sprayed or streamed onto the chain under pressure. This approach is often used for applications that run at higher speeds. An external oil cooler may be needed if the drive generates a significant amount of heat.

For the automated approaches to lubrication, maintenance primarily consists of maintaining the correct oil level. The oil also needs to be changed periodically, according to the equipment manufacturer's guidelines. For drip lubrication, the drip rate needs to be checked periodically. Pressurized systems need periodic inspection of the spray nozzles and service of the oil strainer or filter on the inlet side of the pump.

Chain Inspection

The inspection of a chain drive includes the following tasks, along with any others recommended by the equipment manufacturer:

- *Applying lubricant or checking the lubricant level* — Oil changes are generally scheduled based on hours of equipment operation.
- *Checking for chain wear* — If excessive wear is noted on the inside surfaces of the chain plates, ensure that the sprockets are properly aligned. Chain elongation is a common factor for many drives. Roller chain is usually replaced when it reaches roughly 3 percent elongation. One easy way to determine elongation is with a wear gauge like the one shown in *Figure 58*. Each step of the gauge is designed for a different chain pitch. The gauge is simply inserted between the rollers in several locations. If it advances any farther than the correct step for the chain pitch, the chain should be replaced. Some similar tools rely on precise measurements of the links.

- *Checking for sprocket wear* — Look for rough or worn edges around the teeth. Drive chains tend to develop hooked teeth due to excessive loading on the side of the tooth where pressure is applied. This typically occurs due to the chain being too tight (excess tension). Some "hooking" at the teeth is normal, but too much tension causes it to happen much faster. When the wear is excessive, the sprockets are replaced. Do not apply a new chain to excessively worn sprockets, or new sprockets to an excessively worn chain. Ideally, both components are replaced when either one is excessively worn. However, it is more common for sprockets to be replaced during every second or third chain replacement.
- *Checking the chain tension* — Chain tension will likely change as wear and elongation occur. The tension drops (resulting in more sag) more quickly in the early days of service for a new chain as the chain breaks in. The rate of change may also increase toward the end of its service life. Chain tension should be monitored consistently, along with the elongation rate.

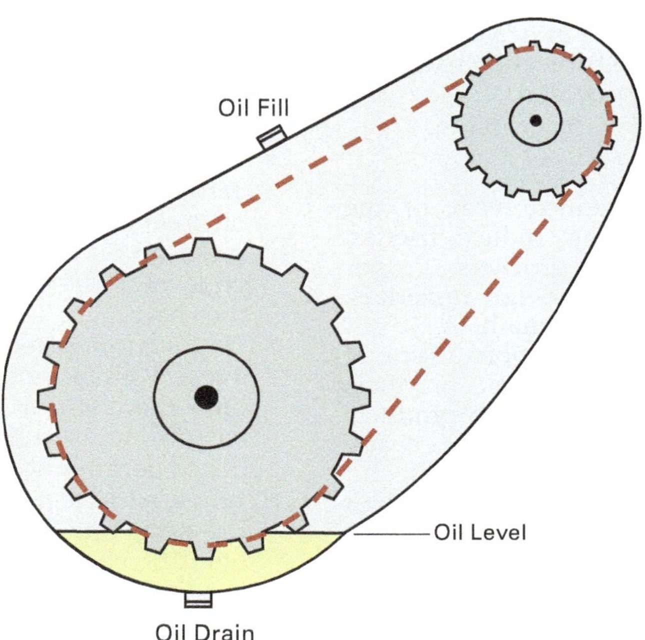

Figure 57 Oil bath lubrication of an enclosed chain drive.

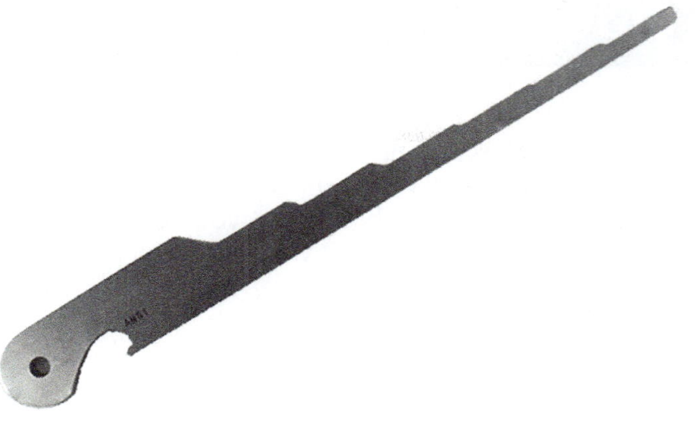

(A) Chain Wear Gauge

(B) Checking for Excessive Elongation

Figure 58 Chain wear gauge.

2.0.0 Section Review

1. ANSI-standardized silent chain is identified with ______.

   a. the letters NF used as a suffix, like #40NF
   b. the numeral 5 placed after a hyphen, like #40-5
   c. the letters SC used as a prefix, like #SC40
   d. an extra zero after the first two digits, like #400

2. Which of the following statements about sprockets is *correct*?

   a. Idler sprockets for chain drives are smooth and have no teeth.
   b. Type A sprockets have hubs on each side.
   c. Type D sprockets are simple flat plates with a fixed bore.
   d. Fixed-bore sprockets fit only one shaft size.

3. When installing a chain master link, ______.

   a. begin by placing the chain on the sprockets
   b. begin by checking the space the link will occupy with a chain gauge
   c. place the two ends in a chain breaker
   d. make sure it is adjacent to an offset link

4. On a chain drive, if the sprocket center-to-center distance is 49" and you wish to set the tension for a 3 percent sag, what would the sag measurement be?

   a. 0.52", or about ½"
   b. 0.73", or about ¾"
   c. 1.47", or about 1½"
   d. 1.78", or about 1¾"

1. The pitch line of a drive belt is commonly known today as the ______.

   a. stress line
   b. datum line
   c. sheave line
   d. drive line

2. Wedge belts can generally be used on the same sheaves that are used for classic and FHP belts.

   a. True
   b. False

3. The length of wedge belts is measured along the ______.

   a. datum line
   b. pitch line
   c. inside circumference
   d. outside circumference

4. The belt type made to US standards that is the *closest* to the metric SP belt series is the ______.

   a. classic belt
   b. FHP belt
   c. banded belt
   d. double-angle belt

5. On a belt drive, the drive sheave is typically smaller than the driven sheave.

   a. True
   b. False

6. One way to address angular misalignment between two horizontal shafts before the sheaves are installed is to ______.

   a. accurately level both shafts
   b. ensure both sheaves are perfectly flat
   c. measure the distance between the shafts at two points
   d. ensure both shafts are the same diameter

7. Even when you check for parallel alignment between two shafts before installing the sheaves for a belt drive, you must still check the installed sheaves for parallel alignment.

   a. True
   b. False

8. When a roller chain has an odd number of links in it, the ends *must* be connected with a(n) ______.

   a. master link
   b. pin link
   c. offset link
   d. cufflink

9. Although the proper amount of chain sag varies by application, the recommended sag typically falls between ______.

   a. 1 percent and 2 percent of the distance between the shaft centers
   b. 2 percent and 4 percent of the diameter of the largest sprocket
   c. 2 percent and 4 percent of the distance between the shaft centers
   d. 2 percent and 6 percent of the diameter of the smallest sprocket

10. A roller chain should generally be replaced when it has elongated ______.

   a. 1 percent
   b. 3 percent
   c. 5 percent
   d. 10 percent

Trade Terms Introduced in This Module

Belt whip: A condition where excess slack in a drive belt causes it to begin riding up and out of the sheave grooves, primarily on the slack side. The slack side is the side exiting the drive pulley as it rotates.

Cut-tooth sprockets: Chain sprockets made by machining the teeth for greater precision.

Idler pulley: A pulley or sheave with no attached load, used to help maintain drive belt tension or alignment.

Master link: A chain-connecting link that is easily assembled and disassembled for repair or changes in the chain length.

Offset link: A specific type of connecting link that is used to connect chain with an odd number of links, designed to connect a roller link to a pin link.

Sprocket: A toothed wheel or disk designed to engage in the gaps between drive or conveyor chain links, typically for power transmission.

Synchronous belts: Belts with teeth that correspond to grooves in matching sheaves, eliminating slippage, and maintaining synchronized rotation of the shafts; also referred to as *timing belts*.

Additional Resources

This module presents thorough resources for task training. The following reference material is suggested for further study.

Electric Motors and Drives: Fundamentals, Types and Applications. Austin Hughes and Bill Drury. 5th Edition. London, UK: Newnes.

Plant Engineer's Handbook. R. Keith Mobley. Latest Edition. Burlington, MA: Butterworth-Heinemann.

Timken Belts. **https://timkenbelts.com/**.

USA Roller Chain and Sprockets. **https://www.usarollerchain.com/**.

Figure Credits

Section Review Answer Key

SECTION 1.0.0

Answer	Section Reference	Objective
1. b	1.1.0; *Figure 5*	1a
2. a	1.2.4	1b
3. b	1.3.1	1c
4. d	1.4.2	1d

SECTION 2.0.0

Answer	Section Reference	Objective
1. c	2.1.2	2a
2. d	2.2.0	2b
3. a	2.3.4; *Figure 55*	2c
4. c	2.3.5	2c

Section Review Calculations

Section 1.0.0

Question 3

$$\text{Driver pitch diameter} = \frac{S_{driven} \times P_{driven}}{S_{driver}}$$

$$\text{Driver pitch diameter} = \frac{500 \text{ rpm} \times 14"}{1{,}200 \text{ rpm}}$$

$$\text{Driver pitch diameter} = \frac{7{,}000}{1{,}200}$$

$$\text{Driver pitch diameter} = 5.83"$$

Question 4

Belt length = $2c + 1.57(d_L + d_S)$
Belt length = $(2 \times 26") + 1.57(6.25" + 14")$
Belt length = $(2 \times 26") + 1.57(20.25")$
Belt length = $52" + 31.8"$
Belt length = **83.8" (round to 84")**

Section 2.0.0

Question 4

$49" \times 0.03 =$ **1.47"**

User Update

NCCER makes every effort to keep its textbooks up-to-date and free of technical errors. We appreciate your help in this process. If you find an error, a typographical mistake, or an inaccuracy in NCCER's curricula, please submit a User Update form by visiting **https://www.nccer.org/olf**. You can also scan the QR code using the camera on your phone or mobile device to access the form.

Introduction to Conveyors

OVERVIEW

Conveyors transport materials from point to point in virtually every industry. Indeed, there are very few components or products that do not travel on a conveyor of some sort as they are manufactured or distributed. There are many types, as well as many subtypes, each designed to meet a specific application. Some systems must handle tiny or fragile items, while others must move heavy equipment or loaded pallets. Conveyor systems offer a fascinating example of mechanical components working with technology to serve very specific needs.

Module 15401

Trainees with successful module completions may be eligible for credentialing through the NCCER Registry. To learn more, go to **www.nccer.org** or contact us at 1.888.622.3720. Our website, **www.nccer.org**, has information on the latest product releases and training.

Your feedback is welcome. You may email your comments to **curriculum@nccer.org**, send general comments and inquiries to **info@nccer.org**, or fill in the User Update form at the back of this module.

This information is general in nature and intended for training purposes only. Actual performance of activities described in this manual requires compliance with all applicable operating, service, maintenance, and safety procedures under the direction of qualified personnel. References in this manual to patented or proprietary devices do not constitute a recommendation of their use.

15401 V4.0

From *Millwright, Trainee Guide*. NCCER.
Copyright © 2023 by NCCER. Published by Pearson. All rights reserved.

15401
INTRODUCTION TO CONVEYORS

Objective

Successful completion of this module prepares you to do the following:

1. Identify and describe the construction of various conveyor systems.
   a. Identify and describe the construction of roller conveyors.
   b. Identify and describe the construction of belt conveyors.
   c. Identify and describe the construction of chain conveyors.
   d. Identify and describe the construction of screw conveyors.
   e. Identify and describe the construction of pneumatic conveyors.

Performance Tasks

This is a knowledge-based module. There are no Performance Tasks.

Trade Terms

Accumulation roller chain
Line shaft
Live-roller conveyor
Mechatronics

Rotary-lobe blower
Servomotors
Thermoplastics

Industry Recognized Credentials

If you are training through an NCCER-accredited sponsor, you may be eligible for credentials from NCCER's Registry. The ID number for this module is 15401. Note that this module may have been used in other NCCER curricula and may apply to other level completions. Contact NCCER's Registry at 1.888.622.3720 or go to **www.nccer.org** for more information.

You can also show off your industry-recognized credentials online with NCCER's digital badges. Transform your knowledge, skills, and achievements into badges that you can share across social media platforms, send to your network, and add to your resume. For more information, visit **www.nccer.org**.

How to Access Resources

This craft has additional videos and resources to enhance your learning experience. To view these resources, scan the QR below. The videos and resources are separated by module.

You can scan this code using the camera on your phone or mobile device to view these videos and resources.

Contents

1.0.0 INTRODUCTION TO CONVEYORS

Objective

Identify and describe the construction of various conveyor systems.

   a. Identify and describe the construction of roller conveyors.

   b. Identify and describe the construction of belt conveyors.

   c. Identify and describe the construction of chain conveyors.

   d. Identify and describe the construction of screw conveyors.

   e. Identify and describe the construction of pneumatic conveyors.

Trade Terms

Accumulation roller chain: A type of roller chain with rollers that have a larger diameter than the chain side-plate height, allowing the free-spinning rollers to support the conveyed product.

Line shaft: A shaft driven by a power source that is connected to multiple loads through sheaves or sprockets mounted along its length.

Live-roller conveyor: A roller conveyor that maintains direct contact between the rollers and the conveyed product, with some or all the rollers powered to move the product along.

Mechatronics: Technology that combines the power of mechanical systems with electronics.

Rotary-lobe blower: A blower that relies on two lobed impellers spinning at high speed to create airflow. Each of the two impellers has either two or three lobes.

Servomotors: Special electric motors that can start and stop very precisely, as well as rotate to a specific position.

Thermoplastics: Describes plastic materials that become more plastic (elastic) when heated and harden again when cooled, allowing them to be reformed. *Thermosets* are plastics that cannot be heated and reformed.

The term *conveyor* covers a lot of ground. Any device or equipment that transports materials from point to point generally qualifies. Conveyors can move materials horizontally, vertically, around turns and spirals, and even through pipes. Conveyor systems must move everything from carrots to cars. *Figure 1* and *Figure 2* provide just two examples of today's unique conveyor systems.

Conveyors can be open or enclosed, and their movement can be constant, varied, or intermittent. They may be portable or permanently fixed in position, and they can be supported by floors, walls, or ceilings (*Figure 3*). Transported materials may ride on a conveyor, be suspended from it, or travel inside a tube that offers protection from the environment. The purpose of any conveyor system is to transport a product in a smooth and controlled manner without damaging it. Timing is also a critical factor since material movement must often be synchronized with other processes to maximize efficiency.

The most common types of conveyors include the following:

- Roller conveyors
- Belt conveyors
- Chain conveyors
- Screw conveyors
- Pneumatic conveyors

There are also many subtypes and hybrid systems, but these broad categories are a good place to begin learning about the conveyor systems that support productivity in every corner of the world.

1.1.0 Roller Conveyors

The simplest conveyor is the gravity-operated roller conveyor (*Figure 4*). Roller conveyors consist of a frame that supports a series of cylindrical metal rollers. They are the simplest and safest conveyors to use and maintain, but they are significantly limited in what they can do to help.

The diameter of gravity conveyor rollers averages around 2" (~5 cm), but smaller and larger sizes are used when they suit the material being moved. The rollers are typically spaced from 3" to 6" (~8 cm to 15 cm) apart. Each roller is replaceable and fitted with ball bearings that allow them to turn freely (*Figure 5*). They may be made from steel, stainless steel, or aluminum. Many are also wrapped in white or colorful plastic sleeves.

Figure 1 Cars move through the assembly process.

Figure 2 Some conveyors must precisely position products, allowing other machinery to target them.

Figure 3 Pork moves through a processing facility.

Conveying Material on a Grand Scale

There are some very large and sophisticated conveyor systems in the world today. But few can compete with the scale of conveying systems used in the mining industry. Per the Guinness Book of World Records, the conveyor belt system that transports bauxite ore from the Mt. Saddleback mine to the Worsley refinery in Western Australia is the longest single conveyor belt in the world. The conveyor, commissioned in 1983, likely has some competitors today. However, it boasts some impressive statistics:

- The total distance traveled is 31.6 miles (51 km), with one segment that is 19.3 miles (31 km) long.
- Every hour, the conveyor moves 2,976 tons (~2,700 metric tons) of bauxite ore, from which aluminum is refined.
- The ore travels at about 16 mph (26 km/h).
- On its way, the ore travels across 10 bridges and through 22 tunnels.

Figure Credit: Shutterstock.com/Valery Shanin

Figure 4 Gravity-operated roller conveyor.

Gravity conveyors must be pitched in the desired direction of travel since the rollers are not powered. Alternatively, external equipment or humans give the materials the push they need to reach their destination or reach a powered conveyor that takes over. Curved sections are often needed in addition to straight sections, and unpowered roller conveyors can also be found in a spiral configuration (*Figure 6*).

The *ball transfer conveyor* (*Figure 7*) and the *skate wheel conveyor* (*Figure 8*) are variations of the gravity roller conveyor. The ball transfer conveyor is simply a table with exposed rollers that enable boxes, pallets, and other bulky items to be pushed in any direction. They are used to manually load materials to a conveyor, transfer materials from one conveyor to another, or move materials off a conveyor at the destination.

Skate wheel conveyors are considerably lighter in weight than roller conveyors. However, they are also less durable and cannot handle the heavy loads that roller conveyors allow. Since they also lack the surface area offered by roller conveyors, they can only be used with loads that have substantial flat, supportive bottoms. The wheels are mounted on axles and are staggered to offer better support. Packages tend to roll more easily across them than on roller conveyors.

The real advantage that skate wheel conveyors offer is portability and quick setup. Sections can be moved by hand, and many of them are designed for rapid assembly. Hooks on one end of a section engage pins on the next section, without the need for tools. Gravity roller conveyor sections are often equipped for quick assembly and connected directly to a compatible section of skate wheel conveyor with pins and hooks.

Figure 5 Nominal 2" replacement roller with a $\frac{7}{16}$" hex axle and a polyurethane coating.

Figure 6 Spiral gravity roller conveyor.

1.1.1 Powered Roller Conveyors

Powered roller conveyors don't need any help from gravity. Powered rollers allow them to move product along with ease, although they can't effectively move materials up significant inclines.

Chain-Driven Live-Roller Conveyors

Chain-driven live-roller conveyors (CDLR) move products by driving the rollers with a series of chains to push the product along. The term **live-roller conveyor** refers to models that have mechanically powered rollers.

Pallets and palletized materials, tires, and drums are common loads for these systems. They are relatively low in cost, but they can move some very heavy loads and are durable with proper maintenance. Conveyors capable of handling heavier loads require more complex drive arrangements and heavier drive chains (*Figure 9*).

Belt-Driven Live-Roller Conveyors

Live-roller conveyors can also be powered with a belt drive. Belt-driven live-roller (BDLR) conveyors are much like chain-driven models, but the chains are replaced by serpentine synchronous drive belts.

There are many variations of this type as well. Some use a series of smaller belts to transfer power from one roller to another. Others may be driven through a common shaft that eliminates the belt sheaves altogether. *Figure 10* shows several examples of drive belt arrangements. As shown, small belts that are little more than large O-rings can be used to drive the rollers directly, transferring power from a **line shaft** or other source. Although line shafts are also used in heavier conveyor designs, systems using small drive belts are limited to handling light loads.

Figure 7 Ball transfer conveyor.

Figure 8 Skate wheel conveyor.

Figure 9 A CDLR conveyor drive arrangement.

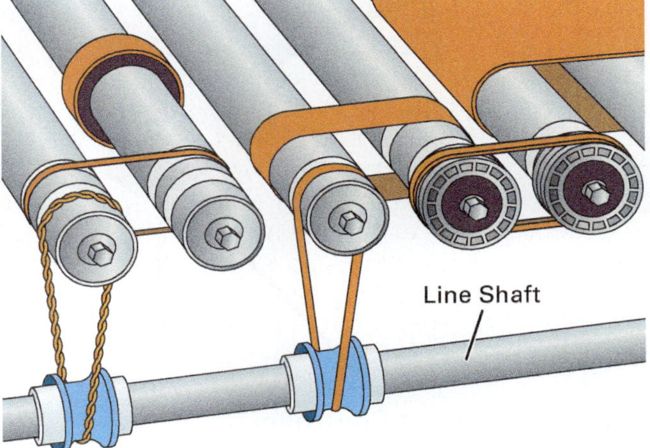

Figure 10 Examples of drive belt arrangements for conveyor rollers using a line shaft.

Independently Powered Roller Conveyors

Chain- and belt-driven roller conveyors are traditional designs that have served us for years. Independently powered roller conveyors are a more recent innovation that represent a state-of-the-art approach.

As the name implies, the rollers themselves are motorized. A DC-powered motor, called a *drum motor*, is integrated into the roller itself. Controllers command and power one or more drum motors (*Figure 11*). The drum motors can operate at variable speeds, reverse their direction, and brake as needed.

Some of these systems are controlled by centralized computers, allowing hundreds or even thousands of rollers to be controlled by a central authority. Sensors monitor material speed, congestion at vital points where material enters and exits the conveyor, and many other operating conditions. All these inputs are sent to a central computer for real-time analysis. The system can monitor material traffic and command controllers and/or rollers as needed to optimize product movement. Decentralized control is also an option, where each controller commands drum motors according to its own programming.

A limited amount of power can be packed into a single drum motor. As a result, these systems are primarily used to move light loads. Some conveyors use a single drum motor to drive several adjacent rollers, using small belts to transfer power, as shown in *Figure 11*. Drum motors are not inexpensive, so using one to power multiple rollers is a practical solution if the load isn't excessive.

The energy efficiency of drum motors, coupled with the elimination of chain and geared drives that require far more maintenance, makes them very popular options today. Millwrights and industrial maintenance personnel are involved in the related mechanical work, but control or instrumentation specialists are generally responsible for wiring and programming.

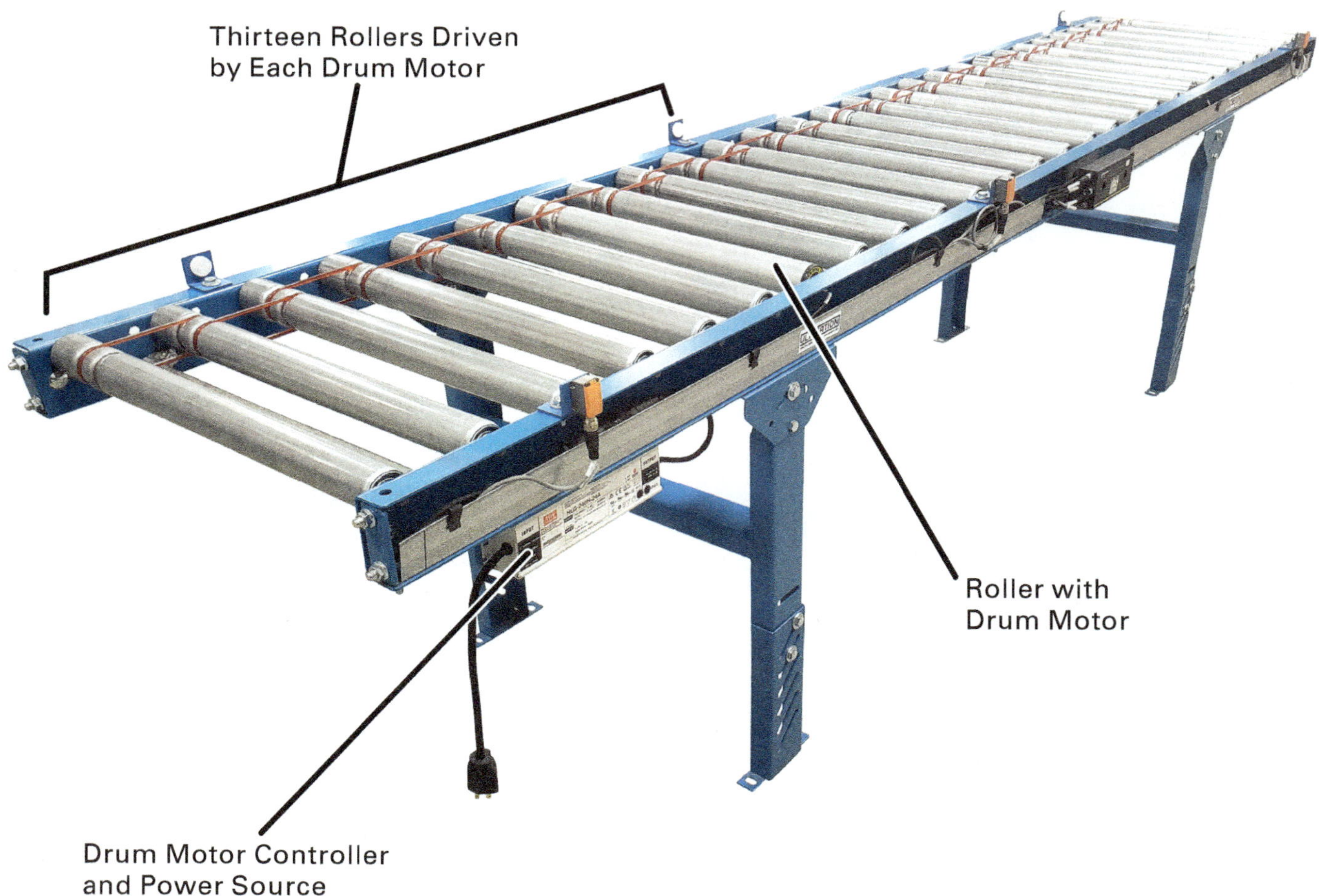

Figure 11 Roller conveyor fitted with drum motors. Each drum motor can drive multiple non-powered rollers.

1.2.0 Belt Conveyors

Belt conveyors are very versatile for moving product from point to point. One advantage they have over roller conveyors is that the belt provides a continuous, solid surface. Roller conveyors obviously have gaps between each roller. This allows belted conveyors to carry materials like soil, rock, and very small items (*Figure 12*). Sanitary belt conveyors handle edible products, such as fruit, vegetables, and even meats (*Figure 13*). Roller conveyors aren't practical for these applications.

A continuous belt also improves traction between the material and the conveyor surface when compared to roller conveyors. Boxes and many other materials can travel up or down reasonable inclines. When the incline is steep, buckets or cleats are added to ensure the material is carried uphill (*Figure 14*). The areas between the cleats are referred to as *flights*.

The belt conveyor components that will be explored in this section include the following:

- Beds
- Belting
- Drive rollers and idlers
- Drive and drive linkage
- Take-ups
- Troughing and training rollers

1.2.1 Beds

The surface beneath a conveyor belt that provides physical support is called the *bed*. A *slider bed conveyor* (*Figure 15*) relies on a rigid bed beneath the moving belt to support the materials. The bed may be made of metal or special plastics. It must be smooth to minimize belt friction when materials are loaded onto the belt.

The bed may serve as a chassis for the entire conveyor assembly. Alternatively, a frame made from heavier material to which the bed is attached provides structural support and points of attachment for other components.

Figure 13 Cherries travel on a belt conveyor.

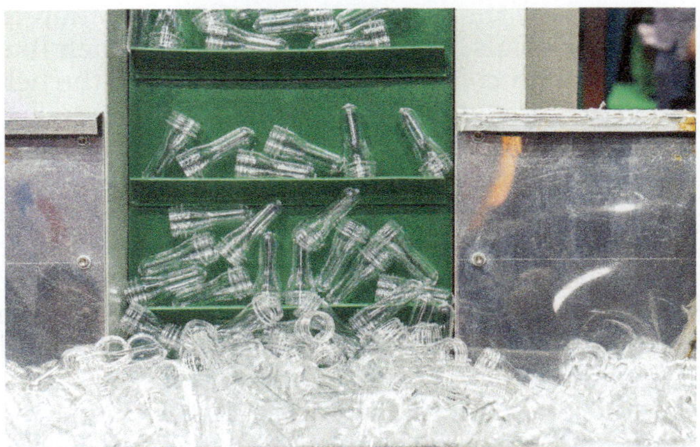

Figure 14 Inclined belt conveyor with troughs in the belt.

Figure 15 Sliding bed conveyor.

Figure 12 Coal in transit by conveyor belt.

Conveyor belts for some applications can also be supported by rollers. These work well for heavier items and those with a large bottom. They are referred to as *roller bed conveyors* (*Figure 16*).

1.2.2 Belting

Conveyor belts have benefited from a lot of innovation over the years. They can be broadly defined as a continuous loop of material used to transport products on a conveyor. But there are many different types, and they can be made from a wide variety of materials. Choosing the belt for a conveyor system is a critical point in the design process. Unique requirements often lead to a new belt design.

Conventional Belting

Conventional conveyor belts that provide a solid surface are made from heavy fabrics, rubber, and various thermoplastics, or a combination of these materials. Many are constructed much like V-belts, with cords running the length of the belt and surrounded by rubber or thermoplastics. The assembly of cords used in some belts to increase strength is referred to as the *carcass*.

All these belts have a relatively smooth bottom and are driven by a large, smooth roller (*Figure 17*). Belts like these can suffer from tracking problems. *Tracking* refers to the tendency of the belt to wander across the roller. If the drive roller and tail roller (see *Section 1.3.3*) aren't perfectly parallel to each other, or the belt is slightly longer on one side than the other, it will wander across the drive roller and try to slip off. *Take-ups*—belt tension and roller adjusting mechanisms—address this problem (see *Section 1.2.5*).

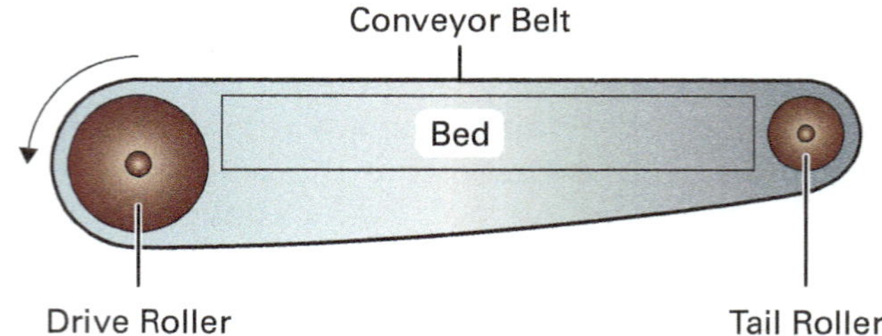

Figure 17 Conventional conveyor belt drive arrangement.

Metal Belting

Metal conveyor belts (*Figure 18*) allow for drainage, and loose product or crumbs can simply fall away. They are the best choice for baking applications and similar situations where the belt is exposed to extreme temperatures. There are many possible configurations. Most are used in food processing and cooking applications, where stainless steel is needed to maintain sanitary conditions and ensure durability. Similar products that allow drainage can also be made from various plastics. Metal belts can be designed to accommodate curves in the conveyor system without binding or bunching on the inside of the turn.

Modular Belting

Modular belting refers to belting that is assembled using interlocking pieces, usually made from plastic (*Figure 19*). Virtually any surface texture and pattern can be created. They allow loose dirt and debris to fall away and liquids to drain. Modular belts are long lasting, easy to clean, and can accommodate tight turns and spirals. Many plastics are also ideal for use with food products.

Figure 16 Roller bed conveyor.

Figure 18 Metal conveyor belt.

Conveyors and Sanitation

Advanced conveyors and new materials are at the center of food processing applications. Sanitation at the highest levels is essential—this is our food supply we're talking about, not a tire for a Jeep. That means conveyors must be built to withstand constant washing with harsh detergents, high-pressure hot water, and steam. This is especially important in the processing of red meats and poultry.

That's a significant challenge, given the many components that come together to create a conveyor. Electronic sensors, motors, bearings, and drive assemblies must be specifically tested and rated for these environments. Motors, for example, must often be certified as having "Wash Down" or "Severe Duty" enclosures. Noncorrosive metals and materials are a must. Every effort must be made in the design of components to keep water out and eliminate small voids and crevices that trap food debris and invite bacterial growth.

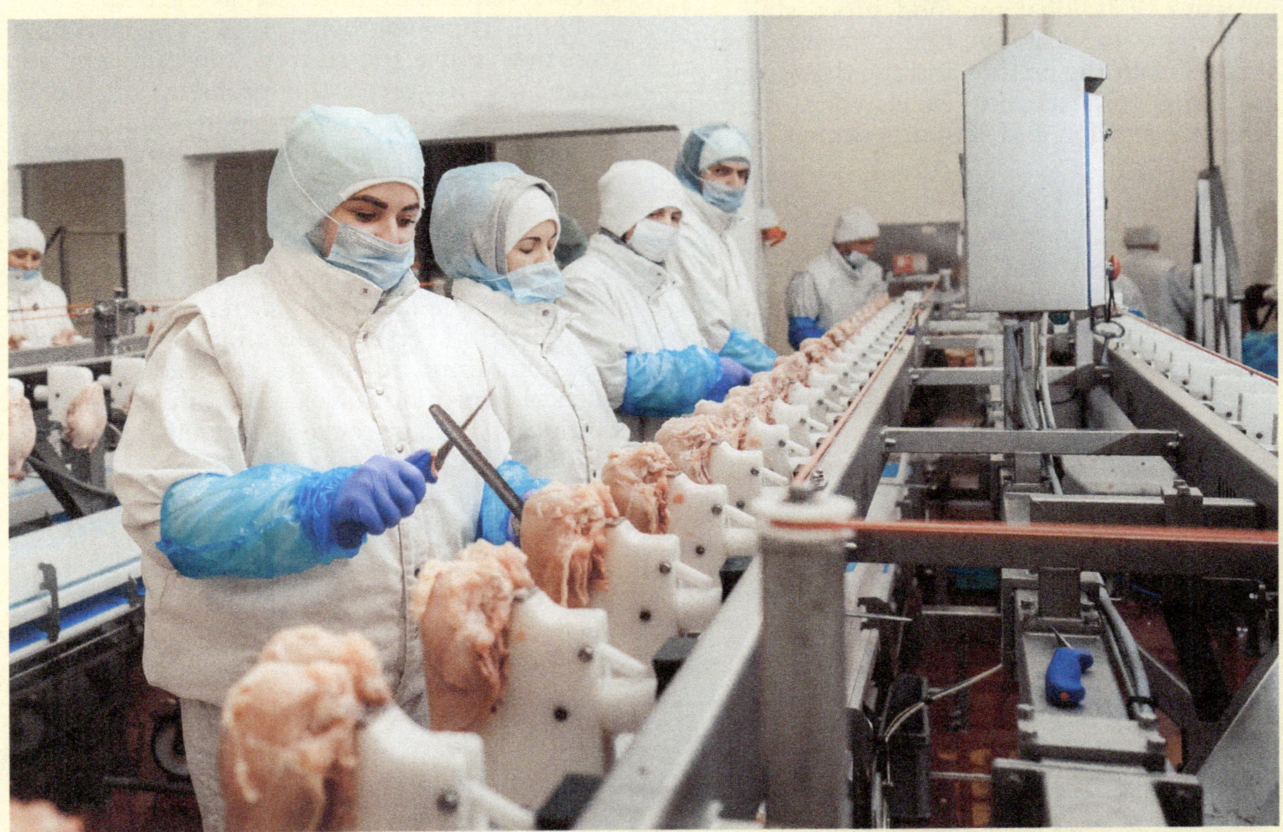

Figure Credit: iStock@Maksymenko Nataliia

(A) Low-Friction Modular Chain

(B) Roller Top Modular Chain

Figure 19 Examples of modular belting.

Most modular belting products share a welcome feature with metal belting. Metal and modular belts are driven in a positive manner. Instead of being stretched taut around two (or more) rollers like a smooth belt, the belts are often driven through mechanical engagement (*Figure 20*). Axles or rollers with toothed sprockets matching the belt design pull the belt along. This helps keep the belt on track naturally, reduces the tension that must be applied to the belt, and eliminates slipping due to poor traction.

Modular belting is very versatile and used in many ways. It is ideal for food processing and other sanitary applications. Using tough, durable plastics for both the belting and the drive components, along with stainless steel where needed, eliminates corrosion and supports sanitation.

Figure 20 Drive sprockets for modular belting.

1.2.3 Drive Rollers and Idlers

Drive rollers used with belt conveyors are simply cylinders with a drive shaft through the center. They are typically larger than any rollers that may act as the bed for the belt. A roller as wide as the bed is mounted at each end of the conveyor. The roller driven by the source of power is called the *drive roller*. The roller at the opposite end, which usually has a smaller diameter than the drive roller, is called the *tail roller* (*Figure 21*). The conveyor belt is wrapped around the outside of each roller and pulled across the bed.

Loose conveyor belts create a safety hazard and may cause the conveyor to bind and move erratically. To correct this problem, small rollers, called *idlers*, are positioned in strategic places to maintain tension and help guide the belt. Their name comes from the fact that they are not rotated by any source other than the belt passing over them.

The small rollers nearest the drive and tail rollers are called *snub idlers*. Snub idlers are designed to keep the belt aligned on the rollers. The remaining idlers are referred to as *return idlers*. Idlers may have a smooth surface or be equipped with sprockets that engage metal or modular belting.

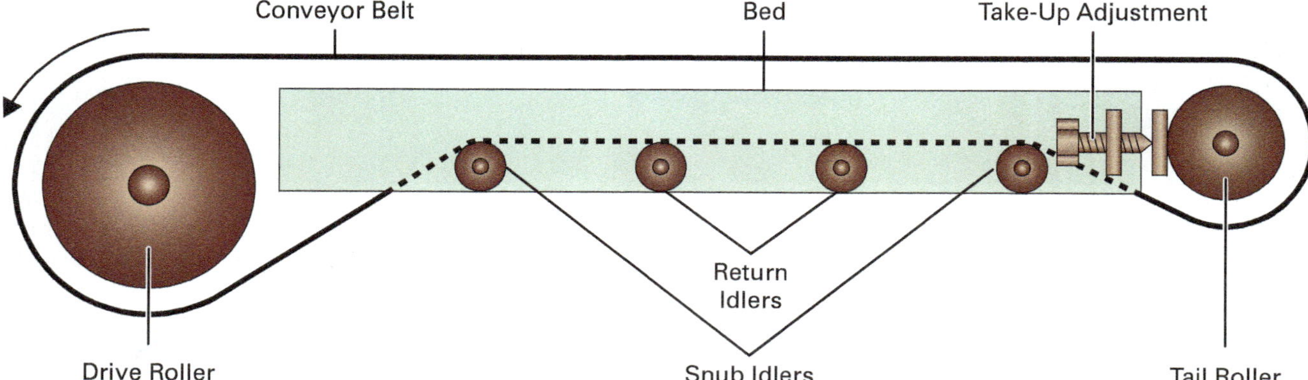

Figure 21 Conventional conveyor belt drive roller and idler arrangement.

NCCER – *Millwright*

1.2.4 Drives and Drive Linkage

The *drive linkage* refers to the components that transfer power from the drive motor to the drive roller and/or belt. Chain and sprocket drives are common, as are belt and sheave arrangements. Direct-drive arrangements are also frequently used. Gearboxes may also be used to change the orientation of the drive shaft, modify the rotational speed, and/or increase torque.

Conveyor belt drives generally fall into one of these categories:

- End drives
- Center, or mid-mount, drives
- Drum motor drives
- Direct drives

End Drives

End drives are the conventional approach. *Figure 21* provides an example. The large drive roller, located at the end of the conveyor, can be driven through a chain, belt, or gearbox arrangement. *Figure 22* shows an end-driven conveyor with a gearbox close-coupled to the motor shaft. The drive shaft of the gearbox exits at a right angle to the motor and drives a sprocket (chain drive) or sheave (belt drive). The driven sprocket or sheave is attached to the drive roller.

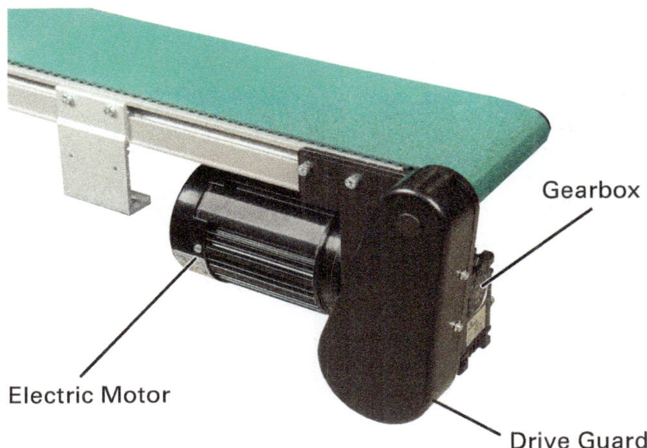

Figure 22 End-driven belt conveyor with a gearbox.

Center Drives

Center, or *mid-mount*, drives are placed away from the end of the conveyor. Although they may be called center drives, the assembly isn't necessarily located in the center.

Figure 23 shows one example of how center drives can be assembled. This type of assembly is sometimes called a *pinch drive* since the belt is "pinched" between the drive roller and idlers. It is very effective with flat, smooth belts as it increases the surface area of the drive roller in contact with the belt. This improves traction without increasing belt tension. Excessive tension causes the belt to stretch and wear more quickly. A pinch drive may be driven by a belt, chain, or drum motor.

Drum Motor Drives

A drum motor drive is another version of the end drive. The same basic drum motors used on roller conveyors can also be used to drive a conveyor belt. All the drive linkage, as well as an external motor, are eliminated. They do not require maintenance and are far more compact. Since the drive roller for a conveyor belt is usually larger than the rollers on a roller conveyor, a larger, more powerful motor can be placed inside.

Direct and Specialty Drives

A direct-drive system couples the motor directly to a drive roller, without chains or belts. Of course, this means the drive roller rotates at the same speed as the motor. Most motors are designed to operate at speeds that are much too fast for a conveyor. This is one of the reasons belt and chain drives, as well as gearboxes, are used—to change the rotational speed applied to the drive roller.

A direct-drive arrangement works fine if you have full control over the motor's movement. Multispeed motors have long been available, but they can only provide a handful of fixed speeds. Variable-frequency drives (VFDs) for motors offer a greater range of speeds than multispeed motors, but older versions were bulky and didn't offer the needed precision in shaft positioning.

Servomotors are a more recent innovation that can provide service in a direct-drive arrangement. A servomotor is a special motor with sensing devices to detect its rotational speed and current shaft position. The sensing component, called an *encoder*, is mated to an electronic driver that uses the data to precisely control the speed and position of the motor shaft (*Figure 24*).

Common and Ganged Drives

There are applications where two conveyor belts can be driven by a single motor and drive. *Common drives* are often adapted to end-driven belts. A single shaft passes through the two drive rollers and is driven by a single motor. The two belts move in unison and at the same speed, but the distance between the two conveyor assemblies is fixed.

A more recent introduction is the *ganged drive*. Ganged drives are usually an adaptation of center drives. Like a common drive, the belts still move at the same speed. The difference is that the distance between the two conveyors can easily be changed at any time. The secret is found in the drive rollers. The drive rollers have a hex-shaped bore through them. With a hex-shaped shaft, one conveyor assembly can easily move left or right with the drive roller sliding along the shaft. The shape eliminates the need to physically lock the roller to the drive shaft. This arrangement works best with modular belts that are positively driven.

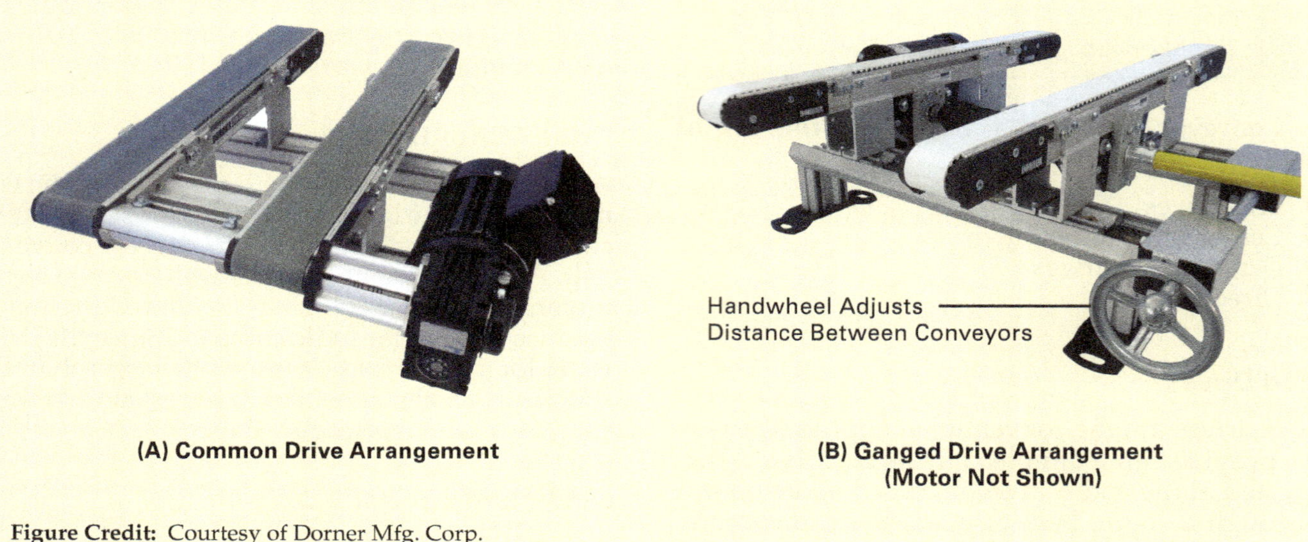

Figure Credit: Courtesy of Dorner Mfg. Corp.

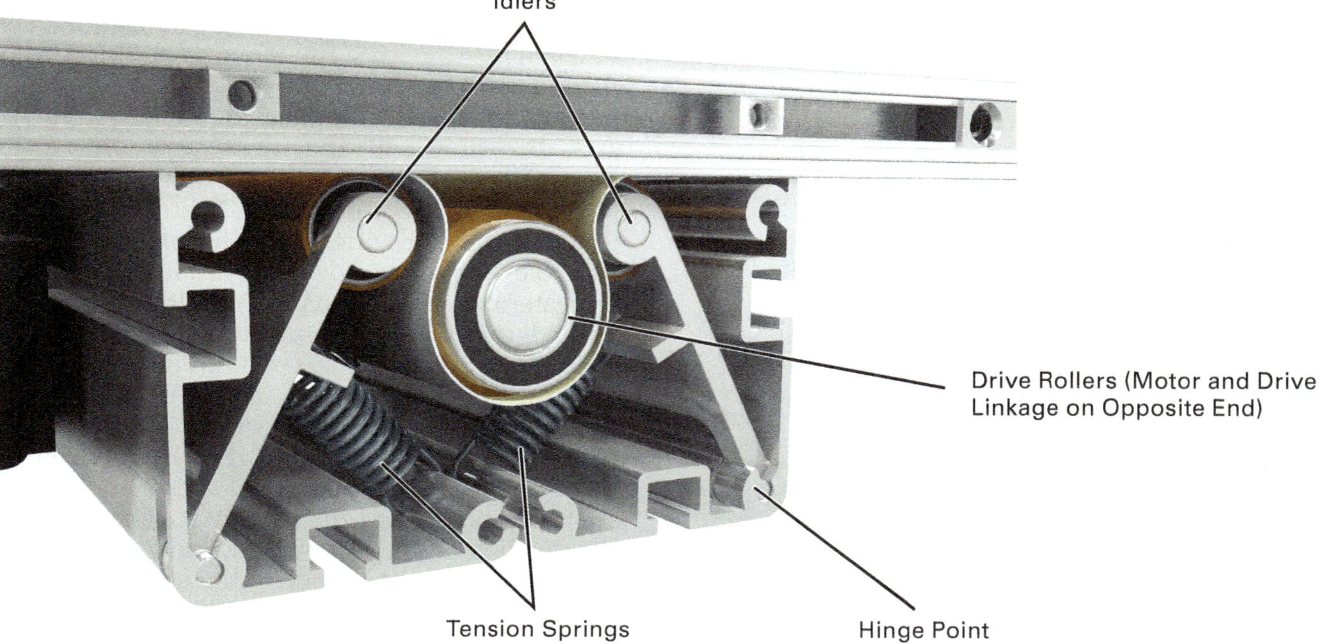

Figure 23 A conveyor belt pinch drive.

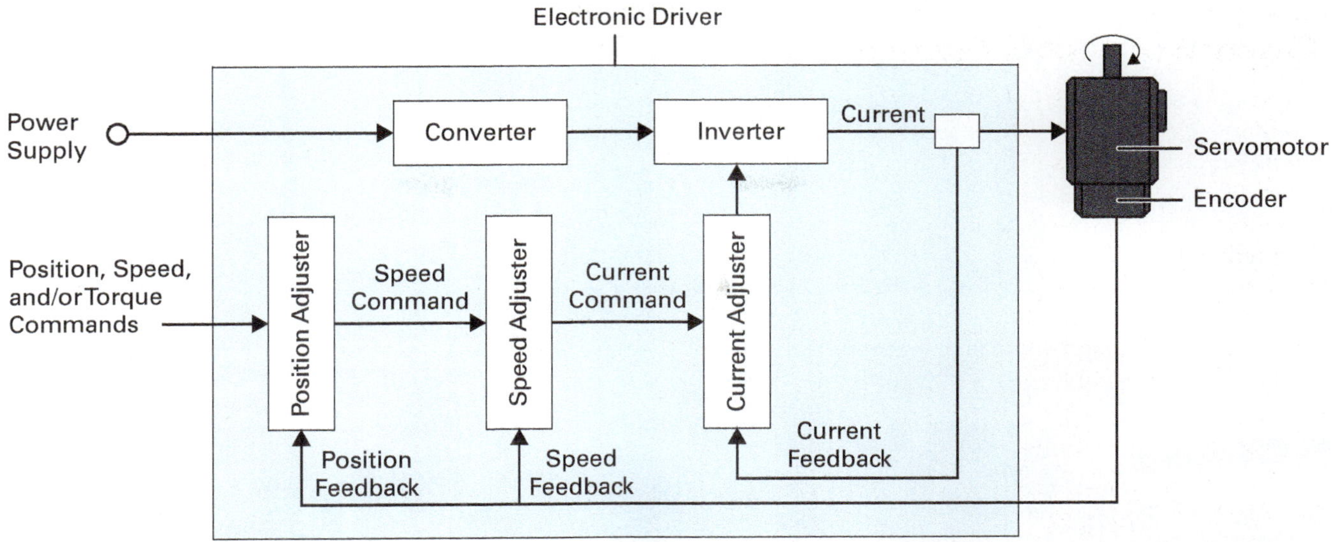

Figure 24 Basic servomotor control scheme.

This type of drive is used when precise speed control and stopping positions are needed. One example is the inspection phase of manufactured components, which often requires the belt to move incrementally and stop as each component reaches a product inspector. Servomotors can also be fitted to gearboxes and other drive linkages (*Figure 25*). True direct-drive applications are relatively rare, since gearboxes also add torque.

Another recent innovation in small, compact drives brings **mechatronics** to conveyors. An electronic gearbox (*Figure 26*) combines three components in a single package—a motor, gearbox, and VFD. Today's compact VFDs, also capable of precise control, enable these three components to be assembled as one.

Millwrights aren't typically responsible for testing or programming servomotor controls and electronic gearboxes. You may, however, be involved in mounting, maintaining, and replacing these devices, so it is important to understand the basic concepts.

1.2.5 *Take-Ups*

Smooth conveyor belts must wrap around the rollers tightly enough to allow the rotating drive roller to pull the belt without it slipping on the roller surface. Belts tend to stretch and wear with age, making them loose. Drive and tail rollers can also wear with use.

Take-ups are mechanical devices that support the bearings of a tail roller shaft and provide a means of adjusting belt tension. Even belts that are positively driven and do not rely on tension for traction must be adjusted to a specified tension.

Most take-ups fall into the category of *screw take-ups*. The bearings supporting the roller ride on a track that is adjusted using a long bolt. *Figure 27* shows several different styles.

Another style of take-up is called a *counterweight take-up* (*Figure 28*). A counterweight is suspended from a hinged frame that hangs below the conveyor. This style is needed to accommodate very long belts because of their substantial change in length as they stretch. Screw take-ups may not have enough range to accommodate a long belt as it breaks in. A counterweight take-up is self-adjusting after the initial setup. Applications for them generally start with conveyors that are at least 150' in length.

Take-ups must be adjusted carefully so there is equal tension applied to the belt cross section. This is more challenging with screw take-ups since there are two points of adjustment, but counterweight take-ups must also be set up properly. Unequal tension will cause the belt to slide off the drive roller.

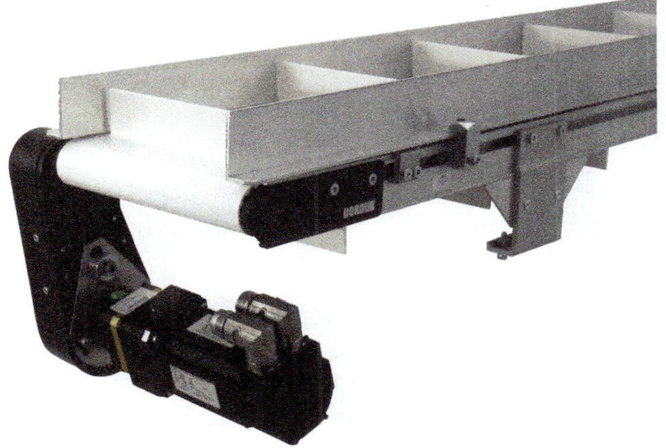

Figure 25 Servomotor mounted to a belt drive.

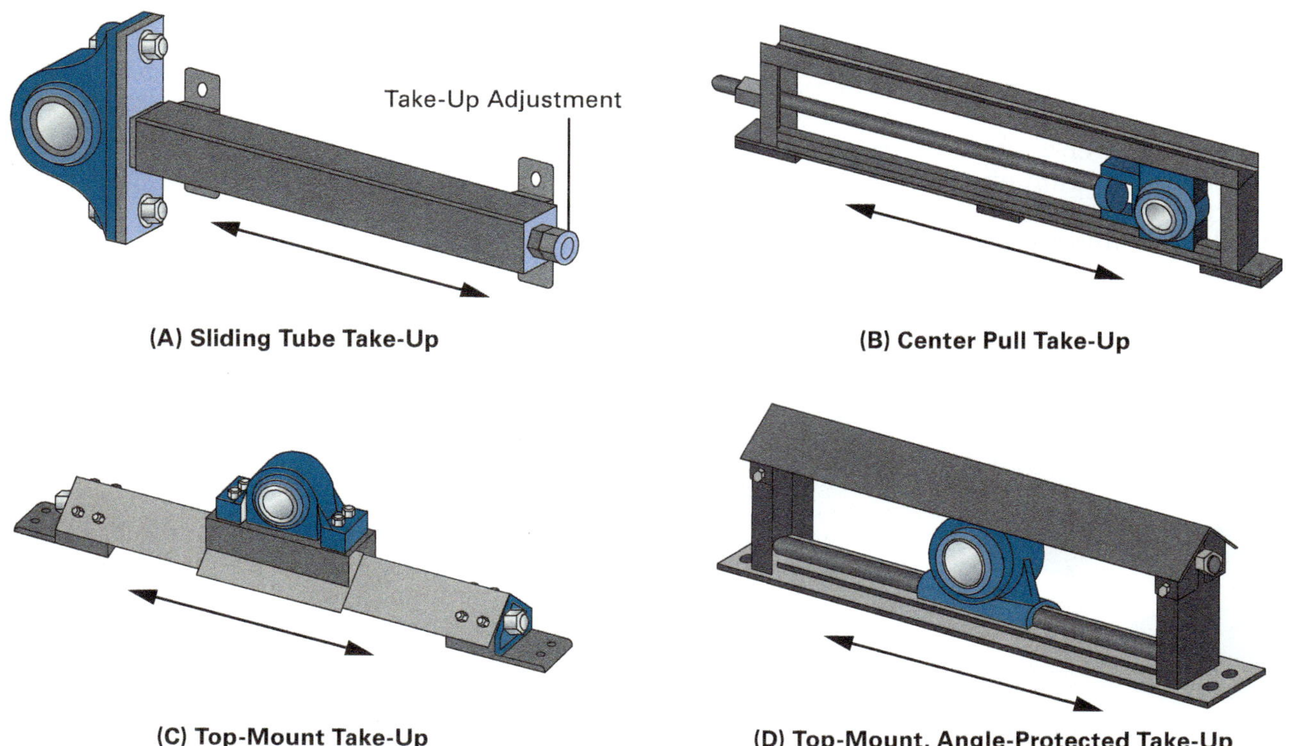

Figure 26 Electronic gearbox drive for a conveyor system.

Figure 27 Examples of screw take-ups.

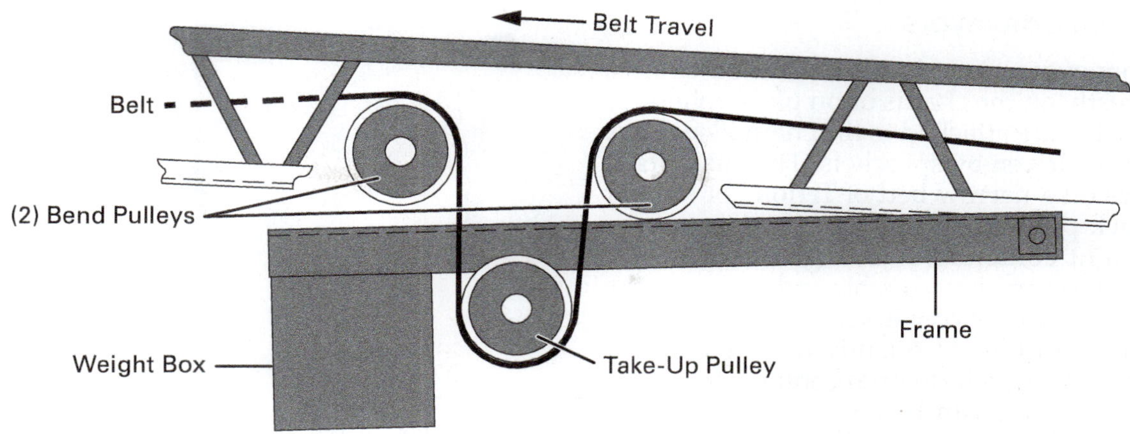

Figure 28 Counterweight take-up assembly.

1.2.6 Troughing and Training Rollers

Troughing and training rollers (*Figure 29*) are located at specific points along some conveyors to help support the belt and guide its movement. Troughing rollers are located underneath the section of belt carrying the load. Training rollers are mounted near the outer edges of the belt.

During the installation process or when a problem occurs, the training rollers guide the belt and prevent it from running off to one side. They should not be relied upon to keep the belt aligned during normal operation, but they do help keep the belt on track when material is being dumped on it. Proper adjustment of the take-ups maintains belt alignment.

The standard angle for troughing rollers has traditionally differed across the globe. Traditional European trough angles are 20, 30, and 40 degrees from horizontal. In the US, trough angles of 20, 35, and 45 degrees have been more common. Due to the extent of today's global economy, you may encounter any of these angles. While the 20-degree trough angle was long considered the most common standard, trough angles have steadily increased over the years, thanks to improvements in belt flexibility and durability. Thicker and heavier belts, though, typically run at lower trough angles and benefit from the reduced stress imposed on the belt.

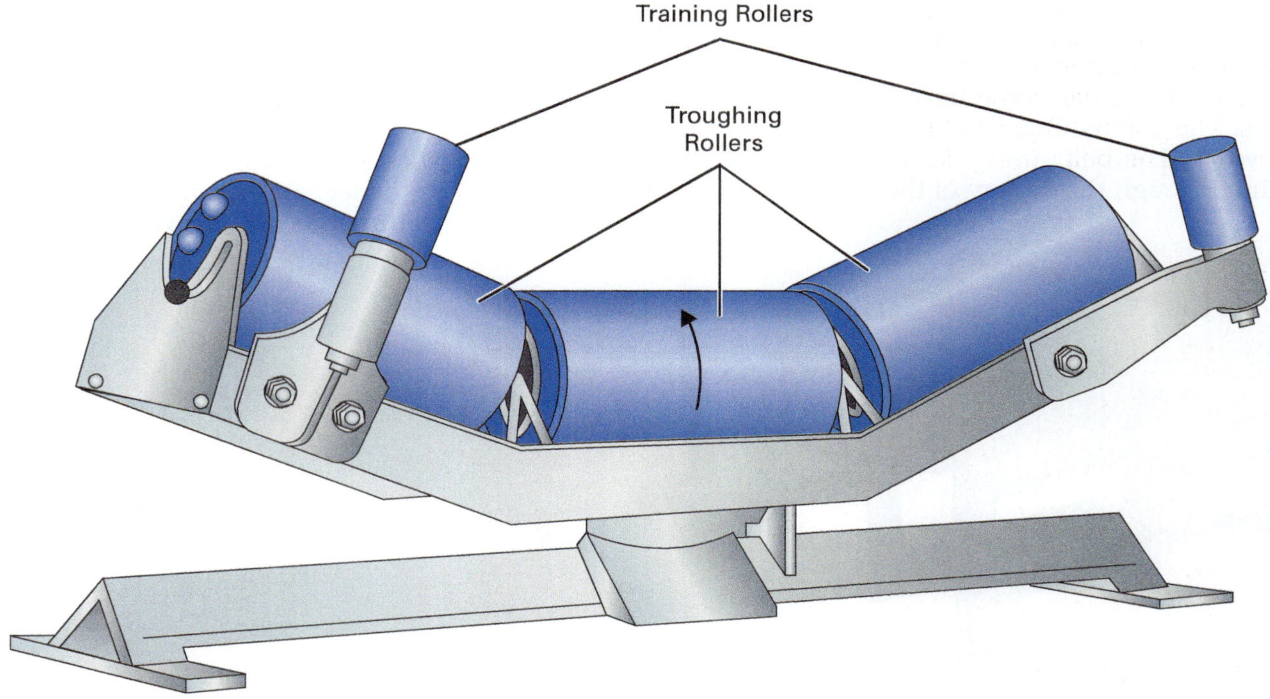

Figure 29 Troughing and training rollers.

1.3.0 Chain Conveyors

Chain conveyors carry loads on linked chains, either directly on the chains or on pads, rollers, or platforms that are attached to the chain (*Figure 30*). The chain is driven by sprockets. The chain itself often rides on a narrow bed of Teflon® or similar tough, slick plastic material. They represent the heavyweight contenders among conveyor systems since they are very durable and can carry the heaviest loads. Chain conveyors can be applied in many ways, but they frequently move palletized materials and heavy industrial containers.

Chain conveyors can be end-driven or center-driven, like belt conveyors. In most cases, a single motor drives all the chains through a gearbox, as shown in *Figure 31*. The chains may also be fitted with pads on top to protect both the chain and the material from damage, and to enhance traction.

Many chain conveyors are fitted with components or accessories to help secure or capture the material being conveyed. They are referred to as *drag chain conveyors*. This category includes several conveyor subtypes that have bars, paddles, and vessels of various sizes and shapes to capture or carry material attached to one or more chains.

Figure 32 shows a drag chain conveyor with a belt attached to the chain and cross ribs that traverse the belt. The ribs are also referred to as *dams* or *feed dogs*, with the spaces between them forming the flights. As you can see in *Figure 32*, conveyors like this can easily move loose materials such as soil and wood chips horizontally as well as up or down an incline.

Although the conveyor in *Figure 32* is open and the chain is visible, some have belts beneath the dams. The chains under the belt, however, do all the work. The belt simply keeps materials from falling through the bottom of the trough.

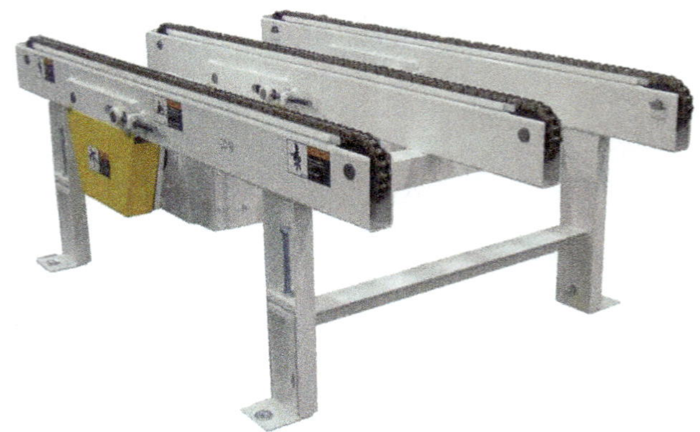

Figure 31 End-driven chain conveyor.

Bucket conveyors are drag chain conveyors that take the concept a bit further. Instead of short cross ribs or bars that create shallow flights, they have hoppers, scoops, or taller cross ribs that create much larger flights than the model shown in *Figure 32*. Instead of each flight carrying several pounds of loose material, the buckets or flights may carry a large volume of material. Bucket conveyors are often referred to as *bucket elevators* when they are highly inclined or vertical.

One unique type of chain conveyor is the *tubular chain conveyor* (*Figure 33*). Lightweight, loose materials can be picked up and rapidly delivered to elevated or distant locations free of damage. Even delicate materials, such as cereal, can be moved this way. The tube protects the contents from contamination during the journey, adding extra value to the concept.

Inside the tube, a continuous series of disks, or *pucks*, are connected by chain links (*Figure 34*). At each end, a special drive sprocket called a *carousel* engages the chain, pulling the pucks around a loop. The pucks are usually made from durable food-safe plastics or stainless steel. Most any kind of nuts, grains, coffee, and similar materials can be moved with this style of conveyor (*Figure 35*).

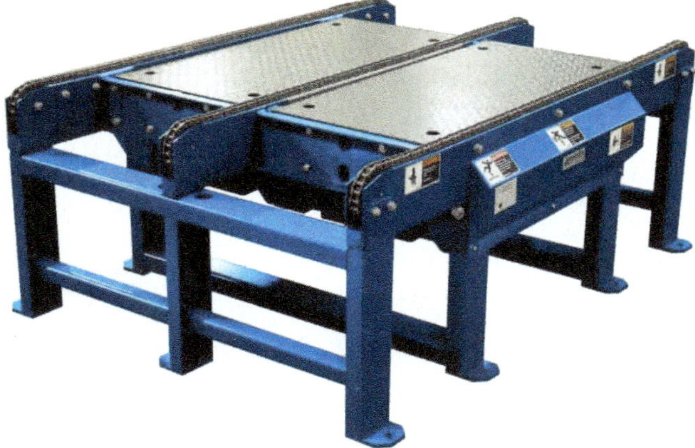

Figure 30 Short section of heavy-duty chain conveyor used to transfer materials.

Figure 32 Typical drag chain conveyor for bulk material.

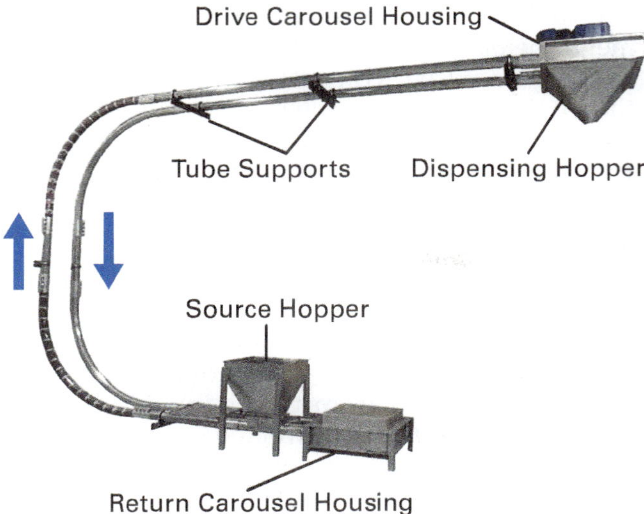

Figure 33 Tubular chain conveyor.

A variation on the tubular chain conveyor is the *tubular cable conveyor*. The design and operation are essentially the same, but the chain is replaced with stainless steel cable.

1.3.1 Chains

Conveyor chains vary widely according to how the conveyor will be used. There are many possible variations and attachments that may be required, and a variety of standards that apply.

Millwrights and industrial maintenance personnel aren't required to select a specific type of chain for an application. The chain is chosen during the manufacturer's design phase. However, you must always ensure that the chain you're installing is precisely what was specified. Lots of mechanical problems can result from using the wrong chain. It is helpful to understand some of the design variations you will encounter.

Roller chain is one common type of chain used, but again, variations are abundant. Roller chain products are covered in detail in NCCER Module 15311, *Installing Belt and Chain Drives*. Silent chain, also presented in Module 15311, is also used. Common roller and silent chain that meets the American National Standards Institute (ANSI) standards are used in many cases, including their variations such as *double-pitch* and *extended-pitch roller chain*, where the normal distance between the rollers is doubled or extended. Roller chain used for conveyance may also have a hollow-pin design (*Figure 36*), as opposed to the solid pin that connects most roller chain. The openings provide a convenient way to attach unique pieces directly to the chain.

One variation of roller chain is used on parts of the conveyor where products accumulate and come to a stop while the chains continue to move. To eliminate the friction between the stalled material and the chain, which increases the load on the drive motor and can damage the product, accumulation roller chain is used (*Figure 37*). This type of chain has rollers with a diameter larger than the chain depth. This places the rollers in contact with the material, instead of the chain surface. The rollers are made from metal or durable plastics. This allows the chain to continue moving without rubbing against product that has come to a stop and accumulated at the end of the line.

Figure 34 Tubular chain conveyor pucks make the trip around the carousel.

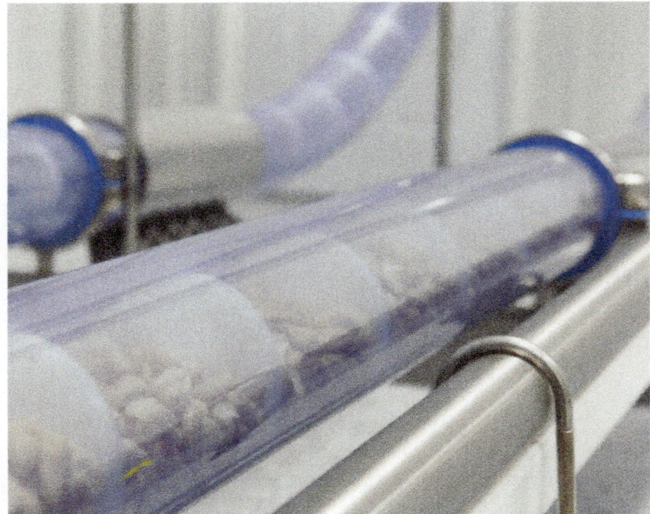

Figure 35 Cashews travel through a tubular conveyor.

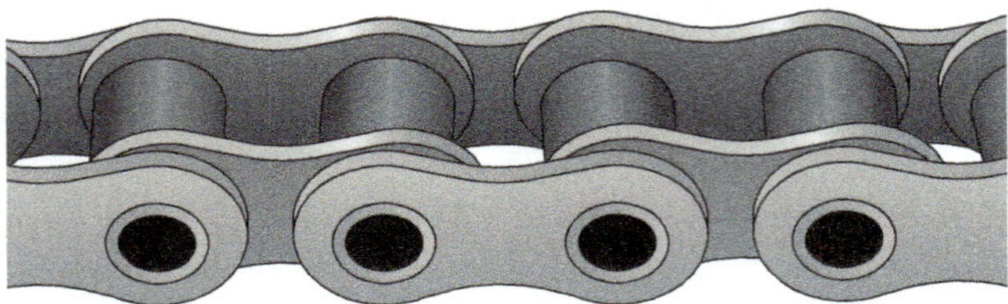

Figure 36 Hollow-pin roller chain.

Figure 37 Accumulation roller chain.

Chain attachments are often required to allow metal belts, modular belt sections, cross ribs, buckets, and other components to be attached to the chain. *Figure 38* shows several examples of attachments. A few are described here. Note that a number after the identifying letter indicates how many holes are placed in the attachment itself. Some attachments can be connected to roller chain with hollow pins, eliminating welds and oddly formed chain side plates.

- *K attachments* provide a flat mounting platform that parallels the chain. The attachment can be integral (formed from the chain side plate, as shown in *Figure 38*), or welded.
- *F attachments* provide a mounting platform at a right angle to the chain. The attachment is usually welded to the chain.
- *L attachments* are formed by lengthening the chain side plate, then bending it and adding holes.
- *Spigot pins* can be installed through hollow-pin chain openings or be welded on center between the pin openings.

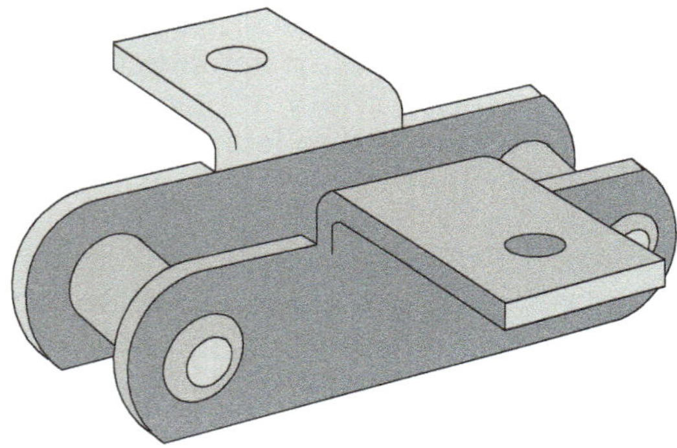

(A) K1 Integral Attachment

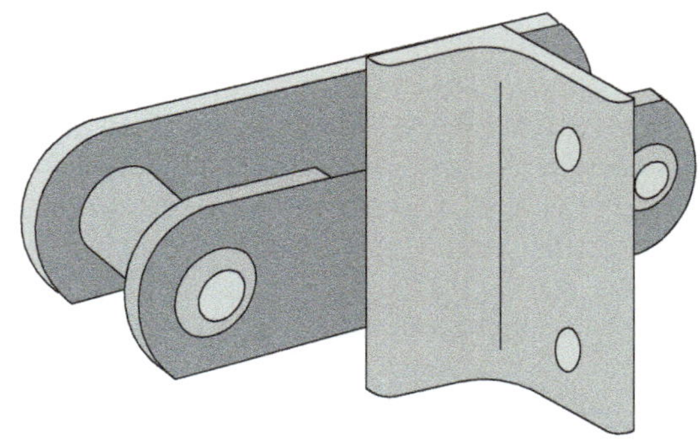

(B) F2 Welded Attachment

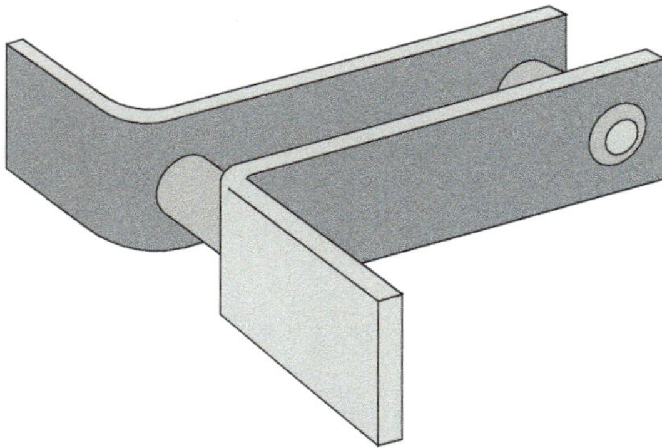

(C) L0 Integral Attachment

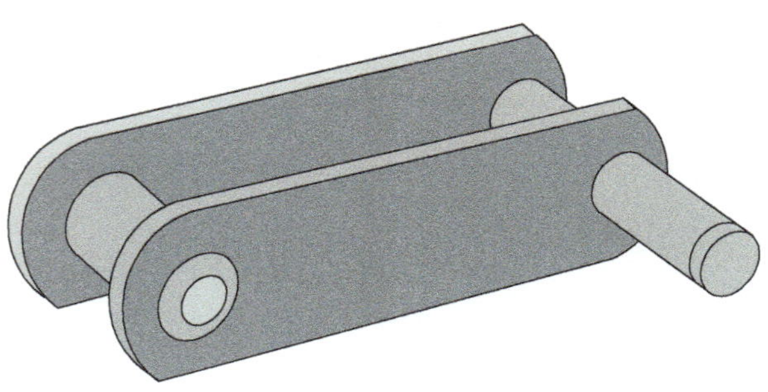

(D) Spigot Pin

Figure 38 Examples of conveyor chain attachments.

The attachments listed here are standardized in the industry, but it is important to understand that there are many possible variations in chain construction. For example, there are at least three unique designs used primarily to engage cotton modules—large cubes of raw, compressed cotton that contain 13–15 standard bales.

Welded-link chain is also used in conveyor applications, especially tubular conveyors. They are simply heavy metal loops linked together in series (*Figure 39*). Once the metal is formed into the shape of a link, the two ends are welded together. The links of a welded-link chain must be cut and then rewelded to repair the chain, although a master link that can be disassembled is often used.

Welded-link chains for tubular conveyors may require specific welding techniques and filler metals, since they are often made of stainless steel or special alloys. Consult the chain vendor for welding specifications.

Figure 39 Welded-link chain.

1.3.2 *Sprockets and Take-Ups*

The teeth of drive shaft sprockets engage links of a conveyor chain to drive it (*Figure 40*). The sprocket is attached to the shaft from a power source, usually a motor and/or a gearbox. The shaft can also be connected directly to a gearbox. Bearings support the shaft and are usually positioned on the outside of the conveyor frame. Locking hubs hold the sprocket(s) in place on the shaft.

Unique chain designs require unique sprockets with teeth that properly engage them. Sprockets that guide and drive common roller chain will likely be identical to those you learned about in NCCER Module 15311, *Installing Belt and Chain Drives*.

Most common chain sprockets are a one-piece design—they must be slipped over the end of a shaft for installation and removal. This is fine for a simple drive arrangement. However, as you can see in *Figure 40*, two sprockets with hubs are installed on the shaft between the conveyor frame rails. To remove a one-piece sprocket, the shaft must be pulled out, at least partially, from one end or the other. For that reason, two other types of sprockets are often used.

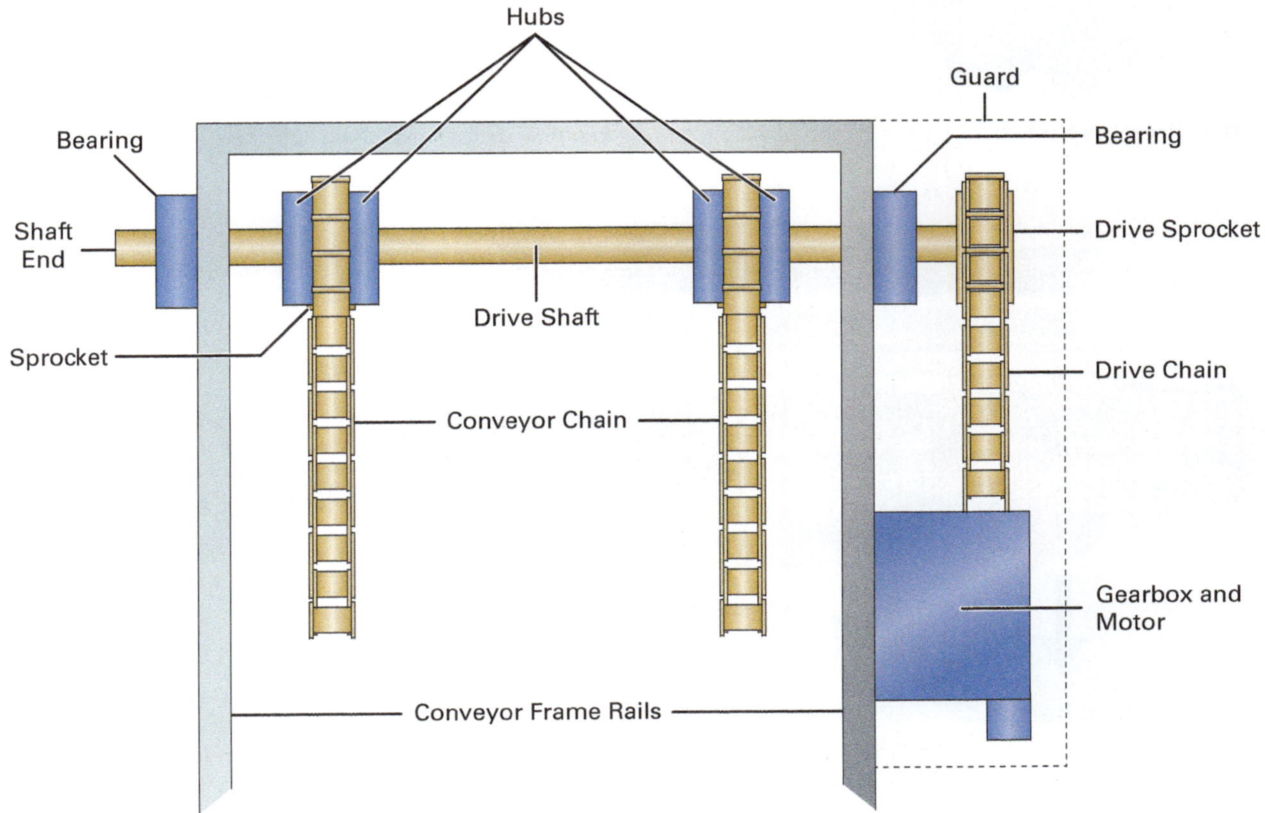

Figure 40 Chain conveyor sprockets, shaft, and bearings.

Split sprockets come in two pieces (*Figure 41*). As a result, they can be removed from the shaft without removing the shaft or bearings from the frame. The hubs (when present) can be loosened and slid to the side, then the two sprocket halves are easily removed or installed. The sprocket shown in *Figure 41* has an integral hub.

Segmented or *modular sprockets* describe most any sprocket that is assembled from more than two pieces (*Figure 42*). Some have three or four segments that require assembly. Like the split sprocket, they can be removed and installed without removing the shaft from the conveyor.

Take-ups for chain conveyors are like those used on belt conveyors. Manufacturers specify the appropriate method of tensioning the chains.

The take-ups are used to position one of the shafts in relation to the other to apply the correct tension and keep the shafts parallel to each other.

1.4.0 Screw Conveyors

Screw conveyors provide smooth, continuous movement of loose products like soil, rock, and crushed ice. Wet materials and slurries can also be moved this way. A screw conveyor (*Figure 43*) has a material entry point, called the *feed*, and an exit point, called the *discharge*. Material can also be moved up or down steep inclines.

Screw conveyors are usually enclosed in a trough or a tube (*Figure 44*). The drive is connected at one end of the conveyor. The screw, or *auger*, can be driven by a belt, chain, or gearbox.

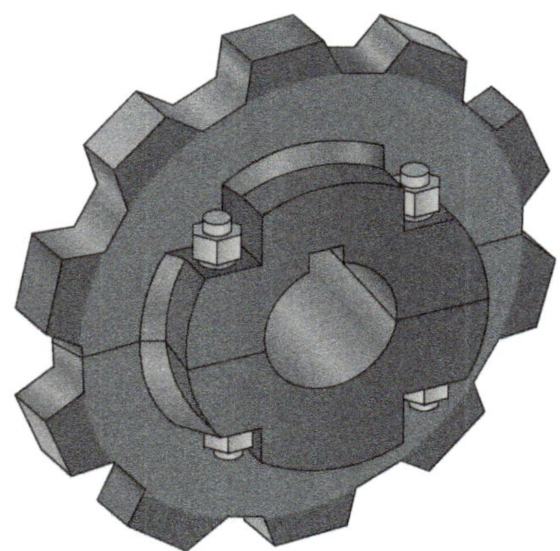

Figure 41 Split chain sprocket.

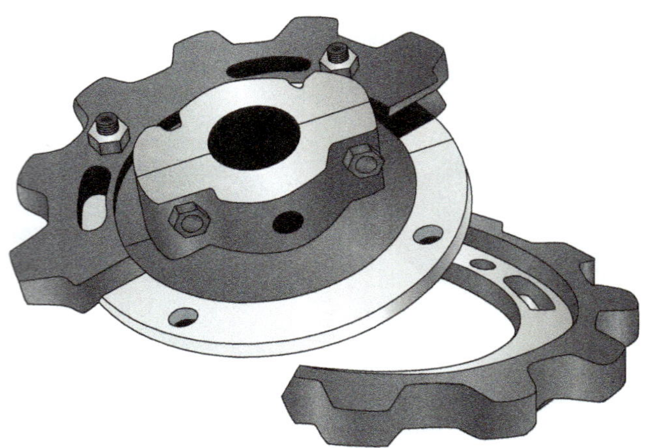

Figure 42 Segmented chain sprocket.

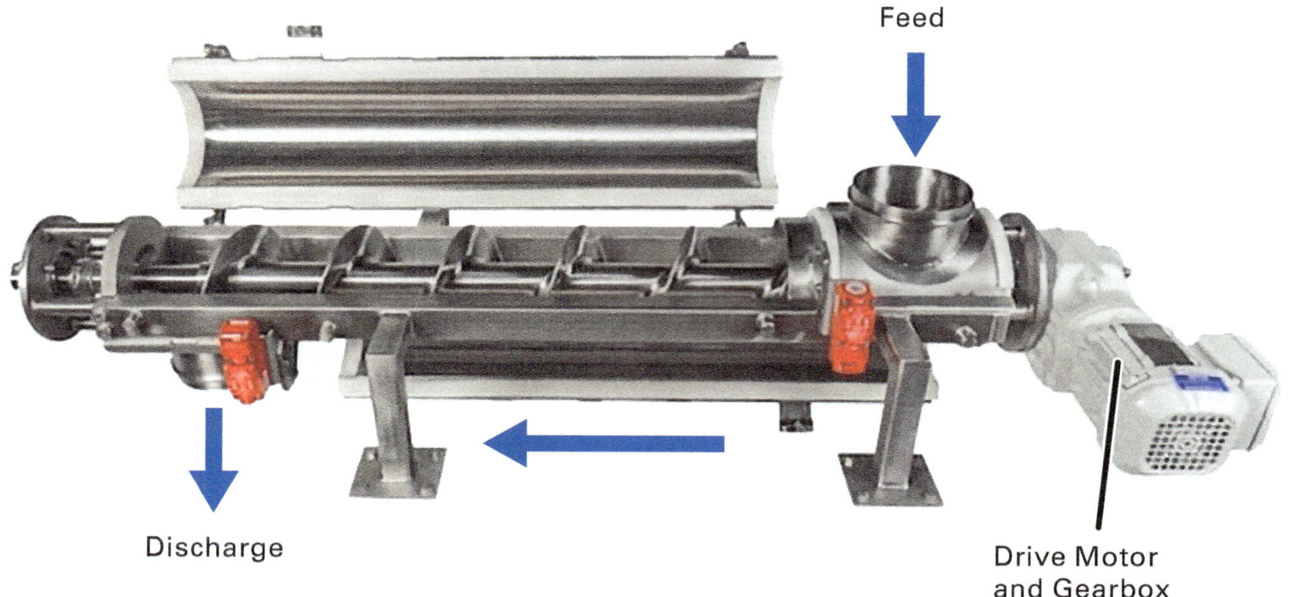

Figure 43 Example screw conveyor.

The auger is fitted with plates called *flighting,* giving it a screw-like (helical) appearance. As the motor turns the shaft, the flighting moves the product from one end of the trough or tube to the other.

Most screw conveyors depend on a rigid shaft and move product in a straight line. Material is transferred to another conveyor section when the direction changes. Some use a flexible metal auger that allows a turn (*Figure 45*), and many can accommodate more than one turn. An example of a flexible auger, called a *flat wire* or *ribbon auger,* is shown in *Figure 46.*

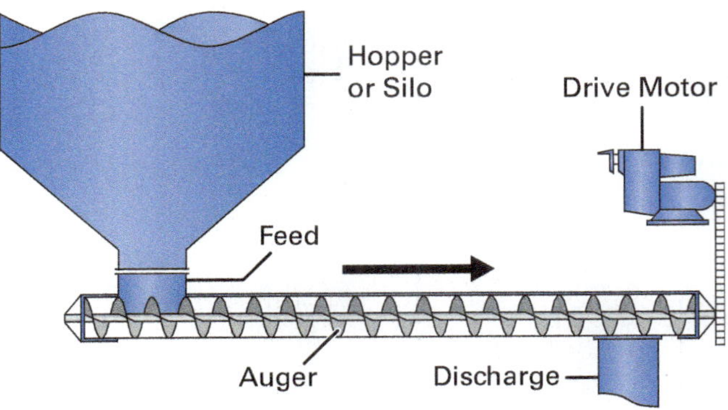

Figure 44 Basic screw conveyor components.

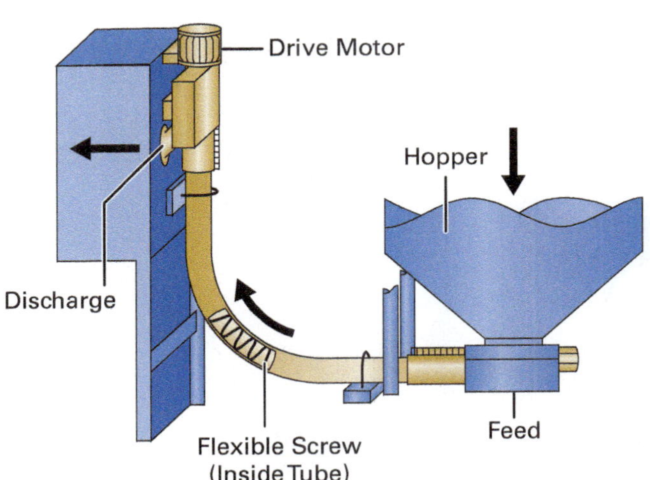

Figure 45 Flexible screw conveyor.

1.4.1 Augers

The auger is the rotating part of the conveyor. The direction in which material moves depends on its direction of rotation. The flights are generally shaped to enhance material movement in one direction only, but some can be reversed.

The auger is placed inside the trough or tube, which is typically closed on both ends. Its shaft protrudes through the end plates and through the bearings mounted on the end plates (*Figure 47*). One end of the shaft is attached to the drive assembly.

Depending on its size and length, the shaft may be supported with one or more hangers along its length. The hangers are bolted to the trough through slotted holes that allow the auger to be adjusted and aligned. The hangers are fitted with bearings, in addition to the bearings located at each end plate.

Unless the conveyor is very short in length, the shaft and auger are assembled from several pieces. The shaft ends must extend through the end plates and fit the bearings precisely. They must also be secured to the auger. The shaft ends are referred to as the *drive shaft* and the *end shaft* (*Figure 48*). The drive shaft likely has a keyway as shown in *Figure 48.*

Figure 46 Flexible flat wire, or ribbon, auger.

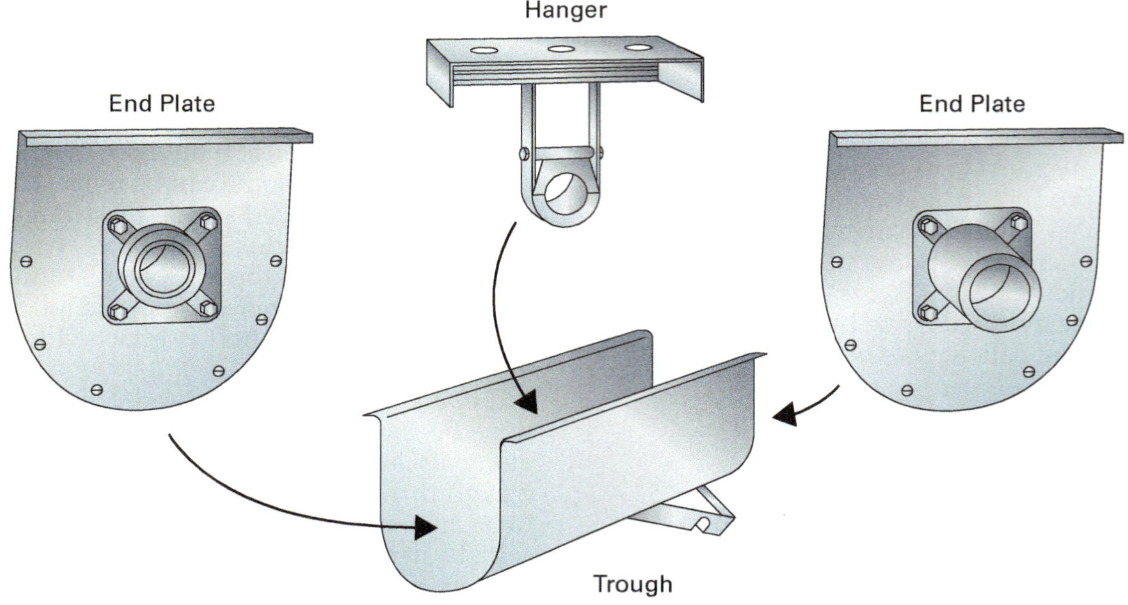

Figure 47 Screw conveyor trough arrangement.

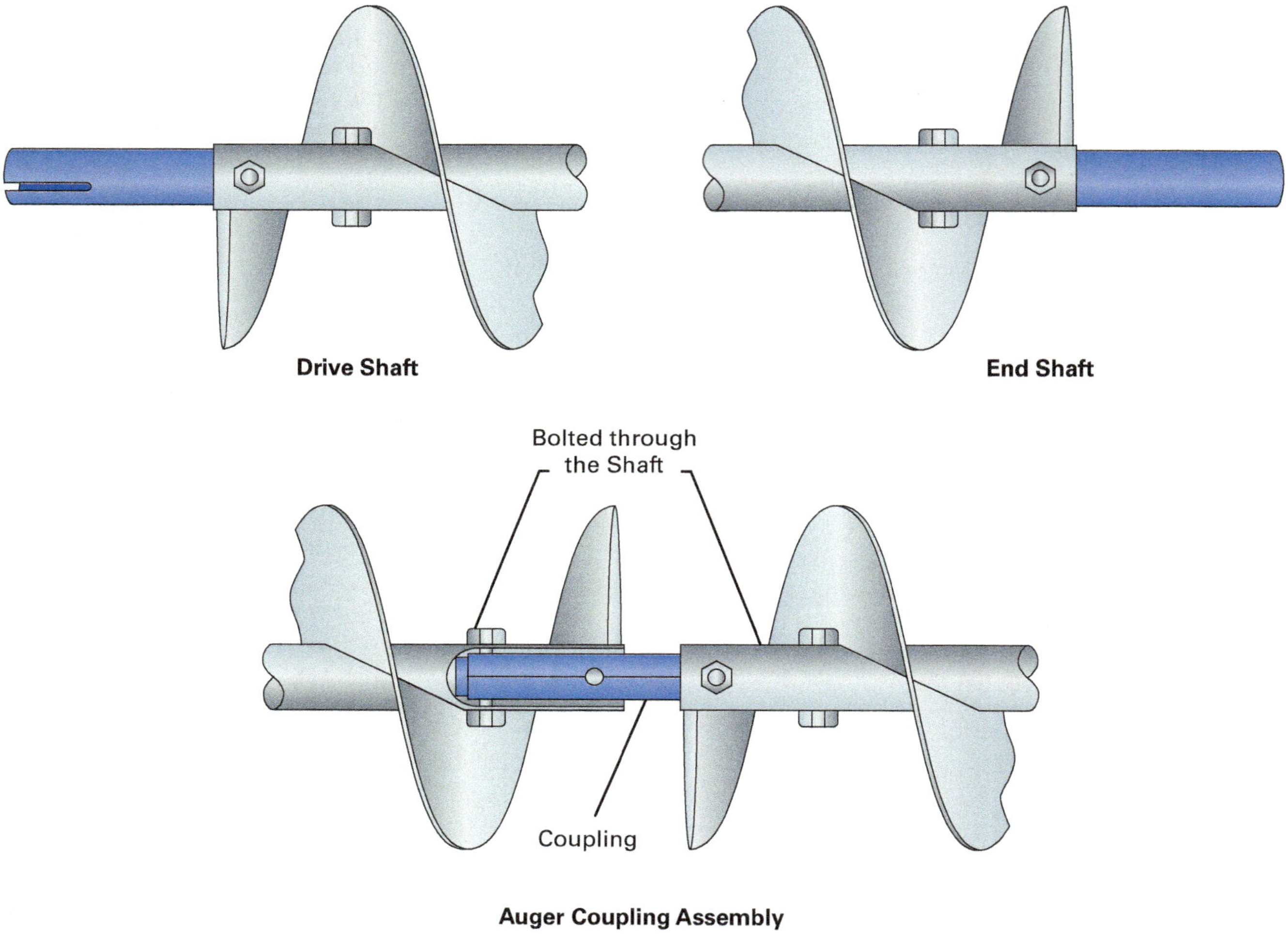

Figure 48 Auger and shaft assembly.

The auger is often assembled in sections to make up the length needed. Sections generally range in length from 8' to 12'. However, they can be made to any custom length needed to accommodate the equipment design. Auger sections are joined by couplings as shown in *Figure 48*.

The shape and design of the auger depends on several factors. The primary factor is the nature of the material being conveyed. Special materials often require special designs.

1.5.0 Pneumatic Conveyors

Pneumatic conveyors (*Figure 49*) move materials by positive or negative airflow. Lightweight granular, dry, and loose materials can be moved this way. Wet materials, due to their extra mass and sticky nature, are not good candidates for pneumatic conveyance. Like tubular chain and cable conveyors, pneumatic conveyors protect the conveyed material from the surrounding environment.

Figure 49 Pneumatic conveyor system, fed by a multisource weighed batching system.

Positive airflow refers to an application where the material is on the discharge side of a blower and is pushed forward (*Figure 50*). Air flowing at a high velocity past the product inlet creates a slight vacuum at the hopper above, drawing material into the airstream. The air discharged from the blower must either leave the system (an open system) or be returned to the blower inlet (a closed system). If fresh air is constantly being drawn in, filtering that air to avoid contamination of the product becomes an important factor.

When the material reaches the collection vessel, the air velocity slows down significantly. The volume of air moving through remains constant, but the velocity is reduced in the larger space. When the product is not moving fast enough to keep it airborne and moving forward, it naturally falls to the bottom of the vessel.

Negative airflow refers to situations where the material is on the inlet side of the fan, and the material is being pulled toward it, like a vacuum cleaner (*Figure 51*).

Pneumatic conveyors are generally designed around one of two concepts—*dense phase* or *dilute phase* conveyance. Dense phase systems rely on establishing a high air pressure difference between the inlet and the outlet to move the material. However, the air velocity is relatively low. The ratio of product to air is very high. In other words, there is a lot of product in motion in a small volume of air—a dense product stream.

Dense phase systems operate intermittently, sending batches, or slugs, of product down the line on each cycle.

Dilute phase systems work best for particles that are less dense. They rely on a lower pressure difference between the inlet and outlet but operate at a higher air velocity. The material-to-air volume ratio is lower than that of dense phase systems; a smaller amount of product is in motion, surrounded by a lot of air. They are best suited for rapidly conveying lightweight materials in relatively low volumes. Unlike dense phase systems, dilute phase systems provide a continuous stream of product.

1.5.1 Blowers

The airflow in a pneumatic conveyor is generated by a powerful fan or blower. Several different types may be used.

Centrifugal fans are used in many systems because they work well against the resistance of the pipe or tubing through which the material flows. Centrifugal fans are typically identified by the design of the wheel. Two centrifugal fan types that often power pneumatic conveyors are *backward-inclined fans* and *radial fans*.

The blades of a backward-inclined centrifugal wheel (*Figure 52*) are inclined away from the direction of rotation. Visually, the wheels might appear to be installed backward.

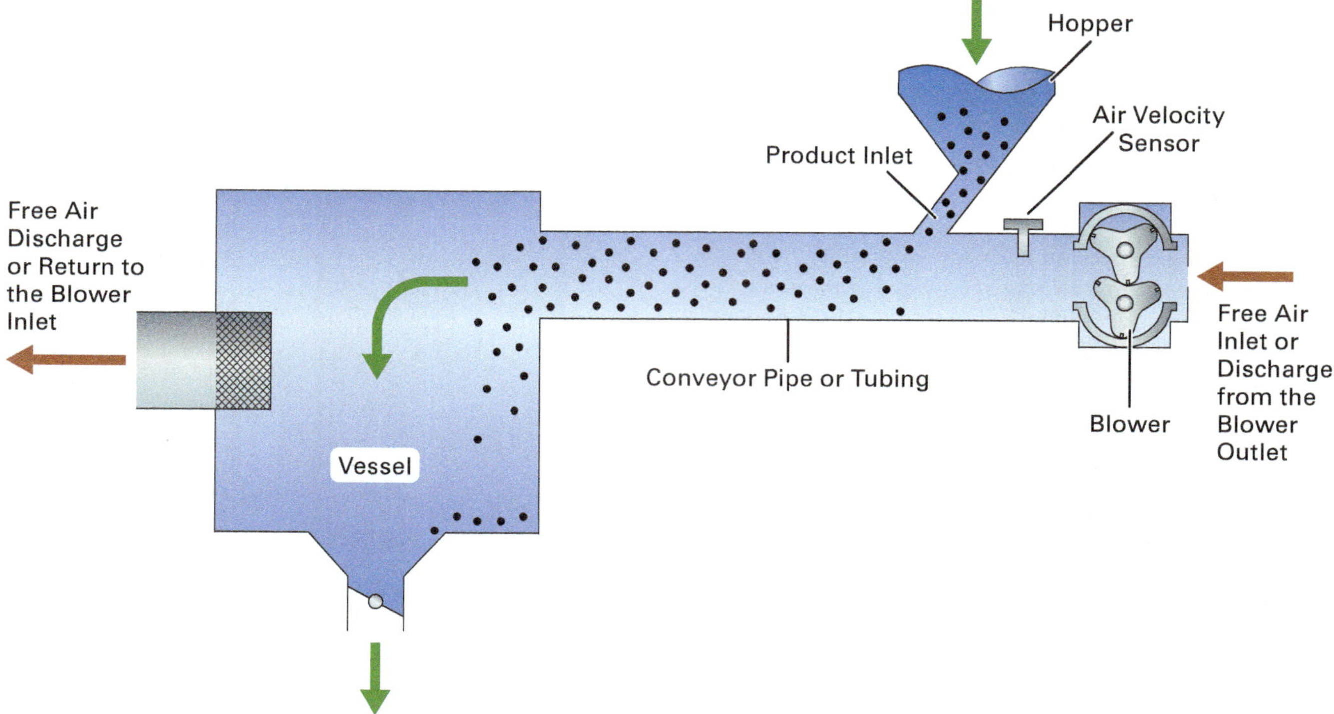

Figure 50 Positive airflow pneumatic conveyance.

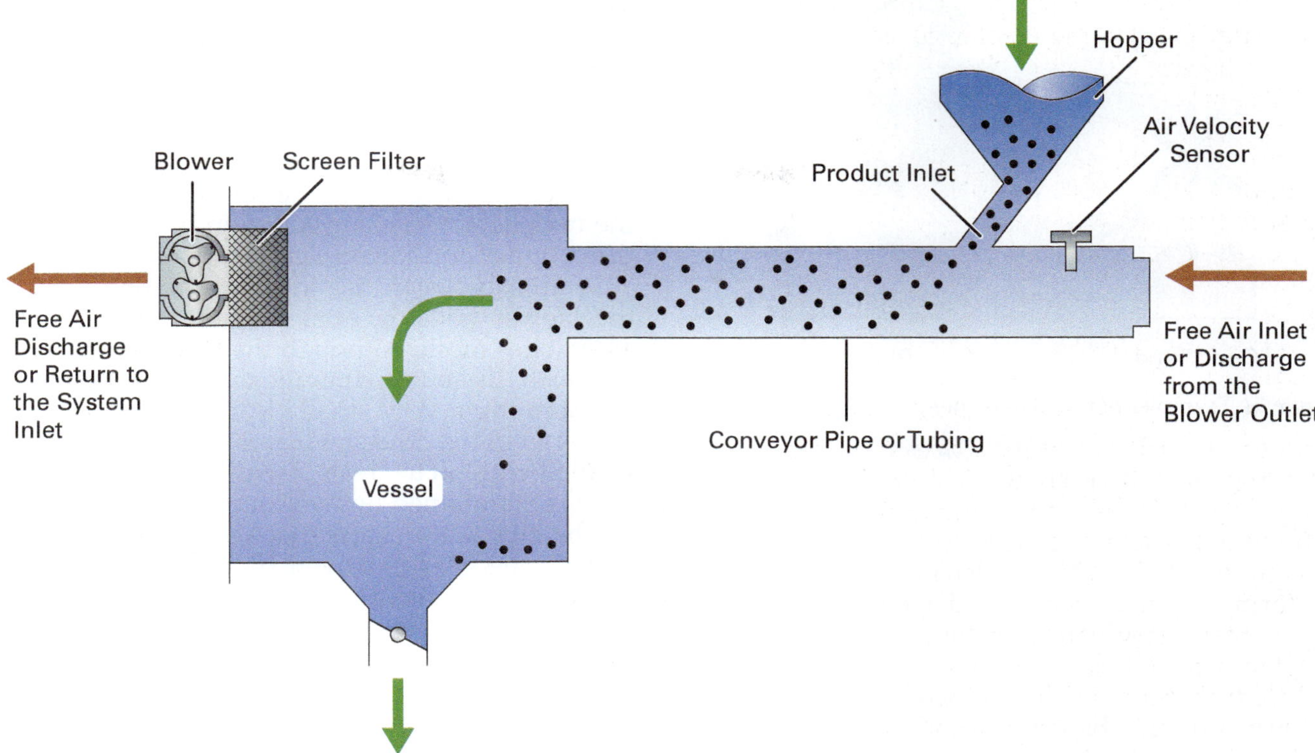

Figure 51 Negative airflow pneumatic conveyance.

Each blade is often welded to the hub. Thicker blades welded in place are required due to the high speeds at which they operate. Faster rotational speeds impart a strong centrifugal force to the blades. Welding the blades ensures that they will remain in place.

Standard backward-inclined wheels have flat blades. Airfoil-shaped blades (*Figure 53*) improve the fan's efficiency and reduce the noise level. Their use has increased over the years due to these two characteristics.

Radial wheels (*Figure 54*) have straight blades that tend to remain clean. This makes radial wheels suitable for air systems that have particles or oils in the air stream. They are used in many applications, including dust collection. Radial wheels are simple in construction, with narrow blades that resemble paddles. They can develop high pressures and operate at high speeds.

You'll note that all the fan wheels shown thus far have one thing in common—the shaft that drives them is perpendicular to the direction of

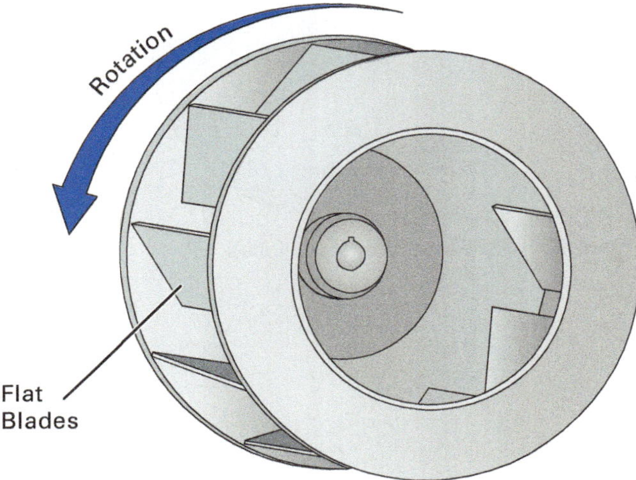

Figure 52 Backward-inclined centrifugal blower wheel.

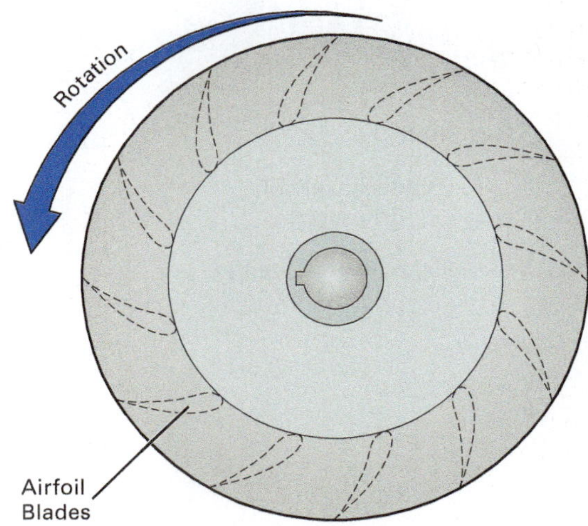

Figure 53 Backward-inclined airfoil fan wheel.

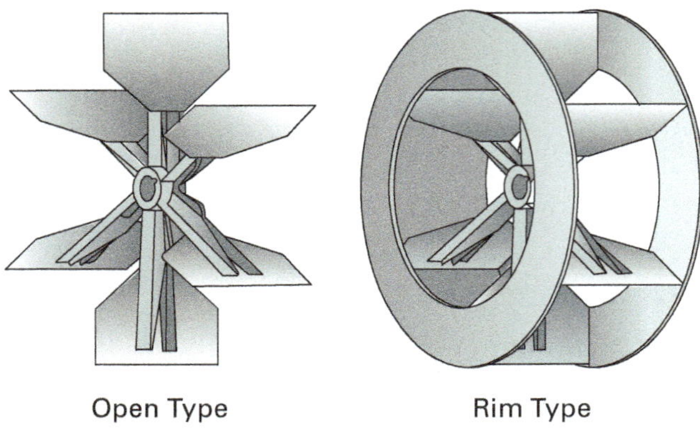

Figure 54 Examples of radial fan wheels.

airflow. The drive of an *axial blower wheel* is parallel to the fan axis, as shown in *Figure 55*. They are used when a large air volume at a low pressure differential is needed, such as in a dilute phase system. Axial blowers can also provide acceptable performance in a smaller package than the other types. Stationary vanes on the discharge side of the fan wheel help straighten the airflow and reduce turbulence as the air exits the fan.

One unique blower found in pneumatic conveyors is the **rotary-lobe blower**. Rotary-lobe blowers (*Figure 56*) have two double-lobe or triple-lobe impellers mounted on parallel shafts.

Manufacturers refer to their products as *bi-lobe* or *tri-lobe* models. Rotary-lobe blowers are also commonly referred to as *Roots blowers*, since the design originated from brothers Philander and Francis Roots in the late 1800s.

The two impellers rotate in opposite directions within a housing that is closed at both ends. As the impellers rotate, air is drawn into one side of the cylinder and forced out the opposite side.

Sealing between the inlet and outlet sides of the blower housing occurs where the two lobe assemblies mesh. Although the lobes may appear to touch in many drawings and photographs, maintaining a very small clearance between the two is essential. The small area between the lobes is filled with oil to create a seal. The precise clearance is maintained by two timing gears mounted on the lobe drive shafts that keep them synchronized. One gear is driven by the blower motor, and it meshes with and drives the second gear.

Rotary-lobe blowers are very durable and require limited maintenance, which primarily consists of gear oil changes. Their construction has changed very little over the years. This makes it easy to replace an old blower with a newer model. In most cases, a comparable replacement will fit neatly into the same mounting location.

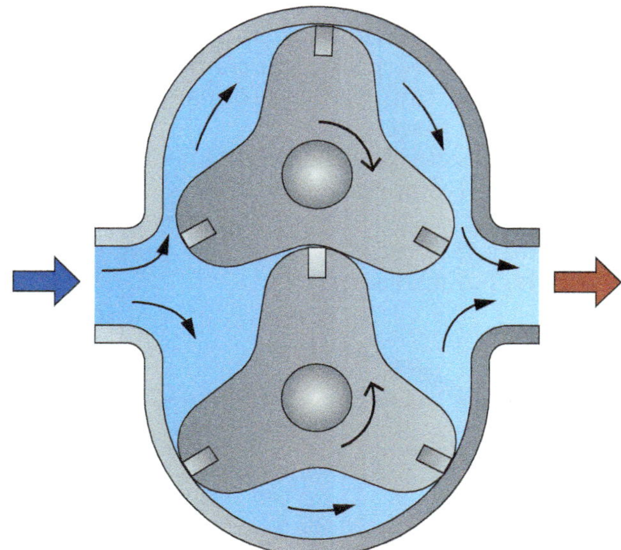

Figure 55 Vane-axial blower assembly.

Figure 56 Rotary-lobe blower (tri-lobe).

1. All maintenance related to chain and geared drives can be eliminated by using ______.

    a. take-ups
    b. line shafts
    c. centralized control systems
    d. independently powered rollers

2. A belt tracking problem refers to marks or damage the belt leaves on conveyed materials.

    a. True
    b. False

3. The conveyor type that is extremely durable and can handle loads such as palletized materials and heavy industrial containers is the ______.

    a. belt conveyor
    b. chain conveyor
    c. tubular cable conveyor
    d. pneumatic conveyor

4. The auger of a screw conveyor looks much like a screw because it is fitted with plates referred to as ______.

    a. wings
    b. waves
    c. flighting
    d. ringlets

5. A pneumatic conveyor that places the material downstream of the blower discharge is a positive airflow system.

    a. True
    b. False

1. The type of gravity conveyor that allows boxes, pallets, and other bulky items to be pushed in any direction is the _______.

   a. roller conveyor
   b. slider bed conveyor
   c. ball transfer conveyor
   d. skate wheel conveyor

2. The term *live-roller conveyor* refers to a roller conveyor that _______.

   a. is powered by a belt drive
   b. depends on accumulation roller chain
   c. is equipped with independently motorized rollers
   d. relies on direct contact between the rollers and the product

3. A belt conveyor moves product up an incline more effectively than powered roller conveyors because _______.

   a. of the improved traction
   b. belt conveyors have a lot more horsepower
   c. the bearings of the rollers can't handle the load
   d. you can only power a few rollers on a roller conveyor

Figure Credit: Courtesy of Dorner Mfg. Corp.

Figure RQ01

4. The belt-driven conveyor arrangement shown in *Figure RQ01* is called a(n) _______.

   a. end drive
   b. pinch drive
   c. spring drive
   d. ganged drive

5. *Pucks* and *carousels* are associated with which type of conveyor?

   a. Tubular chain conveyors
   b. Screw conveyors
   c. Belt conveyors
   d. Skate-wheel conveyors

6. Devices that are used to set and maintain tension on belt and chain conveyors are called _______.

   a. take-ups
   b. bearings
   c. sprockets
   d. couplings

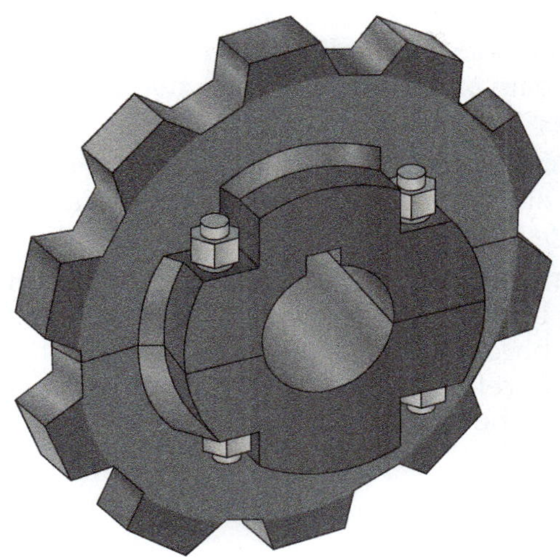

Figure RQ02

7. The component shown in *Figure RQ02* is a
   ______.
   a. take-up
   b. gearbox
   c. carousel
   d. split sprocket

8. Most screw conveyor augers need *at least* two
   bearings located at the ______.
   a. carousels
   b. auger joints
   c. trough end plates
   d. two independent drive assemblies

9. Which of the following materials represents
   a *poor* choice to move with a pneumatic
   conveyor?
   a. Sesame seeds
   b. Fruits and vegetables
   c. Grains such as wheat and rice
   d. Spices such as salt and pepper

10. A dense phase pneumatic conveyor has a
    high ratio of product to air—a lot of product
    in motion in a small volume of air.
    a. True
    b. False

Trade Terms Introduced in This Module

Accumulation roller chain: A type of roller chain with rollers that have a larger diameter than the chain side-plate height, allowing the free-spinning rollers to support the conveyed product.

Line shaft: A shaft driven by a power source that is connected to multiple loads through sheaves or sprockets mounted along its length.

Live-roller conveyor: A roller conveyor that maintains direct contact between the rollers and the conveyed product, with some or all the rollers powered to move the product along.

Mechatronics: Technology that combines the power of mechanical systems with electronics.

Rotary-lobe blower: A blower that relies on two lobed impellers spinning at high speed to create airflow. Each of the two impellers has either two or three lobes.

Servomotors: Special electric motors that can start and stop very precisely, as well as rotate to a specific position.

Thermoplastics: Describes plastic materials that become more plastic (elastic) when heated and harden again when cooled, allowing them to be reformed. *Thermosets* are plastics that cannot be heated and reformed.

Additional Resources

This module presents thorough resources for task training. The following reference material is suggested for further study.

ASME Standard B20.1, Safety Standard for Conveyors and Related Equipment. Latest Edition. New York, NY: American Society of Mechanical Engineers.

The Belt Conveyor: A Concise Basic Course. 1st Edition. 2020. D.V. Subba Rao. Boca Raton, FL: CRC Press.

Figure Credits

iStock@khomsan rakphong, Module Opener, Figure 9
iStock@PhonlamaiPhoto, Figure 1
iStock@cagkansayin, Figure 2
iStock@Dmytro Falkovskyi, Figure 3
Courtesy of Ultimation Industries, LLC, Figures 4–6, 11, 15–16, 30–31
iStock@surasak petchang, Figures 7, 14
iStock@Starkovphoto, Figure 8
iStock@Hermansyah28, Figure 12
iStock@paulacobleigh, Figure 13
iStock@sspopov, Figure 18
Courtesy of Dorner Mfg. Corp., Figures 19–20, 22–23, 25
Courtesy of Rainer Blickle & SEW-EURODRIVE, Figure 26
iStock@Baloncici, Figure 32
iStock@Ekkaluck, Figure 37
iStock@NiroDesign, Figure 39
Anderson Dahlen, Inc., Figure 43
Photo Courtesy of The Flexicon Corporation, all rights reserved, Figure 49

Section Review Answer Key

SECTION 1.0.0

Answer	Section Reference	Objective
1. d	1.1.1	1a
2. b	1.2.2	1b
3. d	1.3.0	1c
4. c	1.4.0	1d
5. a	1.5.0	1e

User Update

NCCER makes every effort to keep its textbooks up-to-date and free of technical errors. We appreciate your help in this process. If you find an error, a typographical mistake, or an inaccuracy in NCCER's curricula, please submit a User Update form by visiting **https://www.nccer.org/olf**. You can also scan the QR code using the camera on your phone or mobile device to access the form.

Troubleshooting and Repairing Conveyors

OVERVIEW

Conveyors represent the bloodstream of many industries. When a conveyor malfunctions or is completely offline, it often affects all aspects of a process. Workers and equipment that are not even within sight of the conveyor are affected when product flow is interrupted.

Millwrights and industrial maintenance workers must approach conveyor issues like a doctor approaches a medical issue—with a broad perspective. Beyond that, it is important to learn how to observe a conveyor problem and quickly develop a mental list of likely causes. Making good calls in that regard, along with applying good troubleshooting and repair techniques, will keep a conveyor system online and the product flowing.

Module 15402

Trainees with successful module completions may be eligible for credentialing through the NCCER Registry. To learn more, go to **www.nccer.org** or contact us at 1.888.622.3720. Our website, **www.nccer.org**, has information on the latest product releases and training.

Your feedback is welcome. You may email your comments to **curriculum@nccer.org**, send general comments and inquiries to **info@nccer.org**, or fill in the User Update form at the back of this module.

This information is general in nature and intended for training purposes only. Actual performance of activities described in this manual requires compliance with all applicable operating, service, maintenance, and safety procedures under the direction of qualified personnel. References in this manual to patented or proprietary devices do not constitute a recommendation of their use.

15402 V4.0

From *Millwright, Trainee Guide*. NCCER.
Copyright © 2023 by NCCER. Published by Pearson. All rights reserved.

Troubleshooting and Repairing Conveyors

Objective

Successful completion of this module prepares you to do the following:

1. Explain how to maintain and repair various types of conveyor systems.
   a. State general considerations and safety practices related to conveyor system maintenance and repair.
   b. Explain how to maintain and repair belt conveyors.
   c. Identify factors that affect conveyor belt tracking and explain how to correct tracking problems.
   d. Explain how to maintain and repair chain conveyors.
   e. Explain how to maintain and repair screw conveyors.
   f. Explain how to maintain and repair pneumatic conveyors.

Performance Tasks

Under supervision, you should be able to do the following:

1. Create a splice between two sections of belting using a mechanical fastening system.
2. Complete an instructor-selected mechanical repair on a belt, chain, screw, or pneumatic conveyor system.

Trade Terms

Carryback
Fugitive material

Skiving
Vulcanizing

Industry Recognized Credentials

If you are training through an NCCER-accredited sponsor, you may be eligible for credentials from NCCER's Registry. The ID number for this module is 15402. Note that this module may have been used in other NCCER curricula and may apply to other level completions. Contact NCCER's Registry at 1.888.622.3720 or go to **www.nccer.org** for more information.

You can also show off your industry-recognized credentials online with NCCER's digital badges. Transform your knowledge, skills, and achievements into badges that you can share across social media platforms, send to your network, and add to your resume. For more information, visit **www.nccer.org**.

> **NOTE**
>
> This module uses US standard and metric units in up to three different ways. This note explains how to interpret them.
>
> **Exact Conversions**
> Exact metric equivalents of US standard units appear in parentheses after the US standard unit. For example: "Measure 18" (45.7 cm) from the end and make a mark."
>
> **Approximate Conversions**
> In some cases, exact metric conversions would be inappropriate or even absurd. In these situations, an approximate metric value appears in parentheses with the ~ symbol in front of the number. For example: "Grip the tool about 3" (~8 cm) from the end."
>
> **Parallel but not Equal Values**
> Certain scenarios include US standard and metric values that are parallel but not equal. In these situations, a slash (/) surrounded by spaces separates the US standard and metric values. For example: "Place the point on the steel rule's 1" / 1 cm mark."

How to Access Resources

This craft has additional videos and resources to enhance your learning experience. To view these resources, scan the QR below. The videos and resources are separated by module.

You can scan this code using the camera on your phone or mobile device to view these videos and resources.

Contents

1.0.0 MAINTAINING AND REPAIRING CONVEYORS

Objective

Explain how to maintain and repair various types of conveyor systems.

a. State general considerations and safety practices related to conveyor system maintenance and repair.
b. Explain how to maintain and repair belt conveyors.
c. Identify factors that affect conveyor belt tracking and explain how to correct tracking problems.
d. Explain how to maintain and repair chain conveyors.
e. Explain how to maintain and repair screw conveyors.
f. Explain how to maintain and repair pneumatic conveyors.

Performance Tasks

1. Create a splice between two sections of belting using a mechanical fastening system.
2. Complete an instructor-selected mechanical repair on a belt, chain, screw, or pneumatic conveyor system.

Trade Terms

Carryback: Conveyed material that fails to unload at the end of a conveyor belt, adhering to or embedding itself in the belt and traveling back to the head of the conveyor on the underside.

Fugitive material: Any material that falls from or escapes a conveyor system, including dust, and doesn't reach the intended destination.

Skiving: The removal of one or more layers of a conveyor belt to accommodate a splice to avoid a significant change in belt thickness.

Vulcanizing: Using heat or chemicals along with pressure to create a conveyor belt splice. Hot vulcanization relies on direct heat, while cold vulcanization relies on chemicals to develop the necessary heat and bond.

Conveyors are essential systems that are very mechanical in nature. Although many of today's conveyors are controlled by sophisticated computer systems and programmable controllers, those devices can't move a peanut from point A to point B without a mechanical partner. Although electronic devices experience their own failures, bits and bytes don't suffer from age, wear, and corrosion like mechanical pieces. That makes the work of millwrights and industrial maintenance specialists essential to reliable conveyor operation and performance.

Over time, mechanical components become worn, loose, or misaligned (*Figure 1*). Worn and misaligned parts quickly become broken parts if they are not addressed. Friction is a constant foe that results in mechanical wear and increased energy consumption. Timely lubrication and the accurate alignment of drive components is necessary to minimize the effects of friction.

Misaligned and poorly lubricated drive components constantly rub and eventually begin to bind. This results in the drive motors taking on greater loads, often leading to overloads and unexpected shutdowns. In other words, small problems tend to become big ones. Problems must be identified and resolved as soon as possible to prevent, or at least minimize, downtime.

In the world of conveyors, you'll find drive couplings, bearings, belts and sheaves, sprockets and chains—the list of mechanical parts is virtually endless. In a sense, if you have completed most of the program modules that precede this one, you have been learning how to service conveyor systems all along. Conveyor systems offer you an opportunity to apply a great deal of what you have learned thus far.

Figure 1 Loose conveyor chain.

1.1.0 General Considerations and Safety Practices

The attention a conveyor system needs largely depends on the type of conveyor, the scope of usage, and the environment in which it is used. Conveyors with fewer moving parts require less maintenance than those with many. Conveyors that carry light loads don't wear out as quickly as those that carry heavy, awkward loads. Conveyors used in wet, dirty, abrasive, or corrosive environments need more attention than those used in cleaner surroundings.

Preventive maintenance (PM), also often referred to as *periodic maintenance,* prolongs the life of the equipment and improves reliability. PM is performed on a scheduled basis and includes cleaning, inspection, lubrication, and visual alignment verification. In some cases, alignment may need to be verified with instruments as well.

PM also includes monitoring the day-to-day operation of the equipment. This is often done through daily walk-arounds. Equipment that is operating normally tends to sound and vibrate a particular way, and it tends to operate at a consistent temperature. Alert craft professionals become attuned to the sound and feel of normal operation. They can often tell when something isn't right while passing by, before measuring or checking anything specific.

Some monitoring makes use of devices such as vibration sensors and other data collectors (*Figure 2*). Many aspects of conveyor operation can be monitored, including vibration, electrical current, rotational speed, and product positions. Some sensors transmit information continuously to a central location, while others remain isolated in place and are connected to handheld devices during walk-arounds that collect their stored data for analysis.

Deficiencies identified during PM activities that can't be corrected on the spot must be documented. The work can then be scheduled based on its nature and priority. Work orders resulting from inspection reports are often grouped into categories based on the risk to workers or the process.

A conveyor belt training roller with a worn bearing, for example, represents a small risk to the conveyor system. On the other hand, a modular belt assembled from interlocking plastic pieces that are breaking apart could cause the conveyor to fail at any moment. That repair would certainly take priority over a training roller. Problems noted during an inspection that are related to the safety of workers nearby must be given the highest priority.

Figure 2 Vibration data collection device.

1.1.1 Troubleshooting and Repair Processes

Troubleshooting represents a very different situation than simple maintenance activities. Once you learn and practice basic troubleshooting strategy, the time it takes to evaluate a problem and determine a course of action begins to shrink.

Troubleshooting and repair activities can be broken down into five basic steps:

- *Verifying or observing the symptoms* — How does the problem reveal itself?
- *Considering probable and possible causes* — What could cause those symptoms to occur?
- *Investigating the possible causes and testing* — Start with what feels like the most likely cause. Based on the symptoms, where is the most effective place to begin? Do I need other crafts to assist in that process?
- *Making the repairs, replacing parts as necessary* — Are the parts being replaced the true cause of the problem, or were they simply damaged due to the failure of something else? Were any other failed or damaged parts discovered that also need replacement? Are there other tasks that need to be done before the conveyor is allowed to operate again?
- *Operational testing and confirming that the problem has been solved* — Does the system now operate as it should? Is there follow-up work to be done later?

A millwright or industrial mechanic always has an advantage when they have observed the operation of a conveyor system while it is operating correctly. Comparing the symptoms to what you know to be correct operation always makes the second step of brainstorming the possible causes much easier.

If a problem were serious, the Emergency Stop button may have already been pushed, and the conveyor is offline when you arrive on the scene. A system safety control also may have stopped the conveyor. If the equipment is not operational, troubleshooting is more difficult because the symptoms are no longer visible or audible. You must then rely on information from the operators, only restarting the conveyor for testing or observation once you are certain that it won't cause more damage.

Ghost problems—those that seem to come and go at random—can be very challenging to resolve. When you can't duplicate the problem, consider the possibilities carefully and take steps to eliminate one or more of them before the next occurrence.

Most conveyors have some form of automation, ranging from a simple On-Off switch to a computer program that uses sensors to monitor various conditions. Sensors are often used to monitor the status of the source (where product is loaded) and the receiver (the product destination). Troubleshooting conveyors with sophisticated and automated control systems usually requires two or even three people with different skill sets. Never hesitate to contact someone who understands and can interface with the electrical and control systems when troubleshooting conveyors.

Replacing a defective part on many conveyors usually requires dismantling at least part of the conveyor. Whenever any part is replaced, ensure all drive components are still aligned before returning the conveyor to service. Components that require alignment for proper and reliable operation may not be the focus of the repair, but even their alignment should be checked before the conveyor is restarted.

1.1.2 Conveyor Safety

Conveyors have many moving parts with powerful drive systems. In many cases, workers are in direct contact with the materials as they move. Serious and even fatal injuries are possible.

The American Society of Mechanical Engineers (ASME) is an essential resource for conveyor safety. ASME publishes and maintains *ASME Standard B20.1, Safety Standard for Conveyors and Related Equipment*. The Occupational Safety and Health Administration (OSHA) also publishes conveyor safety regulations, with the primary resource being *OSHA Standard 1926.555, Helicopters, Hoists, Elevators, and Conveyors*. There are other relevant OSHA standards focused on the maritime environment. Remember that OSHA regulations often include standards from ASME and other entities by incorporation.

The first thing to know about conveyor safety is how to turn it off in an emergency. Emergency Stop controls are required on all powered conveyors. Before working on or near a powered conveyor, locate the Emergency Shutoff controls (*Figure 3*). They should be easy to locate, by design.

On most conveyors, the emergency control is a large, red button labeled EMERGENCY STOP. To shut down the equipment in an emergency, simply press the button. If you are not familiar with the system, ask the operators to review the location of key controls with you, or retrieve and study the installation plans.

Some conveyors have red cords or cables mounted at easily accessible and visible locations around the conveyor, in addition to or instead of a button. Cable or cord arrangements allow workers along the line to quickly stop the conveyor without having to leave their position.

> **CAUTION**
>
> The Emergency Stop control should not be used outside of emergency situations. Many conveyor systems are interlocked with other equipment and systems. In that case, a specific shutdown sequence may be bypassed when the Emergency Stop button is used, in the interest of immediate stoppage. For this reason, it is best to use the normal conveyor controls to shut down a system in the absence of a true emergency.

When performing work on or near a conveyor, always stay alert for potential hazards. Here are some basic safety practices to remember:

- Inform operating personnel when you need to shut down a conveyor. Shutting down a conveyor system without warning can cause problems throughout a facility.

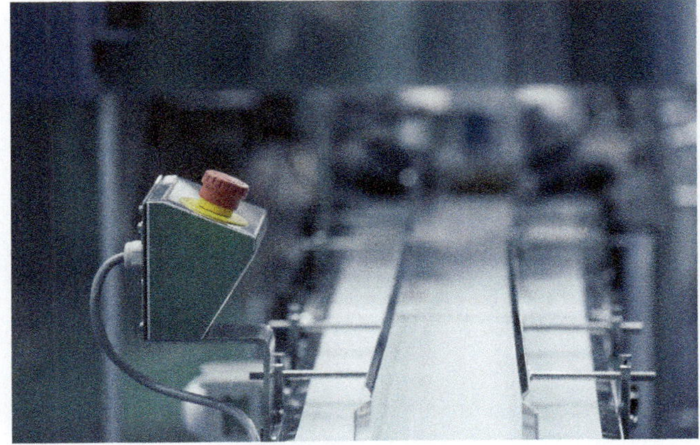

Figure 3 Conveyor Emergency Stop button.

- After turning off the power, lock out and tag (LOTO) the power source according to OSHA requirements and local regulations. Ensure all sources of energy related to the conveyor are disabled, locked, and tagged. Physically confirm that the power source cannot be energized once the locks are in place. Also attempt to start the conveyor with all the safeties in place to further confirm that the correct power sources have been disabled.
- Locking out all sources of external energy is not always enough. Energy can be stored within the conveyor itself. For example, if a belt conveyor is shut down while a significant load is on a portion of the belt that rises vertically, that weight will try to move the belt backward. To avoid unexpected movement, you may need to physically block mechanical components to prevent movement, using safety rods or pins. This is often referred to as *blocking out* the conveyor. Another approach to preventing belt movement during maintenance work is to use belt clamps (*Figure 4*). Don't use clamps along the edge of the belt to secure it to the bed or frame, as this can damage the belt if it is under any stress.
- Keep the work area clean and uncluttered while working on the equipment. Avoid placing tools in locations where they could cause damage if left behind. Place tools back in the toolbox or in a bin as you work, rather than place them in locations where they can fall or be overlooked (*Figure 5*). Tools should either be in your hand or secured, and should never be laid in or on conveyor mechanisms. A screwdriver left in the wrong place can do a lot of damage!
- Collect and inventory all your tools and materials as the work is completed, leaving the work area clean and unobstructed.
- Reinstall all guards and reset all safety devices to their proper conditions before the conveyor is restarted or tested.
- Follow all OSHA and local LOTO procedures as you restore power to the system.
- Pay close attention to how the conveyor operates when it starts. Listen as well as watch.
- Be certain to inform management and the operators of the status of the conveyor before you leave the area.

Specific hazards to be aware of when working around conveyors include the following:

- *Unguarded moving parts* — Conveyors have many moving parts. Generally, moving parts are shielded by some type of guard, but some areas of a conveyor are difficult to isolate. You must always be aware of moving parts, guarded or not. Ideally, conveyor guards require tools for removal, and they are painted a different color than the guarded equipment.
- *Shifting or protruding loads* — Conveyors often move materials or components that protrude beyond the edges of the conveyor, as well as those that may shift as they travel. Keep a close eye on materials that are traveling on the conveyor and stay out of their path. Never work beneath an operating conveyor.
- *Damaged parts* — Moving parts wear out. In addition, conveyors are often damaged by other equipment, such as forklifts or **fugitive material** that finds its way into sensitive areas. Worn and damaged conveyor parts present a hazard to anyone working near them. Any type of conveyor damage should be reported to the operator to ensure that the problem is recognized, and that repairs are scheduled through the proper channels.
- *Overheated components* — Become familiar with the normal sound, smell, and amount of heat produced around the components. Overheated components, especially motors and wiring, tend to produce a significant burning smell. Do not touch a component that you suspect is overheating. Use a thermometer or infrared pyrometer to check the temperature. When necessary, inform the operators or a supervisor, who can initiate a proper shutdown procedure. Initiate an emergency shutdown if a fire, serious damage, or personal injury appears imminent.
- *Moving surfaces and pinch points* — Since most conveyors are constantly moving, it is possible to become entangled at any time. *Pinch points* are defined as points at which a part of the body can be caught between moving parts, or between moving and stationary parts. Conveyor systems have many such points. Avoid loose clothing and be mindful of where each finger and foot are placed when working around an operating conveyor. Never reach over, step onto, or climb over a moving or energized conveyor. The safe way to reach an object or a control located on the opposite side of the conveyor is to simply go around it.

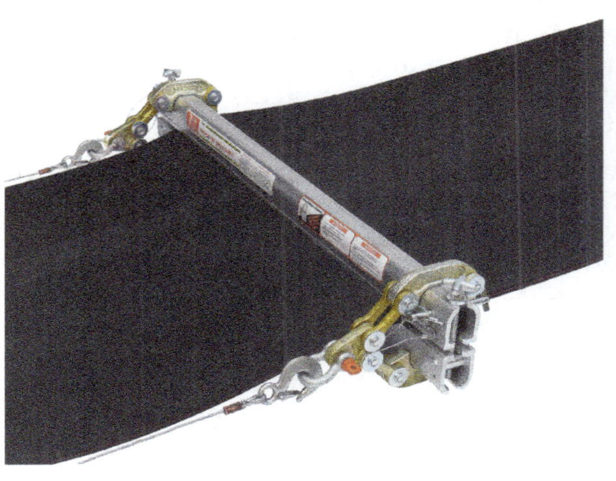

(A) Scissor-Type Belt Clamp

(B) Over-the-Top Belt Clamp

Figure 4 Belt clamps.

Figure 5 Keep your tools organized and confined to a toolbox or bin.

- *Belt tension and stored energy* — During normal operation of a belt conveyor, the highest level of belt tension is found just as the belt enters the drive roller. The lowest level of tension is found where the belt exits the drive roller. Tension remains in the belt even when the conveyor is not running. However, product loading is a factor that can cause the belt tension to change locally. Jams and obstructions that stop or impede the belt cause the tension to change remarkably and quickly. Tension represents stored energy, and this energy can be released very suddenly when you clear a jam or remove an obstruction. These tasks must be done with great care, as it is often hard to predict where and to what extent that energy will be released. Conveyor belts can also break under excessive tension, resulting in a very rapid energy release that can cause serious injuries.

When working on or around conveyors, stop and think about every move you make and where you place your hands, feet, and tools.

1.2.0 Maintaining and Repairing Belt Conveyors

Conveyors are sometimes allowed to operate unattended, and they often operate in harsh environments. Between the lack of attention and the environment, conveyors can easily develop problems that affect production. The easiest way to prevent such problems is to ensure that regular, scheduled PM is performed on the conveyor. Ideally, potential problems are found during PM inspections and resolved before a breakdown occurs.

1.2.1 Belt Conveyor Maintenance

Problems identified during PM activities must either be corrected immediately or scheduled for future repair. To avoid interrupting production, the latter is very common. However, when failure is imminent or the safety of workers is a concern, make sure that this information is made clear to your supervisors so the problem can be addressed quickly.

Remember to observe and analyze each conveyor as it operates, whenever possible, before shutting it down and performing any PM work. The following inspection items are common for belt and roller conveyors:

- If the conveyor is functional before the inspection, test the Emergency Stop switch by activating it with the conveyor running. The best practice is to test the emergency system every 30 days. It is critical for the system to operate as designed. If there is more to it than a single stop switch, test the operation from multiple stations. Proving that the emergency controls work on one side of the conveyor does not prove that they work on the opposite side. Generally, emergency shutdown stations should be no more than 70' apart. However, there are many guidelines applied to these controls and their arrangement.

- Inspect all rollers and idlers. Rollers and idlers that do not rotate properly often show unexpected wear or polishing in one spot. Ensure each roller, driven or passive, rotates smoothly without rough spots and does not have excessive play in the bearings. Listen for unusual noises and look for grease leakage and discoloration from heat on and around bearings.
- Examine all exposed drive shafts on motors and gearboxes for damage. Look for leakage around the gearbox shaft seals. Inspect drive shaft and line shaft couplings to ensure they are aligned and secure.
- Inspect sprockets for excessive tooth wear, wear imbalance (more on one side than another), and damaged teeth. Ensure all interacting sprockets are aligned.

- Brush grit and debris from drive chains. Check for the proper tension as outlined by the manufacturer. Remember that a 3 percent elongation is the typical limit before roller chain used on a drive must be replaced. Lubricate chains as directed by the equipment manufacturer.

- Examine drive sheaves and belts. Sheaves are checked for excessive groove wear and alignment. Check all drive belts, including the very small ones often used to transfer movement from one roller to another, for excessive wear, cracking, or fraying.
- Ensure all bearings that require lubrication are serviced with the proper grease.
- For sliding bed conveyors, inspect the bed surface for flaws that could damage the belt or the product. Look for anything along the length of the conveyor that shouldn't be there, such as pieces of a broken pallet, metal, or glass. Fugitive material and debris in the wrong place are common causes of conveyor problems.

Both roller and belt conveyors may depend on drum motors as a drive option. Drum motors are designed to operate reliably in wet or dusty environments. When modular belts are used, unique sprockets may be attached along the drum motor's surface to engage the conveyor belt modules. Troubleshooting them is typically electrical in nature, and their internal components are not field serviceable.

Talk to Those Operators!

It is rare for millwrights and industrial maintenance mechanics to be present when a conveyor suddenly goes down. In many cases, you must rely on the operators to explain what happened and provide a sequence of events.

When you are responsible for a conveyor system, those operators are your customers. Communicate with them regularly, not just when something is wrong. Many problems can be caused by operator error or a misunderstanding about how things are supposed to work. Train them as necessary and allow them to train you. Do so with the courtesy and respect any vendor should extend to an important customer. Although the operators may not have the authority to determine the pace of their work, it's always a good idea to remind them of limitations in speed and load, and how exceeding those limitations will affect the system.

Having friends along the conveyor means you have multiple eyes and ears that will assist you in monitoring its operation and provide valuable information when the need arises.

One of the advantages of drum motors is simplified maintenance when compared to conventional drives, such as gearboxes and belt or chain drives. However, some maintenance is required, such as the following:

- A buildup of material on the roller surface can interfere with its grip on a belt. Carefully clean any deposits from all rollers, including drum motors.
- Look for signs of damage and ensure the motor rotates freely.
- If the drum motor transfers power through one or more small belts, make sure they are in good condition.
- Examine the drum motor wiring connections to ensure the connections are sound.
- Ensure all mounting hardware is secure.
- Some drum motors have grease fittings and require regular lubrication. Ensure that the manufacturer's lubrication schedule is maintained, and that the correct lubricant is being used. Remember that food-grade lubricants may be required, depending on the environment.

1.2.2 Maintaining and Replacing Rollers

The drive and tail rollers of belt conveyors (*Figure 6*) are critical to the operation of the conveyor. The rollers in a center-drive arrangement (*Figure 7*) are equally important. These rollers have the most influence on the belt, and their position relative to each other and the conveyor frame largely determine whether the belt tracks as it should.

Drive rollers are usually larger than any of the other rollers, as shown in *Figure 6*. This places more surface area against the belt, increasing traction. Some have a smooth metal surface, while others have *lagging* applied to the surface (*Figure 8*). Lagging is simply a textured covering, usually rubbery, that enhances grip on the conveyor belt. Lagging can be replaced if it is worn or damaged.

Drive rollers may have a slight crown in the center, which may help to keep the belt tracking naturally. However, they are generally found on conveyors that do not require a lot of belt tension—those that move lighter loads. In high-tension applications, a crowned drive roller tends to work against consistent tracking.

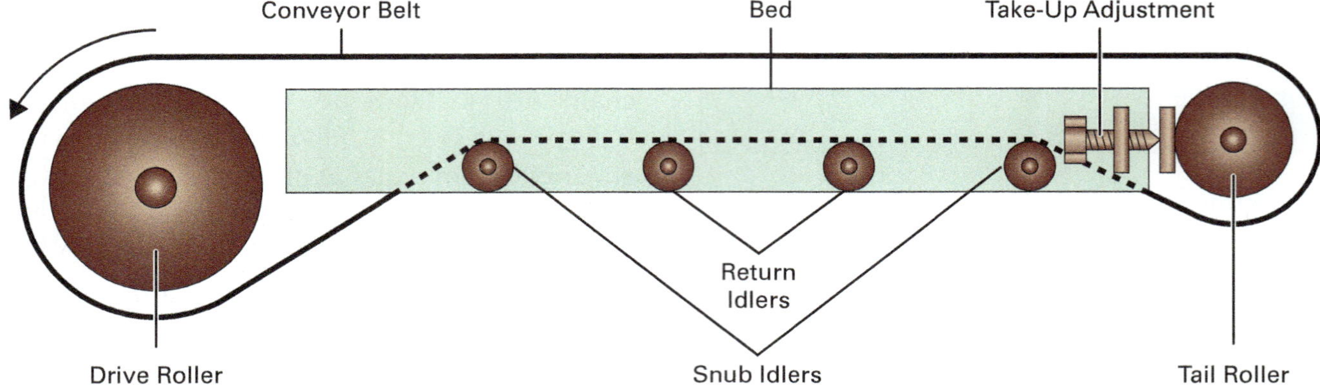

Figure 6 Conventional conveyor belt drive roller and idler arrangement.

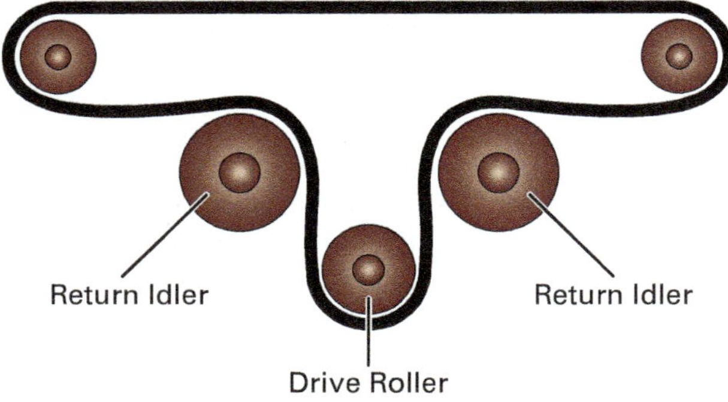

Figure 7 Center-drive arrangement for a belt conveyor.

Tail rollers are often smaller than the drive rollers, but not necessarily. Some have a winged design, as shown in *Figure 9*. The wings help dislodge debris that adheres to the bottom of the belt, called **carryback**. If lumpy or hardened carryback is stuck to the bottom of the belt, a winged roller is less likely to damage the belt as the debris moves over it. Winged rollers, also known as *self-cleaning rollers*, are not used for drive rollers; the reduction of contact area reduces traction. The only way to overcome that weakness is to increase the belt tension, which is never desirable.

From a maintenance perspective, drive and tail rollers are far more likely than other rollers to have large bearings that require periodic greasing. It is also important to ensure the surfaces of the belt and rollers are kept clean.

Take-ups provide the means to properly tension a conveyor belt. Screw take-ups are part of the tail roller mount assembly, as shown in *Figure 10*. They can be much larger in size than the figure suggests. Gravity and counterweight take-ups provide the same service. Tension must be balanced across the full width of the belt to keep it tracking as it should. Assuming the belt is not distorted in some way, keeping the tail roller parallel to the drive roller should provide balanced tension.

Most belt conveyor systems do not have a specified belt tension. The correct tension for the conveyor belt is that which is sufficient to move the maximum design load without slipping on the drive roller. Belt slippage reduces the life of both the belt and the drive roller and slows product flow. There is no need to set the belt tension any higher than the application requires. Excessive tension adds load to the drive train, increasing both wear and energy consumption. Roller bearings are especially affected by the added stress.

When adjusting screw take-ups, start with both the drive and tail roller square to the conveyor frame. Begin with no load on the belt. As you add tension by backing the tail roller away from the drive roller, do so in small increments. Adjust one side a few turns, then adjust the opposite side an equal number of turns. Set the tension so that the belt moves easily as the drive roller rotates without slipping. Then work up to the maximum product load for the belt and adjust the take-ups to eliminate any slipping that develops.

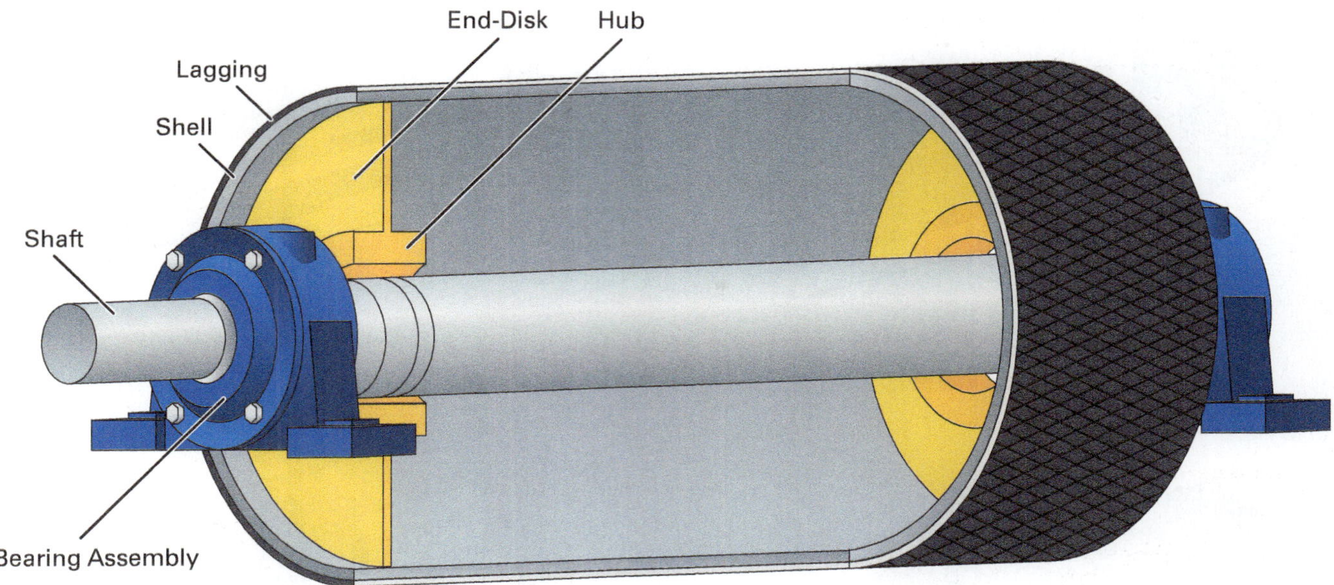

Figure 8 Cutaway of a large drive roller with lagging applied.

Figure 9 Winged tail roller.

For systems that move very light loads, less tension is needed. Far more tension is needed on heavy-duty conveyors, especially when the belt thickness reaches and exceeds 1" (~25 mm). Longer conveyors with thick belts are far more likely to use counterweight take-ups to provide more tension than screw take-ups can reliably provide. Counterweight take-ups also have a much greater range of travel to accommodate the stretching that occurs in long belts before an adjustment is required.

Replacing Rollers

Drive rollers, sprockets, and bearings eventually wear out or become damaged. To replace a drive roller, the drive components must be disassembled and removed. On most conveyors, the task begins with relieving belt tension using the take-ups. The drive chain is then removed from the sprockets and the drive sprocket is removed.

Since the roller is often mounted between the frame rails, with the shaft extending through the frame, flange-mounted bearings may be used. At least one must be removed to free the roller. The roller should then have enough side-to-side clearance to be shifted to the drive side and allow one end of the shaft to clear the inside of the frame rail for removal (*Figure 11*).

As an alternative to the flanged-bearing mounting approach shown, pillow-block bearings may be mounted on the frame instead. In this case, the bearings can be unbolted and removed from the roller shaft.

The tail roller may also be mounted between the frame rails of the conveyor, with the tail roller shaft mounted on bearings carried by the take-up assemblies. A sliding-tube take-up is shown in *Figure 10*. When using it, the take-up assembly position places the tail roller beyond the conveyor frame rails. Regardless, one or both take-up assemblies will need to be removed to replace the tail roller.

Before shutting down the system for roller repairs, be sure to carefully evaluate the task and have everything on hand that should be needed. Poor planning can result in significant losses once the conveyor is offline but can't be returned to service as planned.

Troughing and return idler rollers are usually mounted to brackets attached to the conveyor frame (*Figure 12*). The bearings are housed inside the roller assembly (*Figure 13*). These rollers are very easy to replace quickly, without any special tools. Rollers supported by flange or pillow-block bearings require at least one of the bearings to be removed.

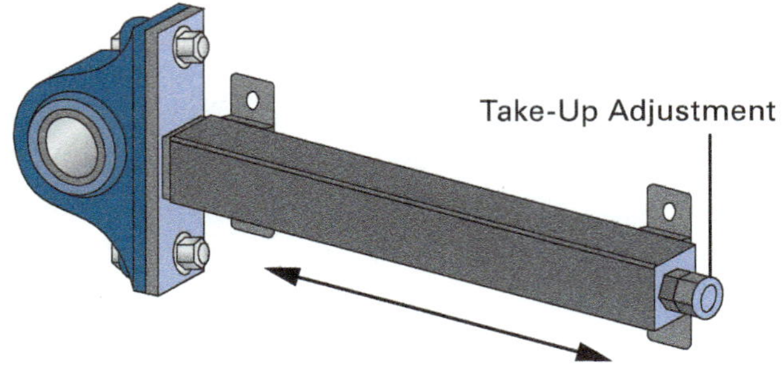

(A) Sliding Tube Take-Up

(B) Center Pull Take-Up

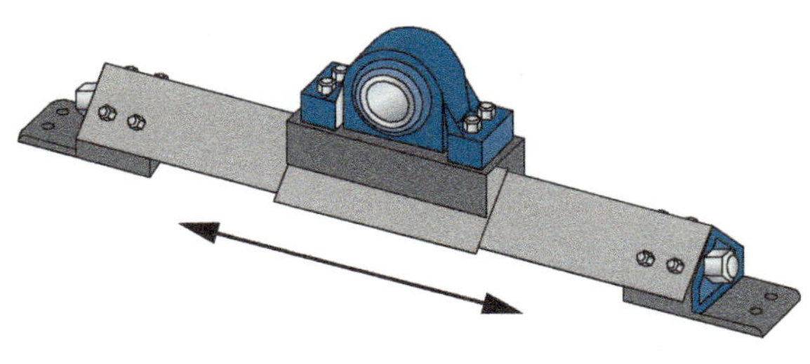
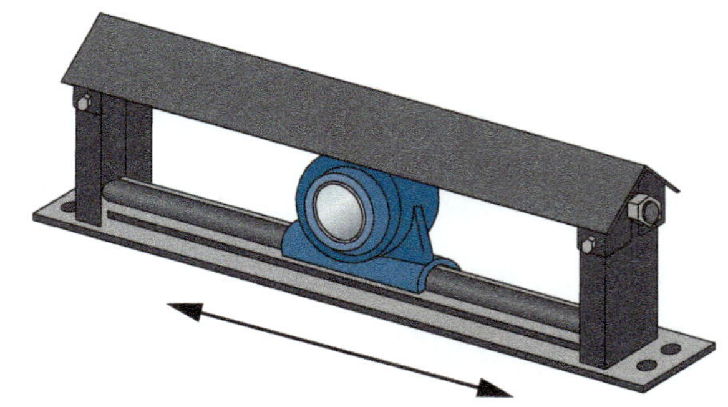

(C) Top-Mount Take-Up

(D) Top-Mount, Angle-Protected Take-Up

Figure 10 Conveyor take-up assemblies.

1.2.3 Belt Repair

Before moving on to belt splicing, it is important to know that some belt damage can be repaired. Splicing in a new section is not always necessary. Damage that can be repaired includes gouges in the center or along the edges, rips and holes, and grooves that come from extended contact against a skirt or other component. However, thin and light belt materials will usually need to be cut and spliced to resolve damage.

Repair kits like the one shown in *Figure 14* are available from a variety of sources. Kits contain a two-part urethane rubber product, cleaning solvent, primer, and simple application tools. It can be used to repair large gouges, holes, or tears. The general sequence for such repairs is as follows, but always remember to follow the directions for the product in hand (refer to *Figure 15*):

WARNING!

Before using solvent-based products and other chemicals, always read and follow the guidelines found on the Safety Data Sheet (SDS) as well as the product directions. Do not work with solvents and similar products in confined areas without the proper breathing protection. Solvents are also flammable; ensure no sources of ignition are present and be prepared with fire safety gear as necessary.

Step 1　Use the solvent to clean the damaged area thoroughly, as well as an area several inches around the damage. Use a rag with a small amount of solvent to rub and clean the surface.

Step 2　Use an abrasive tool to roughen the surface of the cleaned area. Bevel any sharp edges or shoulders around the damage. A file sander (*Figure 16*) can be used for abrading the damaged area, but a hand-held angle grinder with an appropriate sanding disk might also be used. Crimped wire wheels may also be considered, but knotted or beaded wire wheels are generally too aggressive. File sanders—belt sanders with a narrow belt—work better for small areas and are easier to control. Regardless of the tool, use a soft touch to avoid damaging the belt further. Also avoid sanding exposed cords and fabric.

WARNING!

Remember to wear the proper PPE when using any abrading or grinding tool, including eye protection, hearing protection, and a dust mask. A full face shield is often required when using grinding tools. Before plugging the tool in or inserting the battery, ensure all guards and safety features are in place and functional.

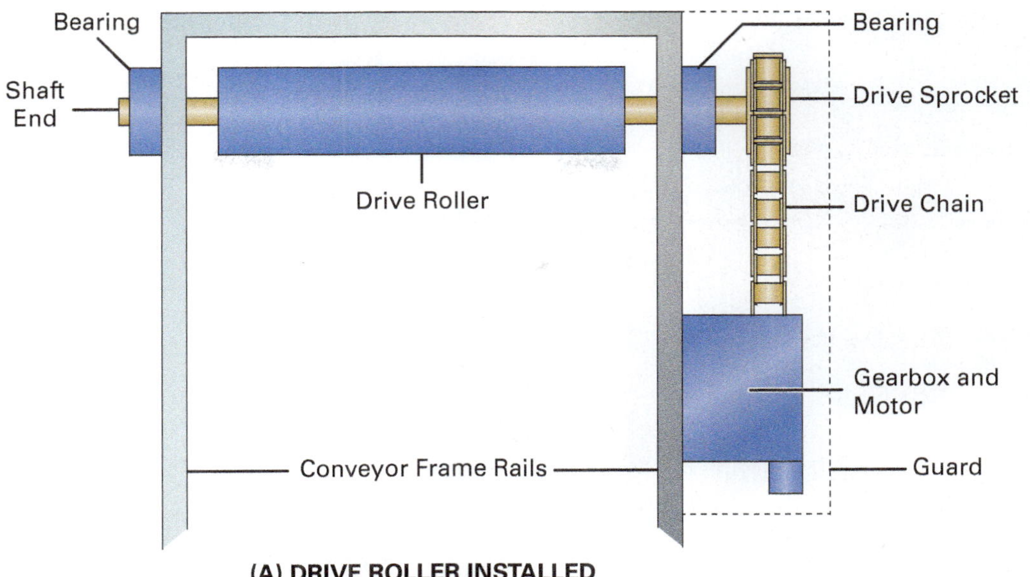

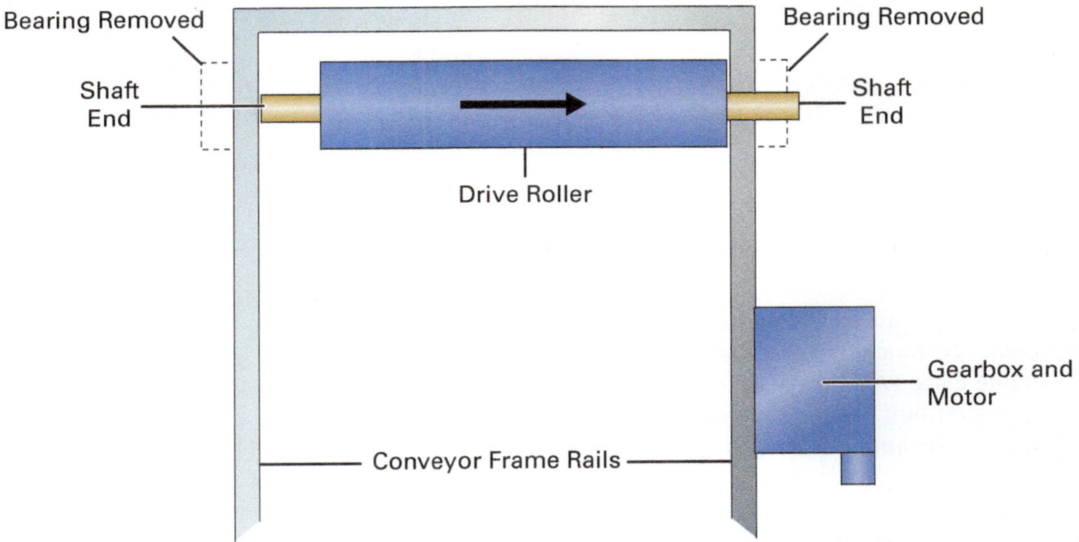

Figure 11 Drive roller removal.

Figure 12 Troughing rollers mounted on simple brackets.

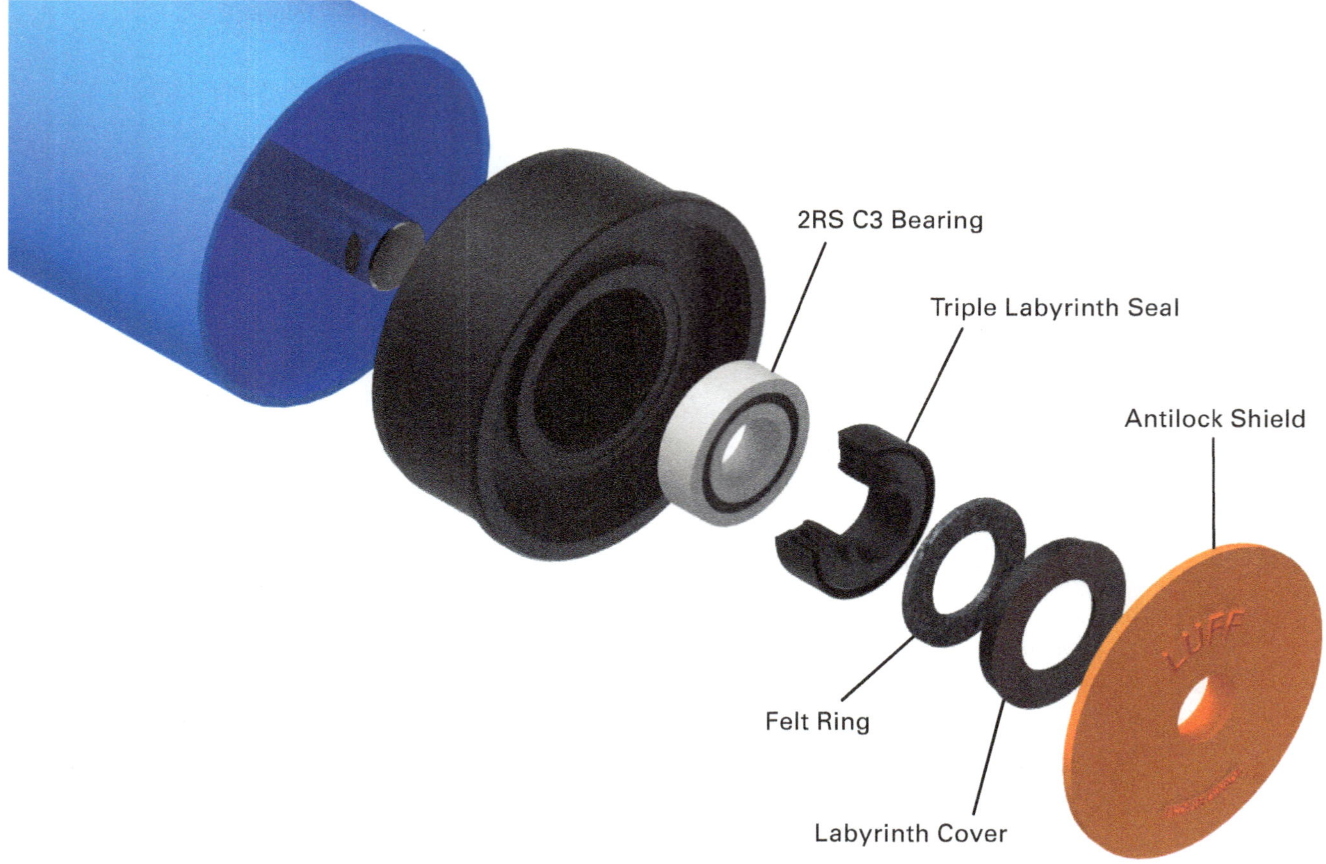

Figure 13 Conveyor roller with integral bearings.

CAUTION

Use a light touch with any powered tool to avoid removing too much material. Do not let it remain in one place while working—keep the tool moving. Never buff or sand exposed fabric or cords, as they are quickly damaged.

Step 3 Clean away the debris and any other remaining particles. Then apply the primer to the entire prepared area.

NOTE

Repair products like this may also be used to fill holes and tears in a belt. If a hole is present, prepare the opposite side of the belt by cleaning it thoroughly, then applying heavy tape over the opening. This prevents the product from leaking through.

Step 4 Mix the hardener into the resin per the package directions, stirring until it is thoroughly mixed. You might also be directed to let the mixture sit for a specified period, to gain consistency before it's applied. This is especially true if you must make a repair while the belt is not horizontal. Temperature and humidity also play a role in the timing. The desired consistency for application can't be sustained for very long.

Step 5 Pour the mixture onto the damaged area to fill it.

Step 6 Use a putty knife or similar tool to smooth the mixture, pushing air bubbles out and tapering the thickness all around the edges. Remain within the boundaries of the prepared area.

Step 7 Allow the material to cure undisturbed for the specified length of time.

Step 8 Once the patch has cured, a light sanding may be required to smooth and level the surface. Check the manufacturer's directions, but many such products can be smoothed or leveled after curing.

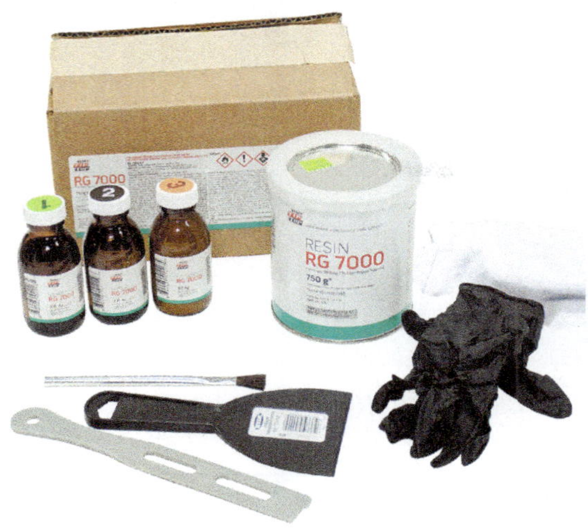

Figure 14 Two-part urethane belt repair kit.

1.2.4 Conveyor Belt Splicing

Conveyor belts are expensive and time-consuming to replace. Therefore, every effort is made to salvage them when they are damaged. Splicing the belt to replace a damaged section is one way to get the expected service life from a belt. The belt type and material usually determine whether the belt can be spliced, and what kind of splice is appropriate.

When **vulcanizing** is a practical approach, it usually represents the best splicing approach for rubber and rubbery materials like EPDM and nitrile. Vulcanizing is often done by specialists that have the necessary equipment and experience.

Hot vulcanizing refers to the process of curing splices using heat and pressure to create a reliable bond (*Figure 17*). This results in a very durable and long-lived splice, but it can also be more complicated and awkward to accomplish in the field. Hot vulcanizing also requires some significant downtime. But when working with very long, heavy belts, such as those used in the mining industry, vulcanizing is a worthwhile investment.

Cold vulcanizing is a simpler process that replaces the heat with chemicals. The process requires less time and equipment, and it is significantly less expensive. However, the service life is shorter, and the failure rate is generally higher.

Both methods of vulcanizing are based on overlapping the two ends of the belt significantly, resulting in a great deal of surface contact in the splice. That feature provides strength and reliability. Mechanical splices, on the other hand, are often done by butting the ends together. Although this works fine in many applications, you can likely see how this would yield a less dependable joint. Mechanical splices are the focal point of this section going forward.

Mechanical Splices

Mechanical splicing offers a much faster option. Although not as strong as a vulcanized splice, it is the most common approach for smaller, thinner belts that do not carry extreme loads. It is also used with belt materials that can't be vulcanized effectively.

When belts are spliced, the belt may need to be cut diagonally, notched, or dovetailed. Cutting the end of the belt in patterns increases the line of contact between the two pieces. For example, cutting a straight line across a 36" (91.4 cm) belt results in 36" of contact along the splice. Cutting it at a 45-degree angle increases the line of contact to nearly 51" (129.5 cm). *Figure 18* shows some of the cuts used in conveyor belt splicing.

Note that *Figure 18* shows both alligator lacing and mechanical fasteners used to splice belts. Today, splices are not made with sewn lacing. There are simply too many faster, more versatile, and more reliable fastening solutions available. Some examples are provided here:

- *Clipper® Wire Hooks* — This product (*Figure 19*) is a machine-applied, hook-style metal fastener for belts up to 0.39" (~10 mm) thick. Hooks are available in a variety of styles, sizes, and materials that are low profile and are easy to install with the Clipper® Roller Lacer®, also shown in *Figure 19*. The Roller Lacer® is a portable installation tool with dual rollers that allow for gradual embedding of the hook points into the belt as the head is moved across the width. Lacers are available in both manually operated and cordless drill-operated models in 24", 36", 48", and 60" widths. All lacers are capable of *indexing* to be able to lace wider belts than the lacer width. This means that the lacer can be shifted across the belt from a laced area to an unlaced area to complete the splice.
- *Alligator® Staple (Figure 20)* — The Alligator® Staple fastening system is ideal for a wide variety of light- and medium-duty fastener applications for belts up to $\frac{1}{4}$" (6.4 mm) thick. The system features one-piece fastener strips with pre-inserted staples that speed installation and keep downtime to a minimum.
- *Bolted solid-plate fastening system (Figure 21)* — Plate fasteners can be used for many belt thicknesses, all the way up to 2" (~50 mm). They also provide a splice that doesn't allow granular material to fall through, but with less flexibility. They can be installed manually or with power tools.

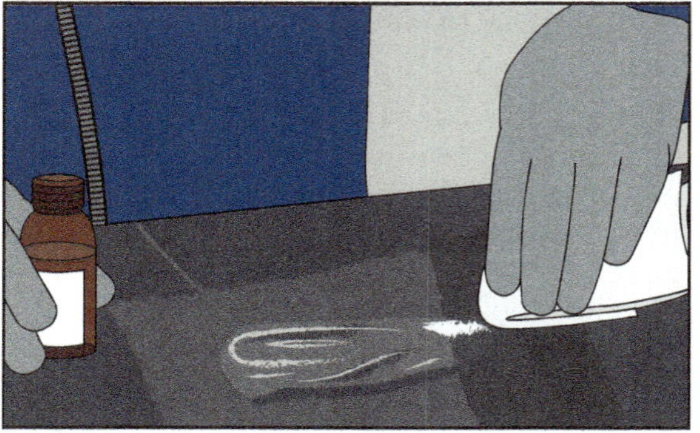
(A) Clean the Area with Solvent

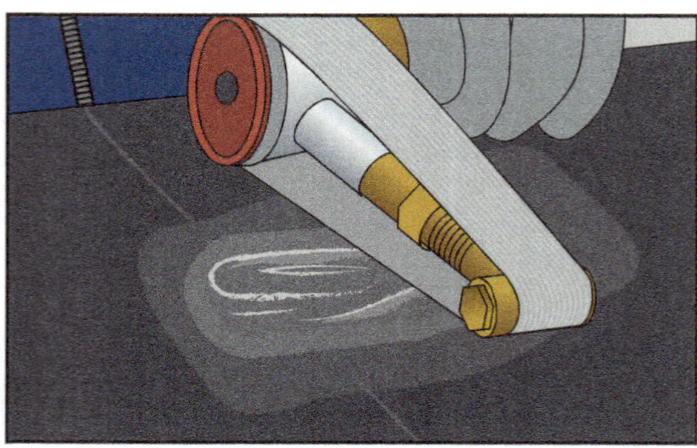
(B) Carefully Buff the Belt Surface

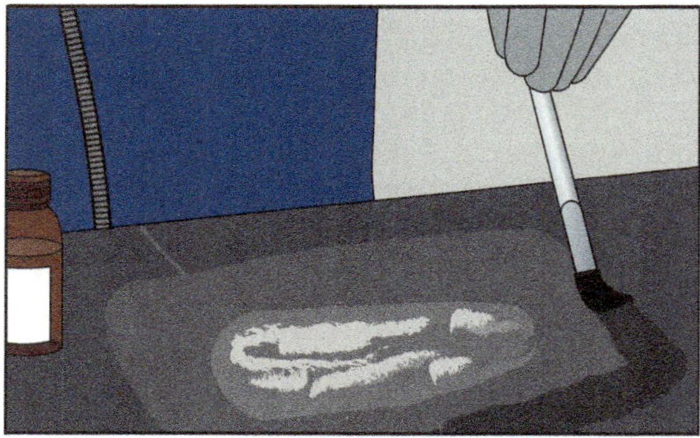
(C) Apply the Primer

(D) Mix the Components and Apply

(E) Work In with a Putty Knife

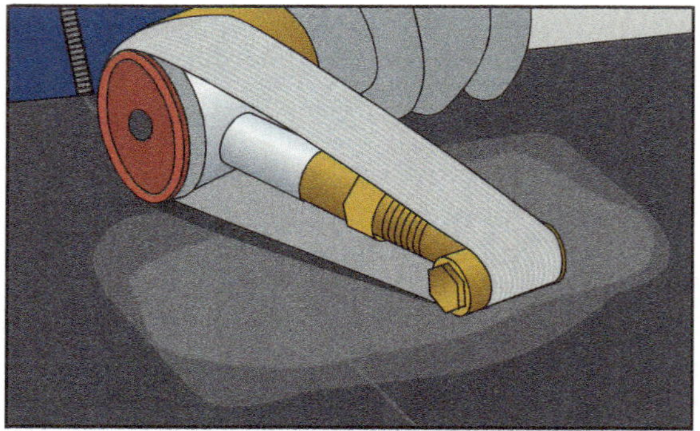
(F) Buff to Level after Curing

Figure 15 Repairing a conveyor belt surface.

Figure 16 File sander.

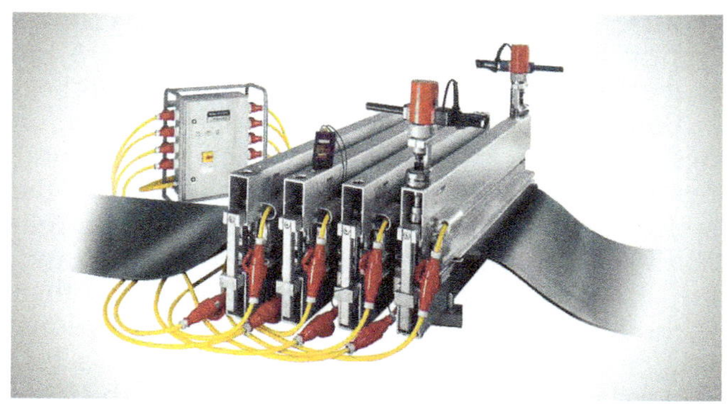

Figure 17 Hot vulcanizing equipment for field use.

NCCER – *Millwright*

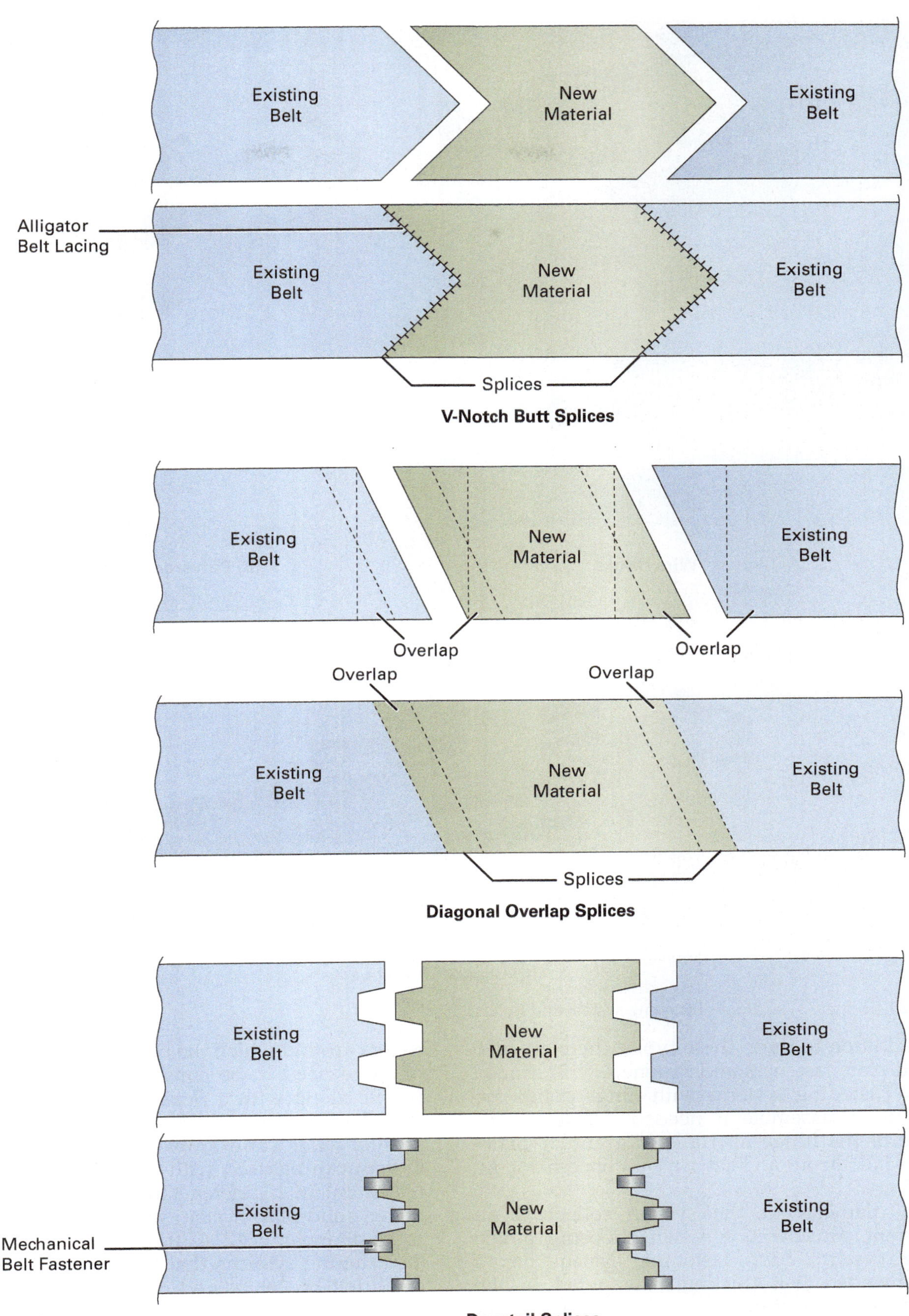

Figure 18 Common belt-splicing cut patterns.

(A) Clipper® Wire Hooks

(B) Powered Roller Lacer®

(C) Clipper® Roller Lacer®

Figure 19 Clipper® Wire Hooks fastening system and Roller Lacer®.

In addition to these three types, there are also riveted-plate fasteners and fasteners with hinged plates. Fastening systems with hinge points are easier to disassemble if needed. However, the nature of the hinge also allows granular material to fall through. That isn't a concern for all conveyors.

The diameter of the system rollers is an important consideration when choosing a fastening system. Each fastening system has a recommended belt thickness, as noted in the preceding descriptions. But a minimum roller diameter is also specified for each system. Only rollers around which the belt wraps at 90 degrees or more need to be considered. A low fastener profile along with a flexible joint design means that a fastening system can accommodate a smaller roller. For example, the Clipper® G-Series system can be used with rollers as small as 1.6" (~40 mm) in diameter. On the other hand, the bolted solid-plate system shown has a minimum roller diameter of 12" (~30 cm).

Fastening systems that lack a lot of flexibility shouldn't be considered inferior. In most cases, the belts they are used with require an equally large roller diameter to operate effectively.

Figure 20 Alligator® Staple fastening system.

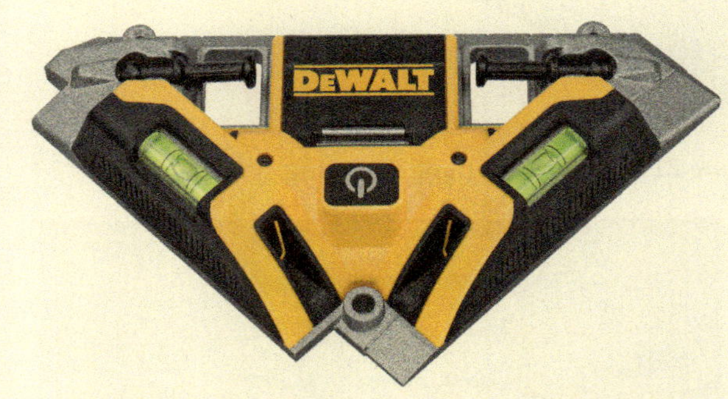

Squaring Laser

Laser squares are available to make quick work of ensuring splicing cuts are precisely square to the belt centerline. It is especially handy when working with belts that are wider than an average framing square. When many splices must be crafted, it can save a significant amount of time while also ensuring accuracy.

Figure Credit: Courtesy of DEWALT Industrial Tool Co.

Determining the thickness of the belt to be joined may seem simple enough. But it is important to remember that the thickness of the belt engaged by the fasteners is what counts. And not every mechanical splice is created on the full thickness of the belt.

Belts may require **skiving** before being joined. Skiving refers to the removal of one or more layers of the belt where the fasteners are installed (*Figure 22*). Skiving must often be done to lower the profile of the splice, making it flush with the belt surface. This prevents snagging of the fasteners by scrapers, also referred to as *cleaners*, that remove carryback. Skiving is usually required for vulcanized splices as well.

If skiving is applied, then it is the remaining thickness of the belt that is important when selecting an appropriate fastening system. Skiving is often recommended by fastener manufacturers unless the outer cover is worn or in poor condition. The fastener manufacturer provides precise dimensions for width and depth of the skive cut.

Another factor in selecting a fastening system is the tension rating of the belt. Belt materials are rated for tension in either pounds per inch of width (PIW) or kilonewtons per meter (kN/m). The metric value is an indicator of the overall strength for a given product. Multiply a belt's PIW by its width, in inches, to gauge its overall strength.

When selecting a mechanical splicing system, make sure the tension ratings of the belt and the fasteners are complimentary. They don't need to be the same, but the maximum rating of the fastening system must be equal to or higher than the rating of the belt to be safe.

Cutting and Skiving Belt Material

When a belt is cut prior to splicing, it must be cut square to the centerline of the belt. Marking a cut line by using a framing square against the side of the belt may not produce a square cut. There is no guarantee that the sides are true.

There are several methods to create a square cutting line. An average centerline can be created as shown in *Figure 23*. The cut line can then be drawn using a square or T-square, using the centerline as a reference. In the example shown, a centerline roughly 4' (1.2 m) long has been created.

The approach shown in *Figure 23* doesn't work well if one side of the belt is worn or has been damaged. In this case, work only from a factory edge to make measurements and plot a "centerline." Note that this doesn't necessarily create a true centerline, as the line may not be precisely in the center. But it does create a line near the center that is parallel to the factory (undamaged) edge. It can be used to create a perpendicular cut line.

(A)

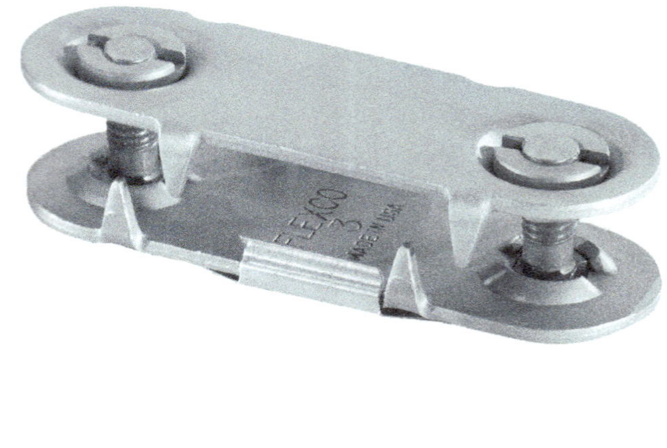

(B)

Figure 21 Bolted solid-plate fastening system.

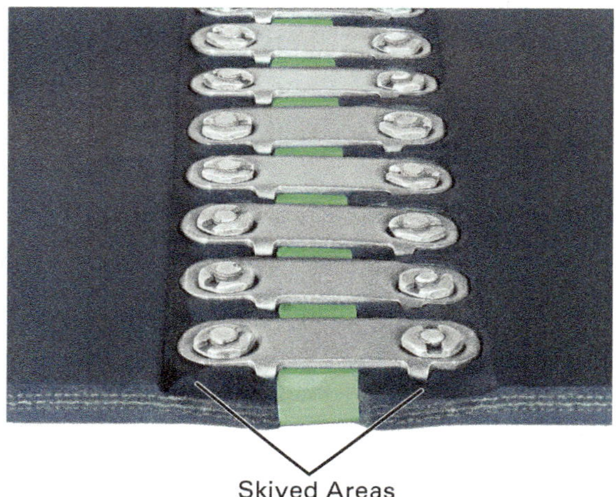

Figure 22 Skived conveyor belt.

Belt manufacturers offer detailed guidance for creating square cutting lines on their products. It is always best to review and follow the belt manufacturer's instructions to ensure good performance and preserve the warranty. Using techniques that are not approved by the manufacturer can result in sizable losses if the belt or splice fails.

Skiving a belt the old-fashioned way, with hand knives, is time-consuming and requires a significant amount of practice. It is essential that the fabric layers are not cut or damaged in the process. This requires a steady hand and a sharp knife. A tool specifically designed for skiving belts is a much safer and faster approach.

A belt skiving tool is shown in *Figure 24*. The tool must be adjusted to ensure it cuts to the proper width and depth. The depth required is dependent upon the fastener being used.

Remember that skiving a belt to accommodate splice fasteners involves only the top cover of the belt. The fabric layer beneath it must not be disturbed. As a precaution, the cover should not be cut to its full depth. Always leave at least $\frac{1}{16}$" (~2 mm) layer of cover, or more, to protect the fabric beneath (*Figure 25*).

Using the tool shown in *Figure 24* involves adjusting the tool for the depth and width of the cut. The ratchet is then used to advance the tool across the belt, removing the cover in a single pass. When a lot of skiving needs to be done, the ratchet can be replaced with a cordless power tool and a special drive linkage (*Figure 26*).

It's clear that there is a lot to know about splicing conveyor belts. Belt products and fastening systems vary widely. It is essential to follow the belt manufacturer's guidance, as well as the instructions provided for the fastening system. While using vulcanizing equipment requires task-specific training, the application of mechanical fastening systems can be learned much more quickly.

No generic splicing procedure can be considered an accurate representation of the steps required. However, splicing a belt using mechanical fasteners generally requires the following basic steps:

Step 1 Identify the belt material and acquire the necessary instructions for splicing the material.

Step 2 Identify and acquire the appropriate replacement belt, splice fasteners, related hardware, and tools.

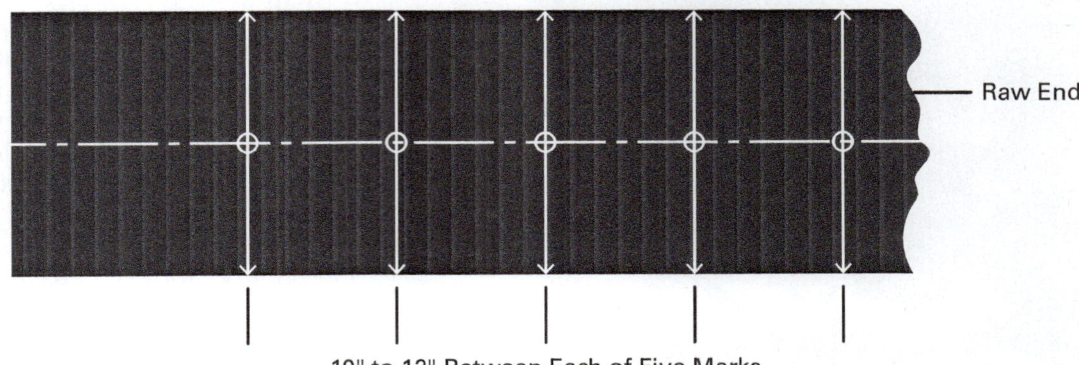

Figure 23 Creating an average centerline on a belt.

Step 3 Shut down the conveyor system, apply the appropriate LOTO procedures, and clamp the belt in place on both sides of the area to be spliced. The belt clamps should be positioned well outside of the work area, so they do not interfere with the work.

WARNING!

Failure to properly lock out the conveyor system and clamp the belt in position can lead to serious personal injury and equipment damage.

Step 4 Adjust the conveyor take-up mechanism(s) to release all tension on the belt.

Step 5 Obtain a sheet of plywood wide enough to place under the belt to be spliced. Carefully slide the plywood under the area of the first cut. Adjust the plywood so that it is squarely positioned under the belt, then secure it to the belt. Clamps or duct tape are both acceptable methods.

Step 6 Determine how much of the existing belt must be removed. If there are existing splices adjacent to the area, it is best to incorporate them into the repair as well, rather than have multiple splices adjacent to each other.

Step 7 Mark and cut the conveyor belt at the required angle. Reposition the plywood as necessary and make the second cut to remove the damaged section.

Step 8 Determine how much new material is needed to cover the damaged area. Use the following formula unless directed otherwise:

New material cut length = removed section length + (splice length × 2) + 4" minimum trim allowance

Step 9 Measure, mark, and cut the new belt material.

Step 10 Splice the new material to the existing belt ends, using vendor-specified procedures. Trim off the end of the new material as necessary before making the final splice.

Step 11 Remove the plywood from under the belt.

Step 12 Carefully remove the belt clamps and adjust the take-up mechanism(s) to reapply tension. Ensure an equal amount of tension is applied to each side of the belt so that it will track correctly. Some adjustments will likely be necessary after observing the conveyor in operation.

Step 13 Reinstall any safety guards removed and make sure that the conveyor area is clear of all tools and unnecessary equipment.

Step 14 Remove the locks and tags from the power sources and start the conveyor.

Step 15 Monitor the conveyor for several belt revolutions to ensure the conveyor belt tracks properly. Then place a normal load on the belt to ensure it moves properly without slipping on the rollers.

Figure 24 Belt skiving tool.

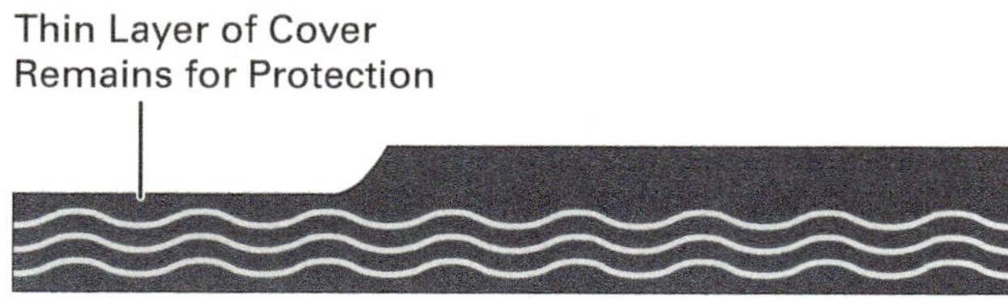

Figure 25 A skive cut should always leave a thin layer of the cover over the fabric.

Figure 26 Skive cutter powered by a cordless power tool.

1.2.5 *Replacing Conveyor Belts*

The method for replacing a conveyor belt is determined primarily by the length of the belt and the complexity of the conveyor. On small, simple conveyors, a factory replacement belt may already be formed into a complete loop when it is received. In this case, one or more rollers may need to be removed to install the new belt. Once the rollers are reinstalled, align the belt and adjust the tension using the take-ups.

Larger and longer belts are more difficult to remove and replace than smaller belts. Conveyors can have belts that are hundreds of feet long. These belts are very heavy and often require extra support from additional return rollers. The extra components needed for belt control add to the challenge of replacing large belts.

Conveyor belts are usually received on rolls. *Figure 27* shows the core of a large roll of conveyor belting. Large rolls are usually wound on a core with a square opening on each end. A shaft with a square profile is inserted, and the roll can then be placed on a rack or suspended from a hoist. Very large conveyors require multiple rolls of belting for a complete replacement.

A roll of new belt material is typically placed near the tail roller, as shown in *Figure 28*. A temporary splice is made to join the old and new belt. Some type of pulling device may be needed to pull the old belt out and the new belt in. After the old belt has been removed, the ends of the new belt are spliced and aligned on the rollers.

Rolls of conveyor belting are rolled at the factory with the load-carrying side of the belt on top (exposed). During installation, the belt's position determines whether the roll is positioned to feed off the top or the bottom. It must feed from the top when being pulled onto troughing rollers, and feed from the bottom if it is being fed onto return idlers. In *Figure 28*, the belt is being properly fed from the top. A braking arrangement is often needed to prevent the belt reel from continuing to feed off belt when the pulling stops.

1.3.0 Conveyor Belt Tracking

Belt tracking is an issue that can keep millwrights and industrial mechanics busy. Some belt conveyors require constant attention to it. Belts that run off-center, commonly referred to as *wandering*, can contact the structure along the sides. This causes excessive belt wear and damage along its edges. The belt can also cause wear and damage to metal components along the edges, due to the constant friction. Of course, the belt gets the worst of it, but the problem takes its toll throughout the system.

Figure 27 Conveyor belt core for suspended storage and handling.

The belt can also be caught by a roller bracket or other component and bring everything to a grinding halt. Making the necessary adjustments so that a belt consistently runs along the center of its bed is referred to as *training a belt*.

Another problem that results from poor belt tracking is product spillage. This is especially true when the product is sand, rock, or similar materials. Not only does it defeat the purpose of moving the product to a destination, but fugitive material represents a serious hazard in conveyor systems that move large volumes of bulk materials. Falling material can cause injuries and damage moving parts.

As noted earlier, tail rollers are generally equipped with take-ups that provide for tension adjustment and roller alignment. All too often, adjusting the tail roller take-ups to correct a tracking problem is the default solution. In reality, it's the last thing you should do to correct a tracking problem! It is one possible solution, but only turn to it after other possible causes have been eliminated or resolved.

1.3.1 Equipment Problems That Affect Belt Tracking

There are several equipment-related causes for conveyor belt wandering and tracking problems. Equipment-related factors include the following:

- Belt curvature
- Belt cupping
- Damaged or out-of-square belt splice
- Conveyor structure that is bent, twisted, or misaligned
- Misaligned or damaged return, idler, and snubber rollers

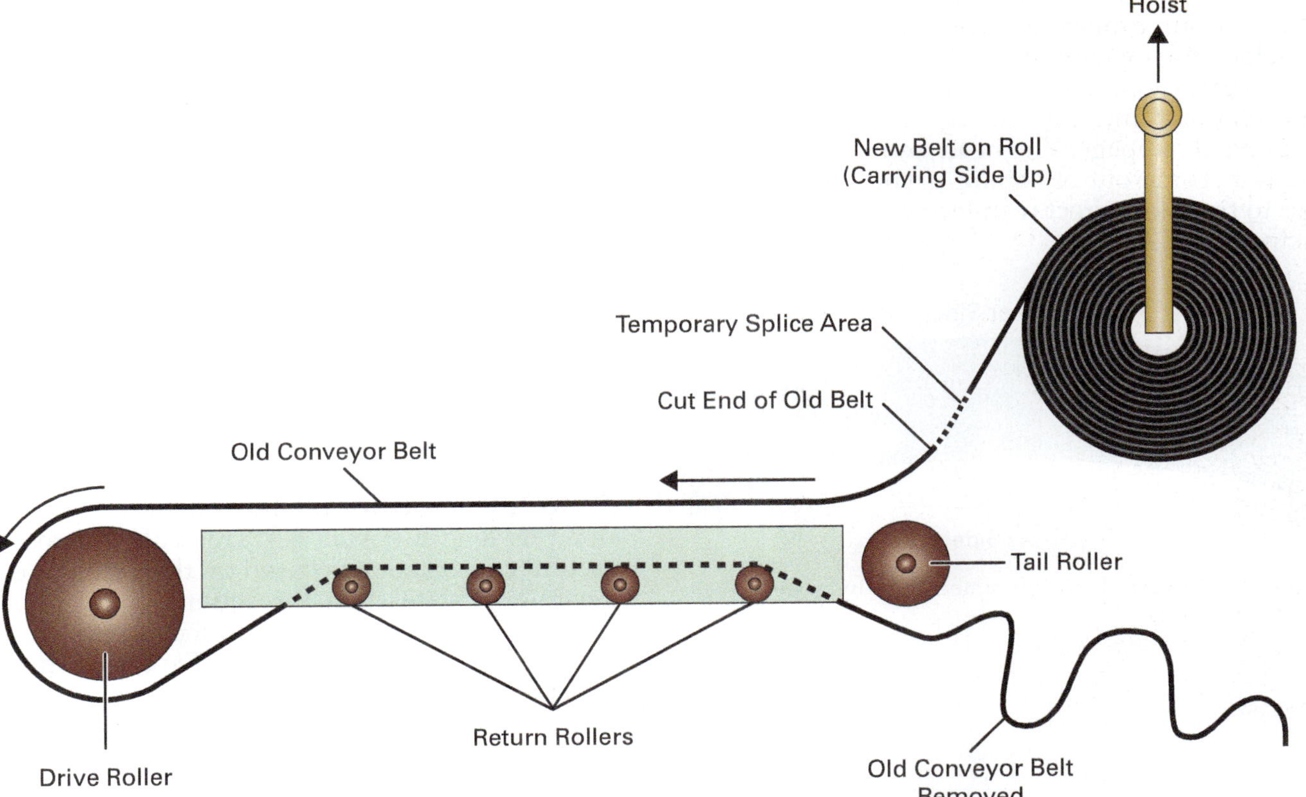

Figure 28 Replacing a conveyor belt from a roll.

Belt wandering isn't necessarily the result of a single problem. In many cases, more than one of these potential causes is present. Each cause must be evaluated and considered on its own before a complete solution can be developed.

Belt Curvature

Belt curvature is often the result of improper storage. Curvature is the result of one side of the belt becoming longer than the other. A belt like the one shown in *Figure 29* is said to have *camber*.

Conveyor belt material can be very heavy, and gravity has a significant effect. Storing a roll on the floor may not hurt a belt for a week or so, but months and certainly years will cause damage. Curvature develops when the belt is stored on its end. Heavier materials develop flaws sooner and to a greater degree. A curved belt will be very difficult, if not impossible, to train.

If a roll of belting can't be suspended by its core, and it must be stored on the floor, do not store it on its end. Place the roll on a dry surface and rotate it 90 degrees every 90 days, rolling it in the same direction as it was wound on the reel. Always limit its exposure to sunlight. The ideal temperature range for belt storage is 40°F to 90°F (4°C to 32°C).

Excessive tension coupled with head and tail roller misalignment can also cause curvature to develop during operation. This is best avoided by ensuring the head and tail rollers are square to each other and only enough tension is present to prevent slippage. The head and tail rollers can easily become out of square if you use the take-ups to try and correct wandering caused by other factors.

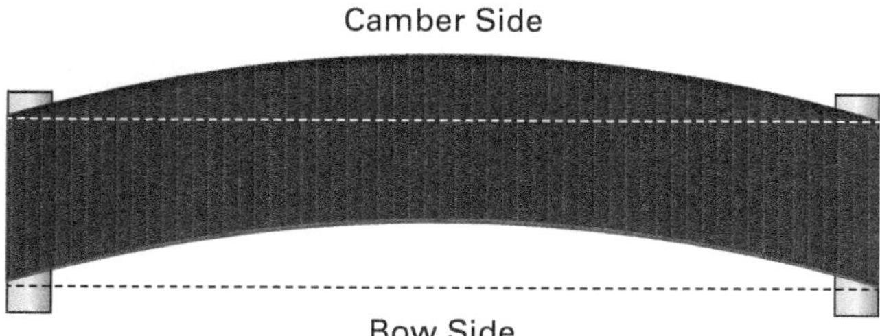

Figure 29 Conveyor belt with camber from improper storage.

Belt Cupping

Belt cupping refers to a condition that results in the belt forming an undesirable trough. Many belts, such as those carrying bulk material like soil or peanuts, are forced to form a trough to keep the materials away from the edge (*Figure 30*). Belts that normally operate flat may cup as well. Cupping is often caused by excessive tension, excessive heat, or chemical attacks.

Cupping can create tracking problems as the belt returns beneath the conveyor structure. The return idlers should make consistent contact across the surface of the idler rollers that support it and guide its return. As shown in *Figure 31*, cupping prevents proper contact. When there is inconsistent contact between the belt and the return rollers, the belt is encouraged to wander. In addition, both the belt and roller experience more wear in the few areas of contact.

Damaged or Out-of-Square Belt Splice

A belt splice that is separating or not square to the belt centerline can cause significant wandering. Applying more tension to one side with the take-ups may seem to help, but this causes more problems over time.

When a belt is cut for splicing, it must be cut square to its centerline. Create a centerline as described previously in this module, working from both sides if the edges are in factory condition. If one edge is damaged, work exclusively from the undamaged edge to create a line near the center that is parallel to the reliable edge.

Conveyor Structure Bent, Twisted, or Misaligned

The conveyor structure must be square in all planes. Assuming that it is not designed for a specific incline, it must also be level from end to end. The structural assemblies at each end that support the head and tail rollers can sag if not properly mounted.

In some cases, you can use the 3-4-5 rule to ensure the structure of the conveyor is square along its length (*Figure 32*). This rule commonly used in construction is based on the Pythagorean theorem. It states that the square of the hypotenuse (*c*) is equal to the sum of the squares of the remaining two sides (*a* and *b*). Expressed mathematically, the theorem looks like this:

$$c^2 = a^2 + b^2$$

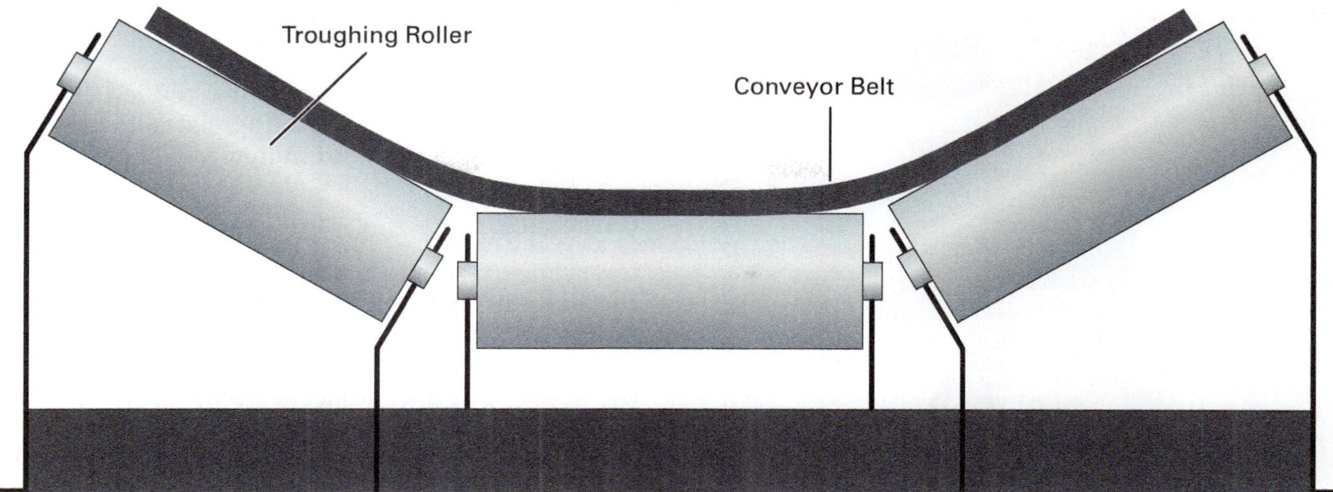

Figure 30 Proper fit of a conveyor belt in troughing rollers.

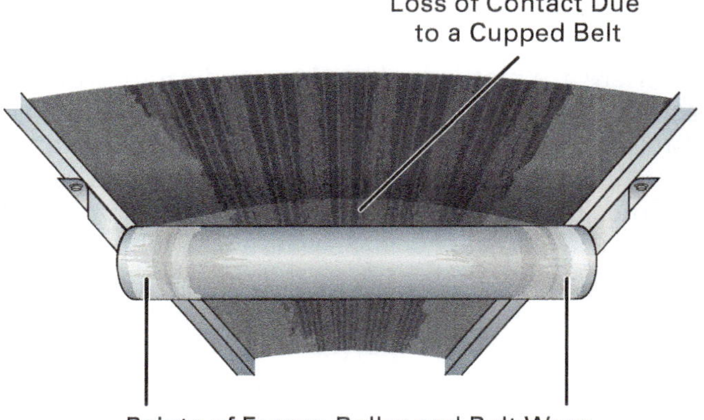

Figure 31 Cupping often results in inconsistent contact with idler rollers.

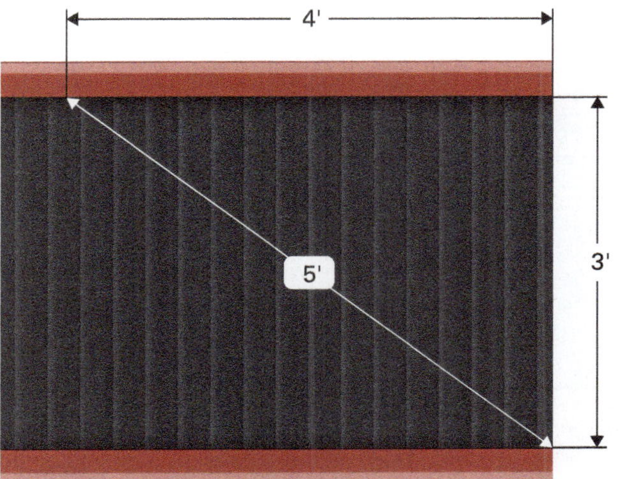

Figure 32 Using the 3-4-5 rule to ensure the sides of a conveyor are square.

The numbers 3, 4, and 5 fit this relationship, since the sum of the squares of 3 and 4 equals the square of 5:

$$5^2 = 3^2 + 4^2$$
$$25 = 9 + 16$$

If the number group 3-4-5 is used, measure and mark the 3' and 4' points. If the diagonal measurement between the points is exactly 5', that section of the conveyor is square. On a long, narrow conveyor, checking to ensure the structure is square using this method is of limited value. But the rule can be applied at multiple points along the conveyor length.

Other number groups that fit the rule include 9-12-15 and 12-16-20. Adjust the numbers as needed to fit the width of the structure, as long as they fit the rule.

Use accurate levels to ensure the structure is level (or inclined to the specified angle). Optical devices such as optical levels (*Figure 33*) and transits offer excellent accuracy for larger and longer conveyor systems. Since some mining conveyors travel great distances, those instruments are a necessity when aligning the frame and rollers.

Misaligned or Damaged Rollers

Every component that contacts the belt affects tracking to some degree. Most components on a conveyor that contact the belt by design are rollers.

Figure 33 Optical level.

Belt tracking is affected by both the drive and tail rollers as well as all the idler and snub rollers it encounters. If any of them are not square to the belt path and parallel to the others, the belt will want to wander offtrack. When the drive and tail roller are not parallel, for example, the belt wanders toward the side with the lesser tension—the side with the shortest distance between the two rollers' axes (*Figure 34*). Troughing rollers must all be set to the same angle to prevent one roller from influencing the belt path more than another (*Figure 35*).

All rollers designed to be in the same plane must be aligned with each other. An optical or laser level is a good choice to ensure a series of rollers are properly aligned with each other. Idlers and training rollers may also be out of position to one side or the other, allowing the belt to move sideways. These conditions must be corrected and monitored by allowing the belt to run empty for several turns before loading it with product.

It is also very important to ensure each roller rotates freely and is kept clean. Even when properly aligned, a roller that isn't rotating freely produces friction against the belt, influencing its path and increasing the load on the drive motor.

1.3.2 Operational Problems That Affect Belt Tracking

Not all tracking problems are caused by the equipment. Some problems are related to how the conveyor is operated and managed.

Carryback

Carryback refers to material remaining stuck to the belt surface. This is far more likely to happen with moist or wet material. As carryback develops, additional material will likely stick to the same spot and adjacent areas. Since the top of the belt becomes the bottom of the belt after it passes over the tail roller, the carryback rolls over the return rollers and idlers. It may then be deposited on them, or simply pass on by. Either way, belt tracking can be affected, and the belt can be damaged. At a minimum, carryback makes a mess under the conveyor and becomes fugitive material.

There are many devices designed exclusively to scrape carryback from conveyor belts. Depending on the application, pre-cleaner, secondary, and even tertiary cleaning devices may be positioned at and beyond the discharge pulley (typically the tail roller). *Figure 36* shows a pre-cleaner with a segmented carbide blade. Polyurethane and carbide-tipped blades are the most common devices used to scrape material off the belt. A solid polyurethane pre-cleaner blade is shown in *Figure 37*. Cleaner designs may feature solid or segmented blades, depending on the application and belt condition. Conveyor manufacturers and engineers can help determine the best approach for a given product and belt design.

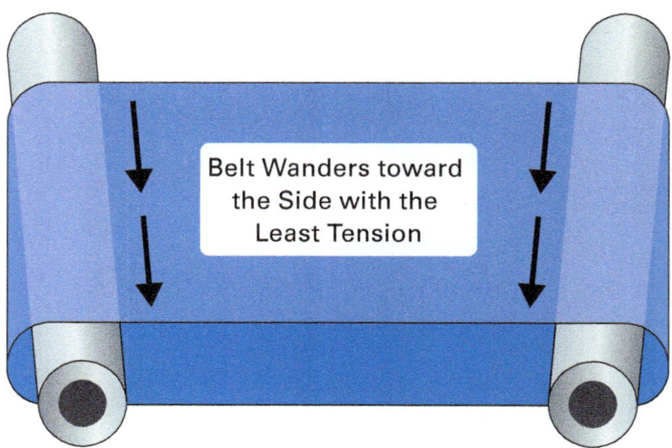

Figure 34 Drive and tail rollers that are not parallel cause the belt to wander.

NCCER – *Millwright*

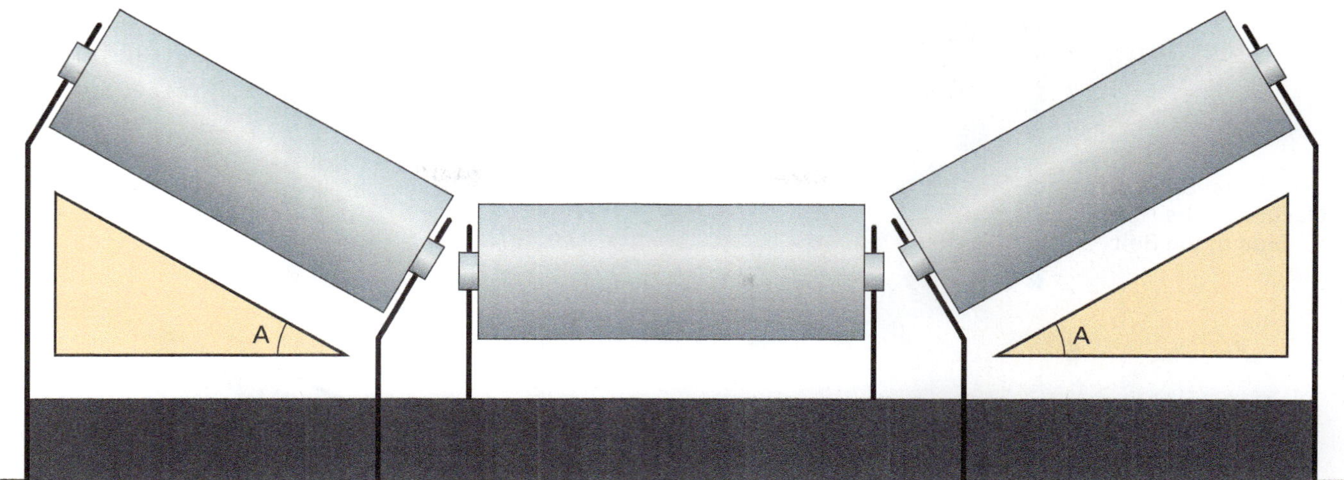

Figure 35 Set all troughing rollers to the specified angle.

Figure 36 Segmented carbide pre-cleaner blade.

Figure 37 Solid polyurethane pre-cleaner blade.

Once installed, scraping devices must be inspected periodically. They must be set relatively close to the belt to be effective. However, a raised splice or other anomaly in the belt can cause it to snag on the scraper, causing serious belt damage and possibly shutting down the entire system.

Belt Loading

Materials to be conveyed must be deposited on the belt at some point. Loading lightweight materials on a belt, such as pasta or potato chips, is not much of a problem, no matter how they are dispersed. There is not enough mass involved to create a problem. However, bulky materials, such as rock, that strike the belt off-center or are poorly dispersed create uneven loading.

Refer to *Figure 38*, which shows how uneven loading affects the belt. While troughing rollers help to keep bulk material on the belt and encourage it toward the center, heavier material that is deposited off-center won't move toward the center immediately. As the material progresses down the line, vibration along with the troughing rollers often improves the situation. But at the point where the material lands and for some distance forward, the belt is encouraged to run offtrack, away from the heavy side. Material spillage on the heavy side may also occur as the belt wanders away.

Uneven belt loading is seldom a problem that can be addressed through adjustments to the conveyor itself. Changes must be made in the chute position or design for the product to land on the belt properly and in a manageable volume.

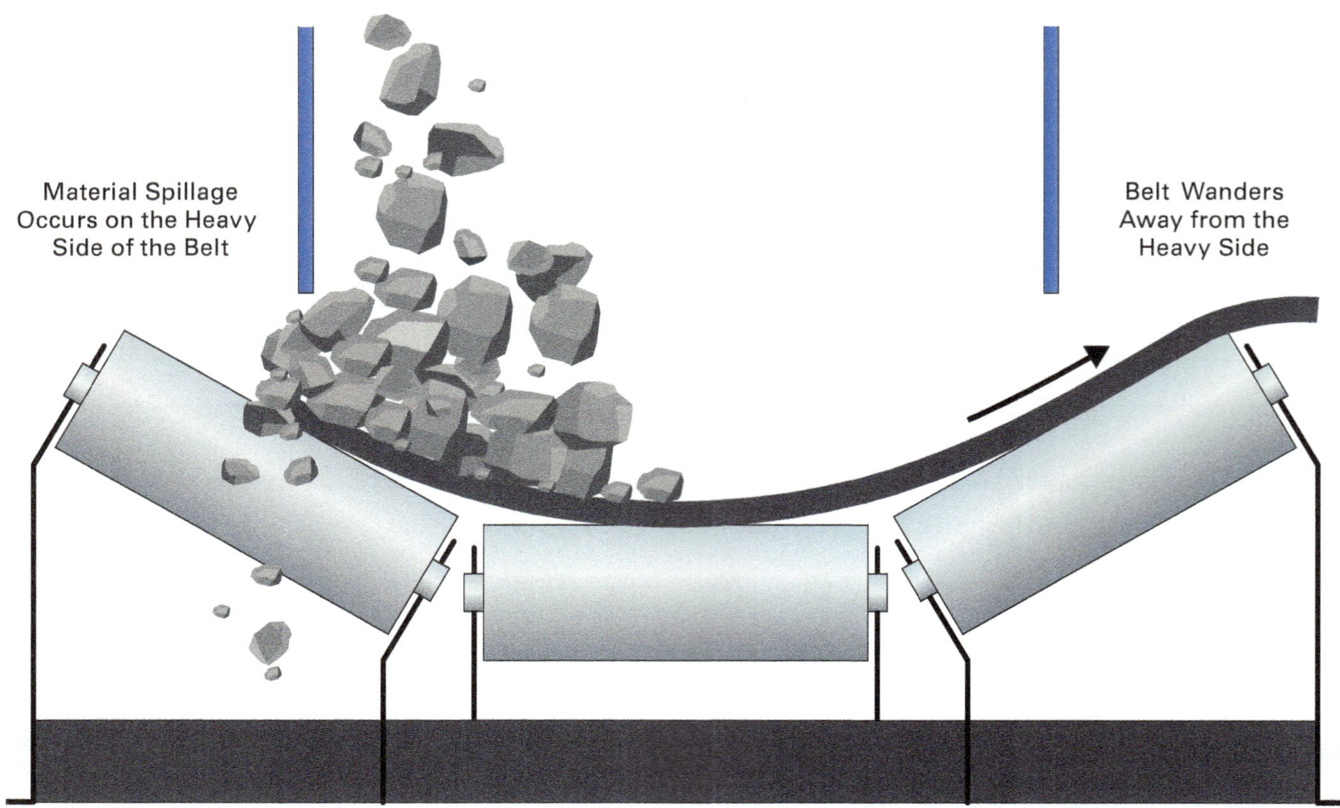

Figure 38 Uneven belt loading causes the belt to move offtrack.

1.4.0 Maintaining and Repairing Chain Conveyors

Chain conveyors are similar to belt conveyors in that they are driven by a power source external to the conveyor and have sprockets, bearings, and take-ups. One major difference, though, is that while a conveyor belt is moved by the friction developed between the belt and a drive roller, the chain conveyor is moved by the teeth of a drive sprocket pulling the chain. This represents a more positive, consistent mechanical force.

While belt conveyors normally carry materials on the top surface of the conveyor, chain conveyors can carry materials above, beside, or below the conveyor. Chain conveyors are extremely versatile, allowing them to move product along a path that rivals the most elaborate roller coasters (*Figure 39*).

One advantage that chain conveyors have over most belt conveyors is the ability to withstand extreme heat and constant temperature changes. Although some belt materials and metal belts can handle relatively high temperatures and may be used for baking foods, chain conveyors are typically used for industrial painting applications, where the paint must be baked on the components. The components can be suspended from the chain to apply paint, in powder or aerosol form, then guided through the oven at a speed that ensures the baking and curing process is complete before they exit (*Figure 40*).

Chain conveyors with a single chain are often used to move suspended product. They may also have buckets attached to the chain, allowing them to carry grains or batches of small components up or down an incline. Others are designed with two or more chains running parallel to each other (*Figure 41*). Most of these conveyors carry the load on the upper surface, with the chain supported along its length by wear strips made from various types of plastics (*Figure 42*). A wide variety of attachments can be fitted to single-chain and multichain conveyors to hold unique components (*Figure 43*).

The key components of a chain conveyor are the chains, carrying devices, sprockets, shafts, bearings, and take-up devices. *Figure 44* shows the main components of a two-chain conveyor drive. You may also find the drive positioned between the chains with a shaft extending in each direction, eliminating the drive sprocket and chain.

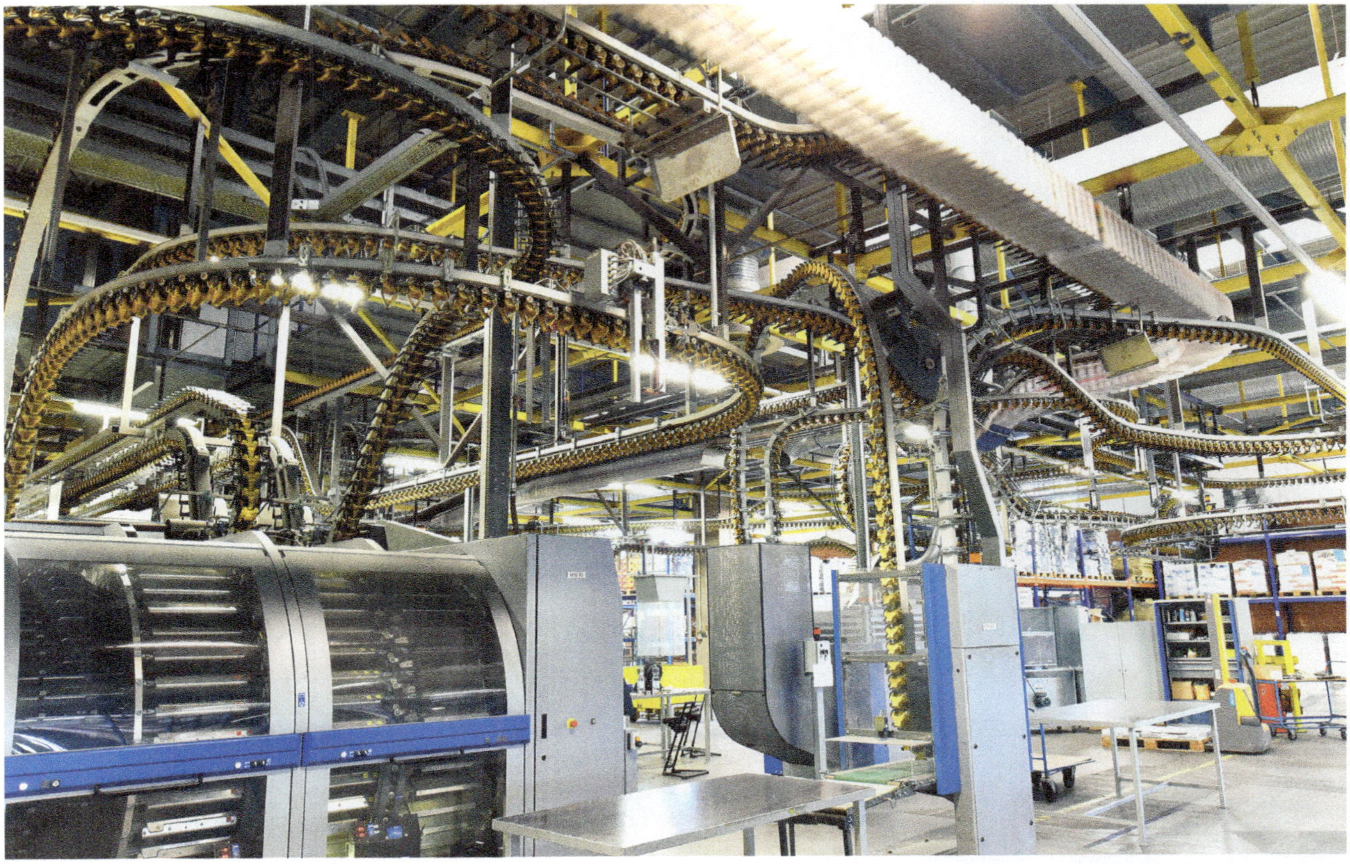

Figure 39 A chain conveyor with a complex path, serving a printing plant.

Figure 40 Parts being routed through a paint oven.

1.4.1 Chain Conveyor Maintenance

The PM required for chain conveyors is much like that required for belt and roller conveyors. Like all conveyors, their design and application vary widely. Each conveyor has its own unique maintenance requirements. General maintenance requirements are discussed in the sections that follow.

Figure 41 Multichain conveyor.

Daily Maintenance

The conveyor chain should be visually inspected daily or, in some cases, at the beginning of each shift. You can safely watch the links go by or shut down and lockout the conveyor for a better look. Listen as well as look for flaws.

Stop the conveyor as needed to remove debris caught in the links or between the chain and wear strips. Lubricate any component that needs daily lubrication. Applying lubricants on the right schedule is the most important thing you can do to ensure the reliability of a chain conveyor.

Figure 42 Conveyor chain wear strips.

Figure 43 Chain conveyors can be adapted to carry unique loads.

Weekly Maintenance

The chains and drive components should be given a closer inspection on a weekly basis. Beyond removing debris, deeper cleaning may also be needed. Apply lubricants as recommended by the conveyor manufacturer and demanded by the application and environment. Oil and grease are not always the answer since both attract dirt and grit.

Since conveyor chain, like roller chain, elongates over time, keep an eye on chain tension. Too much slack usually indicates that it's time to adjust the take-ups. Conveyor performance suffers when the tension is incorrect, whether it is too loose or too tight. Excessive tension increases wear and the rate of elongation. A loose chain also tends to vibrate more, resulting in increased wear.

Remember that the maximum elongation for roller chain is generally 3 percent of its length. Generally, for conveyor chain, elongation is limited to 2 percent. Consider that a section of roller chain on a common drive arrangement may be around 36" (~91 cm) long. If it elongates by 3 percent, its length grows by roughly 1.1" (~28 mm). The motor mount can generally be adjusted to accommodate that.

But a conveyor chain can easily be 100' (~30 m) long. A 3 percent elongation results in the chain increasing in length by 3' (~1 m). Take-ups don't have enough range to accommodate this. Therefore, as the chain elongates, one or more links must be removed to keep the length within the adjustment range of the take-ups.

Chain tends to elongate faster when it is new. Elongation slows down as the chain breaks in. The following schedule for adjusting the tension of new chain is common for conveyors operating eight hours per day. If it runs around the clock, then the schedule would be accelerated by a factor of three:

- During the first week, check and adjust the tension daily.
- During the second through fourth week, check and adjust the tension twice per week.
- For the rest of its service life, check and adjust the tension every two weeks.

When adjusting the tension with take-ups, be sure to adjust them incrementally and alternate from one side to another, just as you do with belt take-ups.

Quarterly Maintenance

More significant maintenance occurs on a quarterly basis. The conveyor should be shut down and locked out long enough for some additional maintenance tasks. The chain should be measured to determine how much elongation has occurred and what steps need to be taken to plan for its replacement. If the elongation is still within reason but the take-ups are approaching the end of their adjustment range, remove one or more links to compensate. Also carefully inspect the sprockets for damage and excess wear. Of course, lubrication that suits the conveyor and its application is always a part of the task.

Chain conveyors differ widely in the types of carrying devices applied. Whether they are hooks, drag plates, or buckets, it is not unusual for them to require more maintenance and repair than the chain itself. This is in part caused by the fact that the attachments are the components consistently in contact with the conveyed material. You should always be on the lookout for a chain attachment that doesn't look or move as expected, but they need a closer look during the quarterly maintenance inspection.

Quarterly inspections should also provide an opportunity to closely inspect all drive components. Look for excessive or uneven wear on the sprockets, damaged or bent drive shafts, and loose hardware. Wear strips beneath the chains should be replaced when worn. They serve two important functions: to provide a low-friction surface and isolate the chain from other metal components. PTFE, also known as Teflon®, is a popular material due to its durable, slick surface. Ultra-high-molecular-weight polyethylene (UHMW) is another type of plastic used for this purpose.

Some manufacturers provide wear strips with a thin layer of a contrasting color beneath the upper layer. When the wear strip has reached the end of its service, the color of the bottom layer is revealed.

1.4.2 Conveyor Chain

There are many types of conveyor chain. While most chain products in the United States are built to American National Standard Institute (ANSI) standards, many more are unique, nonstandard products. Most products are assembled in a similar fashion—by inserting a pin through two links, then securing the pin with a clip, cotter pin, or similar hardware. Threaded hardware may also be used to assemble the heaviest chain products.

ANSI-standard chain products have an assigned number for identification. The first one or two digits in the number denote the pitch in $\frac{1}{8}$" increments. For example, #40 chain has a $\frac{4}{8}$" ($\frac{1}{2}$") pitch, while a #120 chain has a $\frac{12}{8}$" ($1\frac{1}{2}$") pitch.

> **NOTE**
>
> ISO-standard chain products are made to metric dimensions and, although built to similar standards, some dimensions differ. As a result, they are not directly interchangeable. For that reason, no metric conversions were offered where chain dimensions are provided. Metric chain and its standard dimensions are covered in greater detail in NCCER Module 15311, *Installing Belt and Chain Drives*.

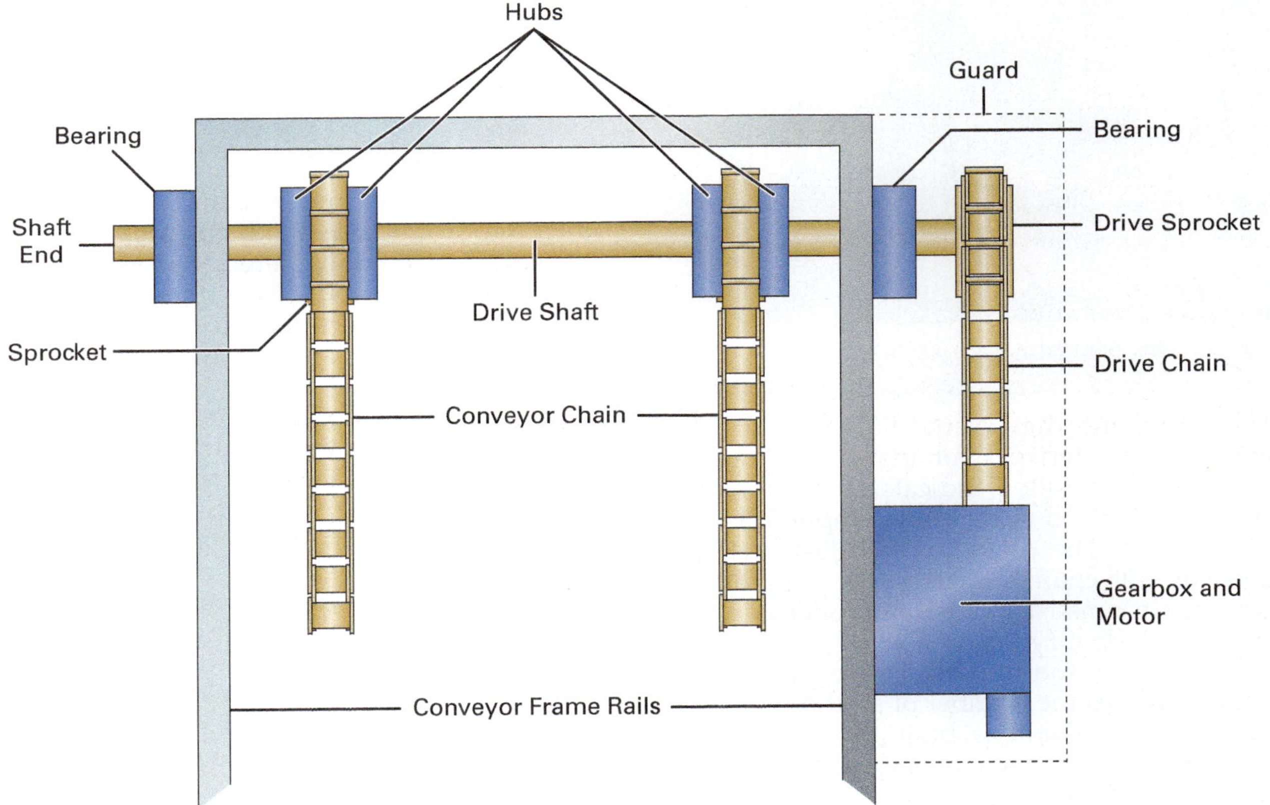

Figure 44 Chain conveyor drive components.

The right-hand digit of the number identifies a specific characteristic. For instance, a zero in the right-hand position indicates that the roller chain is constructed to standard proportions and characteristics. The digit 5 in the last position, e.g., #45 or #125 chain, indicates that it is bushing chain—chain constructed without rollers.

When the identifying number is hyphenated, e.g., #40-3 chain, the number to the right of the hyphen indicates the number of strands. To summarize, a #40-3 chain is built to standardized proportions, has a pitch of $\frac{1}{2}$", and has three strands.

Chain attachments are often required to allow metal belts, modular belt sections, cross ribs, buckets, hooks, and other components to be attached to the chain. *Figure 45* shows several examples of attachments. Note that a number after an identifying letter indicates how many holes are placed in the attachment itself. Some attachments can be connected to roller chain that has hollow pins, eliminating welds and oddly formed side plates. A few standardized attachments are described here:

- K attachments provide a flat mounting platform that parallels the chain. The attachment can be integral (formed from the chain side plate, as shown in *Figure 45*), or welded to a base chain.
- F attachments provide a mounting platform at a right angle to the chain. These attachments are usually welded to a base chain.
- L attachments are formed by lengthening the chain side plate, then bending it and adding holes.
- Spigot pin attachments can be installed through hollow-pin chain openings or welded on center between the pin openings.

The attachments listed here are standardized in the industry, but it is important to understand that there are many possible variations in chain construction. For example, there are at least three unique designs used primarily to engage cotton modules—large cubes of raw, compressed cotton that contain 13–15 standard bales.

Measuring Elongation

Determining how much a chain has elongated is an important task that helps millwrights and industrial mechanics determine when a chain needs to be replaced. Since replacing an entire run of chain can be a time-consuming task that interferes with production, it must be planned accordingly.

One way to determine elongation is by direct measurement and a little math. To prepare for the math, you'll need to measure across 10–12 pitches. You'll recall that pitch is the distance between the pin centers of a chain link (*Figure 46*).

The measurement must be taken accurately. Working with millimeters may be easier and more accurate than working with fractional inches, but the calculation works regardless of what units are chosen. Decimal inches work well enough, but measuring tapes marked in decimal inches are not common on the job.

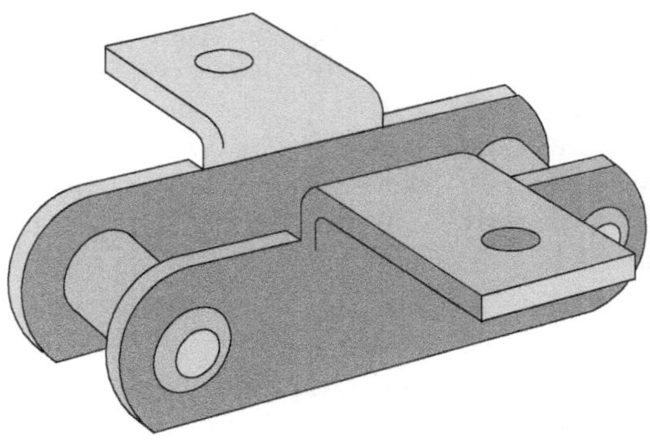

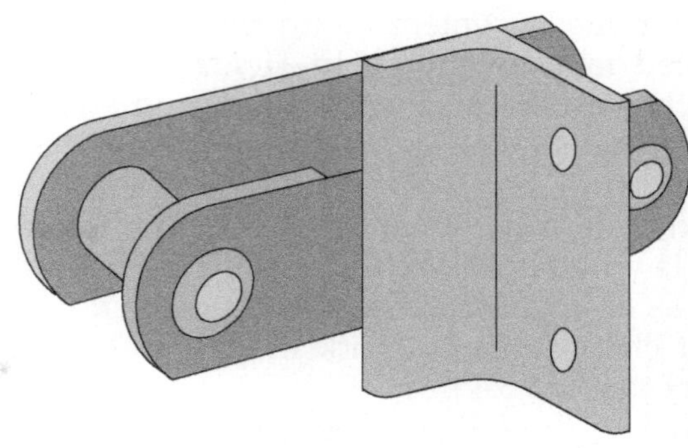

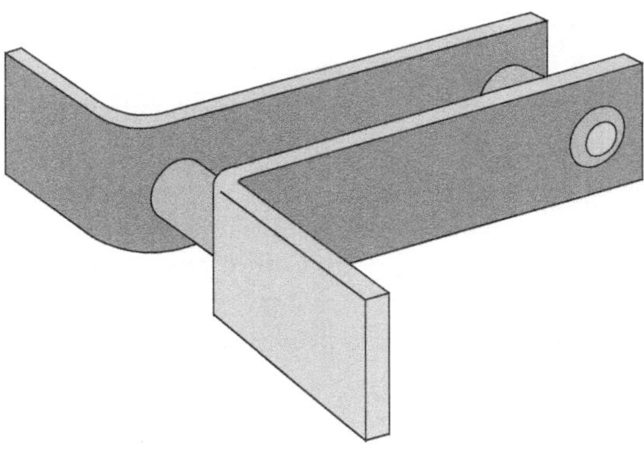

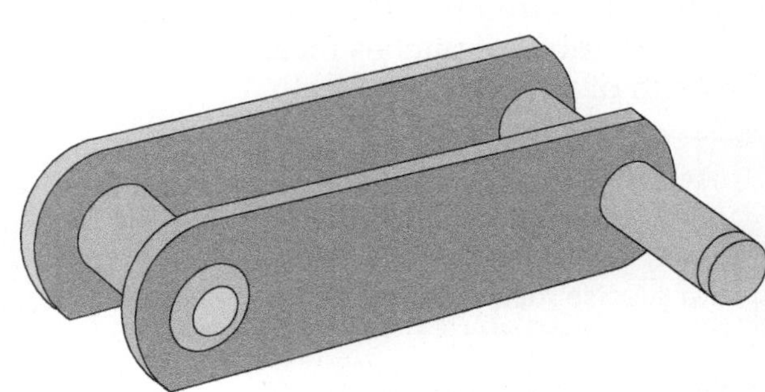

Figure 45 Examples of conveyor chain attachments.

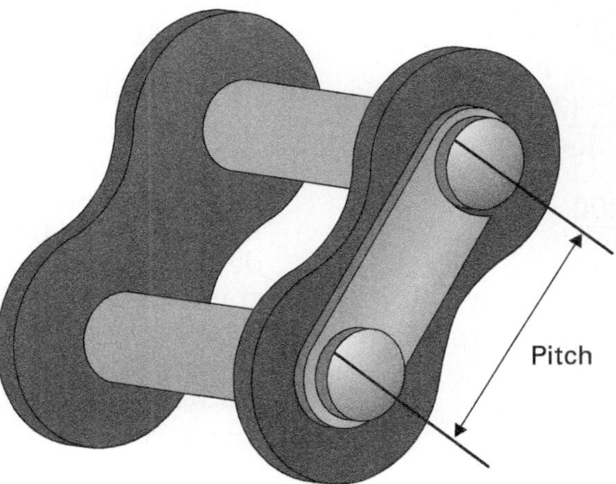

Figure 46 Chain pitch measurement.

Take a measurement along the chain while it is pulled taut, as shown in *Figure 47*. Note that 10 pitches are being measured. Assume that the measurement taken across the 10 pitches is 260 mm.

Next, determine what the specified pitch of the chain is when new. We'll use #80 ANSI-standard chain as an example. The specified pitch for this size of chain is 1". To work in millimeters, we'll convert that to 25.4 mm.

Now use the following equation to determine the elongation, as a percentage:

$$\text{Elongation (\%)} = \frac{[M - (X \times P)] \times 100}{X \times P}$$

Where:
M = the measured length of the pitches (mm)
X = the number of pitches measured
P = pitch of new chain (mm)

Determine the percentage of elongation by inserting the gathered information and completing the math, as follows:

$$\text{Elongation (\%)} =$$

$$\frac{[260 \text{ mm} - (10 \times 25.4 \text{ mm})] \times 100}{100 \times 25.4 \text{ mm}}$$

$$\text{Elongation (\%)} = \frac{[260 \text{ mm} - (254 \text{ mm})] \times 100}{254 \text{ mm}}$$

$$\text{Elongation (\%)} = \frac{6 \text{ mm} \times 100}{254 \text{ mm}}$$

$$\text{Elongation (\%)} = \frac{600 \text{ mm}}{254 \text{ mm}}$$

$$\text{Elongation (\%)} = 2.36\%$$

In this case, the chain is reaching the end of its service life and should be replaced soon. Remember that, if this chain is 100' (~30 m) long, it has stretched 2.36' (~0.7 m). The take-ups would have likely been adjusted a number of times already to maintain tension, and some links would have been removed to accommodate that much elongation.

Chain Assembly and Disassembly

Conveyor chain is often much larger and heavier than standard roller chain used on drives. Smaller sizes can be taken apart like drive chain, using a chain breaker as outlined in NCCER Module 15311, *Installing Belt and Chain Drives*. However, larger sizes may require a different approach. In many cases, it must be done while the chain remains on the conveyor, rather than on a workbench.

To take the chain apart, you'll need to have some slack in the chain. Maybe you are lucky enough that slack exists already where you need to work. But even then, you need to restrain the chain on both sides of the work area. This prevents the chain from retracting away from you once a link is disconnected. This can be done using a chain puller like the one shown in *Figure 48*.

To use the device, place the fixed hook in one link of the chain, then extend the cable out as desired to hook into another link. Turning the crank pulls the chain links toward each other, creating a section of chain with slack. Having a long section of slack chain is an advantage when working on mounted conveyor chain.

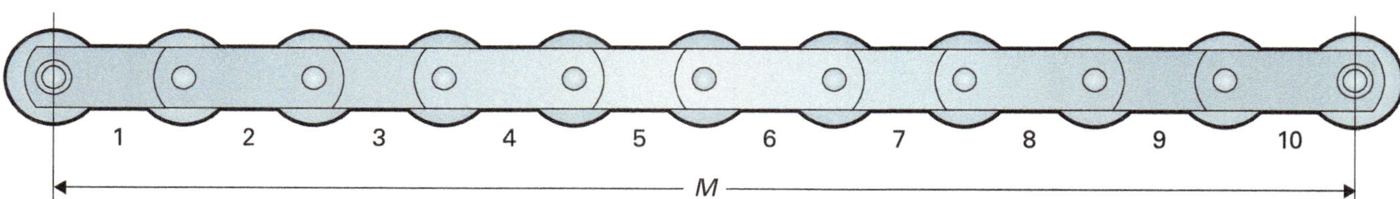

Figure 47 Measuring the length of 10 chain pitches.

Nonstandard?

Many types of drive and conveyor chain products are built to standards developed by ANSI. All manufacturers of ANSI-standard chain agree to make the chain precisely to specification, gaining ANSI certification. This results in products that are largely compatible—one manufacturer's product can be substituted for another.

Although the term *nonstandard* might imply that a chain product is completely unique, that's not usually the case. It simply means that it isn't governed by an ANSI standard. 81X chain, for example, is considered nonstandard, but it is manufactured by a variety of companies to an agreed-upon specification for compatibility.

An alternative to the cable-operated chain puller is a hand-operated ratcheting chain hoist (*Figure 49*). For smaller chain, you can use a simpler tool that only provides slack at a single link (*Figure 50*).

> Common cable-equipped come-alongs are not safe to pull and hold heavy chain. They should not be used for this purpose to avoid possible injury from a sudden release. Ratcheting chain hoists have a superior braking and holding mechanism. The cable-equipped device shown in *Figure 48* is designed specifically for pulling chain and is rated to handle ANSI roller chain sizes #80 through #240.

With the chain under control, you can disassemble a link. The key is removing the pins that connect one link to another. The pins must be secured so they don't work their way out. They are usually secured one of four ways:

- *Riveted links* — In this case, one or both ends of the pins have been mushroomed or pinched to secure them. One end will need to be ground off nearly flush with the side plate. The pin can then be removed with a hammer and punch. If it's not too tight, the pin may be pried loose from the link plate.

- *Pin clips* — Pin clips are also referred to as *circlips*, *retaining rings*, and *snap rings*. Round clips fit on the end of a single pin, but many of those used on chain are elongated and capture both pins at once (*Figure 51*). Be sure to install these pins as shown, relative to the chain's direction of travel. The closed end is oriented toward the direction of travel. If the side of the chain strikes something as it moves, the obstruction will not be able to push the clip off.

- *Cotter pins* — Cotter pins (*Figure 52*) are also commonly used. They are easily removed with pliers by closing the legs together with pliers, then pulling the pin free from the opposite end. When installing new cotter pins, open the legs about 60 degrees.

- *Nuts and bolts* — Heavy chain may be assembled with special threaded, hardened hardware. The link pin is threaded on one end and secured with a nut, like a bolt. The hardware is not the same as standard nuts and bolts.

Once the device retaining a link pin is removed, it may slide out easily. However, it is not unusual to need a hammer and punch to move the pin out. Wear and tear on the chain can add to the difficulty of removal if the pin is deformed in some way. Cutting the pin with an oxyfuel torch or saw may be required. But you must avoid damaging the side plates of a link in the process, or you'll need to remove the link you're working on too.

1.4.3 Chain Conveyor Sprockets

The sprockets on a chain conveyor constantly rub against the chain rollers and experience wear. They may wear faster than the chain. The sprockets are mounted onto bearing-supported shafts. Chain conveyors may have sprockets mounted both inside and outside of the conveyor frame—one outside driving the conveyor sprocket shaft, and one or more between the rails driving the conveyor chains. Others are designed with both the drive motor and sprocket(s) between the rails. More work and downtime are usually required to replace a sprocket mounted between the rails.

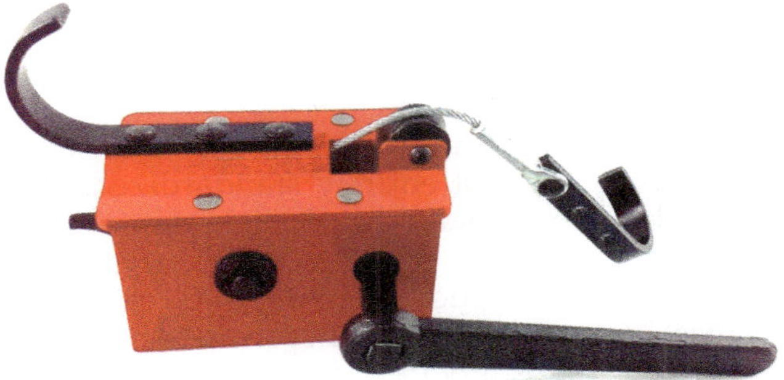

Figure 48 Cable-operated chain puller.

Figure 49 Ratcheting chain hoist.

Figure 50 Chain puller.

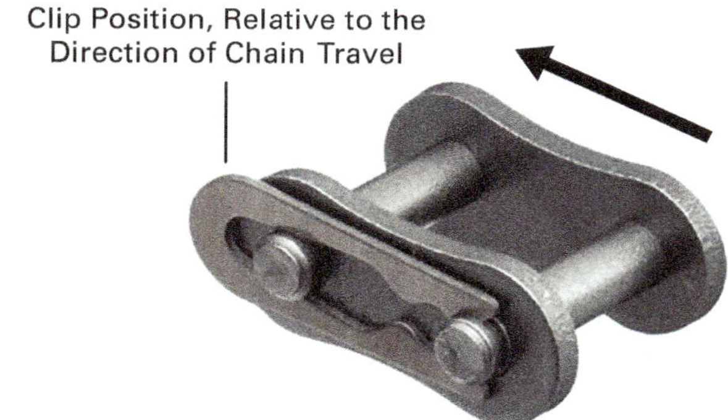

Figure 51 Chain pin clip.

Figure 52 Chain assembly with a cotter pin.

Standard cast iron or steel sprockets are common. But there are also some unique sprockets used on chain conveyors that are not normally seen in power-transmission chain drives. Split sprockets (*Figure 53*) can take a lot of the work out of replacing a sprocket mounted between the conveyor rails. Simply remove the hardware holding them together and separate the two halves.

Another style of conveyor sprocket that makes maintenance and repair easier is the segmented sprocket, also shown in *Figure 53*. The teeth of the sprocket are in three separate segments around the perimeter, each one mounted to the hub with four bolts. The teeth can be replaced without even disturbing the hub on the shaft.

Sprocket shafts do not normally need replacement unless they are bent. However, those that operate in corrosive or other harsh environments may be in poor condition, making it difficult, if not impossible, to remove the sprocket hub from the shaft. In this case, if the sprocket needs to come off, it is often best to replace both the shaft and the sprocket. Shaft stock is relatively inexpensive. The reduced downtime and labor cost usually makes the additional cost of the parts worthwhile.

Measuring Sprocket Wear

Sprockets wear in two common locations: on the drive side of each tooth or along the sides of the teeth. If the sprocket is properly aligned with the chain, the sides should not wear too rapidly. Excess wear on one side is usually a sign that the sprocket is not well aligned. Balanced wear on both sides is considered normal.

The teeth of the sprocket experience significant wear at the point where the chain roller or bushing makes contact—on the flank of each tooth (*Figure 54*).

If the chain tension isn't maintained and it becomes slack, a new wear pattern develops near the top of the tooth (*Figure 55*). This is the result of the chain trying to "jump the teeth," sliding back and up the face of the teeth that are trying to move it forward. Maintaining the proper tension is the cure for this.

Criteria to determine when the sprocket needs to be replaced is not entirely standardized. It is always best to consult the chain manufacturer to determine what is considered excessive wear. One general rule indicates that, if the wear depth reaches 3 mm to 6 mm, the sprocket should be replaced. Perhaps a better way is to compare the wear depth to the width of the sprocket tooth at the point of highest wear, as shown in *Figure 56*. If the depth of the wear exceeds 10 percent of the width, it is time to replace the sprocket.

NCCER – *Millwright*

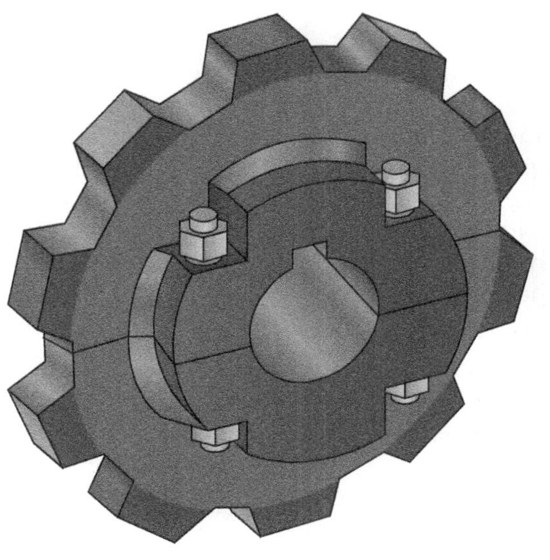

(A) Split Sprocket

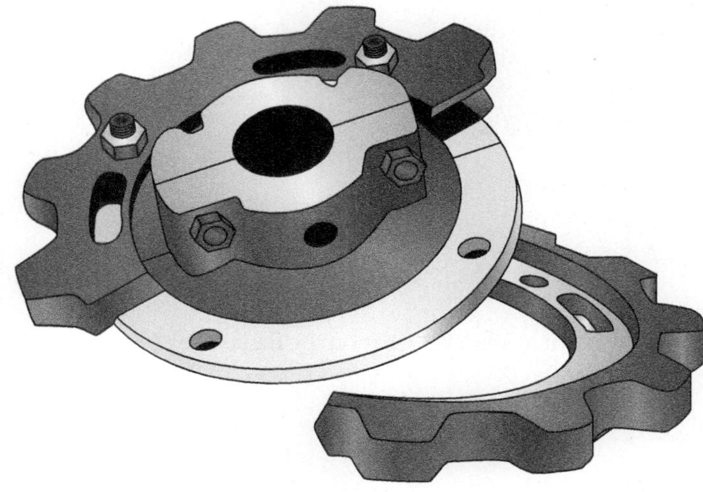

(B) Segmented Sprocket

Figure 53 Split and segmented chain sprockets.

Remember that worn sprockets left in place too long also increase chain wear. Many sprockets are challenging to replace, so they may be ignored until the damage is done. Many facilities consider it a best practice to change the sprockets when the chain is replaced. But as mentioned previously, sprockets may wear faster than the chain.

Significant wear occurs on one flank of the chain teeth. Most manufacturers do allow the sprocket to be reversed though, placing the fresh side of the teeth against the chain. Check with the manufacturer to determine whether that is an option. Reversing the sprocket can nearly double its service life. This can also apply to split and segmented sprockets.

After completing repairs on the chain, sprockets, and other drive components, testing is required. Remember to remove all pins and other safety devices that were used to block the conveyor and reinstall all guards. After the locks and tags are removed, be prepared to stop the conveyor immediately if problems develop. Monitor the operation of the conveyor for multiple revolutions to ensure it operates as expected. Continue to monitor it during scheduled walk-arounds and inspections.

1.5.0 Maintaining and Repairing Screw Conveyors

A basic screw conveyor consists of a drive motor, an auger that turns inside the trough, and the trough itself. *Figure 57* shows the layout of a simple screw conveyor.

Screw conveyors have far fewer moving parts than belt and chain conveyors. In both rigid and flexible screw conveyors, the primary moving parts are the auger, or screw, and its drive. Mechanical maintenance and repair, then, is usually related to those components.

Due to the confined nature of the trough, the conveyor tends to become clogged when the product being moved is too wet or is being pushed through the conveyor too quickly. Clogs and jams are the most common problem with screw conveyors. Although the product may stop moving due to the clog, the drive motor continues turning the auger. The clog may break up and clear on its own. On the other hand, the motor may overload and shut down, or the auger might be damaged. For this reason, a clogged screw conveyor should be attended to immediately.

Augers can be driven by belts, chains, or gearboxes. Direct-drive arrangements are also available but less common. A direct-drive arrangement is more likely when the rotational speed is consistently modulated to support the process.

Screw conveyor maintenance is relatively simple when compared to belt and chain conveyors. Screw conveyors are typically smaller and not as long as other types. The sections that follow present some of the most common inspection points as well as maintenance and repair tasks.

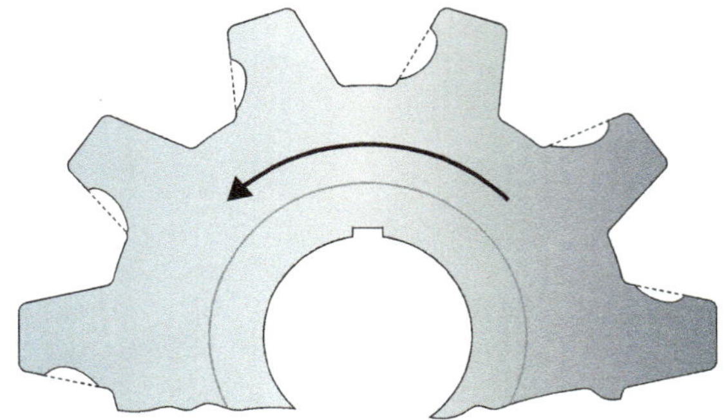

Figure 54 Normal sprocket wear on the flank side of the tooth.

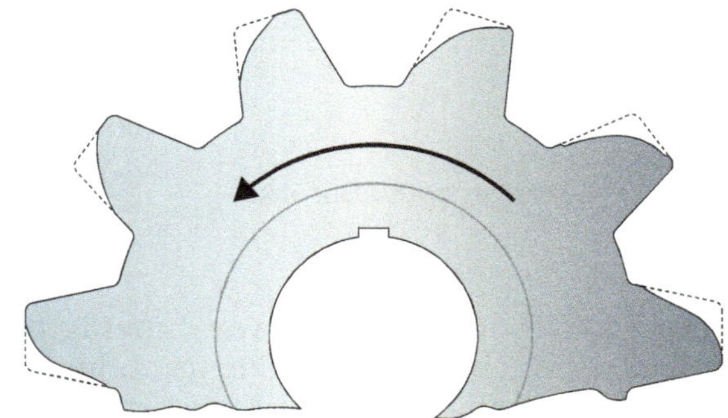

Figure 55 Sprocket wear related to a slack chain.

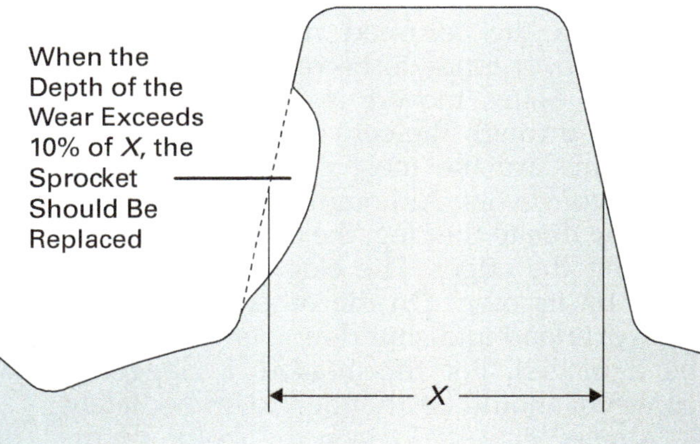

Figure 56 Evaluating sprocket wear.

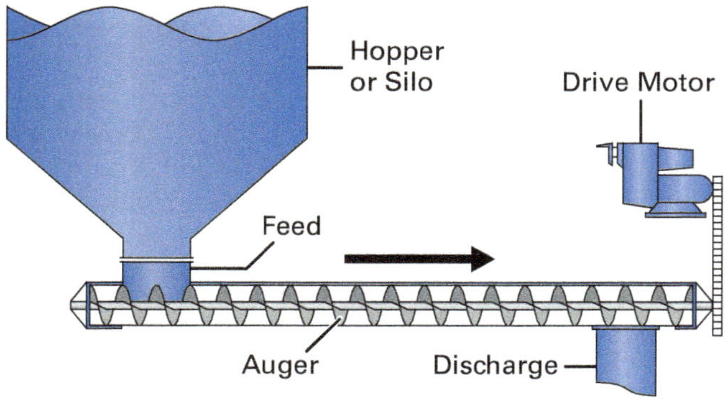

Figure 57 Basic screw conveyor.

1.5.1 Lubrication

Bearings at each end of the auger shaft need proper lubrication. Many augers also have one or more hanger bearings that require lubrication as well (*Figure 58*). If the conveyor is chain-driven, the drive chain also requires periodic lubrication. The lubricant in gearboxes should be checked regularly and changed or topped off as directed by the manufacturer.

> **CAUTION**
>
> Gearboxes are often shipped without lubricant. Before a new conveyor or new gearbox is operated, ensure the correct lubricant has been added.

Be sure to use the oil or grease product recommended for each component. Since screw conveyors are often used in food processing applications, the product may need to be food safe. Different components may also have different lubrication schedules.

1.5.2 Drive Components

As mentioned previously, screw conveyors use a variety of drive arrangements. Service and inspect belts, pulleys, drive chains, and sprockets according to the manufacturer's guidance and NCCER Module 15311, *Installing Belt and Chain Drives*. All bearings need to be inspected to ensure they rotate freely without any significant play. Service and replace bearings per the guidance provided in NCCER Module 15209, *Introduction to Bearings*, and NCCER Module 15306, *Removing and Installing Bearings*.

1.5.3 Augers and Auger Shafts

Abnormal loads and clogs can place a lot of stress on the auger and shafts that pass through the trough end plates. Look for bent shafts and screws. Check the flights of the auger for excessive wear, damage, and adhered material that needs to be removed.

Augers are often shipped in multiple pieces, depending on the length of the conveyor. They are assembled using compatible couplings as shown in *Figure 59*. Ensure any shaft couplings and hardware are not damaged or distorted, indicating they have been overstressed. Coupling bolts typically have a specified torque value. Overtightening them will distort the coupling. A lot of stress can be applied to the bolts as the shaft rotates. It's not uncommon to replace the coupling hardware periodically due to normal wear.

NCCER – *Millwright*

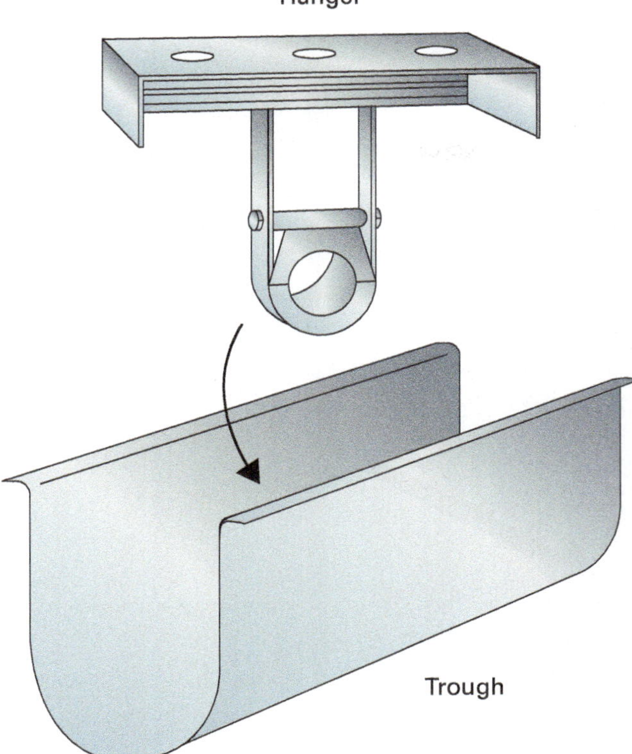

Figure 58 Screw conveyor hanger bearing.

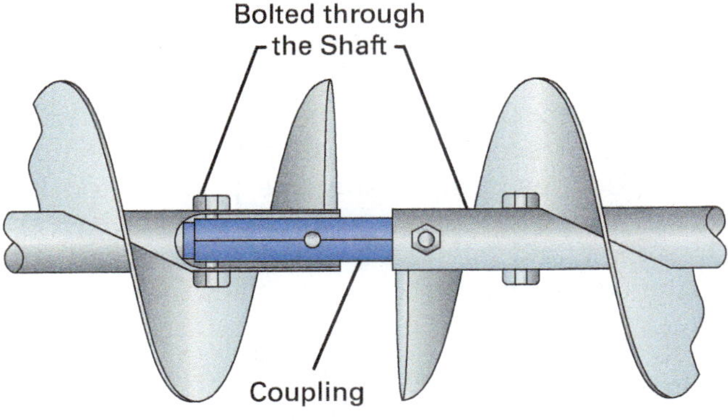

Figure 59 Auger shaft coupling.

The outer edge of the flights is a critical area. The clearance between the flights and the trough is considered carefully in the design phase and varies with the product. As the edges of the flights wear, the clearance to the trough wall increases. This often leads to jams as materials find their way into the wider space. A small change in the clearance can have a surprising impact on performance.

Removal and replacement of an auger, or a section of it, begins at the opposite end from the drive (*Figure 60*). Once the bearing is free of the shaft and the trough end plate is removed, the auger shaft is free to move out and up.

Continue to disassemble the auger couplings and hanger bearings until you reach the section(s) to be replaced.

> **WARNING!**
>
> Before working on a screw conveyor, ensure all sources of energy are locked out and tagged, and any stored energy in the drive is relieved. Removing the drive coupling, belt, or chain before work begins provides an additional measure of protection from unexpected movement.

Once a repaired conveyor has been reassembled, start it up and check the operation of the auger without a load. Once you are satisfied with the results, begin adding the load.

> **WARNING!**
>
> While observing an operating screw conveyor, remain clear of the auger and all other moving parts.

Clearing a Clogged Auger

Screw conveyors are used for a wide variety of products. One common use is to move materials such as plastic and aluminum cans for recycling operations. Materials like this can become caught between the auger flighting and trough, jamming the conveyor.

A jam often needs to be cleared manually. When that is the case, shut down and lock out the conveyor. Don some heavy gloves, remove the trough covers, and clear the jam. Be mindful of the auger and do not pry against the flighting to clear the jam.

Clogs in screw conveyors moving granular materials is another matter. The product may be coal dust, ash, grains, cement, or similar materials. Clogs related to these materials are often due to a change in their characteristics. If so, clogs may occur regularly until the product returns to normal.

Moisture is often the culprit. Dry, granular material can move through a screw conveyor smoothly until the moisture content rises. With cement, the results of an elevated moisture content are fairly obvious. But other materials, such as grains, can also clump together and are difficult to remove when they become damp.

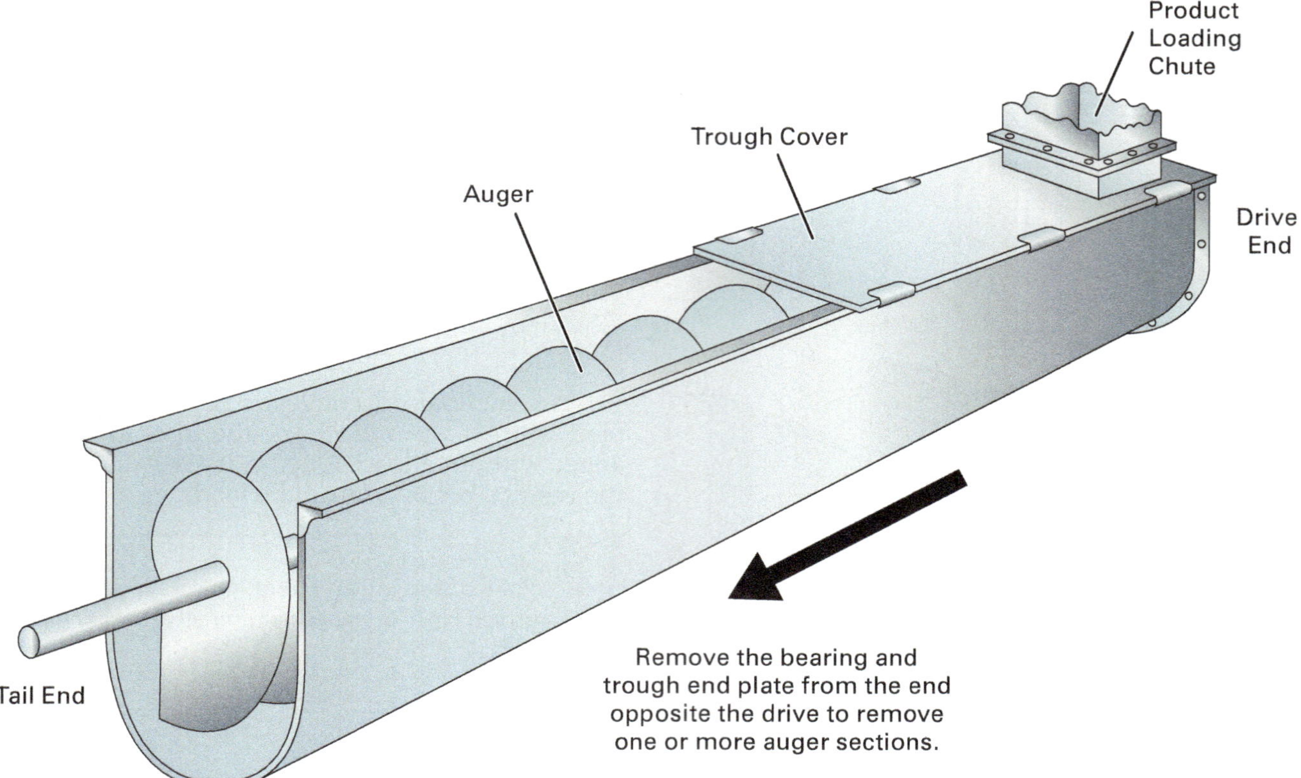

Figure 60 Auger removal.

In some cases, a simple rubber mallet can be used to help dislodge material. By tapping the sides of the trough, material will often fall away from the sides and back into the flowing material. However, you must be careful about striking the trough hard enough to buckle it. Some conveyors have built-in striking points, designated for this purpose. When striking points are not marked, it is best to strike the trough near or on the flanges, where it is strongest.

Leave the trough cover in place while striking the conveyor. After a few strikes, check the discharge and see if the material is moving again. If this doesn't work, the conveyor will need to be shut down and the trough covers removed to gain direct access to the problem.

1.5.4 Shaft Seals and Stuffing Boxes

Auger shafts pass through the trough end plates, with the bearings mounted on the outboard side. Since the product must remain in the trough, the penetrations through the end plates may be fitted with seals, much like pump seals. However, conveyors that move products such as plastic beads don't require seals.

Conveyors that require shaft seals may be equipped with traditional stuffing boxes, packed with two or three rings of packing (*Figure 61*). Like a pump, tighten the packing gland only as needed to prevent leakage. Overtightening must be avoided, as compressing the packing too far creates excess friction and increases shaft wear. Once the gland follower bottoms out and can't be tightened further, it's time to replace the packing.

> **NOTE**
> Refer to NCCER Module 15405, *Troubleshooting and Repairing Pumps*, for guidance in maintaining and replacing shaft packing.

Seals with Lantern Rings

Some screw conveyors are equipped with a lantern ring as well as packing rings in the stuffing box (*Figure 62*). Again, like a pump, the lantern ring provides a path for a cooling liquid or gas to enter and flow around the shaft. The fluid escapes slowly around the packing rings. Air or nitrogen is generally used on screw conveyors, instead of liquid coolants. Adding a fluid under pressure helps reduce drag while improving cooling and increasing the quality of the seal. When there is no liquid involved, there is no runoff to capture.

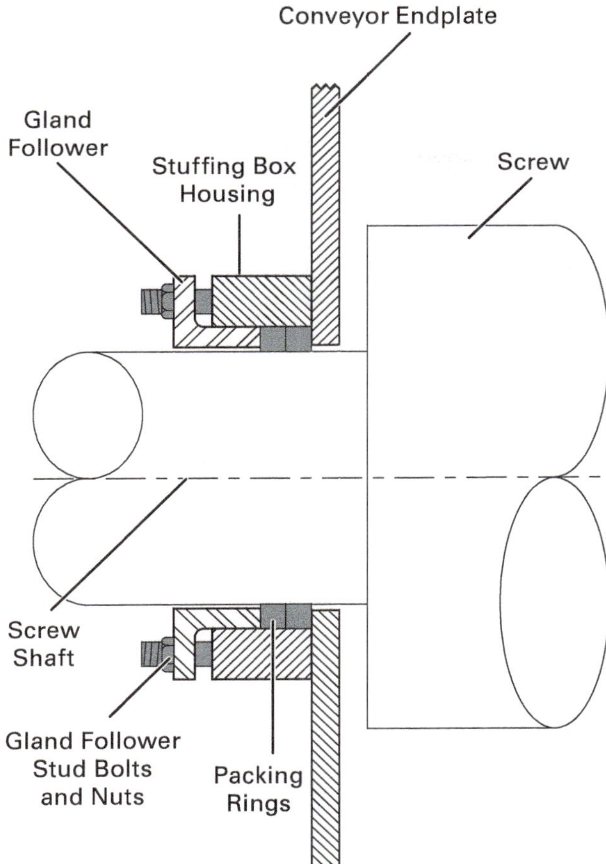

Figure 61 Cross section of a screw conveyor end-plate penetration.

1.5.5 Troughs

The trough must be kept clean and well aligned along its entire length. When it isn't aligned, the clearance between the flights and the trough wall is affected, perhaps enough so that they make contact. Once the trough is aligned and anchored to a supporting surface, it should remain in alignment unless an external force, such as a forklift, enters the picture.

Trough alignment should be checked before the flange bolts are tightened and certainly before the trough is anchored in place. Using piano wire is one simple way to do it. Stretch the wire along the upper flanges of multiple sections. You can also stretch the wire down the side of the trough. The maximum deviation for most screw conveyors is about $\frac{1}{8}$" (~3 mm), but that depends on the conveyor. Some screw conveyors operate with the auger very close to the trough. The tolerance for trough alignment is specified by the manufacturer.

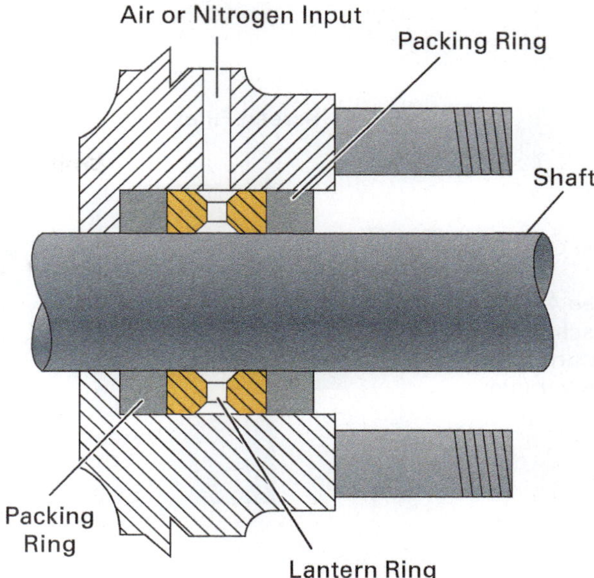

Figure 62 Lantern ring arrangement for a screw conveyor seal.

1.6.0 Maintaining and Repairing Pneumatic Conveyors

Pneumatic conveyors use air to either blow (push) or vacuum (pull) a product from one point to another. Systems that push the product are called *positive systems*, while those that pull the material toward a blower are called *negative systems*. Simplified versions of these systems are shown in *Figure 63*.

The overall design of positive and negative systems is similar. However, more significant differences are seen in the two primary classes of pneumatic conveyance—*dilute phase* systems and *dense phase* systems.

1.6.1 Dilute Phase Systems

Dilute phase systems generate a continuous airstream, consistently pushing airborne material down the line. The material-to-air volume ratio is low compared to the ratio of dense phase systems; a smaller amount of product is in motion, surrounded by a lot of air. They generate a lower pressure difference between the inlet and outlet than dense phase systems, depending on a blower to generate continuous airflow. However, the air velocity moving through the system is much higher, with product moving along at around 40 mph (~65 kph). They are best suited for rapidly conveying lightweight materials in relatively low volumes.

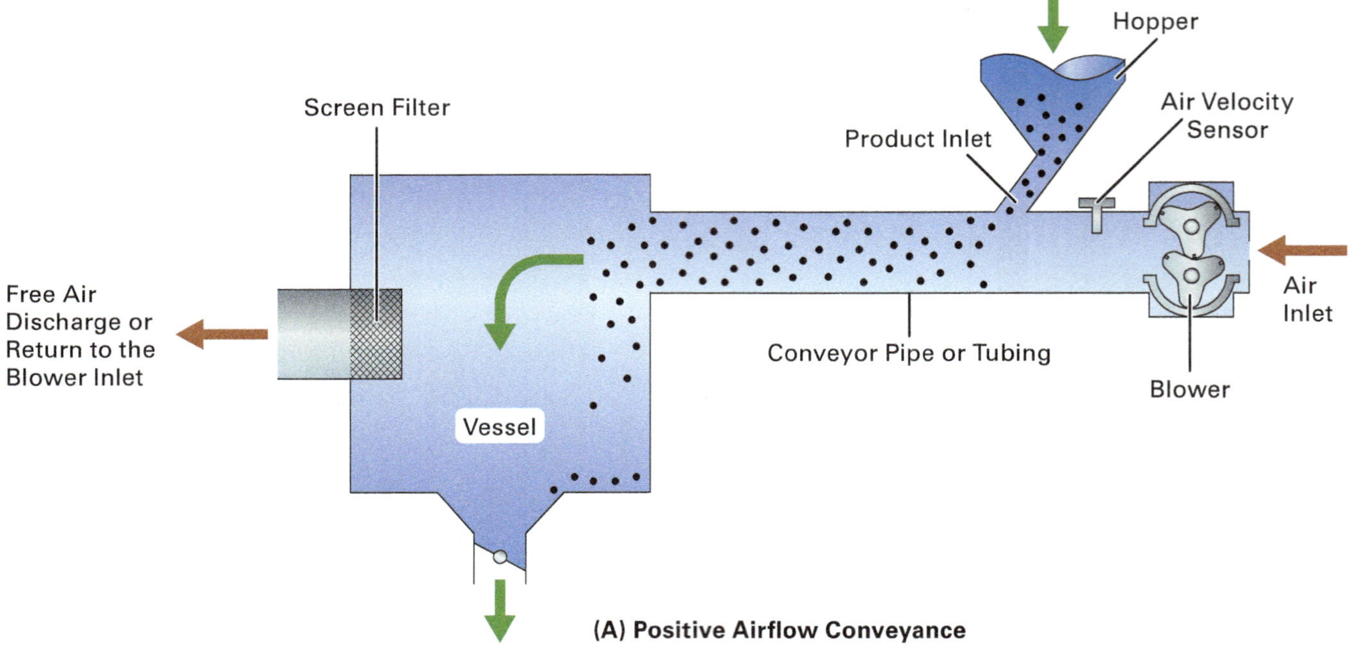

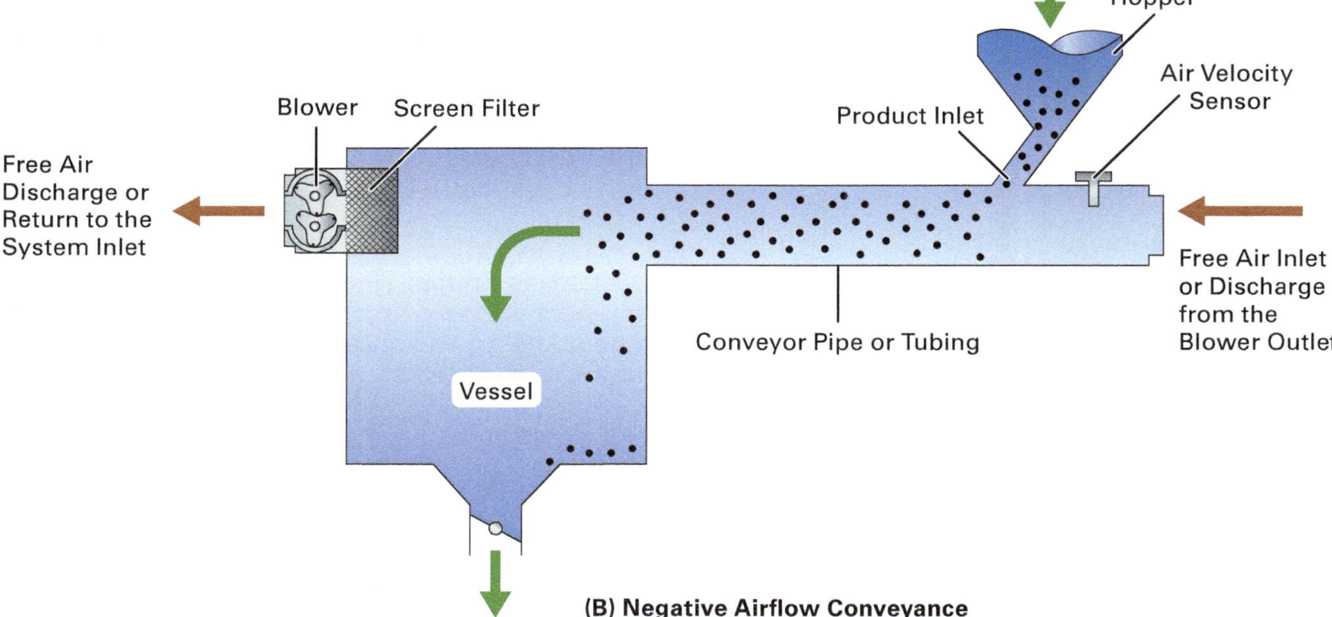

Figure 63 Positive and negative airflow pneumatic conveyance.

Dilute phase systems can operate at a positive pressure or a negative pressure. They can also incorporate both principles, creating what is called a *push-pull system*.

Dilute phase systems usually move the product through what is best described as tubing, as opposed to pipe. To make both assembly and disassembly easy, bolt-on couplings are used to join elbows and sections of tubing.

1.6.2 Dense Phase Systems

Dense phase systems (*Figure 64*) rely on a much higher pressure to propel the product down the line in batches called *slugs*. Product movement is not continuous. A precise volume of product is first charged into a *transporter*, shown in both *Figure 64* and *Figure 65*. The transporter is then closed off, and a blast of compressed air is released into the vessel. Compressed air may also be released directly into the conveyor tubing to ensure the product moves away from the transporter efficiently.

This propels the product down the line at about 3 mph (~5 kph). A human can walk at a higher speed than the product travels. They are called *dense phase systems* since there is a lot of product in motion in a small volume of air—a dense product stream.

All dense phase systems have a compressor instead of a blower, due to the greater pressure difference required. Most operate in the range of 15 psig to 50 psig (~100 kPag to 350 kPag), but some operate at pressures as high as 90 psig (~620 kPag). The compressor can be dedicated to the operation, or the air can be provided by a plant compressed-air system.

They are also equipped with an *accumulator* (may be referred to as a *receiver*) that stores a sufficient volume of compressed air to meet the demand. The air compressor must be capable of refilling the accumulator to the proper pressure before the next cycle occurs. A dedicated air compressor system is generally better than using air from a plant system, as plant systems can be affected by other demands in the facility.

In some cases, the pulse of air that sends each batch of product down the line isn't quite enough, especially with longer systems. In this case, pressurized air may be admitted to the line at various points along the route to boost and maintain the pressure (*Figure 66*). This air quite often comes from a different source. For example, a dedicated air compressor may be the primary source of air, while the booster air comes from a plant system.

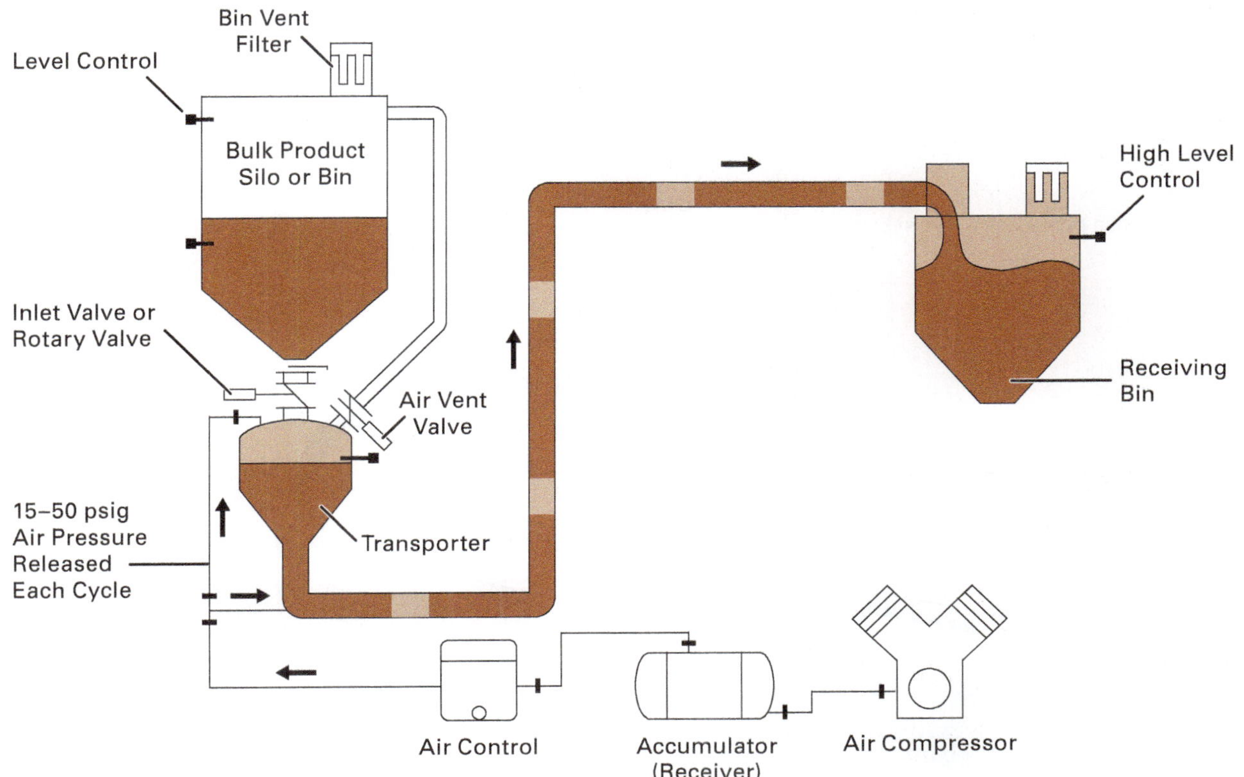

Figure 64 Dense phase pneumatic conveyor system.

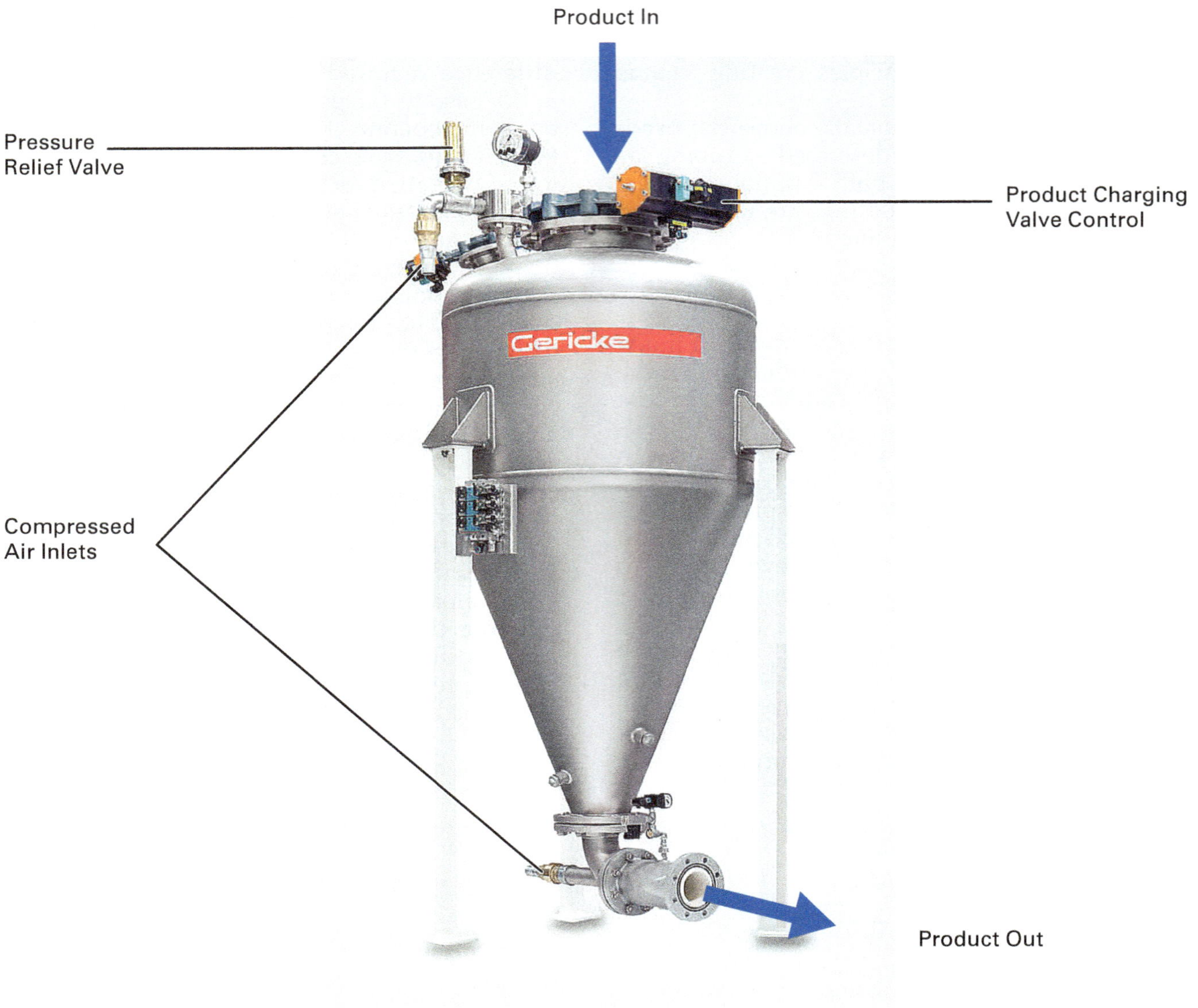

Figure 65 A dense phase conveyor system transporter.

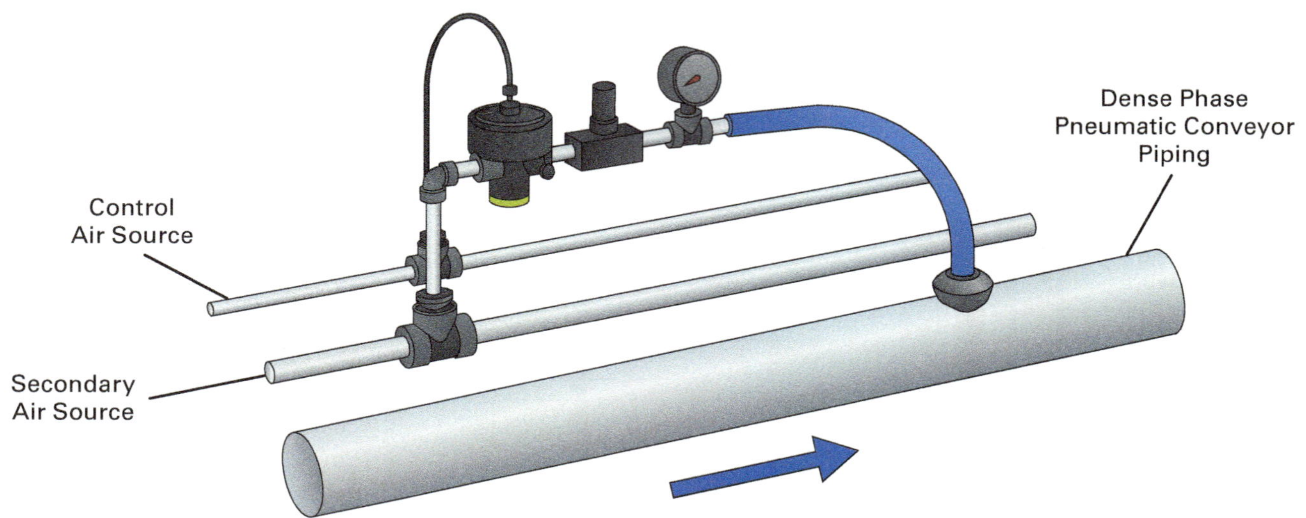

Figure 66 Air booster arrangement for a dense phase pneumatic conveyor.

NCCER – *Millwright*

Due to the nature of dense phase systems, and even though the product moves more slowly, the line experiences more abrasion and wear. For this reason, and due to the higher pressures involved, pipe is used instead of tubing to convey the product. The slugs tend to strike any obstruction hard, including elbows and diverter valves that direct the product to different vessels. Thus, any change in direction needs extra support opposing the direction of flow to withstand the blows as each slug arrives. For ease of disassembly, grooved pipe fittings or flanges are used to assemble the system.

1.6.3 Pneumatic Conveyor Maintenance

Pneumatic conveyor system maintenance largely focuses on two areas: the blower or air compressor(s), and the receiving vessel. Each system is unique and has other minor periodic maintenance requirements, but these two areas are common to all systems.

The maintenance and repair of blowers, air compressors, and pneumatic systems are topics presented in a variety of NCCER modules. For your convenience, they are listed at the end of this module in the *Additional Resources*.

Filter receivers generally represent the destination of the conveyed product. They might also be referred to as *baghouses*, in reference to similar vessels used in industrial dust collection. Think of them as a very wide spot in a river. Although river water may be moving along very quickly, the same volume of water moves more slowly where the river widens. Inside the filter receiver then, which is much larger than the tubing or piping, the air velocity slows. Product that enters slows down too and falls to the bottom, where it is dispensed to a process or packaged. But what about the air?

The air must be allowed to exit the vessel, but it must be filtered on the way out. In this case, the air is not filtered to ensure it leaves clean, although that may be a consideration if the product isn't completely harmless. The primary purpose of filtration here is to ensure the product doesn't leave the vessel along with the air.

To keep the system running effectively, a lot of filter surface area is needed in relation to the air volume. Compared to air filtration in HVACR systems, there is an enormous volume of material to be separated from the airstream.

As a result, the filters can load very quickly. Blocked filters diminish the airflow considerably. When the airflow is reduced below the design volume, blockages begin to develop in the conveyor as the product struggles to stay in motion. If the filters were replaced each time they became fouled, the system would spend most of its time shut down while the task is done numerous times each day.

For that reason, filter receivers are equipped with an automated filter cleaning system. The system is controlled either by a timer or by sensors that monitor the differential pressure across the filter bank. As filters collect material, the pressure drop through them increases steadily. To clean the filters, a blast of compressed air is directed into them, from the inside out. This pushes the debris off the face of the filters, where it can fall to the bottom of the vessel.

It is important to understand that the cleaning cycle is not always based on the premise of simply blowing the debris from the face of the materials. When cartridge filters are used, a blast of compressed air does dislodge much of the debris from the surface. However, many systems use bag filters instead (*Figure 67*). Bag filters used for this purpose often have stiff, heavy wire frames to help maintain its shape. When a burst of high-pressure air is directed into the bag, it causes the bag to "snap," much like snapping a rug, to send the dust flying. The snapping action is very quick and effective for cleaning bag filters. But it does require a quick burst of high-pressure compressed air.

Figure 67 Typical bag filter.

The filters will need to be replaced eventually. They can generally remain in service until they literally begin to come apart. Changing the filters simply because they look soiled is a waste of both time and money. Only replace the filters when the pressure drop through them remains high following the cleaning cycles (a maximum value specified by the manufacturer), or when they are obviously leaking or coming apart at the seams. Note the pressure drop across a new set of filters at startup for future reference.

Periodic maintenance also includes inspecting the entire system for air leaks. Air leaks anywhere in the system can cause significant problems. Leaks cause pressure loss and problems keeping the product in motion. One location that needs significant attention is the filter receiver access doors. The doors are gasketed, and the gaskets often do not receive proper attention. Take care when closing them, always ensuring they are properly positioned, and the gaskets are in good condition. When the filter receiver is under positive pressure, it is fairly easy to see and feel air leakage around the doors. It is far more difficult to tell when the filter receiver is under a negative pressure.

1.6.4 Pneumatic Conveyor Troubleshooting and Repair

Most of the problems that occur are related to one of four areas:

- Filter receivers
- Conveyance tubing or pipe
- Blower and system pressure
- Inlet/Rotary valves

Filter Receivers

You've already learned about filter receivers and the filtration inside. When the filters do not seem to be cleaning as they should, there are several possibilities. The cleaning cycle will be based on either time or differential pressure. Check the differential pressure settings against the gauge reading. One reason the differential pressure might be lower than expected, preventing the cycle from starting, is a reduction in system airflow. As the air volume drops, so does the differential pressure across the filters. When the differential pressure is lower than expected, check the system gauges in other areas to ensure the blower or compressor is producing the needed air volume.

The pulse of air released to dislodge debris is sharp and quick, and often loud. If it's not, check the air pressure provided to the control valves (*Figure 68*). The valves are connected to an air manifold outside of the enclosure where they are easy to access. Also ensure each valve is opening when commanded.

Doors and access panels on filter receivers are common sources of air leaks. Make sure gaskets are secure and in good shape; replace them as needed to ensure they remain soft and pliable. All connections made to the vessel have the potential to leak.

Conveyance Tubing or Pipe

The tubing or pipe used for conveyance must be simple to assemble and disassemble. Clogs do develop, but they are most often caused by system problems, assuming the conveyor was well designed. It's common for pneumatic conveyors to move product both horizontally and vertically. Oddly enough, most products are more challenging to move horizontally than vertically. Systems that attempt to move product up at a 45-degree angle are generally avoided altogether, as this seems to be the most challenging application.

Dense phase systems use pipe instead of tubing for conveyance. This is due to the increased abrasion as well as the impact forces generated. As a slug impacts the back of an elbow to change direction, a great deal of force is applied. Poor assembly techniques can result in elbows being literally blown from the end of the pipe. Abrasion is also highest at the elbows, as the product tends to hug the back of the elbow tightly around the corner. If a blowout is going to occur, it will likely be at an elbow.

A diverter valve also forces a change in direction unless it is positioned for straight-through flow. There are many different styles. Flapper-type diverter valves (*Figure 69*) are subjected to more wear than some other designs. The flapper can't be inspected without disassembly of the system, so they are often left in place until a problem develops. When the flapper is worn or is binding, it does not close off the dead leg of the system effectively. Some product gets by the flapper and promptly stops. If enough gets by, the path is blocked by the fugitive material and a clog develops when product flow is diverted in that direction. A worn flapper also causes pressure loss in the system, just as any leak does, further impacting product flow in the system.

Figure 68 Filter receiver air-pulse cleaning valves for the filters.

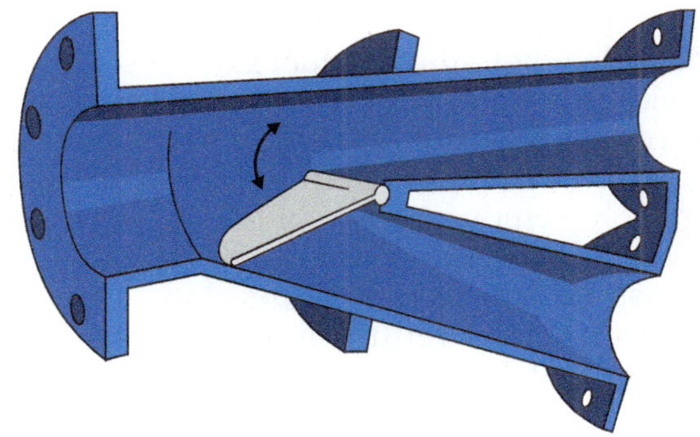

Figure 69 Flapper-type diverter valve.

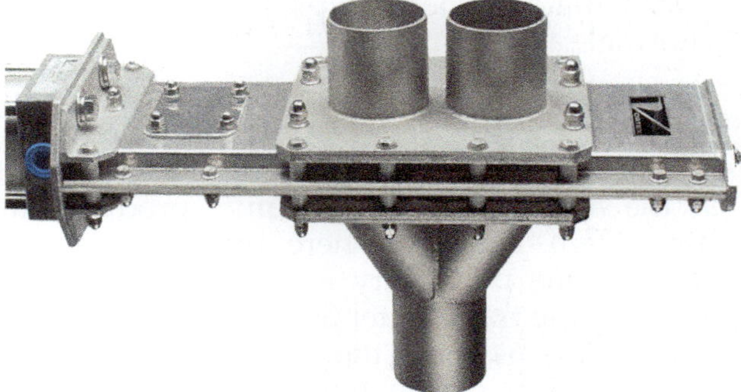

Figure 70 Sliding diverter valve.

Sliding diverter valves (*Figure 70*) eliminate the problems with flapper-type diverters. The sliding action aligns the incoming and outgoing lines to minimize friction, wear, and pressure loss. Sliding diverter valves can also be used to create unique arrangements in complex systems (*Figure 71*). They do generally require some periodic maintenance and inspection, but unlike flapper valves, they do not need to be removed from the system to see if they are operating properly. Although they are better than flapper valves, cost is often a factor in diverter valve selection.

When a leak develops on systems operating at a negative pressure, air is being sucked in rather than blown out. It is very difficult to locate leaks in a negative-pressure system as a result. Leaks also affect product travel. On a positive-pressure system, product may collect around the leak as it tries to follow the escaping air. On a negative-pressure system, the product path becomes chaotic near a significant leak.

Clogs occur occasionally. They can develop from improper operation and control, or from a component failure. Disassembly of the tubing or pipe is required to clear significant clogs. As the tubing or pipe is reassembled, ensure the couplings are properly assembled with fresh gaskets to prevent leaks.

Clogs and blockages may also develop due to changes in the product. Even the best design can't accommodate product that deviates from the norm. Moisture content is a major factor. When blockages don't seem to have a clear cause, check the characteristics of the product to see if something has changed.

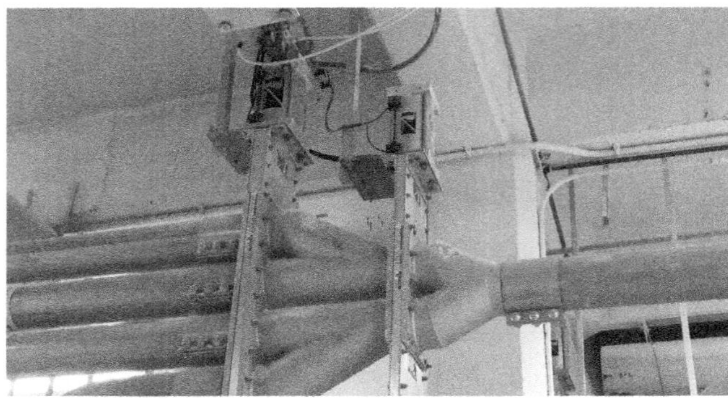

Figure 71 Diverter valves combined to accommodate complex product flow.

Blower and System Pressure

Blowers serving dilute phase systems are very dependable and can operate for years with simple maintenance provided. Direct-drive blowers must be properly aligned, while belt-driven blowers need periodic attention to the belts and sheaves.

The system pressure gauges are the best place to begin for all but the most obvious problems. It is a good idea to mark the gauges so that you can tell immediately when the pressure is outside of the normal range.

- A steady but low-pressure reading may indicate that there isn't enough product entering the system. This often leads back to problems at the rotary valve that admits product into the system. However, there are other possible causes. One possibility is that product is not entering the transporter as it should.

  In *Figure 64*, note the air vent line leading from the top of the transporter to the bulk product bin. This line allows air to escape the transporter as product enters to displace it. If the vent valve is not opening when it should (it must close before compressed air is admitted), the air must move up through the falling product. This interferes with product flow into the top of the transporter.
- A steady but high-pressure reading usually indicates a blockage somewhere. However, it may also be an indication of increased moisture in the product, which causes a change in the density. Note that changing density is rarely a problem with products such as plastic pellets, but it is a common problem when handling powders.

  Pressure gauges at various points throughout the system can help determine if the line is blocked. If a number of gauges show an elevated pressure followed by gauges that show a reduced pressure, the line is likely blocked between the two areas.

- A pressure reading that tends to fluctuate, or *hunt*, up and down is often an indication of wear and air leakage through the rotary valve. The fluctuations come from the valve's inability to stop air from leaking past the vanes.

Rotary Valves

The problem areas discussed thus far are responsible for some of the problems that occur in pneumatic conveyors. But rotary valves (*Figure 72*) generally cause as many problems as the others combined, if not more.

The size of the individual compartments and the rotational speed of the valve determine the volume of product that passes through. Rotary valves are built to precise dimensions internally. The clearance between the vanes and the valve walls is usually just a few thousandths of an inch. The valve must be constructed to minimize *blowby*, which refers to air leaking around the vanes and up into the product feed line. Blowby reduces the volume of material entering the conveyor and robs air from the system.

Wear occurs on the vanes and walls of the valve on the side where the product flows through. The opposite side is usually free of wear. The problem with rotary valves is that they aren't accessible for inspection when installed. The valve must be completely removed for evaluation. Wise operators learn from experience how long the valve will last before problems develop. Thus, they are scheduled for refurbishment or replacement based on that knowledge. Planning is essential, as rotary valves are not components that are commonly in stock, due to the many unique features and characteristics.

A rotary valve serving a dilute phase system is shown in *Figure 73*. The valve is driven using an electric motor and gearbox arrangement. Note the sliding mount for the valve drive. Although it is still challenging to fully remove the valve from the system for evaluation, the sliding mount at least simplifies removal and reinstallation of the drive.

A steady reduction in the volume of product conveyed is one clue that the valve is wearing out. If air forces its way past worn vanes, it interferes with product flow. Extensive wear may result in blockages instead, as the valve is unable to control the volume and too much is dumped into the airstream.

Remember that system pressure fluctuations, or hunting, when the pressure is normally very consistent is a common indication that air is being lost around worn vanes in the rotary valve.

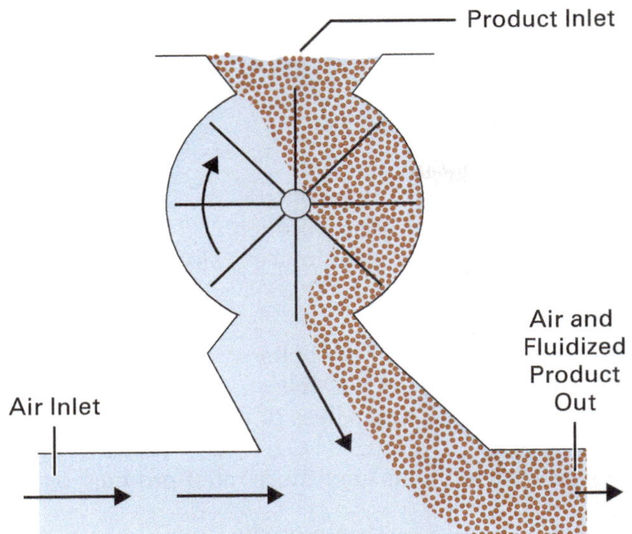

Figure 72 Pneumatic conveyor rotary valve operation.

Figure 73 Rotary valve controlling product inflow to a dilute phase pneumatic conveyor.

Converger Valves

Although they are not as common as diverter valves, *converger valves* are occasionally encountered. While a diverter valve diverts flow from one main line to two or more branch lines, converger valves accept incoming flow from two or more sources and route the product to a single line.

1.0.0 Section Review

1. Which of the following statements about Emergency Stop controls is *correct*?

    a. An Emergency Stop control should only stop the conveyor for a few seconds.
    b. For consistency, only a large red button can be used as an Emergency Stop control.
    c. An Emergency Stop control may bypass important interlocks with other equipment.
    d. Using the Emergency Stop control is the best way to shut down a conveyor in every situation.

2. Which of the following statements about belt conveyors is *correct*?

    a. Counterweight take-ups are usually found on longer conveyors with heavy belts.
    b. Belt conveyors perform at their best with the belt tension set as high as possible.
    c. The correct belt tension for all belt conveyors is roughly the same, regardless of the load or application.
    d. When adjusting belt tension, begin with the conveyor belt loaded to its maximum rated product load.

3. Which of the following steps is *best* to protect rolls of belting that must be stored on the floor?

    a. Rotate the roll 90 degrees every 90 days.
    b. Unroll and then roll the belt back up in the opposite direction every 90 days.
    c. Stand the roll on its end, changing ends every 90 days.
    d. Alternate between standing the roll on its end and laying it on the floor every 90 days.

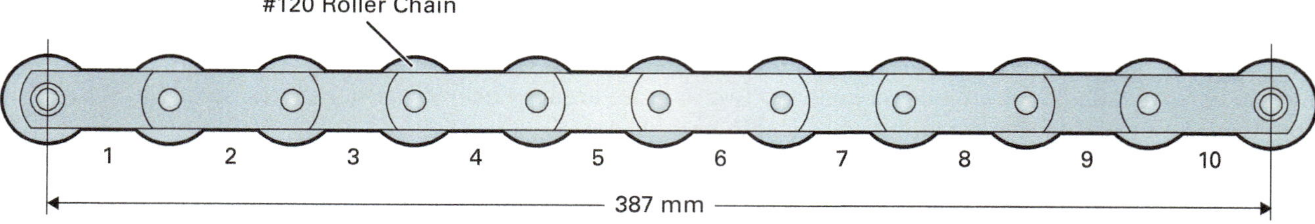

Figure SR01

4. What is the percentage of elongation for an ANSI-standard #120 conveyor chain that measures 387 mm across 10 pitches, as shown in *Figure SR01*?

    a. 3.72 percent
    b. 2.62 percent
    c. 2.04 percent
    d. 1.57 percent

5. Screw conveyor shaft seals that require a cooling fluid introduce the fluid into the seal through a ______.

    a. labyrinth seal
    b. secondary seal
    c. lantern ring
    d. perforated packing ring

6. A dilute phase pneumatic conveyor generates a constant stream of product moving at speeds up to 40 mph (~65 kph).

    a. True
    b. False

1. Troubleshooting conveyors with sophisticated and automated control systems typically requires ______.
   a. weeks of trial and error
   b. two or three people with different skill sets
   c. a degree in mechanical engineering
   d. rare and unique tools and instruments

2. When you need to shut down a conveyor for normal service and maintenance, it's *best* to use the Emergency Stop controls.
   a. True
   b. False

3. Crowned drive rollers are usually found only on belt conveyors that ______.
   a. move the heaviest loads
   b. travel only a short distance
   c. also require lagging on the drive roller
   d. do not require a lot of belt tension

4. Mechanical splices are the most durable splices and are the preferred approach to splicing all belt materials.
   a. True
   b. False

5. When the drive and tail roller are *not* parallel to each other, the belt wanders toward the side with the lesser tension.
   a. True
   b. False

6. Conveyor chain that does *not* have rollers is referred to as ______.
   a. bushing chain
   b. friction chain
   c. nonstandard chain
   d. naked chain

7. To properly secure a chain cotter pin, bend the legs to a ______.
   a. 30-degree angle
   b. 45-degree angle
   c. 60-degree angle
   d. 90-degree angle

8. The primary compressed air source for a dense phase pneumatic conveyor *must* be able to ______.
   a. provide more than 150 psig of pressure
   b. provide enough compressed air for nonstop product flow
   c. recharge the accumulator between cycles
   d. also provide the air for line boosters

9. You note that the system pressure reading on a pneumatic conveyor is steady, but unusually low. The *most likely* cause is that ______.
   a. the system filters are clogged with product
   b. there isn't enough product entering the system
   c. the rotary valve is rotating too fast
   d. the diverter valve is clogged and can't move

10. When a clog develops downstream of a pneumatic conveyor flapper-type diverter valve repeatedly after it is repositioned, it *most likely* indicates ______.
    a. the diverter valve is too large
    b. the flapper is worn and leaking
    c. the blower or air compressor isn't delivering enough air
    d. the transporter air vent valve is remaining closed

Trade Terms Introduced in This Module

Carryback: Conveyed material that fails to unload at the end of a conveyor belt, adhering to or embedding itself in the belt and traveling back to the head of the conveyor on the underside.

Fugitive material: Any material that falls from or escapes a conveyor system, including dust, and doesn't reach the intended destination.

Skiving: The removal of one or more layers of a conveyor belt to accommodate a splice to avoid a significant change in belt thickness.

Vulcanizing: Using heat or chemicals along with pressure to create a conveyor belt splice. Hot vulcanization relies on direct heat, while cold vulcanization relies on chemicals to develop the necessary heat and bond.

Additional Resources

This module presents thorough resources for task training. The following reference material is suggested for further study.

Flexco. With over 100 years of experience and leadership in the belted conveyor industry, Flexco offers a wide array of learning resources and guidance. For millwrights and industrial maintenance trainees who will work with belt conveyors in the future, check out Flexco's offerings, including their new training program, Flexco Essentials™. **https://www.flexco.com/NA/EN/Flexco.htm**.

Foundations™, The Practical Resource for Cleaner, Safer, More Productive Dust and Material Control. Todd Swinderman, Andrew D. Marti, Larry J. Goldbeck, Daniel Marshall, and Mark Strebel. 4th Edition. 2009. Neponset, IL: Martin Engineering.

Martin Engineering Foundations™ Belt Conveyor Training Resources. **https://foundations.martin-eng.com/en-us/training-options**.

NCCER Module 15209, *Introduction to Bearings*. 4th Edition. Alachua, FL: National Center for Construction Education and Research.

NCCER Module 15306, *Removing and Installing Bearings*. 4th Edition. Alachua, FL: National Center for Construction Education and Research.

NCCER Module 15307, *Couplings and Alignment Fundamentals*. 4th Edition. Alachua, FL: National Center for Construction Education and Research.

NCCER Module 15311, *Installing Belt and Chain Drives*. 4th Edition. Alachua, FL: National Center for Construction Education and Research.

NCCER Module 15405, *Troubleshooting and Repairing Pumps*. 4th Edition. Alachua, FL: National Center for Construction Education and Research.

NCCER Module 15406, *Compressors and Compressor Maintenance*. 4th Edition. Alachua, FL: National Center for Construction Education and Research.

NCCER Module 15407, *Basic Pneumatic Systems*. 4th Edition. Alachua, FL: National Center for Construction Education and Research.

NCCER Module 15408, *Troubleshooting and Repairing Pneumatic Equipment*. 4th Edition. Alachua, FL: National Center for Construction Education and Research.

Figure Credits

iStock@Ekkaluck, Module Opener, Figures 1, 5
Reproduced with Permission, Fluke Reliability Corporation, owner of Prüftechnik, Figure 2
Shutterstock.com/MOLPIX, Figure 3
Courtesy of Flexco / Flexible Steel Lacing Company, Figures 4, 19–22, 24, 26, 36–37
Luff Industries' Wing Tail Pulley, Figure 9
Luff Industries' Idlers, Figures 12–13
Courtesy of REMA TIP TOP/North America, Inc., Figure 14
Courtesy of DEWALT®, Figure 16
iStock@Cveja, Figure 27
Courtesy of DEWALT Industrial Tool Co., Figure 33
iStock@industryview, Figures 39, 43
Shutterstock.com/Alba_alioth, Figure 40
iStock@khomsan rakphong, Figure 41
iStock@Afriadi Afriadi, Figure 42
Courtesy of USA Roller Chain & Sprockets, Figures 48, 50–52
Shutterstock.com/N_Sakarin, Figure 49
Parker HVAC Filtration, Figure 67
Salina Vortex Corporation, Figures 70–71

Section Review Answer Key

SECTION 1.0.0

Answer	Section Reference	Objective
1. c	1.1.2	1a
2. a	1.2.2	1b
3. a	1.3.1	1c
4. d	1.4.2	1d
5. c	1.5.4	1e
6. a	1.6.1	1f

Section Review Calculations

SECTION 1.0.0

QUESTION 4

Convert chain pitch in fractional inches to millimeters: $1\frac{1}{2}" = 38.1$ mm

$$\text{Elongation (\%)} = \frac{[M - (X \times P)] \times 100}{X \times P}$$

$$\text{Elongation (\%)} = \frac{[387 \text{ mm} - (10 \times 38.1 \text{ mm})] \times 100}{10 \times 38.1 \text{ mm}}$$

$$\text{Elongation (\%)} = \frac{[387 \text{ mm} - (381 \text{ mm})] \times 100}{381 \text{ mm}}$$

$$\text{Elongation (\%)} = \frac{6 \text{ mm} \times 100}{381 \text{ mm}}$$

$$\text{Elongation (\%)} = \frac{600 \text{ mm}}{381 \text{ mm}}$$

$$\text{Elongation (\%)} = 1.57\%$$

User Update

NCCER makes every effort to keep its textbooks up-to-date and free of technical errors. We appreciate your help in this process. If you find an error, a typographical mistake, or an inaccuracy in NCCER's curricula, please submit a User Update form by visiting **https://www.nccer.org/olf**. You can also scan the QR code using the camera on your phone or mobile device to access the form.

Laser Alignment

Overview

Once installed and roughly aligned, direct-coupled equipment is almost ready to run. Traditionally, millwrights and industrial mechanics finished the job by performing a dial indicator precision alignment. If they were skillful, they got excellent results, but the process could be slow and tricky. In the last few decades, however, they've had another choice—*laser alignment*. This technique gives excellent and quick results. Better still, trainee craftworkers can master it easily.

Module 15502

Trainees with successful module completions may be eligible for credentialing through the NCCER Registry. To learn more, go to **www.nccer.org** or contact us at 1.888.622.3720. Our website, **www.nccer.org**, has information on the latest product releases and training.

Your feedback is welcome. You may email your comments to **curriculum@nccer.org**, send general comments and inquiries to **info@nccer.org**, or fill in the User Update form at the back of this module.

This information is general in nature and intended for training purposes only. Actual performance of activities described in this manual requires compliance with all applicable operating, service, maintenance, and safety procedures under the direction of qualified personnel. References in this manual to patented or proprietary devices do not constitute a recommendation of their use.

15502 V4.0

From *Millwright, Trainee Guide*. NCCER.

15502
LASER ALIGNMENT

Objectives

Successful completion of this module prepares you to do the following:

1. Summarize the laser alignment method and its tools.
   a. Describe laser alignment equipment and principles.
   b. Summarize preparing for a laser alignment.

2. Outline laser alignment procedures.
   a. Summarize checking and correcting soft foot with a laser alignment tool.
   b. Summarize performing a horizontal shaft laser alignment procedure.
   c. Summarize performing a vertical shaft laser alignment procedure.
   d. Summarize thermal growth and its role in alignment.

Performance Tasks

Under supervision, you should be able to do the following:

1. Set up a laser alignment tool.
2. Use a laser alignment tool to check for and correct soft foot.
3. Perform a horizontal shaft laser alignment procedure.

Trade Terms

Collinear
Coupling stresses
Laser
Motor bell

Precision alignment
Soft foot
Thermal growth

Industry Recognized Credentials

If you are training through an NCCER-accredited sponsor, you may be eligible for credentials from NCCER's Registry. The ID number for this module is 15502. Note that this module may have been used in other NCCER curricula and may apply to other level completions. Contact NCCER's Registry at 1.888.622.3720 or go to **www.nccer.org** for more information.

You can also show off your industry-recognized credentials online with NCCER's digital badges. Transform your knowledge, skills, and achievements into badges that you can share across social media platforms, send to your network, and add to your resume. For more information, visit **www.nccer.org**.

This module uses US standard and metric units in up to three different ways. This note explains how to interpret them.

Exact Conversions

Exact metric equivalents of US standard units appear in parentheses after the US standard unit. For example: "Measure 18" (45.7 cm) from the end and make a mark."

Approximate Conversions

In some cases, exact metric conversions would be inappropriate or even absurd. In these situations, an approximate metric value appears in parentheses with the ~ symbol in front of the number. For example: "Grip the tool about 3" (~8 cm) from the end."

Parallel but not Equal Values

Certain scenarios include US standard and metric values that are parallel but not equal. In these situations, a slash (/) surrounded by spaces separates the US standard and metric values. For example: "Place the point on the steel rule's 1" / 1 cm mark."

How to Access Resources

This craft has additional videos and resources to enhance your learning experience. To view these resources, scan the QR below. The videos and resources are separated by module.

You can scan this code using the camera on your phone or mobile device to view these videos and resources.

Contents

1.0.0 METHODS, TOOLS, AND PREPARATION

Objective

Summarize the laser alignment method and its tools.

a. Describe laser alignment equipment and principles.
b. Summarize preparing for a laser alignment.

Performance Task

1. Set up a laser alignment tool.

Trade Terms

Collinear: Two shafts so well aligned that a single, unbroken line could pass through their centers.

Laser: A device that emits a single-color light beam that doesn't spread out quickly.

Motor bell: A flanged cylindrical component that links a flange-equipped motor to another machine. Also called a *motor stand* or *distance piece*.

Precision alignment: Procedures designed to eliminate nearly all misalignment, often down to 0.002" or better.

Soft foot: A coupling stress created by a machine's feet not all resting firmly on the baseplate.

As you've learned in other modules, direct-coupled equipment works best when its shafts are properly aligned. Ideally, you could draw a single, unbroken line through both shafts' centers. If this condition is true, millwrights say that the shafts are collinear (*Figure 1*). Bearings

and seals will last a long time with shafts aligned this accurately.

The procedures described in NCCER Module 15313, *Prealignment and Shim Fabrication*, bring the shafts into *rough alignment*—typically within 0.010" to 0.015" of being collinear. For some applications, particularly those with flexible couplings, this may be acceptable.

> **NOTE**
>
> Rough alignment serves two purposes. First, it eliminates obvious misalignment and factors that make achieving alignment difficult. Second, it reduces the remaining misalignment to a relatively small amount. Rough-aligned equipment won't require major adjustments (thick shims or major repositioning) to bring it into final alignment.

But project specifications often require better alignment. For applications with rigid couplings, nearly perfect alignment *isn't* optional. **Precision alignment** procedures bring the shafts into the best possible alignment.

Always remember that rough-aligned shafts look properly aligned. But they're still misaligned. You just can't see it. For this reason, all precision alignment techniques use instruments to detect the remaining misalignment.

> **NOTE**
>
> Unless the project specifications indicate otherwise, align shafts to 0.002" or better. Millwrights and industrial mechanics usually treat this value as the standard for precision alignment.

Precision alignment techniques reduce the following misalignment types:

- Angular
- Parallel (offset)

Foot-mounted equipment with coupled horizontal shafts usually contains both misalignment types. It's often present in both the vertical and

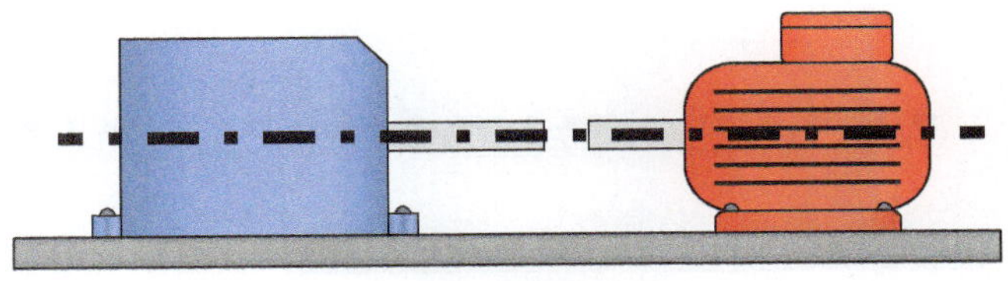

Figure 1 Collinear shafts.

horizontal planes. Vertical and horizontal angularity (VA and HA) bend the line that passes through the shafts, turning it into a pair of crossed lines. Vertical and horizontal offset (VO and HO) split the line into two parallel lines (*Figure 2*). Precision alignment procedures correct both problems, making the shafts collinear.

Most vertical machines mount the motor above the equipment. A flange on the motor bolts to a matching flange on the machine's **motor bell**. Inside the motor bell, a coupling links the shafts (*Figure 3*).

By their very nature, the flanges eliminate major misalignment problems. They don't guarantee precision alignment, however, since both angular and offset misalignments are still possible.

If the flange faces aren't perfectly flat, the slight "tilt" they create will produce angular misalignment (*Figure 4*). As the diagram shows, angular misalignment acts in a three-dimensional space, so it can be quite complex. Similarly, the slight "play" between the flange bolts and their holes can introduce offset misalignment. This acts in just one plane (*Figure 4*).

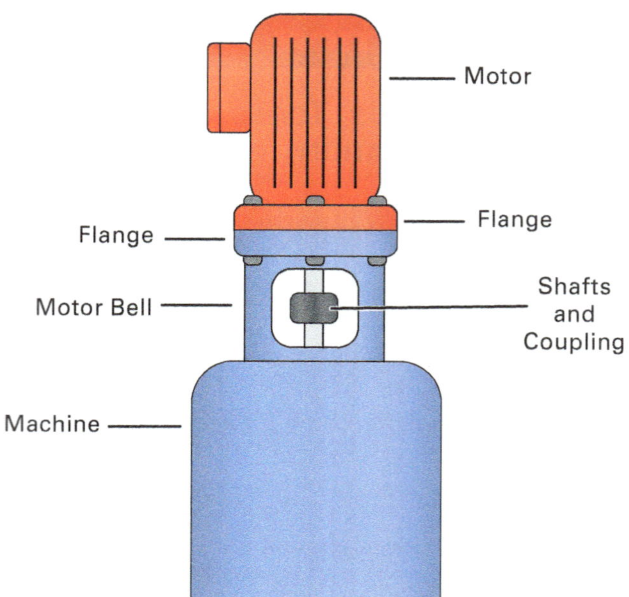

Figure 3 Vertical installation.

1.1.0 Method and Tools

Instead of mechanical measuring instruments, the laser alignment method uses a light beam and sensor to measure misalignment. While laser alignment tools are far more expensive than dial indicator alignment kits, they offer several advantages. First, the beam always travels in a straight line, so it doesn't sag like a rod-mounted dial indicator. Second, the beam can span relatively long distances. This quality makes aligning big machines much easier. Laser alignment tools use a special kind of light that has some unique qualities.

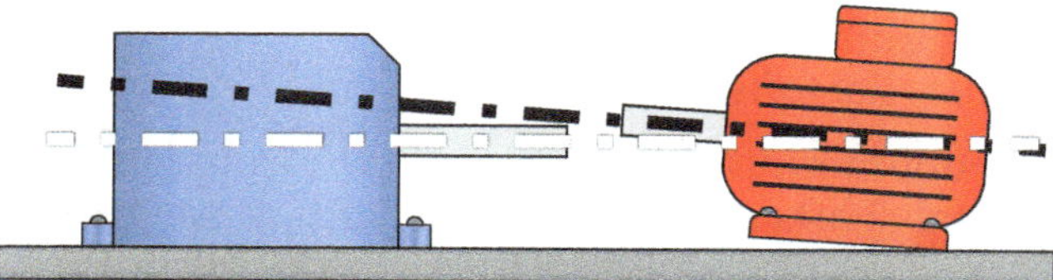

Vertical Angularity (VA)

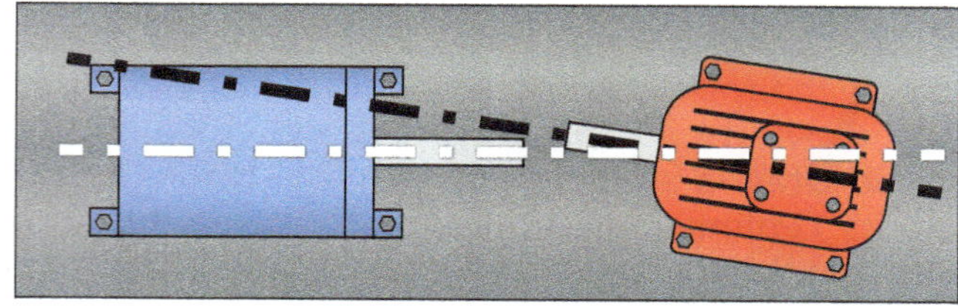

Horizontal Angularity (HA)

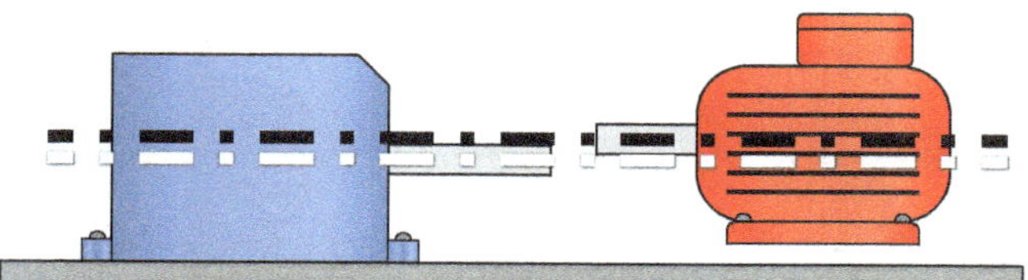

Vertical Offset (VO)

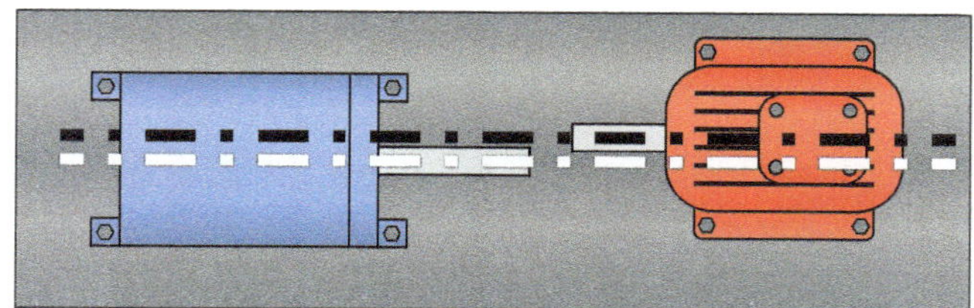

Horizontal Offset (HO)

Figure 2 Vertical and horizontal misalignments.

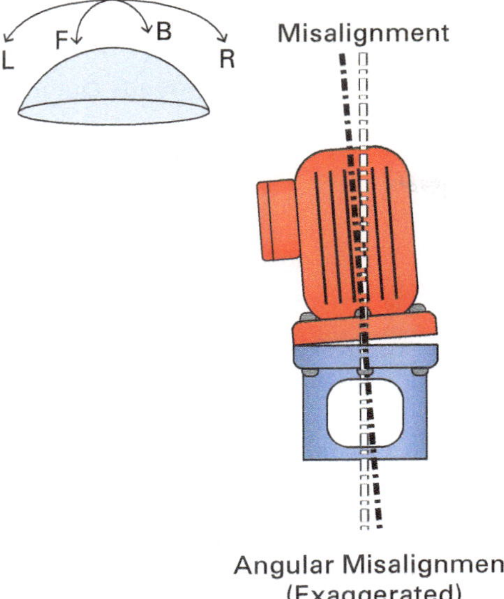

Angular Misalignment
(Exaggerated)

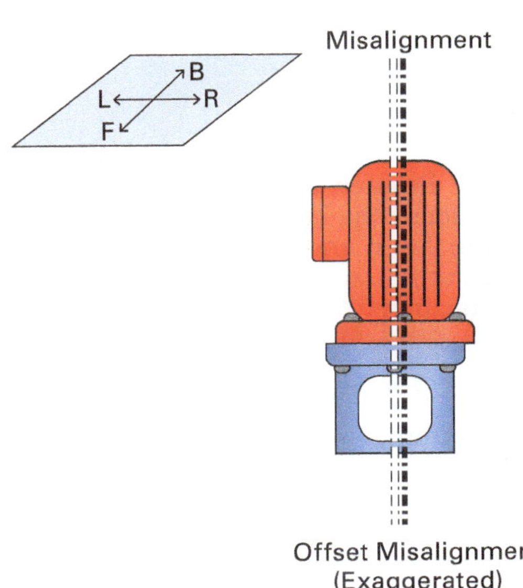

Offset Misalignment
(Exaggerated)

Figure 4 Misalignment in vertical equipment.

1.1.1 Laser Light

An ordinary white light source, like a flashlight, emits a beam that quickly spreads out with distance (*Figure 5*). White light is also a mixture of colors rather than a single hue. A laser, by contrast, emits a special kind of light. It travels in a very tight beam that barely spreads out, even over great distances. It's also a single color—often red or green.

Laser light is perfect for measuring tasks. Because it can be focused into a very thin beam that doesn't spread out, sensors can measure its position very precisely. They can detect it in ordinary indoor lighting and even through light fog, smoke, or fumes.

> **NOTE**
>
> Heavy smoke or fog can prevent a laser alignment tool from working over long distances. The tool will alert the operator if it can't detect the laser beam. Strong vibration from nearby machinery can also affect the laser alignment tool.

1.1.2 Laser Safety

Both a laser's output power and the way it focuses the beam affect how dangerous it is. Laser pointers and pet toys are relatively safe. By contrast, a large industrial laser can cut metal. Regulatory bodies require manufacturers to identify laser equipment by *class* (*Figure 6*). This is a number/letter combination that indicates how hazardous the laser is to eyes and skin. Classes are 1, 1M, 2, 2M, 3R, 3B, and 4.

Laser Bounce

Since the 1960s, scientists have been demonstrating how tight a laser beam really is by bouncing one off the moon. During the Apollo program, astronauts left several special reflectors on the lunar surface. Lasers on Earth shoot a beam at the reflectors. The light travels the approximately 240,000-mile distance (~386,000 km), hits the reflector, and returns to Earth in about 2.5 seconds. Using the transit time and some math, scientists calculate the distance between Earth and moon with millimeter precision. Over several decades, they've learned that the moon is slowly moving away from Earth at the rate of about 1.5" (~4 cm) per year.

Figure Credit: NASA

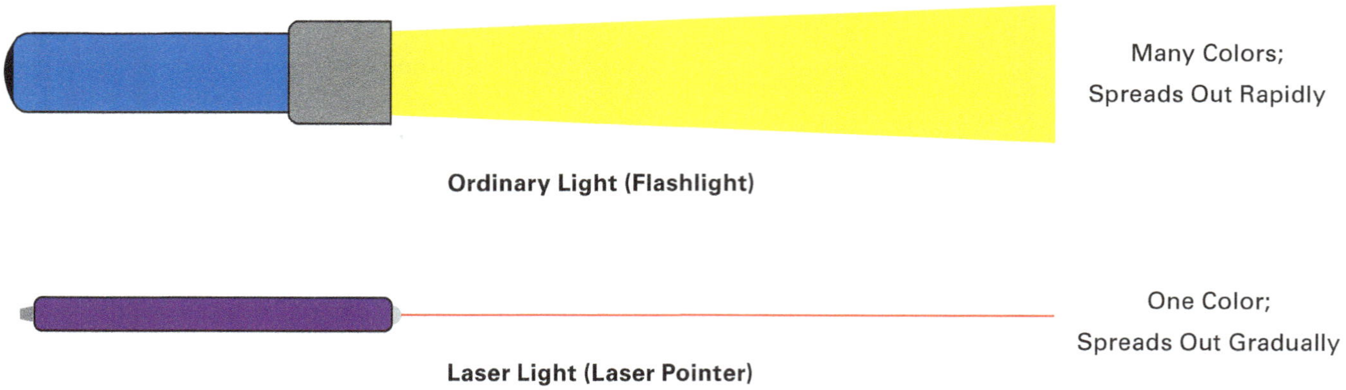

Figure 5 Ordinary light vs. laser light.

Most newer laser alignment tools are Class 2, the same as many laser pointers. They're relatively safe, provided you don't stare directly into the beam. Unless the manufacturer specifies it, you won't need special eye protection.

Never point an active laser alignment tool at someone. Also, be careful not to let the beam reflect off a shiny surface into another worker's eyes. While the beam probably won't do any damage, it could startle the worker, causing an accident.

Prior to 2002, manufacturers classified lasers differently than they do today. Classes were roman numeral/letter combinations—I, II, IIa, IIIa, IIIb, and IV. The current class numbers are close but not identical to their roman numeral equivalents. Older laser alignment tools will have safety labels based on the old system. Many will be Class II.

> **WARNING!**
>
> Before using *any* laser alignment tool, read its warning label and manual. Wear special laser eye protection if the manufacturer recommends it. Never look directly into the beam or allow it to reflect directly into your eyes.

Figure 6 Laser safety label.

1.1.3 Laser Alignment Tools

Laser alignment tools usually come as a kit containing everything necessary for performing an alignment (*Figure 7*). While some tools are easier to use than others, all have the same parts and basic operating principles.

Laser Unit (Transmitter)

The laser unit mounts on one shaft and emits the laser beam. Besides the laser itself, it contains lenses that focus the beam. Integrated electronics manage the laser and handle communications. Most laser units contain a rechargeable battery. Some use ordinary disposable batteries.

Sensor Unit (Receiver)

The sensor unit mounts on the other shaft and detects the laser beam. It contains the laser sensor and its associated electronics. It also includes an *inclinometer*—a sensor that detects the unit's rotational angle. Most sensor units contain a rechargeable battery. Newer laser alignment tools send data between the laser and sensor units over the laser beam itself. This eliminates the connecting cables required on older units.

Fixtures

Every kit includes clamps, fixtures, and rods for mounting the laser and sensor units on the shafts. Roller chain clamps are popular. Other styles, such as magnetic brackets, are available as well.

Computer (Touch Panel)

The operator interacts with the alignment tool through a handheld computer and its touchscreen. The computer communicates with the laser and sensor units, collecting data and performing calculations. Newer models are wireless. Older models use cables.

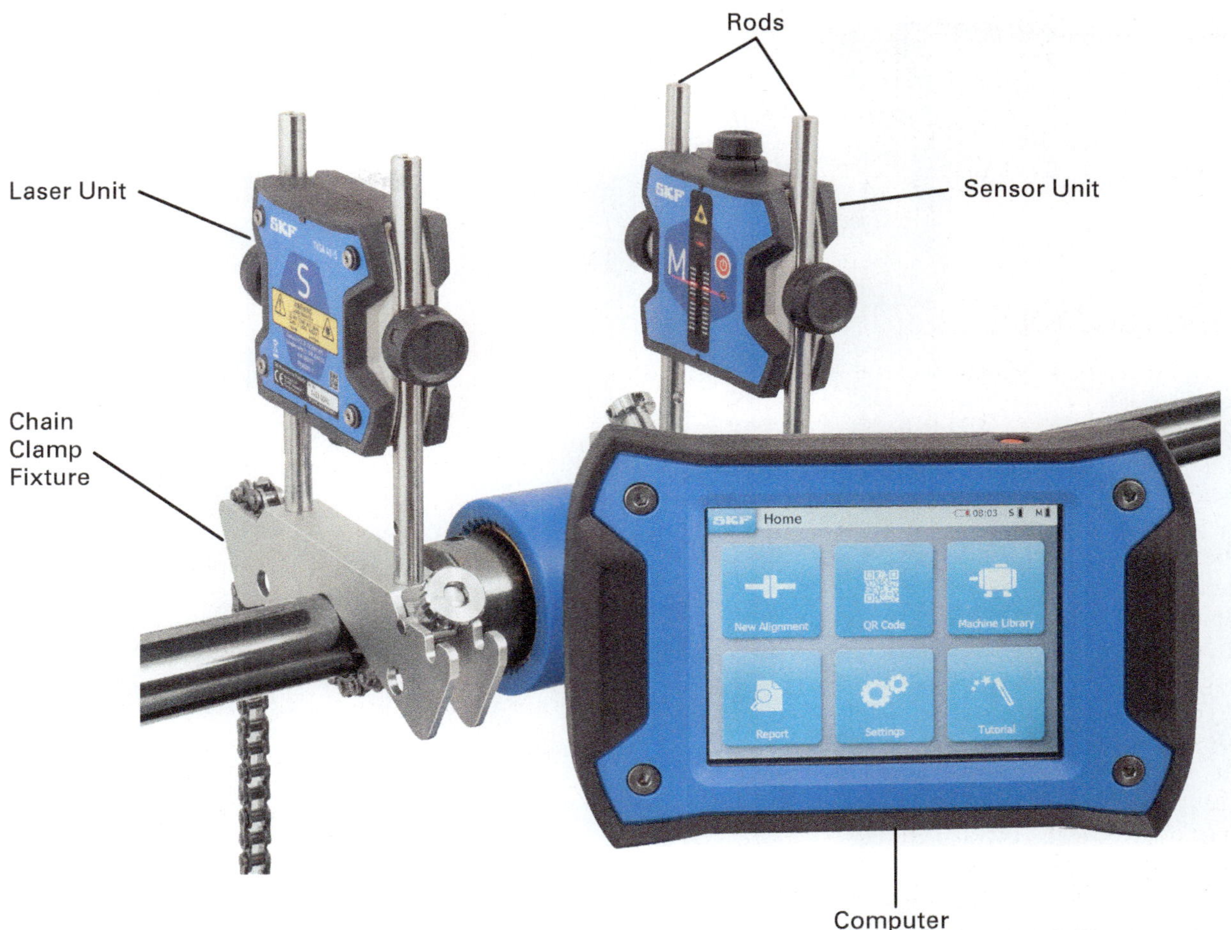

Figure 7 Laser alignment kit.

Recent alignment tools are very well designed. They guide the operator step by step towards eliminating misalignment. Most computers support multiple alignment methods. Many can check for and eliminate **soft foot**. The computer usually contains a rechargeable battery.

Besides their alignment capabilities, many newer computers include advanced features to make managing and maintaining machines easier. The computer may contain an RFID tag reader for identifying machines. Some include a camera for documenting equipment.

A few models are even voice controlled, freeing up the operator's hands for handling tools. Some units can communicate with cloud-based databases to store alignment results. These databases, in turn, can communicate with the plant management software to automate maintenance tasks.

> **NOTE**
>
> Older laser alignment tools won't have as many features. To understand a particular tool's capabilities, consult its manual or visit the manufacturer's website. Many manufacturers offer tutorial videos.

1.1.4 Laser Alignment Principles

All laser alignment tools have similar operating principles. The laser and sensor units mount on opposite shafts. The beam travels from the laser to the sensor, striking it somewhere near the middle (*Figure 8*). The sensor reports the light spot's location to the computer.

As instructed by the computer, the operator rotates the coupled shafts. The sensor unit's inclinometer reports the rotational position to the computer. If the shafts are properly aligned (collinear), the light spot won't move significantly during rotation. On the other hand, if the shafts are misaligned, the spot will move across the sensor during rotation.

The computer records the rotational angles and the moving spot's positions on the sensor. It then does some math. Based on this information, it reports how much angular and offset misalignment are present. *Figure 9* summarizes each alignment situation.

The computer can then guide the operator to correct the misalignment. Newer alignment tools will specify the shim thicknesses and foot

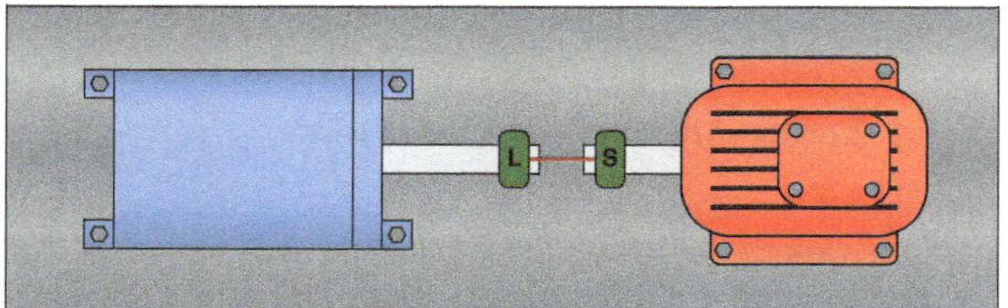

Figure 8 Laser and sensor units.

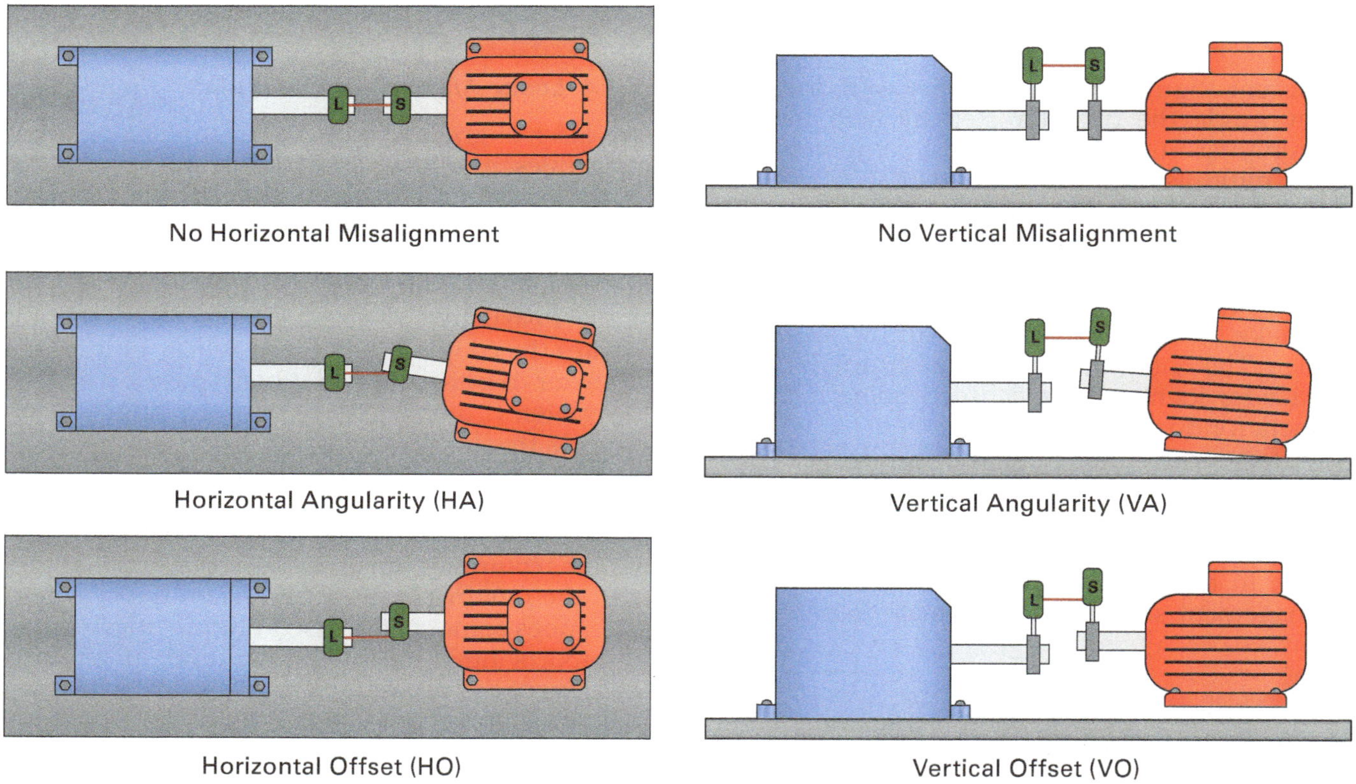

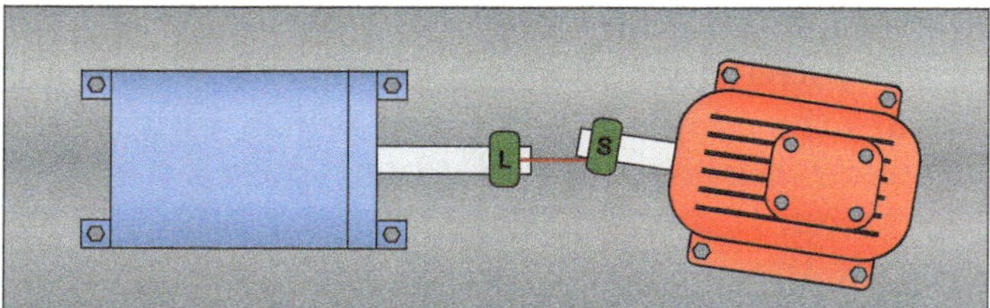

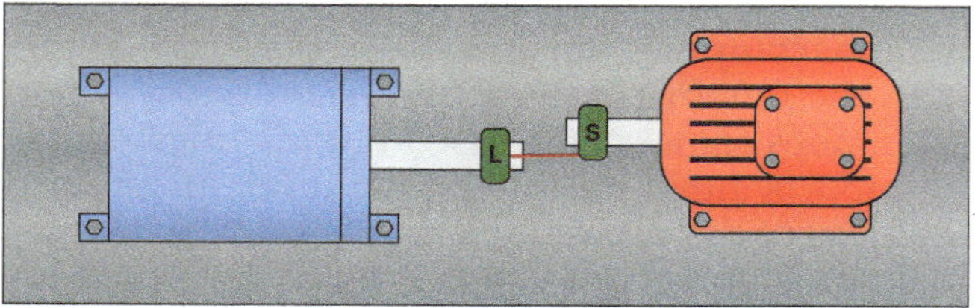

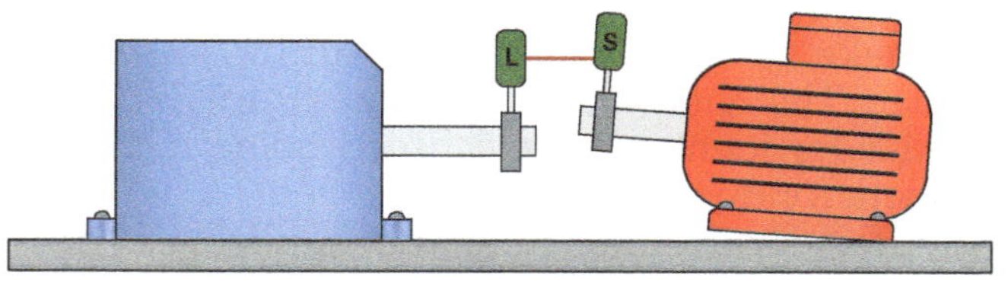

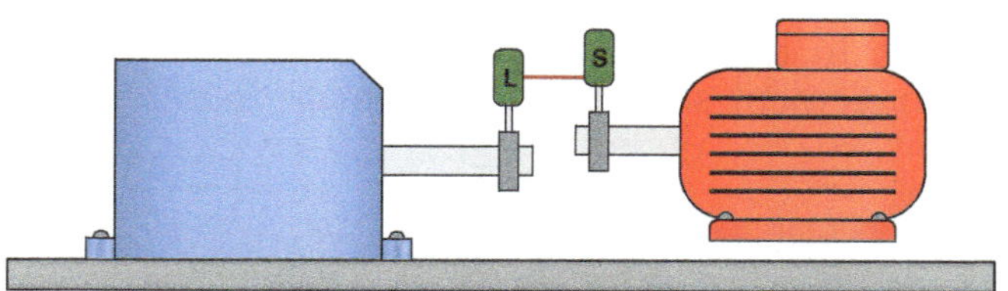

Figure 9 Laser alignment scenarios.

locations needed to adjust the driver's height. The computer may also provide live guidance as the operator tweaks the baseplate. The tool will alert the operator once it confirms acceptable alignment—often with a cheerful smiley face.

1.2.0 Preparation

Every laser alignment tool is slightly different. You should always read its manual before using it. This module uses the Prüftechnik ROTALIGN® touch for all examples (*Figure 10*). If you use a different tool, the overall procedure should be similar.

1.2.1 Equipment Preparation

The following procedure outlines preparing the equipment for precision alignment:

Step 1 Check the equipment and confirm that it's correctly installed. Also verify that its rough alignment is complete.

Figure 10 ROTALIGN® touch.

Step 2 Check both shafts for smoothness. Remove corrosion or roughness with emery paper so the alignment fixtures will attach firmly.

Step 3 If it's not already in place, install the coupling using the appropriate procedure.

Step 4 Collect all required tools—the alignment kit, a shim kit, suitable wrenches, a tape measure, and a dead-blow hammer.

Step 5 Confirm that the laser and sensor units' batteries are charged/fresh by powering up each unit. Check the alignment computer's batteries too. If necessary, recharge or replace them.

1.2.2 Installing the Laser and Sensor Units

The following procedure outlines installing the mounting fixtures and their associated units:

Step 1 Attach a clamping mechanism to each shaft. Position them so the laser and sensor units will line up when installed. Tighten the chains or bolts until everything is snug.

Step 2 Select and attach appropriate supporting rods. Use the shortest rods that will still allow the laser beam to pass over the coupling.

Step 3 Slide the sensor unit over the rods on the driver side. Adjust its height so the sensor isn't blocked by the coupling. Lock it in place.

Step 4 Slide the laser unit over the rods on the driven side. Open its yellow dust cover.

Step 5 Switch on the laser unit by pressing its Power button. Slide it up and down the rods until the red laser dot is approximately centered on the sensor unit's red dust cover (*Figure 11*). Lock the unit in place.

Step 6 Rotate the laser unit's yellow adjustment dials to center the laser dot. These move the unit up/down and left/right. Once the dot is centered, switch off the laser unit. Close the yellow dust cover.

The previous two steps roughly center the laser beam on the sensor unit. Later, you'll use the computer to precisely center the beam.

Step 7 Slowly rotate the linked shafts 360 degrees to confirm that the alignment assembly is attached correctly and doesn't hit anything.

Always turn the shafts to rotate the alignment assembly. Don't use the assembly itself as a handle. You could loosen it or affect the readings.

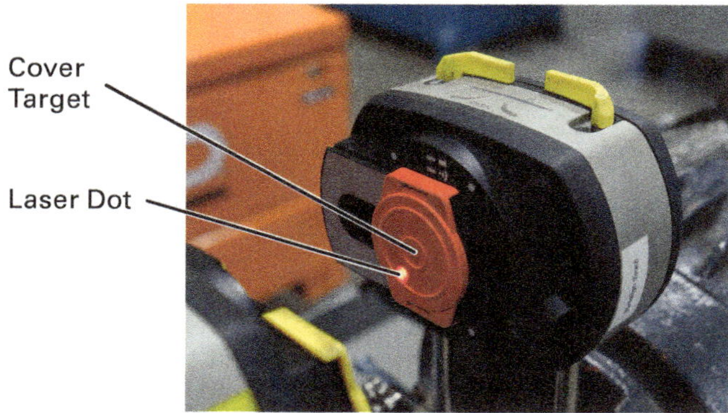

Figure 11 Centering the laser.

When rotating the shafts, always turn them in the same direction that they will turn when operating. Turning the shafts the wrong way can cause components like impellers to come off. If the equipment can operate in either direction, pick a direction and use it consistently throughout the alignment procedure.

When aligning machines with horizontal shafts, the ROTALIGN® touch can determine the misalignment with as little as 70 degrees of rotation. In unusual or tight conditions, confirm that you can rotate the alignment assembly by at least this amount. Whenever possible, however, a full 360-degree rotation gives the best results. Aligning machines with vertical shafts requires a full 360-degree rotation.

1.2.3 Measuring Key Distances

For each alignment procedure, the ROTALIGN® touch needs to know several key distances. It uses these to calculate misalignment values and their corrections. The distances that you'll measure depend on the machine configuration.

The following procedure outlines measuring key distances (*Figure 12*) for horizontally mounted machines with feet:

Step 1 Measure the distance between the coupling center and the reference groove on top of the sensor unit (*Figure 13*). Round your result to the nearest $\frac{1}{8}$".

Step 2 Measure the distance between the coupling center and the driver's front feet. Measure to the bolt hole's center. Round your result to the nearest $\frac{1}{8}$".

Step 3 Measure the distance between the driver's front and back feet. Measure between the bolt holes' centers. Round your result to the nearest $\frac{1}{8}$".

The following procedure outlines measuring key distances (*Figure 14*) for vertically mounted machines with flanges:

Step 1 Measure the distance between the coupling center and the reference groove on top of the sensor unit. Round your result to the nearest $\frac{1}{8}$".

NCCER – *Millwright*

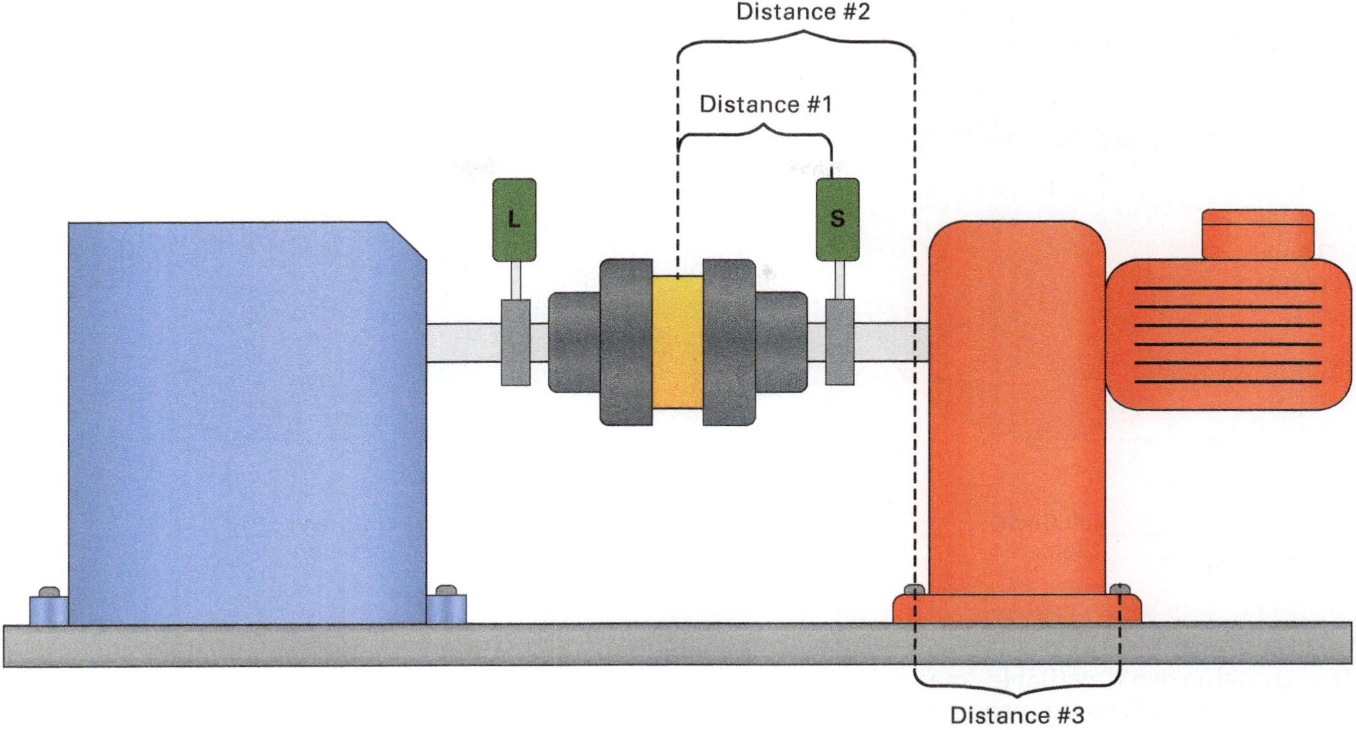

Figure 12 Key distance measurements (horizontal with feet).

Step 2 Measure the distance between the coupling center and the driver's flange. Measure to the flange center. Round your result to the nearest $\frac{1}{8}$".

You'll also need some information about the driver's flange, such as its shape, measurements, and bolt hole count. A manufacturer-supplied mechanical drawing is the best way to find this information. *Figure 15* shows the needed dimensions for both square and round flanges.

Figure 13 Measurement reference groove.

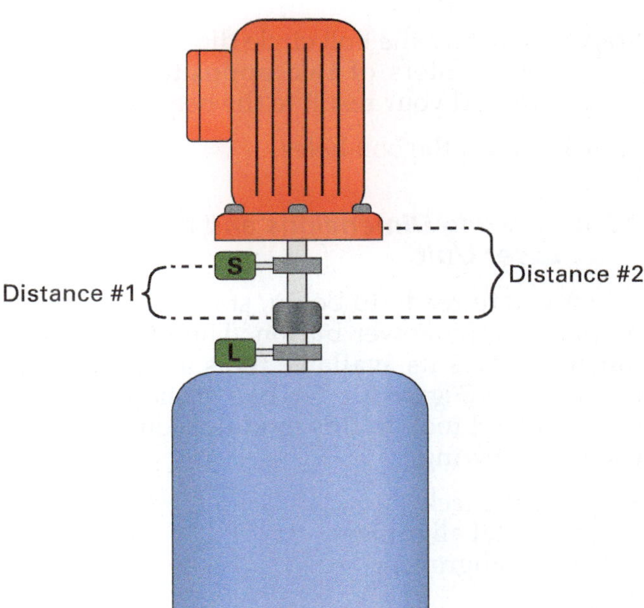

Figure 14 Key distance measurements (vertical with flange).

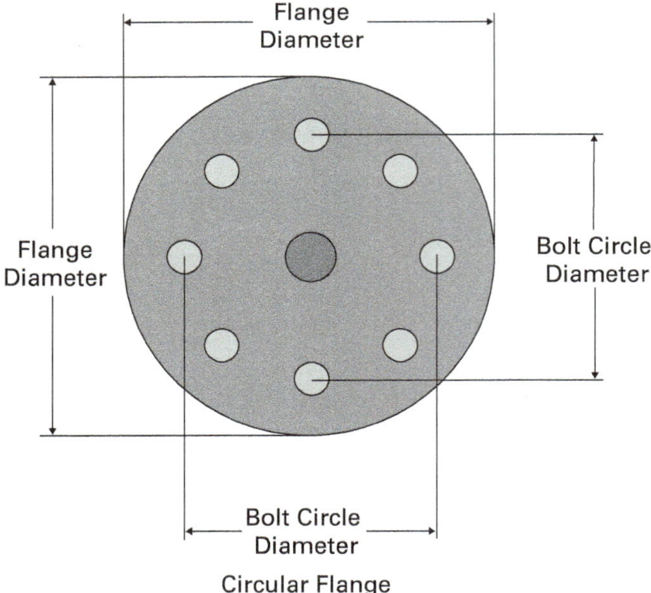

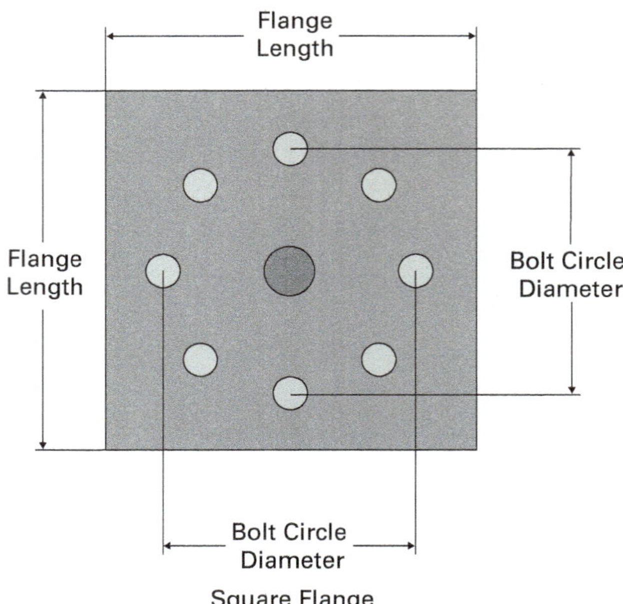

Figure 15 Flange measurements.

If a drawing isn't available, measure the flange instead. The following procedure outlines this process:

Step 3 For circular flanges, measure the diameter. For square flanges, measure one side's length. Round your result to the nearest ⅛".

> **NOTE**
>
> If the flange is elliptical, measure the widest and narrowest diameters. If the flange is rectangular, measure its length and width. Round your results to the nearest ⅛".

Step 4 Measure the bolt circle diameter between the centers of two opposite bolt holes. Round your result to the nearest ⅛".

Step 5 Count the bolt holes.

1.2.4 Entering Dimensions and Centering the Laser Unit

When you're ready to begin, start the computer by pressing its Power button. The ROTALIGN® touch displays its available tools as tiles on the main screen (*Figure 16*). Tap one of these to select its associated tool. In this module, you'll learn to use the following:

- Soft foot check
- Horizontal alignment
- Vertical alignment

Before starting any procedure, you'll need to enter the dimensions that you've just measured. The following steps are for machines with coupled horizontal shafts and feet:

Step 1 On the main screen, tap the **Horizontal alignment** tool tile.

Step 2 You should be on the **Dimensions** page (*Figure 17*). If you're not, tap the **DIM** button.

Step 3 Check the **Units** button in the upper right corner. If it isn't showing **inch**, tap it to change the units.

Step 4 Key in the first measured dimension (coupling center to sensor). Tap the > button.

Step 5 Key in the second measured dimension (coupling center to front feet). Tap the > button.

Step 6 Key in the third measured dimension (distance between the feet). Tap the > button.

> **NOTE**
>
> The ROTALIGN® touch can accept dimensions with either decimal or standard fractions. Round decimal fractions to three places and enter them in the usual way. To enter a standard fraction, key in the whole number part first. Next, hit the + button. Finally, enter the fraction as two numbers, hitting the / button in between.

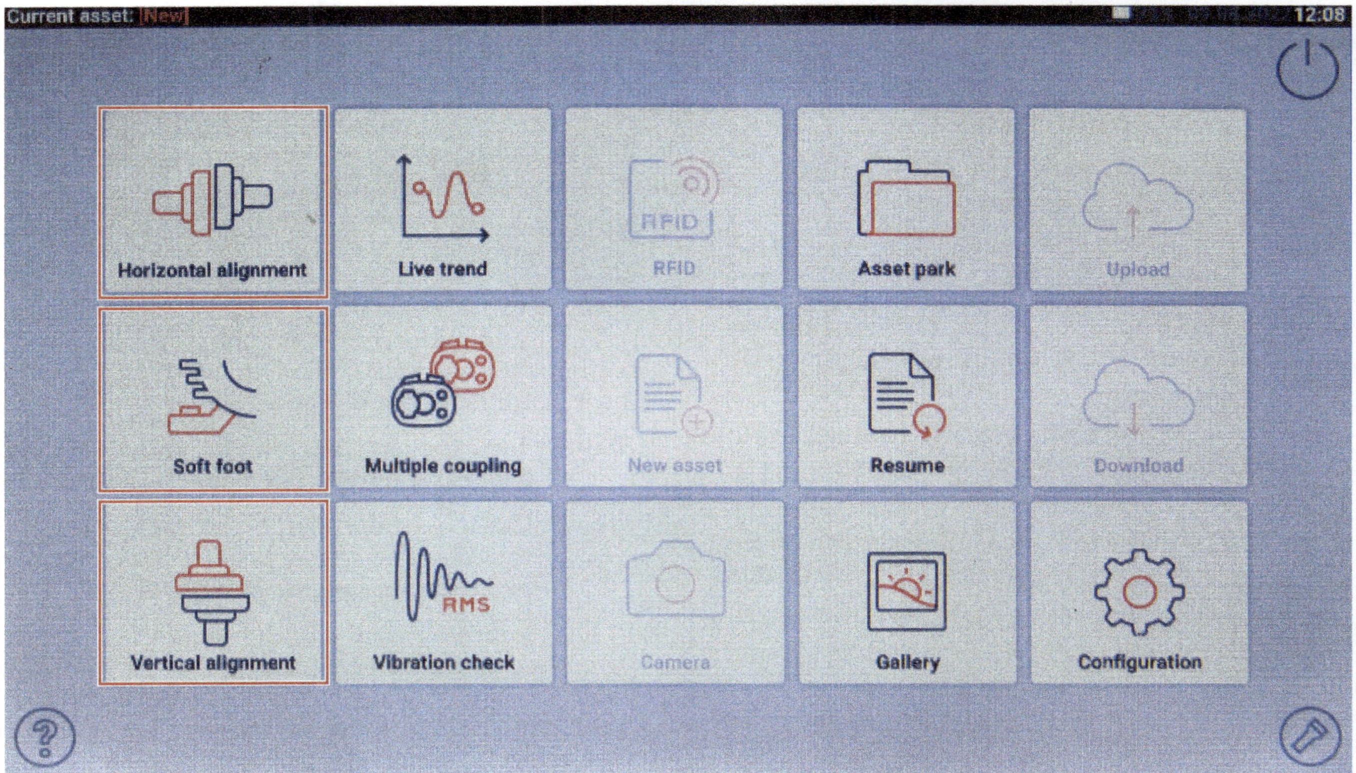

Figure 16 ROTALIGN® touch main screen.

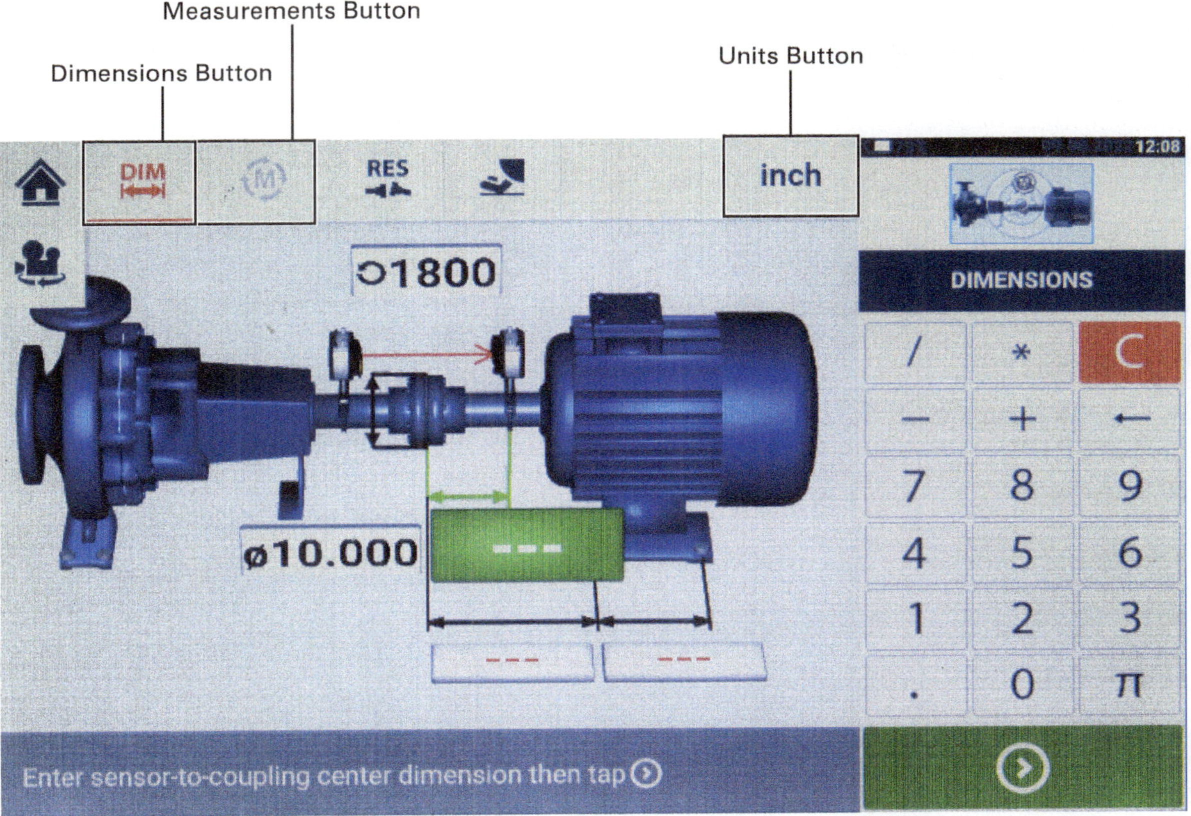

Figure 17 Dimensions page (horizontal shafts).

Step 7 Accept the default coupling diameter value (10"). Tap the > button.

Step 8 Enter the shaft's maximum rotational speed (rpm). Tap the > button.

The following steps are for machines with coupled vertical shafts and flanges:

Step 1 On the main screen, tap the **Vertical alignment** tool tile.

Step 2 You should be on the **Dimensions** page (*Figure 18*). If you're not, tap the **DIM** button.

Step 3 Check the **Units** button in the upper right corner. If it isn't showing **inch**, tap it to change the units.

Step 4 Key in the first measured dimension (coupling center to sensor). Tap the > button.

Step 5 Key in the second measured dimension (coupling center to driver flange). Tap the > button.

The ROTALIGN® touch can accept dimensions with either decimal or standard fractions. Round decimal fractions to three places and enter them in the usual way. To enter a standard fraction, key in the whole number part first. Next, hit the **+** button. Finally, enter the fraction as two numbers, hitting the **/** button in between.

Step 6 Accept the default coupling diameter value (10"). Tap the > button.

Step 7 Enter the shaft's maximum rotational speed (rpm). Tap the > button.

Step 8 Tap the driver in the equipment diagram (*Figure 18*). The driver configuration page will appear (*Figure 19*).

Step 9 Tap the **Flange** button. The flange configuration page will appear (*Figure 20*).

Step 10 Tap the **Shape** button. Select the flange shape.

Step 11 Tap the **Flange details** button. Enter the measured dimensions. Also enter the number of bolt holes in the flange.

For circular or square flanges, enter the diameter (or length) value twice. For elliptical or rectangular flanges, enter the separate diameter (or length/width) values.

Finally, for either horizontal or vertical machine configurations, you'll need to confirm that the laser beam is centered on the sensor.

Step 1 Tap the **M** button to move to the **Measurements** page.

Step 2 Open the yellow and red dust covers on the laser and sensor units. Turn both units on by pressing their Power buttons.

The computer will check whether the laser beam is centered on the sensor. It will show the beam's location by a red dot on a target (*Figure 21*). If the dot isn't within the small box in the middle, you'll have to adjust the laser unit's position.

Step 3 Rotate the side yellow dial to move the beam up or down until the dot is centered vertically.

Step 4 Rotate the top yellow dial to move the beam left or right until the dot is centered horizontally. When the dot is correctly centered, the message **Laser centered** will replace the **Laser OK** message.

The ROTALIGN® touch can perform a successful alignment if the dot is anywhere within the large target box. Centering it within the small box ensures best results, so it's wise to perform this step.

At this point, you're ready to take measurements or perform an alignment procedure.

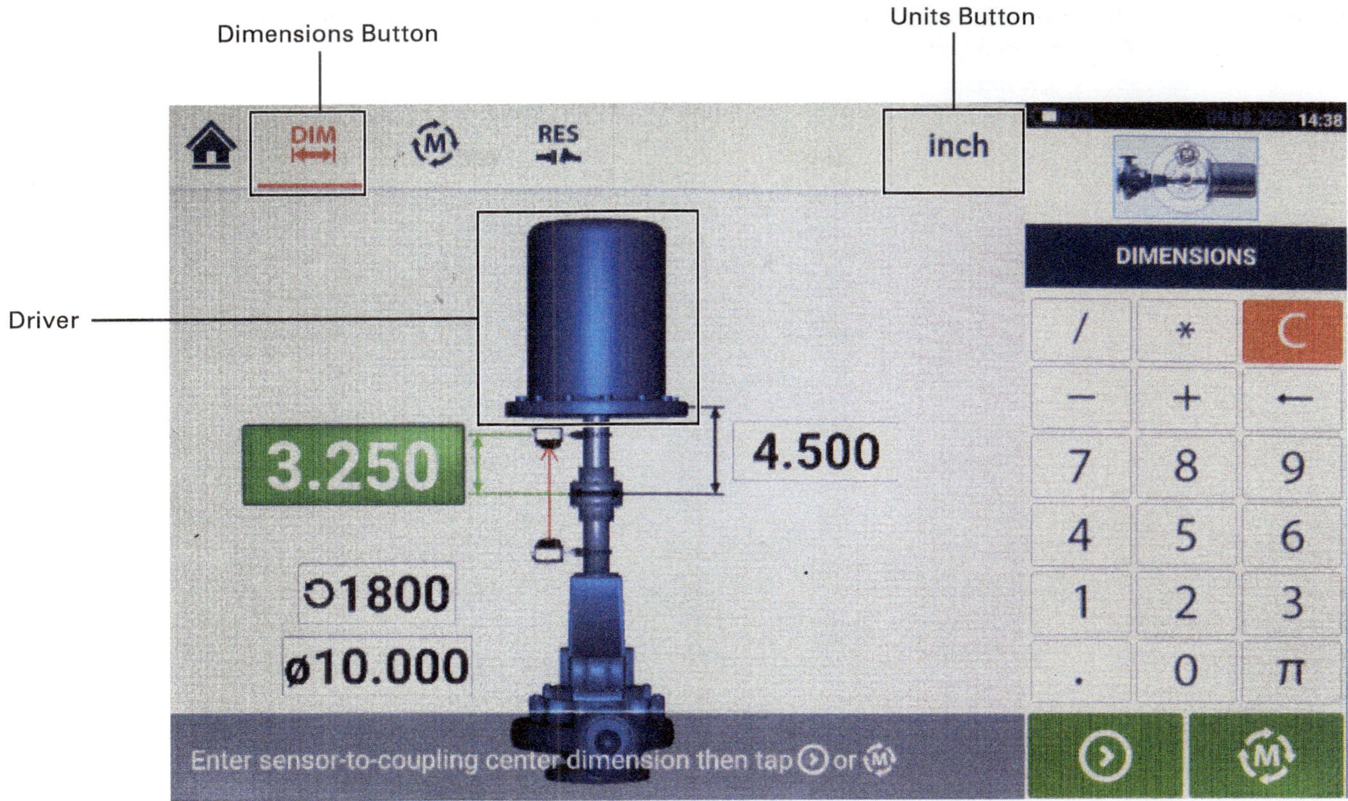

Figure 18 Dimensions page (vertical shafts).

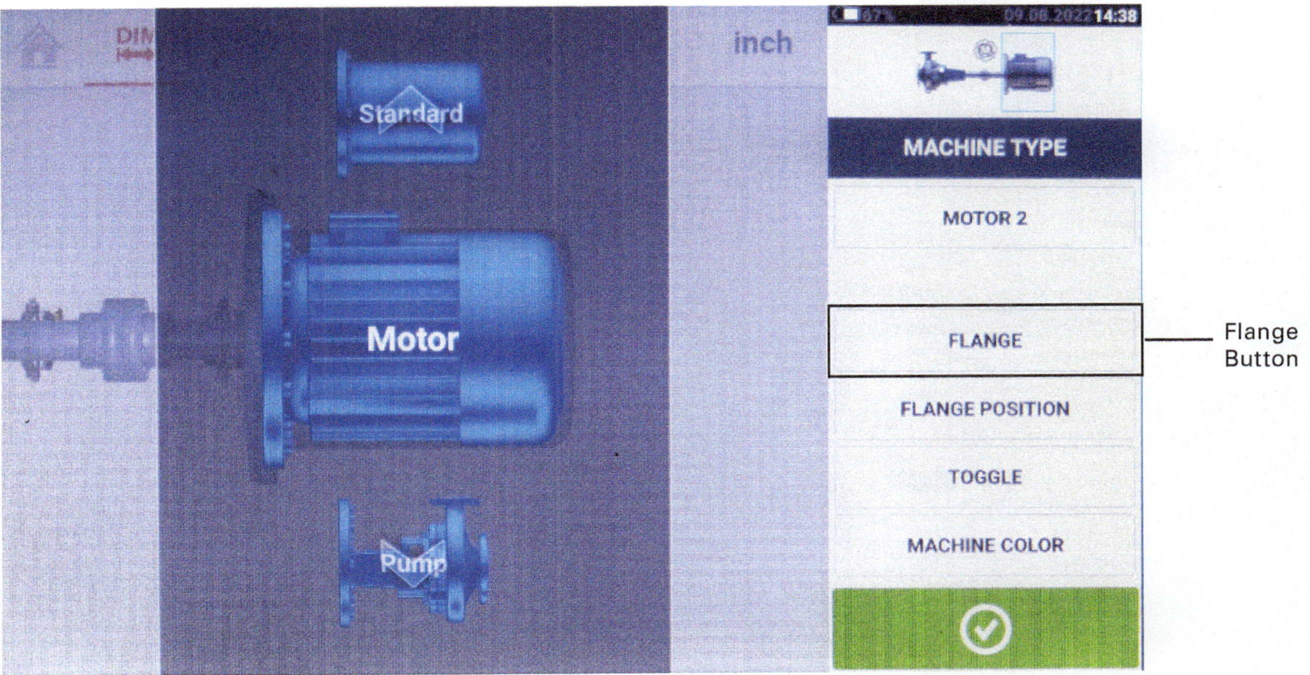

Figure 19 Driver configuration page.

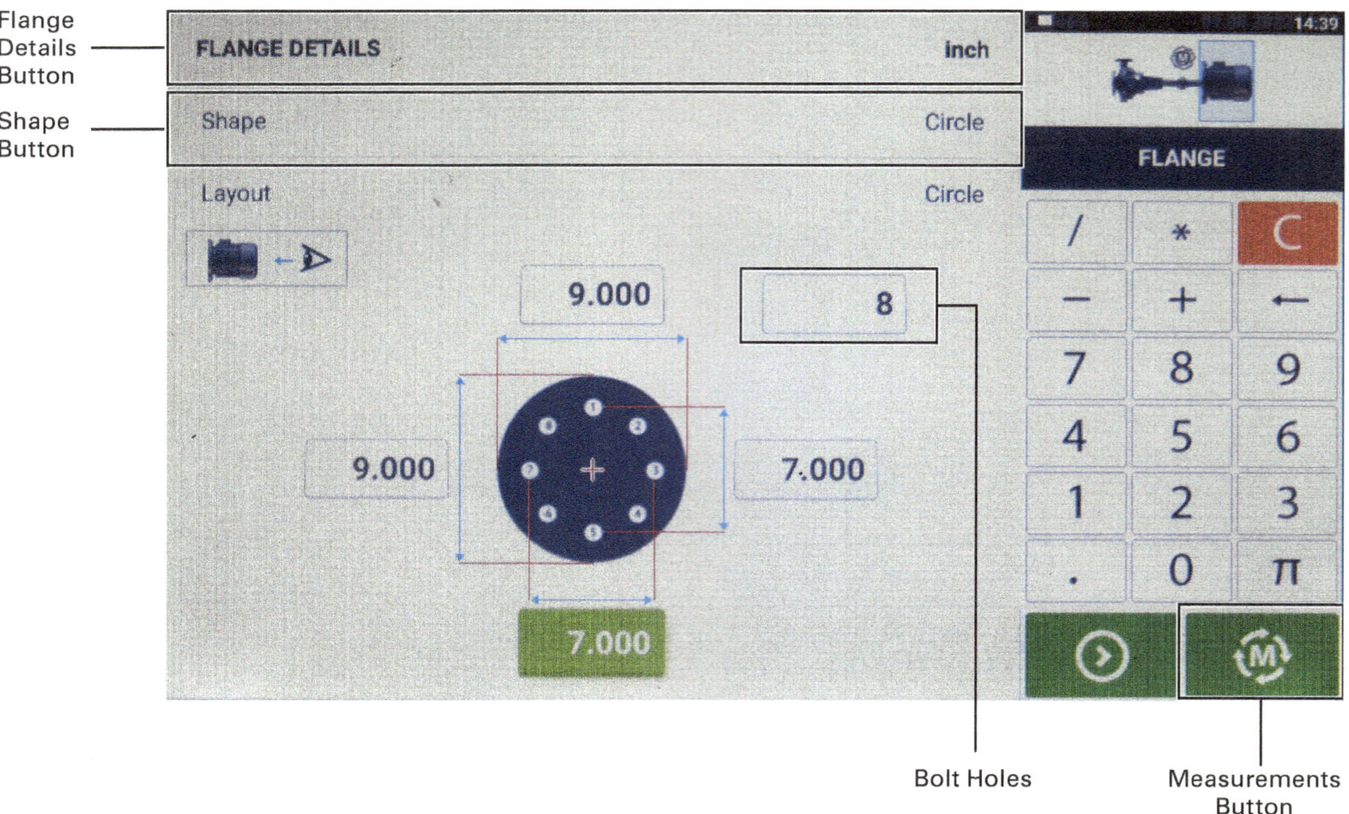

Figure 20 Flange configuration page.

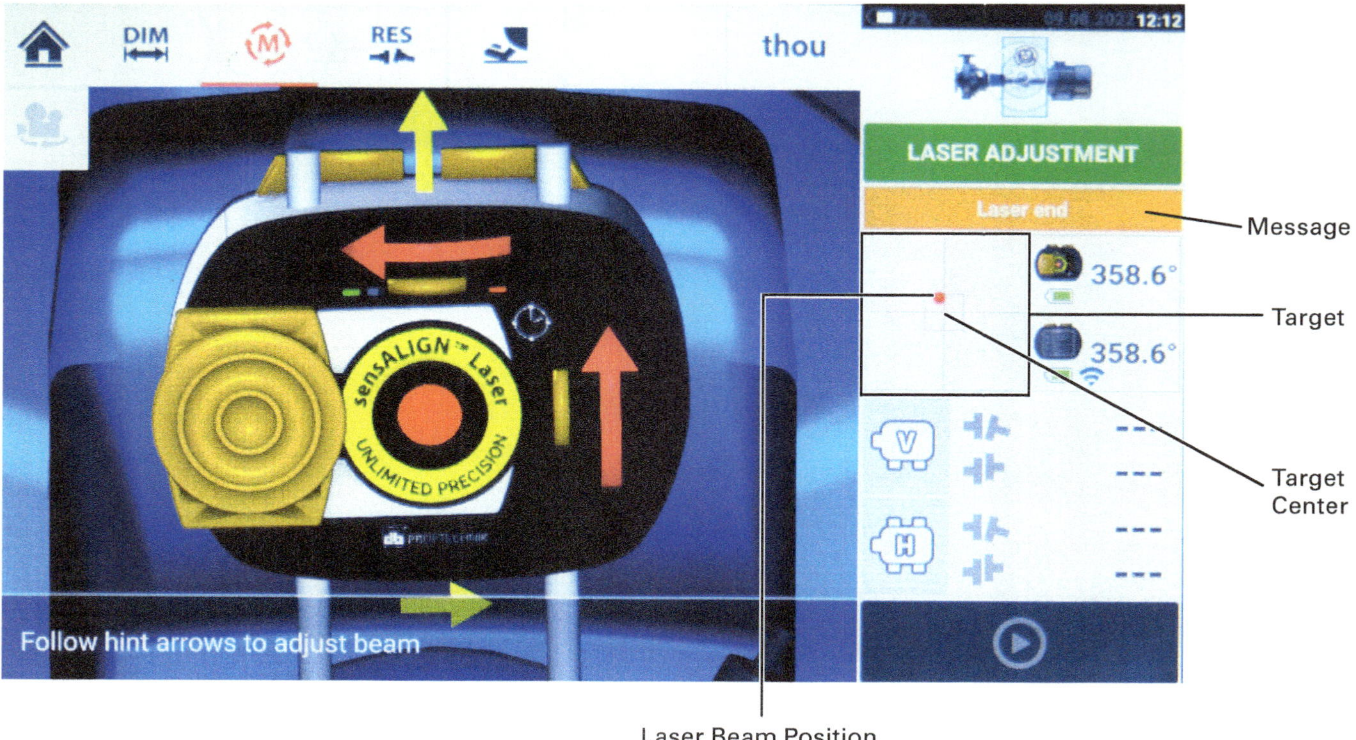

Figure 21 Centering the laser beam.

1.0.0 Section Review

1. Class 2 laser devices, like laser alignment tools, require special laser goggles to protect the eyes.

   a. True
   b. False

2. While the newer laser alignment tools can successfully perform a precision alignment without a preliminary rough alignment, it's still wise to do the rough alignment.

   a. True
   b. False

2.0.0 PROCEDURES

Objective

Outline laser alignment procedures.

a. Summarize checking and correcting soft foot with a laser alignment tool.

b. Summarize performing a horizontal shaft laser alignment procedure.

c. Summarize performing a vertical shaft laser alignment procedure.

d. Summarize thermal growth and its role in alignment.

Performance Tasks

2. Use a laser alignment tool to check for and correct soft foot.

3. Perform a horizontal shaft laser alignment procedure.

Trade Terms

Coupling stresses: Forces that create misalignment.

Thermal growth: Changes in a component's dimensions due to temperature change.

Millwrights and industrial mechanics commonly use laser alignment tools to align machines with horizontal shafts. Newer tools can do other tasks as well, so millwrights use them to solve many problems. For example, most tools can check for soft foot and provide correction guidance. Some can do other alignment procedures, as well, such as vertical shaft alignments. Advanced tools can help millwrights identify and manage thermal growth patterns.

2.1.0 Checking for and Correcting Soft Foot

As you may recall from NCCER Module 15313, *Prealignment and Shim Fabrication*, soft foot is a very common and challenging problem. Unless you correct it early, it will be difficult or impossible to achieve acceptable alignment. Normally, millwrights deal with it before tackling other coupling stresses.

Some millwrights use dial indicator methods for detecting soft foot. They measure it with thickness gauges or shims and estimate corrections. These procedures work well but can be very tedious. Other problems can mimic soft foot, which complicates the situation. Happily, many laser alignment tools will measure soft foot and provide guidance for fixing the problem.

> **NOTE**
>
> The following procedures outline checking the driver for soft foot. During new equipment installation, you should check the driven machine as well. Use the same procedures.

2.1.1 Measuring Soft Foot

The ROTALIGN® touch includes tools for measuring and correcting soft foot. The following steps outline the process:

Step 1 As a preliminary check, loosen the driver's foot bolts. Use a thickness gauge to check for obvious gaps under any foot. If you detect significant foot problems, it might be appropriate to contact the manufacturer for repair or replacement rather than continuing.

Step 2 Retighten all foot bolts.

Step 3 Set up the laser alignment tool as explained earlier. Turn on the computer.

Step 4 Tap the **Soft foot** tile on the main screen (*Figure 16*).

Step 5 Enter the measured equipment dimensions as explained earlier. Also be sure that you've centered the laser unit.

Step 6 Tap the **Soft foot** button. A diagram of the driver will appear (*Figure 22*).

Step 7 Tap any of the four foot buttons on the diagram. An animated wrench will appear next to the bolt, indicating that you should loosen it. The soft foot reading will appear. Tap the reading to record it (*Figure 23*).

Step 8 Retighten the foot bolt.

Step 9 Repeat *Steps 7* and *8* for the remaining feet.

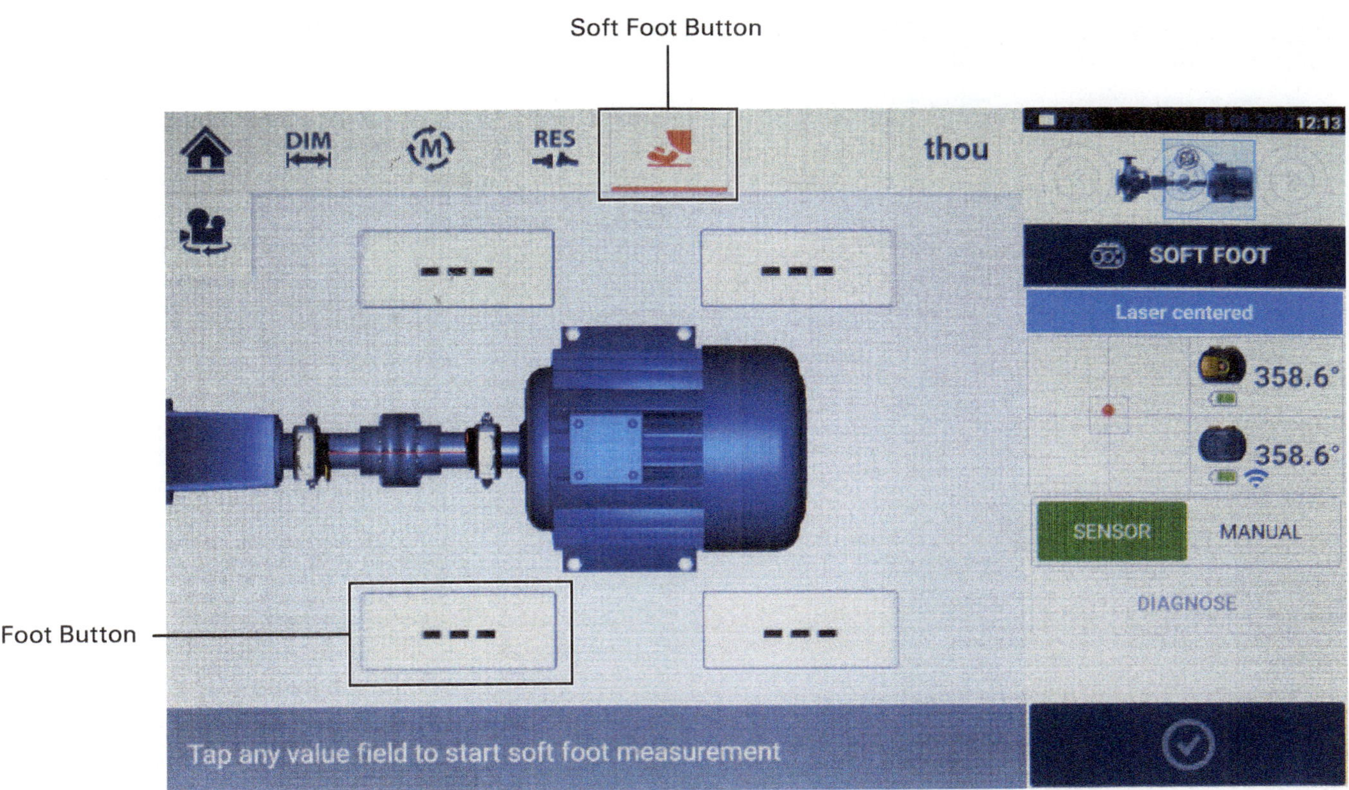

Figure 22 The soft foot tool.

Once you've completed all four measurements, the screen will show the results. If the soft foot results are within acceptable levels, a smiley face will appear (*Figure 24*). If not, a frowning face will appear instead.

If the soft foot level is unacceptable, determine the soft foot type and correct it. The ROTALIGN® touch includes a diagnostic tool that helps with this task. To access the tool, tap the **Diagnose** button (*Figure 25*).

Once you've identified the soft foot type, correct it using appropriate measures. You may wish to review NCCER Module 15313, *Prealignment and Shim Fabrication*, for guidance.

> **NOTE**
>
> Many millwrights check for soft foot several times: at prealignment, after rough alignment, and after precision alignment. Whether or not you do this depends on the application.

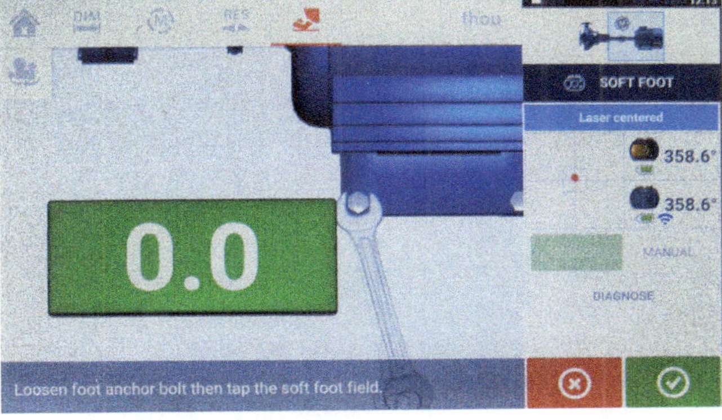

Figure 23 Soft foot reading.

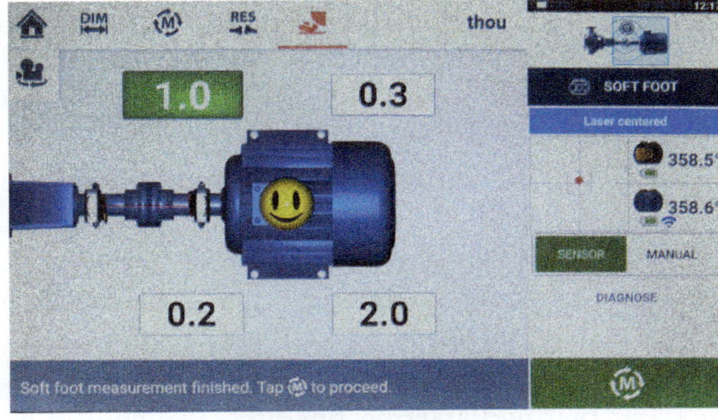

Figure 24 Acceptable soft foot results.

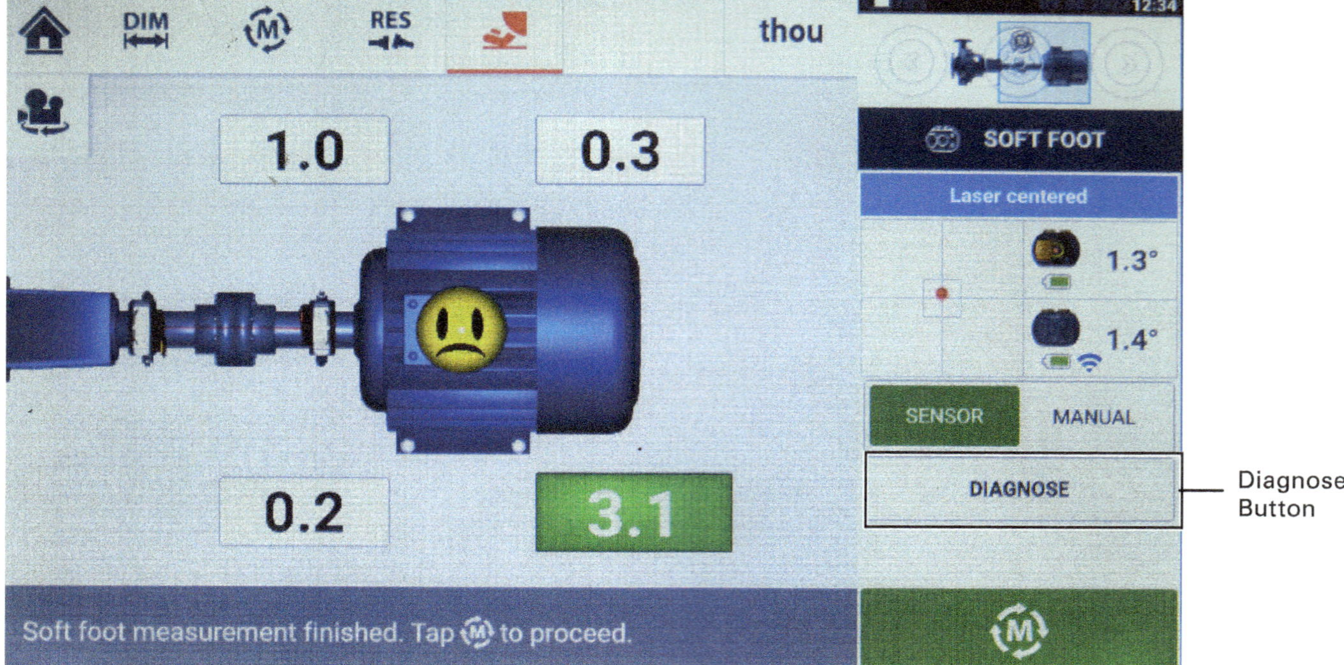

Diagnose Button

Figure 25 Unacceptable soft foot results.

2.2.0 Horizontal Shaft Laser Alignment Procedure

Millwrights and industrial mechanics most frequently align two horizontal shafts linked by a coupling. An electric motor and pump is a common example. The ROTALIGN® touch includes tools for measuring the misalignment and reducing it to acceptable levels.

2.2.1 Measuring Misalignment

The laser alignment procedure begins by measuring the existing misalignment. The following steps outline the process:

Step 1 Confirm that the equipment foot bolts are properly tightened. Set up the laser alignment tool as explained earlier. Turn on the computer.

Step 2 Tap the **Horizontal alignment** tile on the main screen (*Figure 16*).

Step 3 Enter the measured equipment dimensions as explained earlier. Also be sure that you've centered the laser unit.

Step 4 Rotate the alignment assembly to your planned starting position. You should be on the **Measurements** page. If not, tap the **M** button. Tap the **Start** button to begin measuring the misalignment (*Figure 26*).

NOTE

After entering the measured equipment dimensions and switching to the **Measurements** page, the units will change to "thous"—thousandths of an inch (0.001"). This unit is convenient since shims are specified in thousandths.

Step 5 Slowly turn the shafts through one complete rotation. As you turn the shafts, the screen will display a colored circle around the shaft. The circle will change from red to green to blue. The **Start** button will also change colors. This reflects increasingly higher quality readings.

NOTE

In the ROTALIGN® touch's standard IntelliSWEEP mode, you must rotate the shafts at least 70 degrees to measure the misalignment. The rotation circle on the computer screen will turn green when you reach this "minimum" point. The ROTALIGN® touch's limited rotation capability is handy if you can't turn the alignment assembly one full rotation. You'll get better results, however, if you keep rotating the shafts until the circle turns blue. For best results, rotate the shafts a full 360 degrees.

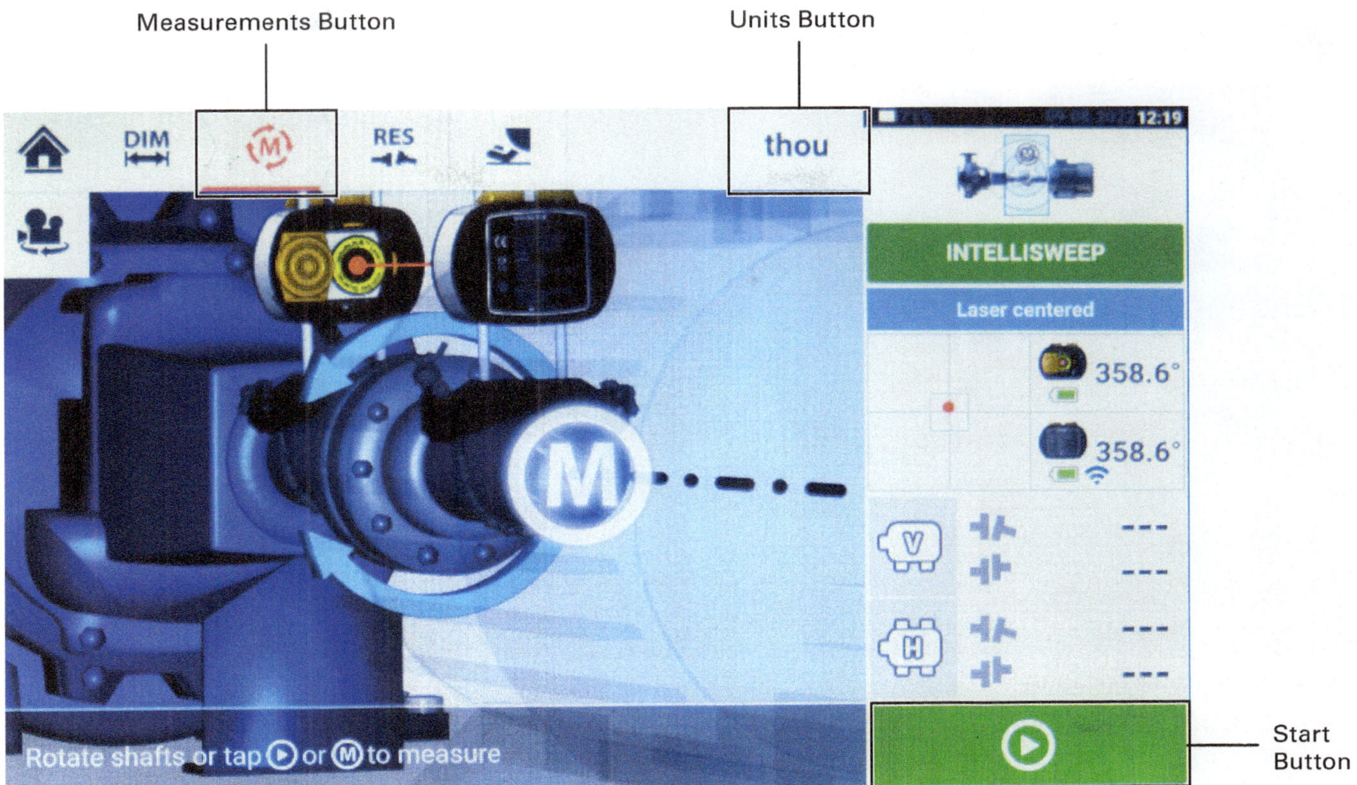

Figure 26 Starting the measurement.

> **CAUTION**
>
> When rotating the shafts, always turn them in the same direction that they will turn when operating. Turning the shafts the wrong way can cause components like impellers to come off. If the equipment can operate in either direction, pick a direction and use it consistently throughout the alignment procedure.

> **NOTE**
>
> Blue values indicate "excellent" alignment, while green values indicate "acceptable" alignment. If all four values are blue, you don't need to make any alignment corrections. If some values are green, you may or may not need to make corrections, depending on the project's specifications. Red values indicate "unacceptable" alignment. You must make corrections if any value is red.

Step 6 When you're finished rotating the shafts, tap the **Start** button to complete the measurement. The VA, VO, HA, and HO results will appear in the lower right corner (*Figure 27*).

Step 7 Repeat *Steps 4–6*.

Step 8 Tap the screen area above the misalignment values. A table showing each test cycle will appear. Confirm that both measurement cycles show the same or very similar results. If they don't, check and tighten the alignment assembly. Repeat the procedure until you get the same results twice in a row.

2.2.2 Correcting Misalignment

Once you've measured the existing misalignment, you can start reducing it in each plane. The ROTALIGN® touch can display the misalignment in either two-dimensional or three-dimensional form. It can show just one plane (vertical or horizontal) at a time, or it can show both at once (*Figure 28*).

Tap the **V/H** button to see both planes at once. Tap the **V** or **H** button to see just the vertical or horizontal plane. Tap the **2D/3D** button to switch between 2D and 3D views. The following examples use the 3D view. Select whichever view you prefer.

Figure 27 Misalignment results.

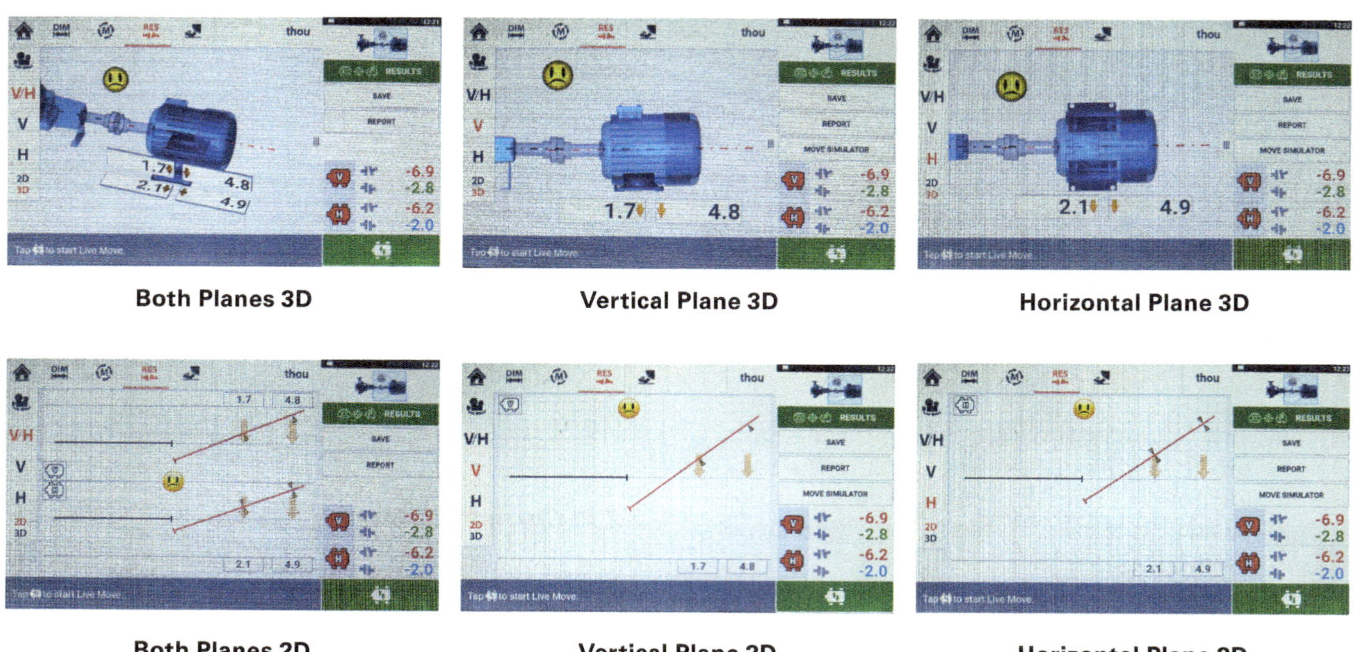

Figure 28 Possible misalignment views.

The following steps outline correcting misalignment:

Step 1 Tap the **RES** button to bring up the **Results** page. Tap the **2D/3D** button to switch to the 3D view.

Step 2 Skip to *Step 6* if the vertical plane doesn't require correction. Otherwise, continue with the next step.

Step 3 Tap the **V** button to view the vertical plane. Examine the front and back feet vertical correction values (*Figure 29*). A negative number indicates that the feet are too low (add shims). A positive number indicates that they're too high (remove shims). The numbers themselves are the shim thickness that you must add or remove.

Step 4 Loosen the foot bolts and add or remove shims as required. Tighten the bolts. When you're finished, tap the **M** button.

Step 5 Perform a new misalignment measurement procedure. Confirm that both vertical misalignment values are now blue. If they're not, repeat *Steps 1–4*.

Step 6 Skip to *Step 11* if the horizontal plane doesn't require correction. Otherwise, continue with the next step.

Step 7 If necessary, tap the **RES** button to bring up the **Results** page. Tap the **2D/3D** button to switch to the 3D view.

Step 8 Tap the **H** button to view the horizontal plane. Examine the front and back feet horizontal correction values (*Figure 30*). The arrows indicate the direction that the baseplate needs to move. The numbers indicate by how much it should move.

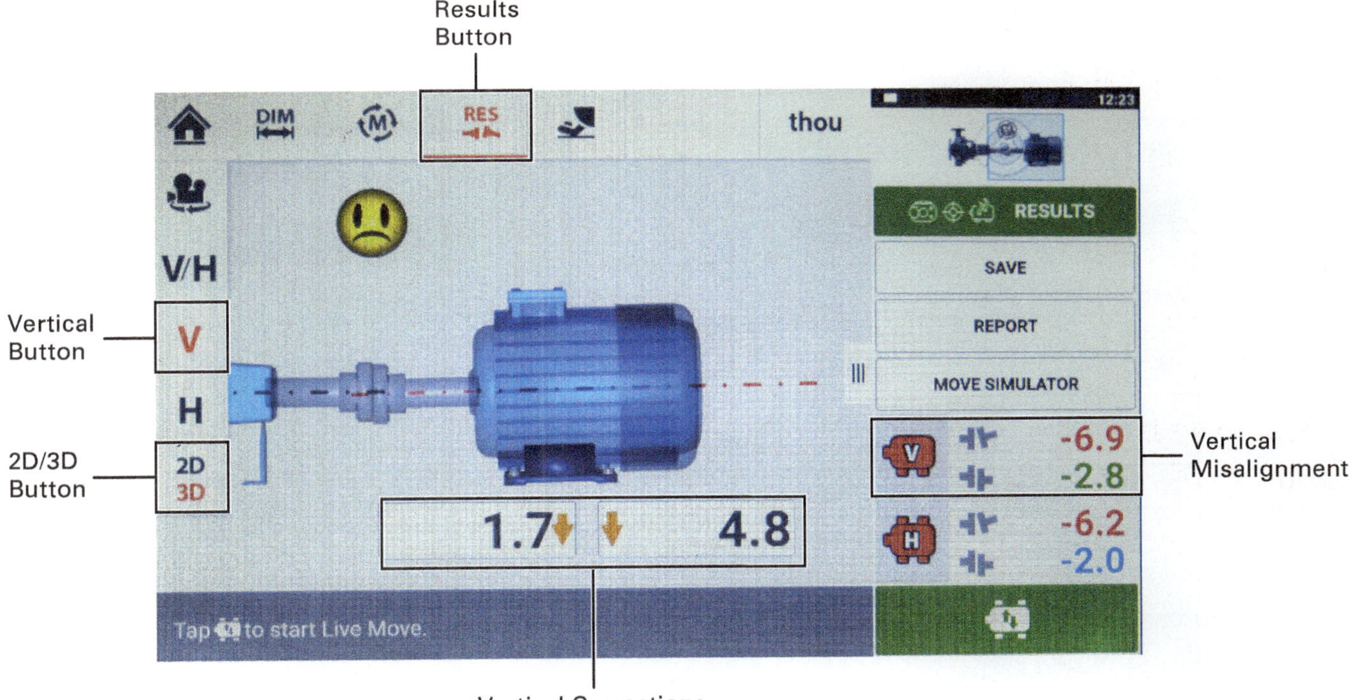

Figure 29 Correcting vertical plane misalignment.

Step 9 Rotate the shafts so the alignment assembly isn't in the way. Tap the **LIVE MOVE** button (*Figure 30*).

Step 10 Loosen the foot bolts. Use a wrench to turn the baseplate's jackbolts in the correct direction. If the installation doesn't include jackbolts, tap the baseplate with a dead-blow hammer. Watch the front and back numbers as they change. Bring them as close to 0 as possible. Tighten the foot bolts. Confirm values close to 0. When you're finished, tap the **M** button.

> **NOTE**
>
> Jackbolts greatly simplify horizontal plane adjustments. It's easy to bring a jackbolt-equipped machine into horizontal alignment when using an alignment tool with a feature like the ROTALIGN® touch's Live Move. If a machine doesn't have jackbolts, consider installing them to make future alignment tasks quicker and easier. As an experienced millwright once said, "Jackbolts are worth their weight in gold!"

Step 11 Perform a new misalignment measurement procedure. Confirm that all misalignment values are now blue. If they're not, repeat the entire alignment correction procedure.

It may take several adjustments in one or both planes, but eventually all four misalignment values should be blue, indicating excellent alignment (*Figure 31*). A smiley face confirms a successful alignment procedure.

2.2.3 Final Steps

At this point, the equipment should be precisely aligned. The following procedure outlines the final steps needed to confirm this condition:

Step 1 Using a suitable torque wrench, tighten all foot bolts to the specified torque value.

Step 2 Follow the procedures outlined in *Section 2.2.1* to measure the VA, VO, HA, and HO. All misalignment values should be blue.

Step 3 If any measurement is unacceptable, perform the alignment procedures again.

Step 4 Document your work and final measurements. Follow your company's procedures and specifications.

If you wish, you can create an alignment report right on the ROTALIGN® touch. Later, you can transfer it to a PC through the ROTALIGN® touch's software. Facilities using plant-management software often use tool-generated reports to automate keeping track of a machine's status.

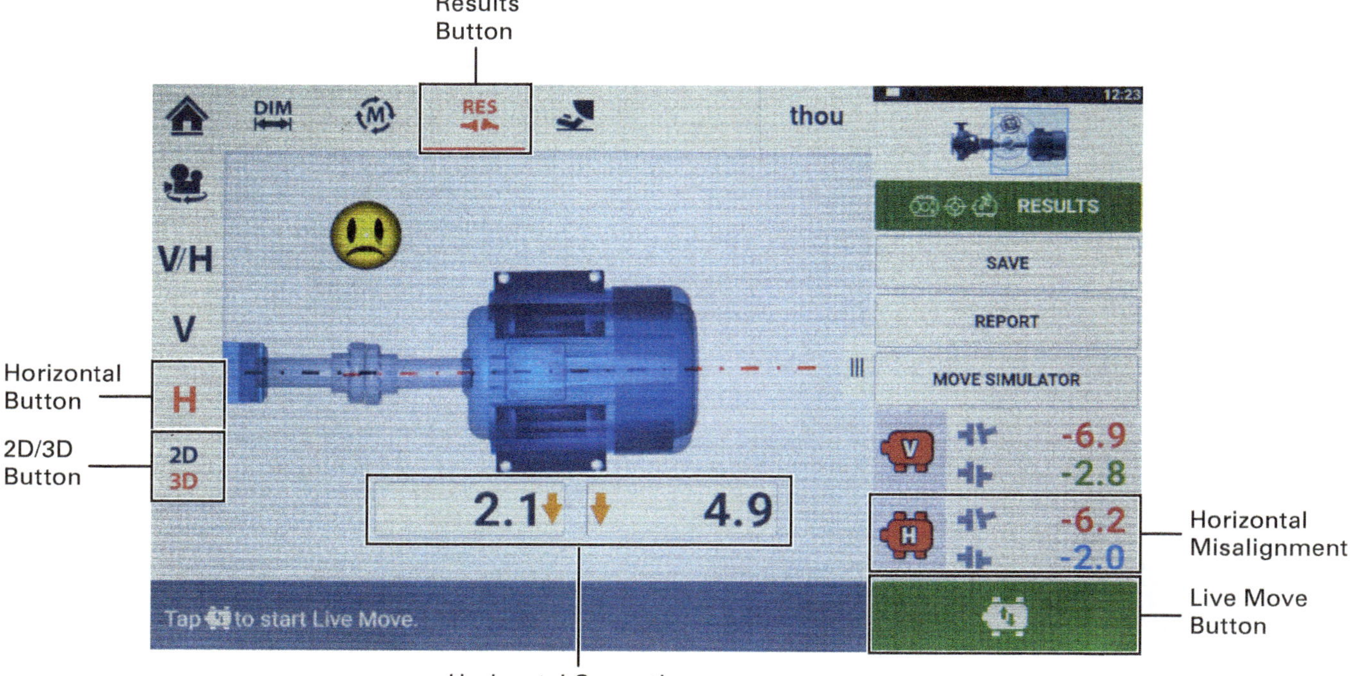

Figure 30 Correcting horizontal plane misalignment.

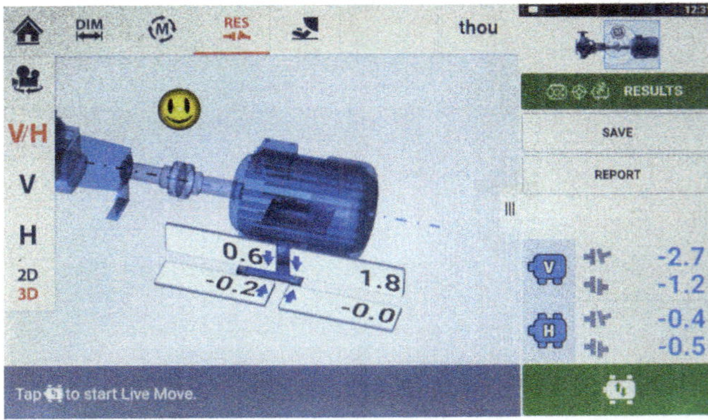

Figure 31 Excellent alignment in both planes.

2.3.0 Vertical Shaft Laser Alignment Procedure

Millwrights and industrial mechanics frequently align equipment coupled by horizontal shafts. Other configurations, such as vertical shaft machines, are less common, but millwrights still encounter them occasionally. Their alignment procedures are similar, although they do have a few significant differences. Most laser alignment tools, including the ROTALIGN® touch, handle vertical alignments without difficulty.

The laser alignment tool measures the angular and offset misalignments. It then specifies the correct shims to add to specific flange bolt locations, which corrects angular misalignment. It also specifies left/right and forward/back adjustments to correct offset misalignment.

Older laser alignment tools are less automated than recent models. In vertical orientations, they can't detect their rotational position as the shafts turn. Instead, the millwright must rotate the alignment assembly to four specific positions and trigger a measurement at each. Some alignment tool manufacturers call this method "multi-point measurement."

Newer laser alignment tools, like the ROTALIGN® touch, *can* detect rotation in the vertical orientation. When performing a vertical alignment, the computer switches to VertiSWEEP mode. This feature makes a vertical alignment nearly as simple and automated as a horizontal one.

2.3.1 Measuring Misalignment

The laser alignment procedure begins by measuring the existing misalignment. The following steps outline the process:

Step 1 Confirm that the equipment flange bolts are properly tightened. Set up the laser alignment tool as explained earlier. Turn on the computer.

Step 2 Tap the **Vertical alignment** tile on the main screen (*Figure 16*).

Step 3 Enter the measured equipment dimensions as explained earlier. Also be sure that you've centered the laser unit.

Before measuring the misalignment, you must choose a flange bolt to become the "0 bolt." When the ROTALIGN® touch provides correction guidance, it uses clockface terms to specify locations. The "0 bolt" position is 12 o'clock (*Figure 32*). Any bolt can be the "0 bolt," but once you select it, all position references depend on that location.

Step 4 Choose a flange bolt to be the "0 bolt" and mark it. If you wish, you may mark the 3 o'clock, 6 o'clock, and 9 o'clock positions as well.

Step 5 Rotate the alignment assembly to the "0 bolt" position (12 o'clock).

Step 6 You should be on the **Measurements** page. If not, tap the **M** button. Tap the **Rotation Direction** button that matches the direction you plan to turn the shafts. Tap the **Start** button to begin measuring the misalignment (*Figure 33*).

> **NOTE**
>
> After entering the measured equipment dimensions and switching to the **Measurements** page, the units will change to "thous" — thousandths of an inch (0.001"). This unit is convenient since shims are specified in thousandths.

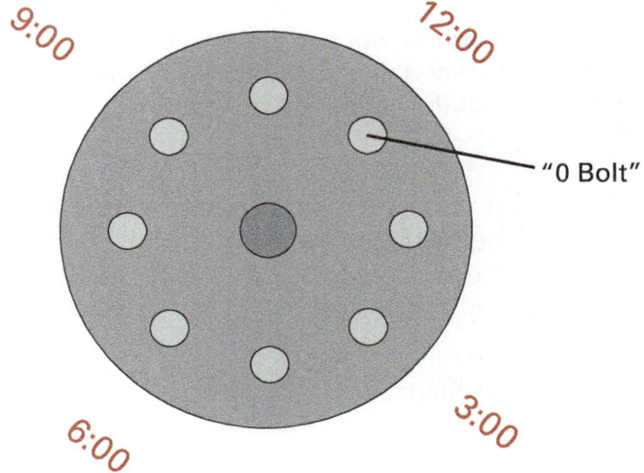

Figure 32 Example "0 bolt" location and clock positions.

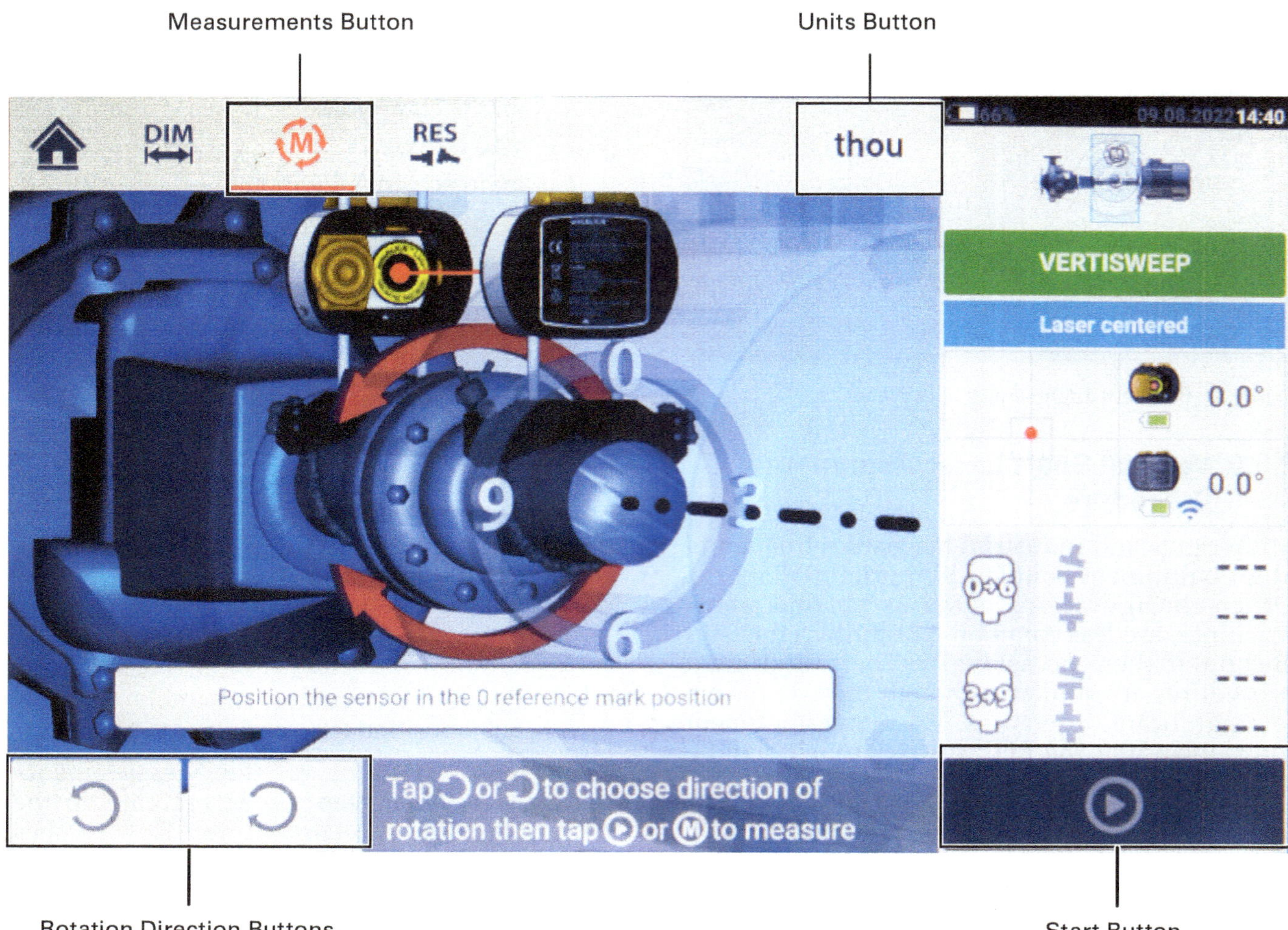

Figure 33 Starting the measurement.

Step 7 Slowly and smoothly rotate the shafts through one complete rotation.

> **CAUTION**
>
> When rotating the shafts, always turn them in the same direction that they will turn when operating. Turning the shafts the wrong way can cause components like impellers to come off. If the equipment can operate in either direction, pick a direction and use it consistently throughout the alignment procedure.

Step 8 When you're finished rotating the shafts, tap the **Stop** button to complete the measurement. The misalignment results will appear in the lower right corner (*Figure 34*).

Step 9 Repeat *Steps 5–8*.

Step 10 Tap the screen area above the misalignment values. A table showing each test cycle will appear. Confirm that both measurement cycles show the same or very similar results. If they don't, check and tighten the alignment assembly. Repeat the procedure until you get the same results twice in a row.

> **NOTE**
>
> Blue values indicate "excellent" alignment, while green values indicate "acceptable" alignment. If all values are blue, you don't need to make any alignment corrections. If some values are green, you may or may not need to make corrections, depending on the project's specifications. Red values indicate "unacceptable" alignment. You must make corrections if any value is red.

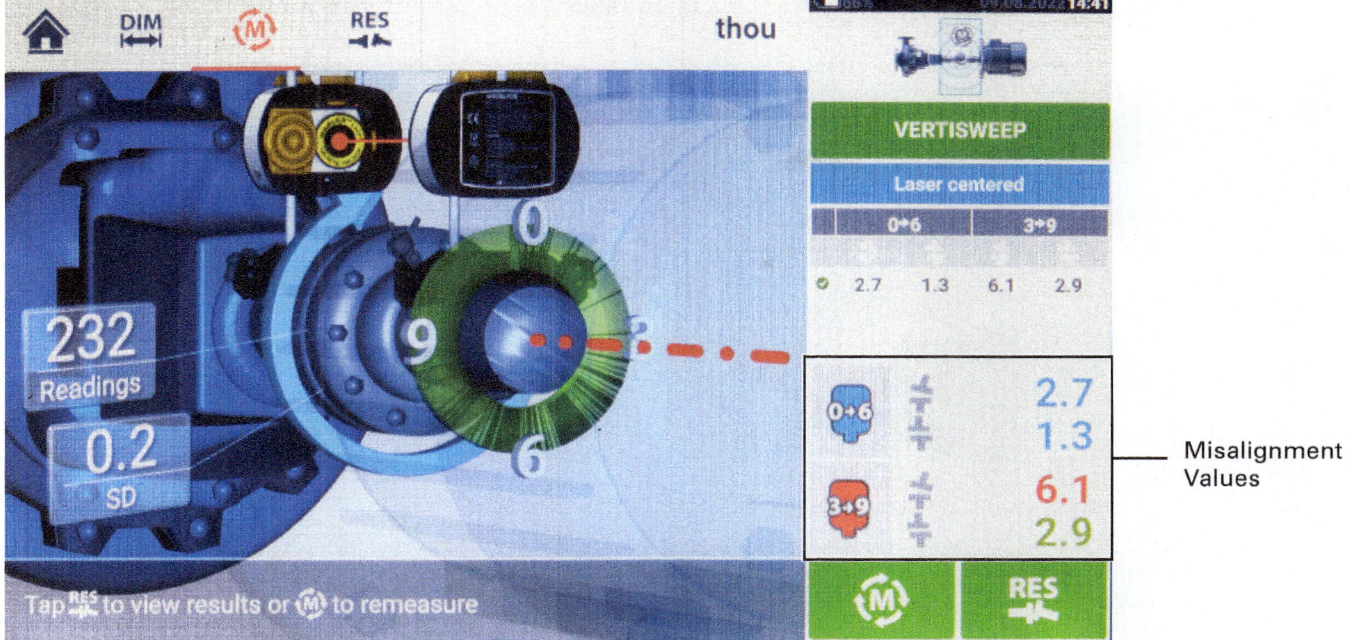

Figure 34 Misalignment results.

2.3.2 Correcting Misalignment

Once you've measured the existing misalignment, you can start reducing it. You'll correct angular misalignment by placing shims between the flanges at specific locations. You'll then deal with offset misalignment by moving the driver flange left/right and forward/back. The ROTALIGN® touch will guide you in each of these adjustments.

The following steps outline correcting angular misalignment:

Step 1 Tap the **RES** button to bring up the **Results** page (*Figure 35*).

Step 2 Examine the two angular misalignment values. Based on their color, decide whether angular misalignment requires correcting or not. Skip to *Step 8* if angular misalignment doesn't require correction. Otherwise, continue with the next step.

Step 3 Tap the leftmost **Shim Mode** button.

> **NOTE**
> The leftmost button activates "positive shims only" mode. In this mode, the ROTALIGN® touch corrects angular misalignment by adding shims rather than by adding and/or removing them. This method is the simplest way to correct misalignment. The other buttons select alternative correction methods. Read the ROTALIGN® touch manual to learn about them.

Step 4 Examine the shim table (*Figure 35*). It indicates which bolt locations require shims. It also specifies the shim thickness for each location. Assemble the required shim collection.

Step 5 Loosen the flange bolts and insert the correct shims at the specified locations.

> **NOTE**
> Remember that 0 on the diagram corresponds to the "0 bolt" location on the actual flange. Be sure to correctly match the flange's bolt locations to the corresponding ones on the diagram.

Step 6 Tighten the flange bolts in the correct sequence. When you're finished, tap the **M** button.

Step 7 Perform a new misalignment measurement procedure. Confirm that both angular misalignment values are now blue. If they're not, repeat *Steps 1–6*.

Step 8 If necessary, tap the **RES** button to bring up the **Results** page (*Figure 36*).

Step 9 Examine the two offset misalignment values. Based on their color, decide whether offset misalignment requires correcting or not. Skip to *Step 14* if offset misalignment doesn't require correction. Otherwise, continue with the next step.

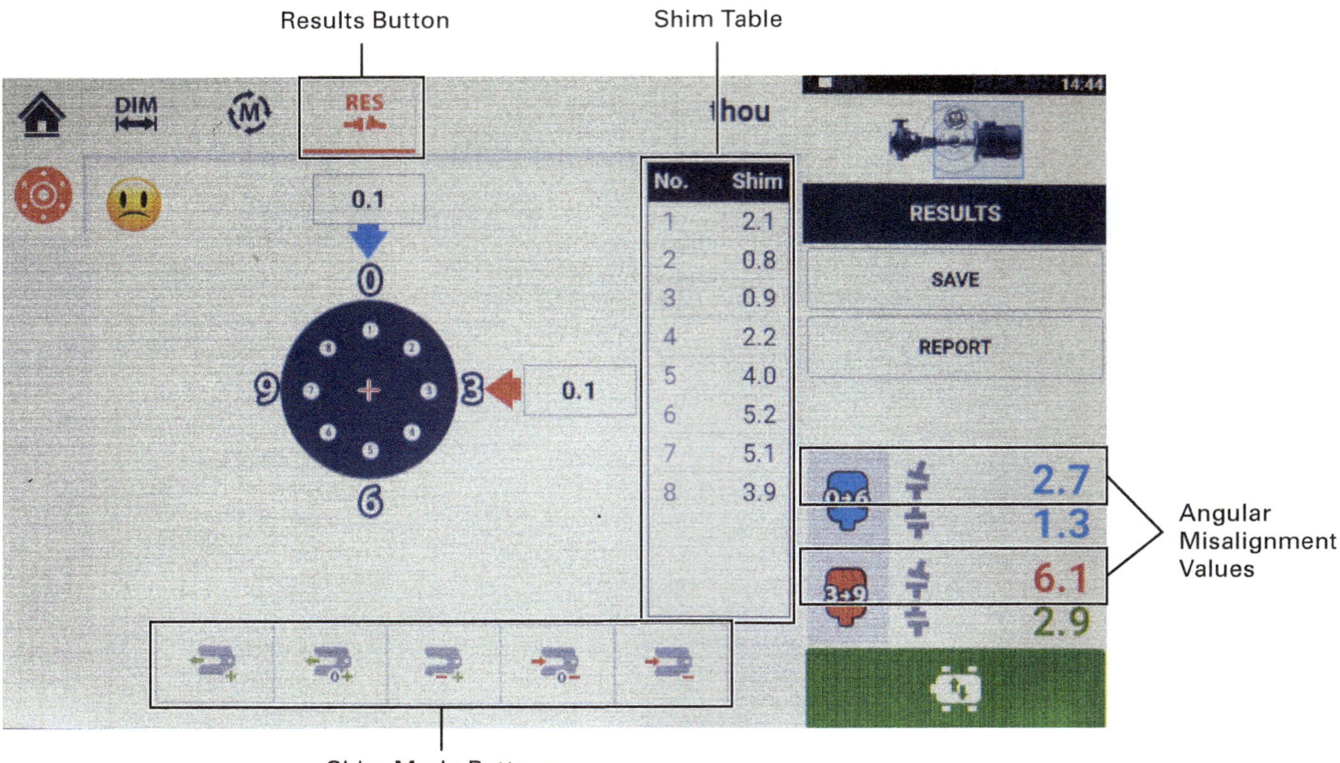

Figure 35 Correcting angular misalignment.

> **NOTE**
> The ROTALIGN® touch has a handy feature called *Live Move* that collects and displays measurements while you adjust the driver. You can use this feature to monitor your adjustments as you make them. Live Move can save a lot of time, particularly when you're making horizontal plane corrections.

Step 10 Examine the offset corrections (*Figure 36*). They indicate the left/right and forward/back movements required to reduce offset misalignment. Tap the **LIVE MOVE** button.

Step 11 A diagram of the flange will appear. Tap the location that matches the alignment assembly's current position. If necessary, move the assembly to the closest position first.

> **NOTE**
> To make the 0–6 correction, move the driver flange forward/back. To make the 3–6 correction, move the driver flange left/right. Remember that 0 (12 o'clock) on the diagram corresponds to the "0 bolt" location on the actual flange. Be sure to correctly match the clockface locations on the actual flange to the corresponding ones on the diagram.

Step 12 Loosen the flange bolts. Adjust the driver flange left/right. Bring the 3–9 value as close to 0 as possible. Adjust the driver flange forward/back. Bring the 0–6 value as close to 0 as possible.

> **NOTE**
> If the machine has an alignment adjustment mechanism, use it to move the driver flange. If not, tap the flange with a dead-blow hammer.

Step 13 Tighten the flange bolts in the correct sequence. Confirm values close to 0. When you're finished, tap the **M** button.

Step 14 Perform a new misalignment measurement procedure. Confirm that all misalignment values are blue. If they're not, repeat the entire alignment correction procedure.

It may take several adjustments, but eventually all misalignment values should be blue, indicating excellent alignment. A smiley face confirms a successful alignment procedure.

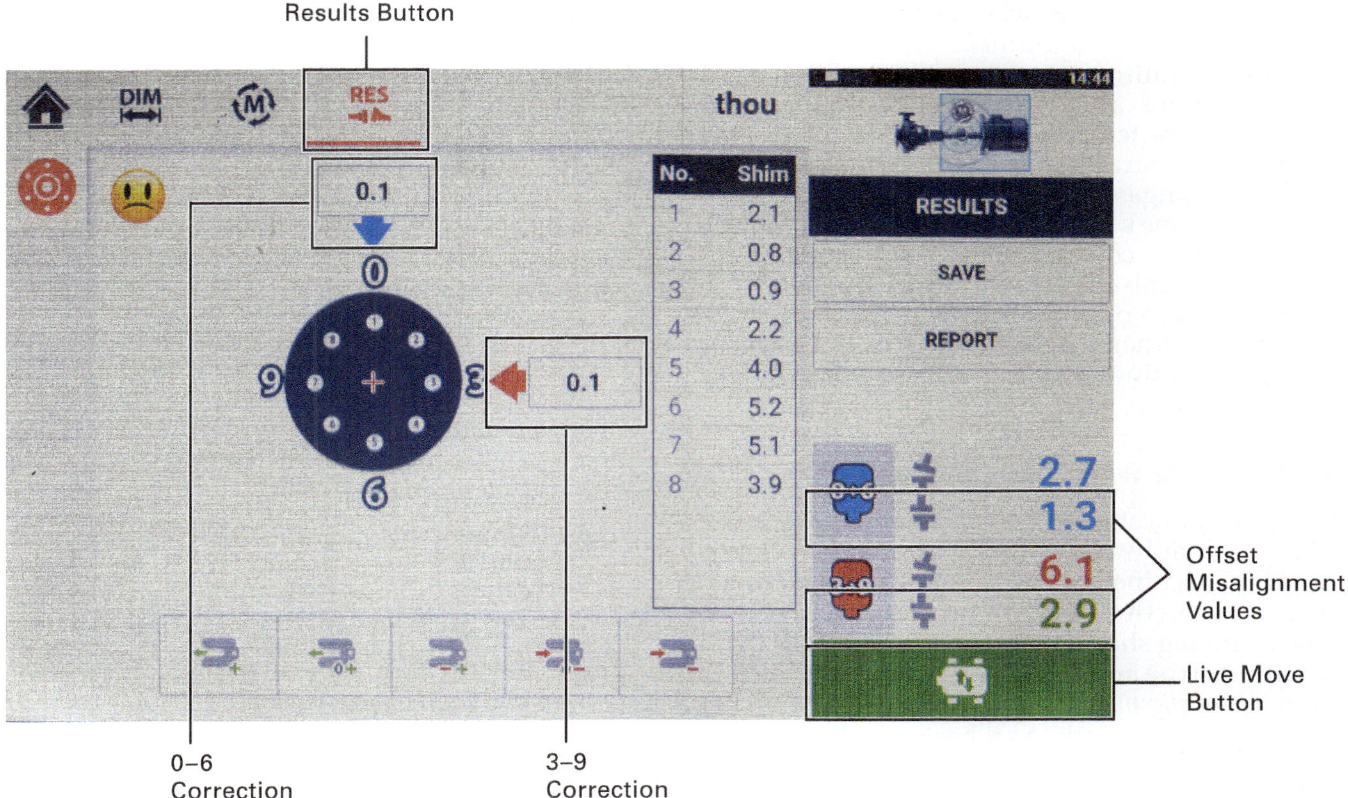

Figure 36 Correcting offset misalignment.

2.3.3 *Final Steps*

At this point, the equipment should be precisely aligned. The following procedure outlines the final steps needed to confirm this condition:

Step 1 Using a suitable torque wrench, tighten all bolts to the specified torque value. Follow the correct tightening sequence.

Step 2 Follow the procedures outlined in *Section 2.3.1* to measure the angular and offset misalignment. All misalignment values should be blue.

Step 3 If any measurement is unacceptable, perform the alignment procedures again.

Step 4 Document your work and final measurements. Follow your company's procedures and specifications.

If you wish, you can create an alignment report right on the ROTALIGN® touch. Later, you can transfer it to a PC through the ROTALIGN® touch's software. Facilities using plant-management software often use tool-generated reports to automate keeping track of a machine's status.

2.4.0 **Thermal Growth**

Temperature changes affect all materials. The metal bar in *Figure 37* has a specific length, width, and height at room temperature. If you heat the bar, it *expands* (becomes larger) along each dimension. Its proportions remain the same, but its size changes. If you cool the bar, it *contracts* (shrinks) along each dimension. Again, its size changes, but its proportions remain the same. These dimensional changes are thermal growth.

Each material has a different thermal growth rate. Metals, for example, respond to temperature changes more dramatically than wood or glass. To determine how much a material changes,

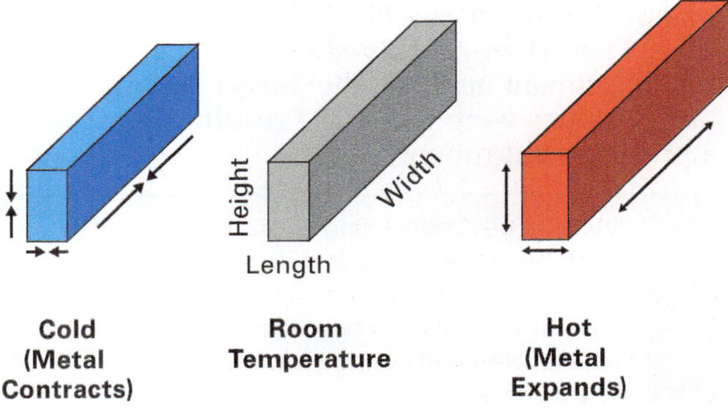

Figure 37 Thermal growth.

craftworkers can look up its *coefficient of thermal expansion*. This is a number that indicates by how many millimeters the material will expand or contract for a 1°C temperature change. For example, if the temperature changes by 1°C, steel expands or contracts by 0.000012 mm.

These changes may seem trivial, but they can alter a machine's alignment. If a motor or pump's feet expand or contract, they could create angular or offset misalignment. Similarly, shafts can become longer or shorter, producing axial misalignment. Other machine parts can change or move, generating coupling stresses that induce misalignment.

2.4.1 Dealing with Thermal Growth

In many applications, thermal changes are insignificant, so millwrights can ignore them. When a running machine heats up significantly, however, thermal growth can cause problems. Large turbines with big shafts are a good example. In these situations, the machine's *cold alignment* differs from its *hot alignment*. Aligning the machine in the usual way won't work. As it heats up, the properly aligned machine will go out of alignment.

Millwrights and industrial mechanics use a special technique to deal with this problem. They deliberately misalign the machine at room temperature (cold) so it will come into proper alignment at its operating temperature (hot). To do this, they program an *alignment target* into their laser alignment tool. This is a set of numbers that produces the required misalignment.

Ideally, the equipment manufacturer provides the alignment target's values. The millwright just enters them into the laser alignment tool and aligns the machine as usual. If the manufacturer can't provide a target, however, the millwright will have to measure or calculate it by hand. Some laser alignment tools can assist with this challenging task.

Experienced millwrights confirm their results when aligning with a target. After completing the cold alignment with the target, they run the machine until it reaches its operating temperature. They then quickly shut it down and check the alignment *without* the target values. If the target values were good, the results should show a precision alignment.

Calculating or determining an alignment target isn't a job for beginners. It's a skill that novices usually learn from an experienced millwright or industrial mechanic. Similarly, aligning a machine with a target is an "expert" task as well. The following section summarizes the process, so you'll understand the key ideas before you learn to do it in the workplace.

2.4.2 Programming an Alignment Target

The ROTALIGN® touch can easily incorporate a target into its normal alignment process. Once you've entered the target, just align the equipment as usual. The following steps outline entering the alignment target when aligning a machine with coupled horizontal shafts:

Step 1 Obtain the alignment target values for the machine. Targets are a set of four numbers that create the required angular and offset misalignment in both planes.

Step 2 Set up the laser alignment tool as explained earlier. Turn on the computer.

Step 3 Tap the **Horizontal alignment** tile on the main screen (*Figure 16*).

Step 4 Enter the measured equipment dimensions as explained earlier.

Step 5 Tap the coupling in the equipment diagram. Tap the **Targets** button (*Figure 38*).

Step 6 The target page will appear (*Figure 39*). Enter the four target values. Be sure to include their signs (+/−).

Step 7 Enable the target by sliding the **Target Enable** switch to the right.

Step 8 Once you've entered the target values and closed the target page, tap the **M** button to move to the **Measurements** page. Center the laser unit.

Step 9 Align the shafts by following the normal procedure.

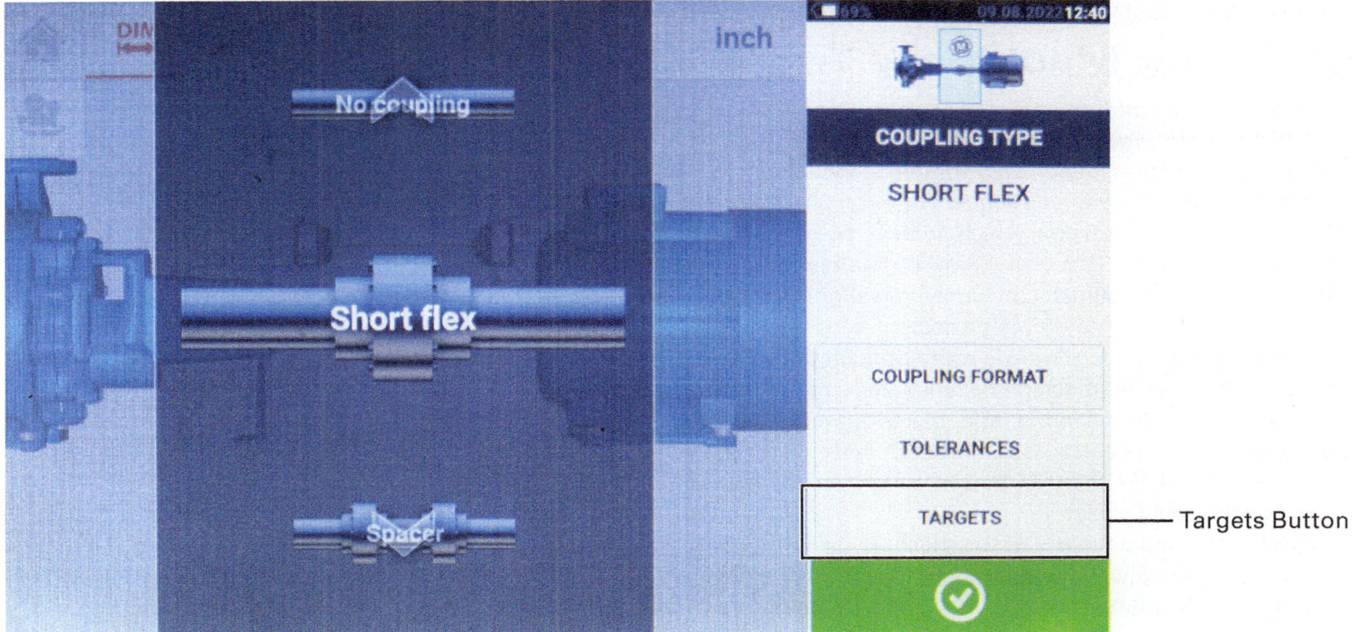

Figure 38 Setting up an alignment target.

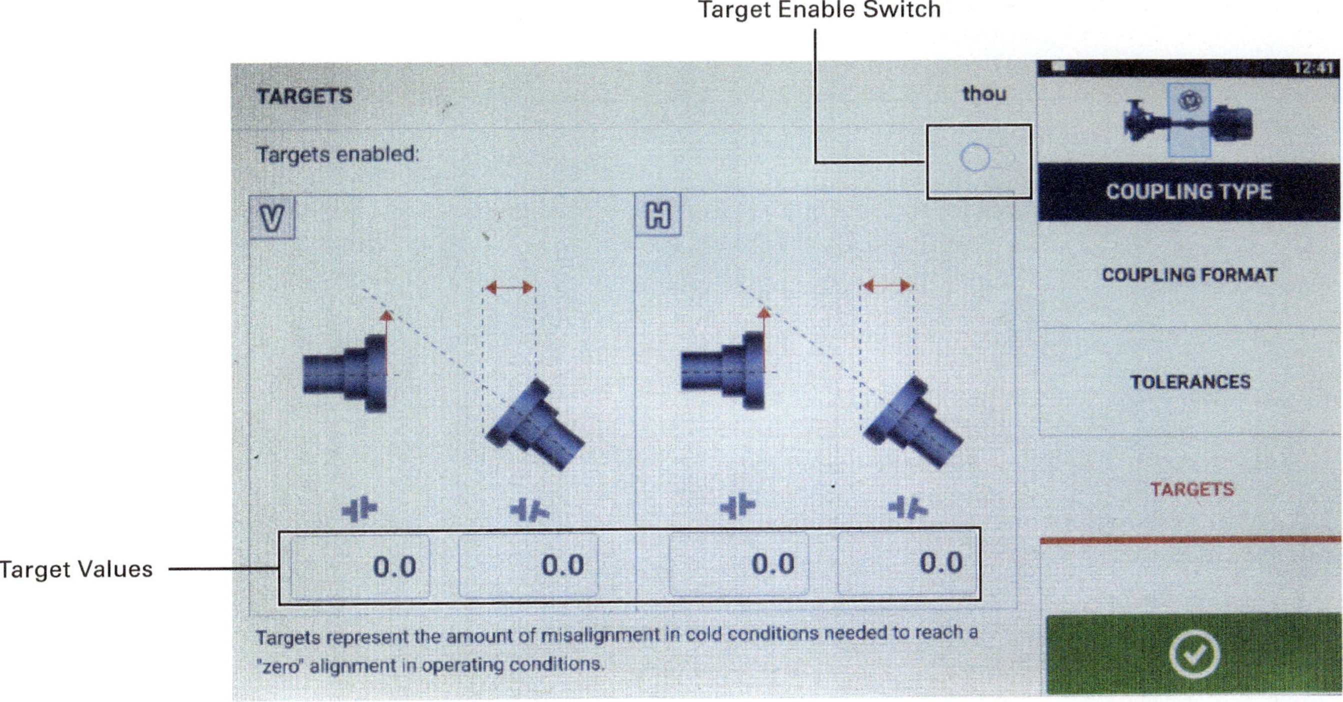

Figure 39 Target page.

Aligning Machinery Trains

Some machines offer millwrights sophisticated alignment challenges. Instead of a simple driver/driven combination, they have multiple stages and shafts linked by several couplings. For example, the driver may spin a gearbox, which, in turn, powers the driven machine. This arrangement requires four shafts and two couplings. Obviously, misalignment is possible and likely in multiple places.

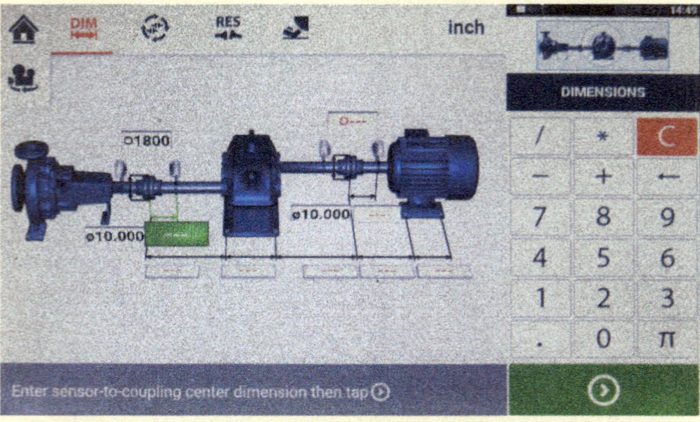

Aligning a *machinery train* is more difficult than a simple driver/driven machine because there are more things to move. At the same time, the alignment process is essentially the same. Modern laser alignment tools like the ROTALIGN® touch make the task considerably easier.

First, you build a picture of the machine by selecting each component. Then you provide all the required dimensions. Finally, you measure and correct the alignment at each shaft pair. The laser alignment tool displays the entire machinery train with its different misalignment values. This feature helps you stay organized and know what to adjust.

Aligning a machinery train is an expert task that requires practice to do well. This is a skill that you'll probably acquire on the jobsite as you work with experienced millwrights.

2.0.0 Section Review

1. Millwrights rarely check for soft foot more than once in the alignment process.

   a. True
   b. False

2. A laser alignment tool instructs you to raise a foot with a 2 thou shim. How thick is this shim?

   a. 0.2000"
   b. 0.0200"
   c. 0.0020"
   d. 0.0002"

3. When performing a vertical shaft alignment with a ROTALIGN® touch, the "0 bolt" location corresponds to ______.

   a. 3 o'clock
   b. 6 o'clock
   c. 9 o'clock
   d. 12 o'clock

4. A pump/motor combination always runs smoothly when first started. After it has been running for a while, however, it starts to vibrate. Over time, the coupling develops significant wear. Finally, both the pump and motor bearings require replacement. What *most likely* happened?

   a. The craftworker forgot to rough-align the shafts at installation.
   b. Thermal growth caused the machine to go out of alignment when it warmed up.
   c. The coupling wasn't sized correctly for the shafts.
   d. The craftworker didn't align the shafts to 0.0002" or better.

---

1. If two shafts are collinear, _____.
   a. two parallel lines could pass through the centers of the shafts
   b. two crossed lines could pass through the centers of the shafts
   c. a single line could pass through the centers of the shafts
   d. a single line that moves back and forth could pass through the centers of the shafts

2. You're aligning a pump and motor linked by a rigid coupling. The project specifications don't mention an alignment standard. To what value should you align the shafts?
   a. 0.2000"
   b. 0.0200"
   c. 0.0020"
   d. 0.0002"

3. A laser beam is useful as an alignment tool because _____.
   a. the beam can travel a long distance without spreading out
   b. the beam's red or green color is easy to see when setting up the tool
   c. the beam can curve around obstructions like large couplings
   d. the beam always sags by a fixed amount, so you don't have to measure bar sag

4. A brand-new laser alignment tool will probably be rated _____.
   a. Class I
   b. Class 2
   c. Class IIa
   d. Class 3R

5. A laser alignment tool's sensor unit measures rotation automatically with a(n) _____.
   a. optical interferometer
   b. sonic rangefinder
   c. GPS
   d. inclinometer

6. To align a vertical machine with flanges, what details does the laser alignment tool need to know about the driver flange?
   a. The flange thickness, the bolt hole diameter, and the number of bolts
   b. The flange diameter/length, the bolt circle diameter, and the number of bolts
   c. The shaft opening diameter, the flange diameter/length, and the flange thickness
   d. The flange radius/major axis, the bolt circle diameter, and the bolt hole diameter

7. What should you do as a *preliminary* step when checking for soft foot?
   a. Check the shaft for spinout and replace the seals if necessary.
   b. Measure each foot's thermal growth coefficient.
   c. Check for obvious gaps under each foot.
   d. Test the shaft for end-to-end play.

8. What is the *minimum* shaft rotation that the ROTALIGN® touch requires to measure horizontal shaft misalignment?
   a. 30 degrees
   b. 70 degrees
   c. 120 degrees
   d. 270 degrees

9. What must you do to reduce angular misalignment in vertical shaft machines with flanges?
   a. Shift the flange from side to side.
   b. Shim specific bolt hole locations around the flange.
   c. Tighten specific flange bolts to higher torques than others.
   d. Add an elastomeric spacer between the flanges.

10. If a machine's shaft changes length due to thermal growth, it can create _____.
    a. angular misalignment
    b. parallel misalignment
    c. offset misalignment
    d. axial misalignment

Collinear: Two shafts so well aligned that a single, unbroken line could pass through their centers.

Coupling stresses: Forces that create misalignment.

Laser: A device that emits a single-color light beam that doesn't spread out quickly.

Motor bell: A flanged cylindrical component that links a flange-equipped motor to another machine. Also called a *motor stand* or *distance piece*.

Precision alignment: Procedures designed to eliminate nearly all misalignment, often down to 0.002" or better.

Soft foot: A coupling stress created by a machine's feet not all resting firmly on the baseplate.

Thermal growth: Changes in a component's dimensions due to temperature change.

Additional Resources

This module presents thorough resources for task training. The following reference material is suggested for further study.

Prüftechnik. **www.pruftechnik.com**.
SKF. **www.skf.com**.

Figure Credits

Courtesy of Prüftechnik/Fluke, Module Opener
iStock@Seetwo, Figure 6
Courtesy of SJKF, Figure 7

Section Review Answer Key

SECTION 1.0.0

Answer	Section Reference	Objective
1. b	1.1.2	1a
2. a	1.2.1	1b

SECTION 2.0.0

Answer	Section Reference	Objective
1. b	2.1.1	2a
2. c	2.2.1	2b
3. d	2.3.1	2c
4. b	2.4.1	2d

User Update

NCCER makes every effort to keep its textbooks up-to-date and free of technical errors. We appreciate your help in this process. If you find an error, a typographical mistake, or an inaccuracy in NCCER's curricula, please submit a User Update form by visiting **https://www.nccer.org/olf**. You can also scan the QR code using the camera on your phone or mobile device to access the form.

Optical Layout and Alignment

OVERVIEW

Whenever new factories go up, millwrights immediately get involved. They work with the construction crew to lay out future machines' locations. Later, they help install those machines, positioning heavy equipment with great precision. Similarly, millwrights are important during plant renovations, helping to move and reinstall equipment. In many cases, they'll use optical instruments to perform these tasks.

Module 15504

Trainees with successful module completions may be eligible for credentialing through the NCCER Registry. To learn more, go to **www.nccer.org** or contact us at 1.888.622.3720. Our website, **www.nccer.org**, has information on the latest product releases and training.

Your feedback is welcome. You may email your comments to **curriculum@nccer.org**, send general comments and inquiries to **info@nccer.org**, or fill in the User Update form at the back of this module.

This information is general in nature and intended for training purposes only. Actual performance of activities described in this manual requires compliance with all applicable operating, service, maintenance, and safety procedures under the direction of qualified personnel. References in this manual to patented or proprietary devices do not constitute a recommendation of their use.

15504 V4.0

From *Millwright, Trainee Guide*. NCCER.
Copyright © 2023 by NCCER. Published by Pearson. All rights reserved.

Optical Layout and Alignment

Objective

Successful completion of this module prepares you to do the following:

1. Identify optical instruments and summarize their roles in layout and alignment.
   a. Summarize optical layout and alignment concepts.
   b. Describe optical instruments and auxiliary equipment.
   c. Describe optical levels and the techniques associated with them.
   d. Describe laser levels and the techniques associated with them.

Performance Tasks

Under supervision, you should be able to do the following:

1. Set up a tripod and mount an optical instrument.
2. Prepare an optical level for taking elevation measurements.
3. Use an optical level to determine a location's elevation.

Trade Terms

Benchmarks	Laser level	References
Calibration	Leveling	Reticle
Elevation	Line of sight	Theodolite
Height	Optical level	Total station

Industry Recognized Credentials

If you are training through an NCCER-accredited sponsor, you may be eligible for credentials from NCCER's Registry. The ID number for this module is 15504. Note that this module may have been used in other NCCER curricula and may apply to other level completions. Contact NCCER's Registry at 1.888.622.3720 or go to **www.nccer.org** for more information.

You can also show off your industry-recognized credentials online with NCCER's digital badges. Transform your knowledge, skills, and achievements into badges that you can share across social media platforms, send to your network, and add to your resume. For more information, visit **www.nccer.org**.

This module uses US standard and metric units in up to three different ways. This note explains how to interpret them.

Exact Conversions

Exact metric equivalents of US standard units appear in parentheses after the US standard unit. For example: "Measure 18" (45.7 cm) from the end and make a mark."

Approximate Conversions

In some cases, exact metric conversions would be inappropriate or even absurd. In these situations, an approximate metric value appears in parentheses with the ~ symbol in front of the number. For example: "Grip the tool about 3" (~8 cm) from the end."

Parallel but not Equal Values

Certain scenarios include US standard and metric values that are parallel but not equal. In these situations, a slash (/) surrounded by spaces separates the US standard and metric values. For example: "Place the point on the steel rule's 1" / 1 cm mark."

VIDEOS AND DIGITAL RESOURCES

How to Access Resources

This craft has additional videos and resources to enhance your learning experience. To view these resources, scan the QR below. The videos and resources are separated by module.

You can scan this code using the camera on your phone or mobile device to view these videos and resources.

Contents

1.0.0 OPTICAL EQUIPMENT AND TECHNIQUES

Objective

Identify optical instruments and summarize their roles in layout and alignment.

a. Summarize optical layout and alignment concepts.
b. Describe optical instruments and auxiliary equipment.
c. Describe optical levels and the techniques associated with them.
d. Describe laser levels and the techniques associated with them.

Performance Tasks

1. Set up a tripod and mount an optical instrument.
2. Prepare an optical level for taking elevation measurements.
3. Use an optical level to determine a location's elevation.

Trade Terms

Benchmarks: Metal markers that precisely identify specific locations.

Calibration: Checking and adjusting an instrument so it can be certified as giving results that meet its specifications.

Elevation: An object's vertical distance above or below a standard reference, such as sea level.

Height: An object's vertical distance above or below a location.

Laser level: An optical instrument that uses a laser beam for measuring heights.

Leveling: Determining an object's elevation by measuring its vertical position relative to a known elevation.

Line of sight: An imaginary horizontal line between an optical instrument and a distant target.

Optical level: An optical instrument that measures heights, horizontal angles, and distances.

References: Locations whose positions and/or elevations are precisely documented.

Reticle: A clear disk engraved with lines or a set of fine wires placed inside an optical instrument.

Theodolite: An optical instrument that precisely measures horizontal and vertical angles.

Total station: An optical instrument that precisely measures horizontal and vertical angles, as well as distances.

If you were to fly a drone over an industrial plant floor, you'd notice something right away. All the machines, pipes, conduits, connections, and supporting equipment are precisely laid out and aligned. Perhaps you'd see a row of pumps and their driving motors (*Figure 1*). Notice the overhead pipes. Each connects to its matching pump in exactly the right place. These details make machinery work correctly and reliably. How did the construction workers place everything so perfectly?

Layout is a three-dimensional task. Not only must machines sit in the right places, but each must sit at the right **height**. Pipes and conduits must connect without pulling or pushing on their machines. Flanges must line up perfectly. When driven machines and their drivers sit on separate baseplates, they too must line up correctly. Otherwise, aligning their shafts won't be possible.

Optical instruments assist millwrights with many layout and alignment tasks (*Figure 2*). These precision devices use lenses, mirrors, and prisms to produce images in the operator's eye. Most sit on a tripod and rotate or tilt. The craftworker carefully points the instrument at a distant location and measures its distance, angle, or height. The measured information helps the craftworker perform layout and alignment tasks.

> **WARNING!**
>
> Never look at the sun through an optical instrument. You could injure your eyes. Pointing an instrument directly at the sun can damage the instrument.

1.1.0 Optical Layout and Alignment

Millwrights help with layout during construction. Using optical instruments and specialized techniques, they create equipment layouts on the empty plant floor. When the machines arrive, they help align them. Millwrights also produce documentation that other craftworkers will someday use when working on these machines (*Figure 3*).

Figure 1 Pumps on a plant floor.

Figure 2 Craftworker using an optical instrument.

NCCER – *Millwright*

Many of the tools and techniques that millwrights use for these tasks are like those that land surveyors use. Some optical layout and alignment techniques are easy to learn. Others require extensive training and practice. Companies usually hire specialists for those tasks. This module introduces the optical instruments that you may encounter in your workplace. It also introduces the more common techniques.

1.1.1 Layout and Alignment Concepts

In NCCER Module 15104, *Basic Layout*, you learned about *baselines*. These are reference lines that millwrights use to create machine centerlines and other layout lines. Frequently, these new lines are either perpendicular or parallel to the baselines. Eventually, workers use these lines to position the concrete pads and baseplates that support machines.

To locate and create baselines, millwrights use references within the plant. These are specific, well-documented locations. Columns are common references since the building's plans document them precisely. Some plants have brass plugs or small metal markers called benchmarks installed in the floor. These too have well-documented locations.

Millwrights can use existing references to create new ones. For example, the plant floor in *Figure 4* shows an existing machine positioned on two centerlines. During its installation, a millwright created the centerlines by using two nearby baselines as references. Those baselines, in turn, use the benchmark in the floor as a reference point.

Suppose the company is about to install a new machine. A millwright will need to create baselines near the new machine's future location. The machine's centerlines will depend on these baselines for their positions. The first step in the process is installing a new reference marker in the plant floor.

The new reference marker must be 150'-8" from the existing one. An imaginary line drawn between the markers should form a 35-degree angle with the existing horizontal baseline. An optical instrument will help the craftworker locate the correct position. After identifying the spot, the worker installs a brass reference marker in the concrete (*Figure 5*).

Sometimes, millwrights must mount a machine's baseplate at a specific vertical position (height or elevation). Simply measuring with a tape measure isn't accurate enough. Instead, they use references with known elevations and "transfer" them to the new locations. They can then establish the machine's vertical position from these.

Leveling is an important concept in surveying. Most people think of leveling as ensuring that something isn't tilted but is sitting or hanging straight. That idea is correct but isn't complete. In surveying, leveling refers to determining an object's elevation by measuring its height relative to a reference with a known elevation.

Figure 6 shows a measuring rod sitting on a location with a known elevation. A craftworker uses an optical instrument to read the marks on the rod. The worker then rotates the instrument and reads a rod sitting on the second location. These measurements, along with the known elevation and some simple math, give the second location's elevation.

In plant layout, leveling measurements help establish new locations at specific heights or elevations. They also ensure that equipment mounted at those positions is truly horizontal rather than tilted. Leveling is the most common optical layout and alignment technique.

1.2.0 Optical Equipment

Many layout and alignment techniques require millwrights to measure angles, distances, and heights. They must do this with great accuracy and precision. In most cases, they use optical instruments instead of ordinary measuring tools.

Many optical instruments include a small telescope for aligning them with distant locations. The telescope contains a reticle inside its tube. This is a clear disk with black lines etched on it or a set of fine wires. The operator positions one or more of these lines on a target. *Figure 7* shows a reticle with *crosshairs* and *stadia lines*. The crosshairs are for positioning, while the stadia lines are for measuring distances.

Some optical instruments contain lasers that project a dot or line onto an object. These may help the operator position the tool. Other instruments use the laser for measuring. These instruments usually include sensors that detect the laser beam or reflectors that bounce it to another instrument.

Older optical tools had scales that the operator read and interpreted. Most current tools have electronic readouts that display results directly. As with all precision equipment, you should read the manual before using the tool. The manual will include useful setup information and explain how to check the instrument for correct operation. Manufacturers usually offer electronic versions of the instrument's manual on their websites.

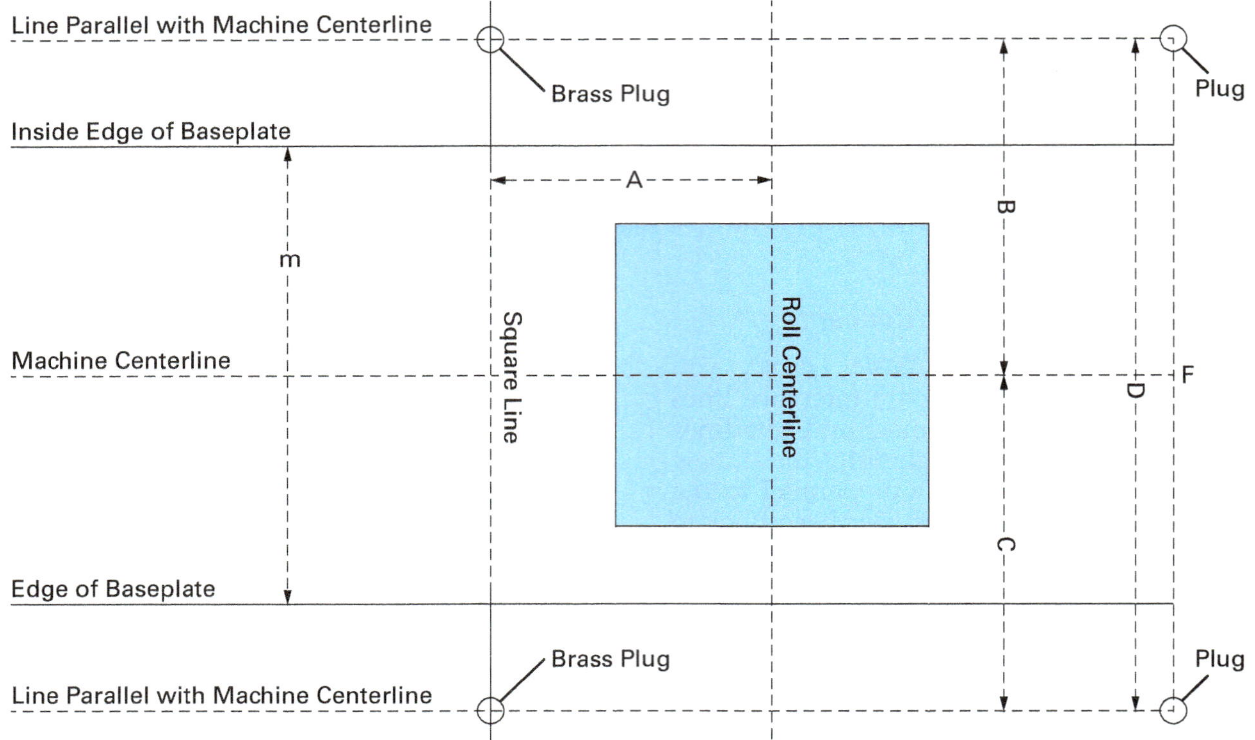

Figure 3 Alignment record.

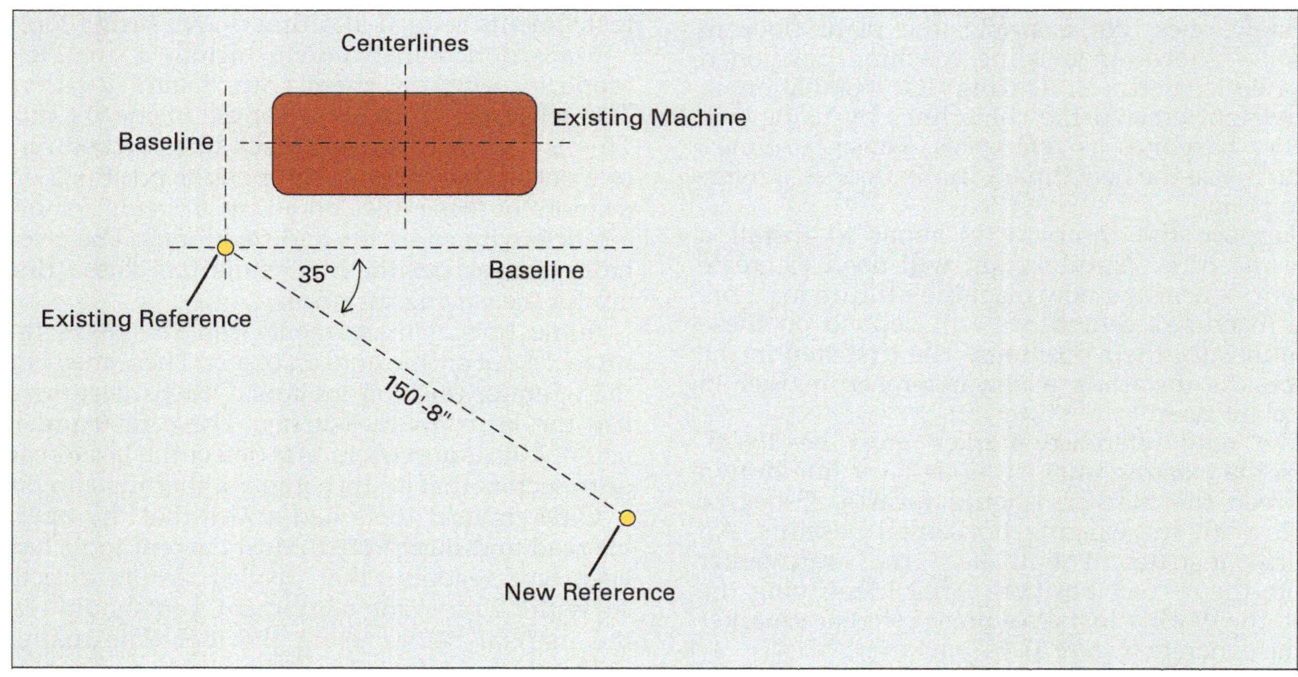

Figure 4 Creating a new reference.

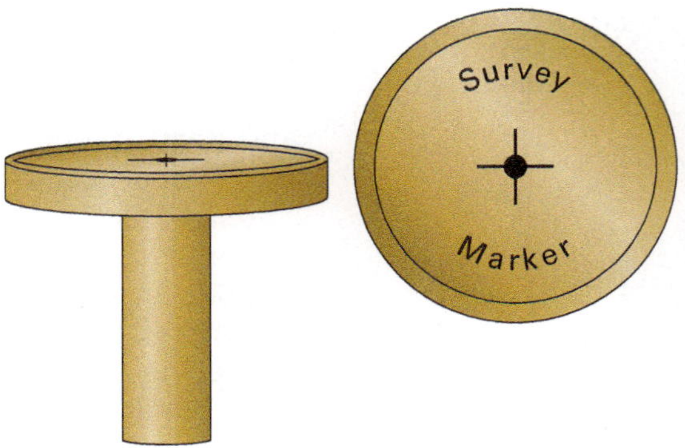

Figure 5 Reference marker.

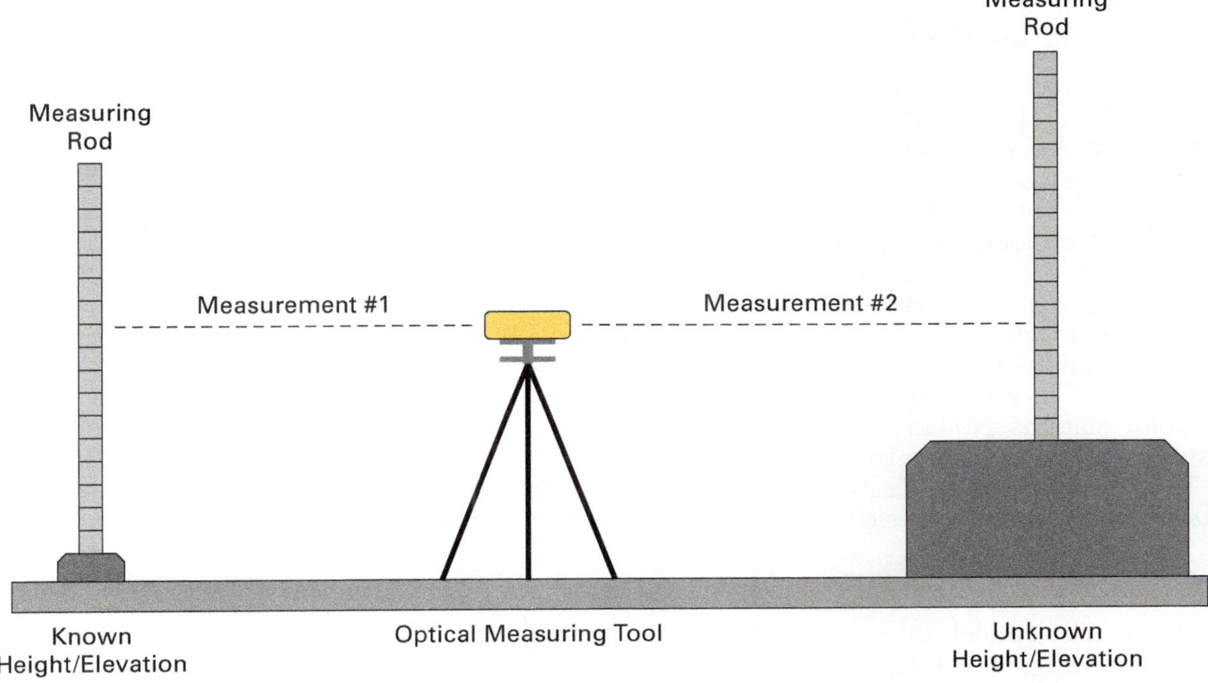

Figure 6 Leveling.

1.2.1 Optical Instruments

The following sections summarize the most common optical instruments (*Figure 8*). Later sections will explore optical and laser levels in more detail.

Optical Levels

An **optical level** has a small telescope that rotates a full 360 degrees. It can measure angles in the horizontal plane only. Optical levels also measure distances. Both measurements are only moderately accurate. The optical level's main purpose is measuring heights. Once properly set up, most align themselves with the horizontal plane and stay level. When the operator looks through the telescope, the horizontal crosshair represents the horizontal plane.

Laser Levels

A **laser level** does the same task as an optical level but doesn't require the operator to look through a telescope. Instead, the level projects a horizontal laser beam. The operator carries a detector attached to a measuring rod. When the detector senses the laser beam, it beeps and flashes a light. The operator then reads the rod to determine the height.

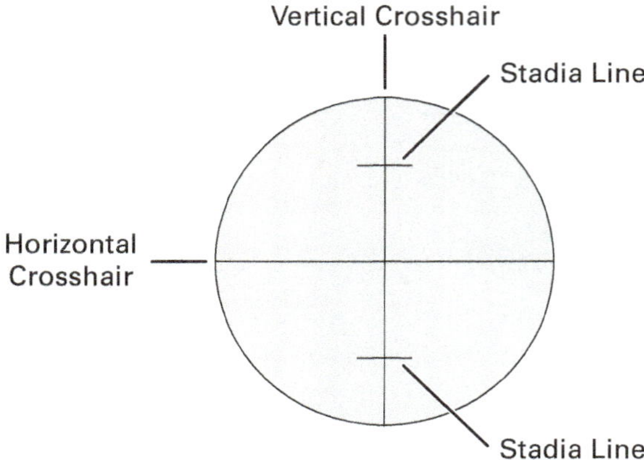

Figure 7 Telescope reticle.

Theodolites and Total Stations

A theodolite precisely measures angles in both the horizontal and vertical planes. Millwrights can use them for many layout and alignment tasks. They're particularly useful for positioning new reference points and benchmarks.

A total station looks like a theodolite. It does everything that a theodolite can do. It also measures distances very accurately with a technique called *electronic distance measurement (EDM)*. Millwrights can use a total station to establish the coordinates of multiple locations on a plant floor. Total stations contain built-in computers that store results and do calculations automatically. They also include an electronic mechanism that keeps them precisely leveled.

1.2.2 Auxiliary Equipment

Millwrights use optical instruments on many surfaces, including concrete, asphalt, and soil. The surface may be level or tilted. Instruments require a solid support and careful positioning to give valid results. Millwrights also need devices to help them take measurements at a distance. The following auxiliary equipment meets these requirements and works with each instrument type.

Bubble Levels

Optical instruments must be perfectly horizontal (level) to take accurate measurements. Many contain a compensating mechanism that automatically keeps the internal assembly horizontal. However, the instrument itself must be relatively level for this mechanism to work correctly. After setting up the instrument, the operator levels it with the aid of a leveling device. Provided the instrument stays reasonably level, the compensator can adjust to minor changes.

Leveling devices use gravity to identify what's truly horizontal. Gravity pulls downward on all objects. Think of it as a line between the object and Earth's center. True horizontal is perpendicular (90 degrees) to this gravity line (*Figure 9*).

Bubble levels (*spirit levels*) are liquid-filled glass tubes or capsules containing an air bubble. The bubble always rises to the highest spot in the container, lining itself up with gravity's pull. Centering the bubble aligns the container with true horizontal. Optical instruments usually include one or more bubble levels. *Figure 10* shows two bubble level types.

Tubular levels are slightly curved glass tubes with lines etched on either side of the center. When the bubble is between the marks, the tube is level. These levels can detect the horizontal position in just one direction—along the axis passing lengthwise through the tube.

Circular levels (*bullseye levels*) are round glass capsules with a curved top. They have a small circle etched in the middle. When the bubble is inside the circle, the capsule is level. Unlike tubular levels, a circular level detects the entire horizontal plane at once.

Optical instruments must be level in both directions (left/right and front/back) within the horizontal plane. Leveling an instrument equipped with a tubular level requires two steps. Adjust the instrument in one direction to center the bubble. Then, rotate the instrument 90 degrees and center the bubble again. Leveling an instrument equipped with a circular level is simpler. Just center the bubble inside the small circle.

Tripods and Tribrachs

Tripods solidly support optical instruments on different surfaces (*Figure 11*). Each leg's length is individually adjustable and ends in a sharp point equipped with a step. Standing on the step forces the point into the ground or surface. Legs have latches or locking screws to hold them in place. Most tripods are made of aluminum or fiberglass so they're relatively lightweight.

The tripod head is triangular with a large hole in the center. A hollow bolt slides back and forth in a track spanning the hole. The bolt threads into the instrument's base to hold it firmly on the tripod. Bolts have a large knob to make tightening and loosening easier.

> **NOTE**
>
> Be sure the tripod you select is rated for the instrument that you plan to use. Tripods for optical levels are usually less sturdy and have fewer adjustments than those intended for theodolites and total stations.

(A) Optical Level

(B) Laser Level

(C) Theodolite

Figure 8 Optical instruments.

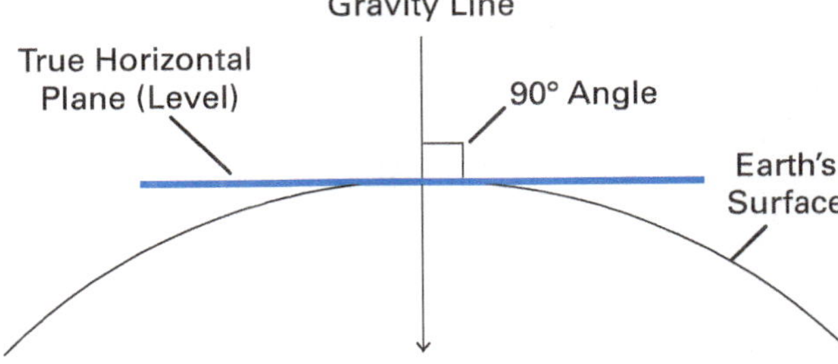

Figure 9 Gravity and true horizontal.

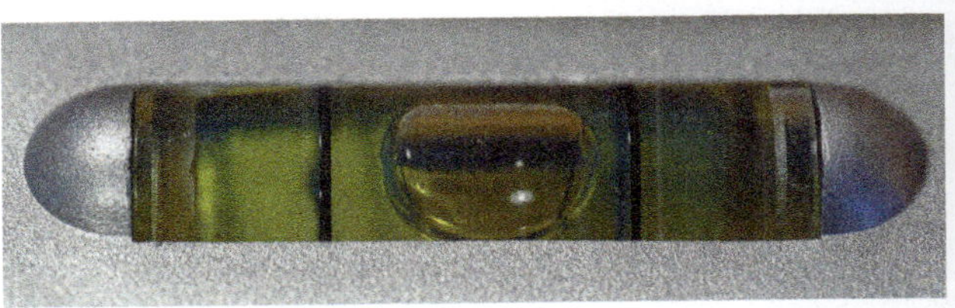
(A) Tubular Level

(B) Circular Level

Figure 10 Bubble levels.

> **CAUTION**
> Never lean on a tripod. You could alter its position or levelness and ruin your measurements.

> **NOTE**
> Instruments like optical levels may come with a permanently attached tribrach. Other instruments attach to a separate unit.

Many optical instruments sit on top of a special platform called a *tribrach* (*Figure 12*). The tribrach's baseplate rests on the tripod head, while its top platform supports the instrument. Three *leveling screws* fit between the baseplate and top platform. The craftworker turns the screws to tilt the platform until it's level. Tribrachs have a circular level mounted on top. Some tribrachs have a small mirror near the level so the operator can see it from the side.

Tribrachs may include extra features. An *optical plummet* lets the craftworker position the instrument precisely over a marker in the floor. This device uses mirrors and lenses to relay the view through the tripod's hollow bolt to an eyepiece on the tribrach's side. The millwright looks through the eyepiece and adjusts the tribrach's position until the marker is centered.

Figure 11 Optical instrument tripod.

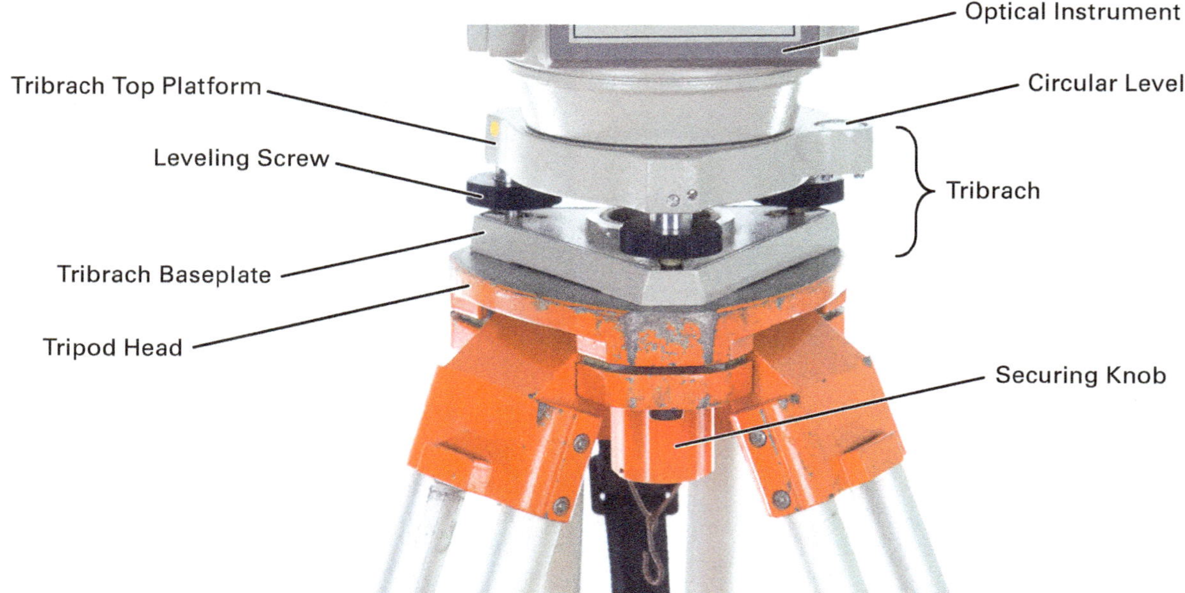

Figure 12 Tripod with an attached tribrach.

Laser plummets are alternatives to optical plummets. They shoot a laser beam through the tripod's hollow bolt onto the floor beneath. The millwright adjusts the tribrach until the dot is centered on the reference marker.

Leveling Rods

A *leveling rod* (*grade rod* or *leveling staff*) looks like a giant aluminum or fiberglass ruler (*Figure 13*). They're usually 10' to 25' (~3 m to 8 m) long and collapse for easier transport. Leveling rods have large numbers and markings to make them easy to read through an optical instrument's telescope. Some include a grip with a circular level to help the worker hold the rod vertically.

Millwrights use leveling rods to measure heights. They're also useful for measuring distances. Finally, a leveling rod can be a visual target for measuring angles and establishing a location's coordinates.

Some US standard rods give readings in feet, inches, and fractions of an inch. Others give readings in feet with decimal fractions. Metric rods give readings in meters and centimeters.

Leveling rods used with laser-equipped instruments include a detector that clips onto the edge (*Figure 13*). The operator slides the detector up and down until it beeps and flashes a light. This indicates that it's aligned on the laser beam. The operator then reads the rod's markings next to the detector's pointer.

(A) Rod   (B) Detector

Figure 13 Leveling rod (collapsed) with laser detector.

1.2.3 Basic Equipment Techniques

Millwrights begin optical layout and alignment tasks by setting up the equipment and readying it for taking measurements. Many of the required processes are common to all procedures. The following sections describe them.

Setting up the Instrument

The tripod supports the instrument, so setting it up correctly is crucial. Mistakes could lead to poor measurements or the tripod falling over. The following steps outline the process:

Step 1 Remove the tripod from its carrying case. Confirm that it's in good condition and appropriate for the instrument you plan to use. The instrument should be at eye level when the tripod is in position. Unlock and extend each leg to the correct length. Lock each leg.

Step 2 Spread the legs equally so they're about 3' (~1 m) apart. If the legs are too close together, the tripod can tip over.

Step 3 Position the tripod in the correct location. If the surface isn't flat, place two legs on the low (downhill) side.

Step 4 Force the leg points into the ground or asphalt by briefly putting your full weight on each leg's step. On smooth or hard surfaces, like concrete, block the legs to keep the tripod positioned. Install leg chains to prevent the legs from sliding apart.

Step 5 Visually check the tripod head for levelness. Adjust the leg lengths as required until the head appears level.

Step 6 Remove the optical instrument from its case. Confirm that it's in good condition.

Step 7 If the optical instrument doesn't have an attached tribrach, remove the tribrach from its case. Confirm that it's in good condition. Attach the instrument to the tribrach.

Step 8 Support the instrument and tribrach over the tripod head. Thread the mounting bolt into the tribrach's baseplate. Center the tribrach on the tripod head. Align its three leveling screws with the tripod's legs. Tighten the mounting bolt snugly, but don't overtighten.

Step 9 Turn each leveling screw until it's in the middle position, indicated by the groove in the shaft (*Figure 14*).

Leveling the Instrument

Optical instruments must be level before you can start taking measurements. Many instruments include an automatic compensator or electronic leveling mechanism that keeps the instrument internally level. This device requires the tripod and tribrach to be reasonably level, or it won't work.

Tribrachs have a circular level on their top platform to help level them. Look at it from above as you make changes. If the level has a mirror, look at it from the side. Some optical instruments include their own levels as well.

The following procedure explains how to level the tripod and tribrach with the aid of the circular level:

Step 1 Move the bubble as close to the center as possible by lengthening or shortening one tripod leg. Grip the leg firmly so it can't collapse. Unlock the leg. Slightly adjust the length to move the bubble in the right direction. Lock the leg.

To move the bubble toward the center, tilt the tripod downward in the *same* direction as the bubble's current location. The arrows in *Figure 15* show the correct direction to tilt the tripod for different situations.

Step 2 If necessary, adjust a second leg to move the bubble closer to the center.

Step 3 If the bubble is centered, skip to *Step 8*. If not, rotate the instrument so its axis is parallel to two of the tribrach's leveling screws (*Figure 16*). Stand behind the two screws.

Step 4 Turn the two leveling screws equally and in *opposite* directions to move the bubble. Bring it as close to the center as possible.

Step 5 Rotate the instrument 90 degrees so it's in line with the third leveling screw. Remain standing in the same position (*Figure 16*).

Step 6 Turn the third leveling screw to move the bubble.

Step 7 If necessary, repeat *Steps 3–6* until the bubble is centered.

Step 8 Slowly rotate the instrument a full 360 degrees while watching the level. The bubble should remain in the center. If not, repeat the leveling procedure.

Focusing Optical Equipment

Properly focusing an optical instrument is crucial to obtaining accurate measurements. Instruments have *two* focus adjustments. The eyepiece focus ring adjusts the eyepiece's optics to match your vision. The instrument's reticle will come into sharp focus when you focus the eyepiece. The main focus knob on the instrument's side adjusts the telescope to form a sharp image. *Figure 17* shows both adjustments on an optical level.

When you look through a properly focused optical instrument, you should see the reticle clearly. The image itself should also be sharp. If either is fuzzy, the instrument isn't focused correctly (*Figure 18*).

Figure 14 Tribrach leveling screws.

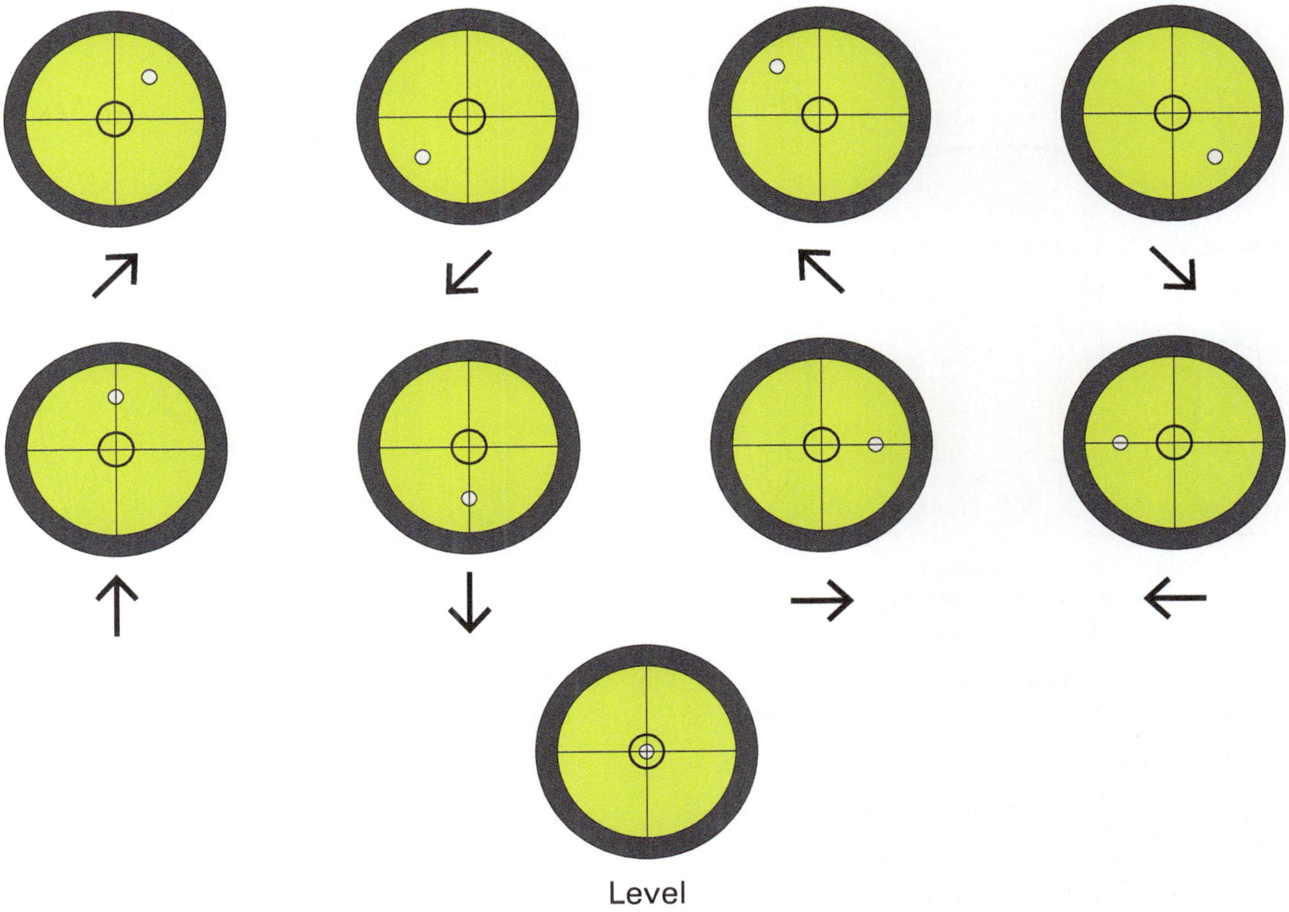

Figure 15 Using a circular level.

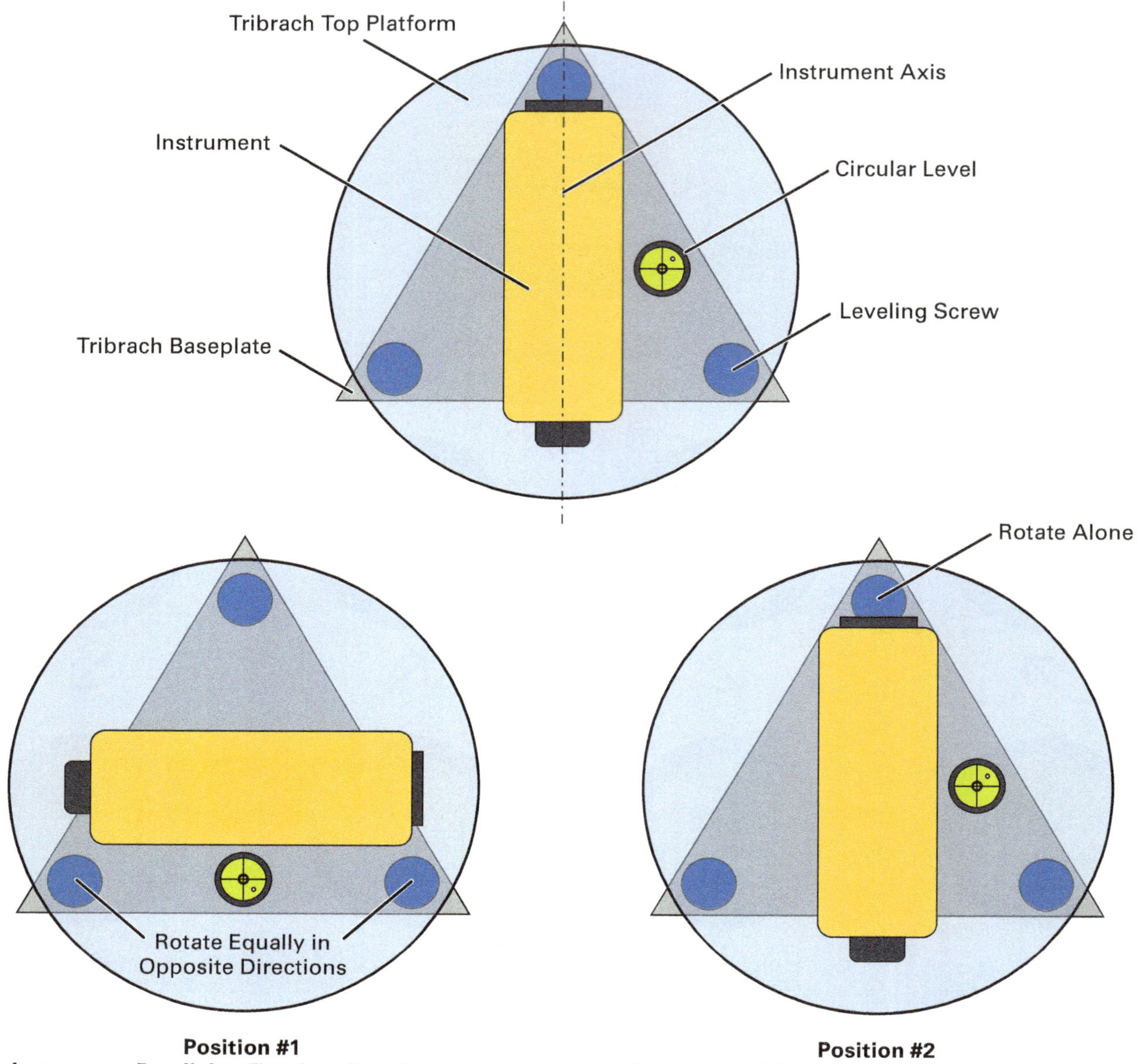

Figure 16 Leveling the tribrach.

The following steps outline focusing an optical instrument:

Step 1   Point the instrument at a light-colored surface, like a wall. Look straight into the eyepiece and relax your eye.

Step 2   Rotate the eyepiece focus ring until the reticle lines are sharp.

> **NOTE**
>
> If the eyepiece is badly out of focus, the reticle lines may not be visible. Rotate the focus ring until they appear. Then tweak the ring to sharpen them.

Step 3   Point the instrument at a distant object. Look straight into the eyepiece and relax your eye.

Step 4   Rotate the main focus knob until the object is sharp.

Next check the telescope for *parallax*—slight focusing differences between the two adjustments. Parallax makes the reticle appear to move against the background when you move your head. This motion can cause inaccurate measurements.

Figure 17 Focusing adjustments.

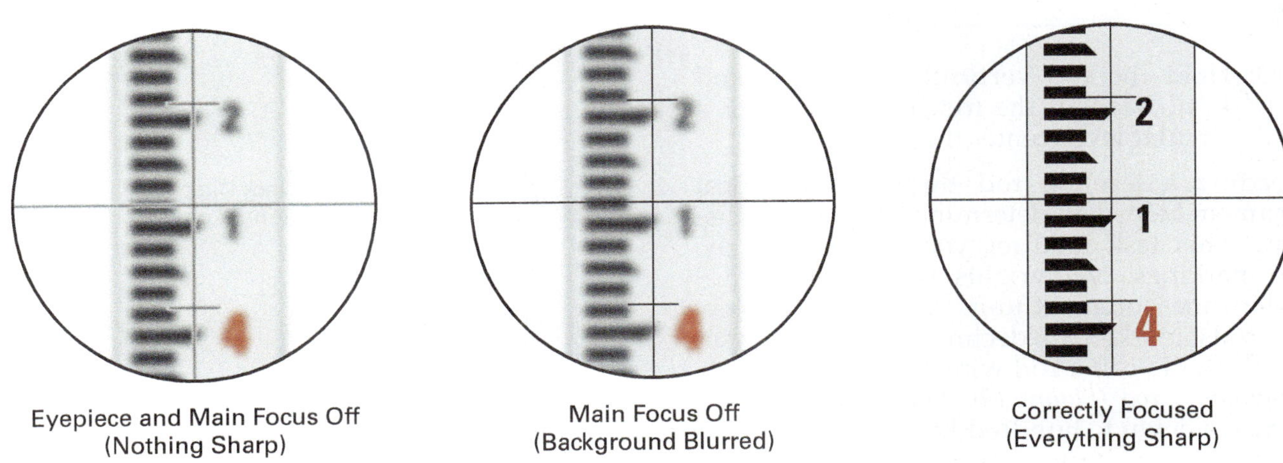

Figure 18 Correct and incorrect focus.

Step 5 Move your head slightly up/down and left/right while you look through the eyepiece.

Step 6 If the reticle appears to move against the background, rotate the eyepiece focus ring slightly. If necessary, adjust the main focus knob to keep the background sharp. Repeat *Step 5* until you don't see any motion.

> **NOTE**
>
> If you wear very strong glasses, you may find it difficult to see through the instrument's eyepiece. Try removing your glasses. You will need to readjust the eyepiece focus and the main focus, as well as check for parallax.

As you use the instrument to take measurements, adjust the main focus as required. Don't touch the eyepiece focus ring again unless the reticle lines become blurred. If you must readjust the eyepiece focus, repeat the entire adjustment procedure.

Using a Leveling Rod

Many optical layout and alignment procedures require you to work with a leveling rod. Sometimes, you'll assist another millwright by holding the leveling rod in position. Alternatively, you'll be the one reading it through the optical instrument's telescope.

The following steps outline holding a leveling rod properly:

Step 1 Extend the rod's sections until it's long enough for the task. You can leave some sections collapsed, but all extended sections must be fully extended.

Step 2 Position the rod's lower end squarely on the ground, floor, or surface.

> **NOTE**
>
> On soft ground, drive a flat-topped stake into the ground until the top is flush with the ground. Place the leveling rod on the stake.

Step 3 Hold the rod vertically (left/right and front/back). If the rod has a grip with a circular level, center the bubble.

Reading a leveling rod through an optical instrument helps you determine heights and distances. This task requires you to interpret the rod's markings. Millwrights working with US standard measurement units commonly use leveling rods marked in decimal feet. Equipment manufacturers call a rod with this marking style an *engineer's rod* (*Figure 19*). They provide measurements down to hundredths of a foot (0.01').

The following procedure outlines reading an engineer's rod through an optical instrument's telescope:

Step 1 Align the instrument with the distant rod.

Step 2 Look through the eyepiece and adjust the main focus until the image is sharp. Center the rod's image.

Step 3 Locate the horizontal crosshair and note where it crosses the rod (*Figure 20*).

To determine the crosshair's location on the rod, identify the closest red number below or adjacent to the crosshair. In *Figure 20*, the red 4 is just below the crosshair. Next, identify the closest black number below or adjacent to the crosshair. In *Figure 20*, the black 1 is just below the crosshair.

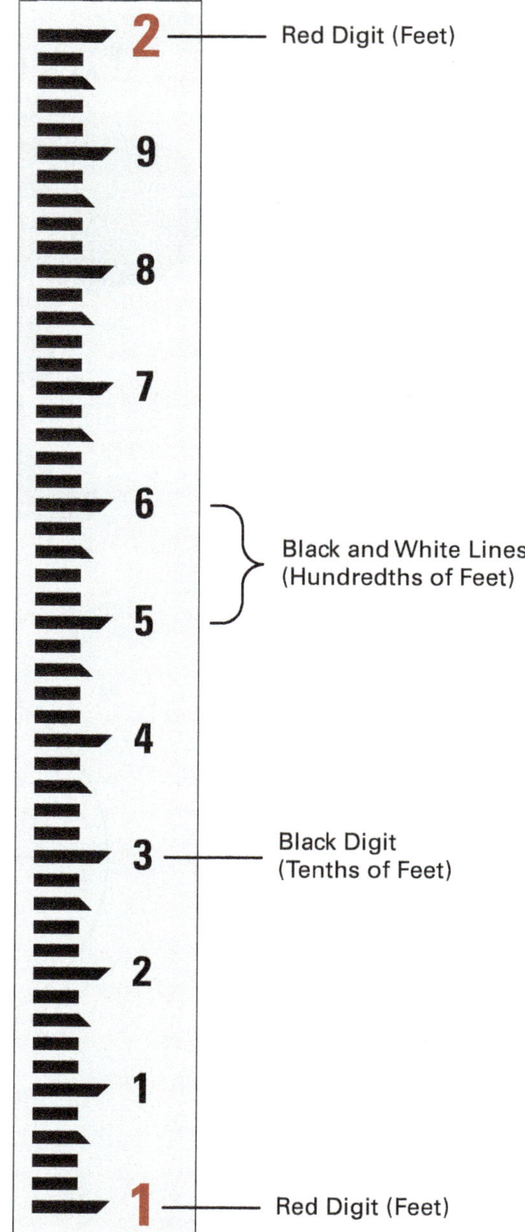

Figure 19 Markings on an engineer's rod.

Red numbers identify whole feet (1'). The smaller black numbers identify tenths of a foot (0.1'). So, the crosshair in *Figure 20* is slightly above the 4.1' location. To complete the measurement, you must interpret the unnumbered marks between the numbers. These identify the crosshair's location to the nearest hundredth of a foot (0.01').

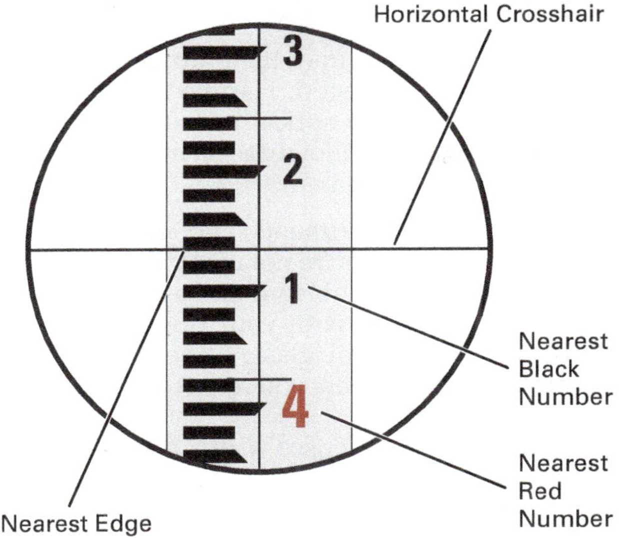

Figure 20 Reading an engineer's rod.

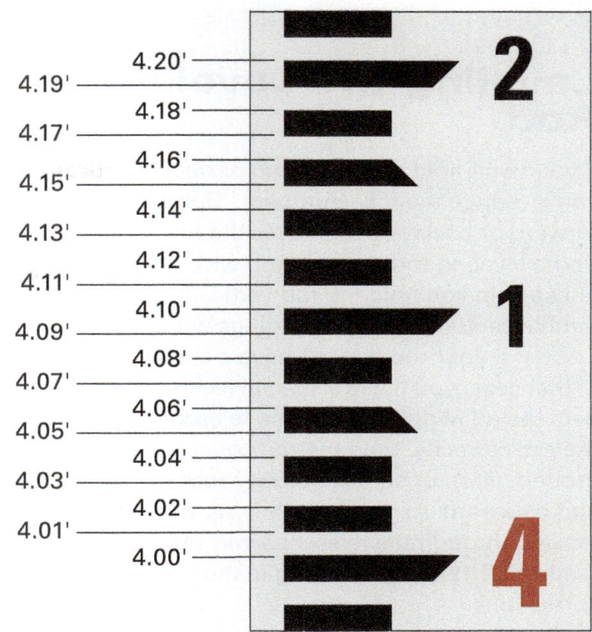

Figure 21 Interpreting the edges on an engineer's rod.

The marks can be confusing, however, since they don't work like the marks on a ruler. Every *edge* between a black mark and the white space around it represents 0.01'. Each black mark has two edges (lower and upper). They identify two locations 0.01' apart. Lower edges identify odd-numbered hundredths. Upper edges identify even-numbered hundredths. *Figure 21* shows how to interpret each edge.

Notice that some black marks have an upward-facing beveled end. These are always next to numbers. The bevel indicates that the mark's upper edge is associated with the number. For example, the 4.00' location is along the upper edge of the beveled mark across from the red 4. Marks with a downward-facing beveled end identify the location midway between numbers (0.05'). The bevel indicates that the mark's lower edge is the halfway point.

By using *Figure 21*, you should be able to work out the final digit for the crosshair's location in *Figure 20*. Notice that the crosshair is along the bottom edge of the second mark above the black 1's beveled mark. This location equals 0.03'. So, the crosshair's location is 4.13' (4.1' + 0.03' = 4.13').

Figure 22 shows another example. See if you can read the rod correctly.

After finding the horizontal crosshair's location, you should have identified the closest red and black numbers adjacent to or below the line as 3 and 2. The crosshair is just above 3.2'. The crosshair is resting on the top edge of the second mark above the black 2. This location is 0.04' above the 2. The crosshair's location is 3.24' (3.2' + 0.04' = 3.24').

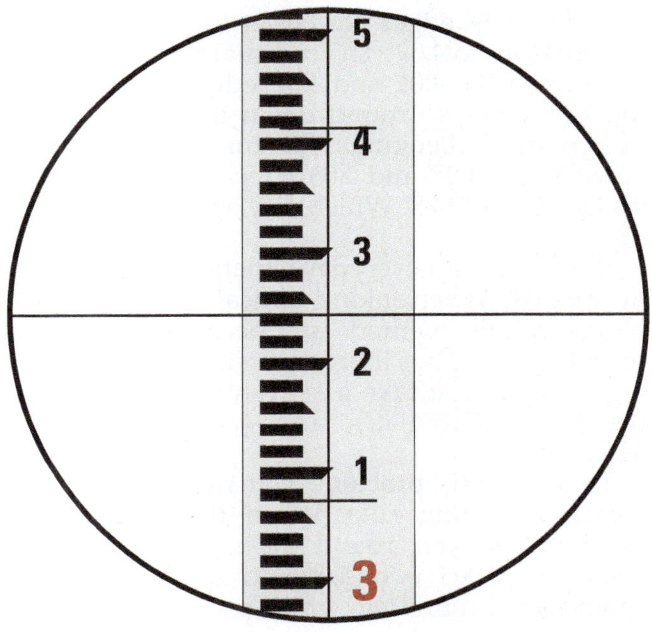

Figure 22 Leveling rod example.

Rounding Leveling Rod Readings

Perhaps you're wondering what to do if the crosshair isn't over an edge. It might be somewhere within a black mark or the white space. In these cases, you must round up or down to the nearest 0.01'. *Figure 23* shows three examples to illustrate this.

In Example #1, the crosshair is between the 4.08' and 4.09' edges. It's closer to the 4.09' edge, so round up to 4.09'. The crosshair in Example #2 is between the 4.01' and 4.02' edges. It's closer to the 4.01' edge, so round down to 4.01'. Example #3 is more challenging. The crosshair is centered between the 4.07' and 4.08' edges. In other words, it's located at 4.075'. Which way should you round it?

If this were an everyday situation, you'd round up to 4.08'. When taking optical measurements, however, this method isn't acceptable. Always rounding up biases the measurements toward the high side. If you take a series of measurements, the bias accumulates and causes significant inaccuracy.

To avoid this problem, you need to follow a special rounding rule. When the digit before the 0.005' is even, round *down*. When the digit before the 0.005' is odd, round *up*. This strategy balances the rounding, which prevents bias from accumulating.

Figure 24 illustrates this rounding method. In the left measurement, the crosshair is at 4.145'. The digit to the left of the 5 is a 4, which is even. Round down to 4.14'. In the right measurement, the crosshair is at 4.115'. The digit to the left of the 5 is a 1, which is odd. Round up to 4.12'. To correctly round Example #3 in *Figure 23*, round up to 4.08'.

> **NOTE**
> Treat 0s as even numbers.

1.2.4 Caring for Optical Equipment

Optical instruments and their auxiliary equipment are easily damaged. Handle all equipment carefully, particularly optical instruments, which are expensive. The following general guidelines apply to optical equipment:

- Keep optical instruments and equipment in their cases when you're not using them. Always transport instruments in their cases.
- Don't touch lenses with your fingers. Skin oils will damage optical glass. Cover lenses with their lens caps when you're not using the instrument.
- If necessary, clean lenses with a disposable wet lens wipe. Lightly brush off dust and grit first. Clean lenses with a circular motion, working from the center outward.
- Don't use a dropped or badly jolted instrument. It could give invalid results. Send it to the manufacturer for inspection and repair. Never repair an optical instrument yourself.
- Always carry the tripod upright when an instrument is attached. Never carry it over your shoulder. Doing this can damage the instrument's automatic compensation mechanism.
- Collapse and fold tripods when you're not using them. Protect their legs so they don't get bent.
- Collapse leveling rods when you're not using them. Protect them so they don't get bent.
- Don't overtighten locking screws or clamps. If a locking mechanism isn't working correctly, don't use the equipment.
- Maintain optical equipment by following the manufacturer's recommended procedures. Read the equipment's manual for guidance.

Optical instruments require regular **calibration** to ensure that they give accurate measurements. The equipment manufacturer or an instrument calibration service performs this task. Send instruments for calibration at least once per year. Instruments used in demanding environments require more frequent calibration. Don't use an instrument whose calibration is out of date.

> **NOTE**
> Never remove official calibration stickers from instruments. Store calibration certificates and records in a safe place. Most companies require millwrights to keep records of their instruments' calibration status. Some layout tasks require millwrights to record their instrument's calibration date on the layout documentation.

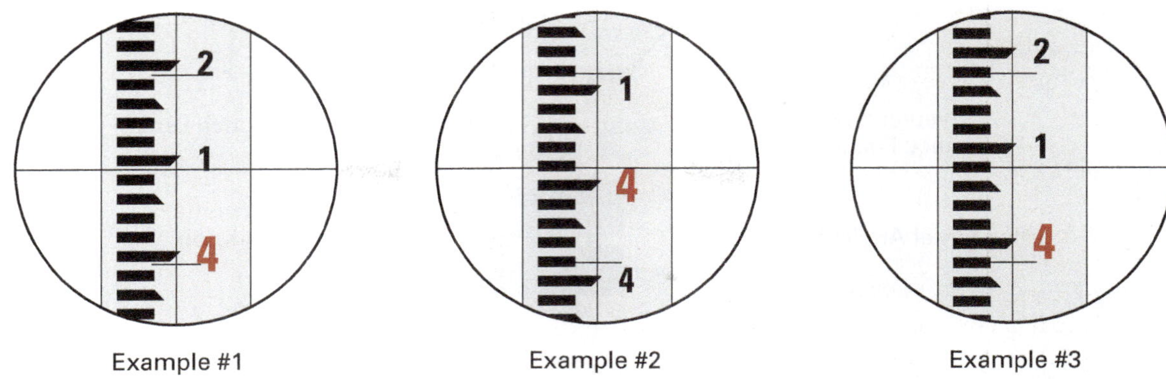

Figure 23 Leveling rod rounding examples.

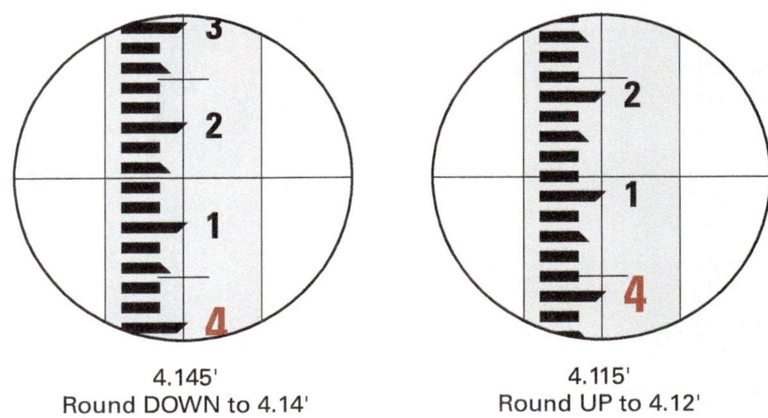

Figure 24 Special rounding rule.

1.3.0 Optical Levels

Of the different optical instruments, the optical level is probably the most useful for millwrights. They're simple to use for measuring horizontal angles, distances, and heights. They're also relatively inexpensive. This module explores standard optical levels rather than precision models, which require a modified operating technique.

1.3.1 Optical Level Features

Most optical levels are *auto-levels*. They contain a compensator mechanism that automatically keeps them level. If the tripod/tribrach is reasonably level, the mechanism can correct for minor changes. Older optical levels don't include this feature, so millwrights must periodically check that they're still level. *Figure 25* shows an auto-level with its key features identified.

Many optical levels have a built-in tribrach. It attaches to the tripod in the usual way. Auto-levels have a circular level on the tribrach. The level in *Figure 25* has this feature, although it's not visible in the picture. The *peep sight* on top is for pointing the level in the right direction. Some optical levels have a sighting groove or two sights, like a rifle instead.

The *horizontal angle scale* measures angles between different locations. It rotates with the instrument. The *fine horizontal motion knob* slowly rotates the optical level in the horizontal plane. It's useful for precisely positioning the telescope.

Optical levels have a reticle like the one in *Figure 7*. The horizontal crosshair represents the instrument's **line of sight**. This is an imaginary horizontal line stretching between the instrument's *objective lens* and the target (*Figure 26*). The vertical crosshair helps the operator center the telescope on the target. It's also helpful for measuring angles. The two horizontal stadia lines are for measuring distances.

> **NOTE**
>
> Before using an unfamiliar optical level, read its manual. If you don't have the manual, download the electronic version from the manufacturer's website.

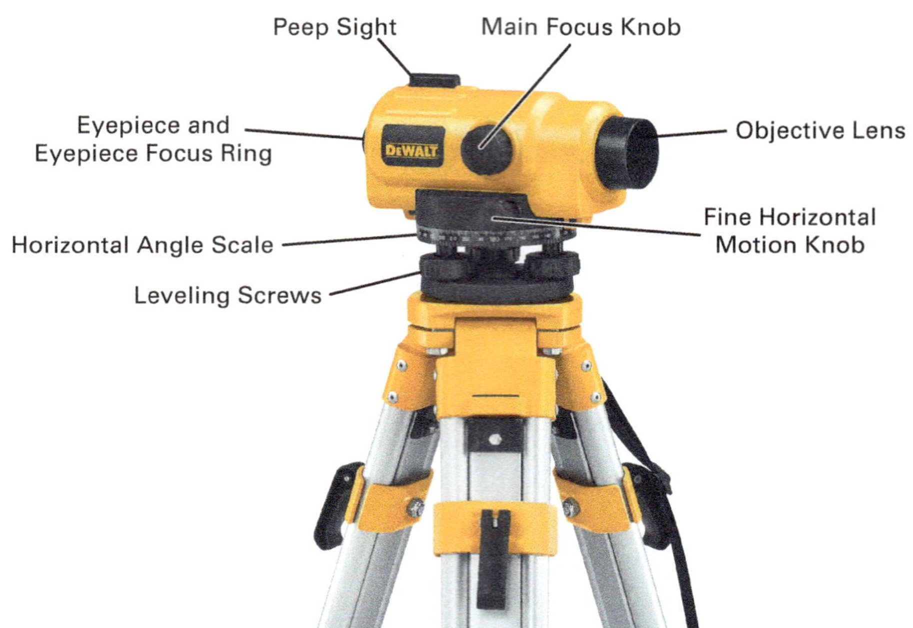

Figure 25 Auto-level.

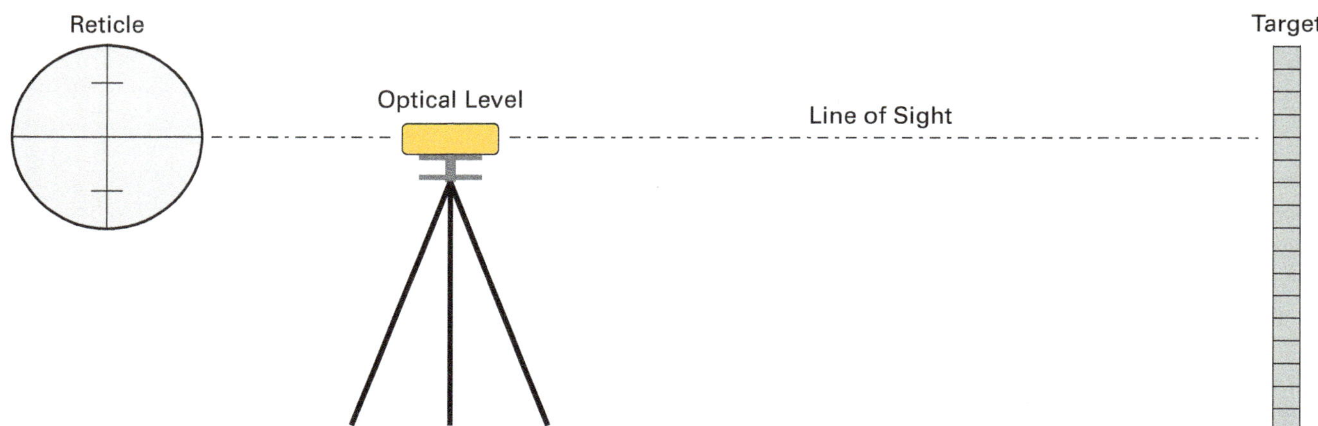

Figure 26 Line of sight.

1.3.2 Measuring Angles

Optical levels can measure the angle between two locations as viewed from a reference location. These measurements are only moderately accurate, but they're quick and easy to perform. The following steps outline the process:

Step 1 Set up the tripod and optical level at the reference location. Level the tripod/tribrach.

Step 2 Adjust the optical level's focus and eliminate parallax.

Step 3 Have an assistant hold a leveling rod vertically at the first location.

Step 4 Use the optical level's peep sight to point the telescope at the leveling rod.

Step 5 Look through the eyepiece. Adjust the main focus knob until the leveling rod is sharp.

Step 6 Use the vertical crosshair and fine horizontal motion knob to center the telescope on the leveling rod.

Step 7 Locate the pointer on the level's horizontal angle scale. Read and record the value under the pointer.

Step 8 Have an assistant hold a leveling rod vertically at the second location.

Step 9 Use the optical level's peep sight to point the telescope at the leveling rod.

Step 10 Look through the eyepiece. Adjust the main focus knob until the leveling rod is sharp.

Step 11 Use the vertical crosshair and fine horizontal motion knob to center the telescope on the leveling rod.

Step 12 Locate the pointer on the level's horizontal angle scale. Read and record the value under the pointer.

Step 13 Subtract the smaller value from the larger. The result is the angle between the two points as viewed from the reference location.

Figure 27 shows an example angle measurement. The optical level sits above the reference location. After pointing the telescope at the leveling rod over the first location, the horizontal angle scale reads 286 degrees. After pointing the telescope at the leveling rod over the second location, the horizontal angle scale reads 233 degrees. The following calculation determines the angle between these locations:

$$\text{angle} = \text{angle \#1} - \text{angle \#2}$$
$$\text{angle} = 286° - 233°$$
$$\text{angle} = 53°$$

1.3.3 Measuring Distances

Optical levels can measure the distance between the tripod and a distant point. These measurements are only moderately accurate, but they're quick and easy to perform. The following steps outline the process:

Step 1 Set up the tripod and optical level at the desired location. Level the tripod/tribrach.

Step 2 Adjust the optical level's focus and eliminate parallax.

Step 3 Have an assistant hold a leveling rod vertically at the distant location.

Step 4 Use the optical level's peep sight to point the telescope at the leveling rod.

Step 5 Look through the eyepiece. Adjust the main focus knob until the leveling rod is sharp.

Step 6 Use the vertical crosshair and fine horizontal motion knob to center the telescope on the leveling rod.

Step 7 Read the leveling rod where the top stadia line crosses it. Record the value.

Step 8 Read the leveling rod where the bottom stadia line crosses it. Record the value.

Step 9 Subtract the bottom reading from the top one. Multiply the result by the *stadia constant*, which is usually 100. The result is the distance between the optical level and the leveling rod.

Figure 28 shows an example distance measurement. The top stadia line crosses the leveling rod at 4.75'. The bottom stadia line crosses the leveling rod at 4.17'. The following calculation determines the distance:

$$\text{distance} = (\text{top} - \text{bottom}) \times \text{stadia constant}$$
$$\text{distance} = (4.75' - 4.17') \times 100$$
$$\text{distance} = 58'$$

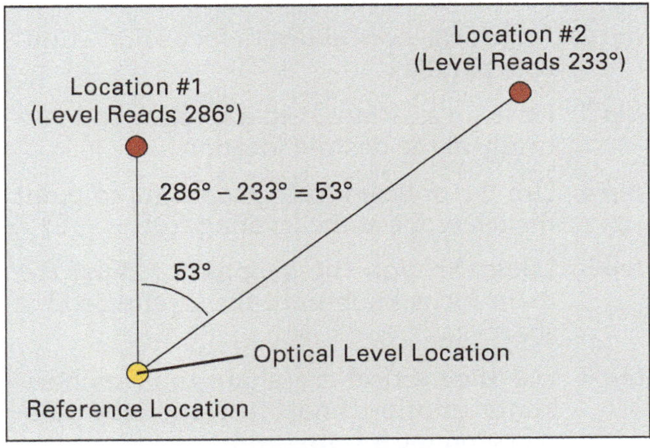

Figure 27 Measuring an angle with an optical level.

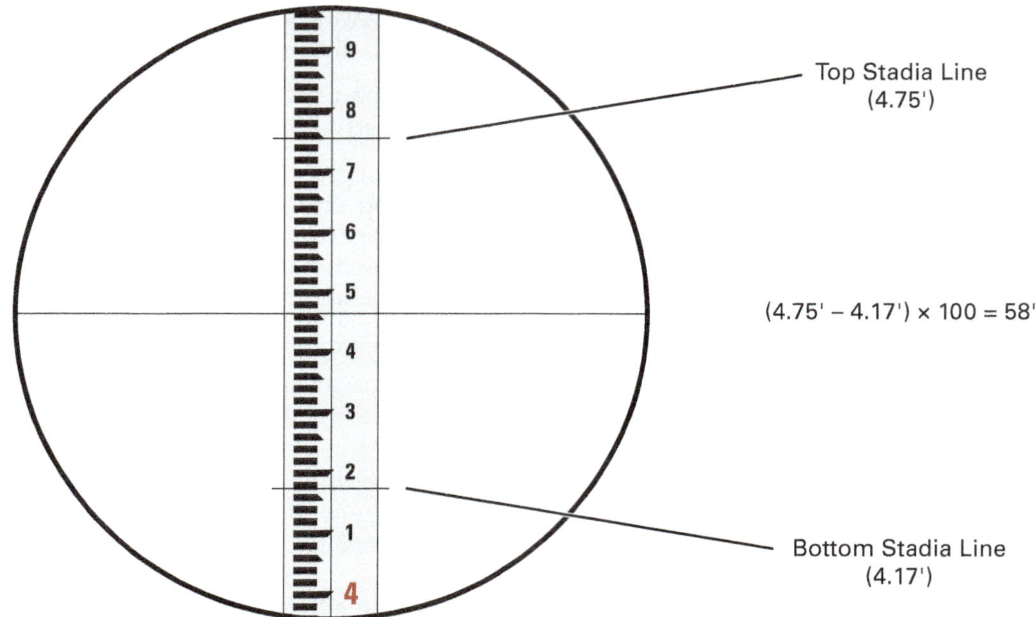

Figure 28 Measuring distance with an optical level.

1.3.4 *Measuring Heights and Determining Elevations*

An optical level's main purpose is measuring heights. By relating these to reference points with known elevations, they can help you determine elevations. Millwrights often use optical levels to set or check a machine's vertical position. The following steps outline measuring height with an optical level:

Step 1 Set up the tripod and optical level at the desired location. Level the tripod/tribrach.

Step 2 Adjust the optical level's focus and eliminate parallax.

Step 3 Have an assistant hold a leveling rod vertically at the desired location.

Step 4 Use the optical level's peep sight to point the telescope at the leveling rod.

Step 5 Look through the eyepiece. Adjust the main focus knob until the leveling rod is sharp.

Step 6 Use the vertical crosshair and fine horizontal motion knob to center the telescope on the leveling rod.

Step 7 Read the leveling rod where the horizontal crosshair passes through it. Record the value.

The value that you've just determined is a height. By itself, however, it's not useful because it isn't referenced to anything. It's simply the vertical distance between the optical level's line of sight and the surface on which the leveling rod is resting.

To turn the height into a useful value, you must reference it to a known height or elevation. A benchmark in the floor is a good reference. The following steps outline using a benchmark to determine another location's height or elevation:

Step 1 Record the benchmark's known height or elevation.

Step 2 Set up the tripod and optical level about midway between the benchmark and the location whose height you're measuring (*Figure 29*). Level the tripod/tribrach.

Step 3 Adjust the optical level's focus and eliminate parallax.

Step 4 Have an assistant hold a leveling rod vertically on top of the benchmark.

Step 5 Follow *Steps 4–7* of the previous procedure to determine the leveling rod's height. Record the value.

Step 6 Have an assistant hold a leveling rod vertically on top of the location whose height you're measuring.

Step 7 Follow *Steps 4–7* of the previous procedure to determine the leveling rod's height. Record the value.

NCCER – *Millwright*

As *Figure 29* shows, the benchmark's elevation is 437' above sea level. The leveling rod reads 5.62' at this location. Using this information, you can determine the optical level's elevation since its line of sight is 5.62' above the benchmark. Add this value to the benchmark's elevation to get the instrument's elevation:

instrument elevation = benchmark elevation + height #1
instrument elevation = 437' + 5.62'
instrument elevation = 442.62'

The leveling rod reads 3.15' at the location whose height you're measuring. Subtract this value from the instrument's elevation to determine the unknown elevation:

unknown elevation = instrument elevation – height #2
unknown elevation = 442.62' – 3.15'
unknown elevation = 439.47'

This method works well if the benchmark and the second location aren't more than about 200' (~60 m) apart. If the distance is greater, you won't be able to read the leveling rod. The solution is to break up the distance with a series of intermediate points. By determining the elevation at each point, you can eventually determine the final location's elevation.

The intermediate points are called *turning points*. *Figure 30* illustrates the measuring process with a single turning point. As you can see, it requires four measurements, with the optical level in two positions.

This process works over very long distances as well. Just add more turning points. Take careful measurements and keep good records. Land surveyors use this strategy to survey over distances of many miles.

Whenever you perform many linked measurements, small variations called *error* creep into your results. If they aren't too large, they're not a problem. Sometimes, however, they can become significant and ruin your results. How do you know if error is acceptably low?

Millwrights check for error by measuring a second time in the opposite direction. To check the measurements of *Figure 30*, a millwright would start at the final location and measure back to the original benchmark. Surveyors call this second measurement sequence *closing the loop*.

Subtracting the benchmark's calculated elevation from its known elevation gives the error. For example, suppose the second set of measurements gave the benchmark a calculated elevation of 436.91'. Its official elevation is 437'. The error is 0.09' (437' – 436.91' = 0.09'), which is probably acceptable.

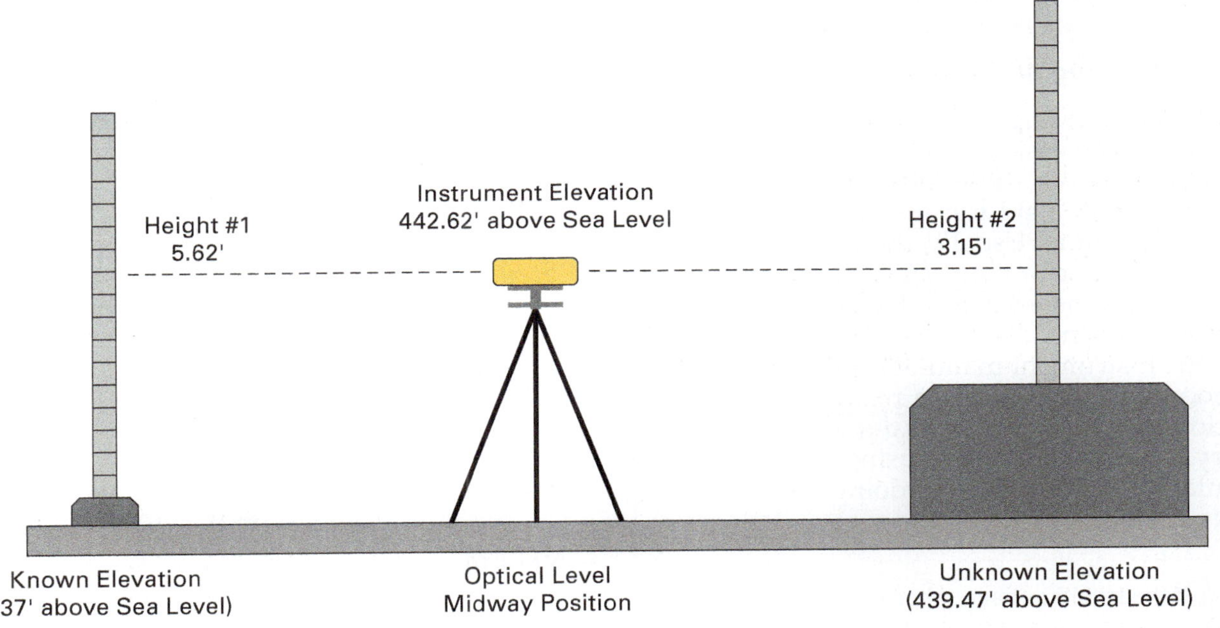

Figure 29 Determining an elevation with an optical level.

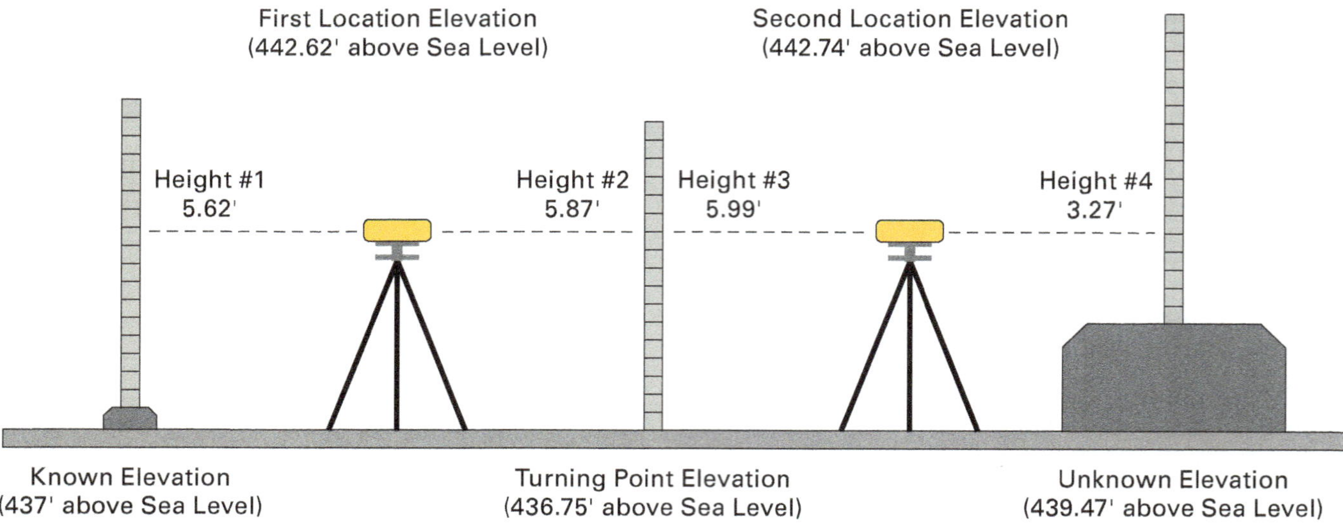

Figure 30 Measuring over longer distances.

Surveying Terminology

Surveyors use special terms and abbreviations to identify their measurements. A *backsight* (*BS*) is a measurement taken on a known reference point or benchmark. A *foresight* (*FS*) is a measurement taken on a point with an unknown elevation. Turning points are commonly labeled *TP* and numbered. Calculated instrument heights are abbreviated *HI* (height of the instrument).

1.3.5 Checking an Optical Level's Calibration

Normally, millwrights send their optical instruments for professional calibration at least once per year. Between these "official" checkups, however, they may field test instruments to confirm correct operation. Usually, the instrument's manual includes one or more procedures for checking calibration. Whenever possible, use these to check your instrument.

If the instrument manufacturer doesn't specify a procedure, you can use a relatively simple calibration check called the *two-peg test*. Perform it every few weeks if you're using the optical level regularly. Perform it before doing critical leveling tasks as well.

CAUTION

If the level has been jolted during transportation, perform a calibration check immediately. Don't use the level if it fails the test.

The following steps outline the two-peg test:

Step 1 Mark two locations on the ground or floor 100' apart. Use a tape measure and measure to the nearest foot. Label the locations A and B.

Step 2 Set up the tripod and optical level midway between the two points (*Figure 31*). Level the tripod/tribrach.

Step 3 Adjust the optical level's focus and eliminate parallax.

Step 4 Have an assistant hold a leveling rod vertically at location A.

Step 5 Use the optical level's peep sight to point the telescope at the leveling rod.

Step 6 Look through the eyepiece. Adjust the main focus knob until the leveling rod is sharp.

Step 7 Use the vertical crosshair and fine horizontal motion knob to center the telescope on the leveling rod.

Step 8 Read the leveling rod where the horizontal crosshair passes through it. Record the value as A1.

Step 9 Have an assistant hold a leveling rod vertically at location B.

Step 10 Read the leveling rod where the horizontal crosshair passes through it. Record the value as B1.

Step 11 Move the tripod to a location about 10' from location A (*Figure 32*). The assistant should stay at location B.

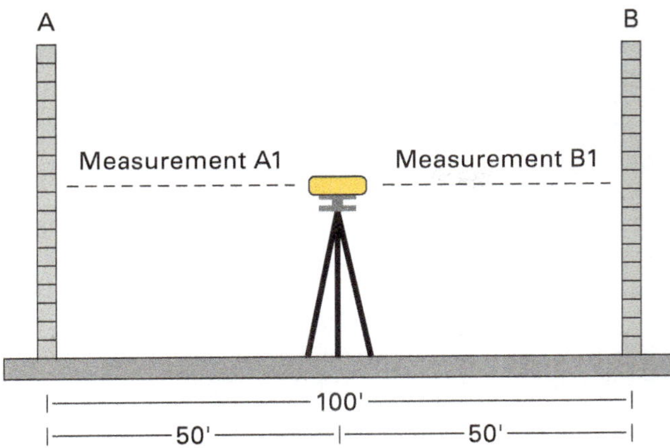

Figure 31 Two-peg test (phase 1).

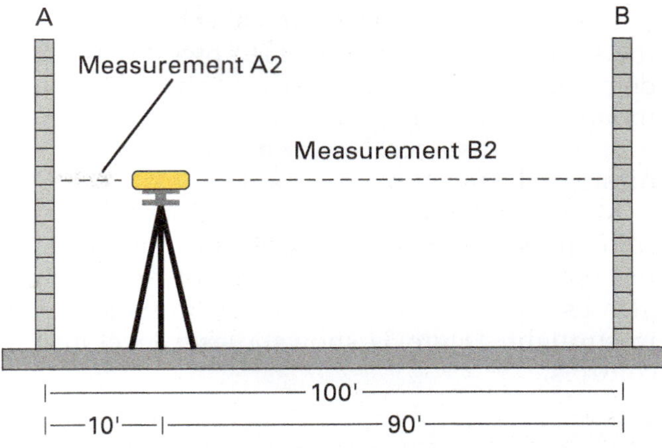

Figure 32 Two-peg test (phase 2).

Step 12 Read the leveling rod where the horizontal crosshair passes through it. Record the value as B2.

Step 13 Have an assistant hold a leveling rod vertically at location A.

Step 14 Read the leveling rod where the horizontal crosshair passes through it. Record the value as A2.

Calculate the instrument error with the following formula:

$$error = [(A2 - B2) - (A1 - B1)] \div 100$$

If the error is 0.01 or less, the optical level's calibration is still good. If it's larger, don't use it. Use another instrument and send the optical level for calibration.

> **NOTE**
>
> An error of 0.01 indicates that the optical level's line of sight is off by 0.01' for each 100' of distance between the instrument and the target. The metric equivalent of this error is 1 mm over a 10 m distance.

1.4.0 Laser Levels

Using an optical level requires two workers. One holds the leveling rod, while the other takes the readings. Laser levels offer an alternative that requires just one craftworker. They're more expensive than optical levels, but they're easier to use. Most can help with other layout tasks as well.

Laser levels are usually Class 2 or 3R. They're relatively safe, provided you don't stare directly into the beam. Unless the manufacturer specifies it, you won't need special eye protection. Never point a laser level at someone. Also, be careful not to let the beam reflect off a shiny surface into another worker's eyes. While the beam probably won't do any damage, it could startle the worker, causing an accident.

> **NOTE**
>
> NCCER Module 15502, *Laser Alignment*, explains laser classifications and safety guidelines.

> **WARNING!**
>
> Before using *any* laser level, read its warning label and manual. Wear special laser eye protection if the manufacturer recommends it. Never look directly into the beam or allow it to reflect directly into your eyes.

1.4.1 Laser Level Features

The level's laser emitter self-levels when first powered. Once leveled, it starts to spin in the horizontal plane, projecting a red or green dot that sweeps around in a circle. Effectively, it paints a horizontal line on any surface that it touches. This line is truly horizontal, so it functions as the instrument's line of sight.

The craftworker clips a laser detector onto a leveling rod (*Figure 33*). When the detector senses the beam sweeping across its surface, it beeps and flashes a light. After positioning the leveling rod vertically at the desired location, the worker slides the detector up and down the rod. When the detector beeps and flashes, its pointer's position against the rod indicates the height.

Besides measuring heights, many laser levels can perform other tasks as well. They can sweep the beam back and forth in an arc (scan mode). This creates a short, highly visible line on nearby surfaces. Craftworkers use this feature to level equipment mounted on walls.

Some laser levels can project vertical lines onto surfaces. These will be perpendicular to the horizontal plane. Craftworkers use them to check vertical structures for plumbness. Some levels can generate vertical and horizontal lines simultaneously, projecting a cross.

Laser levels run on rechargeable batteries, often the same ones as rechargeable power tools. Laser detectors usually have replaceable batteries. Some models include a remote control for operating the unit from a distance. Newer models may communicate with smartphone apps.

Manufacturers often sell laser levels as kits containing the level, the detector, and a leveling rod. Kits may include a pair of red or green glasses. These make the laser beam more visible in sunlight. *Figure 34* shows a laser level and its controls.

1.4.2 *Measuring Heights and Determining Elevations*

Using a laser level to determine an elevation isn't much different from using an optical level. You'll use a reference point, such as a benchmark, to determine the instrument's elevation. From this information, you can determine other locations' elevations. The following steps outline measuring heights and determining elevations with a laser level:

Step 1 Record the benchmark's known height or elevation.

Step 2 Set up the tripod. Position it about midway between the benchmark and the location whose height you're measuring (*Figure 35*). Visually adjust it so the top is level.

Step 3 Remove the laser level from its case. Confirm that it's in good condition. If necessary, install the battery.

Step 4 Support the laser level's baseplate over the tripod head. Thread the mounting bolt into the baseplate. Center the instrument on the tripod head. Tighten the mounting bolt snugly, but don't overtighten.

Step 5 Turn on the laser level and give it time to level itself. It will start spinning when it's ready.

Step 6 Confirm that the laser is sweeping horizontally. If necessary, adjust the rotation speed (rpm). Slower speeds make the beam more visible.

Step 7 Attach the laser detector to the leveling rod using the included bracket. Turn it on. Confirm that it detects the laser beam by holding it in the beam's path. It should beep and flash a light.

Step 8 Hold the leveling rod vertically on top of the benchmark. Slide the laser detector up and down until it senses the beam. When it's aligned on the beam, tighten its clamping screw.

Step 9 The detector will have a line on its case or a pointer on its bracket. Read the leveling rod at the location identified by the line or pointer. Record the value.

Step 10 Hold the leveling rod vertically on top of the location whose height you're measuring. Slide the laser detector up and down until it senses the beam. When it's aligned on the beam, tighten its clamping screw.

Step 11 Read the leveling rod at the location identified by the detector's line or pointer. Record the value.

As *Figure 35* shows, the benchmark's elevation is 255.8' above sea level. The leveling rod reads 4.91' at this location. Using this information, you can determine the laser level's elevation since the laser beam is 4.91' above the benchmark. Add this value to the benchmark's elevation to get the instrument's elevation:

instrument elevation = benchmark elevation + height #1

instrument elevation = 255.8' + 4.91'

instrument elevation = 260.71'

The leveling rod reads 2.29' at the location whose height you're measuring. Subtract this value from the instrument's elevation to determine the unknown elevation:

unknown elevation = instrument elevation –
height #2
unknown elevation = 260.71' – 2.29'
unknown elevation = 258.42'

Laser detectors can sense the laser beam up to several hundred feet away. When working over longer distances, use the same technique outlined for optical levels. Create as many turning points as necessary to span the distance. Check for acceptable error by measuring in reverse (closing the loop) when you've completed the measurement sequence.

1.4.3 Checking a Laser Level's Calibration

Like all optical instruments, laser levels require regular calibration. They're relatively delicate, so a jolt can knock one out of calibration. Like optical levels, you can check their calibration in the field with the two-peg test described in *Section 1.3.5*. Other than setting up the instrument, the procedure is identical. Alternatively, the manufacturer may recommend a different procedure, which you should follow.

Figure 33 Craftworker using a laser detector.

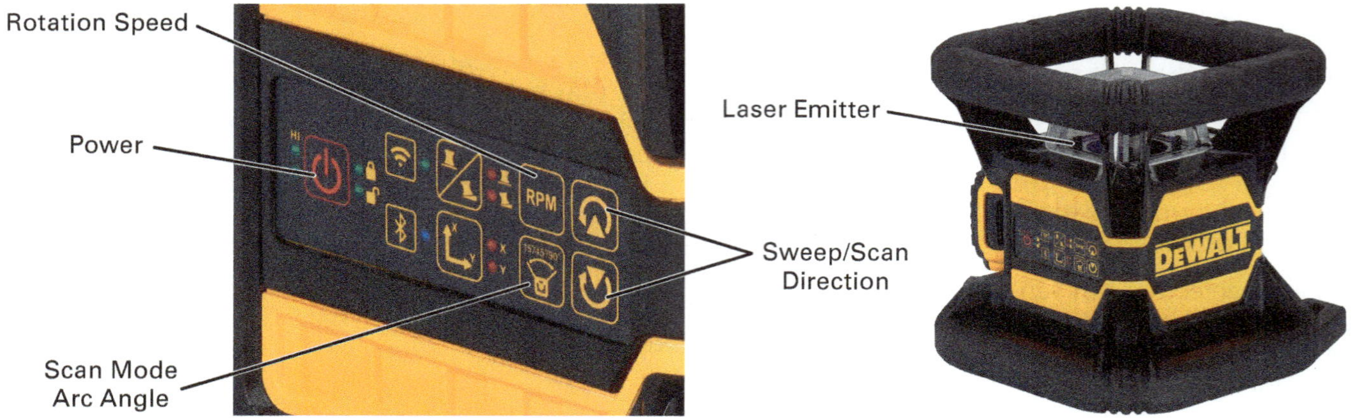

Figure 34 Laser level.

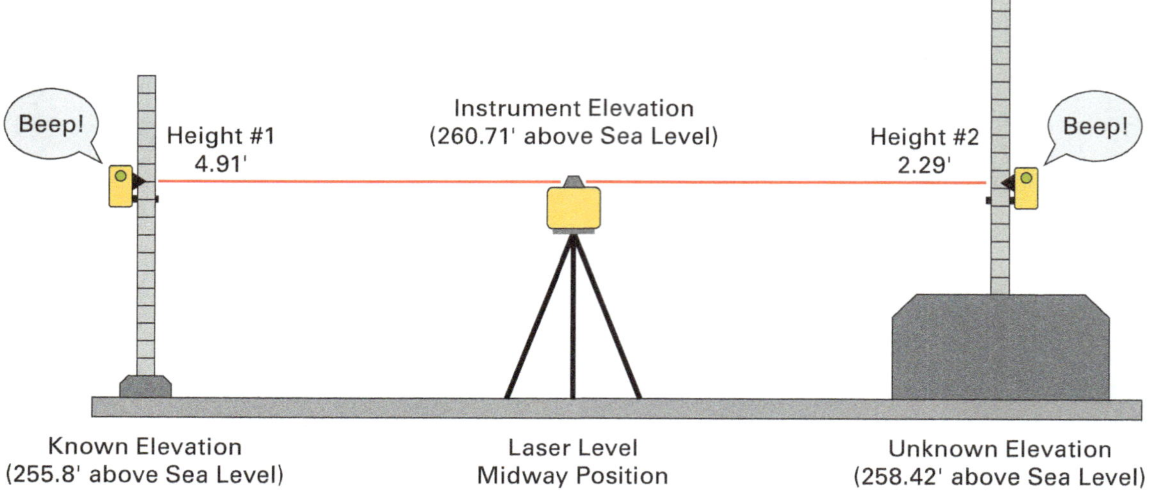

Figure 35 Measuring an elevation with a laser level.

NCCER – *Millwright*

1. Metal markers used as reference points are called ______.

    a. theodolites
    b. circular levels
    c. benchmarks
    d. plummets

2. Which of the following instruments can measure horizontal but *not* vertical angles?

    a. Optical level
    b. Theodolite
    c. Total station
    d. Optical rangefinder

3. Most current model optical levels can keep themselves level provided that the tripod and tribrach are reasonably level.

    a. True
    b. False

4. Most laser levels *don't* require special eye protection.

    a. True
    b. False

1. The techniques that millwrights use during plant layout are like _____.
   a. calibration
   b. surveying
   c. prealignment
   d. shimming

2. An object's distance above or below sea level is its _____.
   a. calibration
   b. height
   c. alignment
   d. elevation

3. Millwrights use references to locate and create _____.
   a. baselines
   b. eye lines
   c. altitude lines
   d. bolt lines

4. In surveying, leveling involves measuring _____.
   a. the plumbness of objects
   b. heights relative to various references
   c. how much the line of sight deviates from true horizontal
   d. the difference between an object's centerline and horizontal

5. The clear disk etched with black lines or the set of wires inside a telescope is a _____.
   a. reticle
   b. stadia
   c. calibration
   d. gradient

6. An optical level's *main* function is _____.
   a. measuring vertical angles
   b. centering shafts
   c. measuring heights
   d. establishing coordinates

7. What do millwrights use to align a tripod's head with true horizontal?
   a. A theodolite
   b. A laser level
   c. An optical level
   d. A bubble level

8. Which auxiliary tool do millwrights read through an optical level when measuring heights?
   a. A tubular level
   b. A leveling rod
   c. A laser plummet
   d. An optical plummet

9. An optical level's horizontal crosshair represents the _____.
   a. stadia difference
   b. horizontal angle
   c. true perpendicular
   d. line of sight

10. What does a laser level do when first powered?
    a. It starts to spin.
    b. It projects a horizontal line in a full circle.
    c. It levels itself.
    d. It sweeps a short arc.

Trade Terms Introduced in This Module

Benchmarks: Metal markers that precisely identify specific locations.

Calibration: Checking and adjusting an instrument so it can be certified as giving results that meet its specifications.

Elevation: An object's vertical distance above or below a standard reference, such as sea level.

Height: An object's vertical distance above or below a location.

Laser level: An optical instrument that uses a laser beam for measuring heights.

Leveling: Determining an object's elevation by measuring its vertical position relative to a known elevation.

Line of sight: An imaginary horizontal line between an optical instrument and a distant target.

Optical level: An optical instrument that measures heights, horizontal angles, and distances.

References: Locations whose positions and/or elevations are precisely documented.

Reticle: A clear disk engraved with lines or a set of fine wires placed inside an optical instrument.

Theodolite: An optical instrument that precisely measures horizontal and vertical angles.

Total station: An optical instrument that precisely measures horizontal and vertical angles, as well as distances.

Additional Resources

This module presents thorough resources for task training. The following reference material is suggested for further study.

Bosch. **www.boschtools.com**.
DeWalt. **www.dewalt.com**.
Leica Geosystems. **www.leica-geosystems.com**.
Topcon. **www.topcon.co.jp**.
Trimble. **www.geospatial.trimble.com**.

Figure Credits

iStock@sturti, Module Opener
iStock@rparys, Figure 1
iStock@Yuriy Pozdnikov, Figure 2
iStock@supagrit tatongboon, Figures 8 (A), 17
iStock@roman023, Figure 8 (B)
iStock@geargodz, Figures 8 (C), 12
Courtesy of DEWALT Industrial Tool Co., Figures 11, 13, 25, 33–34
Shutterstock.com/Nullaihq, Figure 14

Section Review Answer Key

Section 1.0.0

Answer	Section Reference	Objective
1. c	1.1.1	1a
2. a	1.2.1	1b
3. a	1.3.1	1c
4. a	1.4.0	1d

User Update

NCCER makes every effort to keep its textbooks up-to-date and free of technical errors. We appreciate your help in this process. If you find an error, a typographical mistake, or an inaccuracy in NCCER's curricula, please submit a User Update form by visiting **https://www.nccer.org/olf**. You can also scan the QR code using the camera on your phone or mobile device to access the form.

Gearboxes

OVERVIEW

Nearly all powered machines contain two major sections—the *driver* and the *driven*. The driver supplies the mechanical power that operates the driven. Drivers are usually electric motors or combustion engines. Driven machines can be almost anything, from a conveyor belt to an industrial robot to a gigantic mining machine. In some applications, the driver directly turns the driven. In many applications, however, they're not compatible. Instead, special components called *gearboxes* join them and solve the compatibility problem.

Module 15412

From *Millwright, Trainee Guide*. NCCER.
Copyright © 2023 by NCCER. Published by Pearson. All rights reserved.

15412
GEARBOXES

Objective

Successful completion of this module prepares you to do the following:

1. Recognize gearbox principles, types, and components.
   a. Summarize basic power transmission principles.
   b. Outline gear characteristics, types, and principles.
   c. List and describe gearbox types and their applications.
   d. List and describe gearbox components.

Performance Task

Under supervision, you should be able to do the following:

1. Identify a small gearbox's type and components.

Trade Terms

Backlash	Gears	Rotational speed
Bevel gear	Helical gear	Spur gear
Gear ratio	Overhung loads	Thrust loads
Gearbox	Pinion gear	Torque
Gearmotor	Power	Worm gear

Industry Recognized Credentials

If you are training through an NCCER-accredited sponsor, you may be eligible for credentials from NCCER's Registry. The ID number for this module is 15412. Note that this module may have been used in other NCCER curricula and may apply to other level completions. Contact NCCER's Registry at 1.888.622.3720 or go to **www.nccer.org** for more information.

You can also show off your industry-recognized credentials online with NCCER's digital badges. Transform your knowledge, skills, and achievements into badges that you can share across social media platforms, send to your network, and add to your resume. For more information, visit **www.nccer.org**.

NOTE

This module uses US standard and metric units in up to three different ways. This note explains how to interpret them.

Exact Conversions

Exact metric equivalents of US standard units appear in parentheses after the US standard unit. For example: "Measure 18" (45.7 cm) from the end and make a mark."

Approximate Conversions

In some cases, exact metric conversions would be inappropriate or even absurd. In these situations, an approximate metric value appears in parentheses with the ~ symbol in front of the number. For example: "Grip the tool about 3" (~8 cm) from the end."

Parallel but not Equal Values

Certain scenarios include US standard and metric values that are parallel but not equal. In these situations, a slash (/) surrounded by spaces separates the US standard and metric values. For example: "Place the point on the steel rule's 1" / 1 cm mark."

How to Access Resources

This craft has additional videos and resources to enhance your learning experience. To view these resources, scan the QR below. The videos and resources are separated by module.

You can scan this code using the camera on your phone or mobile device to view these videos and resources.

Contents

Figures

1.0.0 BASIC GEARBOX TECHNOLOGY

Objective

Recognize gearbox principles, types, and components.

a. Summarize basic power transmission principles.
b. Outline gear characteristics, types, and principles.
c. List and describe gearbox types and their applications.
d. List and describe gearbox components.

Performance Task

1. Identify a small gearbox's type and components.

Trade Terms

Backlash: Tiny gaps between meshed gear teeth that cause play between the gears as they turn.

Bevel gear: A gear with teeth machined at an angle to its face.

Gear ratio: A single number or a pair of numbers that identifies the rotational relationship between two meshed gears.

Gearbox: A machine that uses meshed gears to transmit power between driver and driven machines.

Gearmotor: A gearbox with an integrated electric motor.

Gears: Wheel-shaped metal or plastic components with teeth machined on their edge or face.

Helical gear: A gear with angled teeth machined on its outer edge.

Overhung loads: Sideways forces acting on a shaft.

Pinion gear: The smaller gear in a meshed pair, usually the driving gear.

Power: The rate at which a machine uses or delivers energy.

Rotational speed: The rate at which a machine or component is turning.

Spur gear: A gear with straight teeth machined on its outer edge.

Thrust loads: Forces that push or pull along a shaft's axis.

Torque: A twisting force that produces rotary motion.

Worm gear: A cylindrical gear with spiral threads wrapped around its outer surface.

Gearboxes exist to solve problems. Examine the industrial hoist in *Figure 1*. Notice that it can lift 5 tons (10,000 lb / ~4,500 kg), yet the integrated electric motor looks quite small. How can it do this?

If the motor drove the hoist directly, it couldn't lift more than about 60 lb. The motor also has another problem. It turns far too fast. Industrial motors commonly spin at around 1,750 revolutions per minute. At this speed, the motor would wind up the hoist cable in seconds. So, the motor has two problems. It can't generate enough force to lift the load, and it turns far too fast.

A **gearbox** (*Figure 2*) solves both problems by transforming the motor's speed into greater rotating force. The motor turns the gearbox's input shaft at high speed. Components inside the gearbox reduce the speed and increase the force. The gearbox's output shaft turns much more slowly but with much greater force. The hoist now can lift huge loads at an appropriate speed.

Most gearboxes reduce the driver's speed (*speed reducers*). Gearboxes can do the opposite, however, delivering a higher output speed at reduced rotational force (*speed multipliers*). A wind turbine driving a generator is an example. It rotates powerfully but relatively slowly, even on a windy day. The generator must spin rapidly to produce electricity efficiently. A gearbox converts the slow but powerful rotation to a much faster but less powerful motion.

Besides converting speed and rotational force, gearboxes solve other problems. They can change the output shaft's orientation or rotation direction. For example, some gearboxes have input and output shafts at right angles.

Gearboxes are easy to understand but come in many styles and varieties. Each has specific advantages and disadvantages. Manufacturers offer numerous accessories and options. Understanding these will help as you install, maintain, and repair gearboxes. Most important, however, is understanding how gears transmit and transform power.

Figure 1 Industrial hoist.

1.1.0 Power Transmission Principles

Machines do work by transferring energy from a source, like a motor, to the application. A *power transmission* transfers the energy and perhaps changes it into another form. Power transmissions come in many styles (*Figure 3*), some of which you may have already studied. This module explores power transmissions that transfer and transform energy with gears.

1.1.1 Speed and Torque

A rotating machine has two fundamental requirements. First, its shaft must turn at a specific rotational speed. This term refers to the number of times the shaft rotates per minute. The unit for rotational speed is *revolutions per minute (rpm)*. Depending on their design, electric motors commonly turn at speeds between 900 rpm and 3,600 rpm. Many applications require far slower rotational speeds.

Second, the shaft must turn with the right torque, or twisting force. Torque has several possible units. In the United States, the *pound-foot (lb-ft)* and *pound-inch (lb-in)* are common. The pound-foot is larger (1 lb-ft equal = 12 lb-in). Countries that use the metric system express torque in *newton-meters (Nm)*.

NCCER – *Millwright*

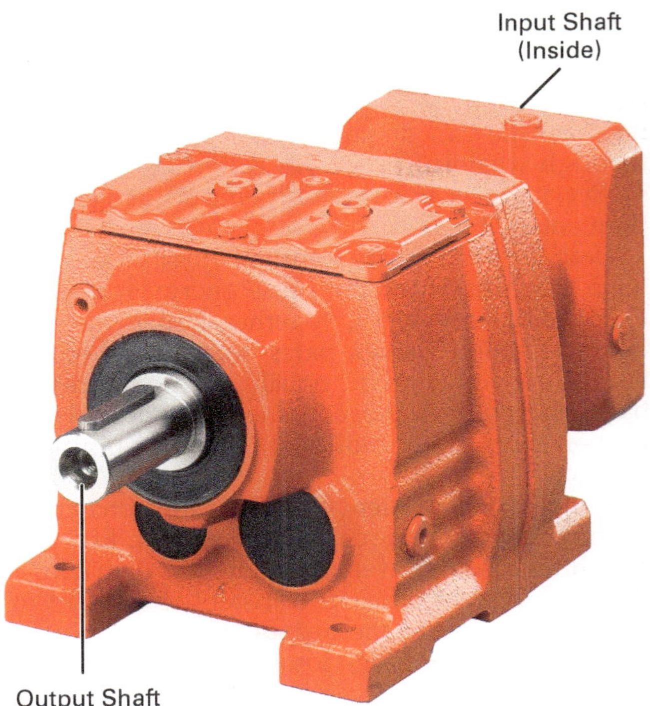

Figure 2 Gearbox.

When engineers design machines, torque is extremely important. Without the proper torque, the machine will slow or stall. For this reason, the driver and power transmission must deliver enough torque. Similarly, supporting components, like shafts and couplings, must have the correct torque ratings so they don't break or wear out quickly.

1.1.2 Power

Most people casually use the term "power" to describe the energy that does work. Scientists and engineers, however, define **power** as the *rate* at which a machine delivers or uses energy. The following example should make this idea clearer.

When you climb a staircase, your body delivers chemical energy to your muscles so they can lift your weight against gravity. The energy required depends on your body weight and the staircase height. It *doesn't* depend on time. Whether you walk or run, you do the same work and use the same energy.

You're probably thinking that this statement can't be true. You feel a lot more tired after running than walking. Surely that means you've used more energy. However, the statement *is* correct. What *isn't* the same is power (*Figure 4*).

Remember, power is the rate at which you deliver or use energy. Running up the stairs requires more power than walking because running uses energy faster. You feel tired because your body had to turn chemical energy into motion very quickly.

In the United States, the unit for mechanical power is the *horsepower (hp)*. In countries that use the metric system, the unit for power is the *kilowatt (kW)*. Manufacturers often rate rotating

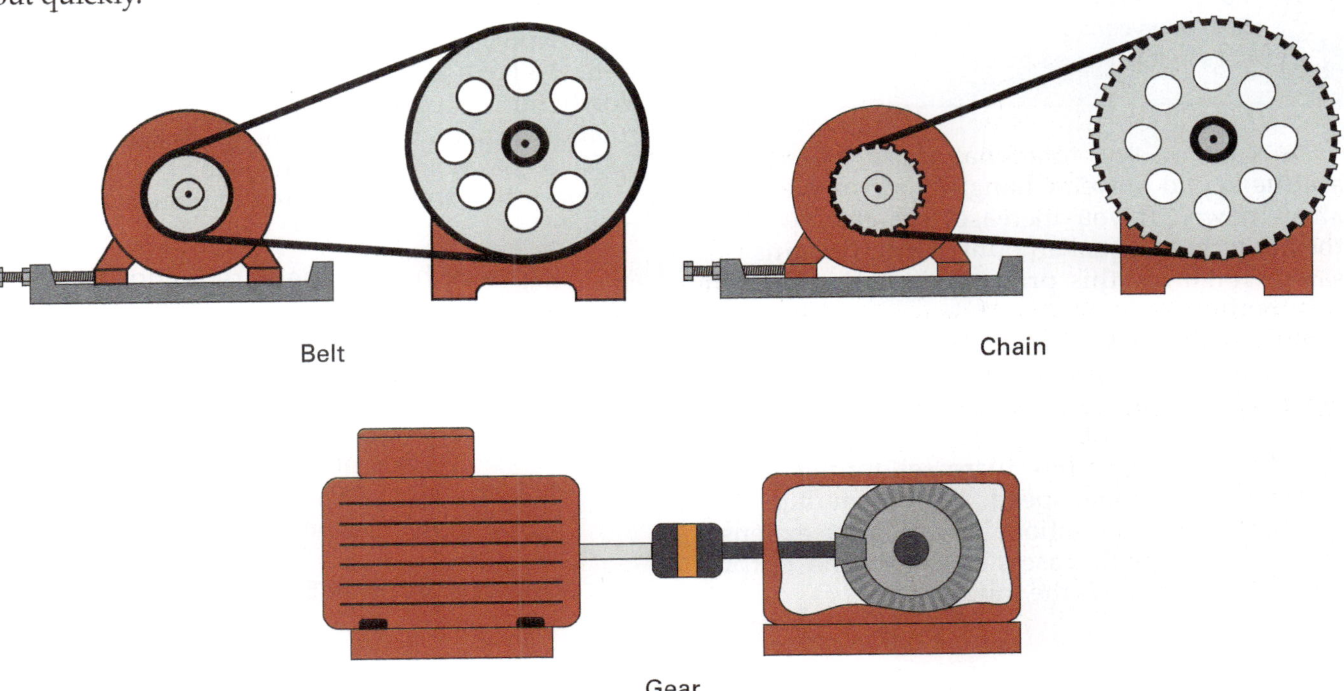

Figure 3 Power transmissions.

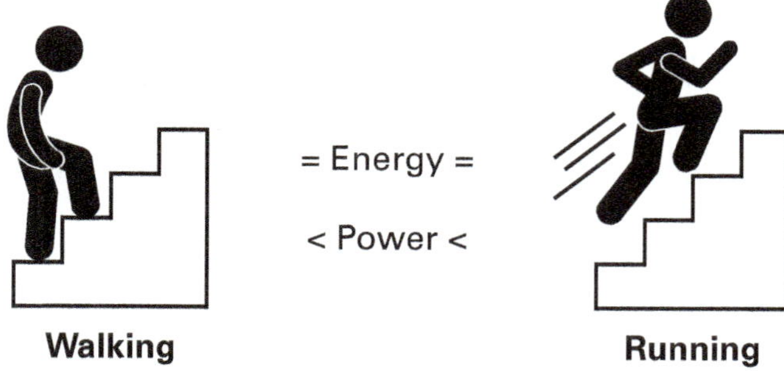

Figure 4 Same energy, different power.

machines by their rotational speed, torque, and power. For example, an electric motor might have a maximum rotational speed of 1,750 rpm, a nominal torque of 15 lb-ft, and a power of 5 hp.

> **NOTE**
> During startup, motors often deliver two to three times their nominal torque. They can't sustain this output for long, however, without being damaged.

The following formulas calculate mechanical power in horsepower:

$$\text{power} = (\text{rotational speed} \times \text{torque supplied in lb-ft}) \div 5{,}250$$

$$\text{power} = (\text{rotational speed} \times \text{torque supplied in lb-in}) \div 63{,}025$$

> **NOTE**
> The 5,250 and 63,025 in the power equations are *conversion constants*. They adjust the answer so it's in the desired power unit (hp).

As you can see, rotational speed and torque are the key to power. Changing one or the other alters power. If you increase one and decrease the other by an equal amount, power remains the same. You'll see this principle in action later in this module.

Another principle to remember is that a machine never outputs more power than it receives through its input. Gearboxes can increase either rotational speed or torque, but they can't increase power. A speed-reducing gearbox increases torque at the expense of rotational speed. A speed-multiplying gearbox increases rotational speed at the expense of torque. In both cases, however, the output power never exceeds the input.

1.1.3 Losses

Ideally, a power transmission transfers all energy from its input to its output. In the real world, no machine can do this. Some energy escapes through wasteful processes called *losses* (*Figure 5*). Every power transmission outputs less energy than enters it.

Heat is the most common loss. The hotter a machine runs, the more energy it wastes. *Friction*, parts rubbing together, causes several losses. Friction makes parts wear out, become hot, and operate more noisily. These processes bleed energy from the machine. Good design and proper lubrication reduce, but can't eliminate, friction.

A machine's **efficiency** rating is the percentage of input energy that reaches the output. Efficient machines lose relatively little energy. A machine that's 95 percent efficient transfers 95 percent of its input energy to the output. The remaining 5 percent escapes through losses.

> **NOTE**
> The machine's efficiency rating added to its losses always equals 100 percent.

1.1.4 Transforming Energy

Sometimes, mechanical energy is in the wrong form. The 5-ton hoist example (*Figure 1*) illustrates this point. Its 10 hp electric motor turns rapidly (1,750 rpm) but with relatively low torque (30 lb-ft). To hoist a 10,000 lb load, it must turn more slowly but with greater torque. Transforming the rotational speed to 10 rpm increases the torque to 5,250 lb-ft—enough to lift the load.

Notice that this transformation doesn't change power:

$$(\text{power before speed reduction})$$

$$\text{power} = (\text{rotational speed} \times \text{torque}) \div 5{,}250$$

$$\text{power} = (1{,}750 \text{ rpm} \times 30 \text{ lb-ft}) \div 5{,}250$$

$$\text{power} = 10 \text{ hp}$$

$$(\text{power after speed reduction})$$

$$\text{power} = (10 \text{ rpm} \times 5{,}250 \text{ lb-ft}) \div 5{,}250$$

$$\text{power} = 10 \text{ hp}$$

Power Transmission Efficiencies

Every power transmission type—gear, chain, or belt—has a typical efficiency value. Yet, an individual transmission's efficiency can vary widely. Much depends on its overall condition and lubrication. Some transmissions gradually lose efficiency as their parts wear out or drift out of adjustment.

Gear transmissions can be extremely efficient—95 percent to 98 percent. One gear transmission type, however, has an efficiency as low as 70 percent. You'll learn about it later in this module.

Chain transmissions reach efficiencies between 94 percent and 98 percent. Their actual efficiency depends on chain type, condition, and lubrication.

Belt transmission efficiencies depend on belt type, condition, and tension. A flat belt can be 99 percent efficient, but this value will drop if the belt starts slipping. V-belts generate more friction, so their best efficiency is around 97 percent. As they age, their efficiency drops steadily, often falling below 90 percent. Synchronous (toothed) belts don't slip and generate less friction than V-belts. Their efficiencies stay around 98 percent.

Properly lubricated and aligned gear transmissions last for years and run very efficiently. Among the different transmission types, they require the least adjustment. Chains, on the other hand, require regular cleaning, lubrication, and adjustment. They also require periodic replacement since they wear out.

Belt transmissions are the most demanding. Flat belts and V-belts are efficient only when new and properly tensioned. As they wear out or lose tension, their efficiency drops sharply. Synchronous belts maintain their efficiency but still require adjusting and replacement.

The transformation exchanges something not needed (rotational speed) for something needed (torque). That's what a gearbox does (*Figure 6*). It converts speed into torque. Gearboxes that do this are often called *torque multipliers*.

1.2.0 Gear Technology

Gears are wheel-shaped parts made from metal or plastic. *Teeth* on their edge or face transfer rotational motion to other gears with matching teeth. Shafts through the gears support them as they turn. Two gears linked by their teeth are *meshed* (*Figure 7*).

1.2.1 Gear Types

Gears come in many styles. Engineers choose gears based on their load-handling ability, performance, and price. The following sections cover gear types that are common in gearboxes.

Spur Gears

A **spur gear** looks like most people's idea of a gear (*Figure 7*). It has straight teeth machined along its outer edge. These mesh with similar teeth on another gear. Spur gears are easy to manufacture, so they're inexpensive. They're noisy, however, and handle only moderate loads.

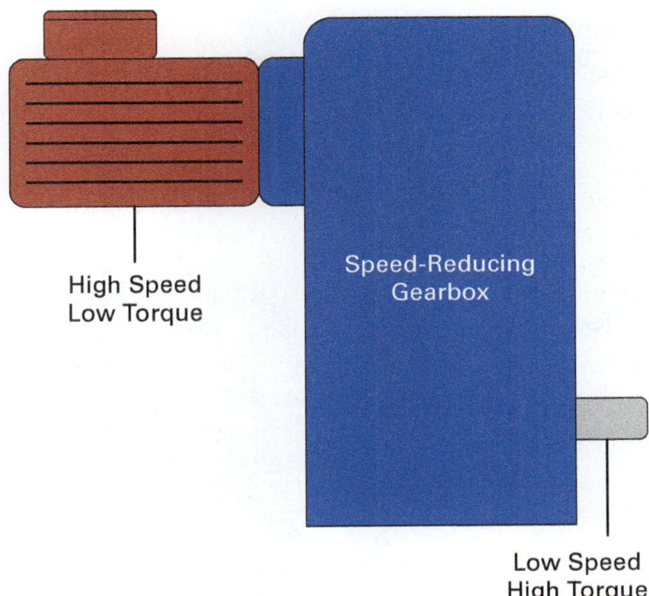

Figure 6 Exchanging speed for torque.

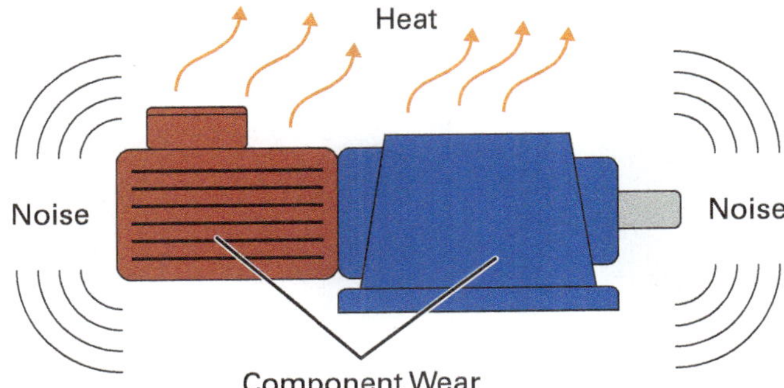

Figure 5 Energy losses.

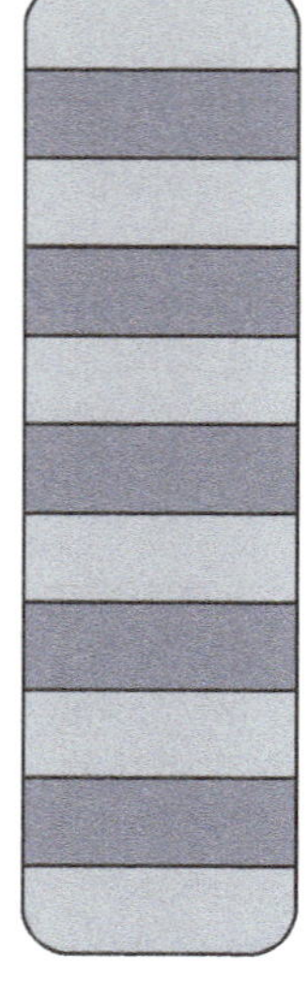

Figure 7 Meshed spur gears.

Helical Gears

A **helical gear** is like a spur gear but with different teeth. Instead of being straight, the teeth are angled (*Figure 8*). This small change gives several advantages. The gears run more quietly with less vibration. They can carry larger loads because the teeth are longer, and more teeth mesh at once. Helical gears are expensive because the teeth are harder to manufacture.

A helical gear is either left- or right-handed, depending on the direction that its teeth face. Meshed helical gears must have the same tooth angle but opposite handedness. Helical gears push against each other as they turn. This *thrust force* stresses the shaft bearings, a definite disadvantage.

Double-helical and *herringbone* gears are specialized helical gears. They have V-shaped teeth. Double-helical gears have a groove running down the middle, while herringbone gears don't. Their specialized tooth shape helps them carry larger loads than regular helical gears. The V-shape generates two thrust forces that push in opposite directions, so they cancel out. These gears are harder to manufacture, so they're expensive.

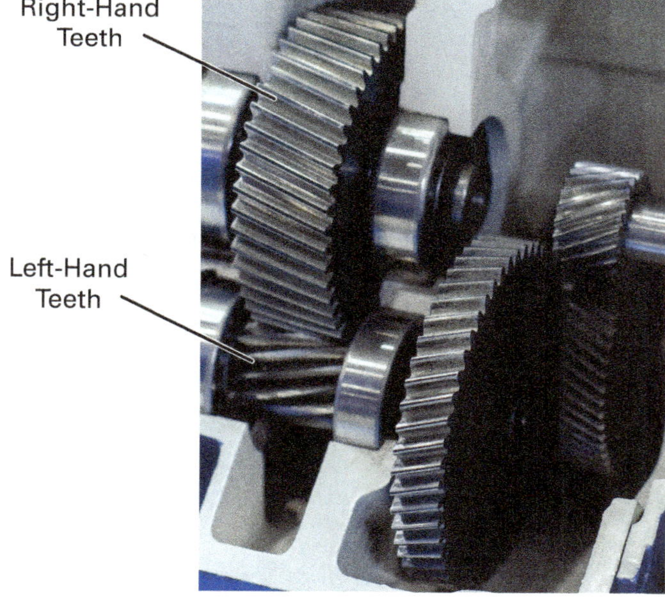

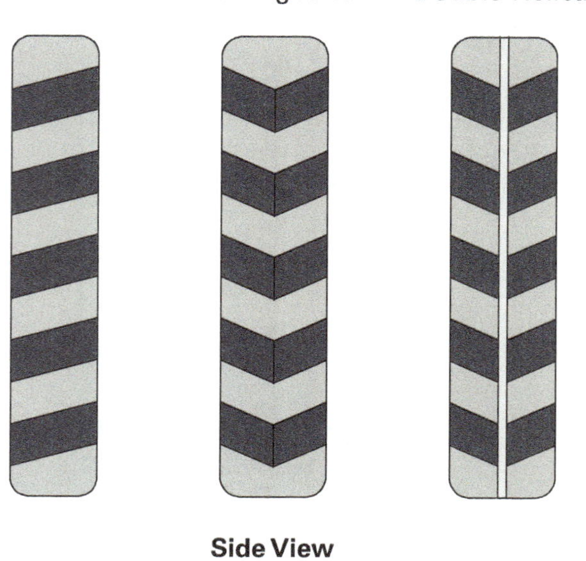

Figure 8 Helical gears.

NCCER – *Millwright*

Bevel Gears

A **bevel gear** has teeth machined on one face at an angle (*Figure 9*). The teeth can be straight, angled, or spiral (angled and curved). Meshed bevel gears change the shaft orientation by 90 degrees. This is useful if the rotary motion must turn a corner.

Straight bevel gears behave like spur gears. They're inexpensive, noisy, and can't carry very large loads. *Skew (angled) bevel gears* are like helical gears. They're more expensive, reasonably quiet, and can carry larger loads. *Spiral bevel gears* are expensive, moderately quiet, and can carry large loads. Both skew and spiral bevel gears generate thrust forces, which stresses their bearings.

Worm Gears

The unusual **worm gear** has some big advantages and disadvantages. It's cylindrical instead of wheel shaped. Rather than teeth, it has screw threads wrapped around its surface. The worm gear meshes with a helical gear—sometimes called the *worm wheel* (*Figure 10*). Like bevel gears, worm gears change the shaft orientation by 90 degrees.

These gears run very smoothly and quietly because the worm gear's threads continuously slide against the worm wheel's teeth. Unfortunately, this quality also generates a lot of friction and heat, which is a major disadvantage. Worm gears are inefficient and wear out much faster than other gears. Usually, the worm gear is steel, while the worm wheel is bronze. This combination reduces friction somewhat. Since the worm wheel is softer, it wears out faster than the worm gear.

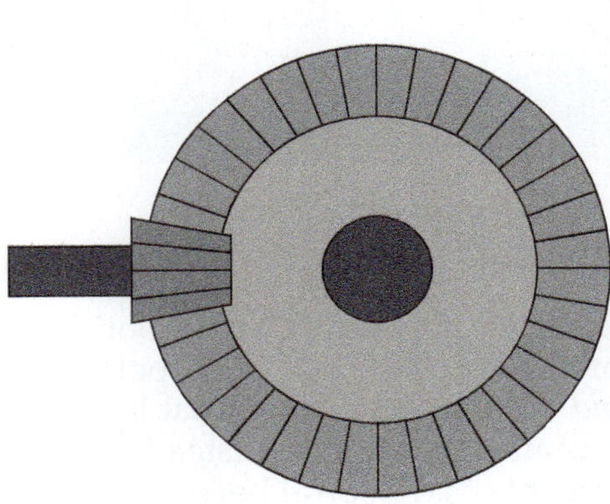

Straight Bevel

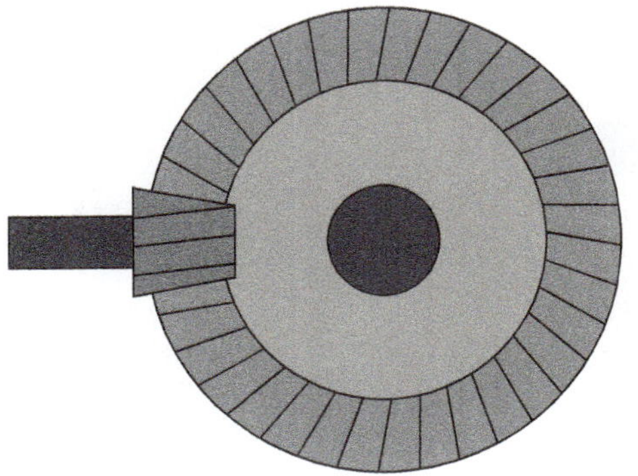

Skew Bevel

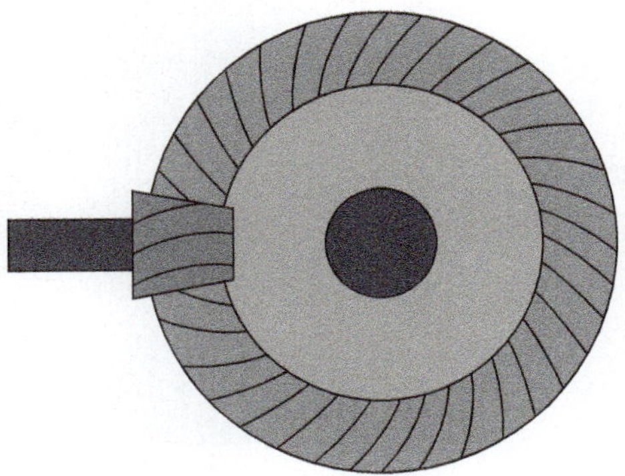

Spiral Bevel

Figure 9 Bevel gears.

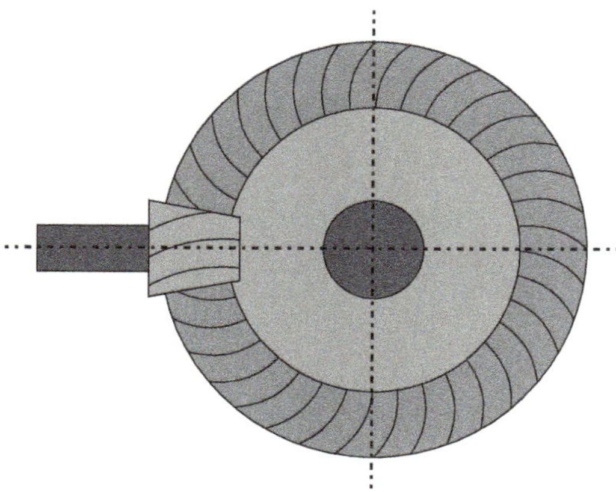

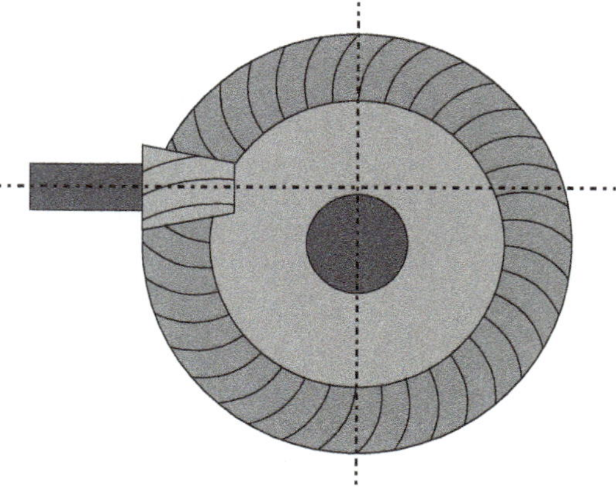

Figure 10 Worm gears and worm wheels.

Hypoid Gears

Some applications require the smooth, quiet operation of a worm gear but need better efficiency. A *hypoid gear* offers an acceptable compromise. It's not another gear type. Instead, it's a modified arrangement of two spiral bevel gears.

Normally, two meshed spiral bevel gears have centerlines that cross in the middle of the larger gear. This arrangement generates little friction and is moderately quiet. Moving the smaller gear so the gear centerlines don't cross in the center creates a hypoid arrangement (*Figure 11*). In this position, the gears run more quietly. They generate more friction as well, but it's less than a worm gear generates.

Figure 11 Hypoid gear arrangement.

Trademarked Gears

Several gear manufacturers offer specialized versions of common designs. These modifications provide advantages or improvements over the originals. The Zerol® gear, for example, is a specialized bevel gear trademarked by Gleason Corporation. It has curved teeth like a spiral bevel gear, but they're not angled. Like straight bevel gears, Zerol® gears don't generate thrust forces. Unlike straight bevels gears, however, they're relatively quiet.

SEW-EURODRIVE offers a specialized hypoid gear design called the SPIROPLAN®. The smaller gear is shaped like a threaded rod instead of a bevel gear. The larger gear has curved and angled teeth like a spiral bevel gear, but it has a flat face. These changes offer technical and economic advantages over traditional hypoid gears.

Figure Credit: Courtesy of Rainer Blickle & SEW-EURODRIVE

1.2.2 Gear Transmission Principles

Gear teeth transfer power by pushing against each other. Usually, they roll rather than slide. Since rolling contact minimizes friction, the process is very efficient—95 percent or better. Low friction also means that the gears wear out slowly. Provided they're properly aligned and lubricated, they'll last for many years. Worm gears are the exception since they slide rather than roll, an inefficient, friction-generating process. Rolling contact can be noisy, however, especially with straight teeth. Angled or curved teeth mesh more gradually, making them quieter.

A gear transmission contains at least two meshed gears supported by shafts and bearings (*Figure 12*). The *driving gear* turns the *driven gear*. In speed-reducing transmissions, the driving gear is smaller and usually goes by the name pinion gear. When two meshed gears rotate, their shafts always turn in opposite directions.

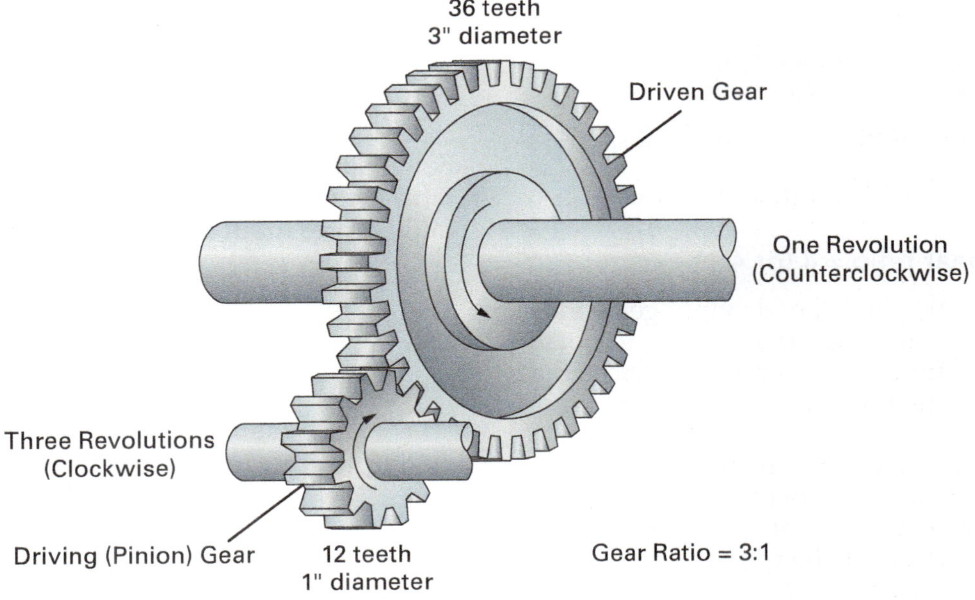

Figure 12 Gear transmission.

1.2.3 Gear Ratio

Normally, the driving and driven gears are different sizes and have a different number of teeth. These qualities cause them to turn at different rotational speeds. This is the way that gear transmissions increase or decrease speed. For example, the driving gear in *Figure 12* is one-third the diameter of the driven gear (1" vs. 3"). It also has one-third as many teeth (12 vs. 36). To turn the driven gear *one* revolution, the driving gear must turn *three* revolutions.

A pair's **gear ratio** identifies the rotational speed difference between the driving and driven gears. The pair in *Figure 12* has a gear ratio of 3:1 because the driving gear must turn three times to make the driven gear turn once.

The second number in a gear ratio is always 1. For this reason, some manufacturers omit it and express the gear ratio with just the first number. Gear ratios bigger than 1, such as 1.25:1, indicate that the gear pair acts as a speed reducer. Gear ratios smaller than 1, such as 0.5:1, indicate that the gear pair acts as a speed multiplier.

The following two formulas calculate the gear ratio:

$$\text{gear ratio} = \text{teeth}_{driven} \div \text{teeth}_{driving}$$

$$\text{gear ratio} = \text{speed}_{driving} \div \text{speed}_{driven}$$

For example, if the driving gear has 10 teeth and the driven gear has 40 teeth, the first formula will give the pair's gear ratio:

$$\text{gear ratio} = \text{teeth}_{driven} \div \text{teeth}_{driving}$$

$$\text{gear ratio} = 40 \text{ teeth} \div 10 \text{ teeth}$$

$$\text{gear ratio} = 4 \text{ (or 4:1)}$$

With this gear pair, the driving gear must rotate four turns for the driven gear to rotate once. The gears function as a speed reducer that cuts the input rotational speed to one-fourth its value.

Alternatively, you can calculate the gear ratio from the gears' rotational speeds. For example, if the driving gear is turning at 1,750 rpm and the driven gear is turning at 500 rpm, the second formula will give the pair's gear ratio:

$$\text{gear ratio} = \text{speed}_{driving} \div \text{speed}_{driven}$$

$$\text{gear ratio} = 1{,}750 \text{ rpm} \div 500 \text{ rpm}$$

$$\text{gear ratio} = 3.5 \text{ (or 3.5:1)}$$

With this gear pair, the driving gear must rotate three and a half turns for the driven gear to rotate once. This gear pair is also a speed reducer. Notice that gear ratios don't have to be whole numbers.

1.2.4 Gears, Rotational Speed, and Torque

If you know the gear ratio and either the input or output rotational speed, you can calculate the other speed. The following two formulas calculate rotational speed:

$$\text{output speed} = \text{input speed} \div \text{gear ratio}$$

$$\text{input speed} = \text{output speed} \times \text{gear ratio}$$

For example, if the input rotational speed is 150 rpm and the gear ratio is 0.25:1, the first formula will give the output rotational speed:

$$\text{output speed} = \text{input speed} \div \text{gear ratio}$$

$$\text{output speed} = 150 \text{ rpm} \div 0.25$$

$$\text{output speed} = 600 \text{ rpm}$$

With this gear pair, the driven gear turns four times faster than the driving gear. The gears function as a speed multiplier that quadruples the input rotational speed.

When a gear pair reduces rotational speed, it *increases* output torque. When it increases rotational speed, it *decreases* output torque. The gear ratio is the key to the change. The following formula relates input and output torque to gear ratio:

$$\text{output torque} = \text{input torque} \times \text{gear ratio}$$

For example, if an electric motor delivering 5 lb-ft of torque drives a gear pair with a 7.5:1 gear ratio, the following calculation gives the output torque:

$$\text{output torque} = \text{input torque} \times \text{gear ratio}$$

$$\text{output torque} = 5 \text{ lb-ft} \times 7.5$$

$$\text{output torque} = 37.5 \text{ lb-ft}$$

Gearboxes use gear ratio to change both torque and speed as the application requires.

1.2.5 Gear Stages

As you can guess, some applications require very large gear ratios. For example, a mining machine might need to turn slowly but with enormous torque. Reducing the motor's speed and multiplying its torque might require a gear ratio of 500:1 or more. Unfortunately, it's not possible to make a gear pair with these huge ratios. The driving gear would be too tiny to mesh with the driven gear.

To solve this problem, gearbox manufacturers combine several gear pairs, called *stages*. The first stage's driven gear turns the second stage's driving gear. Many gearboxes use this strategy to develop very large gear ratios. Some millwrights call these *compound gearboxes*. Typical gearboxes contain two, three, four, or even five stages (*Figure 13*). For even larger ratios, some equipment manufacturers connect several gearboxes together. These develop ratios as high as 4,000:1.

The manufacturer usually doesn't publish the individual stages' gear ratios. Instead, it publishes the gearbox's overall ratio. For example, a mining machine might contain a six-stage gearbox with a 1,500:1 overall ratio. If its driving motor has a rotational speed of 1,750 rpm and a nominal torque of 75 lb-ft, the following formulas give the output rotational speed and torque:

output speed = input speed ÷ gear ratio

output speed = 1,750 rpm ÷ 1,500

output speed = 1.17 rpm

output torque = input torque × gear ratio

output torque = 75 lb-ft × 1,500

output torque = 112,500 lb-ft

1.3.0 Gearbox Applications

Almost every industry uses gearboxes. Manufacturers offer them in many sizes, styles, and configurations. They range from tiny units for precision machines to monsters that power sugar mills and rock crushers. Given their application range, it's no surprise that they come in so many styles.

1.3.1 Gearbox Categories

Gearboxes divide into major categories based on their intended application. *Precision gearboxes* support positioning applications. For example, logistics conveyors move products around automated warehouses at high speed. Gearboxes must start and stop equipment quickly and accurately as it sends products down different paths. Precision electric motors, called *servomotors*, usually drive these gearboxes (*Figure 14*).

General-purpose gearboxes handle everyday applications. They drive conveyors, hoists, pumps, fans, blowers, and mixers. Manufacturers offer them in many sizes and styles. Millwrights and industrial mechanics encounter general-purpose gearboxes most frequently. Some manufacturers combine them with a matched electric motor, producing a **gearmotor** (*Figure 15*).

Industrial gearboxes are specialized machines for demanding applications. Most are very large and extremely durable (*Figure 16*). They drive mining machines and conveyors, giant mixers, ore and rock processing equipment, and sugar mills.

Unlike general-purpose gearboxes, industrial gearboxes are highly customized. Usually, the customer and a gearbox engineer work together to design the gearbox from semi-standard features and options. Many industrial gearboxes include purpose-built features. A typical unit might require months for delivery and cost several hundred thousand dollars.

Figure 13 Three-stage gearbox.

1.3.2 Gearbox Styles

All gearboxes divide into three major styles based on their shaft arrangement. An *inline gearbox* has input and output shafts that share a common centerline. A *parallel-shaft gearbox* has shafts that share the same plane but not a common centerline. A *right-angle gearbox* has shafts that form a 90-degree angle. *Figure 17* illustrates each style.

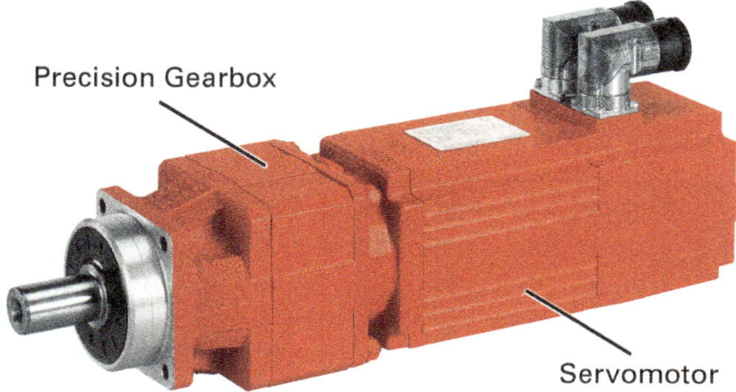

Figure 14 Servomotor and precision gearbox.

Equipment manufacturers select the gearbox style based on the application. For example, right-angle gearboxes are more compact than inline gearboxes. On the other hand, inline and parallel-shaft gearboxes don't change the shaft orientation.

1.3.3 Gearbox Types

A gearbox's type depends on the gears that it contains, as well as their arrangement. Equipment manufacturers may select a gearbox's type based on its torque characteristics, noisiness, compactness, or shaft orientation. The following sections cover common gearbox types found in many machines.

Helical

These gearboxes contain only helical gears (*Figure 18*). They're very popular and versatile, coming in both parallel-shaft and inline styles. Manufacturers offer many sizes and gear ratios. Most contain one to three stages. Helical gearboxes run very efficiently (95 percent to 98 percent) and moderately quietly.

NCCER – *Millwright*

Gearbox

Gearmotor

Figure 15 General-purpose gearbox and gearmotor.

Helical-Bevel

These gearboxes contain both helical and spiral bevel gears (*Figure 19*). They're very popular and versatile, coming in the right-angle style only. Manufacturers offer many sizes and gear ratios. Most contain one to three stages. They run very efficiently (95 percent to 98 percent) and moderately quietly.

Worm Gear

Simple worm gearboxes contain a single worm gear and worm wheel (*Figure 20*). Equipment manufacturers use them in applications that require very smooth, quiet operation. They come in the right-angle style only. They have poor efficiency (85 percent or less) and wear out more quickly than other types. Worm gearboxes can have relatively large gear ratios, but their efficiency drops as the gear ratio rises.

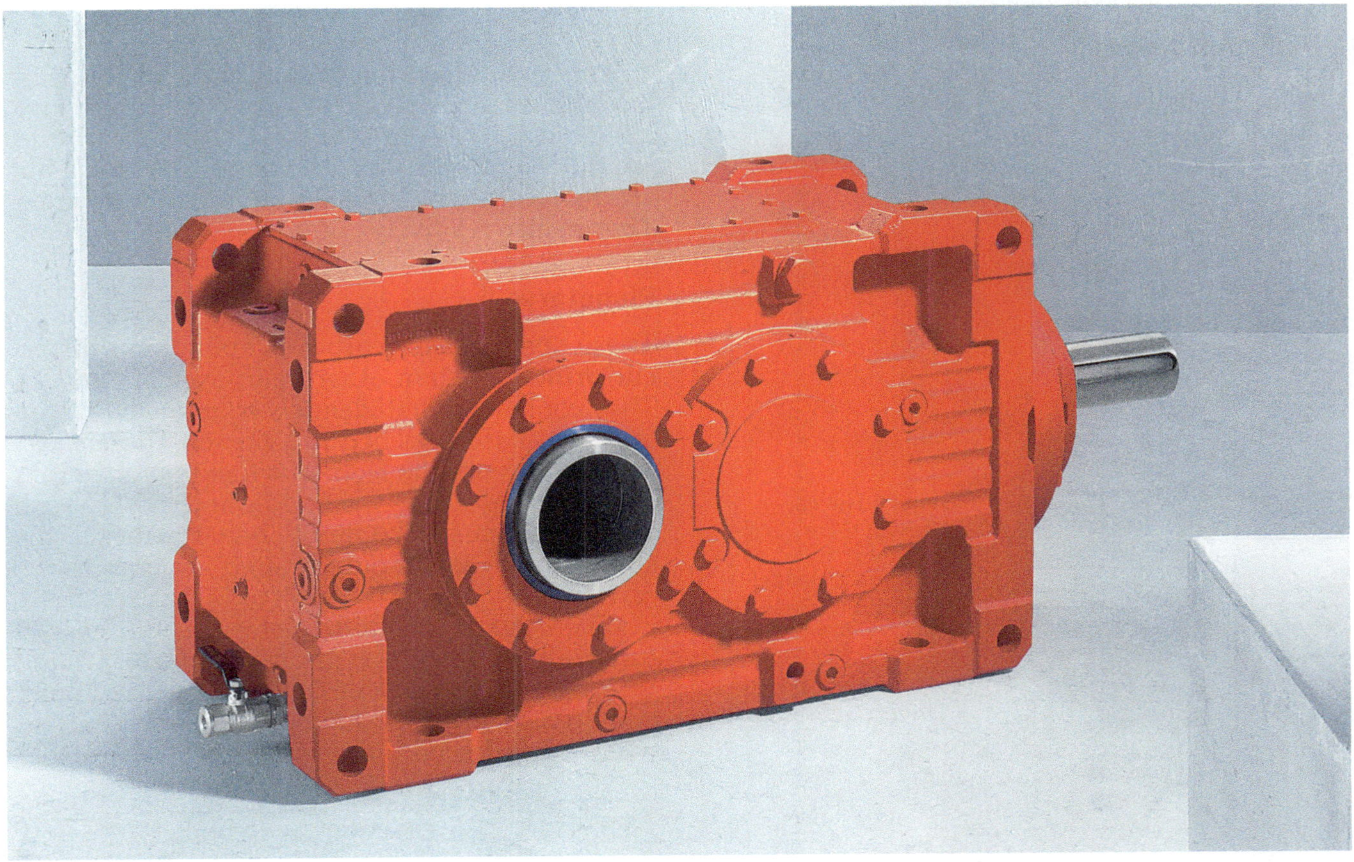

Figure 16 Industrial gearbox.

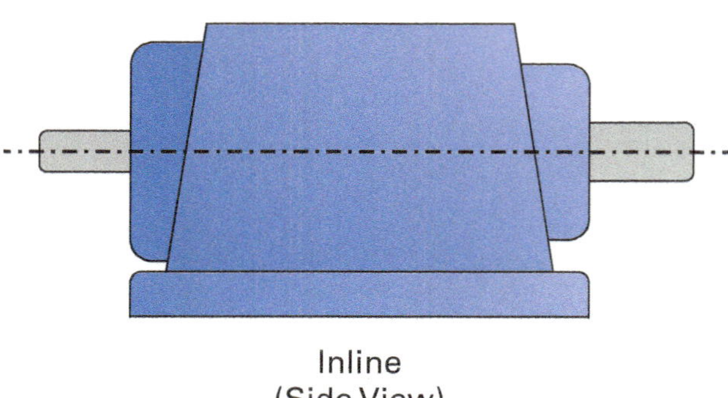

Inline
(Side View)

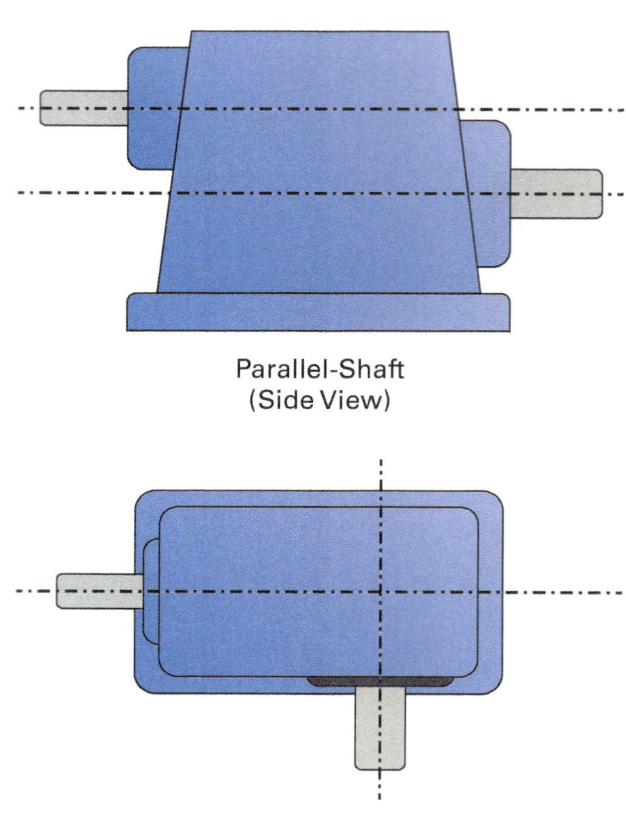

Parallel-Shaft
(Side View)

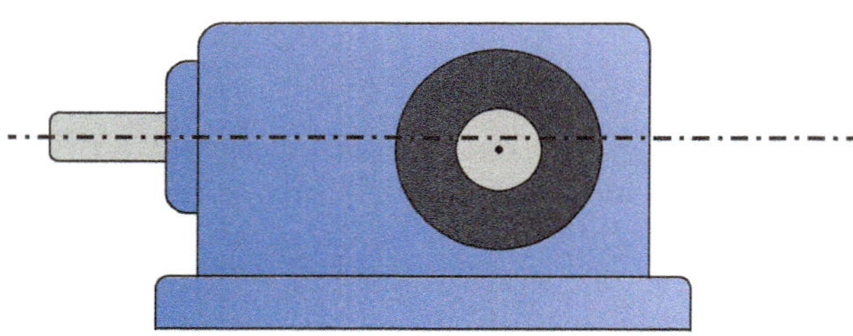

Right-Angle
(Side View)

Right-Angle
(Top View)

Figure 17 Gearbox styles.

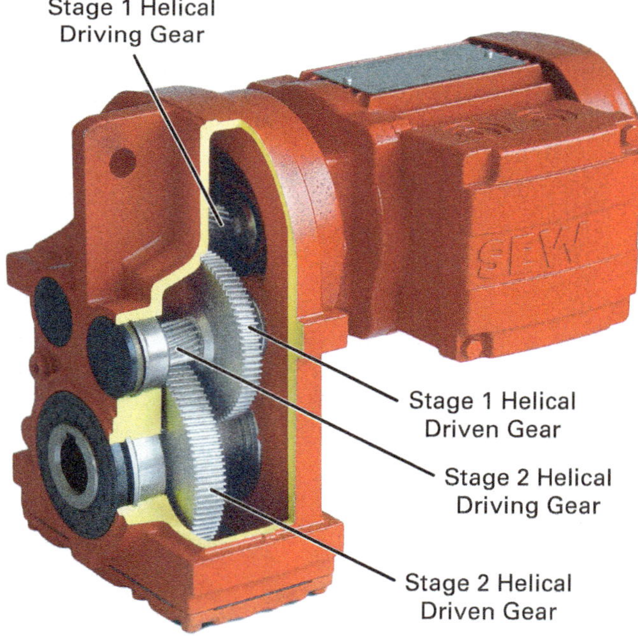

Figure 18 Helical gearbox.

Some manufacturers offer hybrid worm gearboxes that contain a helical stage combined with a low-ratio final worm gear stage. These gearboxes are quiet and have decently large gear ratios but are more efficient than simple worm gearboxes. They're also relatively quiet.

Planetary

These specialized gearboxes operate on different principles than other gearboxes (*Figure 21*). They contain several identical spur gears turning on short shafts attached to a carrier. These *planet gears* mesh with the teeth of a fixed outer ring. A single *sun gear* fits in the middle and meshes with each planet gear. The input shaft attaches to the sun gear, while the output shaft attaches to the carrier.

When the input shaft rotates the sun gear, it turns all the planet gears. They rotate around their shafts as well as orbit inside the fixed outer ring. This complex motion turns the carrier, which turns the output shaft.

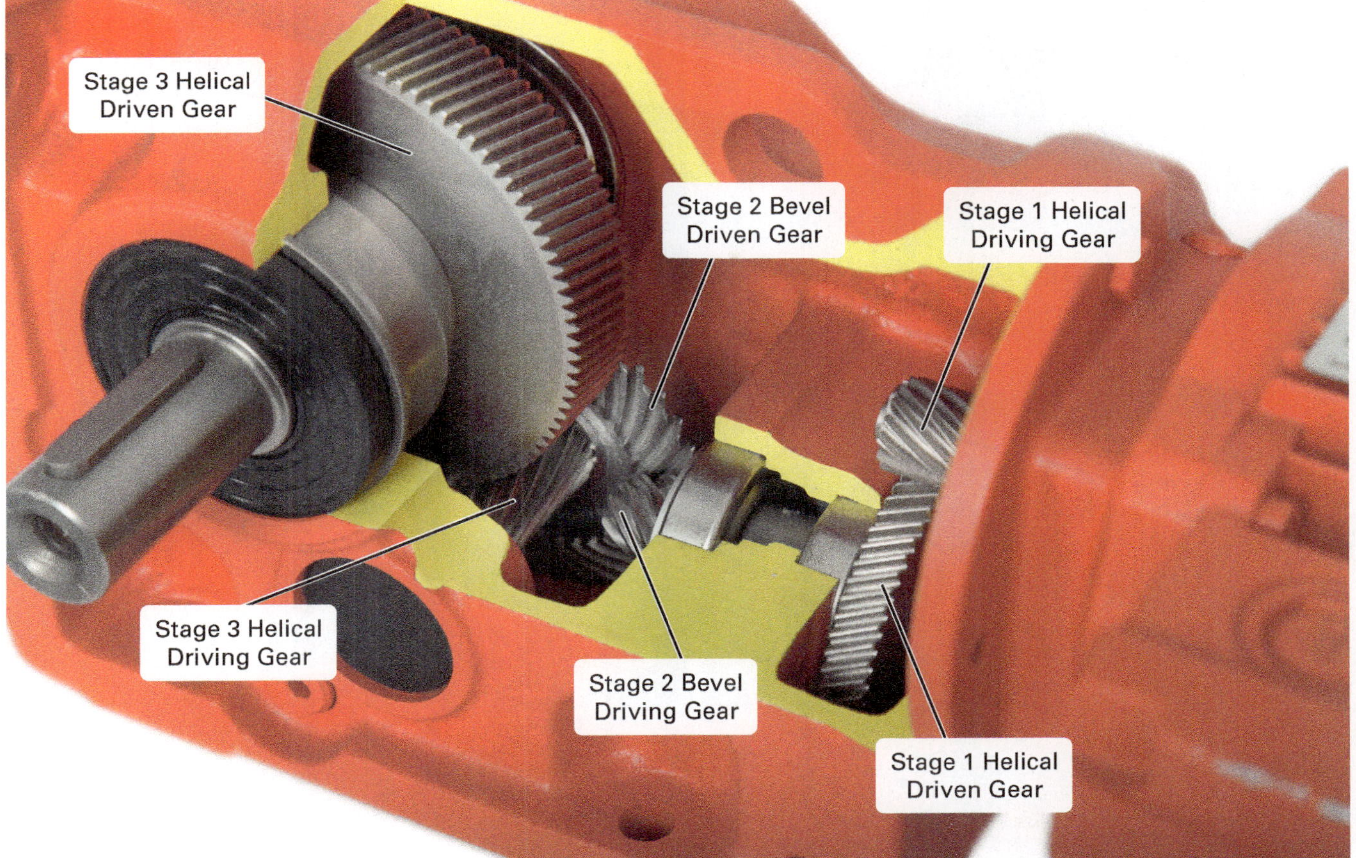

Figure 19 Helical-bevel gearbox.

Planetary gearboxes have several advantages. They can deliver large torques and are very precise. Interestingly, they're popular in both very large, heavy-duty applications and small, precision applications (*Figure 22*). Their complex construction and many gears make them very expensive.

Planetary gearboxes come in the inline style only. Manufacturers offer small or very large units but rarely medium-sized ones. Planetary gearboxes are available in small gear ratios only. Some manufacturers link several planetary stages together to develop larger gear ratios.

1.4.0 Gearbox Components

All gearboxes, regardless of their type or size, share common features and components. Millwrights and industrial mechanics must recognize these since some require maintenance. Others may fail and require replacement. Most gearboxes include optional accessories that meet specific application needs. The manufacturer installs some during the gearbox's assembly. Millwrights can add others later. Craftworkers may have to maintain accessories or replace them if they fail.

1.4.1 Key Components

Every gearbox has the following core components. While they vary in appearance, they're usually easily recognizable. *Figure 23* shows a general-purpose gearbox with many of these features identified. Consult it as you learn about each.

Housing

The gearbox's housing holds everything together. It contains the lubricant and maintains an environment that protects the gears, shafts, and bearings. Most housings are cast iron, steel, or aluminum. Usually, the manufacturer applies paint or a protective coating to the outside. Alternatively, gearboxes that operate in corrosive or harsh environments may have stainless steel housings.

Some housings have mounting feet that bolt onto a baseplate. Others attach to the equipment by flanges or specialized mounting methods. Housings usually have one or more gasketed covers for accessing the internal components. Generally, to prevent leaks from developing, millwrights and industrial mechanics replace the gasket after opening a cover.

Figure 20 Simple worm gearbox.

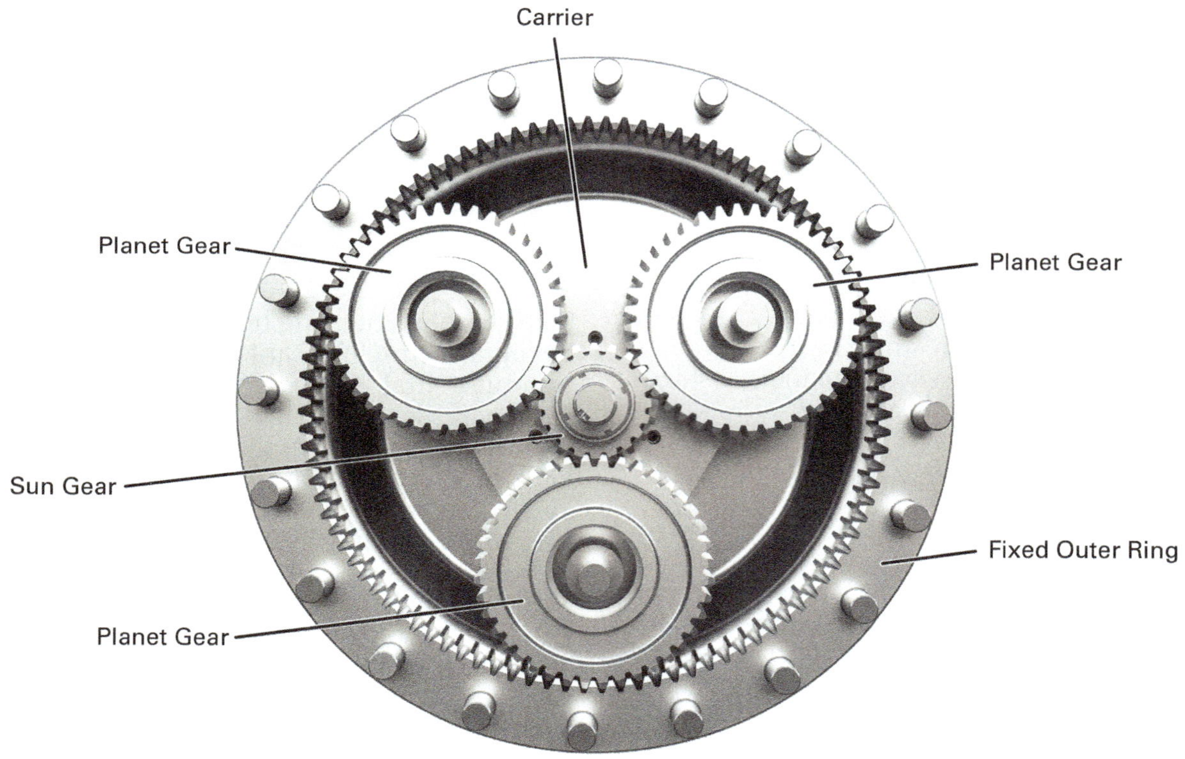

Figure 21 Planetary gear arrangement.

Figure 22 Planetary gearboxes.

Shafts

All gearboxes have at least two shafts. The driver connects to the input shaft and the driven machine connects to the output shaft. Some right-angle gearboxes have two output shafts, one on each side. Shafts are usually steel, although stainless steel is also common.

Solid shafts may be smooth, keyed, or splined. Equipment attaches to smooth shafts with a clamping device that grips the shaft. Keyed shafts have one or more keyways. A metal key rests in each keyway and links the shaft to a matching keyway on the coupling device. Splined shafts slide into a coupling device's matching teeth.

> **NOTE**
>
> NCCER Module 15307, *Couplings and Alignment Fundamentals*, covers shaft attachment methods.

Some gearboxes have *hollow shafts* instead of solid ones (*Figure 18* and *Figure 20*). A matching solid shaft slides into the hollow shaft. A clamping device, keys, or splines link the shafts. The shafts can corrode and become difficult to separate. Some hollow shafts include a built-in mechanism that can free a stuck shaft. Manufacturers may supply an anticorrosion paste to apply to the solid shaft during installation.

Figure 23 Key gearbox components.

Bearings and Seals

Besides the input and output shafts, most gearboxes contain internal shafts for the gear stages. Bearings support all shafts, so they turn freely with minimal friction. Antifriction bearings, usually ball or roller, are the most common style. Bearings fit in "pockets" machined into the housing. Some bearings require regular maintenance, while others are sealed. Millwrights and industrial mechanics may have to replace bearings if they fail.

To keep contaminants from getting inside the gearbox, the input and output shafts have seals around them. *Figure 18*, *Figure 19*, and *Figure 20* all show the seal (black ring) around the gearboxes' output shafts. Manufacturers usually offer several seal material choices at order time. If the gearbox operates in an unusually dirty environment, it may have multiple seals on each shaft. Some industrial gearboxes have highly specialized seals designed to keep out abrasive materials like metallic ore grit.

Millwrights and industrial mechanics may have to remove seals when they maintain gearboxes. Removing a seal often destroys it, so they'll finish the job by installing a new one. Properly installing a seal usually requires a special tool.

Driver Attachment

Manufacturers offer many ways to attach the driver to the gearbox. These include belt or chain drive accessories, fluid couplings, and motor platforms. A flanged motor bell and coupling is the most popular method for electric motor drivers. The motor must have a matching flange that bolts onto the motor bell. The coupling links the motor and gearbox shafts. It's often a jaw-type flexible coupling, which can accommodate limited misalignment.

By design, a gearmotor's electric motor bolts directly onto the gearbox. The motor shaft has an attached pinion gear. It meshes with the first stage driven gear. *Figure 18* and *Figure 19* show directly attached motors and their pinion gears.

Lubrication

All gearboxes have a lubrication system to reduce friction. The lubricant, usually oil, also cools the gearbox and protects its components from corrosion. Lubrication systems may be simple or complex. Gearboxes that operate in cold, hot, or dirty environments may have specialized lubrication accessories.

Most general-purpose gearboxes use a simple system called *splash lubrication*. Oil partially fills the housing, collecting at the bottom. One or more gears dip into the lubricant pool as they turn. The spinning gears collect oil and fling it around the housing where it lands on the other gears, shafts, and bearings. Gravity eventually returns it to the oil pool, where the process repeats.

Since they operate with large loads in demanding environments, industrial gearboxes often have sophisticated lubrication systems. *Spray lubrication* distributes the lubricant with a pump and plumbing system. Spray bars inside the housing direct lubricant onto critical components. This

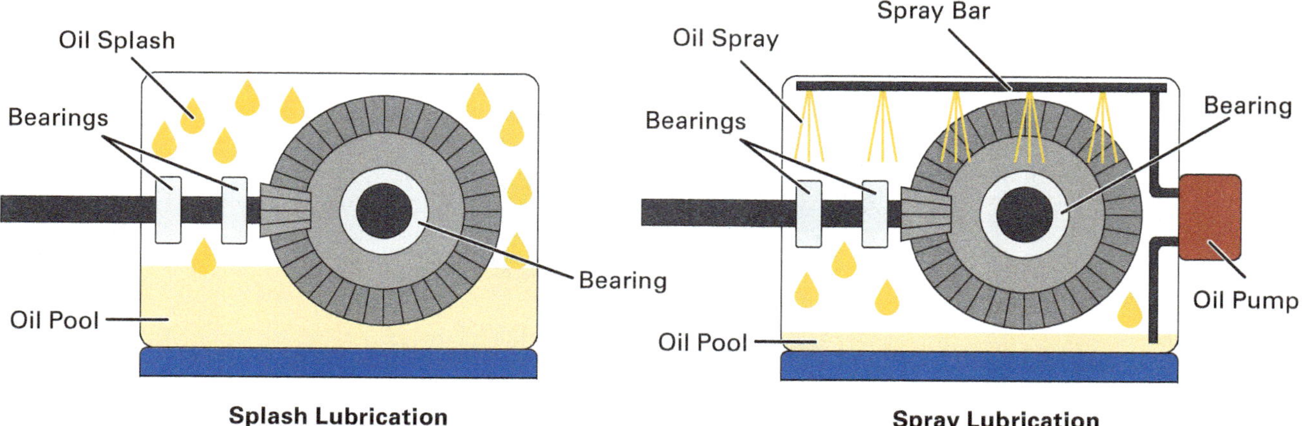

Figure 24 Splash and spray lubrication.

method requires less oil in the pool than does splash lubrication, an important economic factor with large gearboxes. *Figure 24* shows both lubrication methods.

Spray lubrication systems may also include equipment to filter and cool the oil. In very hot environments, cooling is essential. If the gearbox operates in a cold environment, it may include a heater to prevent the oil from becoming too viscous.

Besides oil for general lubrication, most gearboxes use grease to lubricate their bearings. Small bearings may be sealed. Larger bearings usually require periodic relubrication. Often the gearbox oil splashes onto the bearings, keeping their grease from drying out. Millwrights and industrial mechanics regularly change gearbox oil and maintain bearings. They may also maintain and troubleshoot a sophisticated lubrication system.

> **NOTE**
>
> NCCER Module 15411, *Troubleshooting and Repairing Gearboxes*, introduces gearbox lubrication tasks.

1.4.2 Accessories

Most gearboxes include extra features. Some equip the gearbox for special applications or unusual operating conditions. Usually, the customer requests these at order time. Craftworkers can add certain features later. The following sections summarize common accessories.

Plugs, Breathers, and Sight Glasses

Most gearbox housings have a drain so craftworkers can empty the lubricant during maintenance. Usually, this is a simple threaded hole with a matching plug. Since equipment manufacturers may mount the gearbox in various positions, however, a single drain isn't sufficient. Instead, gearbox manufacturers equip the housing with multiple holes. The lowest one becomes the drain. *Figure 25* shows different mounting positions with the drain locations identified.

> **NOTE**
>
> Some gearboxes can't be mounted in every possible orientation. Always consult the gearbox manufacturer for permissible mounting positions. The lubricating oil quantity will be different for each position. Confirm proper lubrication before changing the gearbox's position. Too much or too little oil can cause serious problems.

As the gearbox operates, it warms up, causing the air inside to expand. The increased pressure can damage the seals, or even squirt oil around their edges. To prevent this problem, many gearboxes have a valve called a *breather*. It opens and closes as required to keep the inside pressure equal to the outside pressure. Craftworkers install the breather in the housing's highest hole.

> **NOTE**
>
> Never install a breather below the oil level or oil will squirt from the valve when it opens to relieve pressure.

After maintaining a gearbox, the craftworker refills the housing with the correct amount of lubricating oil. To make this task easier, some gearboxes have a *sight glass* that shows the correct lubricant level. *Figure 26* shows several gearbox lubrication accessories.

Protective Coatings

Unless they're made from stainless steel, most gearboxes have a protective coating applied by the manufacturer. Primer and paint are suitable for clean, dry indoor settings. If the gearbox is exposed to the weather, it will have a more advanced coating. This might include primer, epoxy paint, and a clear, UV-resistant topcoat. Gearboxes that operate in harsh, corrosive, or salty environments often have very sophisticated, multilayer coatings.

Normally, the customer specifies the required coatings at order time. The manufacturer applies them after assembling the gearbox. Some manufacturers sell their gearboxes with only a primer coat applied. The customer can add other coatings later.

Protective coatings must be intact to do their job. If the coating becomes chipped or scratched, the bare metal underneath will corrode. Millwrights and industrial mechanics watch for corrosion spots and deal with them before they become problems.

Electronic Monitoring

Gearboxes require routine maintenance, like oil changes. Craftworkers regularly inspect for unusual behavior, like excessive vibration. In large facilities with thousands of gearboxes, these tasks can become burdensome. To manage them, the company may fit critical gearboxes with *electronic monitoring devices*.

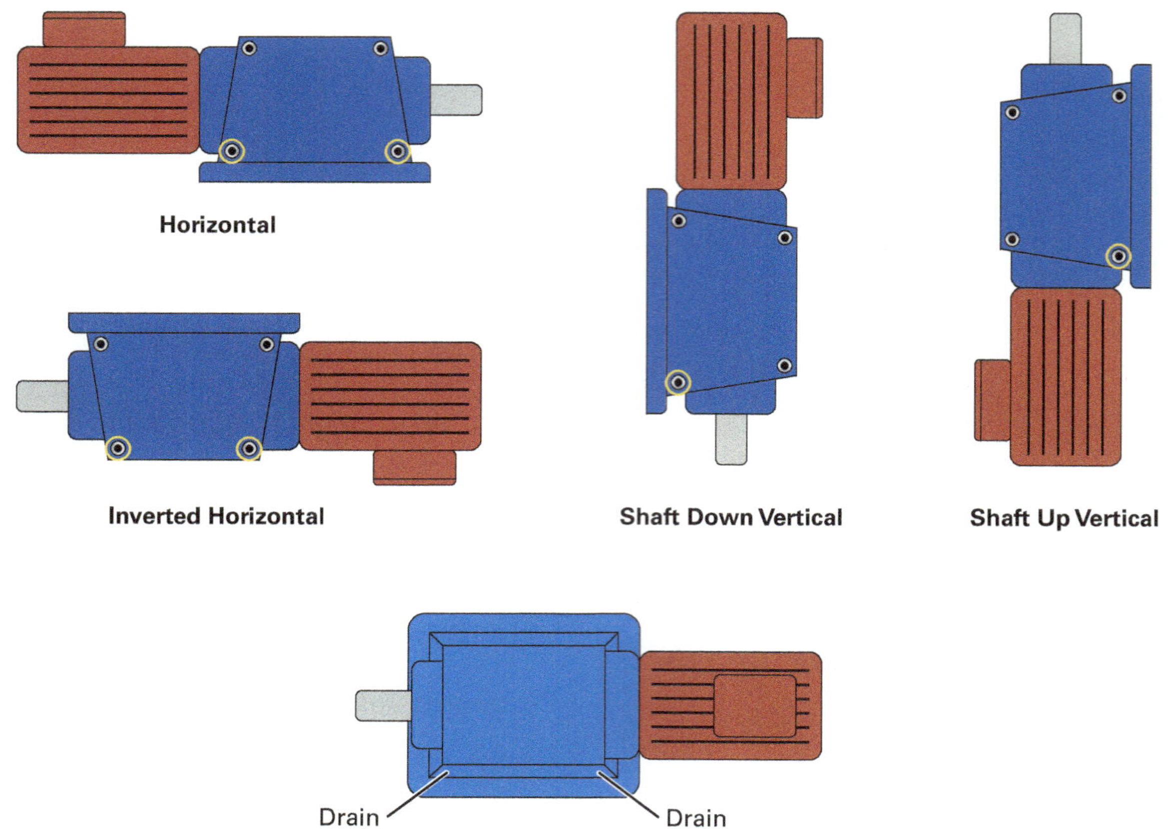

Figure 25 Mounting positions and drain holes.

A monitoring device contains sensors that watch the machine's operating behavior. If the behavior changes, the device automatically requests maintenance through the plant management system.

Oil condition monitoring is a common example (*Figure 27*). Gearbox oil degrades over time. High temperature speeds up the process. An oil condition monitor tracks the gearbox's temperature and its operating hours. It calculates the oil's probable condition and notifies maintenance personnel when they should change it.

Vibration monitors are another example. They contain sensors that detect vibration patterns from the running gearbox. If the gearbox's vibrations match destructive patterns, the monitoring device alerts maintenance personnel. By identifying potential problems before they turn into failures, these devices reduce expensive downtime.

Low Backlash Gears

Meshed gears must have small gaps, called backlash, between their engaged teeth (*Figure 28*). If they didn't, the gears couldn't turn because they'd be locked together. General-purpose gearboxes usually contain gears with moderate backlash. You can feel it by turning the input shaft gently back and forth. It will move a small amount before you feel the gears engage and start to turn.

If backlash is too big, however, the gears will have excessive play. This play prevents the gearbox from starting and stopping precisely. For some applications, like fans and blowers, it's not a problem. On the other hand, a robotic arm must start and stop with no sloppiness. Some manufacturers offer low backlash gears as an upgrade option for customers whose applications need better precision.

Specialized Bearings

All applications generate forces that push or pull on the gearbox's output shaft as it rotates (*Figure 29*). **Overhung loads** act perpendicularly to the shaft. **Thrust loads** act along the shaft's axis. Provided these loads aren't excessive, the shaft's bearings can tolerate them.

Applications with long shafts can develop large overhung loads. Vertical mixing machines that handle thick liquids may develop unacceptable thrust loads. Some applications develop both load types. These loads will damage the shaft bearings over time. To avoid this problem, gearbox manufacturers may offer special heavy-duty bearings that can tolerate the unusual loads. The customer requests them as an upgrade at order time.

Torque Arms

Some applications mount the gearbox to the driven machine by hanging it from that machine's shaft. To be *shaft mounted*, the gearbox must have a hollow shaft. The driven machine's solid shaft slides into the hollow shaft and supports the gearbox. Obviously, the shaft must be strong enough to carry the gearbox's weight, as well as the application torque. Conveyor systems often use this attachment method (*Figure 30*).

To prevent the gearbox from spinning around its own shaft, it must be anchored to the driven machine. A gearbox accessory called a *torque arm* provides a place to secure the gearbox to the driven machine's frame. The torque arm doesn't support the gearbox's weight. It just keeps the gearbox from spinning. Torque arms usually have rubber buffers to dampen vibrations.

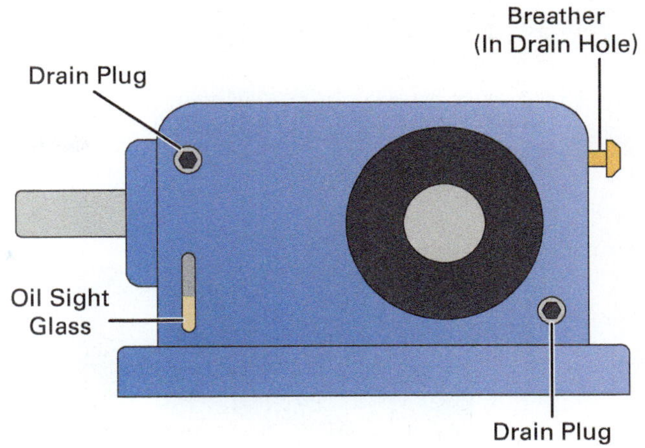

Figure 26 Lubrication accessories.

Figure 27 Oil condition monitoring device.

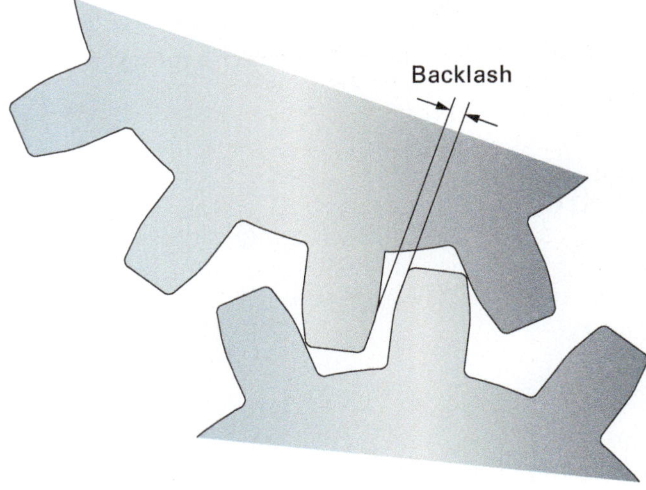

Figure 28 Backlash in gear teeth.

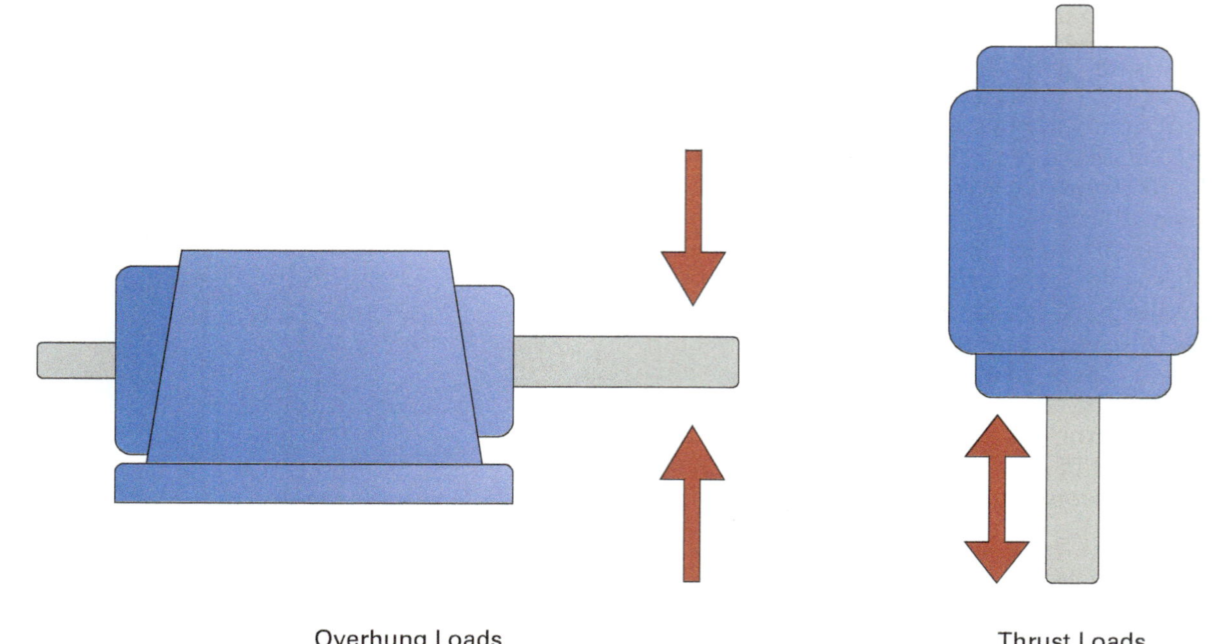

Figure 29 Overhung and thrust loads.

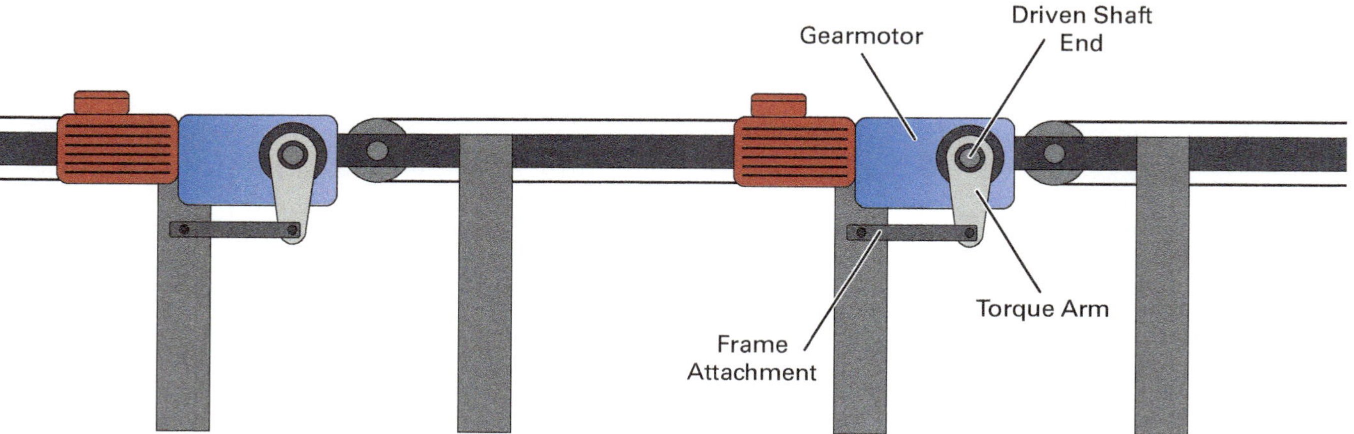

Figure 30 Shaft-mounted gearmotors on a conveyor.

1. A gearbox's output shaft spins at 150 rpm. This is its ______.

   a. torque
   b. rotational speed
   c. gear ratio
   d. power

2. Gears with their teeth machined at an angle on the face are ______.

   a. planetary gears
   b. helical gears
   c. spur gears
   d. bevel gears

3. A gearbox's input shaft is above its output shaft and in the same plane. What is the gearbox style?

   a. Parallel-shaft
   b. Inline
   c. Right-angle
   d. Planetary

4. How does a gearmotor's electric motor attach to the gearbox?

   a. It attaches with a motor bell and coupling.
   b. It bolts directly onto the gearbox.
   c. It attaches through a fluid coupling.
   d. It drives the gearbox through a chain.

1. A speed-reducing gearbox converts ______.
   a. rotational speed into greater power
   b. power into reduced torque
   c. torque into greater power
   d. rotational speed into greater torque

2. A gearbox with a gear ratio greater than 1 will output more power than it receives from the driver.
   a. True
   b. False

3. If a gearbox is 80 percent efficient, how much energy does it *lose*?
   a. 20 percent
   b. 40 percent
   c. 60 percent
   d. 80 percent

4. A gear has angled teeth on its outer edge. It's a ______.
   a. helical gear
   b. spur gear
   c. bevel gear
   d. hypoid gear

5. Which of the following gear types is the *least* efficient?
   a. Spur
   b. Spiral bevel
   c. Worm
   d. Skew bevel

6. A gearbox has an overall gear ratio of 4:1. How many revolutions must the input shaft turn for the output shaft to revolve *twice*?
   a. 1
   b. 2
   c. 4
   d. 8

7. A medium-sized pump *most likely* would be driven by a ______.
   a. general-purpose gearbox
   b. industrial gearbox
   c. precision gearbox
   d. planetary gearbox

8. Which of the following gearboxes is very efficient and comes only in the right-angle style?
   a. Helical-bevel
   b. Simple worm
   c. Helical
   d. Planetary

9. If a gearbox must operate in a harsh environment full of corrosive chemicals, its housing will *most likely* be made from ______.
   a. cast iron
   b. plastic
   c. stainless steel
   d. primed aluminum

10. A customer plans to use a general-purpose gearbox to control a positioning turntable. What will the customer *most likely* request from the gearbox manufacturer at order time to ensure that it starts and stops precisely?
    a. Low backlash gears
    b. Overhung load bearings
    c. An electronic oil monitoring device
    d. A breather valve

Trade Terms Introduced in This Module

Backlash: Tiny gaps between meshed gear teeth that cause play between the gears as they turn.

Bevel gear: A gear with teeth machined at an angle to its face.

Gear ratio: A single number or a pair of numbers that identifies the rotational relationship between two meshed gears.

Gearbox: A machine that uses meshed gears to transmit power between driver and driven machines.

Gearmotor: A gearbox with an integrated electric motor.

Gears: Wheel-shaped metal or plastic components with teeth machined on their edge or face.

Helical gear: A gear with angled teeth machined on its outer edge.

Overhung loads: Sideways forces acting on a shaft.

Pinion gear: The smaller gear in a meshed pair, usually the driving gear.

Power: The rate at which a machine uses or delivers energy.

Rotational speed: The rate at which a machine or component is turning.

Spur gear: A gear with straight teeth machined on its outer edge.

Thrust loads: Forces that push or pull along a shaft's axis.

Torque: A twisting force that produces rotary motion.

Worm gear: A cylindrical gear with spiral threads wrapped around its outer surface.

Additional Resources

This module presents thorough resources for task training. The following reference material is suggested for further study.

Bonfiglioli. **bonfiglioli.com**.
Flender. **flender.com**.
Nord. **nord.com**.
SEW-EURODRIVE. **seweurodrive.com**.
SUMITOMO. **us.sumitomodrive.com**.
Timken. **timken.com**.

Figure Credits

iStock@Pavel Vozmischev, Module Opener
iStock@TongTa, Figure 1
Courtesy of Rainer Blickle & SEW-EURODRIVE, Figures 2, 14–16, 18–19, 22, 27
iStock@NUMAX3D, Figure 7
iStock@artas, Figures 8, 13
iStock@Waldemarus, Figure 9
iStock@Nordroden, Figure 10
iStock@Warut1, Figure 20
iStock@Pixelci, Figure 21
iStock@dja65, Figure 23

SECTION 1.0.0

Answer	Section Reference	Objective
1. b	1.1.1	1a
2. d	1.2.1	1b
3. a	1.3.2	1c
4. b	1.4.1	1d

User Update

NCCER makes every effort to keep its textbooks up-to-date and free of technical errors. We appreciate your help in this process. If you find an error, a typographical mistake, or an inaccuracy in NCCER's curricula, please submit a User Update form by visiting **https://www.nccer.org/olf**. You can also scan the QR code using the camera on your phone or mobile device to access the form.

Troubleshooting and Repairing Gearboxes

OVERVIEW

Gearboxes keep industry turning in countless ways. They transform rotational speed and torque, increasing or decreasing them as the application requires. Most gearboxes are quite robust, with some staying in service for decades. On the other hand, if they're not maintained properly, gearboxes can't do their job and will have short lives. Millwrights and industrial mechanics inspect, maintain, troubleshoot, and repair gearboxes to keep the world moving.

Module 15411

TROUBLESHOOTING AND REPAIRING GEARBOXES

Objective

Successful completion of this module prepares you to do the following:

1. Summarize maintaining, troubleshooting, and repairing gearboxes.
   a. Describe typical gearbox maintenance tasks and procedures.
   b. Outline internally inspecting gearboxes.
   c. Outline troubleshooting gearboxes.
   d. Outline repairing gearboxes.

Performance Tasks

Under supervision, you should be able to do the following:

1. Inspect a gearbox externally.
2. Remove a gearbox and prepare it for internal inspection.
3. Internally inspect a gearbox and perform one or more maintenance tasks.

Trade Terms

Backstop
Churning loss
Food grade

Mineral oil
Shock loads
Synthetic oil

Industry Recognized Credentials

If you are training through an NCCER-accredited sponsor, you may be eligible for credentials from NCCER's Registry. The ID number for this module is 15411. Note that this module may have been used in other NCCER curricula and may apply to other level completions. Contact NCCER's Registry at 1.888.622.3720 or go to **www.nccer.org** for more information.

You can also show off your industry-recognized credentials online with NCCER's digital badges. Transform your knowledge, skills, and achievements into badges that you can share across social media platforms, send to your network, and add to your resume. For more information, visit **www.nccer.org**.

How to Access Resources

This craft has additional videos and resources to enhance your learning experience. To view these resources, scan the QR below. The videos and resources are separated by module.

You can scan this code using the camera on your phone or mobile device to view these videos and resources.

Contents

Figures and Tables

1.0.0 WORKING WITH GEARBOXES

Objective

Summarize maintaining, troubleshooting, and repairing gearboxes.

  a. Describe typical gearbox maintenance tasks and procedures.
  b. Outline internally inspecting gearboxes.
  c. Outline troubleshooting gearboxes.
  d. Outline repairing gearboxes.

Performance Tasks

1. Inspect a gearbox externally.
2. Remove a gearbox and prepare it for internal inspection.
3. Internally inspect a gearbox and perform one or more maintenance tasks.

Trade Terms

Backstop: A device that prevents a shaft from turning in one direction.

Churning loss: Energy wasted by gears plowing through lubricating oil as they rotate.

Food grade: A lubricant meant to be used in food preparation areas.

Mineral oil: A lubricant distilled from crude petroleum that has properties like automobile oil.

Shock loads: Abrupt, brief, and significant increases in a machine's normal load.

Synthetic oil: A chemically engineered lubricant with enhanced properties and a long lifespan.

When working with gearboxes, millwrights and industrial mechanics exercise their senses and skills. They look for damage and leaks. They listen for unusual sounds or vibrations. They notice equipment running hot or giving off odd odors. These clues alert them to problems that may become failures. They deal with these problems to prevent the failures. When something breaks, they troubleshoot the gearbox and repair it. Between repairs, they maintain the gearbox to keep it running smoothly.

1.1.0 Gearbox Maintenance

Gearboxes are simple machines. They're just shaft-mounted, bearing-supported gears in a housing. A well-maintained gearbox will last a long time. Problems usually center upon the gears and bearings since they move and wear out. For this reason, a millwright's major tasks include managing lubrication and dealing with emerging wear.

> **NOTE**
>
> In this module, the term "gearbox" refers to gearboxes and gearmotors. As you recall, a gearmotor is a gearbox with a directly integrated electric motor.

In the average factory environment, millwrights commonly encounter general-purpose gearboxes driven by motors of less than 5 hp (*Figure 1*). These handle many of industry's needs—driving conveyors, pumps, blowers, and production equipment. Since they're relatively small, manipulating them is simple. Most aren't unusually expensive, and they rarely include complicated accessories. Their maintenance is relatively easy.

> **NOTE**
>
> Some facilities replace rather than repair smaller gearboxes. Millwrights mostly manage their lubrication and alignment to maximize their lifespan.

On the other hand, large industrial gearboxes can be extremely heavy and awkward (*Figure 2*). They require hoisting and handling equipment to manipulate. They're also very expensive and usually include specialized accessories. Most are customized, so they can't be replaced quickly. These factors make their maintenance more difficult and complicated.

> **NOTE**
>
> Repairing a large industrial gearbox usually requires guidance from the manufacturer. A service engineer may work directly with the millwright. Some gearbox manufacturers recommend sending the gearbox back to their facility for service since they have specialized tools for handling and repairing it.

Figure 1 General-purpose gearboxes driving a conveyor.

Figure 2 Industrial gearboxes driving a large conveyor.

Most companies use preventive maintenance (PM) strategies to manage their gearboxes. Good PM prevents problems from turning into expensive failures. A facility's PM manager develops a schedule, so maintenance craftworkers can keep gearboxes working reliably.

In facilities with many gearboxes, prioritization is crucial. For example, a gearbox driving an essential machine has a higher maintenance priority than one driving an occasionally used machine.

Replacement time affects priorities too. Obtaining a replacement for a specialized gearbox might require a month. Obviously, keeping that gearbox in good condition has a very high priority. On the other hand, a general-purpose gearbox can be replaced in a day. Even if it's in a crucial location, its failure is probably less consequential than the specialized unit.

The following sections introduce topics associated with gearbox maintenance. They also explore the external inspection process that's part of maintenance.

1.1.1 Lubrication

Proper lubrication is vital to gearbox health. Gears, shafts, and bearings all require the right lubricant to keep turning smoothly. Most gearboxes contain oil as their main lubricant. It partially fills the housing and keeps the gears and shafts lubricated. Grease lubricates bearings. Improper lubrication is the root of many gearbox problems.

Although some smaller gearboxes are sealed for life, most require regular servicing. Checking and changing the lubricant is a standard maintenance task. Gearbox manufacturers specify appropriate lubricant brands and grades. Always follow these recommendations.

Always fill the gearbox with the right amount of oil. The quantity may vary depending on the gearbox's mounting position. Too little oil will cause friction and wear. Too much oil can cause leakage around the shaft seals or through the breather valve. Overfilling the gearbox also increases churning loss, which makes the gearbox run hot.

Consult the gearbox's manual for the correct lubricant amount and filling method (*Figure 3*). Manufacturers may specify it by volume (quarts, gallons, or liters). Some gearboxes have a sight glass or a fill line marked on the housing. Simply add oil up to the mark on the sight glass or the fill line.

Alternatively, manufacturers may specify lubricant quantity by depth. The oil surface must be a specific number of inches or centimeters from a reference point. The access cover seal surface is a common reference. The millwright places a measuring tool against the seal edge at the correct distance and adds oil until it reaches the tool end.

Finally, some manufacturers place drain plugs at the correct oil level for each mounting position. The millwright removes the right drain plug and adds oil until it reaches the lower edge of the hole and starts to "weep" out.

Bearings may or may not require periodic regreasing. Some will be sealed for life. Others will require fresh grease at regular intervals. Large industrial gearboxes operating in harsh, dirty, or abrasive environments may have special fittings for regreasing. Consult the gearbox manual for the correct grease type and lubrication procedure.

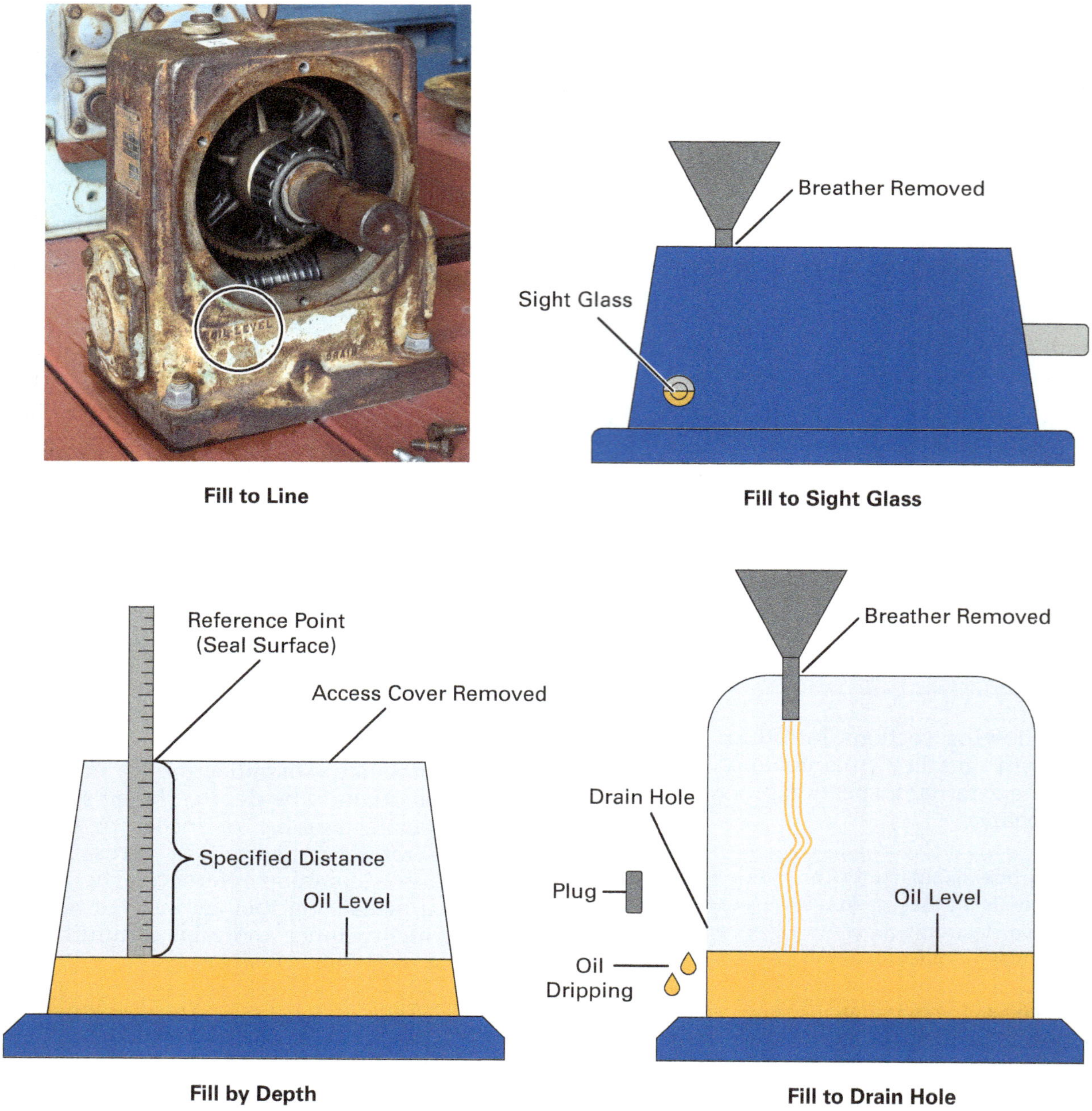

Figure 3 diagrams with labels:

Figure 3 Gearbox oil filling methods.

Gearbox Lubricant Types

Gearbox lubricants fall into three broad categories—mineral oil, synthetic oil, and food grade. Mineral oils come from petroleum and are like the oil used in cars. They work well under ordinary temperatures and have a moderate lifespan. They're also relatively inexpensive. Most mineral oils degrade at high temperatures. Many become too viscous (thick) when cold.

Synthetic oils are chemically like mineral oils but are engineered for better performance. They have a longer lifespan and usually tolerate a broader temperature range. They're also much more expensive—a significant factor with large gearboxes.

Never mix mineral and synthetic oils. If you wish to switch lubricant types, completely remove the old lubricant first.

Food-grade lubricants can be used around food and pharmaceutical products. Most aren't edible, but they aren't toxic in small quantities. Some may routinely contact food. Others are permitted where only accidental contact may happen. Some may not contact food at all but may safely be used near it.

Bearing greases are also rated as mineral, synthetic, or food grade. Usually, the grease type must match the oil type. Again, consult the gearbox manual for guidance.

Factors Affecting Lubricants

All lubricants degrade over time and become less effective. Oxygen and moisture from the air combine with the oil, changing its properties. Heat accelerates this process. Dust, dirt, and contaminants mix with the oil, reducing its effectiveness. Greases attract contaminating particles, which can damage bearings. For these reasons, most gearboxes require regular lubricant changes.

Manufacturers usually specify oil change intervals based on operating hours and temperature. Some publish helpful graphs or tables to guide this process (*Figure 4*). Gearboxes with electronic oil monitoring sensors use the time/temperature method to decide when to request an oil change.

Inspecting Lubricants

The manufacturer's guidelines are just a recommendation. If the oil degrades faster than expected, change it immediately. Fresh oil is clear and amber-colored. Degraded oil is dark and opaque. Foamy or milky oil has water in it.

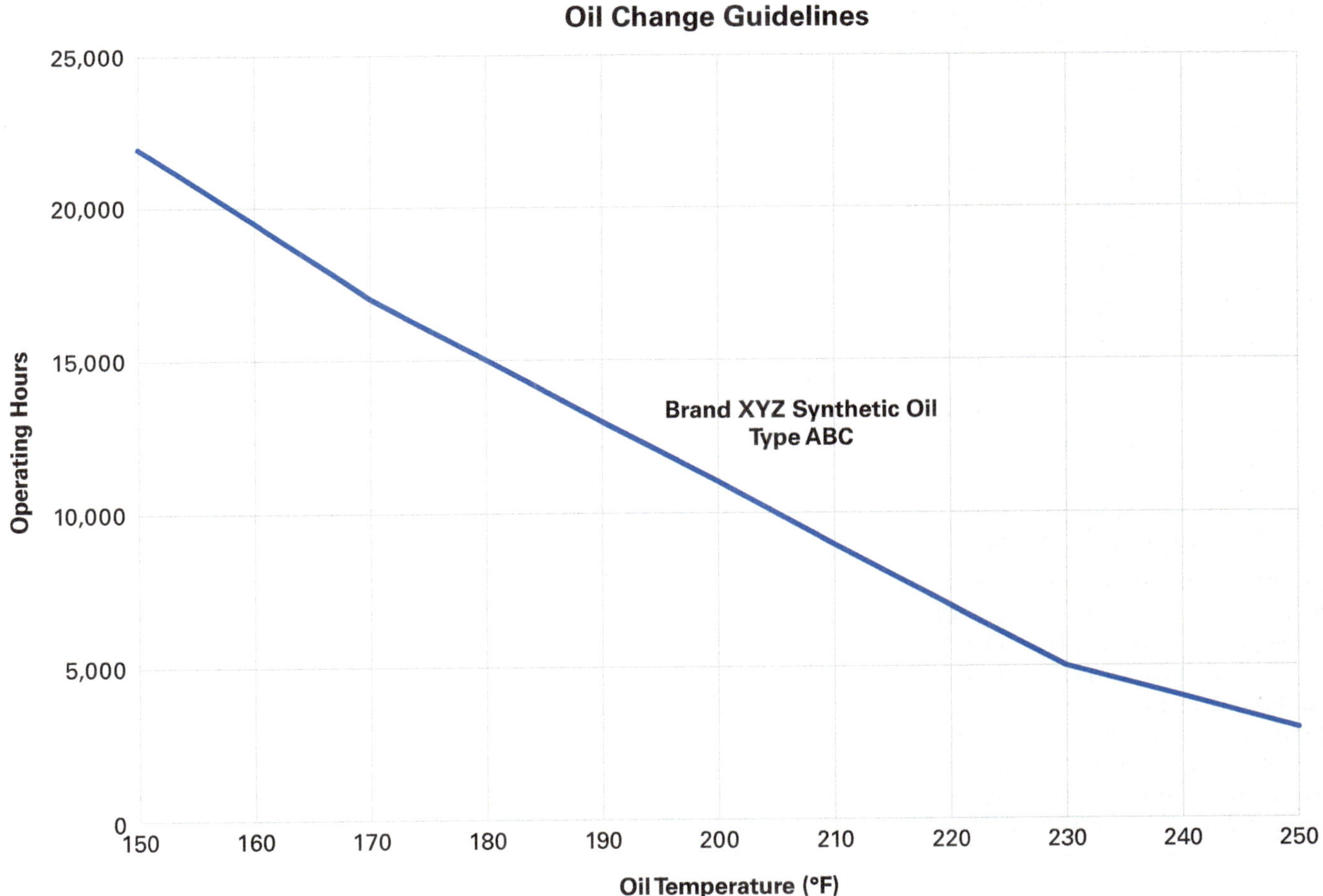

Figure 4 Example oil change graph.

Millwrights and industrial mechanics usually check the gearbox oil during routine inspections. Gearboxes with sight glasses are easy to check. They also make it simple to confirm the correct oil level in the housing. If the gearbox doesn't have a sight glass, remove an upper drain plug. Collect a sample with a clean dipstick. Alternatively, open a lower drain plug to release a sample into a container.

When working with lubricants, wear gloves to protect your skin. Some lubricants are toxic or can cause skin irritation. Prevent slip injuries by cleaning up spilled lubricants. Dispose of rags and old lubricants in the proper containers.

With expensive gearboxes, some PM programs require regular oil sampling and testing. An industrial lab checks the oil for the proper lubricating properties, as well as contaminants.

Bearing grease is harder to inspect than the gearbox oil. With small gearboxes, you usually must open the housing and visually check the bearings. Large industrial gearboxes are easier to manage. Many have two external fittings connected to each key bearing. Forcing fresh grease into one fitting ejects old grease from the other. The gearbox manufacturer will recommend regreasing intervals and specify the correct amount to add.

Clean grease fittings before using them. This prevents contaminants from getting into the bearing.

1.1.2 Damage and Wear

Besides managing lubrication, millwrights check for external damage. Most housings have protective paint or a specialized coating to prevent corrosion. Coatings on outdoor equipment will eventually degrade. An accidental blow can chip a coating, exposing the bare metal underneath. Corrosion will start to creep below the coating, causing it to blister and flake off. Eventually, the gearbox will become badly corroded (*Figure 5*).

Some gearboxes operate in unusually harsh environments (*Figure 6*). Meat processing equipment requires multiple washdowns every day to control biological contamination. These involve

Figure 5 A corroded gearbox.

caustic chemicals and hot water jets. Gearboxes in these environments usually have special epoxy coatings or are made from stainless steel. Even so, they often have relatively short lifespans.

Millwrights inspect the gearbox's coating for damage or early signs of corrosion. Small problems may be corrected with touch-up kits. More serious damage may require swapping the gearbox with a spare and sending the corroded unit for recoating. Badly damaged gearboxes must be replaced.

Besides checking the housing, millwrights check the shafts, seals, couplings, and mounting accessories. Leaking seals require prompt attention. Torque arms usually have rubber buffers to absorb vibration. These can degrade over time and require replacement. Anything that looks abnormal needs investigation. Internal parts starting to wear out or develop problems usually reveal themselves by vibration and noise. A gearbox running hot may have worn parts or a lubrication problem.

1.1.3 External Inspection

Some gearboxes fail without warning, but most show signs that a problem is emerging. External inspections reveal some of these signs. A craftworker can then investigate and schedule repairs. This strategy avoids unexpected and perhaps costly downtime.

Most maintenance workers use inspection checklists to reduce mistakes and omissions. A completed checklist confirms that the worker performed all tasks. Checklists may be paper or electronic. Sophisticated plant management software can automatically schedule maintenance tasks based on inspection checklists.

External inspection has two phases. First, the craftworker examines the gearbox while it's running. Then, the craftworker shuts down the gearbox and performs the second phase.

When inspecting a running machine, be extremely careful. Stay clear of rotating parts and watch out for pinch points. Wear all required PPE, including eye and hearing protection.

The following are typical first phase inspection tasks:

- If the gearbox has sensors with readouts, examine them for abnormal values (temperature, vibration, etc.).
- Listen to the gearbox. Note any vibration or unusual sounds.
- Check the gearbox temperature with a temperature probe or an infrared thermometer. Measure the temperature near bearings as well. Elevated temperatures can indicate internal problems or a lubrication failure.
- Watch a shaft-mounted gearbox. It shouldn't move significantly.
- Watch the shafts. They should turn smoothly and without obvious runout (rotating off-center).

Visible runout indicates a serious shaft or bearing problem. A shaft that looks normal to the eye may still have runout problems, but these require instruments to detect. NCCER Module 15313, *Prealignment and Shim Fabrication*, discusses checking for non-visible runout.

Never perform the second phase without shutting down the gearbox driver. Lock out and tag it. Confirm that you can't restart it. Wear all required PPE, including eye and hearing protection, as well as gloves.

The following are typical second phase inspection tasks:

- Look for signs of leakage around shaft seals, inspection covers, drain plugs, and the breather valve.
- Check the breather valve. Verify that it isn't clogged by paint. Replace a breather valve covered by paint since it can't operate properly.

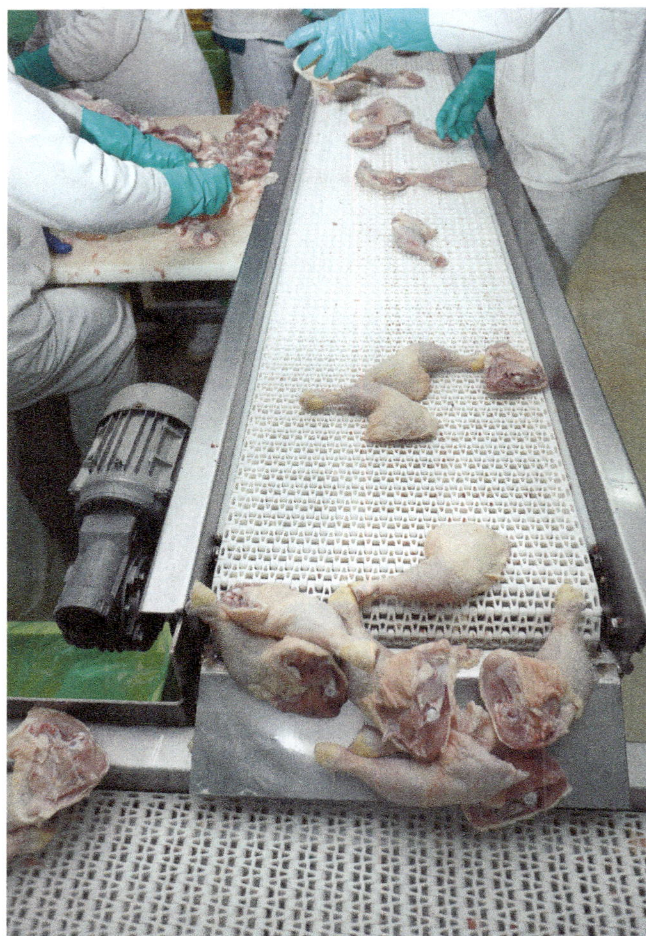

Figure 6 Gearbox on a poultry processing line.

Food-Grade Lubricants

In the United States, food-grade lubricants come in three categories: H1, H2, and H3. H1 lubricants are appropriate for applications in which they may accidentally contact food. Never use them when regular contact is likely. H2 lubricants must never touch food. They're permissible near food since they don't cause cancer or contain highly toxic additives like heavy metals. H3 lubricants are edible and may routinely contact food.

When selecting a food-grade lubricant, don't assume that all types are suitable. Be sure a lubricant's category matches the application. Also be sure that the lubricant is appropriate for the equipment. Using the wrong lubricant shortens a machine's lifespan. The manufacturer will recommend the right oil or grease for the equipment and the application.

- Examine belts, chains, or couplings for damage or unusual wear.
- Examine the gearbox housing for damage, chips, or corrosion.
- Check fasteners for proper tightness. These include foot bolts, setscrews, torque arm attachments, and shaft clamping mechanisms.
- If the gearbox has a torque arm, check the buffers for hardening or cracking.
- Check external gearbox accessories for damage or problems. If they have replaceable parts, like filters, inspect them as well.
- With gearmotors, inspect the electric motor for damage, corrosion, or signs of overheating. Overheated parts often change color or smell burned. Check the cooling fins, fan, and air filter.
- Check the gearbox oil's level and condition.

The gearbox and its oil may be hot. Be careful not to burn yourself.

After completing an external inspection, document your work using whatever system your company specifies. Inspection results affect the maintenance schedule, so be thorough and complete. If you noticed any serious problems, schedule the gearbox for immediate repair.

1.2.0 Internally Inspecting Gearboxes

Normal maintenance inspections examine a gearbox externally. When they uncover possible problems, an internal inspection will follow. Even when all appears well, millwrights still periodically inspect gearboxes internally. Certain components are visible only from the inside. Parts may also be wearing out and require replacement.

An internal inspection takes significant time and effort. The craftworker must shut down the gearbox and possibly remove it from its machine. Small gearboxes are easily handled. Larger units require hoisting equipment (*Figure 7*). Often, the worker must drain the gearbox oil. While a small gearbox holds less than a quart (~1 L), an industrial unit could contain 100 gallons (~400 L) or more.

If possible, before starting an internal inspection, observe the running gearbox. Listen for vibration or odd sounds. Shaft-mounted gearboxes with torque arms shouldn't be moving excessively.

Figure 7 A large gearbox in a challenging location.

Check the gearbox's running temperature with a probe or an infrared thermometer. Check the temperature around the bearings as well. A hot gearbox may have a lubrication problem. Hot bearings may be worn or have lubrication problems. They can also indicate misaligned shafts. Speak to workers who use the equipment. Ask them if they've noticed any recent changes. A few thoughtful questions can save a lot of time later.

Once you've observed the running gearbox, shut it down. Block the driven machine to prevent unexpected movement. Lock out and tag the driver. Confirm that it can't start unexpectedly. If the gearbox is hot, allow it to cool. Obtain appropriate PPE and all required tools.

Gearbox oil can be very hot. A large gearbox will stay hot for a long time. Confirm with a temperature probe or an infrared thermometer that the gearbox is safe to handle.

1.2.1 Removing and Preparing the Gearbox

Sometimes, you can work with the gearbox still attached to the driven machine. If so, your job will be simpler. Often, however, you must remove the gearbox. How you do this depends on the gearbox type, its attachment method, and its size. The following steps outline the general procedure:

Step 1   Remove any protective covers or guards.

Step 2   If the gearbox is too large to safely lift yourself, attach appropriate slings and hoisting equipment. Confirm that you've properly supported the unit.

> **NOTE**
>
> Never work with rigging or hoisting equipment unless you're qualified. NCCER Module 00106, *Basic Rigging*, NCCER Module 53101, *Crane Communications*, and NCCER Module 21106, *Crane Safety and Emergency Procedures*, introduce these topics.

Step 3   If the gearbox is foot-mounted, loosen the foot bolts but don't remove them. If the gearbox is shaft-mounted, disconnect the torque arm from its attachment point.

Step 4   Disconnect the driver from the gearbox's input shaft. Remove the belt, chain, or coupling, as applicable. If the gearbox has a directly integrated motor, leave it attached.

> **NOTE**
>
> For gearmotors, you'll have to disconnect their electrical wiring as well. Unless you're a qualified electrician, do not do this yourself.

Step 5   Disconnect the gearbox's output shaft from the driven machine. Remove the belt, chain, or coupling, as applicable. If the gearbox is shaft-mounted, loosen any clamping devices that secure the gearbox to the driven shaft. Confirm that the driven shaft is free inside the gearbox's hollow shaft.

Step 6   If the gearbox is foot-mounted, remove the foot bolts. Remove any shims and record their number, thickness, and location.

Step 7   Carefully remove the gearbox from the driven machine. Place it on a suitable work surface.

> **WARNING!**
>
> Be sure the gearbox is secure and stable before you start working on it. Large gearboxes can injure or kill if they move unexpectedly. Even small gearboxes can cause injuries if they fall.

Step 8   Clean the gearbox surfaces, particularly around access covers, drain plugs, and removable components.

Step 9   If the gearbox has an access cover, remove it (*Figure 8*).

> **NOTE**
>
> Be as clean as possible when working around an open gearbox. Contaminants that get inside can damage the gears and bearings.

1.2.2 Inspecting the Gearbox

What you do next depends on the reason for the inspection. If the inspection is routine, you may not have to empty the gearbox oil. If you're checking a potential problem or repairing something, drain the housing.

For smaller gearboxes, place a container under the lowest drain hole. Remove the drain plug and allow the oil to run into the container. For large industrial gearboxes, you may have to pump the oil into a drum.

> **NOTE**
>
> For gearboxes without an access cover, you'll have to open a higher drain plug or remove the breather valve. Otherwise, air won't be able to enter the housing as the oil runs out. Be sure to replace the plug or breather when finished.

Examine the oil for contaminants. If you see large particles in the oil, it's possible that the gears may be damaged. Metal in the oil suggests damaged gears or a serious wear problem.

Once the housing is empty, you can inspect the gearbox's internal components. If the gearbox doesn't have an access cover, you'll have to partially disassemble the housing first.

The following sections outline the inspection process.

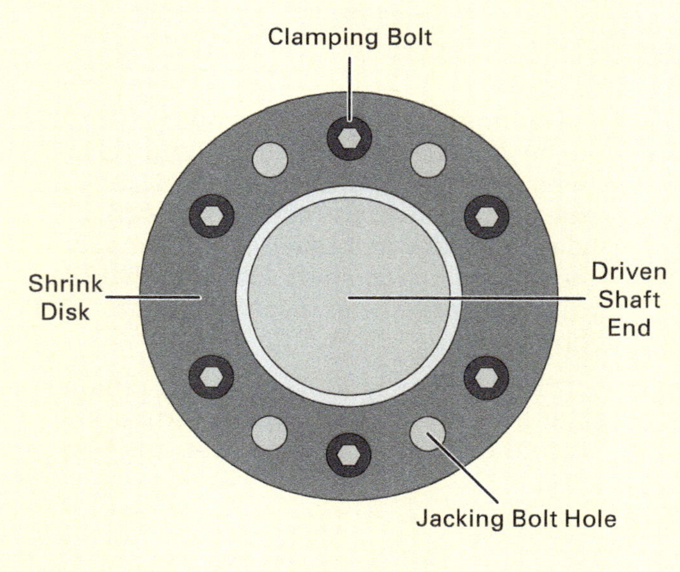

Figure 8 Gearbox with access cover removed.

Stuck Shafts

Gearboxes with hollow shafts have a major challenge. Sometimes the driven shaft gets stuck inside the gearbox's shaft. Usually, corrosion or fretting (vibration-induced sticking) causes the surfaces to bond together. Separating the shafts can be difficult. Gearbox manufacturers offer several solutions to prevent or manage this problem.

Coating the shafts with an anticorrosion paste during installation reduces the likelihood of sticking. Some manufacturers supply a packet with hollow shaft gearboxes. Millwrights can reduce fretting by aligning the gearbox carefully to minimize vibration.

Many shaft-mounted gearboxes use a device called a *shrink disk*. It clamps onto the driven machine's solid shaft. Some manufacturers sell specialized shrink disks with easily removable bushings.

Shrink disks may also include several *jacking holes* to make separation easier. These are threaded holes between the clamping bolts. After removing the bolts, the millwright threads several into the jacking holes and tightens them. The bolts push the shafts apart.

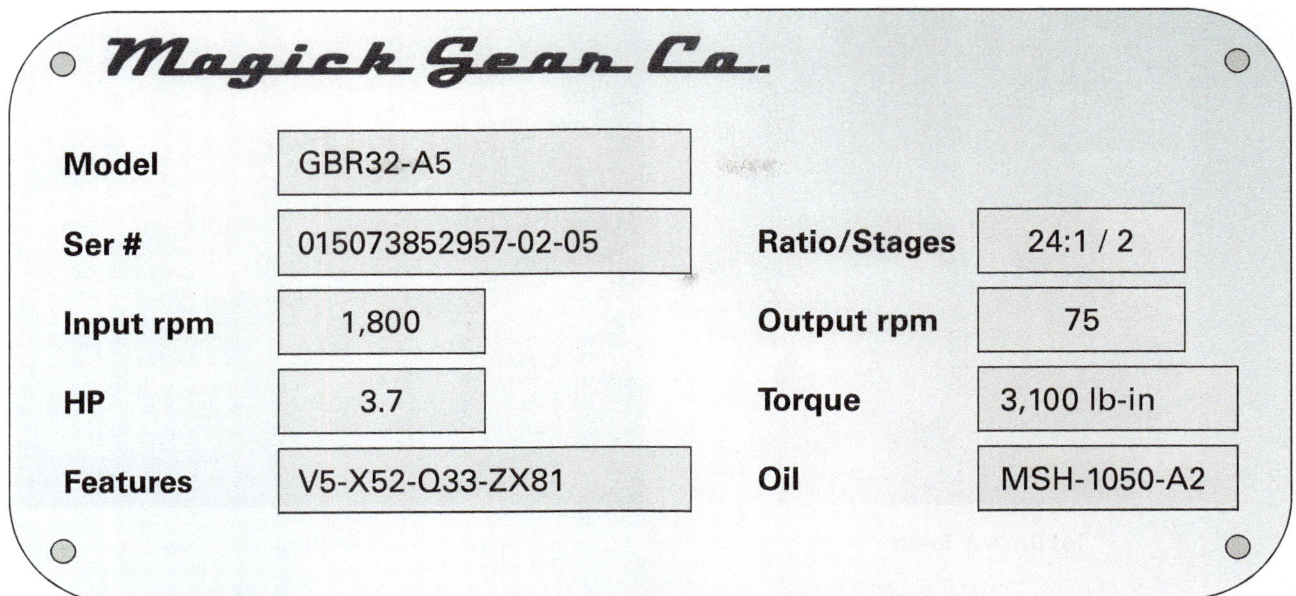

Figure 9 Gearbox nameplate.

Identifying Gearbox Features

Before working with a gearbox, you should know what to expect. While many gearboxes are simple, some are highly customized. For example, a gearbox might include a **backstop** or special bearings to handle overhung loads. It may contain a spray lubrication system with a pump. Lubrication systems may also include oil filters, heaters, or coolers.

Hopefully, your company will have records for each gearbox. If it doesn't, you'll have to work out the gearbox's features. Check the nameplate (*Figure 9*). It may include a feature list. It should also have a serial number or unique identifier. Consult the manufacturer's catalog to learn how to interpret these.

Some manufacturers offer smartphone apps that look up identifiers and return a detailed feature list. Newer nameplates may have a QR code that the app scans to access this information. If you're having trouble identifying features, contact the manufacturer.

Checking the Gears

Most gears last a very long time since they operate with minimal friction. Only worm gears wear out relatively quickly since they generate continuous sliding friction. If non-worm gears show wear patterns or damage, something is wrong.

Carefully examine each gear. Use a flashlight if necessary. Rotate the shafts so you can see all the teeth and each surface. Look for damaged teeth, pitting, spalling, distortion, or uneven wear (*Figure 10*). All indicate serious problems.

Try to determine the causes behind what you observe. Broken teeth may indicate **shock loads**. Continuous overloads can cause bent, cracked, or distorted teeth. Wear patterns suggest insufficient lubrication or misaligned gears. Pitting and spalling may indicate excessive vibration, lubrication problems, or misaligned gears. Abrasive contaminants in the oil can cause scratches, gouges, and chips.

Worm gears wear out relatively quickly through normal operation. When inspecting a worm gearbox, examine the worm gear and worm wheel (*Figure 11*). Regular, consistent wear is acceptable. Note the gears' overall condition since they will eventually require replacement. If you see abnormal or irregular wear patterns, the gears might be misaligned or improperly lubricated.

With large industrial gearboxes, millwrights sometimes use a blue lacquer (bluing) to identify gear alignment problems. First, they clean the gear pair with a solvent to remove oil. Then they paint several teeth with the lacquer and allow it to dry. After running the gearbox under load for several hours, they examine the lacquer. Irregular wear patterns in the color indicate that the gears aren't meshing properly.

Record all observations and identify gears specifically. If possible, take photographs. Badly damaged gears will require replacement. When you catch problems early, you may be able to correct the cause without having to replace the gears.

(A) Broken Teeth

(B) Pitting

(C) Unequal Wear and Damaged Teeth

(D) Unequal Wear and Distortion

Figure 10 Worn and damaged gears.

Checking the Bearings and Shafts

Bearings wear out more quickly than gears because they experience more friction and irregular loading. Shaft misalignment also affects them. Examine each bearing carefully. Check the rolling elements, as well as the inner and outer races (*Figure 12*). Look for obvious signs of damage or abnormal wear. Rotate the shafts, listening and feeling for grittiness. Of course, certain parts won't be visible or easy to inspect.

Large bearings may need their clearances checked. Consult the manufacturer's service manual for values and the proper procedure. Review NCCER Module 15306, *Removing and Installing Bearings*, if you've forgotten how to check clearances. That module also discusses the signs and symptoms of bearing wear and damage.

If the bearing isn't sealed, examine the grease. Confirm its condition and the correct amount. If necessary, add the proper grease type to the bearing. The manufacturer's maintenance manual will indicate the recommended procedure. *Never over-grease bearings.*

Inspect the internal and external shafts for corrosion or damage. If the internal shafts are corroded, suspect a lubrication problem. Remove corrosion with emery paper. Rotate the shafts and confirm that everything moves freely. Bent or seriously damaged shafts should be scheduled for replacement. If the gearbox has a backstop, confirm that it prevents the shaft from turning in one direction.

Figure 11 Worm gear and worm wheel.

Figure 12 Bearing rolling elements.

Checking Internal Accessories

Some gearboxes include internal accessories. Large industrial gearboxes usually contain several since they're more customized than general-purpose units. Specialized bearings, lubrication systems, liquid cooling, and components that manage harsh environments are common. Consult the gearbox's service manual or call the manufacturer's service department for help with these.

1.2.3 Returning the Gearbox to Service

Once you've inspected the gearbox, you'll probably return it to service. If possible, try to deal with minor maintenance issues and repairs immediately. If you discover serious problems or damage, however, you may need to remove the gearbox from service. Put it on the repair schedule. If the gearbox drives critical equipment, swap it with a spare unit to avoid downtime.

The following steps outline returning the gearbox to service:

Step 1 Remove the old gasket from the gearbox's access cover or housing. Install a new gasket.

Step 2 Bolt the cover or housing into place, tightening the fasteners to the correct torque in the proper sequence. Tighten all drain plugs to the proper torque.

Step 3 Return the gearbox to the driven machine. If necessary, use appropriate slings and hoisting equipment to maneuver it.

Step 4 If the gearbox is foot-mounted, return all shims to their original locations. Loosely install the foot bolts. Line up the input and output shafts with the driver and the driven machine.

Step 5 Reconnect any pulleys, sprockets, belts, chains, or couplings. Align the gearbox using the appropriate procedure. Tighten the foot bolts to the correct torque in the proper sequence. Skip to *Step 8*.

> **NOTE**
> NCCER Module 15311, *Installing Belt and Chain Drives*, introduces aligning belt- and chain-driven equipment. NCCER Module 15314, *Dial Indicator Alignment*, and NCCER Module 15502, *Laser Alignment*, introduce aligning directly driven equipment.

Step 6 For shaft-mounted gearboxes, if the manufacturer permits, apply an anticorrosion paste to the shafts. Slide the driven shaft into the gearbox's hollow shaft. Tighten all fasteners or clamping devices to the correct torque in the proper sequence.

> **CAUTION**
> Shrink disks often have unusual tightening sequences. Tightening the shrink disk in the wrong pattern can jam it. Consult the manufacturer's documentation for tightening guidelines.

Step 7 Reconnect the torque arm to its attachment point. Tighten its fasteners to the correct torque in the proper sequence.

Step 8 If you drained the gearbox oil, refill the gearbox. Use the correct amount of the manufacturer-specified oil. Follow the manufacturer's filling procedure. Usually, you'll fill the gearbox from an upper drain hole, or you'll remove the breather valve.

> **NOTE**
> For large gearboxes, you may consider filtering and reusing the oil that you removed earlier. Do this only if the oil is relatively new and in good condition. Never reuse questionable oil. Always refill small gearboxes with fresh oil.

> **NOTE**
> For gearmotors, remember to reconnect their electrical wiring. Unless you're a qualified electrician, do not do this yourself.

Step 9 Reinstall all covers and guards.

Step 10 Confirm that it's safe to restart the equipment. Remove your lock and tag. When other craftworkers have removed theirs, re-energize the equipment.

Step 11 Unblock the driven machine. Start the driver and observe the gearbox. Confirm that it runs smoothly and quietly. Check for leaks. Also confirm that the driven machine is running smoothly.

Step 12 Clean up the workspace. Dispose of old lubricants, gasket materials, and trash in the proper containers.

Step 13 Document your work completely and thoroughly, following whatever system your company specifies.

1.3.0 Troubleshooting Gearboxes

When a gearbox behaves abnormally or fails, it's crucial to troubleshoot and repair it quickly. Broken machines halt productivity and cost a company money. Fortunately, gearboxes are simple machines, so troubleshooting them is relatively easy. As with all troubleshooting tasks, millwrights and industrial mechanics must be logical and systematic. They must also use their senses to identify a problem's likely causes.

1.3.1 Troubleshooting Tools

Whenever possible, obtain the gearbox manufacturer's service manual. These are usually available on the manufacturer's website. While all gearboxes operate similarly, each model has unique features. The manufacturer's documentation makes troubleshooting and repair quicker. It also supplies useful information like adjustment specifications and tolerance values.

With older gearboxes, you might have trouble finding a service manual. In that case, you'll have to use common sense and experience. A generic troubleshooting chart, such as the one in *Table 1*, applies to many gearboxes.

Scan through the problem list and the associated causes. If you identify several problems, look for common factors. Explore these first to avoid wasting time. Good troubleshooters use logic and common sense to identify the most probable causes.

1.4.0 Repairing Gearboxes

After troubleshooting a problem or failure, you're ready to fix it. Repair procedures also apply to problems uncovered during inspection. When possible, consult the manufacturer's service manual. Gearboxes are easier to disassemble if you know the right tips and tricks.

In the past, millwrights and industrial mechanics repaired many gearbox problems. Today, it's less common to do major tasks in-house. Many gearbox manufacturers offer repair and rebuilding services. Some of these have very quick turnaround times.

Servicing customized industrial gearboxes requires specialized equipment and tools that only the manufacturer will have. Since these gearboxes have large and extremely heavy parts, it's often better to send the gearboxes back to the manufacturer.

On the other hand, some repairs are simple. Each usually requires you to remove the gearbox from the driven machine. Follow the procedures outlined in *Section 1.2.1* to remove and prepare the gearbox. Once you have the gearbox drained, you're ready to start repairs. The following procedures outline common repairs.

1.4.1 Replacing Bearings

Gearbox bearings do fail, so millwrights may have to replace one or more. Ball, tapered roller, and spherical roller bearings are the most common. Most gearboxes mount their bearings in "pockets" machined inside the housing (*Figure 13*). These establish accurate alignment between the gearbox's internal shafts.

The following procedure summarizes replacing bearings:

Step 1 Obtain suitable replacement bearings. If possible, consult the service manual's parts list. Alternatively, examine the original bearings for identifiers. Keep the replacement bearings in their packages until you're ready to install them.

Step 2 Open the gearbox housing. Some housings have access covers, while others split into two halves. *Figure 3* includes a gearbox with multiple access covers. *Figure 13* shows a gearbox whose housing splits in half.

Step 3 Carefully unmesh the gears. Remove the appropriate shafts and their attached bearings. Remove any shims from the bearing pockets. Record their number, thickness, and location.

Problem	Possible Causes	Possible Solutions
Excessive noise or vibration	• Worn or damaged bearings	• Replace the affected bearings.
	• Worn or damaged gears	• Send the gearbox to the manufacturer for service.
	• Misaligned gears	• Align the affected gear pairs.
	• Insufficient lubrication	• Add the correct amount of oil or grease.
	• Misaligned driver or driven machine	• Align the driver or driven machine.
	• Loose fasteners, foot bolts, or soleplate anchor bolts	• Tighten fasteners to the correct torque values.
High operating temperature	• Insufficient lubrication	• Add the correct amount of oil or grease.
	• Too much lubricant	• Remove excess lubricant.
	• Failed cooling system	• Repair the cooling system.
	• Excessive load	• Check the driven machine for binding and the gearbox for proper sizing to the application.
	• Excessive speed	• Check the driver's speed.
Oil leaking around the shafts	• Faulty or damaged shaft seal(s)	• Replace the shaft seal(s).
	• Improperly installed shaft seal(s)	• Replace the shaft seal(s).
	• Damaged or corroded shaft	• Correct the shaft problem and replace the shaft seal(s).
	• Breather valve stuck shut or clogged	• Replace the breather valve.
Oil leaking from the breather valve	• Breather valve in the wrong location	• Relocate the breather valve to a higher location on the housing.
	• Too much lubricant	• Remove excess lubricant.
Oil leaking from the access cover	• Access cover gasket faulty	• Replace the cover gasket.
	• Access cover not tightened properly	• Tighten the cover fasteners to the correct torque in the proper sequence.
Metal in the oil	• Damaged gears	• Send the gearbox to the manufacturer for service.
Gearbox moving when shaft mounted	• Bent shaft	• Replace the shaft.
	• Worn or damaged bearings	• Replace the affected bearings.
Shafts not turning smoothly or binding	• Bent shaft	• Replace the shaft.
	• Worn or damaged bearings	• Replace the affected bearings.
	• Damaged gears	• Send the gearbox to the manufacturer for service.
Premature bearing failure	• Misaligned driver or driven machine	• Align the driver or driven machine.
	• Overhung load	• Correct the load position or upgrade the bearings.
	• Lubrication problem	• Confirm the correct type and amount of lubricant.

(A) Ball Bearing

(B) Tapered Roller Bearing

(C) Spherical Roller Bearing

(D) Bearing Pockets in Gearbox Housing

Figure 13 Gearbox bearings.

Step 4 Remove the bearings from the shaft using a puller, press, or heat. Be very careful not to damage the shaft.

> **NOTE**
> NCCER Module 15306, *Removing and Installing Bearings*, outlines the proper way to remove and install bearings.

Step 5 Check the shaft for damage, corrosion, or other problems. Remove corrosion or minor damage with emery paper or a hone. If the shaft is badly damaged, replace it.

Step 6 Install the new bearings on the shaft in the proper locations. Use a press or heat as appropriate. The required procedure depends on the bearing type. Follow the bearing manufacturer's guidelines.

> **NOTE**
> Some bearings require you to set the rolling element clearance. Follow the bearing manufacturer's guidelines. The gearbox manufacturer may specify a clearance value. NCCER Module 15306, *Removing and Installing Bearings*, outlines setting the bearing clearance.

Step 7 If the bearing isn't prelubricated, add the recommended amount of the specified grease. Consult the bearing manufacturer's or the gearbox manufacturer's guidelines. *Never over-grease bearings.*

> **CAUTION**
> Be extremely clean when working with bearings to avoid contaminating the lubricant or rolling elements. Handle new bearings with clean gloves.

Step 8 Reinstall the shaft, seating the bearings in their pockets. Be sure to reinstall any shims that you removed earlier. Carefully re-mesh the gears.

Step 9 Confirm that the shafts turn smoothly.

Step 10 Return the gearbox to service by following the procedure outlined in *Section 1.2.3*.

1.4.2 Replacing Shaft Seals

Gearboxes have one or more seals around their input and output shafts. These keep the oil inside the housing but still allow the shafts to turn freely. Gearboxes used in harsh environments may have complex seals to keep aggressive contaminants out.

> NCCER Module 15304, *O-Rings and Non-Mechanical Seals*, introduces the seals commonly found in gearboxes.

General-purpose gearboxes use simple oil seals (*Figure 14*). Some have just one sealing surface (lip), while others have two. Some manufacturers create a double seal. This is a pair of back-to-back seals that fit inside each other. Seals come in several materials, each appropriate for certain environments. Provided they're correctly installed, seals should work reliably for a long time.

Improperly installed or damaged seals will start leaking almost immediately. A damaged shaft can also cause leaks. A blocked breather valve can indirectly cause leaking seals. If pressure builds up inside the gearbox housing, oil will squirt out around the seals. In each case, the millwright must replace the seals.

> Protect breather valves when painting or touching up the gearbox housing. Paint is the most common cause of clogged breather valves.

Simple seals can't be reused because removing them is destructive. It's crucial, however, not to damage the shaft during seal removal. The following procedure is appropriate for single seals:

Step 1 Place a large flat-bladed screwdriver tip in one of the seal's rectangular indentations.

Step 2 Strike the screwdriver with a dead-blow hammer until the seal starts to bend.

Step 3 Move the screwdriver to the opposite indentation.

Step 4 Strike the screwdriver until the seal starts to bend.

Step 5 Repeat *Steps 1–4* until the seal has bent into a V shape.

Step 6 Place the screwdriver tip under the lifted seal edge and pop the seal free. Slide it off the shaft.

Double seals require a different procedure:

Step 1 Obtain a sharp-pointed sheet metal screw. Place the point in one of the seal's rectangular indentations.

Step 2 Tap the screw with a dead-blow hammer until the point penetrates the seal.

Step 3 Using a screwdriver, turn the screw a few turns into the seal. Don't let it penetrate the second seal.

(A) Oil Seals

(B) Output Shaft Seals

Figure 14 Shaft seals.

Step 4 Using a large pair of pliers, grip the screw. Jerk the screw repeatedly until the seal pops loose. Slide it off the shaft. Hold small gearboxes in place as you pull the seal.

One major gearbox manufacturer recommends using a slide hammer (*Figure 15*) instead of pliers. Use the dent puller tip. Insert the screw into it. After threading the screw into the seal, slide the weight rapidly upwards. A few quick blows should be enough to remove the seal.

After removing the seals, inspect the shaft and the seal pocket. Smooth a corroded, rough, or gouged shaft with emery paper or a hone. Seals work best when the shaft is smooth and undamaged. Clean the shaft and seal pocket.

Installing the new seal is simple but requires the right tools. Gearbox manufacturers recommend a plastic seal installation tool that fits over the seal and shaft (*Figure 16*). Striking the top surface with a dead-blow hammer applies uniform force around the entire seal. This drives it smoothly into its pocket.

Seal installation tools come in various sizes. Some gearbox manufacturers sell them, as do seal manufacturers. Specialty hand tool distributors may also stock them. Never install a seal by striking it with a hammer, metal rod, or wood block.

This strategy will damage the seal or install it crookedly. Poor installation technique causes many seal failures.

The following procedure outlines installing both single and double seals:

Step 1 Obtain the correct replacement seal or seals. Confirm that they're made from the same materials as the old seals. Keep seals in their packages until you're ready to install them.

Step 2 If you're installing a double seal, fit the two seals together if they're not already assembled. Be sure the correct seal is on the inside.

Step 3 If the seal or gearbox manufacturer recommends it, apply a thin film of grease to the seal's inner surface. This helps it slide over the shaft. Use an applicator to apply the grease, not your finger.

> **NOTE**
>
> Some seals shouldn't be greased. Never apply any lubricant unless the seal or gearbox manufacturer recommends it. Be sure to use the correct grease.

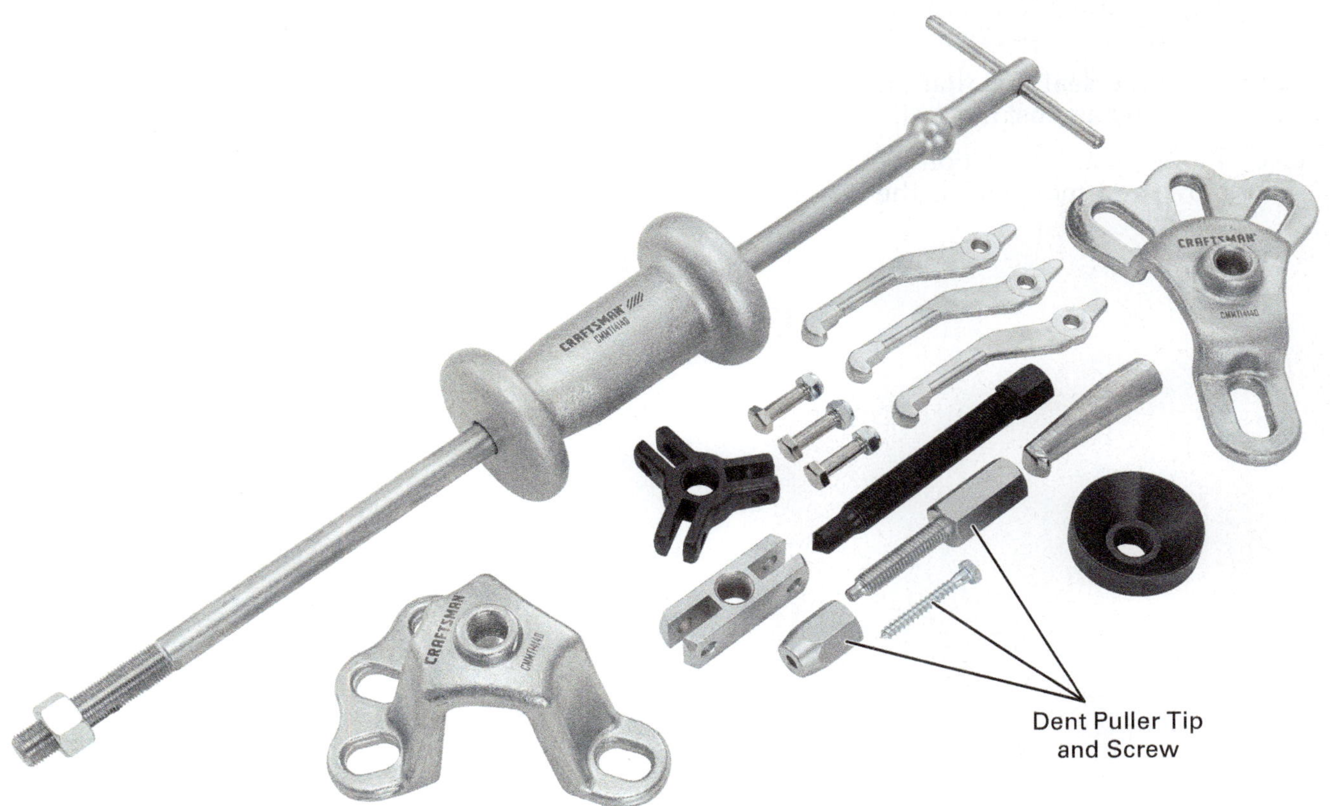

Figure 15 Slide hammer kit.

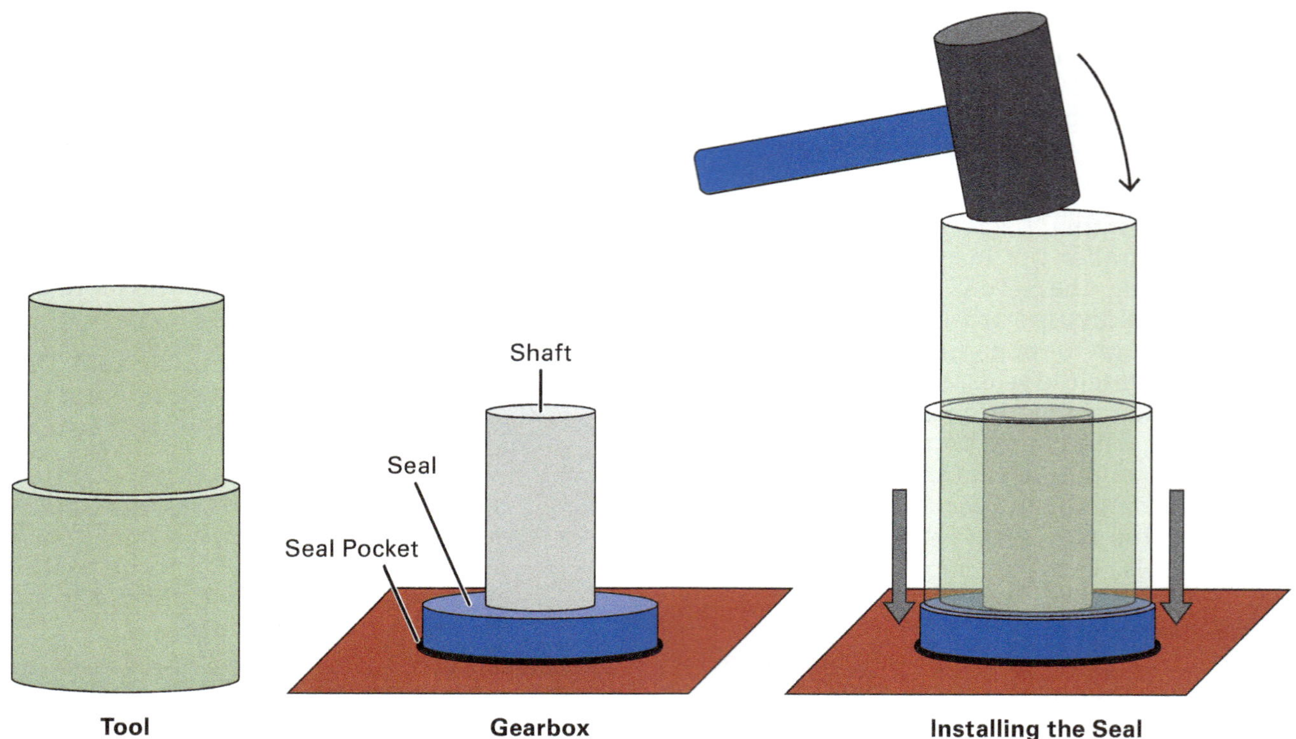

Figure 16 Seal installation tool.

Step 4 Position the seal on the shaft. Confirm that it's facing the correct direction. Tilt it slightly to get it started. Rotate the seal as you slide it down the shaft. Position it squarely in its pocket.

Step 5 Place the seal installation tool over the shaft and against the seal.

Step 6 Tap the seal installation tool with a dead-blow hammer. Drive the seal into its pocket.

Step 7 Confirm that the seal is fully seated in its pocket and not crooked. Confirm that the shaft turns smoothly.

Step 8 Return the gearbox to service by following the procedure outlined in *Section 1.2.3*.

NOTE

Remember that new seals may leak slightly during their run-in period. If they leak excessively or don't stop leaking, investigate the cause. In most cases, you'll have to replace the seal.

1.0.0 Section Review

1. An overfilled gearbox will probably experience _____.

    a. shaft runout
    b. dry bearing
    c. high churning losses
    d. gasket fatigue

2. After draining the oil from a gearbox, you notice that it contains large metal particles. What should you conclude?

    a. A seal may be leaking.
    b. The gearbox has experienced internal damage.
    c. The gearbox is going through an extended run-in period.
    d. The breather valve may be clogged.

3. If a gearbox has gears with badly damaged teeth, you should _____.

    a. cut off the broken teeth with a torch
    b. send the gearbox back to the manufacturer for service
    c. smooth the broken teeth with a file
    d. switch to a high-viscosity synthetic lubricant

4. Millwrights regularly repair almost all gearbox problems in-house.

    a. True
    b. False

1. Conveyors, pumps, blowers, and production machines are usually driven by _____.

   a. specialized industrial gearboxes
   b. precision positioning gearboxes
   c. general-purpose gearboxes
   d. low-ratio planetary gearboxes

2. Most gearbox problems center upon gears and _____.

   a. shafts
   b. bearings
   c. soft foot
   d. breather valves

3. What do most gearboxes use as their *main* lubricant?

   a. Oil
   b. Grease
   c. Silicone
   d. Graphite

4. What is mineral oil's main advantage over synthetic oil?

   a. Low-temperature performance
   b. High-temperature performance
   c. Lifespan
   d. Price

5. Which of the following would be on a gearbox's *external* inspection checklist?

   a. Checking the gears for damage
   b. Checking the breather valve
   c. Checking the bearings' rolling elements.
   d. Checking bearing clearances

6. When removing a shaft-mounted gearbox from the locked out and tagged driven machine, what should you do *first* after removing guards and attaching any required lifting equipment?

   a. Loosen the gearbox foot bolts.
   b. Disconnect the torque arm from its attachment point.
   c. Remove the output shaft pulley, sprocket, or coupling.
   d. If present, remove a directly integrated motor.

7. A gearbox contains a device that prevents its shaft from turning in one direction. What is this device?

   a. A dual-thrust bearing
   b. An overhung load bearing
   c. A torque converter
   d. A backstop

8. A gearbox contains several gears with broken teeth. What is the *most likely* cause?

   a. Shock loads
   b. Too much lubricant
   c. Vibration
   d. Corrosion

9. While troubleshooting a gearbox, you notice that oil has been leaking from the breather valve. What should you do?

   a. See if the breather valve has been painted over accidentally.
   b. Confirm that the shafts aren't binding or jammed.
   c. Switch to a high-viscosity oil.
   d. See if the gearbox has been overfilled with oil.

10. You've just installed a new shaft seal. After putting the gearbox back into service, you notice a very slight leak around the shaft. What should you do?

    a. Don't do anything yet since the seal is probably going through its run-in period.
    b. Replace the seal immediately.
    c. Apply extra grease around the shaft.
    d. Using the seal installation tool, tap the seal several more times to seat it better.

Trade Terms Introduced in This Module

Backstop: A device that prevents a shaft from turning in one direction.

Churning loss: Energy wasted by gears plowing through lubricating oil as they rotate.

Food grade: A lubricant meant to be used in food preparation areas.

Mineral oil: A lubricant distilled from crude petroleum that has properties like automobile oil.

Shock loads: Abrupt, brief, and significant increases in a machine's normal load.

Synthetic oil: A chemically engineered lubricant with enhanced properties and a long lifespan.

Additional Resources

This module presents thorough resources for task training. The following reference material is suggested for further study.

Bonfiglioli. **bonfiglioli.com**.
Flender. **flender.com**.
Nord. **nord.com**.
SEW-EURODRIVE. **seweurodrive.com**.
SUMITOMO. **us.sumitomodrive.com**.
Timken. **timken.com**.

Figure Credits

iStock@Cylonphoto, Figure 1
Shutterstock.com/Goff Designs, Figure 2
iStock@Picsfive, Figure 6
iStock@deyangeorgiev, Figure 7
iStock@2Ban, Figure 10 (A)
Shutterstock.com/pattanachai w, Figure 10 (B)
iStock@pack_zero, Figure 10 (C)
iStock@Kinek00, Figure 10 (D)
iStock@urfinguss, Figure 13 (A)
iStock@surakit sawangchit, Figure 13 (B)
iStock@saliduran, Figure 13 (C)
iStock@SocoXbreed, Figure 13 (D)
iStock@Phantom1311, Figure 14 (A)
iStock@Nordroden, Figure 14 (B)
Courtesy of DEWALT Industrial Tool Co., Figure 15

Section Review Answer Key

SECTION 1.0.0

Answer	Section Reference	Objective
1. c	1.1.1	1a
2. b	1.2.2	1b
3. b	1.3.1; *Table 1*	1c
4. b	1.4.0	1d

User Update

NCCER makes every effort to keep its textbooks up-to-date and free of technical errors. We appreciate your help in this process. If you find an error, a typographical mistake, or an inaccuracy in NCCER's curricula, please submit a User Update form by visiting **https://www.nccer.org/olf**. You can also scan the QR code using the camera on your phone or mobile device to access the form.

Turbines

OVERVIEW

Turbines are machines that we have long depended on to generate electrical power, using other forms of energy as their primary driver. While turbines used for power generation share some similarities, each type also has unique features. This module introduces steam, gas, and hydraulic turbines and presents their basic operating principles.

Module 15505

Trainees with successful module completions may be eligible for credentialing through the NCCER Registry. To learn more, go to **www.nccer.org** or contact us at 1.888.622.3720. Our website, **www.nccer.org**, has information on the latest product releases and training.

Your feedback is welcome. You may email your comments to **curriculum@nccer.org**, send general comments and inquiries to **info@nccer.org** or fill in the User Update form at the back of this module.

This information is general in nature and intended for training purposes only. Actual performance of activities described in this manual requires compliance with all applicable operating, service, maintenance, and safety procedures under the direction of qualified personnel. References in this manual to patented or proprietary devices do not constitute a recommendation of their use.

15505 V4.0

From *Millwright, Trainee Guide*. NCCER.
Copyright © 2023 by NCCER. Published by Pearson. All rights reserved.

Objective

Successful completion of this module prepares you to do the following:

1. Identify and describe common turbine designs and their components.
   a. State the operating principles of common turbine designs.
   b. Identify and describe hydraulic turbines.
   c. Identify and describe steam turbines and their components.
   d. Identify and describe gas turbines and their components.

Performance Tasks

This is a knowledge-based module. There are no Performance Tasks.

Trade Terms

Babbitt
Black starts
Condensing turbine
Generator
Kinetic energy

Mechanical energy
Noncondensing turbine
Penstock
Turbine
Water Hammer

Industry Recognized Credentials

If you are training through an NCCER-accredited sponsor, you may be eligible for credentials from NCCER's Registry. The ID number for this module is 15505. Note that this module may have been used in other NCCER curricula and may apply to other level completions. Contact NCCER's Registry at 1.888.622.3720 or go to **www.nccer.org** for more information.

You can also show off your industry-recognized credentials online with NCCER's digital badges. Transform your knowledge, skills, and achievements into badges that you can share across social media platforms, send to your network, and add to your resume. For more information, visit **www.nccer.org**.

NOTE

This module uses US standard and metric units in up to three different ways. This note explains how to interpret them.

Exact Conversions

Exact metric equivalents of US standard units appear in parentheses after the US standard unit. For example: "Measure 18" (45.7 cm) from the end and make a mark."

Approximate Conversions

In some cases, exact metric conversions would be inappropriate or even absurd. In these situations, an approximate metric value appears in parentheses with the ~ symbol in front of the number. For example: "Grip the tool about 3" (~8 cm) from the end."

Parallel but not Equal Values

Certain scenarios include US standard and metric values that are parallel but not equal. In these situations, a slash (/) surrounded by spaces separates the US standard and metric values. For example: "Place the point on the steel rule's 1" / 1 cm mark."

How to Access Resources

This craft has additional videos and resources to enhance your learning experience. To view these resources, scan the QR below. The videos and resources are separated by module.

You can scan this code using the camera on your phone or mobile device to view these videos and resources.

Contents

Figures

1.0.0 TURBINES

Objective

Identify and describe common turbine designs and their components.

  a. State the operating principles of common turbine designs.
  b. Identify and describe hydraulic turbines.
  c. Identify and describe steam turbines and their components.
  d. Identify and describe gas turbines and their components.

Trade Terms

Babbitt: A soft metal alloy that typically contains tin, copper, lead, and antimony.

Black starts: Startups conducted on turbine systems while there is no power currently available from the grid.

Condensing turbine: A steam turbine that has a condenser in place to condense any remaining steam as it exits the turbine. The resulting condensate returns to the boiler or other steam-generating process.

Generator: An electrical apparatus constructed much like an electric motor that converts mechanical energy into electricity.

Kinetic energy: The energy an object contains resulting from being placed in motion.

Mechanical energy: The stored (potential) energy plus the moving (kinetic) energy associated with a machine.

Noncondensing turbine: A steam turbine that uses any remaining steam exiting the turbine to support other industrial processes.

Penstock: A channel designed to direct water into a hydroelectric turbine rotor.

Turbine: A machine that converts the energy contained in a moving stream of fluid to mechanical energy.

Water hammer: A hydraulic shock that occurs when rapidly moving slugs of water impact pipe walls, especially when the water must change direction.

A basic turbine (*Figure 1*) is a machine that converts kinetic energy into mechanical energy. A turbine receives energy from a moving fluid or gas. This energy is converted to mechanical energy as it causes a shaft to rotate. When the rotating turbine shaft is connected to another machine, that machine can produce useful work. In the case of a power-generation turbine, electricity is produced by a connected generator. Generators convert mechanical energy from the turbine to electrical energy.

Turbines are complex pieces of machinery, built and assembled with great precision. Their design and engineering details vary from one manufacturer to another, and some level of secrecy must be imposed so that any design advantages are maintained as long as possible.

For that reason, it is impossible to provide detailed information about any specific turbine. However, you will learn about their general design and application in this module. If you work with turbines in the future, this introduction will prepare you for more detailed training provided by the manufacturer and your employer.

1.1.0 Basic Turbine Operating Principles

The primary mechanical feature of a turbine is the rotating element, or *rotor*. The rotor consists of a shaft with a series of vanes or blades attached to it. Each rotating assembly of blades is referred to as a *wheel*. The blades of each wheel are angled around the rotor such that, as the moving fluid impacts and moves through them, the energy of the fluid causes the rotor to turn.

The casing surrounding the rotor often has stationary vanes, or *stators*, that direct the moving fluid through the rotor blades at a specific angle. The vanes of some turbines serve as nozzles that increase the velocity of the fluid before it strikes the rotor blades.

The volume of fluid entering the turbine can be controlled so that the energy transferred to the rotor shaft can be managed. This is especially useful when the turbine shaft is connected to an electric generator. It allows the turbine to generate the right amount of power for the current load conditions. Fluids used to rotate turbines include water and steam.

Fluids

Remember that fluids aren't just liquids. The term *fluid* can also include air and similar gases.

Figure 1 A power-generation steam turbine.

Water is a reliable natural resource that is used to power hydroelectric turbines at dams across the country. Steam must be generated from water by the addition of heat. The heat generally comes from burning fossil fuels or controlling a nuclear reaction.

There are two basic classifications of turbines, differing by their operating principles—*impulse turbines* and *reaction turbines*. These two basic designs are often combined in a single turbine. Multistage turbines are also introduced in the sections that follow.

1.1.1 Impulse Turbines

Impulse turbine wheels (*Figure 2*) change the direction of a fluid moving through at a high velocity. The fluid makes the turbine spin by transferring some of its energy to the rotor. The fluid loses energy and slows down as a result.

The pressure doesn't change much as it passes through the turbine rotor. For this reason, impulse turbines are also known as *constant-pressure turbines*. The most significant pressure loss occurs at the nozzles (a stationary ring of blades or vanes). The nozzles exchange pressure for increased velocity. The rotor blades are shaped to capture the maximum amount of energy from the nozzles. Impulse turbines are best applied to situations where the fluid flow is relatively low, but the inlet pressure is high.

Note that the rotor wheels are not submerged in the fluid. In an impulse turbine, the fluid is only in contact with a small number of the blades on a rotor at any moment.

Generally, impulse turbines require less maintenance than reaction turbines, but there are many other factors that affect a turbine's maintenance requirements.

Power to Spare

The largest hydroelectric power plant in the world today operates in China, located at the Three Gorges Dam on the Yangtze River. It currently has an installed capacity of 22,500 megawatts (MW), generated by 32 turbine-driven generators producing 700 MW each. Two smaller generators generate 50 MW each for internal use. Consider that 1 MW of electricity can generally support 500 to 900 homes. Each of the 32 larger generators weighs about 6,000 tons (5,443 metric tons).

Figure Credit: iStock@prill

1.1.2 Reaction Turbines

In reaction turbine wheels (*Figure 3*), the fluid pressure is distributed across all the rotor blades in the turbine wheel at once. In other words, the rotor is immersed in fluid. A windmill is a reasonable example of a basic reaction turbine wheel. Since the fluid is admitted to the turbine wheels around their entire circumference, the wheels are often smaller in diameter than those of an impulse turbine of equal capacity. Like a windmill, the turbine wheel must be fully submerged in the fluid to be most effective.

Reaction turbines develop their power by virtue of the fluid's pressure. Unlike the impulse design, a pressure drop occurs as the fluid flows through the rotor. Reaction turbines are best suited to applications where the flow rate is high, but the inlet pressure is low. This is the opposite of the best condition for an impulse turbine to operate efficiently. Newton's third law outlines how energy is transferred in reaction turbines.

1.1.3 Multistage Turbines

Most turbines in operation today are multistage models (*Figure 4*), meaning there are multiple sets of wheels. They are also referred to as *compounding turbines*. Adding additional stages does not change the principle of operation, but more stages significantly increase turbine efficiency and capacity.

Modern multistage turbines can have as many as 50 stages on a single rotor. One complete stage consists of a set of stationary blades or vanes and an adjacent rotating turbine wheel. As the steam flows through the turbine blades, the steam pressure is reduced. For that reason, the diameter of the rotors increases toward the low-pressure end of the turbine, allowing them to extract the maximum amount of energy.

Multistage turbines do not represent another design class. There are very few single-stage turbines operating in the industrial and power-generating environment, simply because they don't produce enough work. One important thing to remember about multistage turbines, though, is that the various stages do not have to share the same design. Impulse and reaction wheels, as well as wheels designed to take advantage of both the pressure and velocity of the fluid (known as a *Curtis turbine*), can be combined in a single turbine.

1.2.0 Hydraulic Turbines

Hydraulic, or water-driven, turbines are used to drive generators at hydroelectric dams. The source of energy is the water flowing from the base of a reservoir stored behind a dam.

A hydroelectric dam that maintains a column of water 400' (~122 m) high over the turbine, for example, naturally develops a pressure of around 160 psi (~1,100 kPa) that is applied to the nozzles. Pumps to increase the water pressure feeding a hydroelectric turbine are unnecessary. This pressure is applied to the turbine nozzle(s), causing a sharp increase in velocity as the water passes through them, which then impacts the rotor blades.

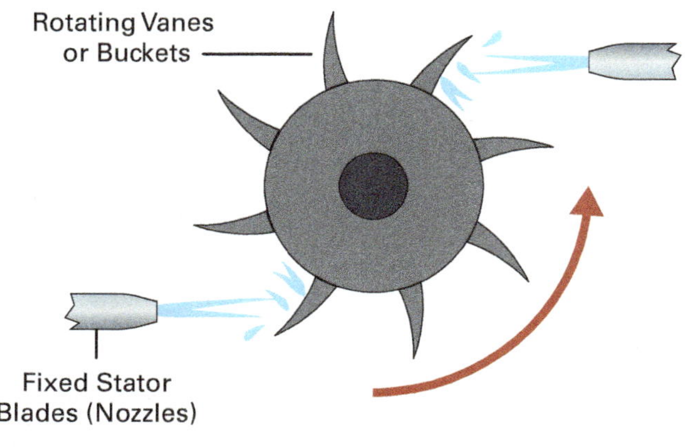

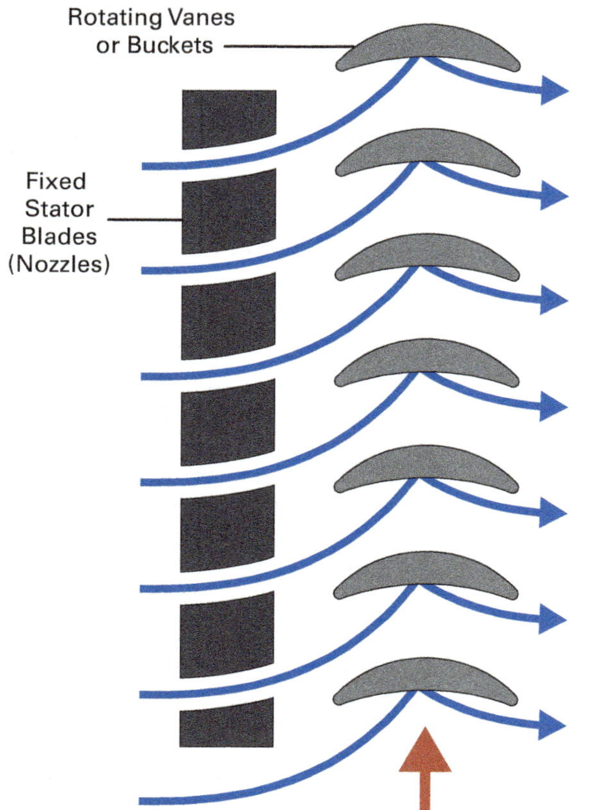

Figure 2 Basic impulse turbine design concept.

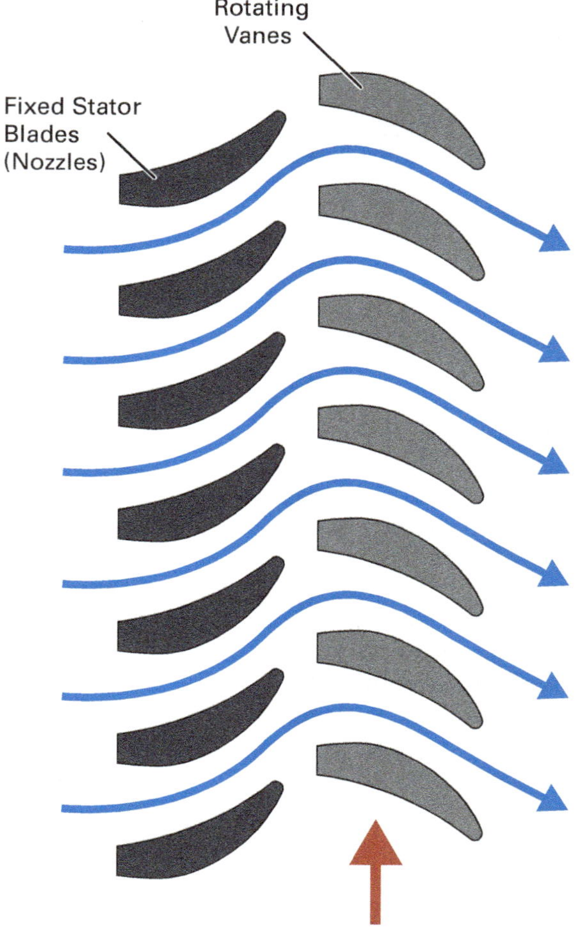

Figure 3 Basic reaction turbine design concept.

The type of turbine used (such as impulse or reaction) depends on the *head* available. The head represents the distance that the water falls before striking the turbine—the height of the water column above the turbine rotor. The height can range from as little as 8' to more than 1,000' (~2.5 m to more than 305 m). The water is generally conveyed to the turbine through a channel known as a penstock.

Some hydroelectric power plants use reversible turbines. These units normally drive an electric generator, as expected. However, when the demand for electrical power is low, such as at night, the generator can be used as a motor to drive the turbine like a pump. This pushes water back to the reservoir above for future use. Facilities that do this by design are referred to as *pumped storage hydropower plants*.

Compared to the wheels found in steam turbines and gas turbines, the wheels of hydraulic turbines are unique. Hydraulic turbines are typically constructed around one or more of the following wheel designs:

- Pelton wheels
- Francis wheels
- Kaplan wheels

1.2.1 Pelton Wheels

Pelton wheels (*Figure 5*), first introduced in the 1870s, are built with rotor vanes resembling bowls that are divided in the center, creating two symmetrical sides. The jet of water strikes the vanes between the two sides. The splitter divides the jet into two equal parts, thus balancing the forces applied to the wheel and its bearings.

There may be several nozzles acting on a single Pelton wheel. The shape of the cups varies somewhat as engineers try to capture as much of the energy from the water stream as possible. The Pelton wheel is considered an impulse turbine design and can be mounted on a horizontal or vertical shaft.

The Pelton wheel requires a significant head to operate efficiently for power generation. However, very small Pelton wheels can be used to draw energy from a mountain stream or similar water source for local use.

Hydraulic turbines generally operate at much lower rotational speeds than steam turbines. This is especially true of turbines equipped with a Pelton wheel. Single-nozzle Pelton turbines, for example, operate at roughly 30 revolutions per minute (rpm). Those with dual nozzles may turn at about 60 rpm.

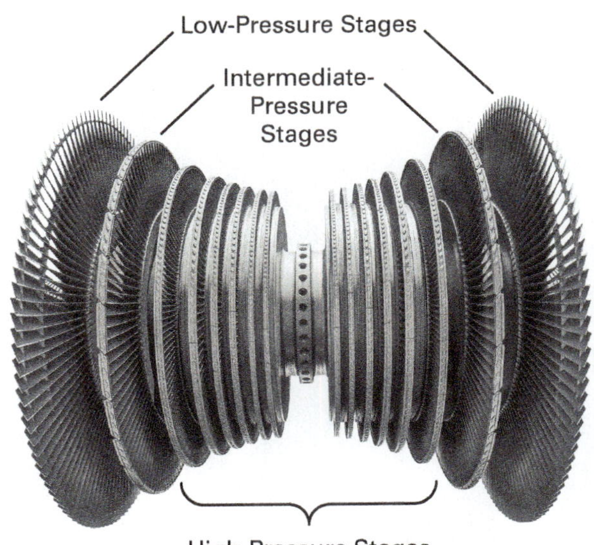

Figure 4 Multistage steam turbine.

Figure 5 Pelton turbine wheel.

1.2.2 Francis Wheels

Most hydroelectric turbines use reaction turbine wheels. Francis and Kaplan wheels are both considered reaction turbine wheels.

The Francis wheel (*Figure 6*) is the most common design used in hydroelectric reaction turbines today. Although it was originally developed in the mid-1800s, the design used today came around 70 years later. *Figure 7* shows a Francis wheel, built by Newport News Shipbuilding in Virginia, being installed at Washington's Grand Coulee dam in 1947. The wheel is typically enclosed in a volute that is similar to the volute of a centrifugal pump (*Figure 8*). Note that this work was done before personal safety became the highest priority on a jobsite.

Francis wheels rotate at speeds ranging from about 60 rpm to 300 rpm and are usually mounted to a vertical shaft. This allows water to enter from all sides while the generator remains well above the water. They typically require a head in the range of 130' to 1,000' (~40 m to 300 m) to be most effective.

1.2.3 Kaplan Wheels

The Kaplan wheel (*Figure 9*) looks like a ship's propeller positioned at the end of a tube. The wheel, a reaction design, is surrounded by guide vanes with water directed around the entire periphery of the turbine. The position and attitude of the guide vanes can be controlled to regulate the flow of water through the turbine.

The Kaplan wheel, when introduced in the early 1900s, enabled power generation where only a low head is available. They require a head of only about 35' to 250' (~10 m to 76 m) for effective power generation. They are exceptionally efficient when the water flow rate is high. The generally rotate at a speed of 300 rpm up to 1,000 rpm, although speeds well below 1,000 rpm are the most common.

1.3.0 Steam Turbines

Steam turbines, like the one shown in *Figure 1*, are used primarily in utility-scale fossil fuel and nuclear power plants to drive electric generators. They are also used to drive generators in large industrial plants to provide the plant's power when necessary, but there must also be a significant steam resource to support it.

In utility plants, the burning of fossil fuels in boilers or the cooling of nuclear reactors heats water to make steam. Nuclear reactors or fossil fuel boilers also provide steam aboard ships and submarines, where steam turbines are used to both generate power and turn the propellers.

Steam can also be generated by *solar thermal systems* that are designed to reflect light from thousands of mirrors toward a single receiver (*Figure 10*). The intense heat from this renewable resource is used to generate steam and drive a

Figure 6 Francis turbine wheel.

Figure 7 Francis turbine wheel being installed at the Grand Coulee Dam.

NCCER – *Millwright*

Pressure Developed from a Column of Water

A column of water exerts a pressure of about 0.43 psig for every foot of height. Thus, a column of water 2.31' high exerts a pressure of about 1 psig.

A column of water 1,000' high exerts a pressure of about 433 psig at its base. In metric values, this equates to a column of water about 305 m high, exerting a pressure of nearly 3,000 kPa.

Figure Credit: iStock@Cristi Croitoru

steam turbine, which is connected to a generator. Since steam can be generated in many ways, steam turbines for power generation will likely remain with us for decades to come.

Steam turbines commonly rotate at speeds of 10,000 rpm to 12,000 rpm. Considering the mass of a rotor and the many wheels that can be attached to it, all turning at such speeds, it is easy to understand why the rotor assembly must be perfectly balanced. Steam turbine vibration characteristics must be consistently monitored for any changes.

> **WARNING!**
>
> Steam turbines commonly operate at pressures ranging from about 600 psi to as high as 5,000 psi (~4,000 kPa to 35,000 kPa). Steam inlet temperatures can be as high as 1,200°F (~650°C). Small steam leaks can be invisible to the naked eye, while physical contact with the escaping steam can cause serious injuries. It is essential that you practice safe working habits and follow all safety directives when working near turbines and steam-generating equipment of this magnitude.

As steam travels through each turbine stage, it expends some of its energy. Therefore, to develop the maximum amount of capacity, each stage is larger in diameter than the one that precedes it. This arrangement is noticeable in *Figure 4*.

A steam turbine may be either a **condensing turbine** or a **noncondensing turbine**, depending on how the steam leaving the turbine is managed. *Condensing* refers to the change of state from steam (a vapor) back to liquid water. Steam naturally condenses as the pressure and temperature fall.

In a condensing turbine, any remaining steam exiting the turbine enters a *condenser* where the heat energy is transferred out, enabling the steam to revert to water. The condenser is simply a heat exchanger, with the cooling medium being air or water. A reduced pressure results, creating a vacuum effect that helps draw fresh steam into the turbine. The water, referred to as *condensate*, is then returned to the boiler or reactor to be converted into steam again. Condensing turbines are usually dedicated solely to power generation.

In a noncondensing turbine, the "used" steam is not intentionally condensed as it exits the turbine. By design, some steam at a usable pressure remains after it passes through the turbine. The design pressure at the exit is referred to as the *back pressure*, which is why they may be referred to as *back-pressure turbines*. The remaining steam is routed to another process in the plant that can make use of the energy. Steam can also be extracted from the turbine at various points along its casing to obtain steam at a higher pressure for a dependent load. This replaces the vacuum effect that results from condensing the steam in a condensing turbine, encouraging steam to flow through more readily. Control valves at each extraction point regulate the extraction process.

There are a lot of variations in steam turbine design though, many of which are related to how the steam resource is to be used. For example, steam at an intermediate pressure can also be extracted to do other work from a condensing turbine. This type of condensing turbine is referred to as an *extraction turbine*. However, when the demand for power is at its peak, steam extraction is disabled so all the energy can be used for

Figure 8 Francis turbine wheels are typically enclosed in a volute.

power generation. An extraction turbine is a form of condensing turbine, but not all condensing turbines are extraction turbines.

The goal of many approaches to steam turbine operation is to use as much energy as possible from the steam; generating steam has a substantial energy cost. If steam that would otherwise be wasted can be extracted and used productively, the plant's overall operating efficiency rises. More steam becomes available when the electrical load is low. There is no advantage to generating maximum electrical power without a matching demand. Generated electrical power is either used or wasted, since we have yet to develop electrical energy storage on a massive scale.

The major working parts and components of a steam turbine can be divided into the following categories for further discussion:

- Casing and associated components
- Rotor and its mounted components
- Auxiliary system components

1.3.1 Steam Turbine Casing Parts

The turbine casing is the outer shell of the steam turbine. The casing is a thick, metal casting with insulation covering the outer surface. The casing is made in upper and lower halves, divided horizontally so that the machine can be opened for maintenance and repair (*Figure 11*). Some of the casing components that are introduced in this section are shown in *Figure 12*.

Common steam turbine components that are considered part of the casing or directly connected to it include the following:

- Steam chest and steam supply lines
- Inlet control valves and nozzle blocks
- Stationary blades and blade carriers
- Extraction and exhaust ports
- Grounding brushes
- Bearings
- Equalizing seals and gland seals
- Rupture disk
- Insulation and lagging

Figure 9 Kaplan turbine wheel.

Figure 10 Solar thermal power-generation facility, with thousands of mirrors focused on a single point.

Figure 11 Steam turbine with the upper casing removed, exposing the rotor.

Steam Chest and Supply Lines

The steam chest is an external pipe-like reservoir and header, or a large chamber in the casing, that supplies steam to the lines feeding the turbine wheels. It is generally located at the smaller end of the turbine where steam at the highest pressure enters. *Figure 13* shows an example of how steam is distributed and controlled in a turbine.

The steam chest itself is fed from the boiler. The steam supply line carries the steam from the source to the chest. A main stop valve controls the flow of steam into the chest. Control valves control the flow of steam from the chest into the turbine. The steam chest must be large enough to accommodate the full flow of steam needed to operate the turbine without a significant pressure drop.

Some turbines have another steam supply line connected to the steam chest, routed from a secondary source and often at a lower pressure than the main steam supply. The line can admit intermediate-pressure steam from the other source during main boiler outages, so that the turbine can still operate. Its capacity will, of course, be reduced due to the reduced pressure. The main stop valve for this line remains closed most of the time.

Inlet Control Valves and Nozzle Blocks

The inlet control valves are also shown in *Figure 13*. They are variable-position valves that regulate the amount of steam admitted into each section of the turbine. The position of the control valves determines the capacity of the turbine and regulates the back pressure in a noncondensing boiler.

Nozzle rings (*Figure 14*) are also called *stators*, *nozzle plates*, *nozzle blocks*, or *nozzle boxes*. They are fixed and don't rotate. The nozzle ports—the spaces between the vanes—direct steam at a high velocity and at the correct angle into the rotating turbine wheels. Each inlet valve controls the flow to one of the nozzle rings.

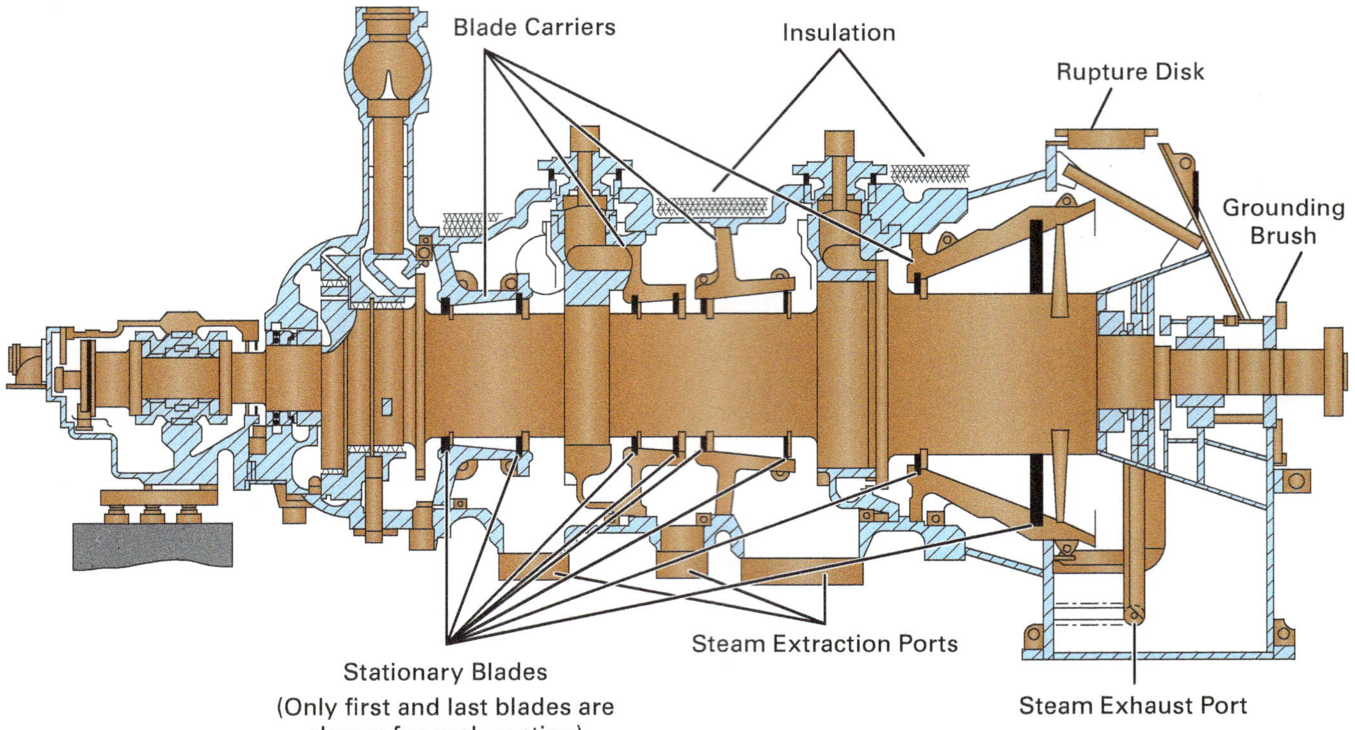

Figure 12 Steam turbine casing components.

Stationary Blades and Blade Carriers

The stationary blades are sets of vanes that direct the steam at the required angle to the turbine wheels. They are attached to the blade carriers, as shown in *Figure 12*.

The blade carriers, also called *diaphragms*, are cylinders mounted inside the turbine casing (*Figure 15*). They secure the stationary blade sets (nozzles) in place. Fixed vanes are attached to the inner surface of the carriers to direct the steam into the wheels at the proper angle for optimum energy transfer. The blade carriers are attached to the casing in a manner that allows them to expand both radially and axially as the turbine warms up.

Extraction and Exhaust Ports

The extraction and exhaust ports, shown at the bottom of *Figure 12*, allow steam to be removed from the turbine. Extraction ports provide steam to other loads at an intermediate pressure. Extraction valves are used at each port to regulate the steam flow. Steam that passes all the way through the turbine exits through the exhaust port. This steam is either routed into a condenser (a condensing turbine), or to other process loads (a noncondensing turbine).

Grounding Brushes

Grounding brushes are simple devices used to ensure that stray current doesn't build up in the turbine shaft. Like static electricity that builds up in your body, stray current in the shaft will eventually arc to some other conductive surface, and the arc usually occurs at bearings. High-voltage electric discharges cause pitting and corrosion of the bearing surfaces.

The grounding brushes provide a continuous path for the current to leave the shaft by keeping conductive carbon elements or copper straps (brushes) in contact with the rotating shaft. A ground wire runs from the brush mounts to conduct any stray current to ground. Grounding brushes are usually positioned adjacent to the turbine rotor main bearing on the end closest to the generator.

Bearings

You may recall that bearings are commonly subjected to two types of loads—axial and radial (*Figure 16*). Like all bearings, turbine bearings must be selected to accommodate the type of loads being applied. Turbine bearing loads often come from different directions, so each bearing must be designed to accommodate the loads unique to its location along the rotor.

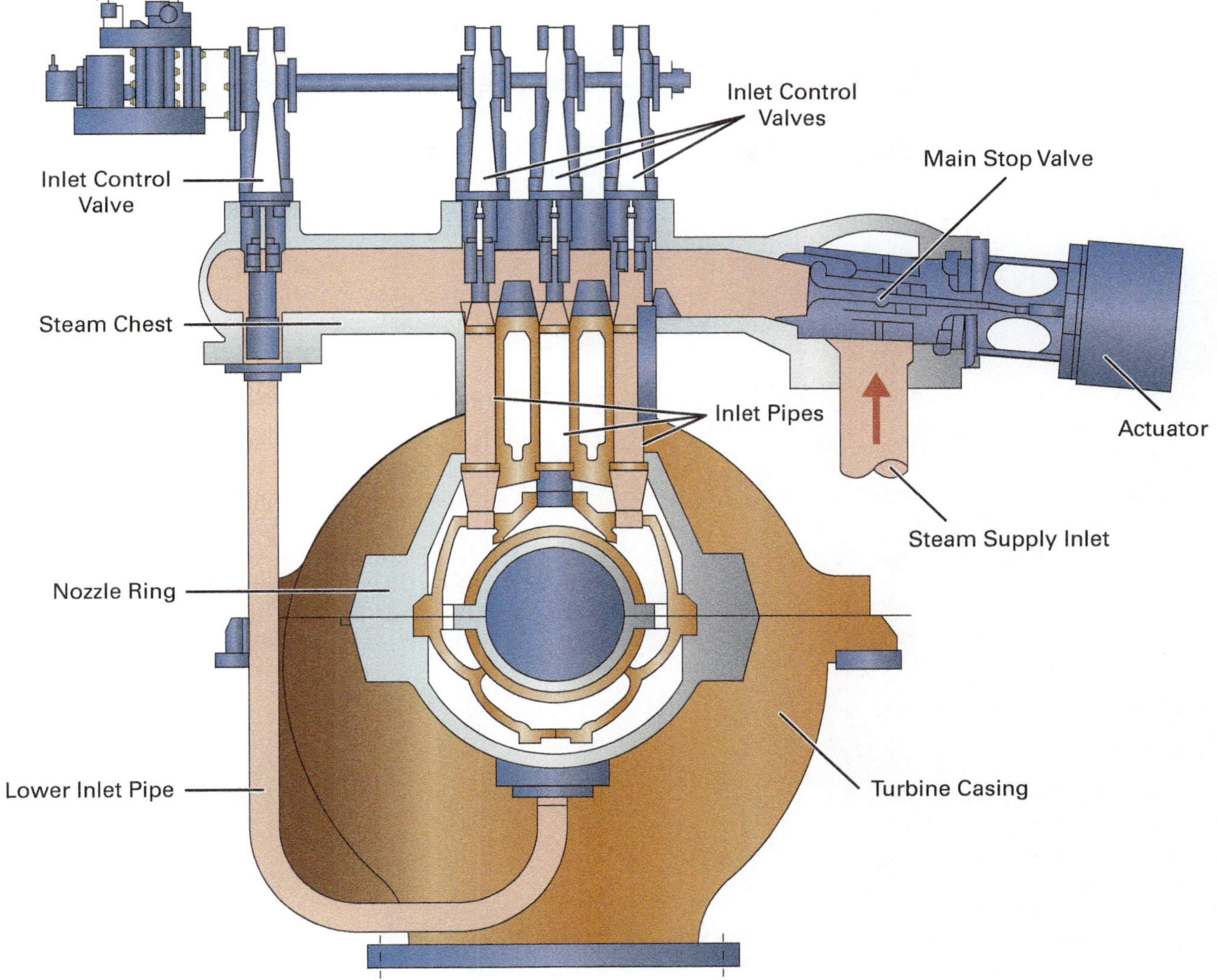

Figure 13 Turbine steam supply and distribution.

Journal bearings are positioned at each end of the shaft, and perhaps at other locations along the length of the rotor. Journal bearings support the shaft, accepting the radial load applied. They generally have a **Babbitt** liner that fits into a machined and precisely fit recess in the casing (*Figure 17*). Journal bearings are made in two halves, allowing them to be replaced without removing the turbine rotor.

Turbine journal bearings, a common type of sleeve bearing, are *hydrodynamic* in design. The term refers to the fact that the shaft, by design, isn't rubbing hard against the Babbitt while rotating but instead rides on a thin layer of lubricant when rotating at its design speed. At that point, the film of oil is well-balanced around the bearing, providing a minute amount of clearance between the metal parts. This is referred to as *full film lubrication*. But during startup and shutdown, when the rotational speed is low, full film lubrication has not developed. This leaves the bearings vulnerable to rapid wear and failure. This problem is addressed by what is referred to as a *jacking oil system*.

NOTE

Jacking oil systems are described in *Section 1.3.3* of this module. General lubrication concepts, including the development of mixed film, boundary, and full film lubrication in bearings, are presented in NCCER Module 15208, *Lubrication*.

An axial load develops in the turbine by the thrust applied by the steam as it enters the rotors. The steam exerts pressure on the rotor, pushing the shaft in the direction of steam flow. A thrust end bearing holds the rotor in place axially, ensuring that the shaft can't move.

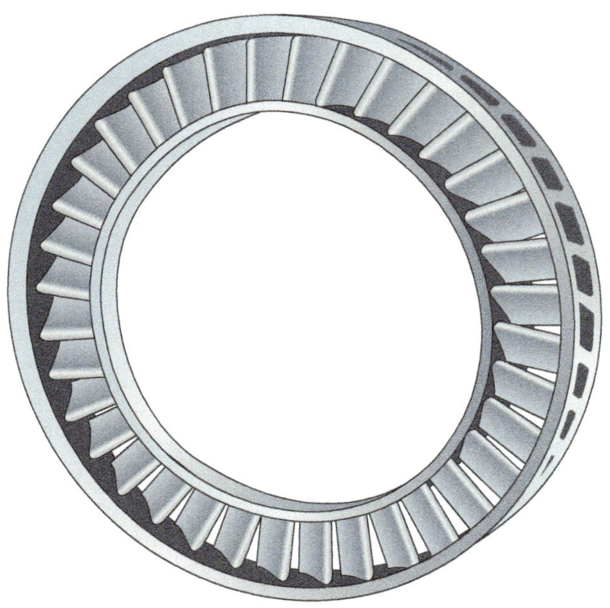

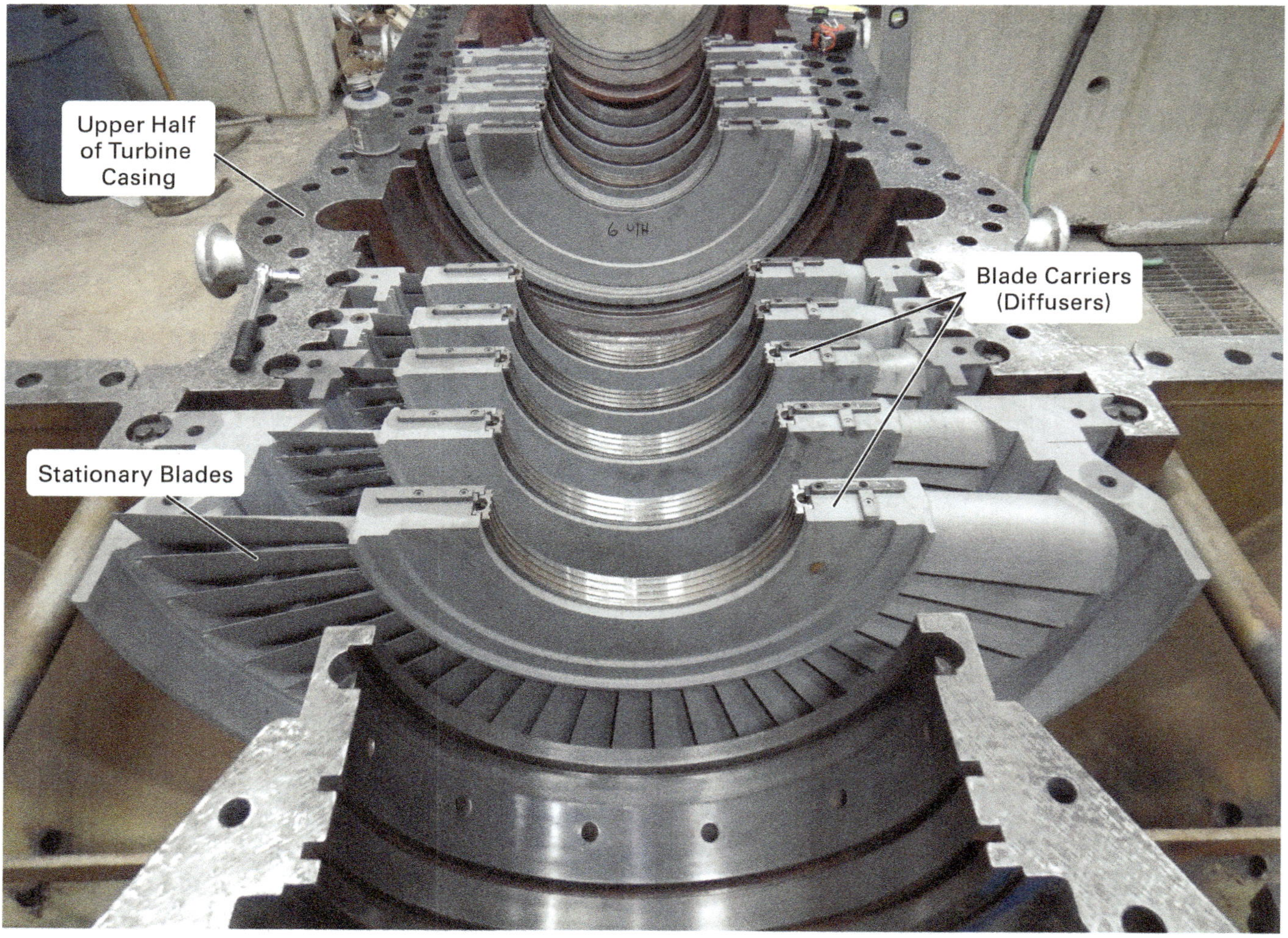

Figure 14 Turbine nozzle ring.

Babbitt-lined, tilting-pad bearings are often used in steam turbines for the thrust end bearing (*Figure 18*). A film of lubricant also develops here, separating the Babbitt pads and the fixed plate mounted on the casing. Each pad is free to tilt, helping the development of a consistent film of lubricant at the design speed.

NOTE

Bearings and their applications are presented in detail in NCCER Module 15209, *Introduction to Bearings*, and Module 15306, *Removing and Installing Bearings.*

Equalizing Seals and Gland Seals

The equalizing seals are placed in recesses that encircle the shaft at the front of each section. *Figure 19* shows the steam path. Equalizing seals divide the steam path and provide backing surfaces against which the steam pressure can react. Labyrinth seals (*Figure 20*) between the equalizing seals and the rotor and turbine housing prevent significant steam leakage between the sections.

Figure 15 Blade carriers and stationary blade halves positioned in an upper turbine casing.

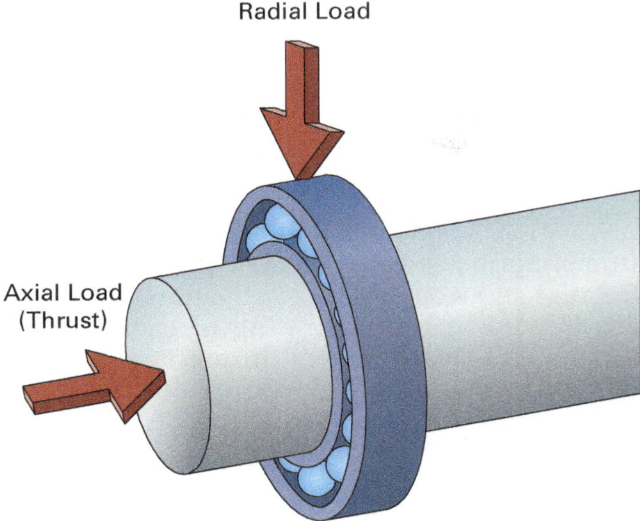

Figure 16 Axial and radial loads on a shaft.

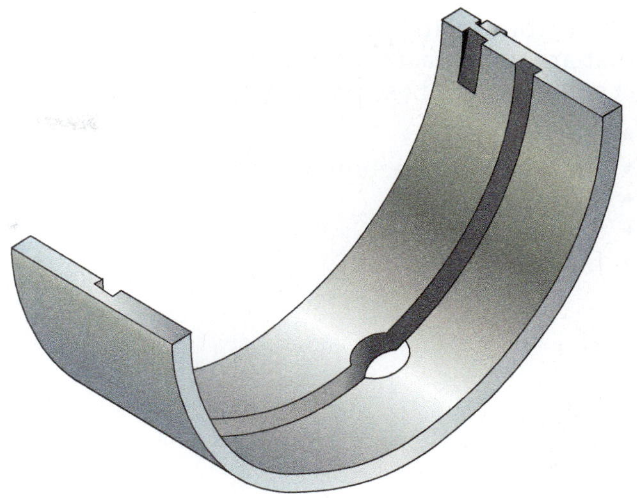

Figure 17 Split journal bearing.

Gland seals are rings that rely on the pressure from the steam supply along with spring tension to hold them close to the shaft and prevent steam leakage. Higher steam pressures serve to push the seal tighter against the shaft.

Rupture Disk

A rupture disk (*Figure 21*) is a thin, soft metal diaphragm across a flanged opening at the top of the low-pressure section. When the pressure in the turbine exceeds the maximum pressure, the rupture disk bursts, allowing the steam to escape. It is designed to open well below the pressure that would be hazardous to the casing.

Unlike pressure relief valves, rupture disks can't be reset or reused. Once the material breaks and relieves the pressure, the assembly must be replaced before the turbine can be restarted. Fortunately, they are designed to be replaced with limited effort.

Insulation and Lagging

The steam turbine casing is covered with insulating material to prevent heat loss and dangerous burns. The insulation may be attached in various ways, and it is often in the form of removable blankets.

(A)

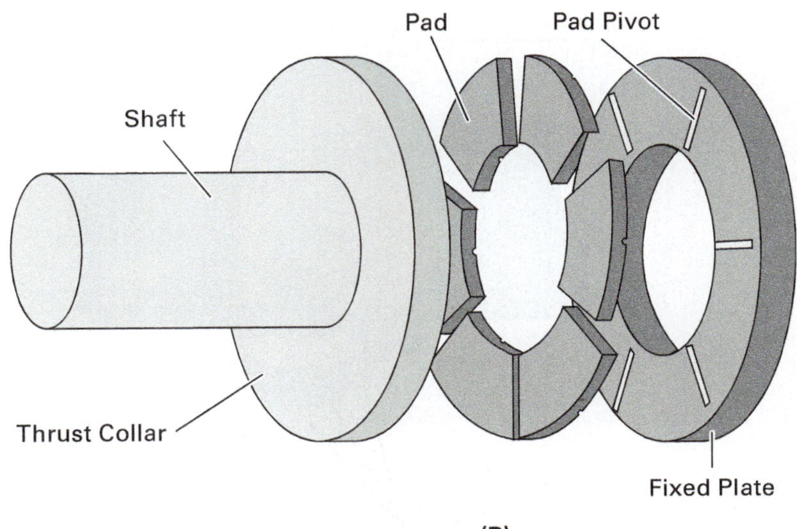

(B)

Figure 18 Tilted-pad thrust bearing.

1.3.2 Turbine Rotor Parts

The turbine rotor parts (*Figure 22*) include those that are in contact with the rotor or central shaft at some point. These parts include the following:

- Turbine shaft
- Impulse and reaction wheels
- Turning gear
- Shaft coupling
- Lube oil gear pump

Turbine Rotor

The turbine shaft is the primary rotating component of the turbine. The shaft is coupled to the generator shaft and transfers the mechanical energy required to produce electricity.

Impulse and Reaction Wheels

In compound steam turbines containing both impulse and reaction wheels, the impulse wheels are located at the beginning of each turbine section. As steam passes through the nozzles upstream of the wheel, a pressure drop occurs in exchange for an increase in velocity. As the steam

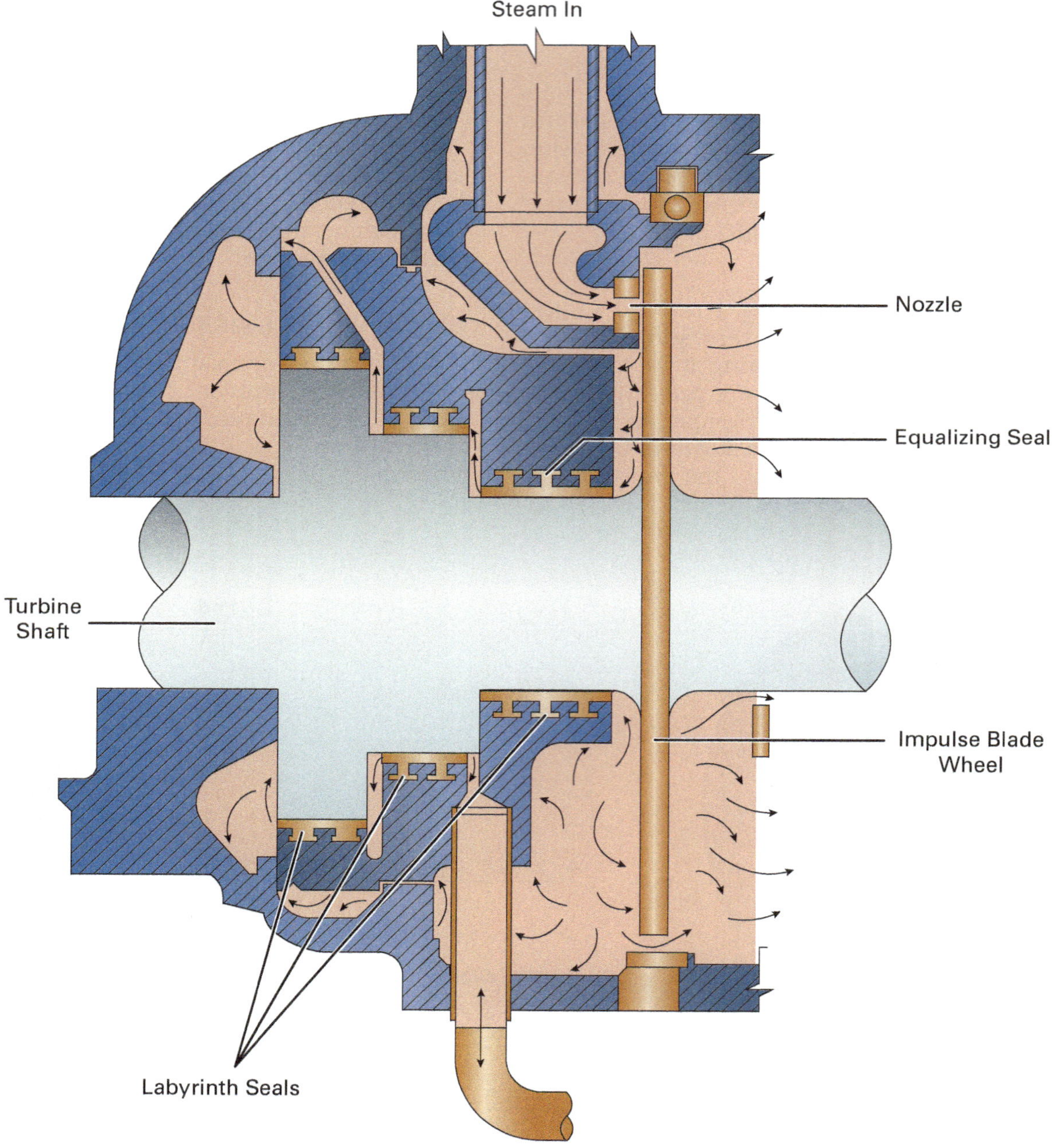

Figure 19 Steam path at high-pressure equalizing seal.

Figure 20 Labyrinth seals.

passes through the impulse wheel, it changes direction and loses some of the velocity. *Figure 23* shows how the path of the steam is affected by the blade.

The steam is directed through a reaction wheel in a different way. *Figure 24* shows the difference. Think of the blades as aircraft wings. There is an aerodynamic shape to them, with the upper surface longer than the lower surface. As the steam flows across the top and bottom, a lower pressure develops across the top of the "wing," resulting in a lifting force from the higher pressure on the opposite side. In the case of a steam turbine, the lift developed by the many blades causes rotation.

Turning Gear

Steam turbines experience a great deal of thermal stress, especially as they start and shut down. They often go through a warm-up period before they are started, and they must be allowed to cool gradually during shutdown. During these warm-up and cooldown cycles, it is best to keep the rotor turning slowly. Otherwise, hot spots can develop along the rotor shaft, and the shaft can sag or otherwise become distorted. Any significant change in the shaft can cause the rotating wheels to contact the stators or the casing due to the small clearances. The shaft and other components must be warmed and cooled slowly and consistently from one end to the other.

The turning gear is a motor-driven, speed-reduction gearbox (*Figure 25*). In this case, the word *gear* in the name can refer to the assembly of motor, gearbox, and controls. The turning gear is connected to the low-pressure end of the turbine shaft. It is normally driven by a small electric motor. The turning gear is used to slowly turn the rotor assembly during turbine warm-up and cooldown. The turning gear may also be used periodically if a turbine is offline for an extended period, again to minimize any chance of distortion along the length of the rotor.

Shaft Coupling

The shaft coupling to the generator (*Figure 26*) is located at the low-pressure end of the turbine. Precision alignment is essential, and thermal growth must be considered in the alignment process.

1.3.3 Steam Turbine Auxiliary System Components

Several auxiliary systems are required to operate the turbine safely and efficiently. These systems include the following:

- Lubrication and jacking oil system
- Electrohydraulic governor
- Condensate drain and injection system

Lubrication and Jacking Oil System

Proper and reliable bearing lubrication is essential for every turbine. The lubrication and jacking oil system (*Figure 27*) consists of the following primary components:

- Main and backup pumps
- A reservoir
- Oil coolers and heaters
- Oil filters
- A centrifugal purifier
- A vapor extractor

Figure 21 Burst rupture disk.

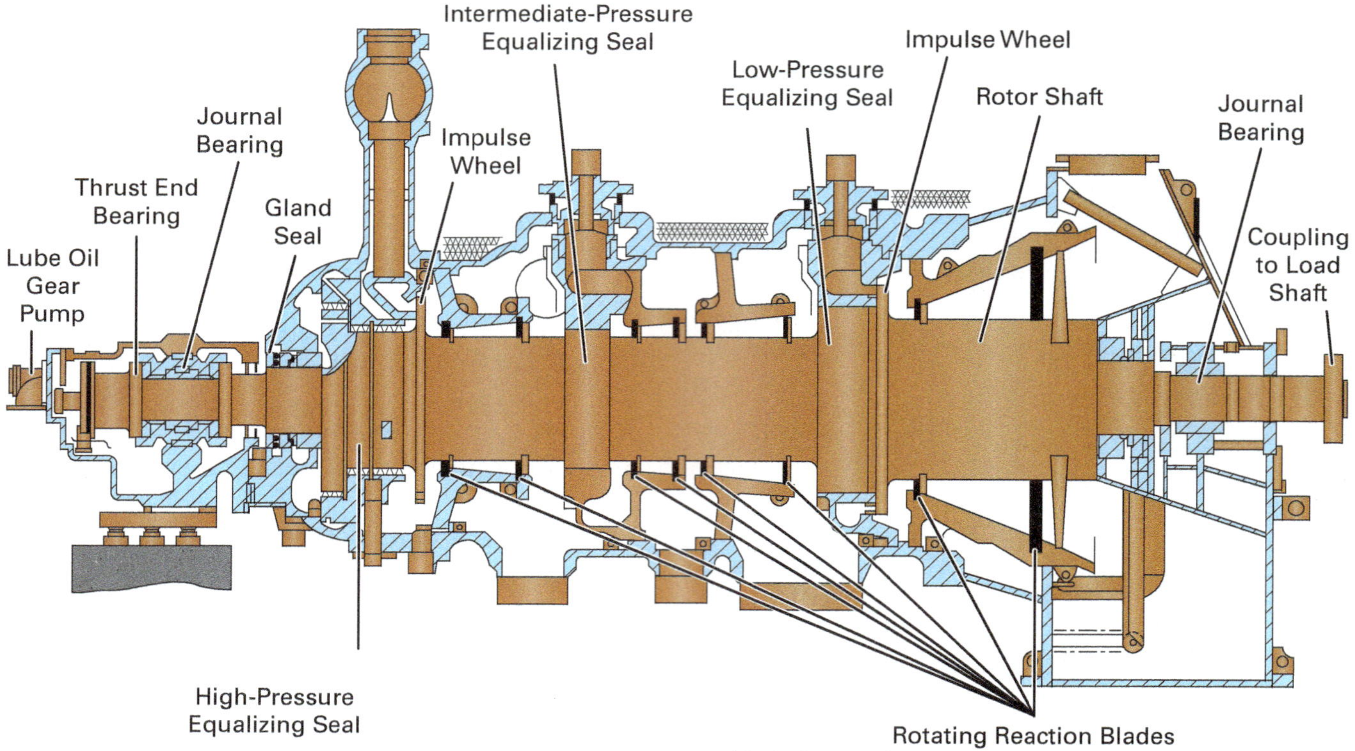

Figure 22 Turbine rotor parts.

The lubrication system provides oil to the turbine bearings and, in some cases, the generator bearings as well.

The main oil pump is typically mounted on the high-pressure end of the turbine shaft, at the opposite end from the generator. It provides lubricant to the bearings when the turbine is at design speed. At that point, the film of oil is well-balanced around the bearing, providing full film lubrication. But during startup and shutdown, when full film lubrication is not active, the metal surfaces still need to be kept apart to minimize wear.

The term *jacking oil system* comes from the unusual function of the system. It is designed to lift the shaft on a thin film of lubricant. The jacking pump delivers very high-pressure oil to the bearings during startup and shutdown. The jacking oil pressure typically ranges from 700 pounds per square inch gauged (psig) to 1,400 psig (~4,800 kPa to 9,600 kPa). The jacking oil pump also operates in unison with the turning gear system to maintain proper lubrication and prevent bearing or shaft damage when the turbine is offline. When the turbine is operating normally, centrifugal force helps lift the shaft and center it in the bearings.

The lubricating oil is warmed by heaters when the turbine is offline, keeping the bearings warm as well. The oil cooling system is enabled when the turbine is running to keep the oil temperature in the ideal range. The vapor extractor, shown on top of the oil reservoir in *Figure 27*, allows any water vapor to exit the reservoir. The centrifugal oil purifier, shown beneath the reservoir in *Figure 27*, collects unwanted contaminants and pollutants from the lube oil using centrifugal force. It has an internal pump that circulates the oil from and to the reservoir.

Electrohydraulic Governor Equipment

The electrohydraulic governor is an electronic controller that regulates the hydraulically positioned servos of the control valves, and thus the valve position. They govern the horsepower developed, regulate extraction and turbine back pressure, control the start-up load rate, and synchronize the shaft speed and frequency output. The governor is never used, however, as a means of shutting the turbine down.

Some turbines are equipped with a turbine control and protection system that can provide hydraulic oil under pressure to operate the rotary drives for the valves, replacing steam as their power source.

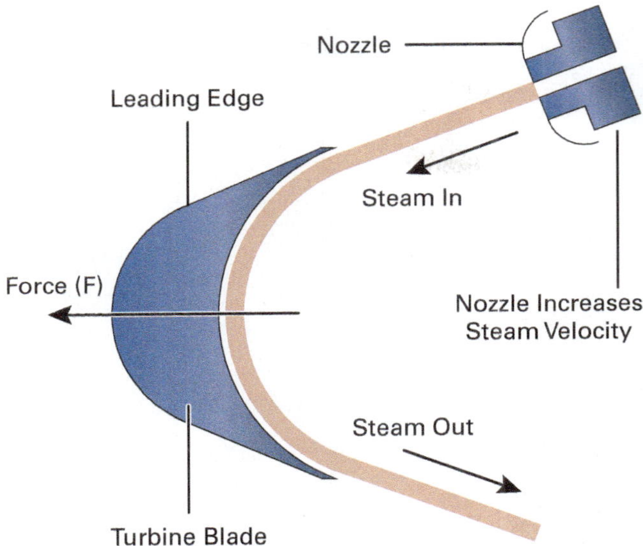

Figure 23 Steam path as it encounters an impulse wheel blade.

Condensate Drain and Injection System

The condensate drain and injection system supplies steam condensate to the turbine for cooling purposes and also provides the path for condensate to leave the turbine. Collected condensate can be sprayed into the low-pressure section of the turbine, serving as a source of cooling for the blades. During normal operation, the condensate flashes to steam upon contact with the blades due to their very high temperature. This reduces the blade temperature significantly.

Residual steam in the turbine during and after shutdown will condense on its own as the turbine cools. Some of the condensate used for cooling may also collect in the turbine as it winds down. Turbine damage and corrosion is often caused by residual moisture in the turbine. The condensate must therefore be drained from all areas following a shutdown. The turbine must also be free of any residual condensate during startup when the steam is first admitted. When rapidly moving steam encounters stagnant or slow-moving water, the resulting water hammer can seriously damage the turbine.

1.4.0 Gas Turbines

Gas turbines (*Figure 28*) are best described as internal-combustion turbines used to power generators and aircraft (jet) engines. Since they are largely self-contained, they are easily stopped and started. Thus, they are often used to generate additional power during peak periods when the steam turbines are unable to meet the extra demand. Smaller versions are used as emergency generators for major facilities.

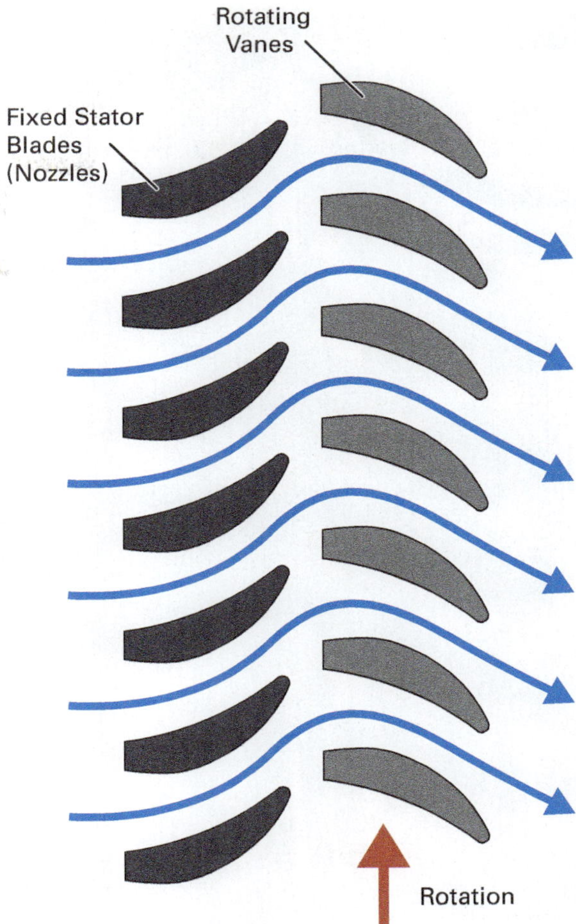

Figure 24 Steam passage through a reaction wheel.

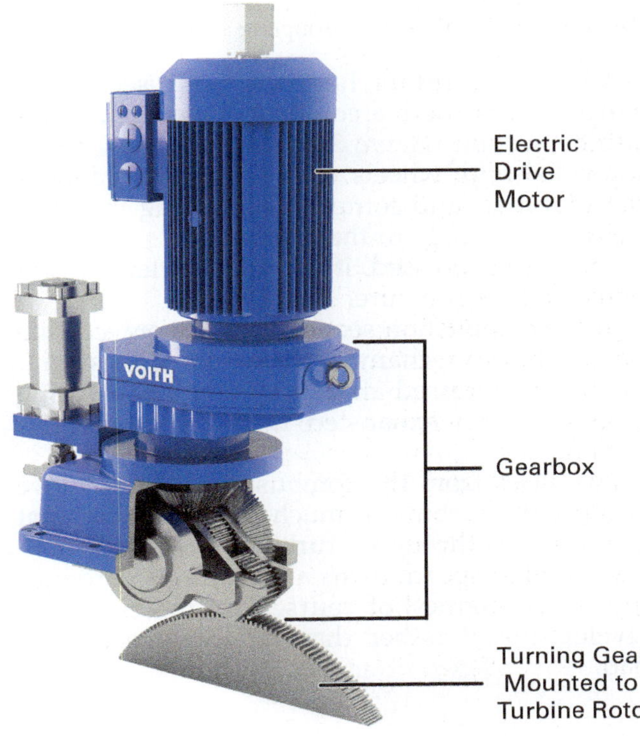

Figure 25 Turning gear and its drive assembly.

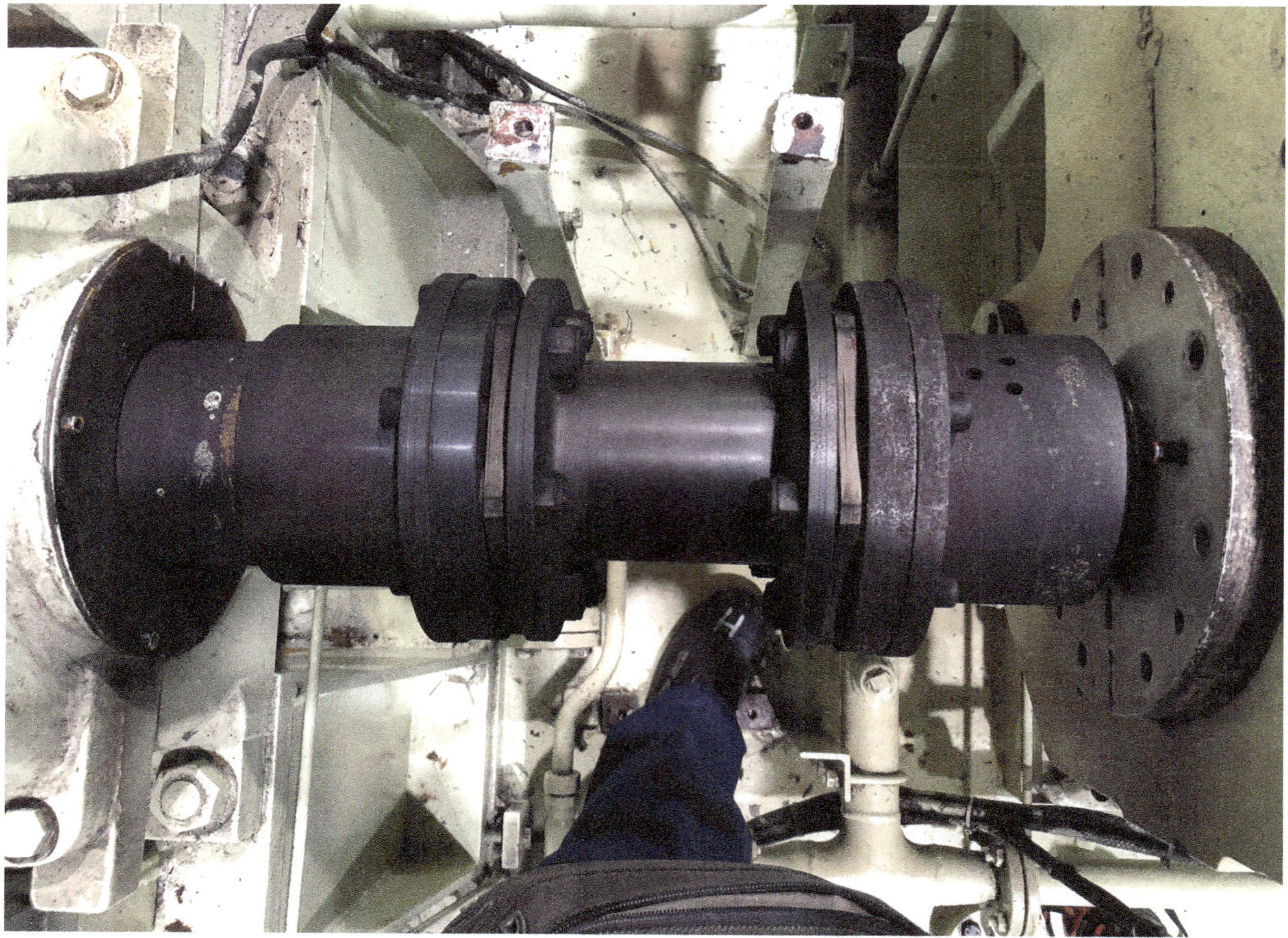

Figure 26 Steam turbine shaft coupling assembly.

A basic gas turbine has three main sections: a compressor section, a combustion section, and a turbine section (*Figure 29*). The compressor section consists of wheels with hundreds of blades that ingest air and compress it, feeding the compressed air supply to the combustion section. As the air is compressed, it becomes hotter, further increasing the pressure.

In the combustion section, fuel is sprayed into the combustion chamber. The fuel mixes with the hot, compressed air and ignites. The burning gases are then exhausted through the turbine section.

The gases from the combustion process move through the turbine in much the same way that steam moves through a turbine. The rotor, rotating at a high speed, turns a generator to produce power. Jet engines, of course, use the energy to develop thrust rather than drive a mechanical load.

Gas turbines used for power generation generally rotate at 3,000 rpm to 4,000 rpm. They burn various fuels, sometimes exposing the combustion components to temperatures exceeding 2,400°F (~1,300°C). The exhaust gases are understandably hot, ranging from about 800°F to 1,100°F (~425°C to 600°C). That is a tremendous amount of energy to waste in the process since it does not contribute to developing mechanical energy. For that reason, various methods to capture the lost heat are implemented. Every effort must be made to conserve and reuse all energy sources to support the growing need for power as efficiently as possible.

Figure 30 shows a typical gas turbine layout in block form. The four major sections of a gas turbine are as follows:

- Compressor section
- Combustion section
- Turbine section
- Auxiliary support systems

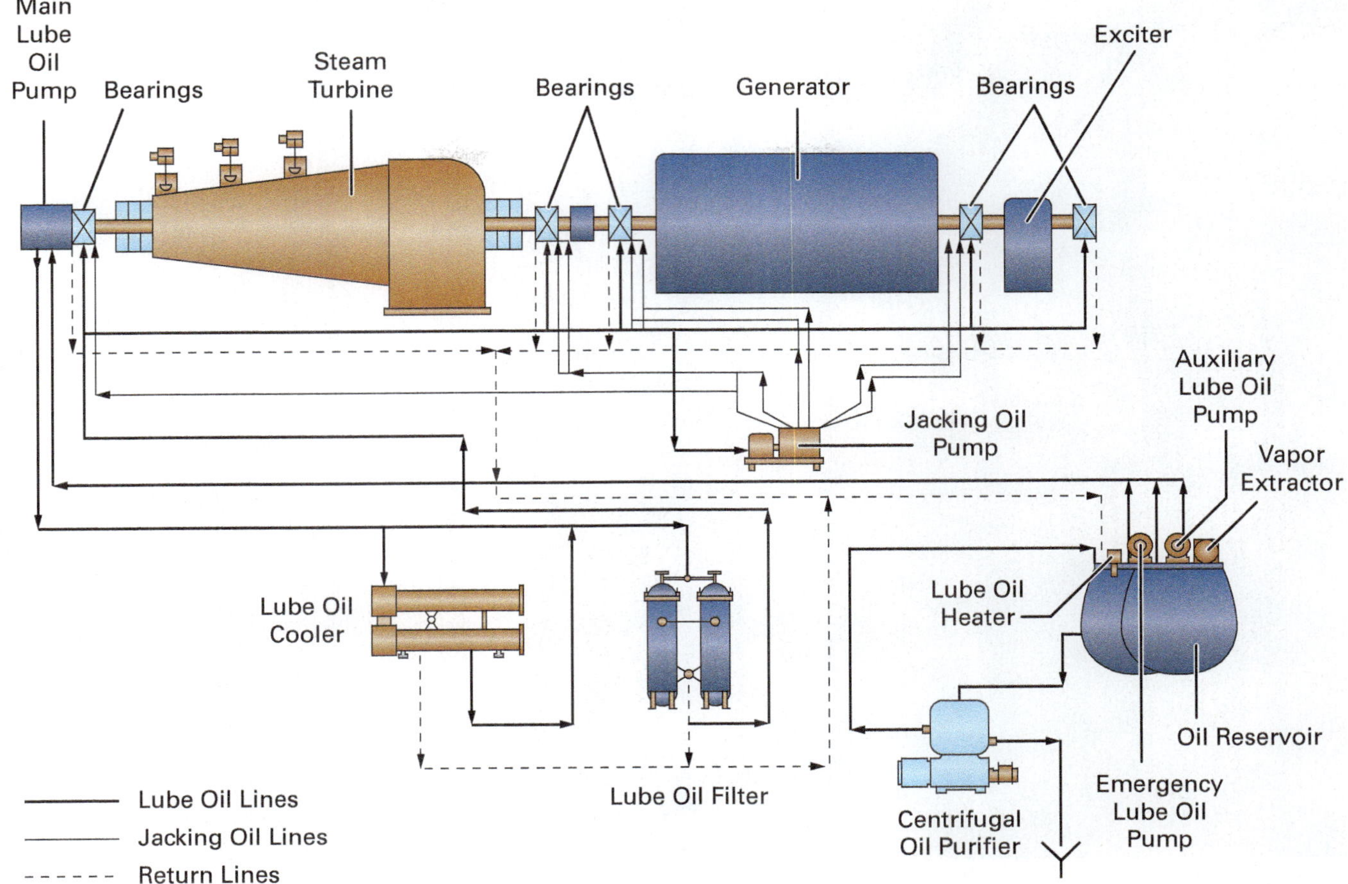

Figure 27 Lubrication and jacking oil system.

1.4.1 Compressor Section

Gas turbine compressors draw in air and compress it, reducing its volume to increase its pressure. The air is then forced into the combustion section. The air provides oxygen to support combustion, and more fuel can be burned using compressed air. Burning more fuel results in more power.

Most power plant turbines use *axial-flow compressors*, meaning that the air flows parallel to the main shaft. The following are the major parts of the compressor section (*Figure 31*):

- Inlet guide vanes
- Rotor and stator blades
- Diffuser section
- Bleed-off lines

Inlet Guide Vanes

The inlet guide vanes do exactly what their name implies—straighten and guide incoming air into the compressor blades at a specific angle. In many cases, the vanes can also rotate to different angles to control the volume of airflow entering the compressor, acting as a valve.

During startup, the vanes are kept partially closed to throttle the air entering the compressor. As the turbine reaches operating speed, the vanes slowly rotate open to allow more air into the compressor.

Rotor and Stator Blades

Rotor blades are mounted on wheels along the rotor throughout the compressor section. The rotor blades accept the air through the inlet guide vanes and force the air to slide along the blade faces. The rotor blades also push the air sideways in the direction the blades are rotating. These two forces cause the air to leave the rotor blades at the proper angle to enter the stator blades.

The stator blades are mounted to the inside of the compressor casing between each row of rotor blades. They direct the airflow to the next set of rotor blades. A row of stator blades and a row of rotor blades make up a stage in the compressor. A typical compressor is made up of 10 or more stages.

Figure 28 Power-generating gas turbine.

Microturbines

The term *microturbine* describes a small, power-generating gas turbine that provides power on a small scale. A single microturbine typically produces between 25 kilowatts (kW) and 1,000 kW of power. As the name implies, they are significantly smaller than a standard turbine. Each turbine/generator pair is fully self-contained inside an enclosure, creating a modular system.

Another feature beyond their physical size and capacity sets them apart from their larger cousins. While utility-scale turbines rotate at around 3,500 rpm, microturbines rotate much faster. Their minimum speed is generally around 40,000 rpm, but some rotate at speeds approaching 120,000 rpm. Due to the extreme speed and the heat from combustion, standard bearings aren't practical. Air-lubricated and magnetic bearings are commonly used instead.

Figure Credit: Capstone Green Energy

Microturbines are used for emergency power in critical applications, or to serve as a primary power source for facilities that are far from the power grid.

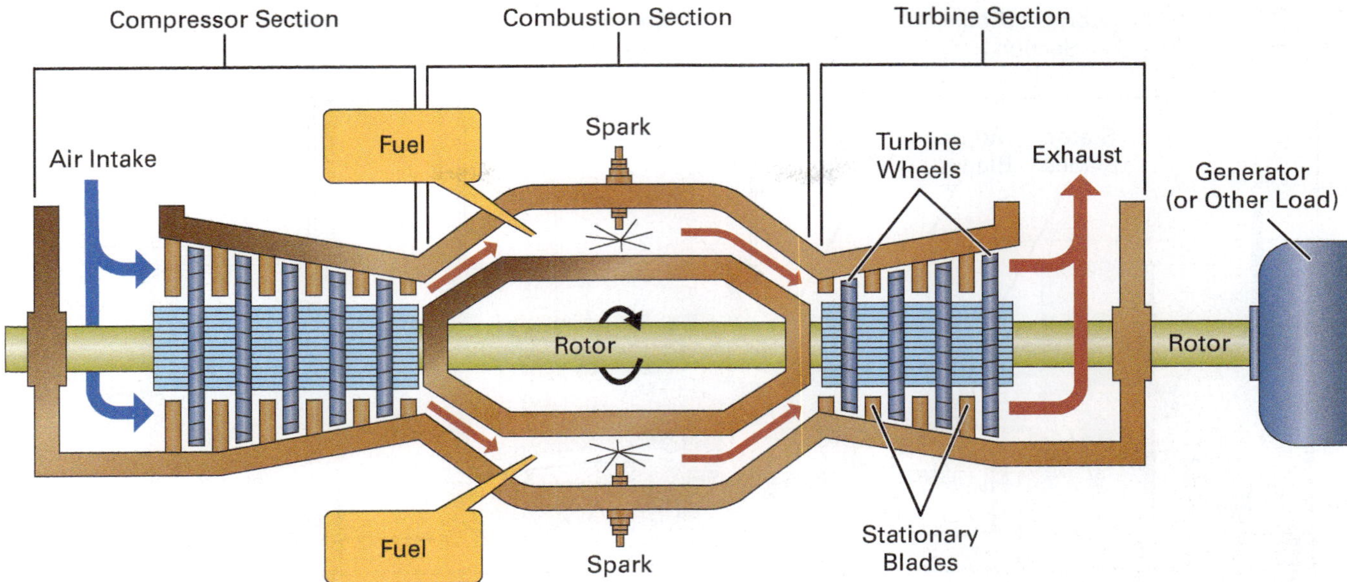

Figure 29 Sections of a gas turbine.

Each stage compresses the air further. The diameter of the rotor and stator assemblies decreases as the air moves toward the discharge of the compressor section. Most gas turbine compressors increase the air pressure to 10 or 14 times the normal atmospheric pressure.

Diffuser Section

The final section of the compressor is known as the diffuser section (*Figure 32*). It captures the compressed air from the final stage of compressor blades. The air velocity slows down here as it passes through due to the increase in free area through which the air can flow. This serves to reduce any pressure losses.

Bleed Lines

The air pressure sometimes increases too rapidly in a compressor and causes a problem known as *compressor surge*. Compressor surge occurs when the air tries to reverse direction and rush back through the compressor toward the inlet. This can result in serious compressor damage. It is more likely to occur during startup than at any other time.

To prevent compressor surge, bleed lines relieve air pressure from ports in the diffuser section, as shown in *Figure 32*. Pressure relief valves open when the air pressure exceeds a setpoint, allowing some of the air to escape through the bleed lines to the exhaust section of the turbine. Once the surge has been controlled, the valves close and the compressor returns to normal operation.

1.4.2 Combustion Section

Gas turbines can use a variety of fuels for combustion. The combustion section mixes compressed air from the compressor with the selected fuel, *atomizing* it. The mixture is ignited by a spark ignition system in the combustion section. The hot, rapidly expanding gases from the burning mixture drive the turbine.

Combustion takes place inside a *combustor*. They are also referred to as *burners*, *cans*, or *combustion chambers*. The combustion section is made up of a ring of connected combustors (*Figure 33*). The air-fuel mixture is burned inside each combustor at temperatures exceeding 2,000°F (~1,100°C). The combustion produces a high-temperature, high-pressure stream of combustion byproducts that is delivered to the turbine section.

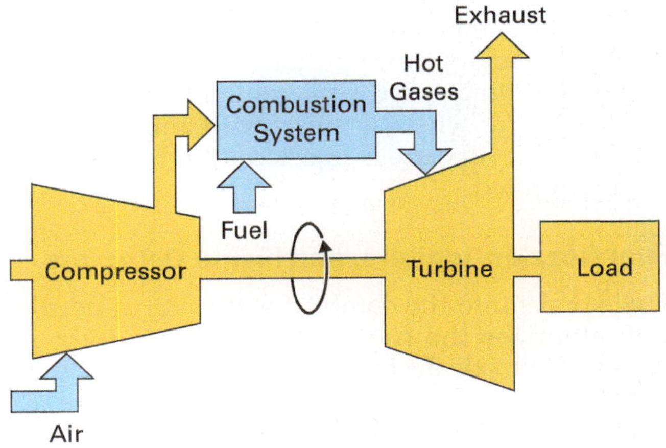

Figure 30 Gas turbine block layout.

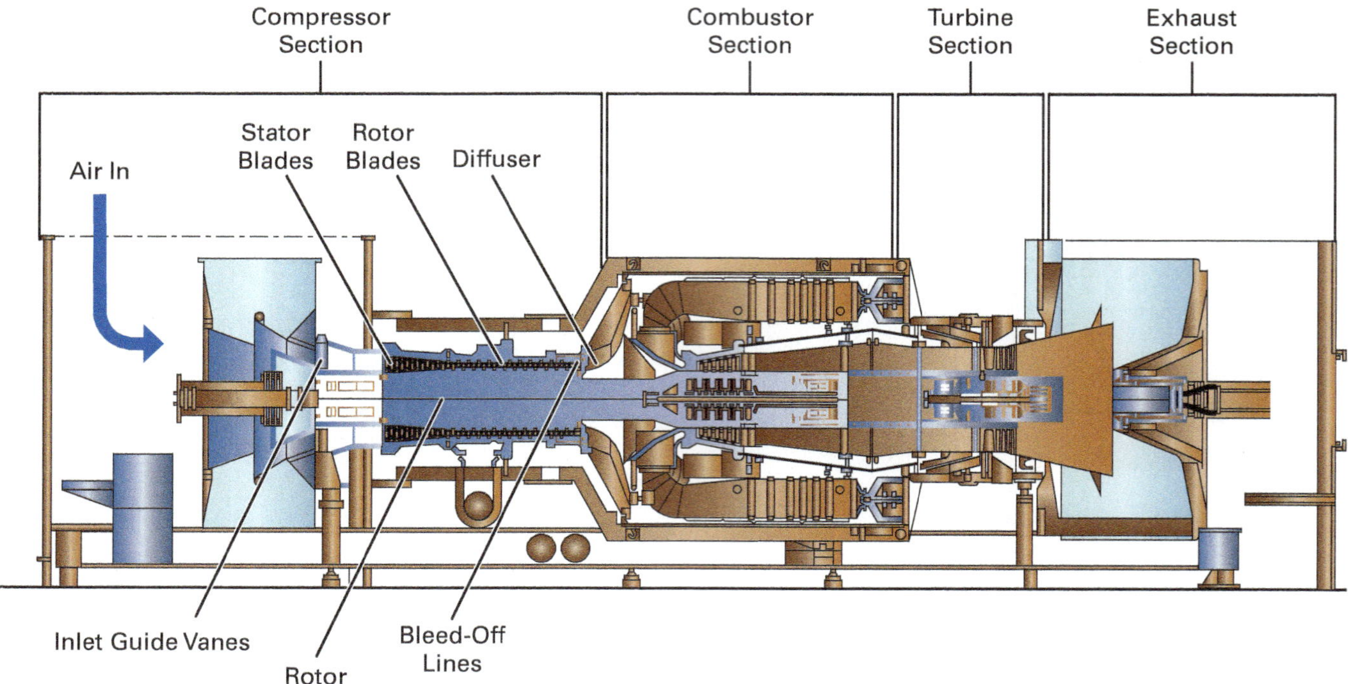

Figure 31 Major gas turbine components.

In what is known as a *can-annular combustor*, compressed air flows in a straight path toward and through the combustors (*Figure 34*). Some air flows through slits in the combustor liner to cool the burning gases. Larger holes in the liner permit compressed air for combustion to enter. Some of the air entering the larger holes is directed back toward and into the fuel-air mixture entering at the front of the combustor. This creates additional turbulence needed to mix the air and fuel more efficiently.

Some combustors use a reverse airflow design (*Figure 35*). In this case, *reverse airflow* means that the compressed air enters the combustion section at the same end at which the combustion gases exit. The air then reverses direction, moving back toward the combustor inlet. The air flows into the combustor liners through holes and slits. A portion of the compressed air is routed to the head of the combustor where it mixes with and atomizes the fuel. The mixture is injected into the combustor and ignited.

Fuel Nozzles, Igniters, and Flame Detectors

Fuel sprays into the combustor through a nozzle that atomizes the fuel with compressed air. A variety of nozzle designs are used in gas turbines today.

Igniters, which can be compared to spark plugs, ignite the fuel-air mixture to get the process started. The igniters are usually installed only in two adjacent combustors, rather than each combustor having its own igniter (*Figure 36*). They receive power from the ignition transformers that create enough voltage for the spark to arc across a gap. The combustors are interconnected by crossfire tubes, as shown in *Figure 36*.

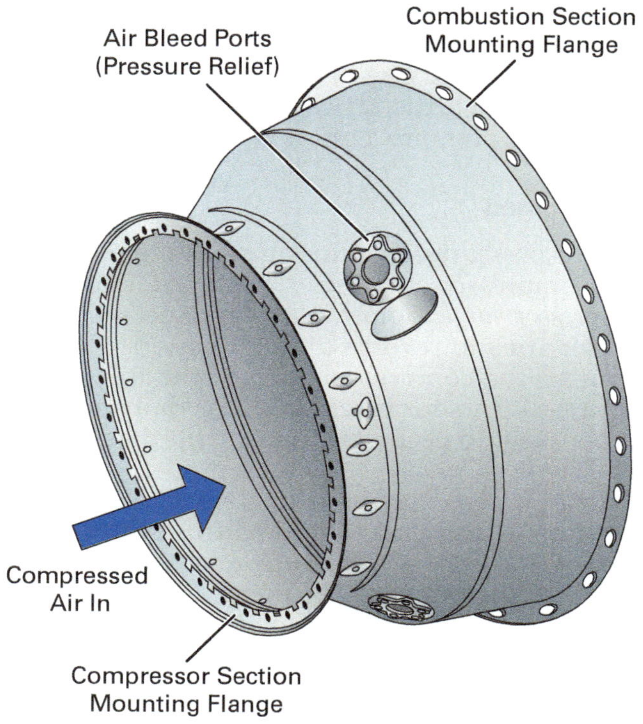

Figure 32 Diffuser section.

The chambers without igniters are ignited by the flames from the two igniter-equipped chambers traveling through the crossfire tubes.

Once combustion begins and stabilizes, it is self-sustaining. The igniters only fire long enough to ensure that a stable flame is established.

Flame detectors are usually located only on two adjacent combustors, like the igniters. But they are located on the opposite side of the ring, on the combustors farthest from the igniters. Detecting proper combustion on the opposite side indicates that all the combustors in between have ignited as expected. The sensors may detect combustion by light, heat, or both. If ignition does not take place or combustion ceases for any reason, the flame detector sends a signal to the fuel system governor to stop the flow of fuel.

The transition pieces, seen at the right end of *Figure 35*, carry the gases from the combustors to the turbine. In a reverse airflow combustor, the compressed combustion air flows around the transition pieces before turning back to the combustion process. The compressed airflow reduces the temperature of the exhaust gases. The air temperature increases as a result, which benefits the combustion process.

1.4.3 Turbine Section Components

The turbine section of a gas turbine is similar to that of a steam turbine. Instead of steam, the gases from the combustors are directed at the turbine blades to apply a rotating force to the turbine shaft. Thus, both gas and steam turbines extract energy from a moving fluid as it flows through.

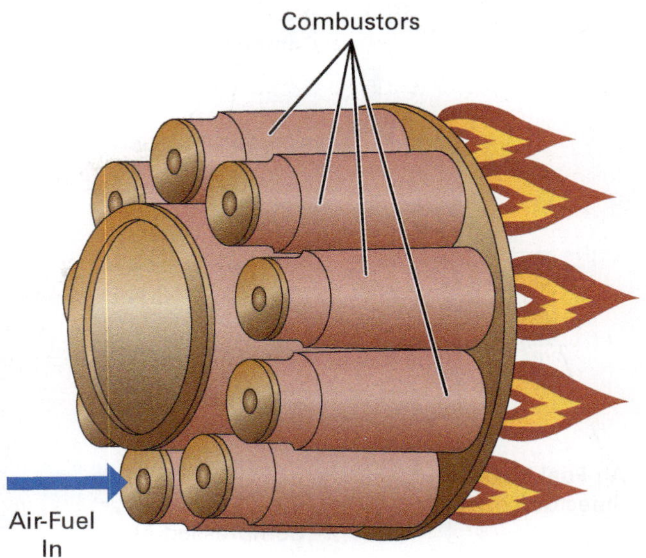

Figure 33 A ring of combustors.

The major parts of the turbine section include the nozzles (stators), rotor wheels, and the exhaust silencer.

Nozzles

Combustion gases enter the turbine through a row of stationary blades referred to as *nozzles*. The nozzles direct the hot gases into the rotor blades, forcing rotation. As in the compressor, one ring of stationary nozzles coupled with a wheel of rotor blades is considered a stage (*Figure 37*).

A ring of nozzles at the beginning of each stage directs the gases into the adjacent rotor blades. Like steam turbines, each stage is larger

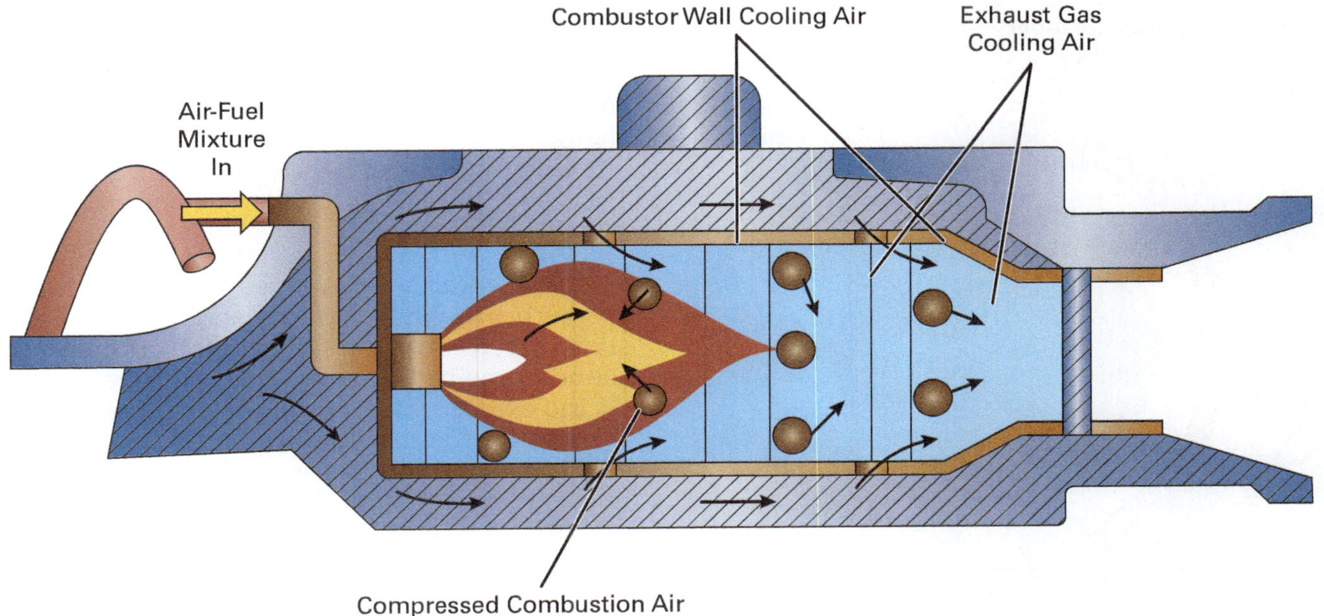

Figure 34 Airflow through a can-annular combustor.

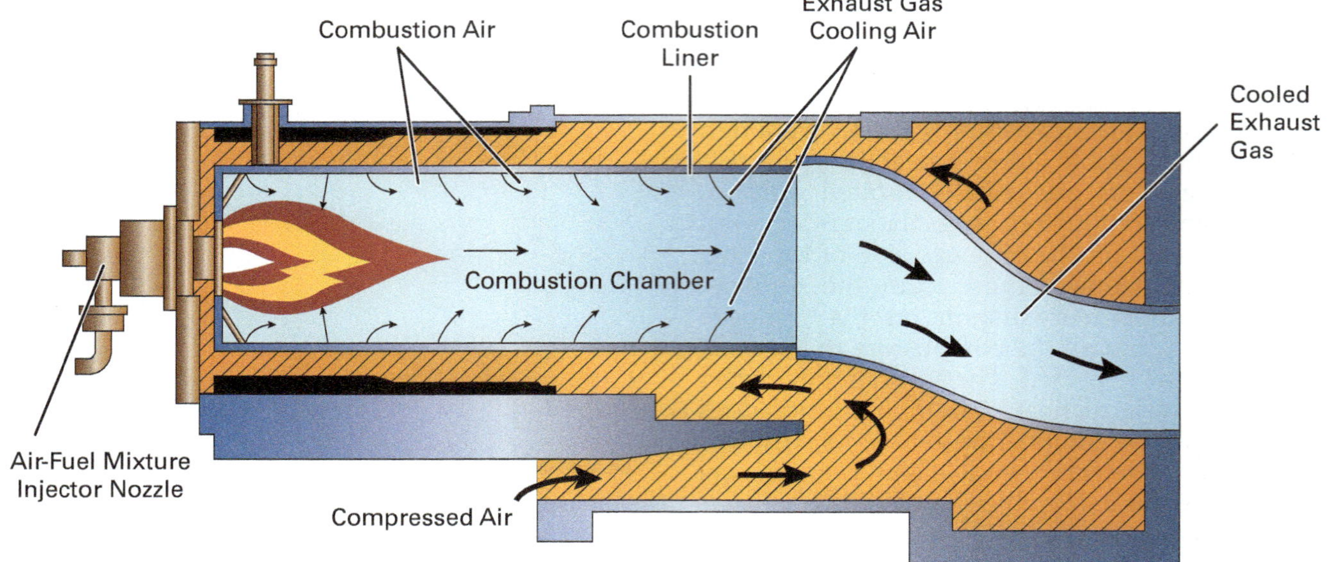

Figure 35 Reverse airflow combustor.

in diameter than the preceding stage to extract the maximum power from the gases passing through. As the gases pass through the early stages and the pressure falls, the remaining stages need larger wheels to use the remaining energy effectively.

Rotor Blades

Like a steam turbine, the rotor blades are attached to a wheel that is attached to the turbine shaft. The turbine shaft passing through the turbine section may be straight or cone-shaped. When cone-shaped, the cone grows in diameter along with the diameter of the wheels. Many turbine

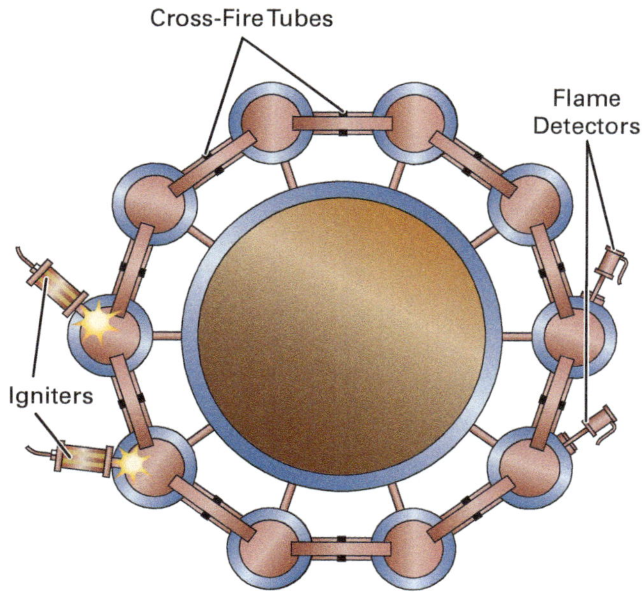

Figure 36 Ignition system layout.

shafts are hollow to allow compressed air from the front to flow through the middle and cool the shaft and rotor hubs.

You'll recall that there are two basic blade shapes found in steam turbines—impulse blades and reaction blades. However, most gas turbine rotor blades are a combination of impulse blades and reaction blades. The base of the rotor blade is shaped like an impulse blade, while the tip is shaped more like a reaction blade (*Figure 38*). The more streamlined reaction shape at the tip allows the gases to move through more efficiently around the outer portion of the rotor.

Engineers and manufacturers consistently conduct research and development on turbine blades to determine the ideal shape for each application. For that reason, do not assume that all gas turbine blades share a common profile. Many subtle changes have been made over the years, and changes will continue in an effort to maximize efficiency and performance.

Exhaust Silencer

The hot combustion gases exit the turbine through an exhaust silencer (*Figure 39*). The silencer contains a series of baffles to quiet the sound of the turbine, like an automotive muffler. As the exhaust gases travel through the silencer, the offset baffles inside absorb sound.

The exhaust diffuser is positioned at the turbine exhaust outlet as shown in *Figure 39*. Like a diffuser used to distribute room air in an air conditioning system, it helps turn the air and reduce turbulence. But its primary function is to lower

NCCER – *Millwright*

the velocity of the escaping gases, which leads to a slight increase in back pressure. This has a positive effect on turbine performance.

1.4.4 Gas Turbine Auxiliary Systems

The major auxiliary systems needed to support gas turbines include the following:

- Starting system
- Lube oil system
- Fuel system
- Water cooling system

Starting Systems

Large gas turbines need powerful, heavy-duty starters to be able to turn the heavy compressor and turbine rotors for several minutes until ignition occurs and the turbine can sustain itself. All starters use a clutch of some sort to disengage the starter motor as the turbine ignites and accelerates. Most industrial gas turbines use either air motors, diesel engines, or electric motors to power the starter. The type of starter used varies from one turbine to the next.

Air-motor starters are generally used for smaller gas turbines and aircraft engines. They are small and rugged and can attain very high speeds. The volume of high-pressure air needed to drive these motors is stored in an accumulator.

Diesel engines are often used to start large power-generation turbines during black starts. They do not require external electrical power to operate, and they can provide the power needed to bring large industrial turbines up to self-sustaining speeds.

Electric motors are used to start the largest gas turbines because they can deliver the most power at the fastest rate. They also require very little maintenance. Electric motors usually start gas turbines that operate intermittently to support peak electrical loads. They are useless during black starts though, unless the plant has diesel-powered emergency generators or similar equipment to provide temporary power. A gearbox is required for speed reduction and to increase the torque applied to the starter.

Lube Oil System

A properly operating lube oil system (*Figure 40*) is essential. The system must reliably provide filtered lubricant at the proper temperature and pressure. A loss of lubrication can bring a turbine to a halt quickly, with significant internal damage

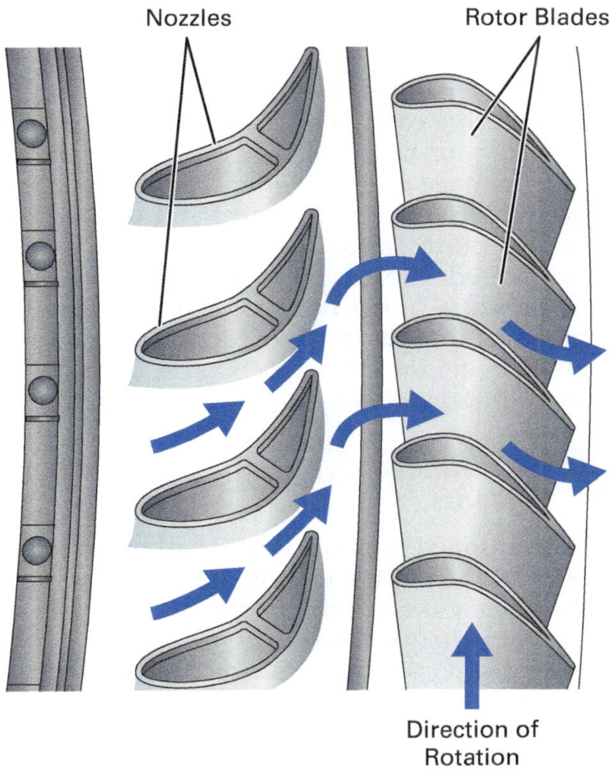

Figure 37 Nozzles and rotor blades.

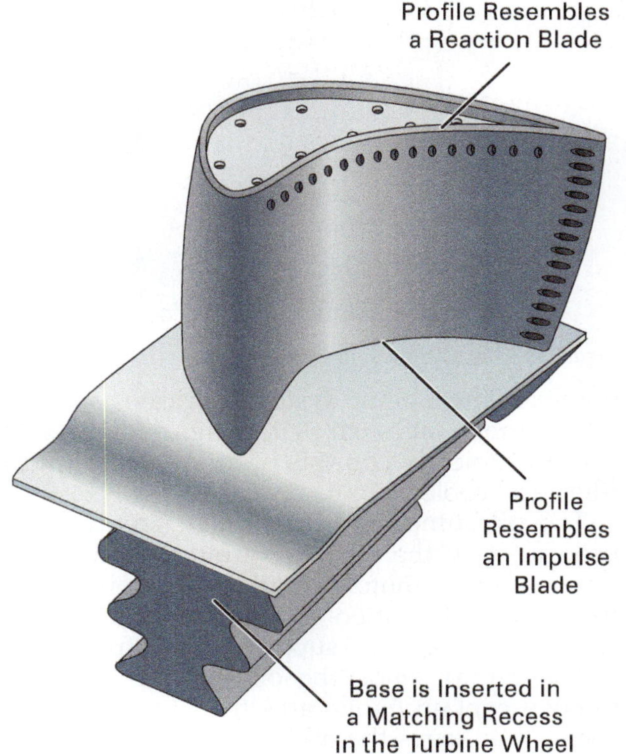

Figure 38 Common rotor blade profile.

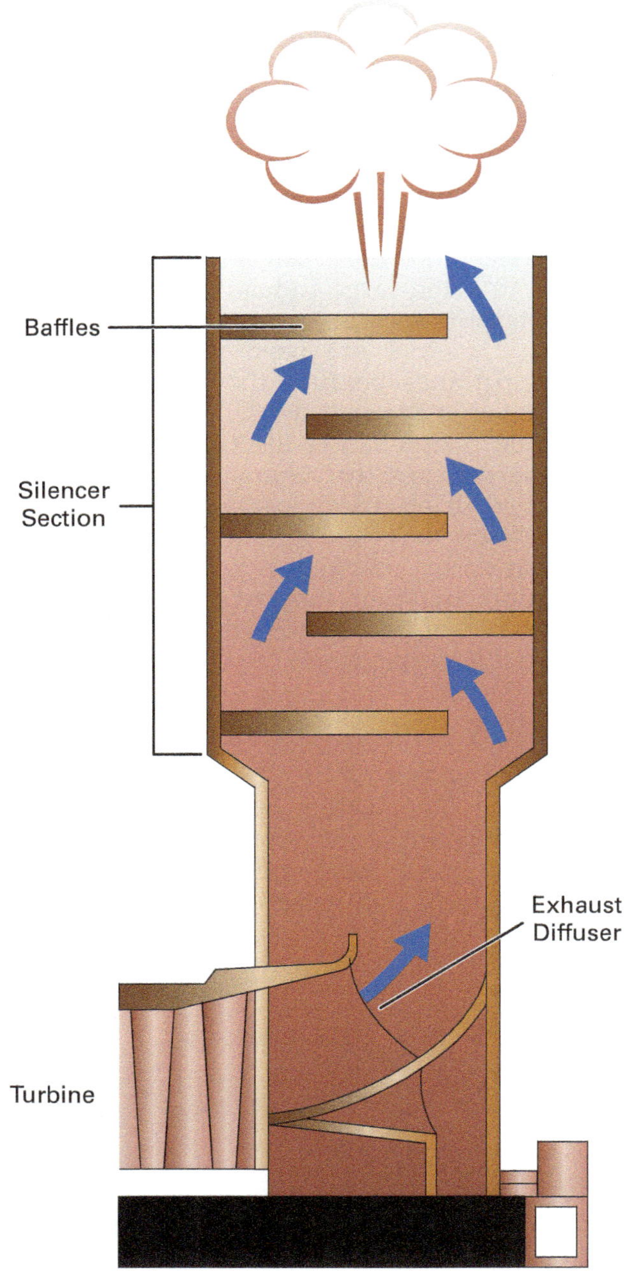

Figure 39 Gas turbine exhaust silencer.

Figure 40 responds to the oil temperature sensor. The valve modulates oil flow through the cooler as necessary to maintain the proper temperature downstream. The oil cooler is a heat exchanger that uses water or air to remove heat from the oil (*Figure 41*).

The cooled oil flows to all lubrication points and then drains back into the sump. Many flow, temperature, and pressure sensors and gauges are installed in the system to closely monitor system operation.

Fuel System

The fuel system must consistently feed fuel to the nozzles on the combustors. The fuel feed rate must also be consistent from one combustor to another. The fuel system construction details vary depending on the type of fuel being used.

A typical light fuel-oil system (*Figure 42*) consists of individual *flow dividers* for each combustor. The flow dividers are constructed like gear pumps, but the fuel flowing through them causes them to rotate; they have no drive mechanism. However, as shown in *Figure 42*, they are all connected to a common shaft. This means that they must all turn at the same rate, called their *frequency match*. The same volume of fuel flows into each combustor as a result.

If the turbine is capable of firing on heavy fuel oil, the same basic system is used. However, the flow dividers in that case are powered by a hydraulic motor driving the common connecting shaft. The result is the same—an equal volume of fuel entering each combustor.

Natural or manufactured gases are much easier to manage and deliver to the combustors. The fuel is stored under pressure and delivered as a gas. No pump is required, but the fuel supply is still filtered. A pressure regulating valve controls the pressure in the fuel manifold. With an equal pressure applied to each fuel nozzle, and each nozzle being the same precise size, consistent and equal flow is delivered to the combustors.

1.4.5 *Combined-Cycle and Cogeneration Plants*

As mentioned previously, gas turbines produce a lot of heat from the combustion process. Ideally, that energy is captured and used in some way. It is a lot of energy to waste.

Combined-cycle systems use the heat from the gas turbine exhaust to generate steam (*Figure 43*). The steam is then used to drive a second turbine. As is the case for most steam systems, the condensate from the steam is captured and reheated.

possible. The lube oil system lubricates and cools vital components such as bearings and gears. The system typically consists of an oil sump, pump, filter, and cooler.

The oil sump, or reservoir, is simply a tank used to store the oil. The pump, usually driven by an electric motor, circulates the oil through the system. It is often mounted on top of the oil sump, drawing its oil supply directly from it.

The pump sends the oil through a filter to remove contaminants, and then through an oil cooler that keeps the oil between 80°F and 120°F (~27°C to 49°C). The three-way valve shown in

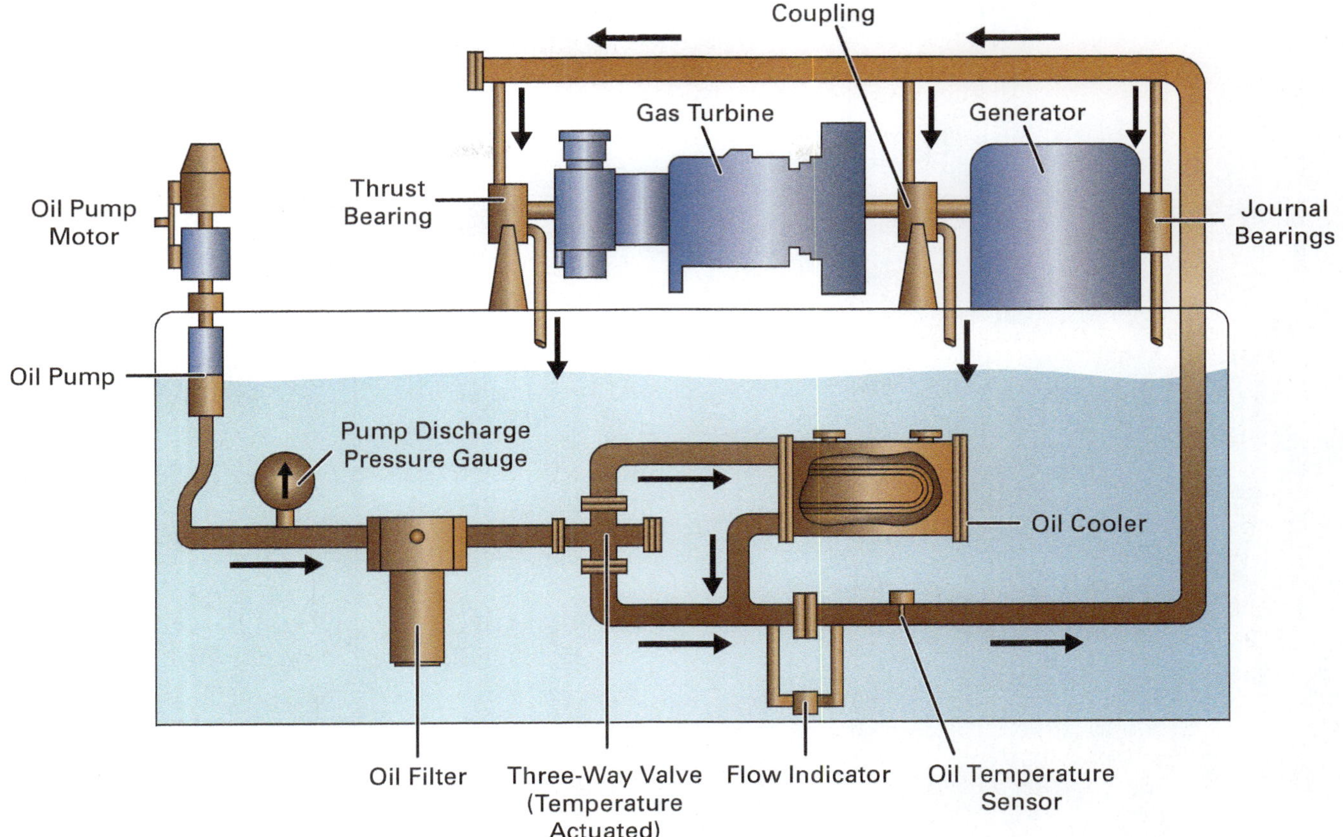

Figure 40 Lube oil system.

A combined-cycle system can generate as much as 50 percent more power than the gas turbine alone, without additional fuel consumption.

Cogeneration plants are also referred to as *combined heat and power (CHP) plants*. The primary difference between a CHP and combined-cycle system is that a CHP system uses the steam generated by the turbine exhaust for purposes other than generating electrical power. In an industrial facility, for example, the steam may be used for heating the plant or in a manufacturing process.

It is important to note that a power plant does not have to be one or the other. In many cases today, steam generated by gas turbines is used to both drive a turbine and provide steam to other processes.

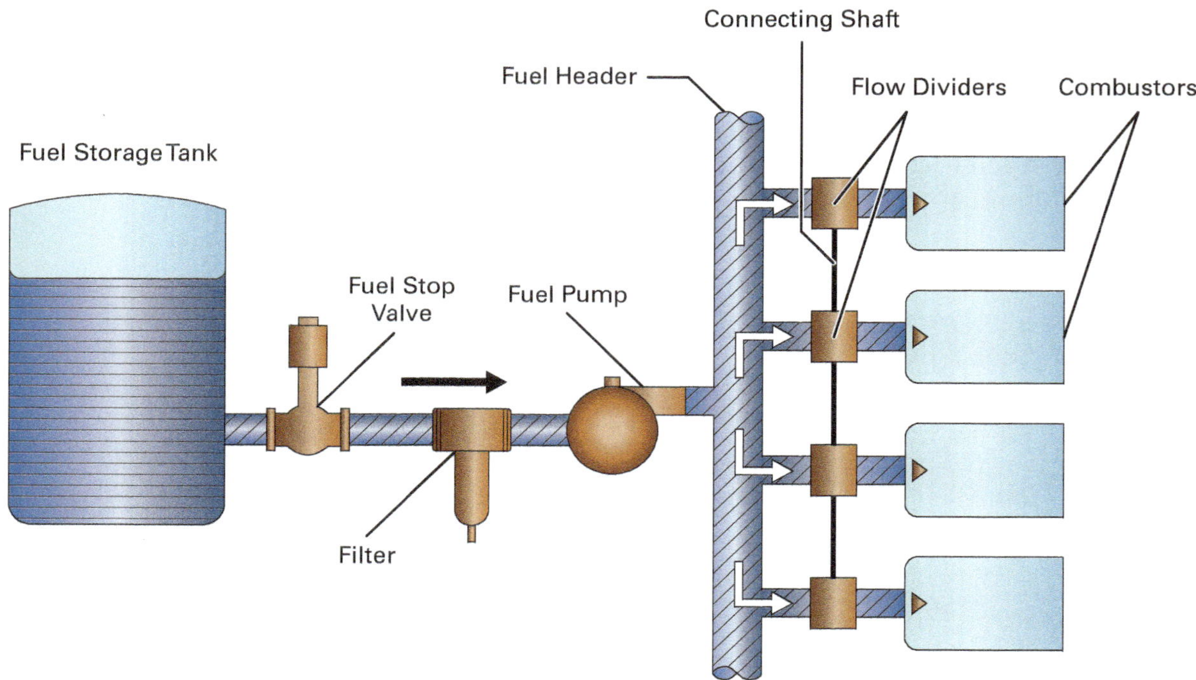

Figure 41 Air-cooled oil cooler serving a power-generation gas turbine aboard an oil platform.

Figure 42 Light fuel-oil delivery system.

NCCER – *Millwright*

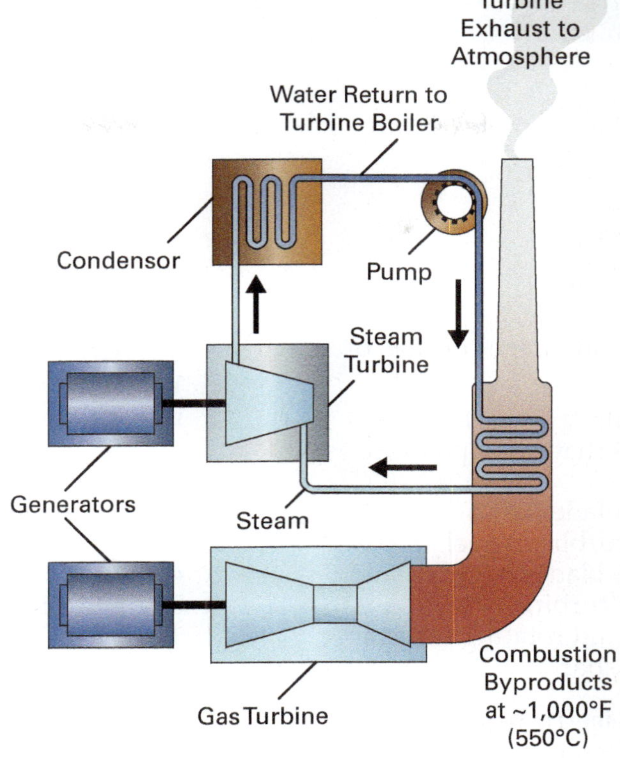

Figure 43 Block diagram of a combined-cycle power plant.

1.0.0 Section Review

1. Reaction turbine wheels are fully immersed in the fluid that forces them to rotate, like a windmill.

   a. True
   b. False

2. Which reaction turbine wheel is the *most* common in today's hydroelectric turbines?

   a. Francis wheel
   b. Pelton wheel
   c. Single-nozzle Pelton wheel
   d. Kaplan wheel

3. The main oil pump for a steam turbine lubrication system is typically located ______.

   a. at the low-pressure end of the shaft, adjacent to the generator
   b. at the high-pressure end of the shaft, opposite the generator
   c. on the generator shaft, opposite the turbine
   d. about midway through the low-pressure section of the turbine

4. Inside a gas turbine can-annular combustor, compressed air is directed through large holes in the combustor liner and directed back toward the entering fuel-air mixture to ______.

   a. reduce the pressure in the combustor
   b. stop the combustion process and shut down the turbine
   c. preheat the combustors prior to ignition
   d. create turbulence and improve the air-fuel mixing action

1. A windmill is a reasonable example of a(n) ______.

    a. reaction turbine wheel
    b. impulse turbine wheel
    c. multistage turbine wheel
    d. conductor turbine wheel

2. On a multistage turbine, one stage consists of ______.

    a. any number of stationary vanes and rotating turbine wheels that are exposed to the same pressure
    b. one set of stationary blades or vanes and an adjacent rotating turbine wheel
    c. one pair of stationary blades or vanes and two adjacent rotating turbine wheels
    d. all stationary blades and rotating wheels attached to the same shaft

3. Pelton wheels for hydroelectric turbines are built with rotor vanes resembling ______.

    a. bags
    b. flat pans with grooves
    c. bowls that are split in the center
    d. aircraft wings

4. Most hydroelectric turbines use ______.

    a. impulse turbine wheels
    b. reaction turbine wheels
    c. condensing turbine wheels
    d. gas turbine wheels

5. Which style of turbine wheel looks like a ship's propeller?

    a. Pelton wheel
    b. Francis wheel
    c. Kaplan wheel
    d. Sirius wheel

6. Steam turbines rotate very slowly, usually no more than 100 rpm.

    a. True
    b. False

7. When are jacking oil systems needed in a steam turbine?

    a. During startup and shutdown, and often when the turning gear is in operation
    b. Consistently, throughout the range of operating speeds
    c. When the main oil pump needs to be serviced while the turbine remains running
    d. When the steam pressure from the source is less than ideal

8. As they exit a gas turbine, the exhaust gases generally range in temperature from ______.

    a. 100°F to 250°F (~38°C to 120°C)
    b. 400°F to 650°F (~200°C to 350°C)
    c. 800°F to 1,100°F (~425°C to 600°C)
    d. 1,800°F to 2,500°F (~1,000°C to 1,400°C)

9. The final section in a gas turbine compressor that captures the compressed air and delivers it to the combustion section is called the ______.

    a. rotor section
    b. diffuser section
    c. turbine section
    d. transition section

10. During black starts, large gas turbines are often rotated for startup by a(n) ______.

    a. air-powered starter
    b. electric motor-driven starter
    c. manually powered starter
    d. diesel engine-driven starter

Trade Terms Introduced in This Module

Babbitt: A soft metal alloy that typically contains tin, copper, lead, and antimony.

Black starts: Startups conducted on turbine systems while there is no power currently available from the grid.

Condensing turbine: A steam turbine that has a condenser in place to condense any remaining steam as it exits the turbine. The resulting condensate returns to the boiler or other steam-generating process.

Generator: An electrical apparatus constructed much like an electric motor that converts mechanical energy into electricity.

Kinetic energy: The energy an object contains resulting from being placed in motion.

Mechanical energy: The stored (potential) energy plus the moving (kinetic) energy associated with a machine.

Noncondensing turbine: A steam turbine that uses any remaining steam exiting the turbine to support other industrial processes.

Penstock: A channel designed to direct water into a hydroelectric turbine rotor.

Turbine: A machine that converts the energy contained in a moving stream of fluid to mechanical energy.

Water hammer: A hydraulic shock that occurs when rapidly moving slugs of water impact pipe walls, especially when the water must change direction.

Additional Resources

This module presents thorough resources for task training. The following reference material is suggested for further study.

Advances in Steam Turbines for Modern Power Plants. 1st Edition. Cambridge, United Kingdom: Woodhead Publishing.

Gas Turbine Design, Components and System Design Integration. 1st Edition. Meinhard T. Schobeiri. New York, NY: Springer International Publishing.

General Electric—Gas Turbines. **https://www.ge.com/gas-power/products/gas-turbines**.

General Electric—Steam Turbines. **https://www.ge.com/gas-power/products/steam-turbines**.

Siemens Energy—Gas Turbines. **https://www.siemens-energy.com/global/en/offerings/power-generation/gas-turbines.html?gclid=EAIaIQobChMIv8Kegd-o-QIVI8LCBB2MQQGaEAAYASABEgIQE_D_BwE**.

Siemens Energy—Steam Turbines **https://www.siemens-energy.com/global/en/offerings/power-generation/steam-turbines.html?gclid=EAIaIQobChMIv8Kegd-o-QIVI8LCBB2MQQGaEAAYASADEgJN6vD_BwE**.

Figure Credits

iStock@photosoup, Module Opener

iStock@Filipp Borshch, Figure 1

iStock@Kinwun, Figure 4

iStock@Satakorn, Figure 5

Shutterstock.com/Mariusz Hajdarowicz, Figure 6

"Francis Runner grandcoulee.jpg" by U.S. Bureau of Reclamation photo archives is licensed under the Public Domain, Figure 7

Shutterstock.com/Jakkrit kladpu, Figure 8

iStock@KarelGallas, Figure 9

iStock@c1a1p1c1o1m1, Figure 10

iStock@industryview, Figure 11

Combined Cycle Journal, Figure 15

Courtesy of Dover Precision Products and Bearings Plus, Figures 18 (B), 20

"Rupture disk used 01.jpg" by Hans-Peter Scholz is licensed under CC BY-SA 3.0, Figure 21

Compliments of the Voith Group, Figure 25

Shutterstock.com/Hafizzuddin, Figure 26

iStock@imantsu, Figure 28

iStock@pichitstocker, Figure 41

Section Review Answer Key

SECTION 1.0.0

Answer	Section Reference	Objective
1. a	1.1.2	1a
2. a	1.2.2	1b
3. b	1.3.3	1c
4. d	1.4.2	1d

User Update

NCCER makes every effort to keep its textbooks up-to-date and free of technical errors. We appreciate your help in this process. If you find an error, a typographical mistake, or an inaccuracy in NCCER's curricula, please submit a User Update form by visiting **https://www.nccer.org/olf**. You can also scan the QR code using the camera on your phone or mobile device to access the form.

Preventive and Predictive Maintenance

OVERVIEW

Machinery must be properly maintained to operate reliably. Preventive and periodic maintenance includes tasks that help keep machines running properly. Predictive maintenance represents a different concept, focusing on data collection and specialized techniques to reveal problems as they develop. Predictive maintenance includes nondestructive evaluation and testing methods such as radiography and vibration analysis. Preventive and predictive maintenance programs work together to support a plant's reliability and productivity.

Module 15508

Trainees with successful module completions may be eligible for credentialing through the NCCER Registry. To learn more, go to **www.nccer.org** or contact us at 1.888.622.3720. Our website, **www.nccer.org**, has information on the latest product releases and training.

Your feedback is welcome. You may email your comments to **curriculum@nccer.org**, send general comments and inquiries to **info@nccer.org** or fill in the User Update form at the back of this module.

This information is general in nature and intended for training purposes only. The actual performance of activities described in this manual requires compliance with all applicable operating, service, maintenance, and safety procedures under the direction of qualified personnel. References in this manual to patented or proprietary devices do not constitute a recommendation of their use.

From *Millwright, Trainee Guide*. NCCER.
Copyright © 2023 by NCCER. Published by Pearson. All rights reserved.

PREVENTIVE AND PREDICTIVE MAINTENANCE

Objective

Successful completion of this module prepares you to do the following:

1. Define and describe preventive and predictive maintenance activities.
   a. Define and describe preventive maintenance activities and benefits.
   b. Define and describe predictive maintenance and its role in maintenance programs.
   c. Identify and describe various nondestructive inspection techniques.

Performance Tasks

This is a knowledge-based module. There are no Performance Tasks.

Trade Terms

Delamination
Eddy current
Ferrography
Pareto principle

Sensory inspection
Tribology
Welding procedure specification (WPS)

Industry Recognized Credentials

If you are training through an NCCER-accredited sponsor, you may be eligible for credentials from NCCER's Registry. The ID number for this module is 15508. Note that this module may have been used in other NCCER curricula and may apply to other level completions. Contact NCCER's Registry at 1.888.622.3720 or go to **www.nccer.org** for more information.

You can also show off your industry-recognized credentials online with NCCER's digital badges. Transform your knowledge, skills, and achievements into badges that you can share across social media platforms, send to your network, and add to your resume. For more information, visit **www.nccer.org**.

How to Access Resources

This craft has additional videos and resources to enhance your learning experience. To view these resources, scan the QR below. The videos and resources are separated by module.

You can scan this code using the camera on your phone or mobile device to view these videos and resources.

Contents

Figures and Tables

1.0.0 Preventive and Predictive Maintenance

Objective

Define and describe preventive and predictive maintenance activities.

a. Define and describe preventive maintenance activities and benefits.
b. Define and describe predictive maintenance and its role in maintenance programs.
c. Identify and describe various nondestructive inspection techniques.

Trade Terms

Delamination: The separation or splitting apart of layers.

Eddy current: An induced electrical current that is generated in a conductive material exposed to a moving magnetic field.

Ferrography: A specific type of oil analysis that focuses on lubricant contaminants, their characteristics, and their sources.

Pareto principle: A theory based on the work of Italian economist Vilfredo Pareto that states, for many outcomes, roughly 80 percent of consequences come from 20 percent of the causes or events. Also referred to as the *80/20 rule*, the theory manifests itself in many fields and applications.

Sensory inspection: A maintenance inspection that incorporates sight, sound, smell, and touch.

Tribology: The study of lubrication, friction, and the wear of interacting surfaces.

Welding procedure specification (WPS): A document specifying all essential procedural details related to project-specific welds.

Machines and mechanical systems need attention. Machines will break down at times, despite your best efforts. But giving them the proper attention can go a long way toward ensuring they operate as designed.

The purpose of an equipment maintenance program is to maximize equipment reliability, which ultimately saves money and enhances productivity. Equipment reliability is maximized by accumulating data through testing, analyzing trends, compiling repair histories, and applying the right maintenance at the right time. Good maintenance programs help reduce equipment downtime and unscheduled work. Predictive maintenance especially allows millwrights and industrial mechanics to stay ahead of problems.

In some facilities, maintenance and testing is performed by specialists and outside contractors rather than the plant staff. However, millwrights and industrial mechanics must understand the processes and tests involved to monitor the work of others. On the other hand, you may be employed by a contractor that specializes in preventive and predictive maintenance and serves a variety of clients. In that case, maintenance-related tasks will be a major part of your workday.

1.1.0 Preventive Maintenance

Preventive maintenance (PM) refers to the periodic inspection and maintenance of plant assets and equipment to avoid or uncover conditions that may lead to equipment failure or shortened life (*Figure 1*). The primary purpose of a PM program is to prevent breakdowns and unscheduled repairs. It is important to identify and prioritize the most critical tasks to ensure they are done at the right time.

PM duties are generally grouped into the following activities:

- Inspecting
- Lubricating
- Replacing consumables and high-wear parts
- Cleaning
- Adjusting
- Documenting and reporting (*Figure 2*)

Figure 1 Inspecting a robotic system.

Figure 2 Documenting inspection data.

Primary PM needs are scheduled according to their priority and recommended interval. The most important PM activities cover items that are critical to safety and/or economics. If a failure could cause loss of life or injury and/or shut down production, preventing it is a high priority. Items that could cause major economic loss are next in priority, although they may be interrelated with higher priority items because of the complexity of the machinery.

Each system and its components must be analyzed and prioritized this way. Labor and material projections can then be made to assess and prepare for both present and future needs. This helps maintenance programs function efficiently, ensuring that the necessary resources are available at the right time.

Another important facet of a good PM program is the careful observation of the equipment while working. **Sensory inspection**, which involves using sight, sound, smell, and touch, is used to determine how systems are performing. Changing a compressor's oil may be the assigned task, but the senses must be used to examine other parts, listen, and recognize when something isn't right. In some cases, the assigned task will be a simple walk-around inspection that largely relies entirely on the senses to evaluate equipment performance.

Some activities are difficult to place in the maintenance category, but they are also difficult to categorize otherwise. While their classification as maintenance may be debatable, the framework of a maintenance program does offer a convenient means of planning for them. These activities include the following:

- Upgrades and engineering-related changes
- Corrective work
- Scheduled overhauls

Upgrades and engineering-related changes aren't generally released on a schedule. They are developed and released as engineers and manufacturers see fit. Even if the improvements are designed to enhance the maintainability of the equipment, the improvement effort isn't generally considered an element of the maintenance program. However, the PM program is often used to plan for them, then collect data that documents the effectiveness of the improvement after changes have been made (*Figure 3*). Although it may not seem like maintenance work, maintenance staff often completes the work.

Corrective work is generally considered to be needed repairs that allow production to continue without a major shutdown. In some cases, the need for these repairs was identified during scheduled maintenance. Corrective maintenance activities do need to be scheduled, and for that reason, the responsibility for them may fall to the maintenance team. An example would be repairing storm-related electrical damage to back-up systems, while the primary systems remain running. In many facilities, redundancy in pumps, compressors, and other critical equipment is a fundamental requirement.

Major overhauls are often conducted during a production shutdown. A significant equipment overhaul may be deemed necessary due to the results of testing, or simply because a specific amount of time has passed. While some see that work as maintenance, others do not. The assignment may also be affected by the skills and resources of the maintenance staff. They must be knowledgeable enough to complete a complex overhaul and have the required equipment. The maintenance team must also be able to handle the work without ignoring other responsibilities. Since the overhaul of complex machinery may require both specialized skills and equipment, contractors or equipment manufacturers are often brought in to complete the work.

Figure 3 Analyzing robotic performance on an assembly line.

Once again, the maintenance program offers the needed structure to schedule and plan the work. Since a PM program requires a significant investment of time and labor, the expenditure must be justified. The benefits used to justify the maintenance effort and its cost generally include the following:

- Reducing reactive and emergency calls
- Increasing equipment availability
- Extending the life cycle of the equipment
- Minimizing spare parts inventory
- Reducing total overtime hours
- Improving product quality

1.1.1 Reducing Reactive and Emergency Calls

Many plant activities for millwrights and mechanics involve reacting to problems as they occur and performing emergency repairs. Some of this is inevitable, but a good PM program can eliminate many problems before they occur, freeing personnel and resources to perform planned maintenance.

1.1.2 Increasing Equipment Availability

PM is planned and scheduled to meet production needs so that potential problems can be detected before they affect production. Scheduled PM activities should be planned in a manner that supports production rather than interfering with it. This ensures that the equipment remains available when needed.

1.1.3 Extending the Life Cycle of the Equipment

Proper cleaning, lubricating, and adjusting adds to the efficiency and life of the equipment. Changing the lubricating oil in a machine at the recommended interval, for example, is expected to extend equipment life. Contaminated oil increases wear in moving parts. If the oil isn't changed on time, it could affect equipment warranties.

A decreased operational demand on the equipment often decreases the frequency of maintenance since many maintenance functions are scheduled based on equipment operating hours. On the other hand, increased production goals require a more aggressive maintenance program to keep up with the tasks.

1.1.4 Minimizing Spare Parts Inventory

Keeping spare parts in inventory is expensive (*Figure 4*). With proper PM, the spare parts inventory can usually be minimized. Having spare parts costing thousands of dollars remain on the shelf for years is not a very good investment. From an economic point of view, expensive and unique components are better purchased as needed instead of maintaining a large inventory of them.

Although minimizing the spare parts inventory can result in reduced costs, it can work against you if the required maintenance tasks are not completed on schedule. The life of the parts must be protected if a reduced inventory is going to work. Minimizing the spare parts inventory requires collecting historical data and using common sense in purchases, but the net gain is worthwhile.

1.1.5 Reducing Total Overtime Hours

The cost for overtime labor to complete repairs cuts directly into profits because it is not generally factored into the product costs. Thus, any reduction of overtime labor enhances a company's profits. As mentioned previously, conducting maintenance on schedule can eliminate many equipment-related emergencies.

1.1.6 Improving Product Quality

To be competitive, most manufacturers follow an extensive quality improvement program. Maintaining equipment at the optimum performance level is often part of the campaign. Quality improvement programs often include maintenance standards that must be met. After all, the condition of the machinery making the products has a great deal to do with the results.

Figure 4 Managing an inventory of industrial parts.

1.2.0 Predictive Maintenance

Predictive maintenance (PDM) involves the testing, measuring, and tracking of physical characteristics or operating performance of equipment. Nondestructive tests and evaluations are the main tools used in predictive maintenance.

Various nondestructive tests measure and identify wear and deterioration and become part of a machine's health records. The same type of testing is also applied to new parts and important welds to ensure there are no flaws that would jeopardize equipment performance and integrity. While PM focuses on mechanical tasks and measures, PDM focuses on testing, data collection, and analysis. PDM enhances and supports a good PM program with actionable information developed from testing.

One example of the difference between PDM and PM is found in oil changes. Changing the oil in a machine after 500 hours of operation is considered PM. However, a sample of the oil drained from the reservoir is often analyzed to better determine the internal condition of the machine. Perhaps the oil has water in it consistently, and a solution to that may become a priority. A high concentration of wear metals may cause concerns about longevity. Oil sampling and testing are part of a PDM program. A sample oil analysis report is shown in *Figure 5*. Oil sampling and testing is part of a field called tribology, which will be discussed later in this module.

Table 1 compares some PM and PDM program characteristics. A PDM program is set up using the same priorities as PM, and it has virtually the same objectives. PDM, though, is often done in the background while the equipment is operating.

Lubricant Condition	GOOD
Machine Condition	OK

Account		Equipment Data		Sample Data	
Account #:	654321	Equipment:	#3701-A	Sample #:	11
Company:	DJK Plastics	Component:	#2 Helical Gear	Lab ID#:	ID5
Address:	651 Plastic Way	Manufacturer:	HexGear	Lab:	Boise, ID
	Greenville, ID	Part #:	HG43-9	Sample Date:	11/07/2022
	69814	Oil Capacity:	4.5 qt	Rec'd Date:	11/14/2022
Contact:	Sam Hill			Test Date:	11/17/2022

Filter Information	Oil Product		Client Notes
<NA>	Manufacturer: Product: Viscosity:	Lube Meister Diablo 320 ISO 320	

Sample #	Wear Metals (ppm)										Multisource Metals (ppm)						Additive Metals (ppm)				
	Iron	Nickel	Chromium	Aluminum	Copper	Lead	Tin	Silver	Cadmium	Vanadium	Antimony	Boron	Lithium	Manganese	Potassium	Sodium	Barium	Calcium	Magnesium	Phosphorus	Zinc
9	9	–	–	–	–	–	–	–	–	–	–	–	–	–	9	–	3	7	1	85	38
10	14	–	–	–	–	–	1	–	2	–	–	3	–	–	6	–	2	9	2	90	55
11	77	–	–	–	–	2	–	–	–	–	–	–	–	1	9	–	3	9	2	76	49

Lab Notes
Increase in iron concentration needs to be monitored

Figure 5 Sample oil analysis report.

Table 1 Comparison of Preventive and Predictive Maintenance

Actions	Preventive Maintenance (PM)	Predictive Maintenance (PDM)
Diagnosis and inspection	Includes standard PM inspections and services to extend equipment life.	Uses diagnostic tools and compares operation and performance to a normal operating profile.
Detecting abnormal conditions	Consists of visual and teardown inspections and estimating potential points of failure.	Consists of monitoring specific characteristics and establishing trends; more accurately predicts points of failure and their timeframe.
Correcting expected deficiencies	Consists of periodic component replacement based on history or a best guess.	Consists of replacing components based on deeper testing and determining when they need to be replaced with greater precision; maximizes the life of parts.
Reduction in repair costs	Chance of replacing sound, serviceable parts through time-based actions; some parts and materials may be overstocked without realizing it.	Predicts the life of operating components based on test data; leads to more timely parts orders, fewer surprises, and a reduced inventory.

As with PM, the primary objective of PDM is to predict and prevent component failures in equipment. However, PDM's secondary objectives help make a PM program more cost-effective. One of the secondary objectives of PDM is to prevent unnecessary replacement of usable parts by singling out only the components that are failing. Another objective is to analyze data and recommend that certain adjustments, calibrations, or changes in procedures be made. These changes lead to better equipment performance and a better product.

1.2.1 Identifying Maintenance Requirements and Priorities

Because no two plants are exactly alike, each PM and PDM program must be customized to fit unique and changing needs. The equipment and machinery must be classified based on function, need, and criticality within the system. These general guidelines are used to produce an efficient and flexible PDM program:

- Develop an equipment list that identifies all required maintenance items for each machine or system.
- Identify all health, safety, and environmental hazards.
- Pinpoint all equipment and maintenance items critical to continued production.
- Determine the significance and priority of each maintenance item and classify them as critical, important, or nonthreatening as they relate to the following:

    - Safety and the environment
    - Lost production and financial losses
    - Production schedules

A wide variety of diagnostic tools to identify abnormalities in equipment are available. Proactively identifying problems before they are obvious allows for preemptive steps to be taken. If accurate charts are maintained and the trends analyzed, diagnostic tests can help predict the life of equipment and key components.

General manufacturing statistics indicate that only 20 percent of equipment or component failures are critical in nature. Critical failures are those that create safety hazards, environmental threats, or severe production and economic loss. Thus, if the top 20 percent are avoided, the remaining 80 percent of the issues can be corrected with minimal loss and handled as routine work. This fact is why a detailed analysis of equipment function, as it relates to the consequences of failure, should be consistently maintained.

The critical failures are sometimes referred to as the *critical few*. Because of their consequences, that 20 percent is said to cause roughly 80 percent of the significant mechanical problems. This principle, that 20 percent of the breakdowns create 80 percent of the significant problems, is an example of the Pareto principle (*Figure 6*). By consistently using PDM techniques, millwrights can address these critical problems before the equipment fails. Then the remaining noncritical problems can be covered by regular maintenance that is done without impacting safety or production.

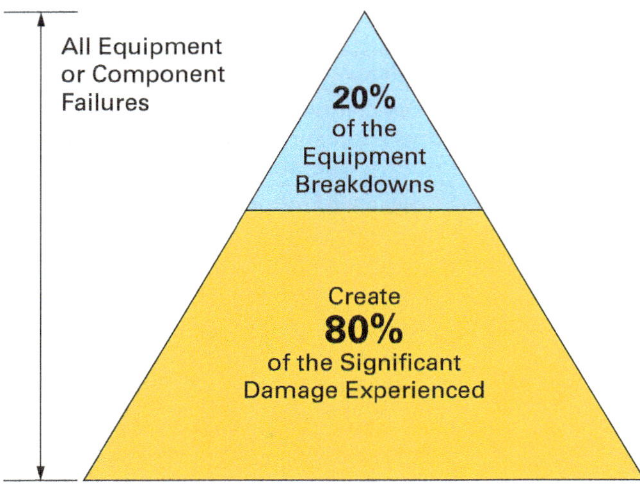

Figure 6 Pareto principle illustrated.

1.2.2 Documenting Equipment Maintenance History

For a complex, multilayered PDM system to work, there must be accurate and consistent documentation of component failures and work performed. Since manufacturing techniques are always evolving, the system must allow for changes and new testing methods to be applied. Each facility must design and modify their PDM to be locally relevant.

There are many computer systems and software packages that can be used to track maintenance, but the key to making it effective is consistent monitoring and the timely analysis of the data. A millwright with basic instruments and a simple documentation method can provide usable results, but the power of computers and software makes documentation easier and provides a means of rapid analysis and trends in the data. PDM-oriented personnel can use the analysis to detect weaknesses and avoid critical failures.

1.3.0 Nondestructive Testing and Evaluation

Nondestructive testing (NDT), or nondestructive inspection (NDI), methods are those used to test equipment and components without damaging them. Important welds, for example, can be inspected using radiography (essentially X-rays) (*Figure 7*). This process has no effect on the weldment. However, some welds must be cut or ground for visual inspection to evaluate the results of the **welding procedure specification (WPS)**. This method of inspection is destructive in nature.

Nondestructive evaluation (NDE) is the process of analyzing test results to quantify defects and predict failures. Most NDT is conducted under actual load conditions, so the equipment does not have to be shut down. NDE is where the results of NDT are compiled into a source of guidance. *Table 2* compares some types of NDT methods that will be examined further in this module.

NDT results can also be used to fine-tune equipment and increase productivity through minor adjustments. Machines may appear to be running fine, but they may not be doing all they can do. NDE can help define the upper limit of a machine's capability without jeopardizing its integrity. Quality control personnel responsible for raw materials can also use NDT and NDE to identify flaws before compromised material reaches the production line.

Although there are certainly exceptions, the life of a component or piece of equipment generally follows a predictable failure pattern. When the equipment is new, its break-in period and the learning curve of the operating personnel may cause problems. Once the machine matures, it runs more smoothly and predictably throughout its life cycle, supported with proper PM. Toward the end of the machine's life cycle, long-term wear sets in, component failures increase, and rebuilding or replacement becomes necessary. This progression is charted on what some refer to as a *bathtub curve* (*Figure 8*).

It's worth pointing out that there is such a thing as too much maintenance, at least from an economic point of view. Excessive maintenance or unnecessary rebuilds waste time and materials without extending a machine's life cycle. Truly successful maintenance programs identify the right level of maintenance to maximize equipment life and avoid costly activities that won't make a measurable difference.

Figure 7 Radiography of a pipeline weld.

NDT Process	Detects...	Advantages	Limitations	Examples of Use
Visual/Optical	Surface flaws such as inconsistent finishes, scratches, cracks, discoloration, and excess strain in transparent materials.	Simple, inexpensive, convenient, and can be automated.	Can only be applied to visibly accessible surfaces, through surface openings, or transparent materials.	The inspection of paper, wood, or metals for surface finish and uniformity.
Ultrasonic	Changes in the way sound passes through a material, caused by cracks, failed bonds, inclusions, and interfaces.	Can penetrate thick materials; excellent for crack detection; can be automated.	Normally requires either surface contact or immersion in a fluid; the orientation or inferior interpretation of a defect can present problems.	Testing adhesive-based assemblies for bond integrity; crack detection; thickness measurement.
Radiography	Changes in material density due to voids, inclusions, material variations, porosity, and positioning of internal parts.	Can be used to inspect a wide range of materials of varying thickness; versatile; resulting X-ray film provides a permanent record of the test.	Safety precautions required; can be expensive and detecting cracks can be difficult.	Pipeline welds for bead penetration, inclusions, and voids; verification of the position of internal components.
Eddy Current Testing	Changes in electrical conductivity or magnetic permeability that can be caused by material variations, cracks, voids, or inclusions.	Can easily be automated and applied at a moderate cost.	Limited to electrically conductive materials and has limited penetration depth; interpretation of the defect signals requires some skill and experience.	Heat exchanger tubes for thinning walls or cracks; verification of a metal's heat treatment success.
Liquid Penetrant	Openings and cracks in surfaces, seams, and folds.	Inexpensive, easy to apply, highly portable, and sensitive to small surface flaws.	Flaws must be open to the material surface; not useful on porous materials or surfaces.	Cast turbine blades for surface defects or defects that reveal themselves on the surface.
Magnetic Particle	Leakage of magnetic flux caused by surface or near-surface cracks, voids, inclusions, and material or geometry changes.	Inexpensive and sensitive to both surface and near-surface flaws.	Limited to use on ferromagnetic materials, such as iron; surface preparation and post-inspection demagnetization may be required.	Railroad car wheels and similar objects for defects; weld defects.
Infrared Imaging	Heat emanating from objects, with substantial precision.	Reasonable cost; portable equipment that can deliver instant results on a display, as well store a permanent image for future reference.	Limited to sensing temperature; unable to detect physical flaws.	Electrical connections, wiring, and switchgear; bearings; pumps and piping systems.
Vibration Analysis	Vibrations and their characteristics, primarily on rotating equipment.	Data can be gathered manually or automatically; provides excellent data to establish trends and pinpoint the cause of unusual vibration.	Unable to detect flaws of any type directly; requires a significant investment to gather and analyze the data, as well as substantial training.	Monitoring all types of rotating equipment, including turbines, pumps, and generators.

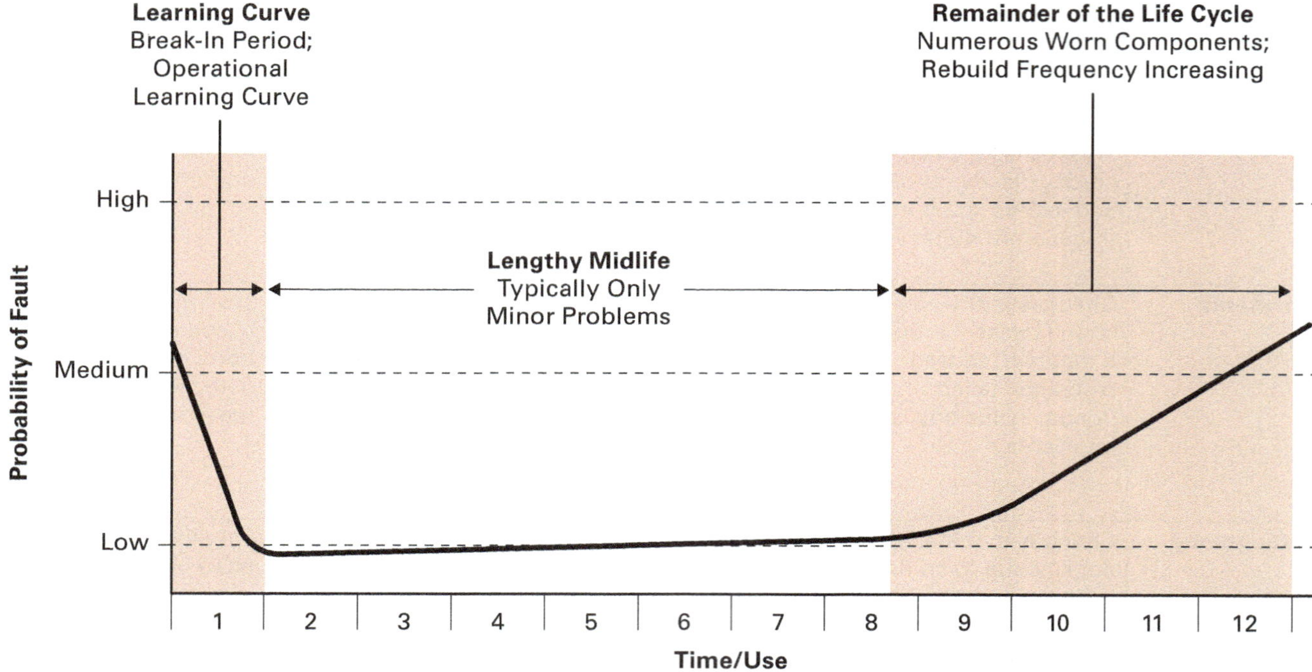

Figure 8 Bathtub curve of machine life.

Computerized Maintenance Management

Many industrial and manufacturing facilities today have disposed of the old ways to manage maintenance activities. In years past, work was simply documented on paper. If any sort of analysis was going to happen, it was going to be done using nothing more than the eyes and an analytical mind. Beyond that, the paper merely went into a drawer for safekeeping, serving only as evidence that the work was done. It would only come out again if something negative happened and questions were asked.

Today's computerized maintenance management systems (CMMSes) have changed all of that. Work orders can be delivered electronically, and craftworkers can document their work using mobile devices. Such systems can analyze a variety of test results and incoming data to identify developing problems and report them. Dashboards provide the user with an overview of equipment health, prioritizing certain information and bringing it to the screen as needed.

CMMSes have revolutionized the maintenance industry and made all that stored paper unnecessary. They also provide the perfect platform to coordinate PM and PDM testing.

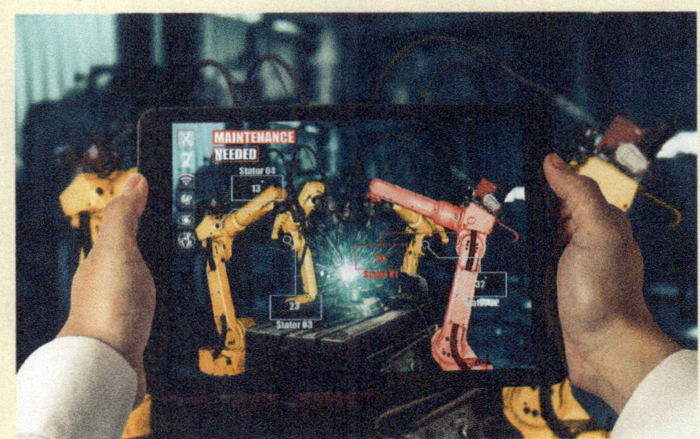

Figure Credit: iStock@NanoStockk

1.3.1 Visual and Optical Inspection

Visual and optical inspection of machinery is the easiest to perform and very common. You already own the most important piece of equipment! However, it is also the most likely to be overlooked as an inspection technique.

It is best to develop a systematic approach to visual inspection so that no details or areas are missed. Surprisingly, detailed observations can be made while the equipment is running. Follow the path of the product, carefully watching every step and noting any abnormalities. Don't forget to listen and smell as well. With the equipment off and secured, look closer for any signs of a problem. Excessive corrosion, bent shafts, minor leaks, and other abnormal conditions should be documented.

Parts of the equipment that are hard or impossible to see directly can be inspected with *optical borescopes* and *fiberscopes*. A flexible optical borescope (*Figure 9*) reaches deep inside a machine and tight areas, magnifies like a microscope, and provides its own light source. Advanced models include those that also provide thermal imaging, like the one shown in *Figure 9*. Probes come in various shapes, sizes, and lengths.

A simpler device, although less versatile, is the *rigid borescope (Figure 10)*. The user observes through an eyepiece. Many rigid models can see both straight ahead and to the side. The probe on most models can be rotated while observing, providing a 360-degree view of the subject.

Flexible fiberscopes (*Figure 11*) work much like a borescope. However, they use fragile optical fibers to illuminate and transfer the image to the display. They are not able to articulate at the end to look in different directions as well as a borescope due to the fragile nature of the fibers. When the fibers experience slight damage, the damage usually causes small black spots to appear on the image. Fiberscopes are also far more expensive to maintain and repair. Although they have their uses, borescopes are generally chosen over fiberscopes for industrial applications.

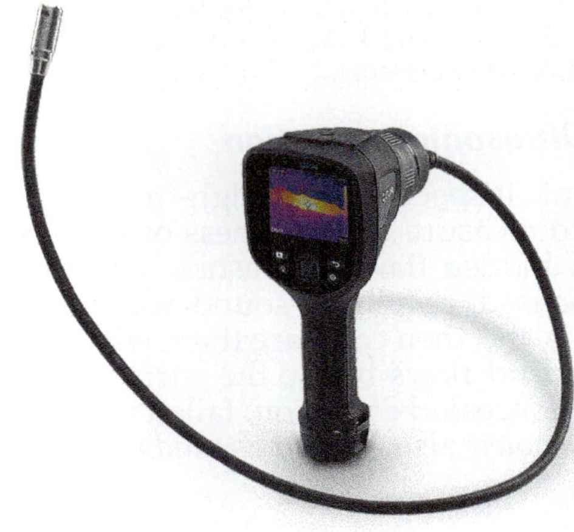

Figure 9 Thermal and visual borescope, or videoscope.

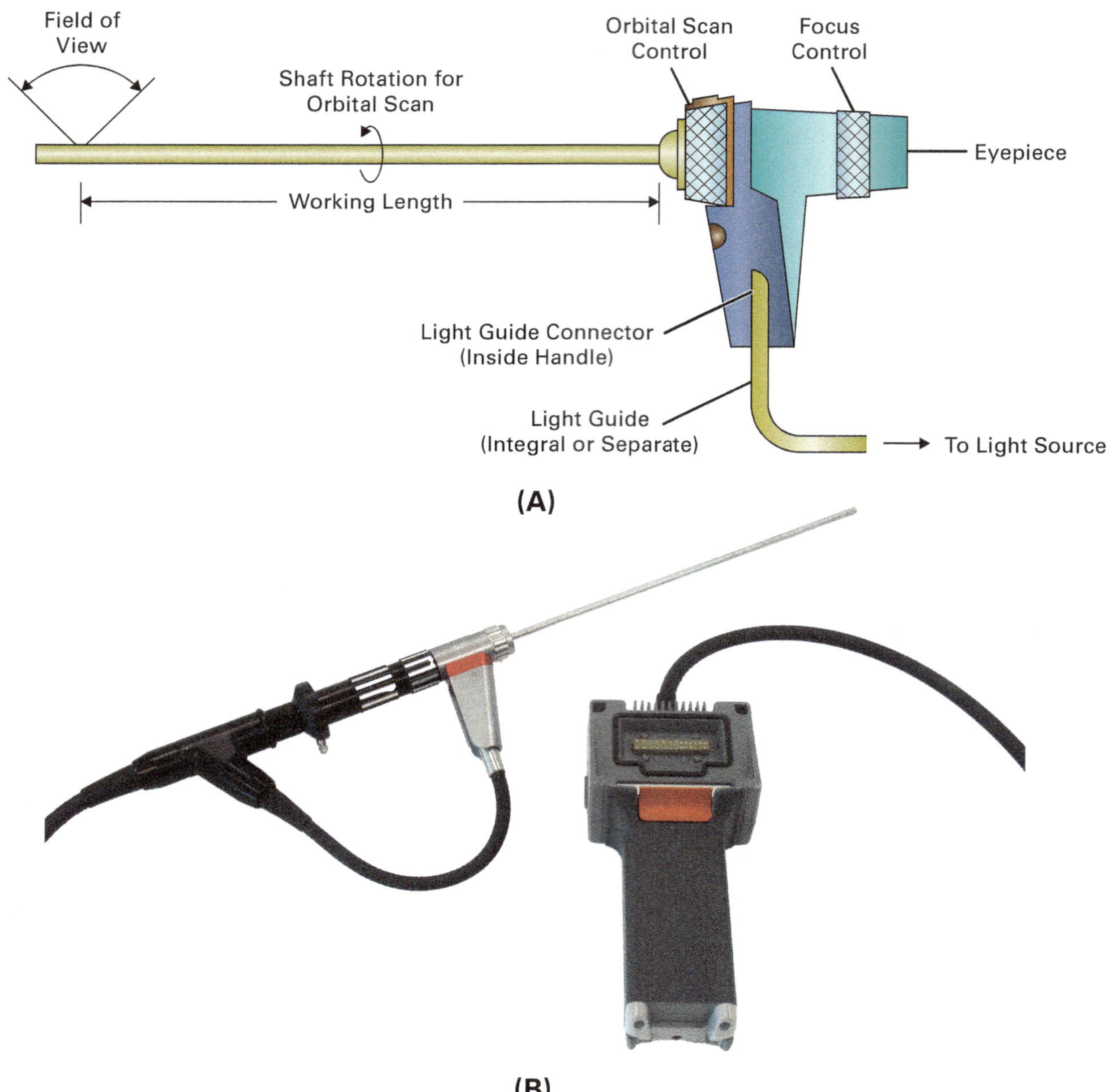

Figure 10 A rigid borescope.

1.3.2 Ultrasonic Inspection

Ultrasonic inspection uses high-frequency sound waves to measure the thickness of materials and look for hidden flaws. Ultrasonic equipment can send focused, amplified sound waves into solid materials and then compare them with the return wave to find flaws below the surface. Flaws can include concealed corrosion, failed welds, or casting blowholes, also known as *sand traps*.

The velocity of the sound waves as they move largely depends on the medium they encounter. Like a beam of light, ultrasonic waves may be reflected from surfaces, or modified as they encounter obstacles or the edges of surfaces. When the beam is reflected toward the instrument, it creates a signature that is interpreted as an image by the ultrasonic monitor.

Sound waves have a frequency, which describes how many waves pass a given point per second. The frequency range for ultrasonic inspection is generally from 0.5 megahertz (MHz) to 25 MHz. However, both higher and lower frequencies may be chosen for specific materials and applications.

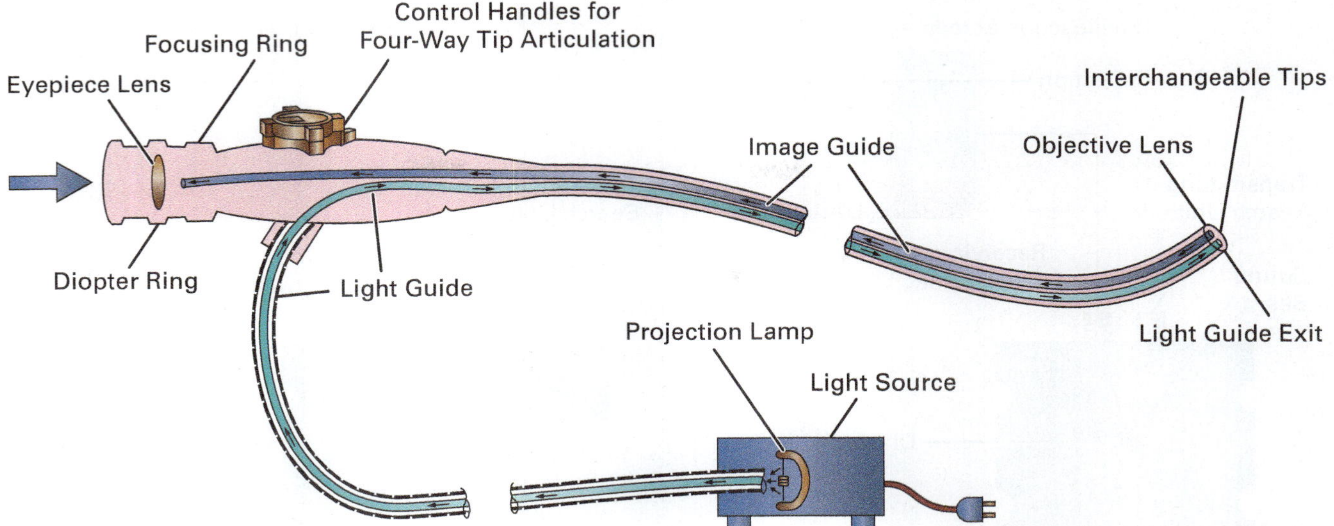

Figure 11 Flexible fiberscope.

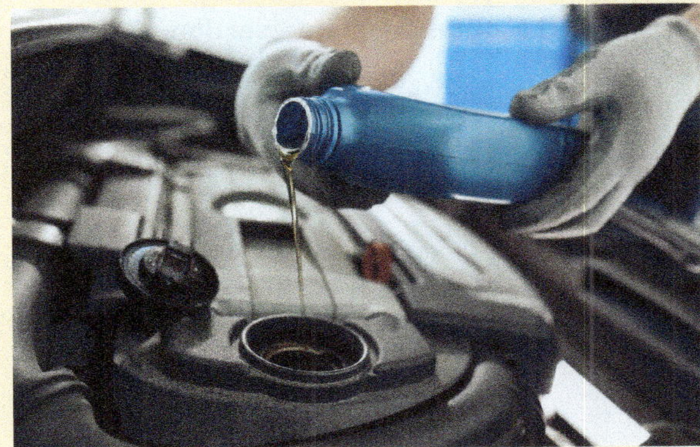

Does That Oil *Really* Need to Be Changed?

For generations, we've changed the oil in automobiles based on a schedule of mileage or time. With the advent of synthetic motor oil, some manufacturers allow a little more time between oil changes.

Food for thought: How much serviceable automotive oil has been drained and replaced over the years? How much more would it be if you added all the industrial applications and oil changes done strictly based on operating hours? In what percentage of cases do you think the oil might remain in service if it was tested and changed only when there are signs that it is no longer serviceable?

Figure Credit: iStock@Drazen Zigic

Ultrasonic sensors (*Figure 12*) can penetrate deeply into materials. They are very sensitive and provide highly accurate information. The test is best used on metals such as steel, but it can be applied to concrete, wood, and composite materials. However, on materials that don't have the density of metals, the results are not as good. There are no significant hazards related to the use of ultrasonic equipment.

Of course, interpreting the signals accurately does require some specific training and practice. *Figure 13* shows how some discontinuities in various orientations and material shapes might respond. Generally, the height of each reflection indicates the distance, such as the distance to the other side or the depth of a void. The width of the reflection at its base represents the width of the flaw. However, various features modify the signal in different ways. The positioning of the probe in relation to those features also changes the characteristics of the reflected signal.

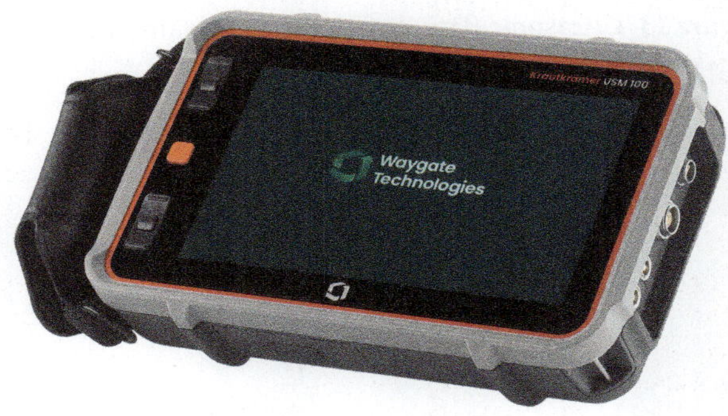

Figure 12 Portable ultrasonic flaw detector.

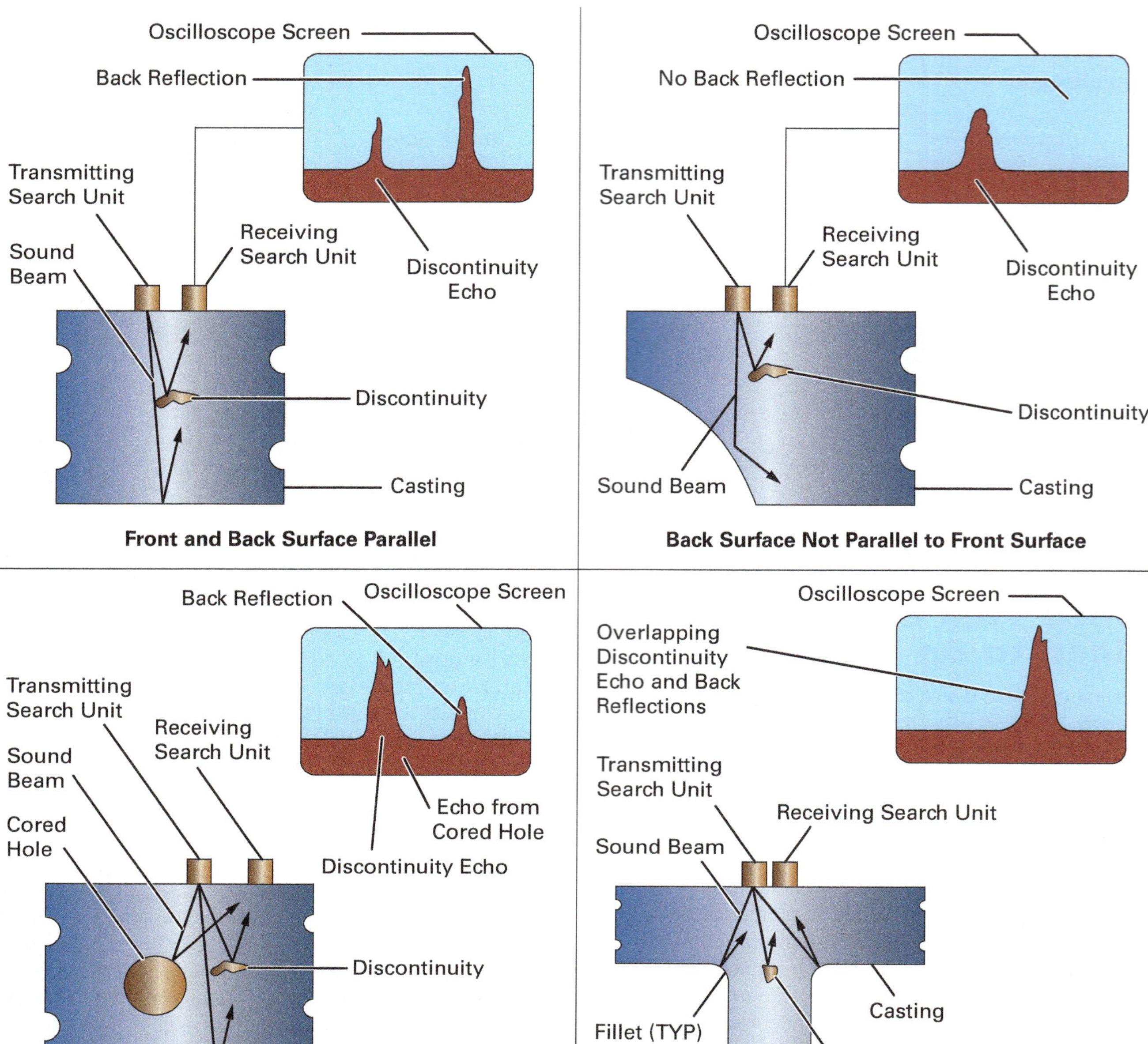

Figure 13 Ultrasonic flaw detector image examples.

1.3.3 Radiography

Traditional radiography uses a source of radiation to beam rays through an object and project the image on a film. The image is formed when the different densities and features of the object create shadows on the film, just as they do in a medical X-ray.

However, digital radiography is now popular. A plate to capture the image is still needed, but the captured image is immediately transferred to a computer. In digital radiography, the plate is referred to as a *digital detector array (DDA)*.

Radiography is one of the favored methods to inspect welds, often using portable equipment (*Figure 14*). Advanced portable equipment allows the images to be displayed in the field for immediate evaluation. In many cases, though, the images are viewed and analyzed in a lab or office (*Figure 15*).

An X-ray image displays the internal structure of intricate machine parts, castings, and weld beads. Industrial radiography was born from medical technology, and it includes computer-aided tomography (CAT or CT) scans and magnetic resonance imaging (MRI). CAT scans advance radiography from two-dimensional to three-dimensional (3D) imaging. Due to the size and complexity of the equipment, MRI and CT scanning equipment are generally limited to use in the laboratory (*Figure 16*). Radiography can be applied to virtually any material.

X-rays can produce a visible image of weld discontinuities, both those on the surface and beneath it. Surface flaws, though, are much better identified through a variety of simpler and more economical tests. X-rays also excel at verifying the alignment of assembled parts.

One disadvantage is related to the orientation of certain flaws. For example, a crack that runs in the same direction as the beam travels is almost impossible to see. Of course, this can be overcome by acquiring images from multiple positions. Delamination in layered materials is also impossible to detect because there is no difference in X-ray absorption.

When a joint is X-rayed, the radiation source is placed on one side of the weld and the film plate (or DDA) is placed on the other side (*Figure 17*). The joint is then momentarily exposed to the radiation source. The radiation penetrates the metal and produces an image, providing a permanent record. X-rays may reveal some flaws that are obvious even to a casual observer, but some flaws are much more difficult to recognize. Well-trained and qualified personnel must analyze them to make the results valid.

Figure 14 Radiography (X-ray) of a gas pipeline weld.

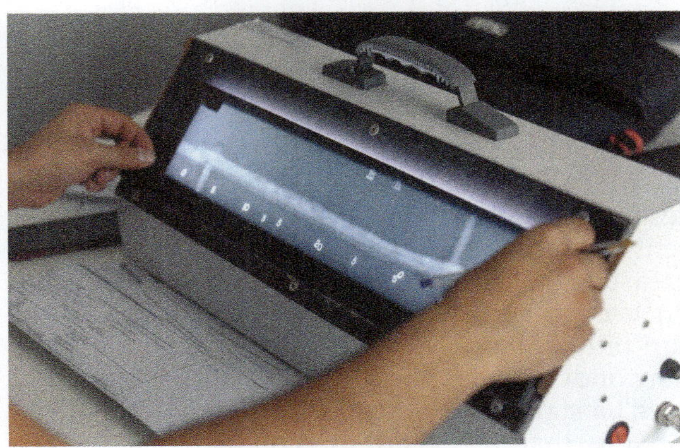

Figure 15 Evaluating weld X-rays.

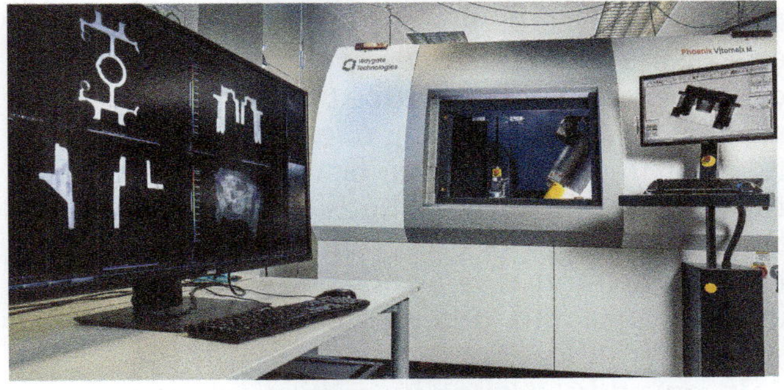

Figure 16 Industrial CT scanner.

Note that, because radiography equipment is radioactive and X-rays can cause damage to human tissue, only qualified technicians can conduct these tests. All safety procedures must be strictly followed. In the field, the area must be properly secured to prevent others from wandering into the test area.

> **WARNING!**
>
> Only certified technicians are permitted to operate radiography equipment due to the radiation hazard. Never cross a radiation barrier unless instructed to do so by a qualified person.

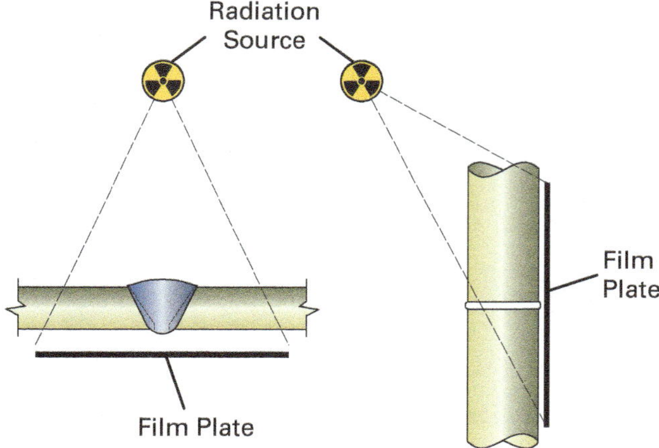

Figure 17 Radiography example.

1.3.4 Eddy Current Testing

Eddy current testing observes the interaction between electromagnetic fields and metals. The inspection can be used to measure electrical conductivity, magnetic permeability, heat treatment results, and even physical dimensions. Eddy current testing can detect seams, cracks, and voids, or measure the thickness of nonconducting coatings on a conductive material. Eddy current testing can only be applied to conductive materials, but nonconductive coatings on conductive materials aren't a significant obstacle.

Note that the need for conductivity doesn't limit the testing to iron-based metals that are magnetic. Indeed, the most common use for eddy current analysis is testing the integrity of boiler and heat exchanger tubes, which are often made of copper. Even when a tube bundle is completely removed from its housing (*Figure 18*), it is still difficult or impossible to see or inspect the tubes at the center of the bundle. Eddy current testing can test the integrity of each tube without removing the bundle, and it is an ideal way to locate and identify pits and other common flaws in heat exchanger tubes.

In an eddy current inspection, electrical currents are induced in the test object by a coil of wire that carries alternating current. When the probe is placed on the test object, electromagnetic energy produced by the coils is partly absorbed and converted into heat (*Figure 19*).

Part of the remaining energy is reflected toward the test coil, but the object being tested has affected the returning signal. The feedback provided by the reflected energy is analyzed and compared to the electrical signature of a reference specimen.

The depth of penetration to identify flaws can be a disadvantage. Flaws closer to the surface are more likely to be identified than those at a significant depth. Eddy current testing also fails to effectively identify flaws that run parallel to the surface. Since heat exchanger tubes are relatively thin, eddy current testing works well.

Figure 18 Heat exchanger tube bundle removed from its housing.

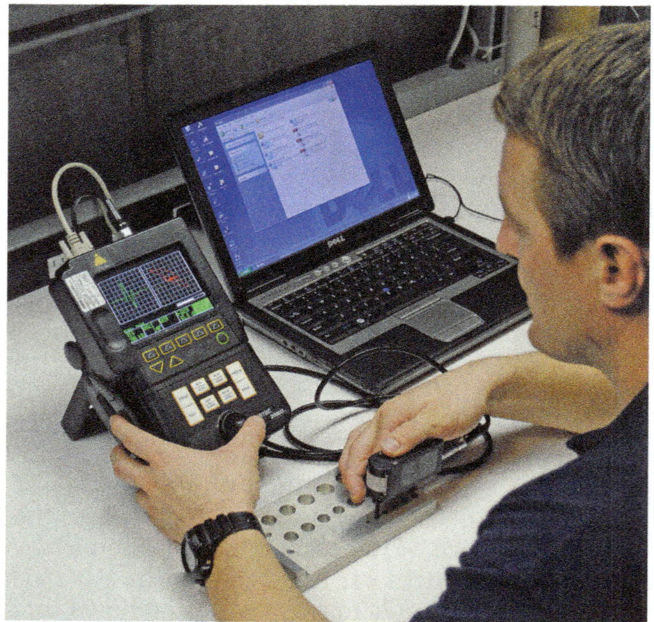

Figure 19 Conducting an eddy current test.

1.3.5 Liquid Penetrant Inspection

Liquid penetrant inspection is used on the surface of smooth and nonporous samples to highlight cracks and gaps. The liquid penetrant seeps into surface cracks, pores, delaminations, or shrinkage areas by capillary action. It can also be used to mark surfaces and evaluate wear patterns. The materials needed are often provided as a kit that includes dye, a dye cleaner, and a developer (*Figure 20*). The products are available in liquid and aerosol forms.

The inspection starts with cleaning common contaminants from the surface. The dye cleaner in the kit serves a different purpose, so this cleaning is done with a general cleaning product or solvent. The dye is then applied to the surface. (*Figure 21*). It flows over the surface to form a continuous, uniform coating that rapidly migrates into cracks and surface defects.

The dye is left for some time, usually from five minutes to an hour. This is called the *penetrant dwell time*. It is then lightly cleaned from the surface using the cleaner in the kit. Finally, the developer is applied. The developer draws the dye to the surface of the defects, producing a highlighted effect. The stained developer is in sharp contrast to "flawless" areas. Good lighting is needed to study the surface, and ultraviolet (UV) light is often used. A magnifying glass can also be used for closer examination.

Many flaws are too small to see normally, since the human eye can't generally identify features that are smaller than about 0.004" (about 0.1 mm). But the natural spread of the penetrant along with the contrast provided by the developer serves to make even tiny flaws stand out. Liquid penetrant testing is popular because it is effective, fast, easy, and not very costly.

Figure 20 Liquid penetrant kit.

(A) Applying the penetrant dye.

(B) Cleaning the dye from the surface.

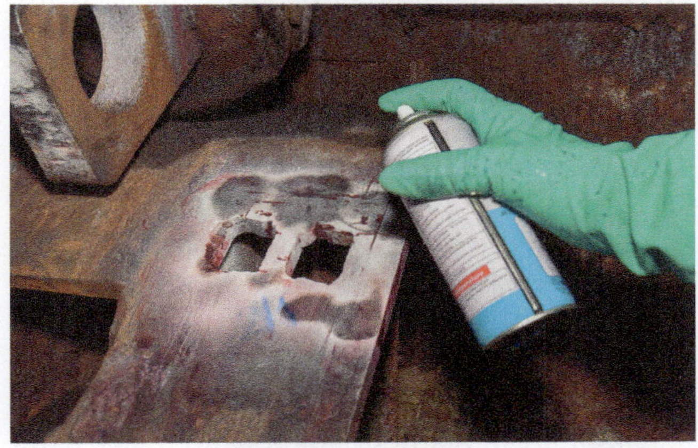

(C) Applying the developer.

Figure 21 Liquid penetrant testing.

The standard defects identified include stress or fatigue cracks, underbead cracks, pits, and porosities. Large stress cracks are indicated by wide lines that become apparent quickly once the developer is applied. Underbead cracks are subsurface cracks that bleed through to the surface. They are often indicated by a line of dots that appears a few minutes after the developer is applied. Porosity produces small dots that come to the surface very quickly. *Figure 22* shows how a longitudinal crack appears in what is known as the *heat-affected zone* of a weld.

There are two basic types of penetrants. Type 1 penetrants are those that are fluorescent in nature. UV light is needed for these products to work well. Type 2 penetrants are simple red dyes. There are also four different classifications for dye cleaners, identified as Method A through Method D. Some involve the use of a solvent, while others are based on water. The dyes are classified into five levels based on their ability to detect the tiniest of cracks:

- Level $\frac{1}{2}$ — Ultra-low sensitivity
- Level 1 — Low sensitivity
- Level 2 — Medium sensitivity
- Level 3 — High sensitivity
- Level 4 — Ultra-high sensitivity

Developers are classified by their method of application. There are six classifications, including dry powder, water soluble, and water suspendable.

Although the testing is relatively easy to conduct, it must be done in a very consistent manner and with careful attention to the specifications provided. The specifications for a test, such as the precise type of dye and developer to be used, are established by specialists in the field who have a complete understanding of the factors involved and the best product for the task.

1.3.6 Magnetic Particle Inspection

A magnetic field can be generated in and around any part made of a *ferromagnetic* (iron-bearing and magnetic) material, such as common steel. Magnetic particle inspection works only for materials that can be magnetized. That means that only some forms of stainless steel (those that are ferritic) can be tested this way.

Before a sample is tested, a contrasting paint with a matte finish is applied. The sample is then magnetized with an electrical current using a *yoke* (*Figure 23*). When the lines of magnetic flux encounter a defect like a crack, detectable magnetic poles are generated on either side of the defect.

Magnetic particles are then applied over the surface. The particles can be applied either dry or in a liquid form, mixed with an oil, solvent, or water. Dry particles can be applied using a simple squeeze bulb. Wet particles are most often applied with a spray can (*Figure 24*).

The flaws on or just under the surface cause the magnetic field to be interrupted. The particles are attracted to the crack or flawed area, which experiences what is known as *magnetic flux leakage*. When the particles arrange themselves in a pattern that allows the flaw to be seen, it is called an *indication*. Maximum sensitivity is generally obtained when a linear target, like a weld bead, is oriented perpendicular to the yoke. However, changing the position one way or the other also helps better identify the extent of the flaws. Magnetic particle testing is done using either alternating current (AC) or direct current (DC).

Magnetic particle inspection is very sensitive to minor surface cracks and flaws that are near the surface (*Figure 25*). Its disadvantages include being limited to magnetic materials and the inability to identify deeper flaws.

Figure 22 Longitudinal crack along a plate weld.

Figure 23 Using a yoke to apply an electrical current to a workpiece weld.

Figure 24 An oil-based magnetic particle suspension in aerosol form.

Figure 25 Cracking along the edge of weld, indicated through magnetic particle inspection.

1.3.7 Infrared Imaging

Infrared test devices detect the heat energy emitted by an object. Detectable heat energy is produced naturally by all materials at temperatures above absolute zero. This method detects and converts the emitted energy into an image of contrasting colors, with each color associated with a range of temperature (*Figure 26*). The technical term for the process is *infrared thermography*. *Figure 27* shows an infrared image of a group of pumps and the connected piping.

The image can be used to locate overheated bearings, abnormal shaft temperatures, or faulty electrical connections.

1.3.8 Vibration Analysis

All machines generate mechanical forces as they operate. These forces create unique vibrations that change as parts wear or begin to fail. These vibration *signatures* can be monitored, recorded, and analyzed to identify problems as they develop.

Vibrations in rotating machinery can be separated into individual vibration cycles (*Figure 28*). Each cycle begins with the shaft centered in the housing. As the shaft rotates, it may travel away from its centered position due to excessive loads, worn bearings, or similar flaws. As the rotational speed increases, the shaft moves away from the centerline until it reaches a peak distance. The shaft then moves back toward and through the centerline until the distance peaks in the opposite direction. The shaft deflection again reverses back to the centerline on the way to the opposite side. As it arrives at its proper centerline, one vibration cycle has been completed.

> **NOTE**
>
> All aspects of mechanical vibration and vibration analysis are presented in NCCER Module 15509, *Vibration Analysis*.

Figure 26 Infrared camera capturing an image.

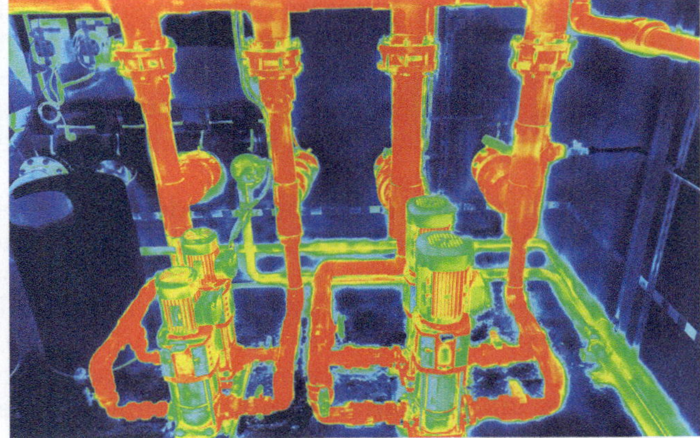

Figure 27 Infrared image of industrial pumps and piping.

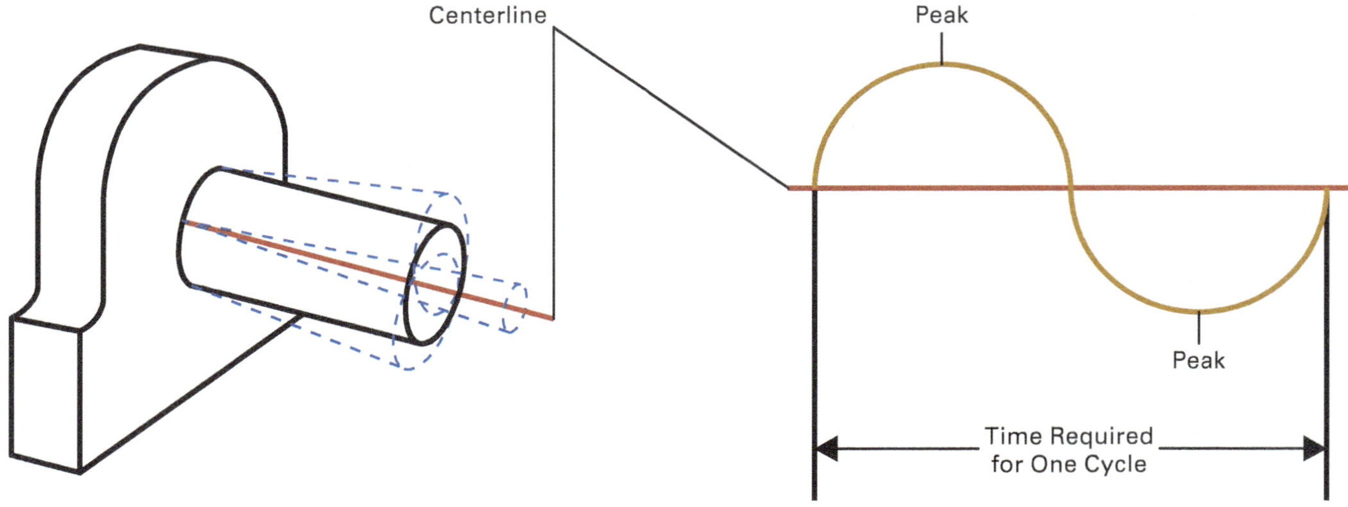

Figure 28 One complete vibration cycle.

The physical vibration we feel is caused by the reversal of direction at each peak of the cycle. Changes in the load or rotational speed change the characteristics of the "wobble," as does a loss of shaft alignment, a bent shaft, or a loose shaft coupling. "Normal" vibration can be monitored, and problems begin to reveal themselves through changes in otherwise steady trends. The signature of the vibration often provides a clue to the exact problem. A bent shaft and a worn bearing, for example, have different vibration signatures.

Vibration monitors and meters can be completely portable and used during maintenance visits to record current data intermittently (*Figure 29*). Vibration analyzers can typically produce an analysis immediately. Stored information can be downloaded and analyzed by software, comparing it to previous results. More sophisticated systems have permanent sensors installed that are either wired to a network or connect wirelessly (*Figure 30*). This allows for continuous monitoring and a dashboard that provides alerts when unusual or damaging vibration trends are detected.

Vibration monitoring is usually done in horizontal radial, vertical radial, and axial planes, as they relate to a rotating shaft (*Figure 31*). Probes of different designs may be used for the radial and axial positions. To get meaningful results, it is very important to ensure each consecutive reading is taken from a common point on the machine. *Figure 32* shows a sample schematic for vibration monitoring points on a boiler feed pump.

Figure 29 Recording vibration data from a motor bearing.

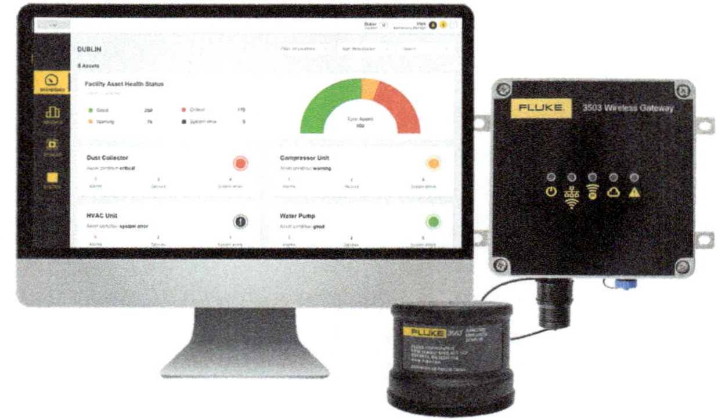

Figure 30 Wireless vibration monitor, data gateway, and software dashboard.

1.3.9 Tribology

Analyzing the condition and content of lubricants drained from compressors and gearboxes is an excellent way to monitor internal health and the condition of moving parts. **Tribology** is the field of science related to the interaction of surfaces in contact with each other. Tribology focuses on lubrication, friction, and the wear experienced by interacting surfaces.

Tribology includes the process of examining the lubricants in a machine to determine the state of the lubricants and the characteristics of any particles found in them. Lubricant analysis determines the condition of a machine's lubricant by analyzing a sample to identify the chemical elements, additives, and the presence of contaminants. A Total Acid Number (TAN) analysis, for example, is used to determine how acidic the oil has become. Acidity generally increases over time and at higher operating temperatures.

Over time, consecutive lubricant samples can reveal wear patterns and developing failures. The condition of the lubricant can also help determine if it is the best choice for the application, needs to be changed at a different frequency, or if different additives may be needed.

Wear particle analysis provides information about the wear of mechanical parts. Particles in the lubricant drained from a machine can provide important information about the internal moving parts. Wear particle analysis considers the size, shape, composition, and volume of particles in the lubricant. The characteristics of the particles indicate which parts are wearing out and how quickly they are deteriorating. This information guides planning for major maintenance or equipment replacement.

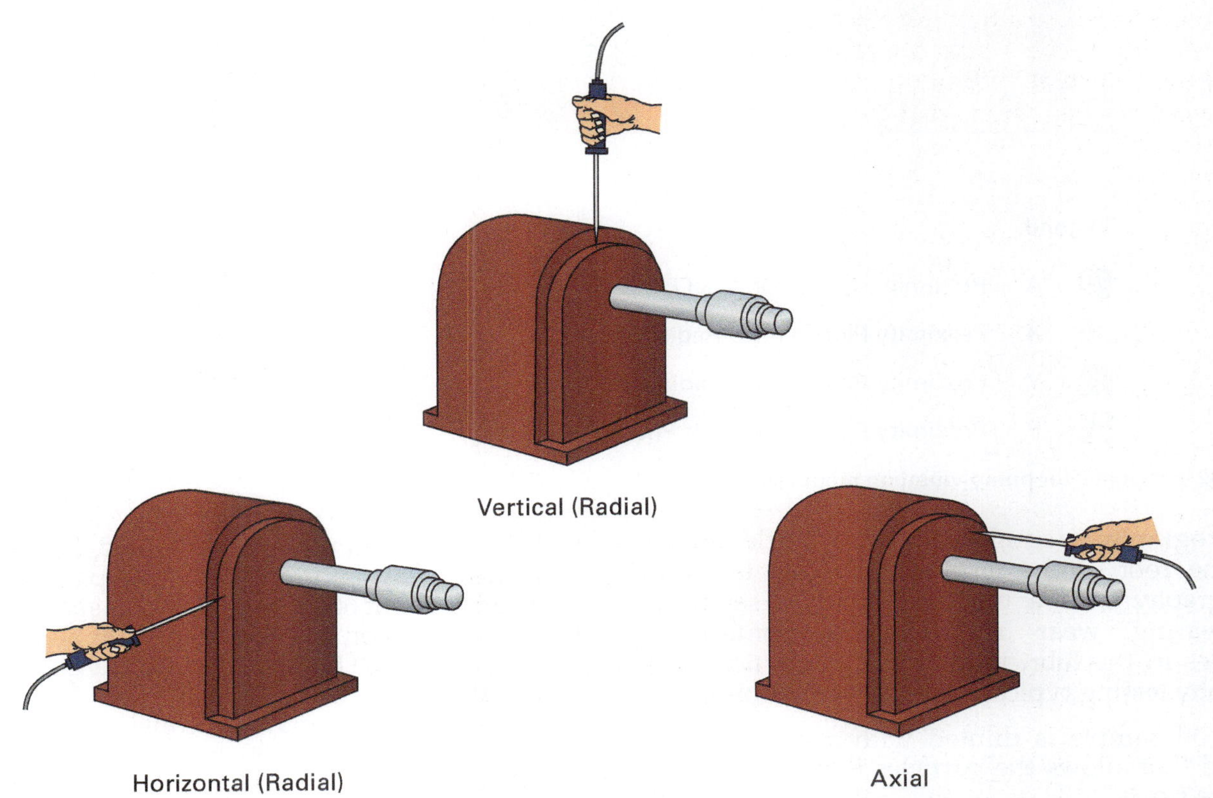

Figure 31 Radial and axial vibration measuring points.

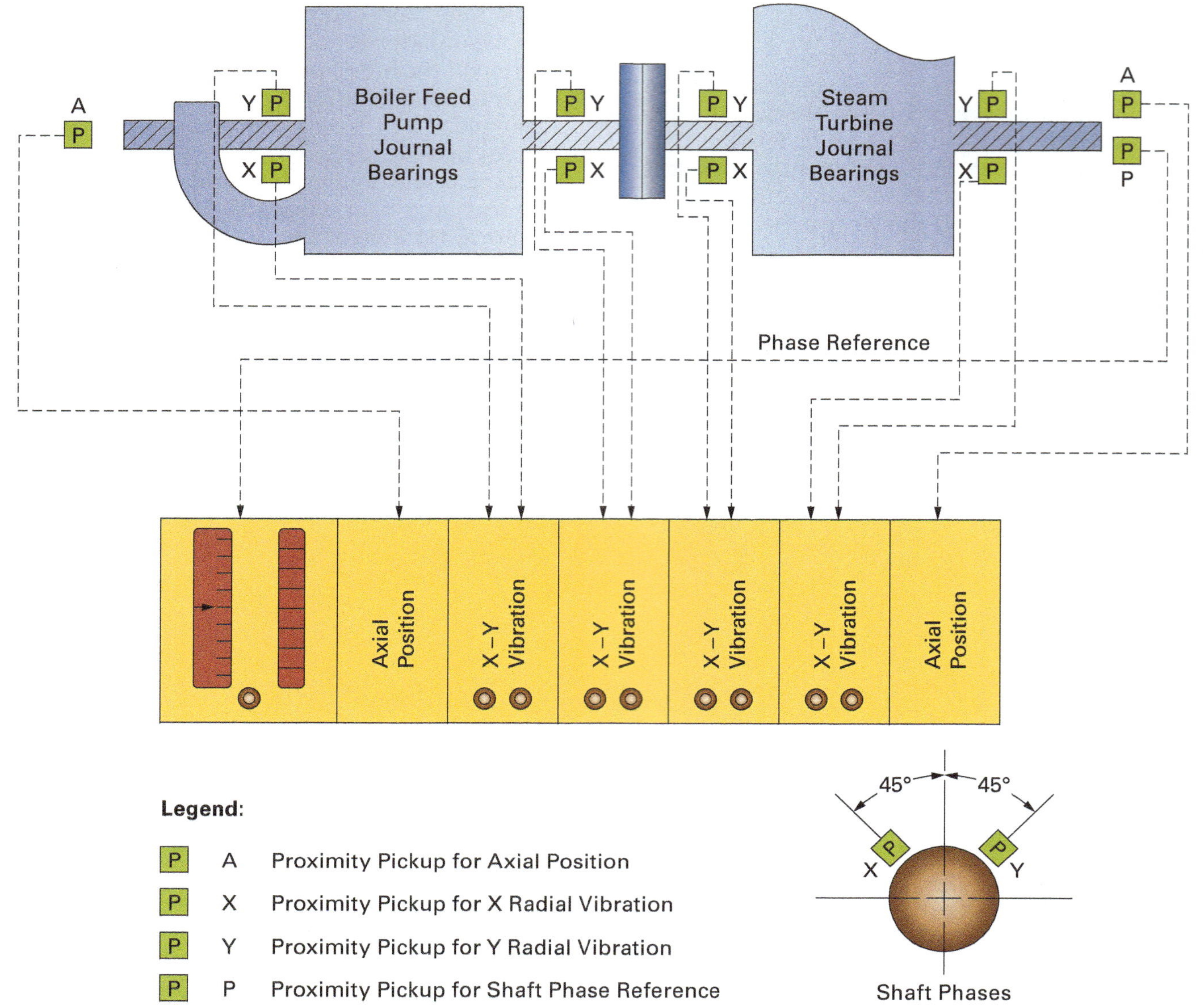

Figure 32 Schematic for pump vibration monitoring points.

Ferrography is similar to wear particle analysis. The root of the term, *ferro*, refers to iron. Ferrography uses a magnetic field to separate iron-bearing wear metals from nonferrous particles in the lubricant sample. Analytical ferrography testing typically progresses as follows:

- An oil sample is diluted with a less viscous fluid that allows the particles to move around more freely.
- The diluted lubricant is applied to a glass slide. The slide is then exposed to a magnetic field that cause the ferrous materials to move into a pattern. Any nonmagnetic contaminants remain in position, unaffected by the magnetic field.
- With the contaminants separated, the oil is washed away, and the remaining particles are baked at about 600°F (~316°C) for a short time.
- The particles on the slide are examined under a microscope. The particles are classified into six categories and ranked by size. While the smaller particles may be considered normal wear, particles over 30 microns across typically indicate unusual and undesirable damage is occurring. However, that standard differs for different types of equipment, and a large volume of smaller particles may also cause concern.

The six categories into which the particles are separated include the following:

- Copper particles
- Babbitt particles, which contain tin and lead, commonly used for bearings in turbines and other applications
- White nonferrous particles, typically consisting of chromium or aluminum
- Fiber particles that may come from filtration materials
- Contaminant particles, including simple dirt
- Ferrous particles, which are further broken down into five categories

Categorizing the different particles and grading them by size can provide valuable information about what components are wearing out and the rate of wear.

Millwrights and industrial maintenance craft-workers must read and follow any guidance provided to gather valid oil samples. The details are very important. Oil sampling bottles (*Figure 33*), for example, are even classified based on their cleanliness as clean, super clean, or ultraclean. When, where, and how samples are taken can substantially affect the results.

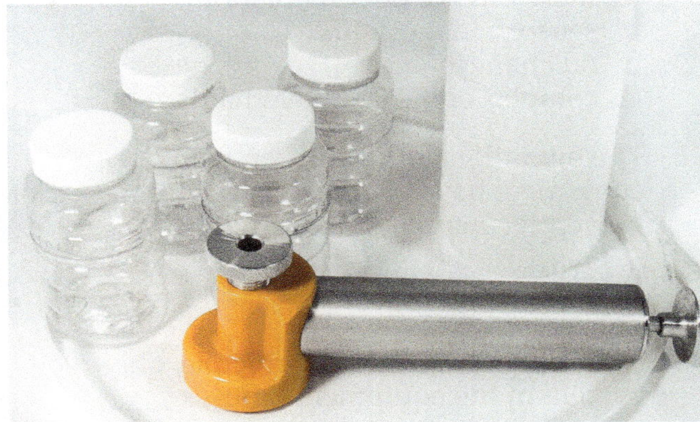

Figure 33 Hand-operated vacuum pump and oil sample bottles.

1.0.0 Section Review

1. Which of the following activities is *not* considered part of PM?

    a. Inspecting
    b. Lubricating
    c. Troubleshooting
    d. Cleaning

2. Changing the oil in an air compressor is considered a PDM task.

    a. True
    b. False

3. Small black spots that show up on the display during an optical inspection are often the result of damage to a(n) ______.

    a. rigid borescope
    b. infrared camera
    c. ultrasonic flaw detector
    d. fiberscope

1. A shortage of knowledgeable staff and the required resources often affects the assignment of responsibility for _______.

   a. maintenance documentation
   b. sensory inspections
   c. oil changes
   d. complex equipment overhauls

2. The operational demands on plant equipment have no effect on the frequency of preventive maintenance activities.

   a. True
   b. False

3. According to the Pareto principle, only 20 percent of the equipment failures _______.

   a. cause 80 percent of the critical problems
   b. are cost effective to repair
   c. should be acknowledged
   d. are maintenance related

4. You need an NDI method that is very sensitive, portable, completely safe, and allows you to see flaws that may be deeply embedded below the surface of a metal workpiece. The *best* choice would be _______.

   a. liquid penetrant inspection
   b. a flexible optical borescope
   c. ultrasonic inspection
   d. radiography

5. Which NDT method works on conductive ferrous and nonferrous metals, and is most often used to test hidden boiler and heat exchanger tubes for pitting?

   a. Magnetic particle inspection
   b. Radiography
   c. Liquid penetrant inspection
   d. Eddy current testing

6. Without assistance, the human eye can't identify features that are smaller than about _______.

   a. 0.0004" (about 0.001 mm)
   b. 0.001" (about 0.025 mm)
   c. 0.004" (about 0.1 mm)
   d. 0.01" (about 0.25 mm)

7. Liquid penetrant inspection dye is an excellent choice to find flaws in the surface of porous materials.

   a. True
   b. False

8. Magnetic particle inspection typically begins with _______.

   a. applying magnetic particles on the workpiece surface
   b. magnetizing the workpiece with a yoke
   c. applying a contrasting paint with a matte finish
   d. wiping the workpiece surface with a developer

9. Detectable heat energy is naturally produced by all materials at temperatures above _______.

   a. freezing
   b. absolute zero
   c. 0°F
   d. 0°C

10. Ferrography is used to separate ferrous and nonferrous particles from each other _______.

    a. in an oil sample
    b. in an air sample
    c. on metal surfaces
    d. on nonconductive surfaces

Trade Terms Introduced in This Module

Delamination: The separation or splitting apart of layers.

Eddy current: An induced electrical current that is generated in a conductive material exposed to a moving magnetic field.

Ferrography: A specific type of oil analysis that focuses on lubricant contaminants, their characteristics, and their sources.

Pareto principle: A theory based on the work of Italian economist Vilfredo Pareto that states, for many outcomes, roughly 80 percent of consequences come from 20 percent of the causes or events. Also referred to as the *80/20 rule*, the theory manifests itself in many fields and applications.

Sensory inspection: A maintenance inspection that incorporates sight, sound, smell, and touch.

Tribology: The study of lubrication, friction, and the wear of interacting surfaces.

Welding procedure specification (WPS): A document specifying all essential procedural details related to project-specific welds.

Additional Resources

This module presents thorough resources for task training. The following reference material is suggested for further study.

An Introduction to Predictive Maintenance. 2nd Edition. R. Keith Mobley. Woburn, MA: Butterworth-Heinemann.

Complete Guide to Preventive and Predictive Maintenance (Volume 1). Latest Edition. Joel Levitt. South Norwalk, CT: Industrial Press, Inc.

Maintenance Fundamentals. 2nd Edition. R. Keith Mobley. Amsterdam, Netherlands: Elsevier.

Welding Inspection Technology. Latest Edition. Doral, FL: American Welding Society.

Figure Credits

Section Review Answer Key

Answer	Section Reference	Objective
1. c	1.1.0	1a
2. b	1.2.0	1b
3. d	1.3.1	1c

User Update

NCCER makes every effort to keep its textbooks up-to-date and free of technical errors. We appreciate your help in this process. If you find an error, a typographical mistake, or an inaccuracy in NCCER's curricula, please submit a User Update form by visiting **https://www.nccer.org/olf**. You can also scan the QR code using the camera on your phone or mobile device to access the form.

Maintaining and Repairing Turbine Components

OVERVIEW

Millwrights may be called upon to work on turbines, especially when working in the power industry. Different types of turbines share some common maintenance requirements, but steam and gas turbines do differ significantly. This module presents some procedures for repairing or replacing steam turbine components. While a single module can't possibly capture all the relevant information you will need to service turbines, some activities common to steam turbines are presented herein. The example procedures in this module are based on those for a Westinghouse Type E steam turbine.

Module 15506

Trainees with successful module completions may be eligible for credentialing through the NCCER Registry. To learn more, go to **www.nccer.org** or contact us at 1.888.622.3720. Our website, **www.nccer.org**, has information on the latest product releases and training.

Your feedback is welcome. You may email your comments to **curriculum@nccer.org**, send general comments and inquiries to **info@nccer.org**, or fill in the User Update form at the back of this module.

This information is general in nature and intended for training purposes only. Actual performance of activities described in this manual requires compliance with all applicable operating, service, maintenance, and safety procedures under the direction of qualified personnel. References in this manual to patented or proprietary devices do not constitute a recommendation of their use.

15506 V4.0

From *Millwright, Trainee Guide*. NCCER.

Maintaining and Repairing Turbine Components

Objective

Successful completion of this module prepares you to do the following:

1. Explain how to remove, install, and maintain various turbine components.
   a. Identify and describe common steam turbine maintenance activities.
   b. Explain how to remove and reinstall turbine casings and rotors.
   c. Explain how to maintain and repair sealing glands and carbon rings.
   d. Explain how to maintain and repair governor systems.
   e. Explain how to replace nozzle rings and reversing blade assemblies.
   f. Explain how to replace rotor locating bearings, pedestals, and housings.
   g. Explain how to maintain overspeed trip mechanisms.

Performance Task

Under supervision, you should be able to do the following:

1. Identify six instructor-selected turbine components.

Trade Terms

Carbon rings
Carryover
Sublimate

Industry Recognized Credentials

If you are training through an NCCER-accredited sponsor, you may be eligible for credentials from NCCER's Registry. The ID number for this module is 15506. Note that this module may have been used in other NCCER curricula and may apply to other level completions. Contact NCCER's Registry at 1.888.622.3720 or go to **www.nccer.org** for more information.

You can also show off your industry-recognized credentials online with NCCER's digital badges. Transform your knowledge, skills, and achievements into badges that you can share across social media platforms, send to your network, and add to your resume. For more information, visit **www.nccer.org**.

How to Access Resources

This craft has additional videos and resources to enhance your learning experience. To view these resources, scan the QR below. The videos and resources are separated by module.

You can scan this code using the camera on your phone or mobile device to view these videos and resources.

Contents

1.0.0 MAINTAINING AND REPAIRING TURBINES

Objective

Explain how to remove, install, and maintain various turbine components.

a. Identify and describe common steam turbine maintenance activities.
b. Explain how to remove and reinstall turbine casings and rotors.
c. Explain how to maintain and repair sealing glands and carbon rings.
d. Explain how to maintain and repair governor systems.
e. Explain how to replace nozzle rings and reversing blade assemblies.
f. Explain how to replace rotor locating bearings, pedestals, and housings.
g. Explain how to maintain overspeed trip mechanisms.

Performance Task

1. Identify six instructor-selected turbine components.

Trade Terms

Carbon rings: Self-lubricating packing rings made of carbon that are used to seal the casing and rotor shaft.

Carryover: Any solid, liquid, or vapor contaminant that is entrained in the steam leaving a boiler.

Sublimate: To change state directly from a solid to a gas, without passing through a liquid state.

Turbines are used to transfer one form of energy, such as steam, into mechanical energy that can be used to drive equipment. Small turbines may be used to drive pumps, compressors, and other rotating equipment. Large steam turbines are primarily used for power generation.

A turbine converts the kinetic energy of a moving fluid into mechanical energy. The fluid may be water or steam, or even a gas such as compressed or heated air. Water is associated with hydraulic turbines, such as those used at dams to generate electrical power. Steam is supplied to a turbine by a boiler or a nuclear reactor. Compressed and heated air are associated with gas turbines.

Turbines must be properly and consistently maintained to ensure safe and efficient operation. Although there are certainly similarities, the procedures for maintaining and repairing turbines vary from one turbine to another. This module presents some common maintenance procedures related to a small Westinghouse Type E steam turbine. When performing maintenance on a turbine, you must follow the procedures in the turbine manufacturer's maintenance manuals specific to that unit. While two turbines may look identical on the outside, important changes are often made from one build to another.

You will undoubtedly require additional training provided by your employer or the turbine manufacturer if you are regularly engaged in turbine service. The procedures here will only serve to familiarize you with common services for a single turbine model.

1.1.0 Basic Steam Turbine Maintenance

Steam turbines are used primarily in fossil fuel and nuclear power plants to drive electric generators. They are also used to drive generators in large industrial plants to provide electricity to the facility when needed. The rotational speed of a steam turbine can exceed 10,000 revolutions per minute (rpm). That is a significant speed for something as massive as a utility-scale turbine rotor assembly.

Modern industrial steam turbines can have 50 or more stages. Each stage consists of a rotating turbine wheel with blades and a stationary wheel with blades, also referred to as *nozzles*. The blades of the stationary wheel are shaped so that the spaces between them act as nozzles that guide the steam and increase its velocity before it enters the turbine wheel.

As steam travels through the turbine, it expands as the pressure drops. Therefore, to extract as much energy as possible, each stage must be larger in diameter than the one before it (*Figure 1*).

Steam turbines may be either *condensing* or *noncondensing*, depending on how the steam exiting the turbine is handled. In a condensing turbine, remaining steam that exits the turbine enters a condenser where the heat is transferred out and the steam is condensed. This creates a vacuum effect that helps draw fresh steam in through the turbine. The water, referred to as *condensate*, is then pumped back to the boiler and

---

Figure 1 The diameter of the stages must increase to extract power as the steam pressure drops on its way through the turbine.

collected along with any other condensate that formed in the turbine.

The steam exiting a noncondensing turbine is not intentionally condensed. The remaining steam is used to do more work before it is condensed and returns to the boiler. It is usually sent to other processes or systems in the plant that require a low-pressure steam supply. In a noncondensing turbine, steam can also be extracted from the turbine at various points to obtain higher pressures. Control valves at each extraction point regulate the volume of steam extracted.

There are many types, sizes, and configurations of steam turbines. The following checklist provides a summary of the periodic maintenance activities often required on large turbines:

- Check all piping and piping connections for leaks as necessary.
- Test, calibrate, or replace instrument probes.
- Remove and replace the governor. Governors are often refurbished or remanufactured to be used again.
- Open and inspect the turning gear and drive motor.
- Inspect and replace exterior insulation as necessary.

- Inspect and check the alignment of the generator coupling. The alignment is checked both when the unit is hot and when it is cold, as thermal growth will no doubt affect the alignment. Due to their accuracy and speed, laser alignment equipment is typically used with today's turbines. Coupling halves may be replaced periodically to ensure their integrity.
- Remove, disassemble, inspect, and repair the turbine's trip and throttle valve (TTV) and steam extraction valves. The TTV modulates the main flow of steam into the turbine, but also serves as a safety device through its ability to close rapidly. Many TTVs can stop the flow of steam in less than half of a second.
- Split the turbine case for major inspections and internal repair. The case bolts may be replaced during reassembly since they can become elongated after being torqued and then exposed to high temperatures for an extended period. The mating surfaces of the two halves are buffed and honed as necessary to ensure a precision fit.
- Remove and inspect the rotor assembly.
- Remove and replace the upper- and lower-case diaphragms.

NCCER – *Millwright*

- Lubricate and recondition all linkages.
- Remove, recondition, and replace all steam- and condensate-related valves.

1.2.0 Removing and Reinstalling Turbine Casings and Rotors

The turbine casing surrounds the complete rotating element of the turbine and supports the stationary steam parts. Most casings are split along a horizontal plane near their midpoint (*Figure 2*).

It is important to prevent steam leakage from the casing seam. At each end of the turbine, the shaft must extend through the casing. As you likely know from working with pumps, maintaining a seal around a rotating shaft isn't easy. For a steam turbine, preventing the steam from escaping is the common challenge. However, remember that, on a condensing turbine, the low-pressure end of the turbine may be below atmospheric pressure (vacuum). In this case, a leak results in air entering the turbine, rather than steam leaking out.

The turbine gland sealing system (TGSS) helps prevent steam from escaping around the turbine shaft and other casing penetrations. The system also helps maintain the seal at major steam control and stop valves. On the low-pressure end of the turbine, in areas where the pressure may be less than the atmospheric pressure (condensing turbines), the TGSS prevents air from leaking in.

Follow these basic steps to remove the turbine casing. Note that many turbines have more than one casing section. It is also important to precisely follow the turbine manufacturer's guidance for all tasks; this text is not intended to replace or supersede those instructions at any level:

> **WARNING!**
>
> Before beginning any turbine service, ensure that you have and don the required PPE. Ensure that all sources of stored energy, including electrical power and control circuits, are locked out and tagged as required by OSHA and facility regulations. When working with turbines, this can be an extensive process that requires multiple crafts to work together.
>
> When working with steam turbines, ensure that all remaining steam pressure inside the turbine system has been released. The turbine must be at atmospheric pressure and at a safe temperature before work begins.

Step 1 Remove the cap screws from the horizontal flanges on the top half of the TGSS sealing glands.

Step 2 Remove the bolts and alignment dowels from the horizontal casing flange.

> **WARNING!**
>
> Ensure that all accessories used for rigging, such as eyebolts and slings, are specifically designed for rigging and have the appropriate working load limit (WLL) capacity for the task.

Step 3 Carefully lift the casing cover until it clears the rotors. Guide pins are in place to maintain the stability of the casing for a short distance until it is lifted above the rotors. Lifting is typically done with gantry cranes or small mobile cranes.

> **CAUTION**
>
> The casing cannot be allowed to swing or move until it clears the rotors to avoid significant damage to the turbine wheels. Steam lines and other significant obstructions are likely to be present as well. Use tag lines as necessary to maintain precise control over the upper casing after it rises above the guide pins.

Step 4 Place the cover in a safe, predetermined location where it can be accessed for service and inspection. Then remove the sealing glands.

> **CAUTION**
>
> Care must be taken to protect the machined surfaces of the casing. Nicks, scratches, and similar flaws can cause leaks that require a substantial amount of work to address after the casing has been reinstalled. Gaskets are not typically used to seal turbine casings, due to the extremely small clearances involved. The thickness of a gasket would interfere with the precise fit required. Therefore, the sealing action depends on precise and consistent contact between the polished surfaces of the casing flange.

Step 5 Carefully clean the mating surfaces between the bottom half of the casing, the casing cover, and the sealing glands while also inspecting for flaws.

Step 6 Apply an appropriate sealing compound according to specification to the sealing surfaces or in the sealant groove, if such a groove is present (*Figure 3*).

Figure 2 Large turbine with the upper casing removed.

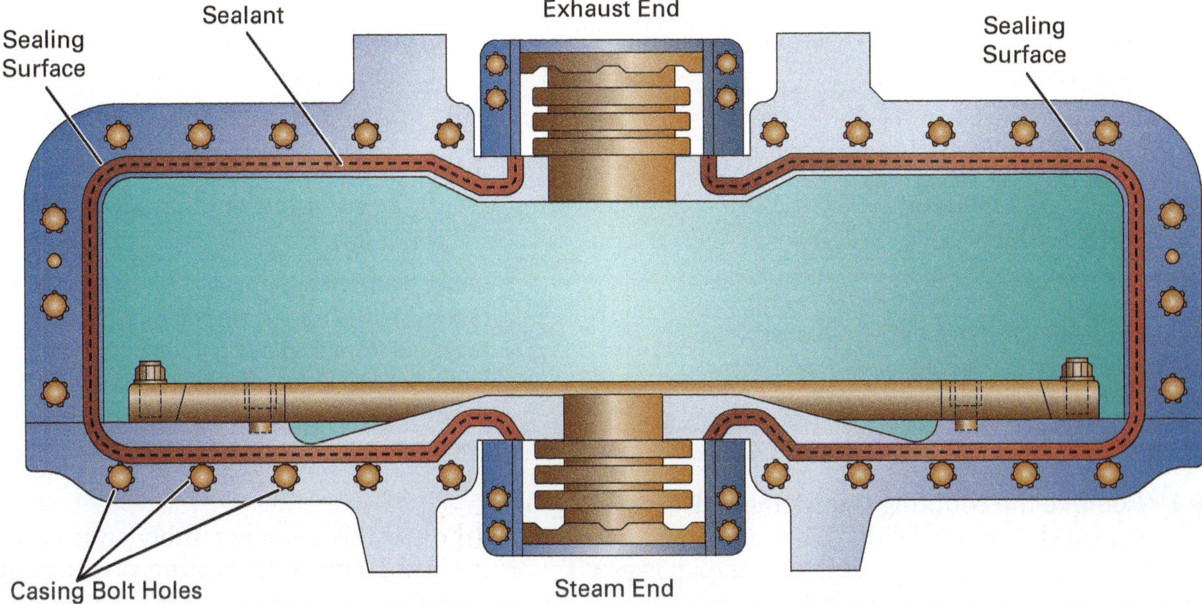

Figure 3 Sealant bead on a turbine casing.

> **NOTE**
> Another popular sealant used for turbine casings is boiled linseed oil. When used, its properties may allow it to be spread across the entire flange face.

> **CAUTION**
> Avoid getting sealant too close to the turbine casing bolt holes. A poor seal may result if the sealant gets in these holes. Always ensure that the manufacturer-recommended sealant is applied.

Step 7 Carefully position and lower the casing cover down onto the bottom half of the casing.

Step 8 Seat the dowel pins to ensure precise alignment.

Step 9 Tighten the bolts on the horizontal casing flange, starting with the bolts located closest to the sealing glands. Check the manufacturer's specifications for torque requirements and the tightening sequence.

> **NOTE**
> Remember that proper torquing typically requires that the torque be applied in 33 percent increments. For example, if a torque of 210 foot-pounds (ft-lb) is specified, tighten each bolt to 70 ft-lb, then 140 ft-lb, and finally to 210 ft-lb. It is also important to determine if the hardware must be torqued wet or dry.

Step 10 Clean the sealing gland flange surfaces and their matching turbine casing surfaces.

Step 11 Use compressed air to blow any debris away from the sealing glands.

> **WARNING!**
> Be sure to wear eye and face protection when working with compressed air.

Step 12 Apply a thin coat of sealing compound, according to manufacturer's instructions, to the horizontal flanges and inside the bolt circles of the vertical flange faces.

> **CAUTION**
> Do not use too much sealant on the sealing gland flanges. Avoid getting the sealant into the sealing glands. Keep the sealant approximately $\frac{3}{16}$" (~5 mm) away from the inside edges of the flanges. On larger turbines, the labyrinth seals must also be protected from the sealant. An example of a labyrinth seal is shown in *Figure 4*.

Step 13 Place the top sealing glands into position.

Step 14 Loosely install all the cap screws.

Step 15 Tighten the cap screws on the vertical flange until they are snug.

Step 16 Tighten the cap screws on the horizontal flange to the torque specified by the manufacturer incrementally, using a star pattern.

Step 17 Tighten the cap screws on the vertical flange to the specified torque incrementally, using a star pattern.

1.2.1 Maintaining Rotor Assemblies

Follow these basic steps to remove and reinstall the rotor assembly:

Step 1 Remove the coupling guard, then disconnect and remove the drive coupling.

Step 2 Remove the turbine casing cover.

Step 3 Remove the top half of the sealing glands and carbon rings.

Step 4 Remove the journal bearing liners.

Step 5 Disconnect the governor linkage.

Step 6 Remove the governor.

Step 7 Lift the rotor approximately 1" (~2.5 cm) using a sling. When lifting the rotor, keep it level and steady to prevent it from binding in the casing or damaging machined surfaces.

Figure 4 Common labyrinth seal profile.

Step 8 Lift the oil rings, also referred to as *slingers*, from the bearing housings and set them aside.

Step 9 Ensure that the rings are free of the bearing housing support casings.

Step 10 Lift the rotor out of the turbine casing.

Step 11 Lower the rotor assembly so it is within 1" (~2.5 cm) of its resting position in the casing.

Step 12 Place the oil rings into the openings between the bearing liner supports in the bottom of the bearing housing.

Step 13 Position the anti-rotation tab on the rotor locating bearing to engage the groove in the steam-end bearing housing.

Step 14 Lower the rotor slowly into the casing. Take your time and guide the rotor carefully into position.

Step 15 Reinstall or replace the journal bearing liners and caps.

Step 16 Reinstall the governor.

Step 17 Connect the governor linkage.

Step 18 Reinstall or replace the carbon rings and the top half of the sealing glands.

Step 19 Reinstall and secure the casing cover.

Step 20 Reinstall the shaft coupling and perform a shaft alignment.

Step 21 Reinstall the coupling guard.

Step 22 Complete a final inspection and ensure that all tasks have been completed before returning the turbine to service.

1.3.0 Maintaining and Repairing Sealing Glands and Carbon Rings

A turbine has either cartridge seals or two horizontally split sealing glands (*Figure 5*). One gland is bolted through a vertical flange to the steam end of the turbine casing and casing cover. The other gland is similarly attached to the exhaust end of the turbine casing.

In smaller turbines, the sealing glands house the carbon rings, which seal both the casing and the rotor shaft. These rings minimize steam leakage along the shaft when the turbine operates in a noncondensing mode. Small turbines operating in a condensing mode employ carbon rings and a sealing steam arrangement to prevent air from leaking into the casing at the low-pressure end. The carbon rings are self-lubricating.

> **WARNING!**
>
> Ensure that all sources of stored energy are disabled, locked out, and tagged before initiating any maintenance activity.

1.3.1 Disassembling Sealing Glands

Follow these basic steps to disassemble a sealing gland. Remember that the manufacturer's guidance supersedes any guidance offered here:

Step 1 Remove the cap screws from the horizontal and vertical flanges on the top half of the sealing glands.

Step 2 Pry the top halves of the sealing glands away from the bottom halves, gently using a pry bar to break the horizontal and vertical joints.

Step 3 Lift the top halves of the sealing glands straight up until the halves are clear of the carbon ring assemblies.

1.3.2 Replacing the Carbon Rings

Carbon rings aren't adjustable to accommodate wear or damage. Replace them if an excessive amount of steam is leaking. When a turbine is reassembled, carbon rings are not typically reused, regardless of their condition or performance prior to disassembly.

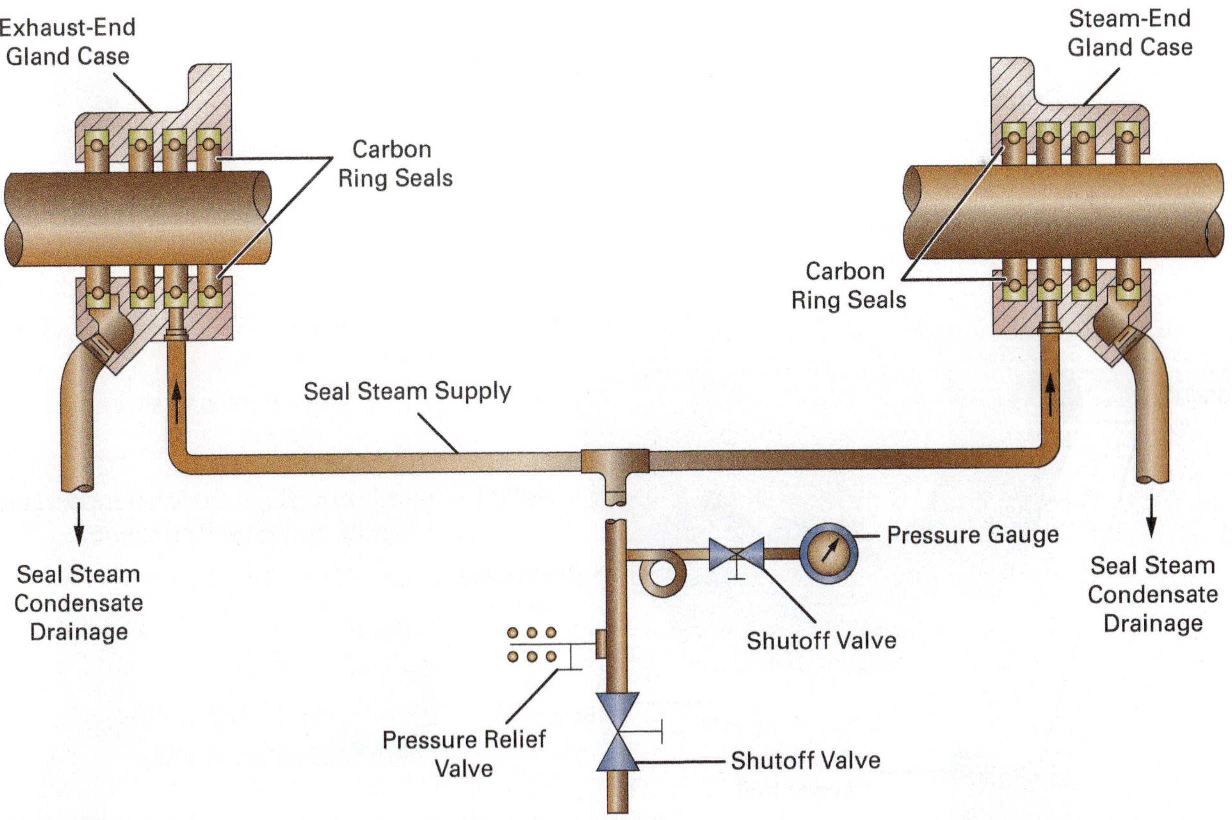

Figure 5 Sealing glands.

Always install new carbon rings in complete sets, rather than individual rings. The carbon rings are typically surrounded by a spring to hold multiple segments together. Three segments is common.

Follow these basic steps to replace the carbon rings:

Step 1   Remove the cylinder cover to provide access to the gland case containing the carbon rings (*Figure 6*).

Step 2   Use a thickness gauge to check the radial clearance of the carbon ring (*Figure 7*). Compare the results to the turbine specifications.

Step 3   Lift the upper half of the gland case (*Figure 8*) from the lower half. The lower half of the gland case is held by a large-headed screw that screws into the cylinder base and clamps the outer edge of the gland case.

Step 4   Unhook the carbon ring spring from around the first carbon ring.

Step 5   Slide the carbon ring stop pin off the carbon ring spring.

Step 6   Remove the top segment of the carbon ring from the lower half of the gland case.

Step 7   Rotate the carbon ring segments around the rotor shaft to access them for removal.

Step 8   Pull the retaining spring from the sealing gland.

Step 9   Clean the sealing gland, rotor shaft, and all sealing surfaces on the sealing gland flanges.

Step 10   Use compressed air to blow out the sealing glands.

Step 11   Place the carbon ring retaining springs under and part of the way around the rotor shaft.

Step 12   Roll the new carbon ring segments around the shaft and into the sealing gland grooves. Ensure the carbon ring

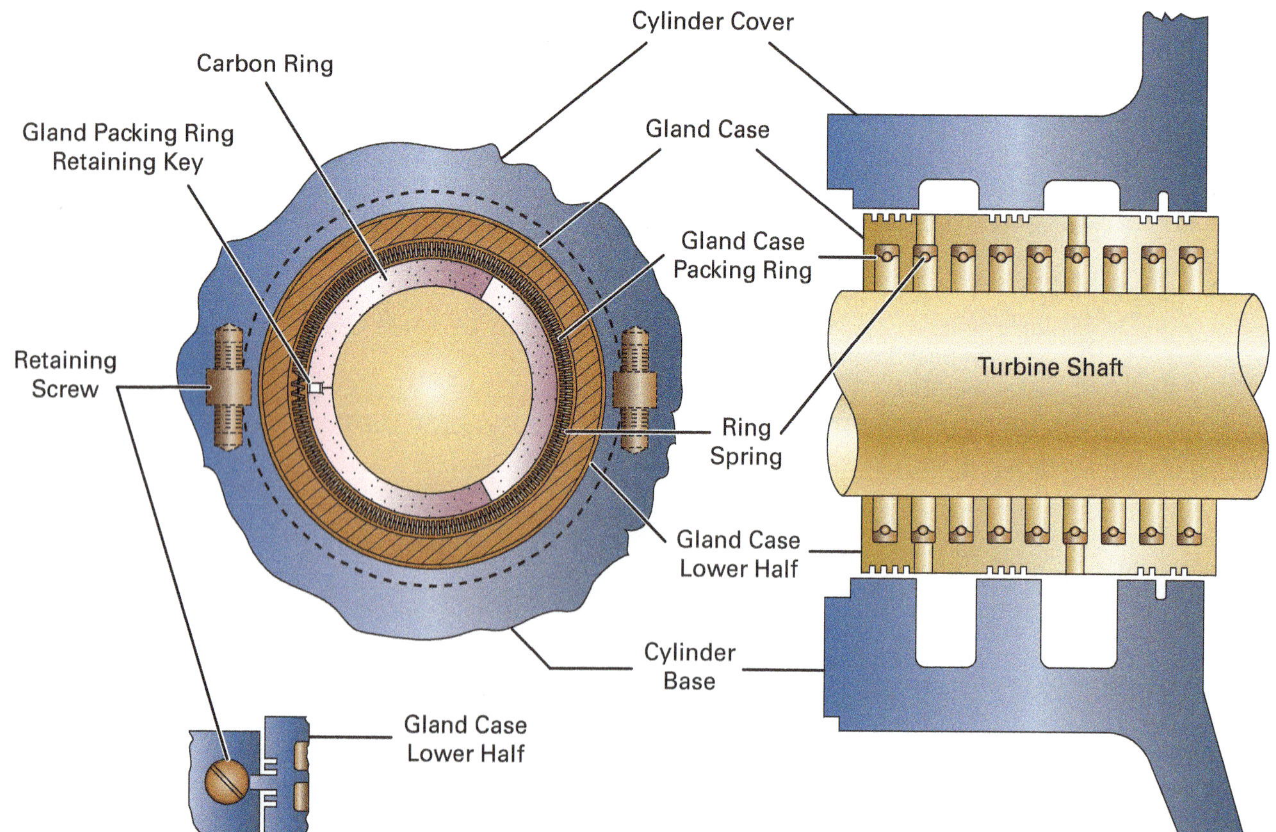

Figure 6 Carbon ring removal.

sealing face is facing the rotor and the flow of steam to properly seal around the shaft. Align the match marks on the carbon ring segments to ensure proper assembly.

Refer to *Figure 8* and note the match marks on the carbon rings. The match marks are typically oriented toward the incoming steam flow.

Step 13 Slide the carbon ring stop pin onto the retaining springs and position the stops in the notched carbon ring segments.

Step 14 Hook the ends of each retaining spring together.

Step 15 Rotate the carbon rings so that the carbon ring stop pins are seated in the notches in the bottom half of the sealing glands.

Step 16 Install the upper half of the gland case.

Step 17 Install the turbine cylinder cover.

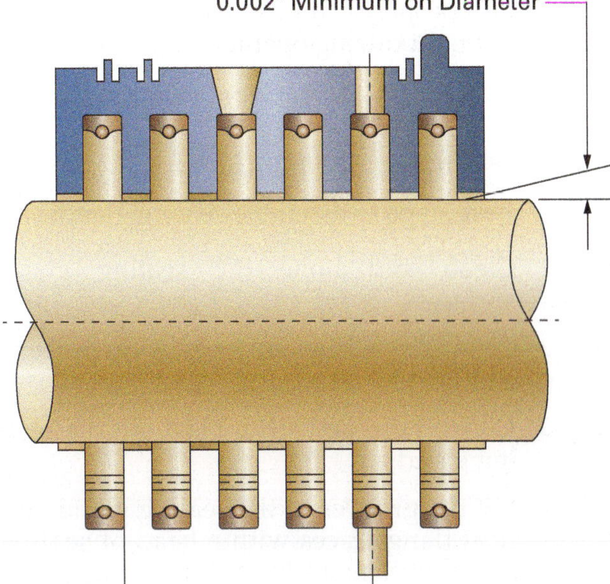

Figure 7 Carbon ring radial clearance.

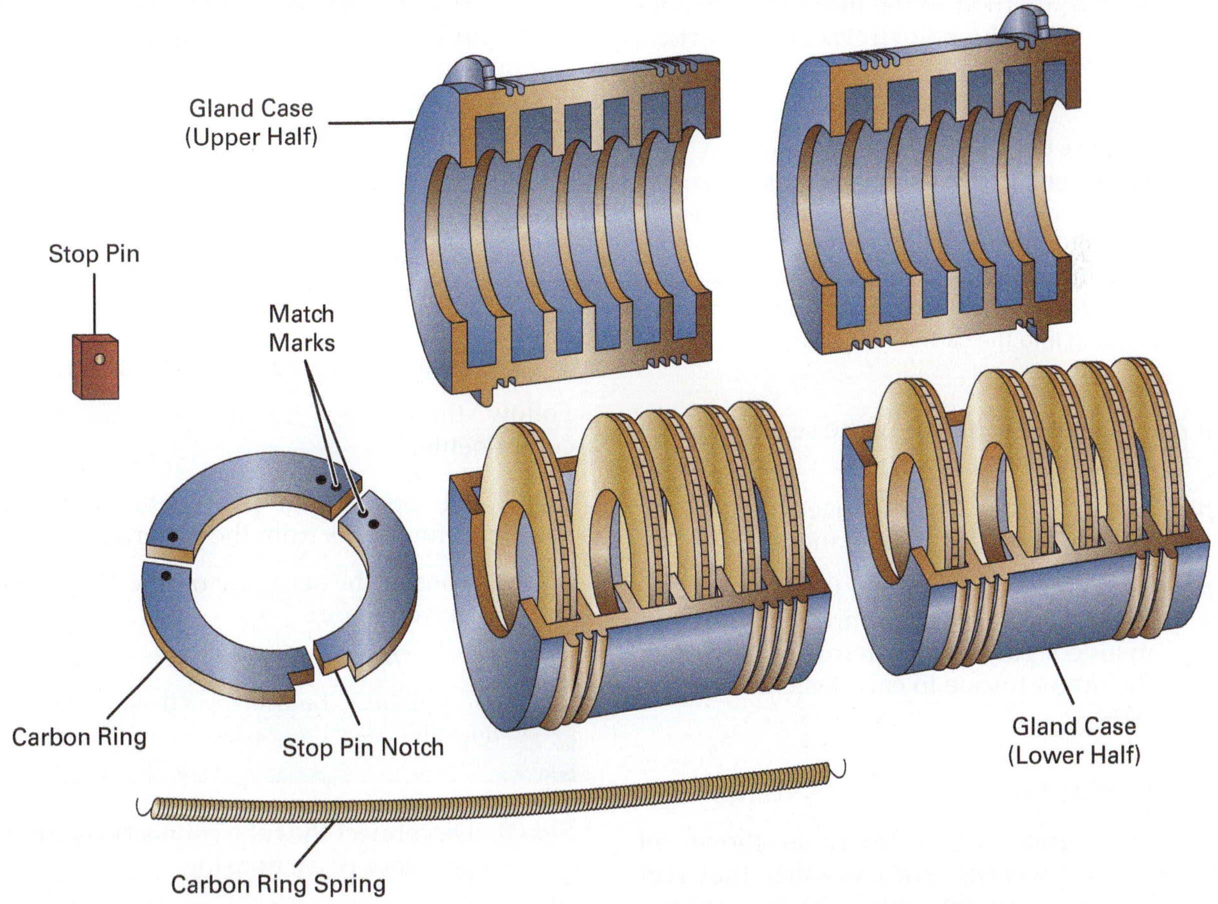

Figure 8 Gland case assembly.

Step 18 After completing all necessary start-up preparations, ensure that the glands function properly and show no signs of being too tight during operation.

Step 19 Return the turbine to service.

1.3.3 Assembling Sealing Glands

Follow these steps to assemble sealing glands:

Step 1 Clean and hone the sealing gland surfaces.

Step 2 Clean the mating surfaces of the turbine casing.

Step 3 Use compressed air to blow out the sealing glands.

Step 4 Fill the grooves in the sealing gland vertical flange faces with a bead of sealing compound about $\frac{3}{16}$" (~5 mm) wide.

Step 5 Cut the sealing compound with a putty knife to prevent it from extending beyond the horizontal flange.

Step 6 Apply the manufacturer's recommended sealing method to the horizontal flanges and inside the bolt circles of the vertical flange areas.

Do not use too much sealant on the sealing gland flanges. Excess sealant may get in the sealing glands and adhere to the carbon rings, interfering with the seal. Keep the sealant approximately $\frac{3}{16}$" (~5 mm) away from the inside edges of the flanges to prevent it from squeezing into the carbon ring chambers.

Step 7 Place the top halves of the sealing glands in position.

Step 8 Install the cap screws (finger-tight) on the horizontal and vertical flanges.

Step 9 Tighten the cap screws to the manufacturer's specified torque and in the recommended pattern, applying one-third of the target torque to each fastener on each pass.

1.4.0 Maintaining Governor Systems

An example governor assembly is shown in *Figure 9*. The governor is a controller that regulates the servos of the steam control valves, and thus the valve positions. They govern the horsepower developed, regulate extraction and turbine back pressure, control the start-up load rate, and synchronize the shaft speed and frequency output. The governor is never used, however, as a means of shutting the turbine down.

The following components are shared by many governor systems:

- A self-contained hydraulic oil system, including a built-in oil pump and relief valve
- A centrifugal flyweight head and pilot valve assembly that control governor oil flow to and from a hydraulic power cylinder assembly
- A power cylinder assembly, also called a *servomotor*, that operates the turbine governor valve linkage
- An internal governor compensation system for control stability
- An external, manually operated governor speed-setting adjustment system

Follow these basic guidelines to maintain the governor system:

- Check the governor oil level daily, and add oil as needed to maintain the oil level at the manufacturer's specified level. Do not overfill the governor reservoir because an excess of oil can lead to foaming. A low oil level causes sluggish governor operation and overheating, which can result in damage to the turbine as well as the governor system.
- Inspect the governor linkage daily for binding, excessive play, and loose hardware.
- Clean and lubricate the governor linkage as needed, using a silicone grease that resists high temperatures and water.

1.4.1 Removing Governor Components

Follow these steps to remove the governor components:

Step 1 Disconnect the pneumatic or electrical connections from the governor.

Step 2 Loosen the setscrew on the lever and remove the pin.

Perform *Steps 3* and *4* only if the turbine is oil-ring lubricated; otherwise, proceed to *Step 5*.

Step 3 Disconnect the tube connections from the governor drive housing.

Step 4 Remove the oil feed tube from the governor drive housing.

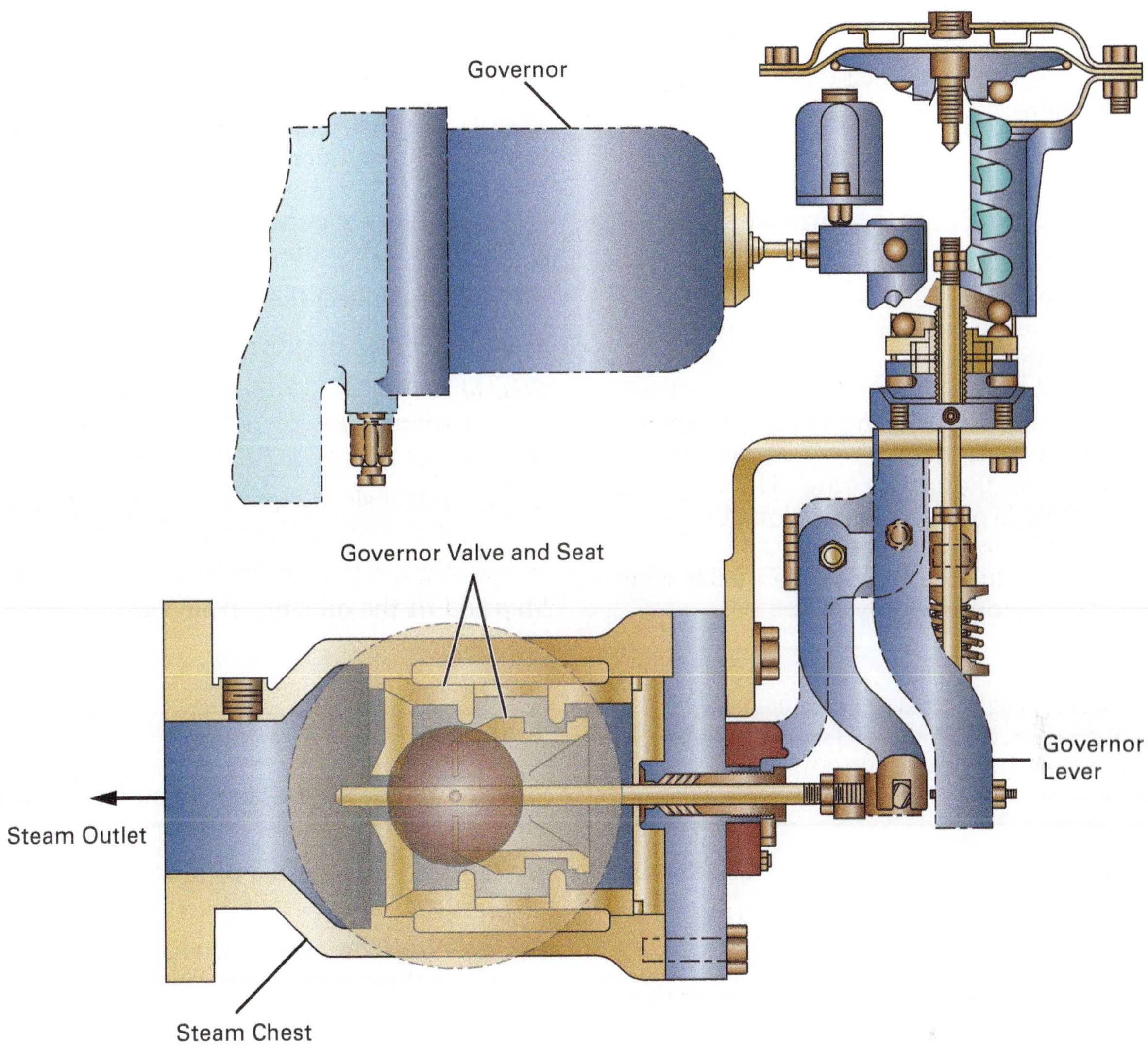

Figure 9 Example governor system.

Step 5 Remove the dowel pins and bolts that secure the governor to the drive housing.

Step 6 Lift the governor off the drive housing. Pay attention as you do so, as shims are likely present.

> **CAUTION**
>
> Be careful to avoid damaging the worm gear and worm wheel.

Step 7 Mark the shims before removing them to ensure that they are returned to their original position.

Step 8 Remove the shims.

1.4.2 Replacing Governor Components

Follow these steps to replace the governor components:

Step 1 Install the shims on the governor drive housing.

Step 2 Place the governor on the governor drive housing.

> **CAUTION**
>
> This unit must be handled carefully to prevent damage.

Step 3 Install the oil feed tube and connect the tube connections if required.

Step 4 Install the bolts and the dowels.

Step 5 Install the pin in the lever.

Step 6 Tighten the setscrew.

Step 7 Connect the pneumatic or electrical connections.

1.5.0 Replacing Nozzle Rings and Reversing Blade Assemblies

The nozzle ring directs the steam flow into the first row of rotor blades or buckets at the proper angle. Steam exits the first row of rotor blades and passes through the stationary reversing blade assembly before entering the second row of rotor blades. The reversing blade assembly is positioned between the two rows of rotor blades and is bolted to the nozzle ring. The reversing blade assembly is accurately positioned by spacers and requires no adjustment.

Follow these steps to replace the nozzle rings and reversing blade assembly:

Step 1 Disconnect the coupling between the turbine and the driven machine.

Step 2 Remove the turbine casing cover.

Step 3 Remove the top halves of the sealing glands.

Step 4 Remove the carbon rings.

Step 5 Remove the cooling water piping from the bearing caps if applicable.

Step 6 Remove the dowels and bolts from the bearing cap joints.

Step 7 Pry the bearing caps away from the bearing housings, gently using a pry bar to break the joints.

Step 8 Raise the caps approximately 1" (~2.5 cm) and pry out the top liners from the bearing caps to release the oil rings from the caps.

Step 9 Remove the bearing caps.

Step 10 Remove the top journal bearing liners.

Step 11 Lift the rotor slightly and roll the bottom bearing liners away from the positioning lugs to remove them. Once the bottom liners are removed, the rotor shaft will be resting on the shaft sleeve seals.

Step 12 Disconnect the governor linkage.

Step 13 Remove the governor.

Step 14 Place a sling either outside or between the rotor disks.

Step 15 Lift the rotor approximately 1" (~2.5 cm). Lift it slowly and keep it level to prevent it from binding in the casing or damaging mechanical surfaces.

Step 16 Lift the oil rings from the bearing housings.

Step 17 Place the rings to the side so that they are free of the bearing housing support casings.

Step 18 Lift the rotor assembly out of the turbine casing.

Step 19 Set the rotor in a rotor stand to prevent it from rolling.

Step 20 Wrap the rotor journals and carbon ring sealing areas with clean rags to protect them from damage.

Step 21 Remove the bolts, lock washers, and spacers that secure the reversing blade assembly. Mark and identify each spacer so that it can be returned to its original location.

Step 22 Remove the nozzle ring bolts and lock washers.

Step 23 Remove the nozzle ring from the casing.

Step 24 Inspect the nozzle ring and the reversing blade assembly for scale or boiler compound deposits. Clean the ring and the reversing blade assembly as necessary. Replace any eroded parts.

Step 25 Clean the casing and nozzle ring sealing surfaces.

Step 26 Apply a thin coat of paste sealant to the nozzle ring sealing surface on the steam-end casing. An example of a suitable sealant is shown in *Figure 10*.

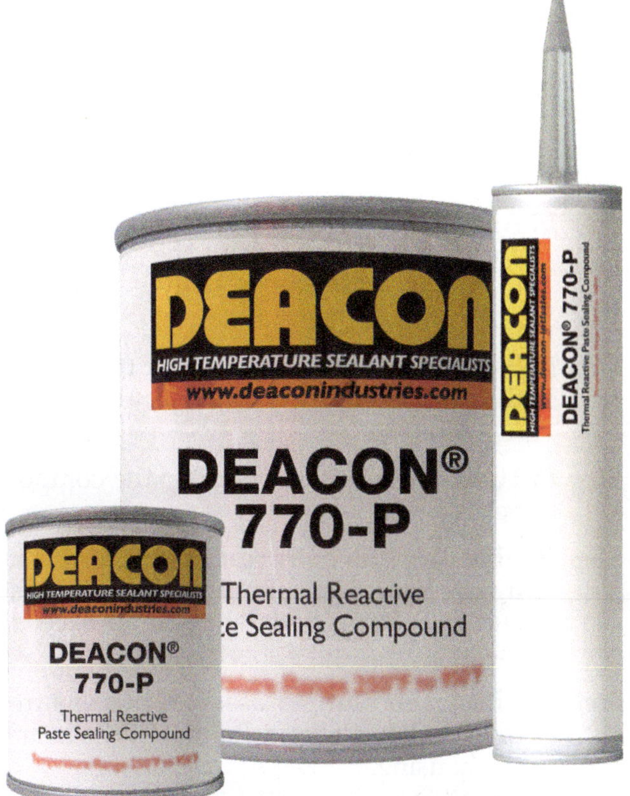

Figure 10 Example of paste sealant suitable for nozzle rings.

Step 27 Apply a high-temperature anti-galling/anti-seize compound to the threads of the nozzle ring bolts.

Anti-galling products that incorporate molybdenum sulfate are generally preferred over those that contain nickel.

Step 28 Bolt the nozzle ring to the turbine casing. Ensure that lock washers are used with all bolts.

Step 29 Place lock washers on the reversing blade assembly bolts.

Step 30 Apply an anti-galling/anti-seize compound to the bolt threads.

Step 31 Insert the bolts into the holes in the reversing blade assembly.

Step 32 Slip the spacers over the bolts.

Step 33 Position the reversing blade assembly in the turbine casing.

Ensure that the reversing blade assembly is installed in the same location from which it was removed. Also ensure that the installation position coincides with the rotation of the turbine to avoid causing damage to the unit.

Step 34 Bolt the reversing blade assembly to the nozzle ring.

Step 35 Lower the rotor assembly to within 1" (~2.5 cm) of its seated position in the casing.

Guide the rotor assembly slowly and carefully into the casing to prevent the disks from contacting the reversing blade assembly, as this will damage the blades.

Step 36 Position the oil rings so that they fall into the openings between the bearing liner supports located in the bottom of the bearing housings.

Step 37 Position the anti-rotation tab on the rotor locating bearing so that it engages the groove in the steam-end bearing housing.

Step 38 Slowly lower the rotor assembly into the casing.

Step 39 Install the journal bearing liners and caps.

Step 40 Install the governor and connect the related linkage.

Step 41 Install the carbon rings and the top halves of the sealing glands as previously outlined.

Step 42 Install the turbine casing cover.

1.6.0 Replacing Rotor Locating Bearings, Pedestals, and Housings

The rotor locating bearing maintains the correct axial position of the rotor assembly in the turbine casing. Follow these basic steps to replace the rotor locating bearing:

Ensure that all sources of stored energy are disabled, locked out, and tagged before initiating any maintenance.

Step 1 Remove the rotor assembly.

Step 2 Remove the setscrews from the overspeed trip body.

Step 3 Heat the overspeed trip body evenly. Apply the heat as quickly as possible, then pull the overspeed trip body from the rotor shaft.

Step 4 Use retaining ring pliers to remove the retainer ring.

Step 5 Remove the rotor locating bearing with a bearing puller.

Step 6 Mount a dial indicator perpendicular to a vertical shaft to check the runout (axial rotor movement).

Step 7 Shift the rotor as far as possible in both axial directions while observing the dial indicator for runout.

Step 8 Install the bearing on the shaft using a sleeve-type bearing driver. The driver must make proper contact with the bearing inner race.

Step 9 Seat the bearing solidly against the machined shoulder on the shaft so that the shielded side of the bearing faces the trip body.

Step 10 Install the retainer ring, seating it firmly in the groove on the rotor shaft. Ensure the beveled edge of the retainer is positioned toward the trip body.

Step 11 Heat the trip body in an oven or bearing heater.

Step 12 Quickly place the heated trip body on the rotor shaft. If it will not slip into place, remove it and continue heating.

Step 13 Align the setscrew holes in the trip body and the shaft and tighten the setscrew(s) to ensure that the trip body is properly positioned on the shaft.

Step 14 Back the setscrew(s) out one or two turns, then allow the trip body to cool to room temperature.

Step 15 Tighten the setscrew(s) after the components have cooled.

Step 16 Check the trip body runout and correct it if necessary. The runout on the outboard end of the trip body should not exceed the manufacturer's specification.

Step 17 Check the plunger assembly to ensure that it is properly positioned in the bearing housing.

Step 18 Install the rotor in the turbine casing.

Step 19 Flush the rotor locating bearing with clean oil.

Step 20 Install the bearing cap.

1.6.1 Replacing Exhaust-End Bearing Pedestals

Follow these steps to replace the exhaust-end bearing pedestal:

Step 1 Remove the rotor assembly.

Step 2 Support the weight of the turbine exhaust-end casing with wooden cribbing or dedicated stands to prevent damaging the casing. Avoid leaving the casing supported by a hydraulic jack.

Step 3 Remove the mounting bolts and the dowel pins from the pedestal support feet.

Step 4 Remove the tapered pins from the combining studs.

Step 5 Loosen the four cap screws three or four turns.

Step 6 Pry the pedestal away from the casing until the spacers are free to move.

Step 7 Remove the cap screws and the spacers, then mark each spacer as it is removed so that it can be returned to the same location.

Step 8 Slide the pedestal off the combining studs and dowel pins.

Step 9 Slide the new pedestal onto the combining studs and dowel pins.

Step 10 Install the spacers and cap screws, ensuring that the spacers are returned to their original positions.

Step 11 Tighten the cap screws.

Step 12 Insert the taper pins into the pedestal and the combining studs.

Step 13 Install the rotor assembly, following the previous guidance.

Step 14 Install the bottom half of the journal bearing liners.

Step 15 Check the bearing alignment and adjust if necessary.

1.6.2 Replacing Steam-End Bearing Housings

Follow these steps to replace the steam-end bearing housing:

Step 1 Remove the rotor assembly.

Step 2 Support the steam end of the turbine casing and steam chest with wooden cribbing or dedicated stands to prevent damage. Avoid leaving the casing supported by a hydraulic jack.

Step 3 Remove the hold-down bolts and dowel pins from the steam-end bearing support.

Step 4 Remove the bolts that secure the support to the bearing housing.

Step 5 Loosen the socket head cap screws.

Step 6 Pry the bearing housing away from the turbine casing with a pry bar until the spacers are free to move.

Step 7 Remove the cap screws and spacers. Mark the spacers as they are removed so that they can be returned to their original positions.

Step 8 Pull the bearing housing off the dowel pins.

Step 9 Push the bearing housing onto the dowel pins in the steam-end turbine casing.

Step 10 Install the cap screws and spacers, ensuring that the spacers are returned to their original positions.

Step 11 Bolt the support to the bearing housing.

Step 12 Install the rotor assembly.

Step 13 Install the bottom halves of the journal bearing liners.

Step 14 Check the bearing alignment and adjust if necessary.

1.6.3 Aligning Exhaust-End Bearing Pedestals and Steam-End Bearing Housings

Follow these steps to align the exhaust-end bearing pedestal and the steam-end bearing housing:

Step 1 Remove the rotor assembly.

Step 2 Clean the shaft journals.

Step 3 Apply a light coat of layout dye containing Prussian blue (*Figure 11*) to both shaft journals.

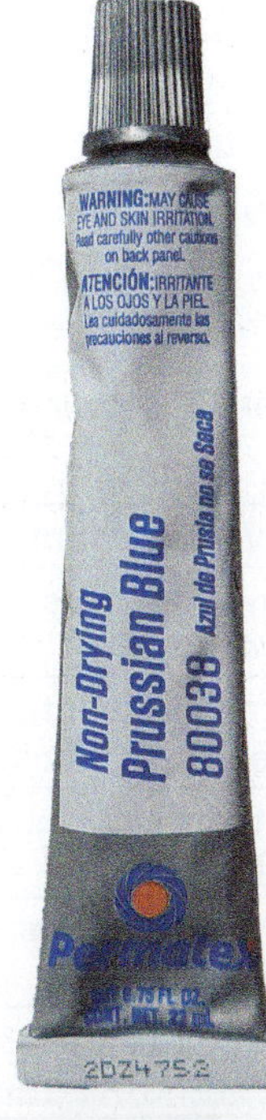

Figure 11 Prussian blue layout dye.

Step 4 Install the bottom-half journal bearing liners in the bearing pedestal and steam-end bearing housing. Ensure that the liners are properly seated to prevent damage.

Step 5 Lower the rotor assembly until the full weight of the rotor is supported by the journal bearing liners.

Step 6 Rotate the rotor assembly one-quarter turn in each direction. While turning the rotor, ensure that the rotor shaft is seated on the bottom of the bearing liners and does not shift sideways or upward while being rotated.

Step 7 Remove the rotor assembly from the turbine casing, then check the bearing contact by examining the wear pattern in the dye.

The exhaust-end bearing pedestal and the steam-end bearing housing are considered aligned when the bearing contact with the shaft journals is at least 85 percent of the surface area along the bottom of the bearing liners. The contact along the sides of the liners must also be parallel with the bearing bore and equal on each side.

Step 8 Place shim stock in increments of 0.002" (use 0.05 mm shims for metric applications) behind the spacers that need shims to correct any misalignment.

Step 9 Recheck the bearing contact and continue to add shims until the bearings display proper alignment in the dye.

Step 10 Remove the shims from each spacer and alter the thickness of the opposite spacer accordingly. Surface grinding is the preferred method for adjusting the thickness of the spacers.

Step 11 Recheck the bearing contact a final time.

1.7.0 Maintaining Mechanical Overspeed Trip Mechanisms

All turbines have a specified maximum rotational speed. While they can typically endure speeds as much as 10 percent higher, a significant overspeed condition can result in the destruction of the turbine. On many of today's turbines, overspeed protection is electronic.

Table 1 provides a comparison in performance between mechanical and electronic overspeed protection. Electronic systems offer a significant advantage. However, mechanical overspeed systems are still often encountered.

The mechanical overspeed trip device is mounted in a housing carried on the governor end of the rotor shaft. It is actuated by centrifugal force when the turbine reaches a predetermined speed. The predetermined speed is typically 10 percent above the normal full-load turbine speed.

The linkage is arranged to control not only the governor valve but also the emergency quick-closing valve, located ahead of the governor valve. The overspeed trip mechanism (*Figure 12*) should be checked regularly to ensure correction operation.

Two factors should be considered when maintaining a mechanical overspeed trip system. One is the potential for valve stems to become sticky due to scale deposits or carryover. Another issue

Table 1 Comparison of Mechanical and Electronic Overspeed Systems

Mechanical Overspeed Protection	Electronic Overspeed Protection
Trip speed generally accurate to only ±50 rpm.	Overspeed accuracy to setpoint is precise.
Trip speed tends to vary over time.	No variance in trip speed over time.
A mechanical trip-lever interface that responds to centrifugal force is required.	No levers or physical contact with the shaft is required.
Can only be interfaced with controls and alarm circuits using mechanical devices and linkage.	Provides an easy electronic interface with control systems and alarms without mechanical devices.
Tendency of valve stems and plungers to stick due to accumulated deposits.	No vulnerability to accumulated deposits.
Must be decoupled from the turbine for testing (turbine shutdown required).	Systems can be tested using a signal generator with little or no effect or risk to the turbine.
Adjusting the trip setpoint requires several turbine starts and stops.	No extra turbine cycles are needed to adjust the setpoint.

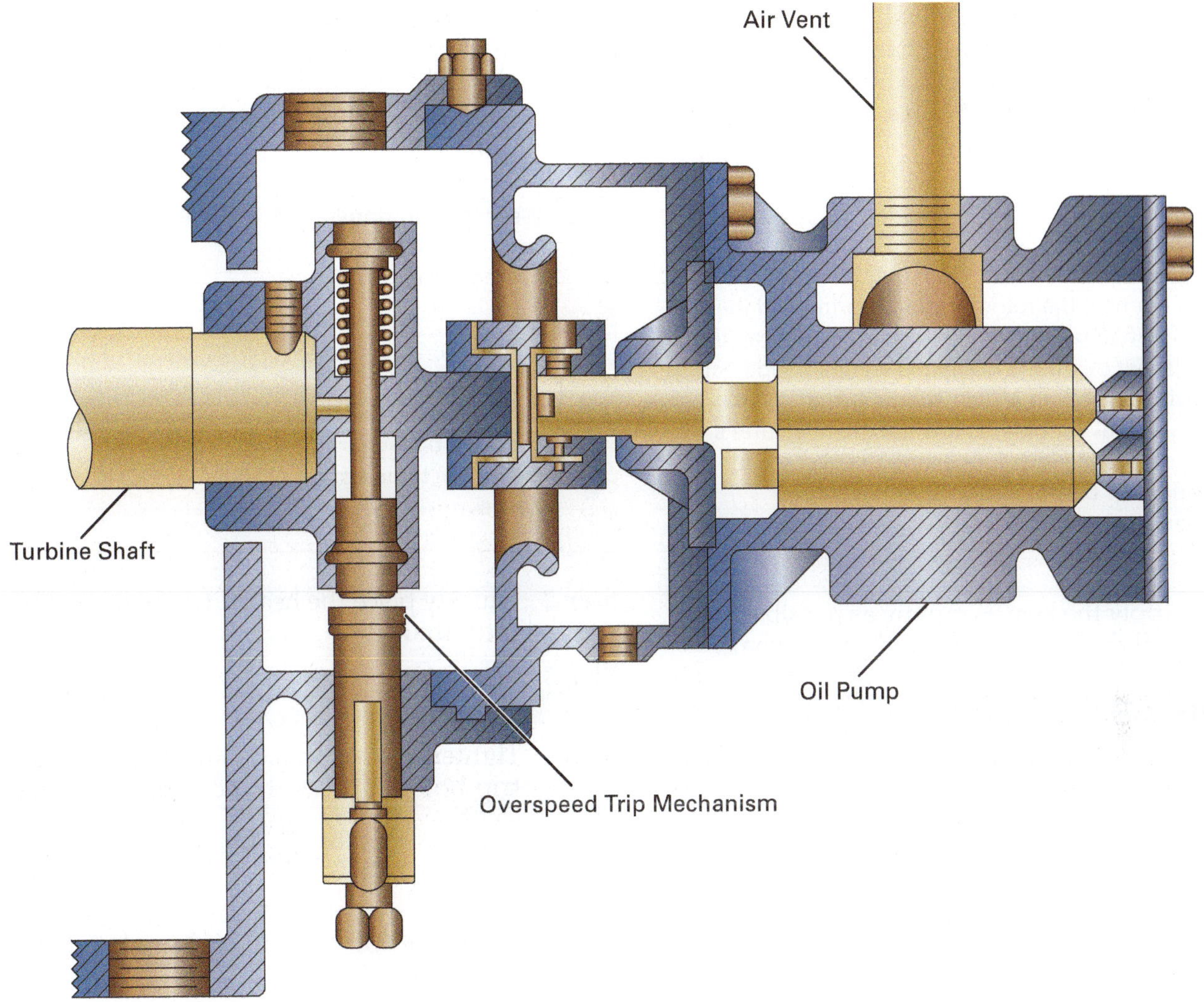

Figure 12 Overspeed trip mechanism.

to look for is excessive clearance between the turbine shaft and the trip lever due to wear or incorrect adjustment.

> **WARNING!**
>
> Ensure that all sources of stored energy are disabled, locked out, and tagged before initiating any maintenance.

1.7.1 Disassembling Overspeed Trip Mechanisms

Follow these steps to disassemble the overspeed trip mechanism:

> **NOTE**
>
> In many cases, overspeed mechanisms may only be adjusted or tested by certified specialists.

Step 1 Remove the steam-end bearing cap.

Step 2 Remove the retaining ring surrounding the adjustment nut out of the trip body.

Step 3 Remove the adjusting nut, trip spring, and washers. Record the number of turns required to remove the adjusting nut so that it can be returned to the original setting during assembly.

Step 4 Rotate the rotor shaft 180 degrees, then remove the retaining ring surrounding the weighted end of the trip pin.

Step 5 Remove the trip pin from the trip body.

Step 6 Remove the auxiliary weight, if present.

Step 7 Remove the oil pump.

Step 8 Remove the rotor assembly from the turbine casing.

Step 9 Remove the setscrew from the trip body.

Step 10 Heat the trip body evenly using a torch.

Wear the appropriate PPE, including heavy heat-resistant gloves. Avoid direct contact with heated components.

Do not heat the rotor locating bearing and the rotor shaft while heating the trip body. Wrap the adjacent bearing and shaft in an approved heat-resistant cloth to protect them from the heat. To prevent warping, follow the manufacturer's recommendations for heating the overspeed trip body. Do not exceed the specified maximum temperature.

Step 11 Apply the heat as rapidly as possible, then pull the trip body from the rotor shaft.

1.7.2 Replacing Plunger Assemblies

Follow these steps to replace the plunger assembly:

Step 1 Remove the steam-end bearing.

Step 2 Remove the governor and adapter piece from the steam-end bearing housing.

Step 3 Loosen the jam nut.

Step 4 Remove the setscrew from the side of the bearing housing.

Step 5 Remove the setscrew from the plunger assembly.

Step 6 Separate the two halves of the plunger.

Step 7 Remove the two plunger halves from the bearing housing.

Step 8 Install the two new plunger halves into the bearing housing, making sure that they fit together tightly.

Step 9 Install the setscrew into the plunger assembly to ensure proper alignment.

Step 10 Secure the setscrew into the side of the bearing housing.

Step 11 Tighten the jam nut.

Step 12 Install the governor and adapter piece into the steam-end bearing housing.

Step 13 Install the steam-end bearing, taking care not to damage it.

1.7.3 Replacing Trip Bodies

Follow these steps to replace a trip body:

Step 1 Heat the trip body in an oven.

Wear the appropriate PPE, including heavy heat-resistant gloves. Avoid direct contact with heated components.

Do not exceed the maximum temperature specified by the turbine manufacturer. A maximum temperature of 500°F (260°C) is typical.

Step 2 Quickly place the heated trip body on the rotor shaft.

Step 3 Align the setscrew holes in the trip body and the shaft.

Step 4 Tighten the setscrew to ensure that the trip body is properly positioned on the shaft.

Step 5 Back the setscrew out of the body one or two turns.

Step 6 Allow the trip body to cool to room temperature.

Step 7 Tighten the setscrew.

Step 8 Check the trip body runout and correct if necessary. The runout should not exceed the manufacturer's specification on the outboard end of the trip body.

Step 9 Lock the setscrew.

Step 10 Ensure that the plunger assembly is properly positioned in the bearing housing.

Step 11 Return the rotor to the turbine casing.

1.7.4 Assembling Overspeed Trip Mechanisms

Follow these steps to assemble the overspeed trip mechanism:

Step 1 Place the auxiliary weight on the trip pin.

Step 2 Insert the trip pin into the trip body.

Step 3 Position the weighted end of the pin on the opposite side of the trip body setscrew.

Step 4 Press the retaining ring into the trip body to secure the weighted end of the trip pin. The staple must be fully seated in the circular groove in the trip body.

Step 5 Place the trip spring in the trip body.

Step 6 Install the washers.

Step 7 Return the adjusting nut to the original setting. Tighten the nut the same number of turns that were made during disassembly.

Step 8 Press the retaining ring into the trip body to lock the adjusting nut. Ensure that the staple is fully seated in the circular groove in the trip body.

1.7.5 Adjusting the Trip Pin and Plunger Clearance

Follow these steps to adjust the trip pin and plunger clearance:

Step 1 Remove the inspection plug from the steam-end bearing cap.

Step 2 Rotate the rotor shaft by hand until the adjusting nut can be seen through the inspection hole. This positions the weighted end of the trip pin directly above the plunger assembly.

Step 3 Latch the resetting lever.

Step 4 Loosen the jam nut on the trip-lever jackscrew.

Step 5 Push the plunger assembly upward and into the bearing housing. Ensure that the plunger assembly is in solid contact with the trip pin.

Step 6 Adjust the jackscrew to obtain $\frac{1}{16}$" (~1.6 mm) of clearance between the plunger and the jackscrew.

Step 7 Tighten the jam nut and lock it in place.

> **CAUTION**
>
> The jam nut must be properly tightened to prevent the jackscrew from vibrating loose during operation. A loose jackscrew can prevent the overspeed trip system from shutting down the turbine.

Step 8 Recheck the clearance of the trip pin and plunger.

1.7.6 Adjusting Turbine Trip Speeds

Follow these steps to adjust the turbine trip speed:

Step 1 Remove the inspection plug from the steam-end bearing cap.

Step 2 Rotate the rotor shaft by hand until the adjusting nut can be viewed through the inspection hole.

Step 3 Latch the resetting lever.

Step 4 Place a nonferrous drift pin (brass or bronze) on the adjusting nut.

Step 5 Strike the drift pin sharply to ensure that the trip pin, trip valve, and trip linkage function properly.

Step 6 Latch the resetting lever.

Step 7 Start the turbine and monitor the speed.

> **WARNING!**
>
> Starting the turbine requires all energy sources to be enabled. All relevant start-up procedures for the turbine being serviced must be completed. Only qualified personnel should conduct and manage the start-up process.

Step 8 Override the governor and gradually overspeed the turbine until it trips or approaches an unsafe speed.

Step 9 Close the steam inlet shutoff valve and again disable, lock out, and tag all energy sources.

Step 10 Turn the shaft by hand after the rotor shaft stops rotating until the adjusting nut is visible through the bearing cap inspection hole.

Step 11 Pry the retaining ring partially away from the trip body until the adjusting nut is free to turn.

Step 12 Turn the adjusting nut to change the trip speed. To decrease the trip speed, turn the nut counterclockwise. To increase the trip speed, turn the nut clockwise.

Step 13 Push the retaining ring back into the trip body, making sure that the staple is firmly seated.

Step 14 Check that the trip pin moves freely.

Step 15 Restart the turbine.

Step 16 Override the governor once again and gradually overspeed the turbine until it trips or approaches an unsafe speed.

Step 17 Repeat these steps as necessary until the turbine shuts down at the specified trip speed. Several starts and stops are generally required to ensure that it works properly and at the required trip speed.

Remember that mechanical overspeed trip systems rarely remain accurate over time. Ensure that the mechanism is tested and adjusted periodically, according to an established maintenance schedule.

1.7.7 Disassembling and Assembling Trip Valves

Follow these steps to disassemble and assemble the trip valve:

Step 1 Place the trip valve in the "tripped" position.

Step 2 Disconnect the closing spring from the resetting lever.

Step 3 Remove the cap screws from the valve cover.

Step 4 Lift the trip valve assembly and cover from the steam chest body.

Step 5 Remove the nut, the spring, the bushing, and the spring seats from the valve stem.

Step 6 Remove the valve assembly from the cover.

Step 7 Use a nonferrous (brass or bronze) drift pin to drive the bushings out of the valve cover.

Step 8 Clean the valve cover thoroughly.

Step 9 Press new bushings into the valve cover and lock them in place.

Step 10 Clean the sealing surfaces on the valve cover flange and the steam chest body.

Step 11 Insert the valve stem into the lower guide bushing and to the valve cover. Turn the valve stem into and through the connection.

Step 12 Install the spring seats, bushings, spring, and locknut.

Step 13 Apply the specified sealant to the sealing surfaces of the steam chest valve cover flange.

Step 14 Return the valve assembly and cover to the steam chest body.

Step 15 Tighten the cap screws.

Step 16 Backseat the trip valve.

Follow the procedure in the next section to backseat the trip valve.

Step 17 After the valve is properly backseated, connect the closing spring to the resetting lever.

1.7.8 Backseating Trip Valves

Follow these steps to backseat the trip valve:

Step 1 Disassemble the trip valve and linkage. Clean all the removed components.

Step 2 Replace any worn linkage pins, guide bushings, valve stems, knife edges, and latches.

Step 3 Reassemble the trip valve and linkage.

Step 4 Disconnect the closing spring from the resetting lever.

Step 5 Remove the locknut from the trip valve stem.

While removing the locknut, firmly grasp and maintain control of the spring the locknut secures to prevent it from striking someone as it decompresses.

Step 6 Pry against the bottom of the connection and the valve cover with a small pry bar to raise the connection. This backseats the valve against the lower guide bushing. *Figure 13* shows how this is done.

Step 7 Release pressure on the pry bar slightly, then turn the valve stem until the bottom of the resetting lever knife edge is the specified distance (for example, 0.12", or 3.05 mm, for this turbine) below the top edge of the hand-trip lever latch. Turning the valve stem clockwise decreases the dimension; turning the valve stem counterclockwise increases the dimension.

Step 8 Reinstall and fully tighten the locknut until the upper spring seal is seated against the bushing.

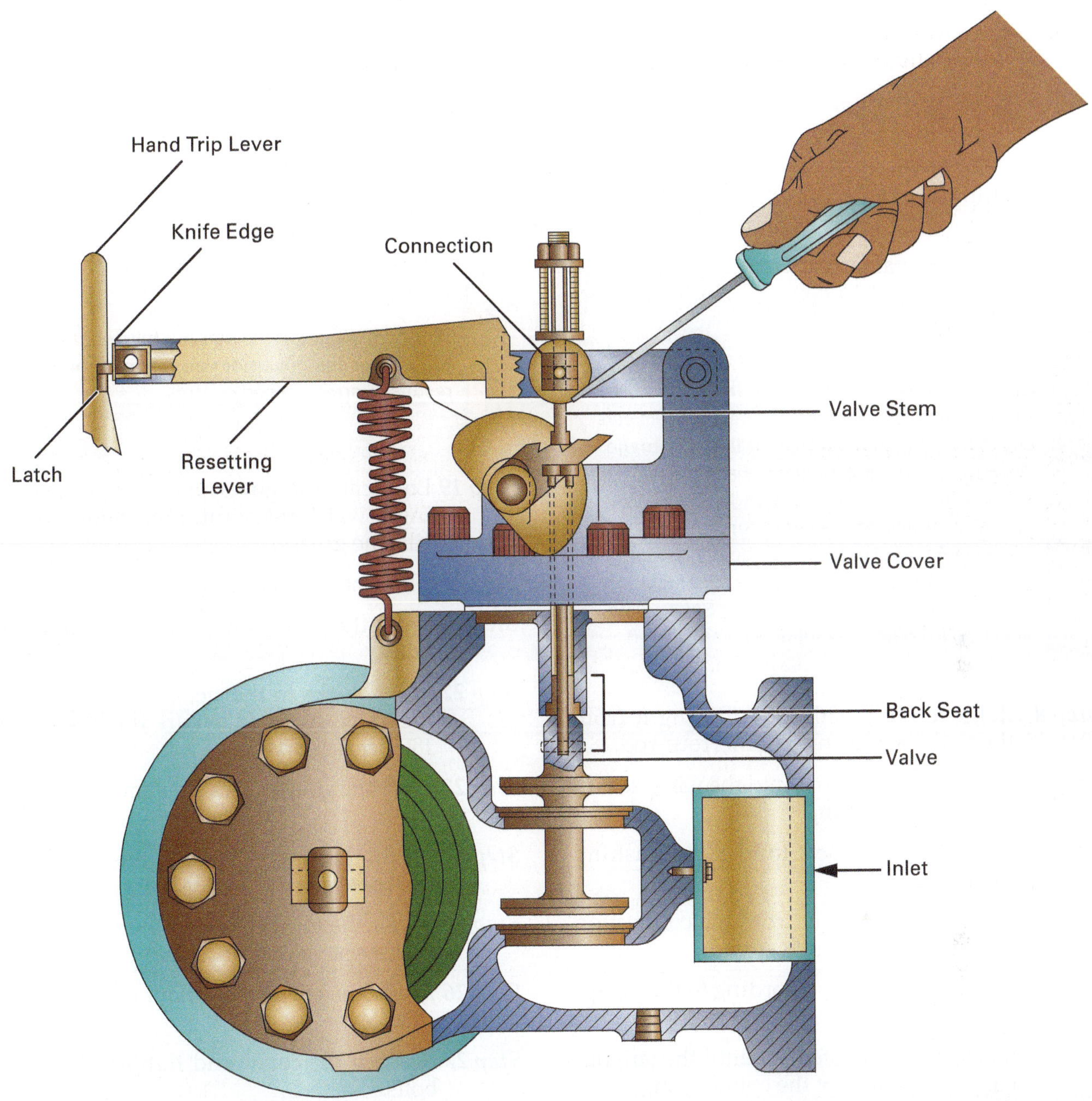

Figure 13 Backseating the trip valve.

Step 9 Place a wrench on the valve stem flats below the connection to prevent the valve stem from turning.

Step 10 Raise the resetting liner until the valve backseats against the bushing.

Step 11 Check to ensure that the bottom of the resetting lever knife edge is still at the correct distance below the top of the hand-trip lever latch.

Step 12 Latch the resetting lever. Verify that the spring compresses. If the spring does not compress, adjustments are required.

Step 13 Connect the closing spring.

Step 14 Complete the necessary procedures to check the trip valve operation.

1.7.9 Maintaining Governor Valves

Follow these steps to maintain the governor valve:

Step 1 Remove the linkage that connects the governor valve to the governor.

Step 2 Remove the bolts from the valve cover.

Step 3 Pull the cover and the valve away from the steam chest body.

Step 4 Remove the valve stem connection and the jam nut from the valve stem.

Step 5 Remove the valve stem from the cover assembly.

Step 6 Chip or grind the welded blocks, using a chipping hammer or a hand grinder, to remove the blocks from the steam chest.

Step 7 Pack the valve seat with dry ice to chill it, causing it to contract slightly before removal.

Dry ice is carbon dioxide (CO_2) in its solid form. Only a few seconds of direct contact can cause frostbite and permanent tissue damage. Wear goggles or safety glasses and a face shield when in the presence of dry ice. Heavily insulated gloves are required for handling. Any remaining dry ice should be left outdoors in a ventilated area where it can **sublimate** at its own pace. Refer to the product Safety Data Sheet (SDS) before handling and as needed.

Step 8 Remove the bushing by driving it from the valve seat using a nonferrous rod.

Step 9 Press a new bushing into the valve seat to replace the bushing.

Step 10 Stake the valve seat to lock the bushing in place.

Step 11 Turn the valve stem from the connection until the valve is fully seated.

Step 12 Adjust the jam nut according to the equipment specifications.

Step 13 Screw the valve stem in until the jam nut contacts the face of the connection.

Step 14 Tighten the jam nut against the connection to lock the jam nut.

Step 15 Install the governor linkage pins and bushings.

Step 16 Inspect the governor valve stem and guide bushings. Replace any worn valve stem and bushings if necessary.

Step 17 After steam pressure has been restored, inspect the valve for excessive steam leakage.

Step 18 Remove the packing follower and replace the valve stem packing.

Do not overtighten the packing follower because this causes the governor valve stem to bind and results in erratic speed control.

Step 19 Lubricate the governor linkage pins using a water-resistant, high-temperature silicone grease.

Step 20 Chill the valve seat again using dry ice.

Step 21 Press the valve seat into the steam chest body.

Step 22 Weld blocks to the steam chest to secure the valve seat. Make sure the blocks are 180 degrees apart.

Step 23 Place the governor valve stem in the valve cover.

Step 24 Install the connection and the jam nut on the valve stem.

Step 25 Clean the joint between the valve cover and the steam chest body.

Step 26 Apply the specified sealant to the sealing surfaces.

Step 27 Replace the cover and tighten the cover bolts.

Step 28 Connect the governor valve linkage.

Step 29 Adjust the valve travel.

1. In a noncondensing steam turbine, the amount of steam extracted from the turbine is regulated by _____.

    a. control valves
    b. the governor
    c. oil pressure
    d. the boiler

2. One material commonly used to seal turbine casings is _____.

    a. mortar
    b. lithium grease
    c. white glue
    d. boiled linseed oil

3. In smaller turbines, the carbon rings are housed in the _____.

    a. rotor shaft
    b. sealing glands
    c. upper casing
    d. cartridge seals

4. Which of the following causes the oil in the self-contained governor oil reservoir to foam?

    a. Operating the turbine without a load
    b. Normal operation of the governor system
    c. An overfilled oil reservoir
    d. Excessive oil pressure in the turbine's oil reservoir

5. When replacing the nozzle rings or reversing blade assembly, once the bottom bearing liners are removed, the rotor shaft rests on the _____.

    a. oil rings
    b. casing gaskets
    c. shaft sleeve seals
    d. governor linkage

6. The rotor locating bearing maintains the correct rotor _____.

    a. tension
    b. axial position
    c. timing
    d. rotational speed

7. Before pulling the governor valve seat from the governor, force it to contract by packing it with _____.

    a. insulation
    b. lamb's wool
    c. extruded polystyrene
    d. dry ice

1. What form of energy does a turbine convert into mechanical energy?

    a. Potential energy
    b. Kinetic energy
    c. Thermal energy
    d. Electrical energy

2. When installing and tightening the bolts along the horizontal casing flange, start with the bolts closest to the ______.

    a. rotors
    b. generator
    c. sealing glands
    d. steam chest

3. The *first* step toward working on the rotor assembly after the lockout/tagout process is complete is to ______.

    a. disconnect the coupling between the turbine and the driven machine
    b. lift the rotor out of the turbine casing
    c. remove the governor
    d. remove the journal bearing liners

4. New carbon rings should *always* be installed in complete sets.

    a. True
    b. False

5. Check the radial clearance of a carbon ring using a ______.

    a. micrometer
    b. taper gauge
    c. ruler
    d. thickness gauge

6. The governor oil level is checked ______.

    a. daily
    b. weekly
    c. monthly
    d. annually

7. The governor system is the *primary* means of control to shut down a steam turbine.

    a. True
    b. False

8. The steam flowing into the first row of rotor blades is directed by the ______.

    a. nozzle ring
    b. steam chest
    c. carbon rings
    d. governor linkage

9. When heating the overspeed trip body for removal, do *not* heat the adjacent rotor locating bearing or the ______.

    a. valve linkage
    b. retainer ring
    c. servomotor
    d. rotor shaft

10. The overspeed trip device is actuated when the turbine reaches a predetermined speed, which is typically ______.

    a. 10 percent above normal full-load speed
    b. 20 percent above normal full-load speed
    c. 30 percent above normal full-load speed
    d. 50 percent above normal full-load speed

Trade Terms Introduced in This Module

Carbon rings: Self-lubricating packing rings made of carbon that are used to seal the casing and rotor shaft.

Carryover: Any solid, liquid, or vapor contaminant that is entrained in the steam leaving a boiler.

Sublimate: To change state directly from a solid to a gas, without passing through a liquid state.

Additional Resources

This module presents thorough resources for task training. The following reference material is suggested for further study.

Advances in Steam Turbines for Modern Power Plants. 1st Edition. Cambridge, United Kingdom: Woodhead Publishing.

Gas Turbine Design, Components and System Design Integration. 1st Edition. Meinhard T. Schobeiri. New York, NY: Springer International Publishing.

General Electric — Gas Turbines. **https://www.ge.com/gas-power/products/gas-turbines**.

General Electric — Steam Turbines. **https://www.ge.com/gas-power/products/steam-turbines**.

Siemens Energy — Gas Turbines. **https://www.siemens-energy.com/global/en/offerings/power-generation/gas-turbines.html?gclid=EAIaIQobChMIv8Kegd-o-QIVI8LCBB2MQQGaEAAY ASABEgIQE_D_BwE**.

Siemens Energy — Steam Turbines. **https://www.siemens-energy.com/global/en/offerings/power-generation/steam-turbines.html?gclid=EAIaIQobChMIv8Kegd-o-QIVI8LCBB2MQQGaEAAYAS ADEgJN6vD_BwE**.

Figure Credits

Section Review Answer Key

Answer	Section Reference	Objective
1. a	1.1.0	1a
2. d	1.2.0	1b
3. b	1.3.0	1c
4. c	1.4.0	1d
5. c	1.5.0	1e
6. b	1.6.0	1f
7. d	1.7.9	1g

User Update

NCCER makes every effort to keep its textbooks up-to-date and free of technical errors. We appreciate your help in this process. If you find an error, a typographical mistake, or an inaccuracy in NCCER's curricula, please submit a User Update form by visiting **https://www.nccer.org/olf**. You can also scan the QR code using the camera on your phone or mobile device to access the form.

Crane Communications

OVERVIEW

This module focuses on the methods and modes of communication required in crane operations. General information about the communication process is also presented to help workers better understand the mechanics of communication in all environments. Signal persons are relied upon to properly communicate both verbally and nonverbally with crane operators, and crane operators must learn how to interpret verbal messages and hand signals provided by a signal person.

Module 53101

Trainees with successful module completions may be eligible for credentialing through the NCCER Registry. To learn more, go to **www.nccer.org** or contact us at 1.888.622.3720. Our website, **www.nccer.org**, has information on the latest product releases and training.

Your feedback is welcome. You may email your comments to **curriculum@nccer.org**, send general comments and inquiries to **info@nccer.org**, or fill in the User Update form at the back of this module.

This information is general in nature and intended for training purposes only. Actual performance of activities described in this manual requires compliance with all applicable operating, service, maintenance, and safety procedures under the direction of qualified personnel. References in this manual to patented or proprietary devices do not constitute a recommendation of their use.

53101 V2.0

From *Mobile Crane Operations, Trainee Guide*. NCCER.
Copyright © 2018 by NCCER. Published by Pearson. All rights reserved.

53101

CRANE COMMUNICATIONS

Objectives

When you have completed this module, you will be able to do the following:

1. Describe the communication process and identify barriers to effective communication.
   a. Describe the basic communication process.
   b. Identify common barriers to effective communication.
2. Identify and interpret the OSHA regulations related to crane communications and explain how to communicate with crane operators verbally and nonverbally.
   a. Identify and interpret construction-related OSHA regulations associated with crane communications and signaling.
   b. Describe the equipment used for verbal communications and how to communicate with and direct a crane operator verbally.
   c. Explain how to communicate with and direct a crane operator nonverbally.

Performance Tasks

Under the supervision of your instructor, you should be able to do the following:

1. Demonstrate proper crane-communication techniques using a handheld radio or another acceptable verbal-signaling device.
2. Demonstrate each standard hand signal depicted in 29 *CFR* 1926.1400, Subpart CC, Appendix A.
3. Direct an operator to move and place a load using the appropriate hand signals.
4. Direct an operator to move and place a load using voice communication.

Trade Terms

Abstraction
Blind lift
Bridge
Consensus standard
Dedicated spotter
Diver tender

Line of sight
Nonverbal communication
Open mike
Paraphrasing
Trucks

Industry Recognized Credentials

If you are training through an NCCER-accredited sponsor, you may be eligible for credentials from NCCER's Registry. The ID number for this module is 53101. Note that this module may have been used in other NCCER curricula and may apply to other level completions. Contact NCCER's Registry at 1.888.622.3720 or go to **www.nccer.org** for more information.

You can also show off your industry-recognized credentials online with NCCER's digital badges. Transform your knowledge, skills, and achievements into badges that you can share across social media platforms, send to your network, and add to your resume. For more information, visit **www.nccer.org**.

> **NOTE**
>
> This is an elective module and is not required for successful completion of *Millwright Level Four*, nor for the successful completion of the Millwright craft credential.

Contents

Figures

1.0.0 THE COMMUNICATION PROCESS

Objective

Describe the communication process and identify barriers to effective communication.

a. Describe the basic communication process.
b. Identify common barriers to effective communication.

Trade Terms

Abstraction: Any form of verbal, graphical, or written communication representing a generalized and nonspecific idea or quality of a thing, action, or event.

Nonverbal communication: All communication that does not use words. This includes appearance, personal environment, use of time, and body language.

Paraphrasing: Expressing the perceived meaning of something read or heard in one's own words, generally to ensure clarity. Paraphrasing is an important component of active listening.

The ability of workers to communicate effectively is essential to the safe operation of cranes. The clarity of the information being exchanged is very important, and can be difficult to maintain due to distractions and noise that accompany crane operation and other construction activities. The techniques presented in this module can assist anyone that provides or responds to crane operating signals in strengthening their ability to communicate effectively.

Before presenting the detailed requirements of crane signaling and communication, it is beneficial to understand the general communication process. This knowledge helps workers understand how and why information may not be accurately transferred and take the necessary steps to avoid problems. The sections that follow provide general information about communication that are valuable both on and off the job.

1.1.0 Exchanging a Message

The communication process (*Figure 1*) consists of a message being sent and, ideally, received and interpreted precisely as intended. A message may be sent verbally or through **nonverbal communication**.

The challenge for those involved in operating cranes is not only to communicate the right information to co-workers, but to do so effectively.

The communication process consists of the following three general components:

- Sending the message
- Receiving the message
- Feedback

1.1.1 Sending the Message

There are four elements involved in sending a message. First, the sender prepares the message that is intended for communication. Next, the sender considers possible internal barriers that may affect the message. This includes the sender's own experiences, the terms used, and even the sender's feelings toward the receiver. External barriers, such as noise, must also be considered. Third, the sender encodes the message; that is, the sender puts the message into spoken words (verbal), written words (nonverbal), or gestures (nonverbal) that he or she wants to use. Finally, the sender sends the message through the chosen method.

1.1.2 Receiving the Message

There are also four elements involved in receiving a message. The receiver will first hear and/or see the message that was sent. Second, the influence of any active external or internal barriers takes effect. Possible internal barriers, for example, may include the receiver's experience level, the receiver's understanding of the terms used by the sender, the receiver's attitude toward the job, or even the way the receiver feels about the sender. Third, the receiver often decodes the

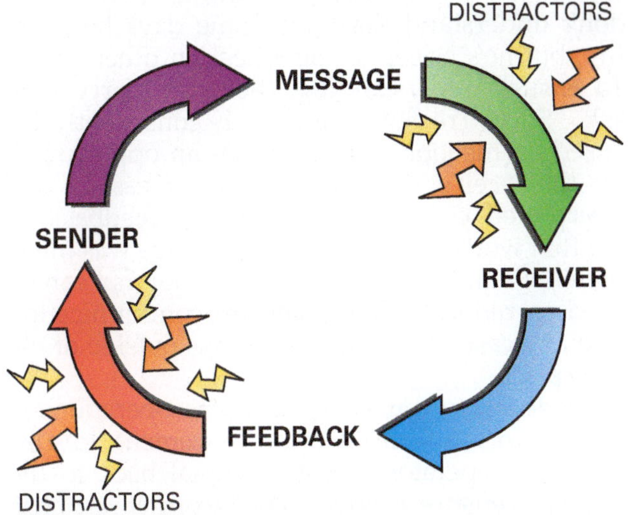

Figure 1 The communication process.

message through a rapid set of mental images. For instance, when a sender speaks the term *two-block*, a receiver does not generally imagine the letters that form the word. Instead, a mental image represented by the words appears. Many different mental images might arise among those who hear this word—perhaps a crane boom, a wire rope, or a load block might be briefly pictured. Fourth, the message is interpreted from the receiver's perspective. At this point in the process, there is no way to determine that the message was received as intended. To determine this, the receiver must provide feedback to the sender.

1.1.3 Feedback

Feedback, which may take several forms in general communication, provides essential information about the success in communicating a message. To get feedback, ask or look for a response. A simple yes or no may be all that is needed for simpler messages. Other times, a question may be asked in response to the message, indicating a lack of understanding or a need to verify the information. Nonverbal behaviors can also provide important clues about the clear reception of a message. Facial expressions and body language often indicate when the receiver clearly understands the message or is unsure of its meaning. Even a nonverbal response such as a nod of the head or a thumbs-up signal can be considered feedback.

Paraphrasing is a communication tool that often helps ensure clear communication between a sender and a receiver. It can be used when the message is not clear, or when verification is desired to avoid a mistake. Paraphrasing means to express the perceived meaning of something read or heard back to the sender using different words. For example, another worker may say, "I don't understand that guy. Some days he is on fire, but he's asleep at the wheel on other days." To ensure understanding, the other party may ask, "So you're not sure if he is consistently focused on his job?" This provides an opportunity for the receiver to find out if the message was interpreted correctly, and provides feedback to the first worker about how the message was interpreted. Paraphrasing is a valuable tool that can be used to reduce or eliminate miscommunication in many cases, including situations outside of the workplace.

Feedback to a message in crane operations is usually in the form of crane movement. Ideally, the crane operator repeats a signal back to the sender to ensure accuracy. The incorrect response to a signal may be uneventful, but it can also be disastrous. For this reason, crane signaling goes further to formally close the communication loop with a three-step process:

- The signal person signals the crane operator.
- The operator repeats the signal back to the signal person.
- The signal person confirms that the crane operator has interpreted the signal correctly.

The terms and signals used to communicate with crane operators must be learned and practiced until they are deeply embedded in memory and are as natural to use as any other part of speech.

1.2.0 Communication Barriers

The purpose of effective communication in any environment is to ensure that the receiver accurately understands the material or information provided by the sender. The existence of certain barriers or filters increases the potential for poor communication. A barrier is something that can halt communication altogether. An example would be a jackhammer starting up nearby when you are speaking to someone. A filter is an internal, personal screening mechanism that receives a message and alters its meaning in some way. A filter can be a person's knowledge or prior experience, or even emotions. For example, if a signal person has sent the same signal incorrectly to a crane operator seven times in a row, the operator most likely will develop a filter that renders future uses of the same signal untrustworthy. By being aware of barriers and filters, lift teams can avoid them and ensure clear understanding of the information they are attempting to communicate. The following sections describe some of the barriers and filters that can damage effective communications, including those related to crane operations.

1.2.1 Lack of Common Experience

One potential barrier to effective communication is the lack of common experience. Operators are likely to find that their co-workers have many different backgrounds. Some individuals may have worked exclusively in one type of construction, such as bridge/road, structural steel, or residential, and are unable to immediately relate to another area of construction. To prevent misunderstandings, the sender and receiver first need to determine their experience level. Then, the sender should develop comparisons between the different types of work. For example, an operator who is accustomed to working on a building construction site might not understand some of the terminology used on bridge projects. Indeed, the word *bridge* itself has a completely different meaning in the world of overhead cranes than it does in bridge construction.

1.2.2 Language

Today's construction workplace is a reflection of the global marketplace. Some employees may not be fluent in the principal language of the jobsite or organization. A language barrier can certainly complicate the process of communication in any environment. The challenge of clear communication between individuals that do not share a native language is very common today, and a challenge that will likely continue to grow. Even when a non-native speaker has advanced knowledge of the vocabulary in a language, their pronunciation of some words may be difficult for a native speaker to understand.

One option is for all workers to become fluent in all the languages spoken on the job. Of course, that is an impractical solution. However, it is beneficial to understand some of the basic concepts and words of the language(s) you hear on the job regularly. A few words spoken in the language of the listener may be all it takes to clarify the instruction or statement.

Signal persons and crane operators must be fluent in a standardized language that is commonly understood by both. Using the standardized crane hand signals as outlined in 29 *CFR* 1926, Subpart CC, Appendix A is a reliable method of bridging language barriers in crane operations.

1.2.3 Overuse of Abstractions

An **abstraction** is a generalized, nonspecific concept or idea. To avoid confusion, speak in common, accepted, standardized terms, and be specific. Many abstractions are too general in nature, and therefore do not provide enough detail to the receiver. Be aware of the abilities of your co-workers and use appropriate terms and examples that suit their communication needs. Remember that signal persons are also responsible for the safe operation of the crane, so it is crucial that all communications between the operator and signal person are clearly understood. For example, if a signal person tells an operator to move a load "a little to the left"—an example of an abstraction—one operator may move it a few inches while another may move it several feet. The correct verbal instruction would include how far the load needs to be moved to the left. This removes the abstraction.

1.2.4 Fear

Fear may be one of the greatest barriers to effective communication. The fear of showing ignorance, the fear of disapproval, the fear of losing status, and the fear of judgment are all common barriers. Co-workers may have hidden anxieties or fears about their own abilities. They may lack confidence or be afraid of appearing ignorant, thus avoiding communication when they should speak out.

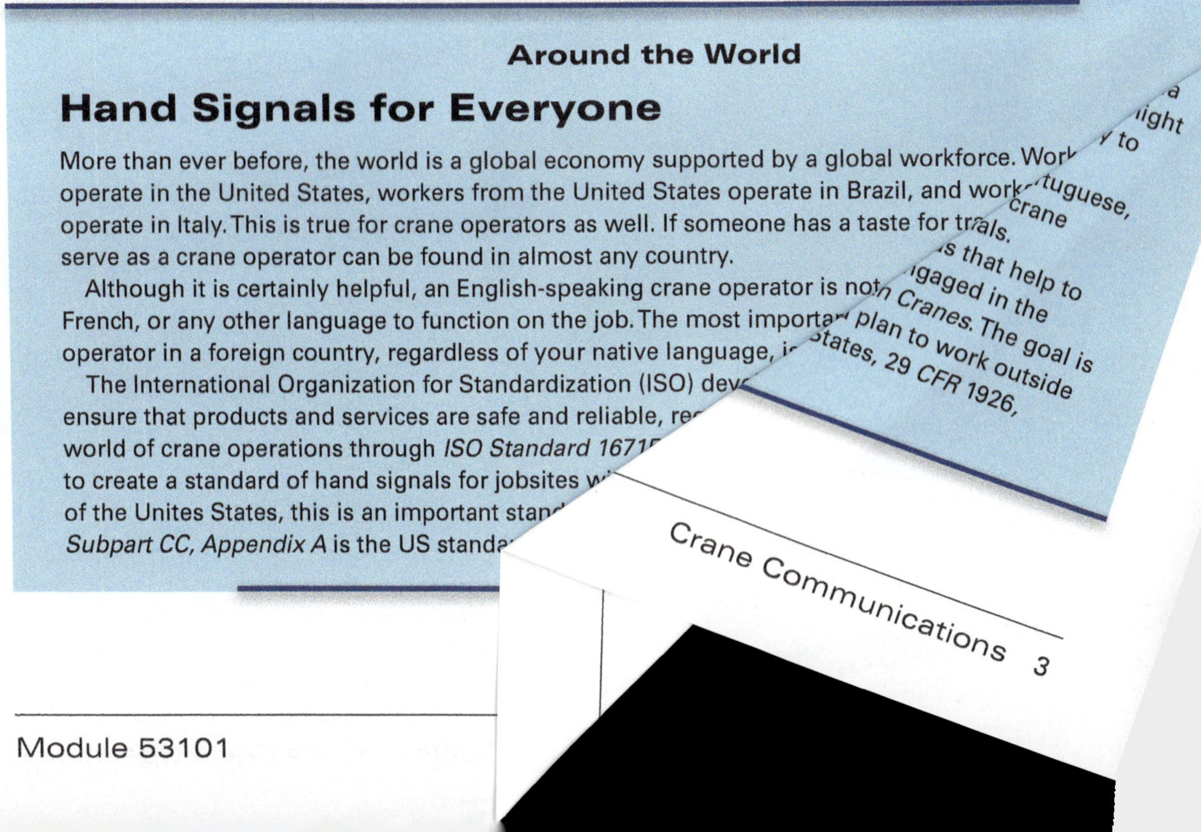

Provide a threat-free environment by being encouraging and nonjudgmental. It is important that communication flow smoothly. During meetings of all kinds, including pre-lift meetings, encourage everyone to ask questions without fear of judgment and ridicule.

Fear can affect communication in crane operations as well. When confidence is lacking, a worker may avoid displaying the Stop or Emergency Stop signal on the job when a hazard clearly exists or is developing. A signal person may also hesitate to display a common signal because the worker is not confident it is the correct signal. This is yet another reason why crane signals must be learned and practiced until they become second nature. Signal persons must be prepared to stop a lift at any time if things are not progressing as expected.

1.2.5 Environmental Factors

Environmental factors such as noise and weather often interfere with the communication process on the job. Pile-driving operations (*Figure 2*) are a perfect example because the noise involved can be a barrier to hearing what is being said. In inclement weather, it may be difficult to see clearly or listen attentively. In good weather, environmental factors such as the sun in your eyes can pose a problem. However, subtle factors may also affect the communication process. The background color of a wall or structure, the position of the signal person, and the location of the load in relation to the signal person can all interfere with effective communication.

Both signal persons and crane operators should constantly strive to identify and eliminate interference from the communication process. As stated earlier, clarity in communication and adhering to standard signal sets is a crucial part of crane operations, since the feedback is usually in the form of crane movement. As a result, miscommunication can lead to equipment damage and/or personal injury.

Figure 2 Pile-driving operations.

SECTION TWO

2.0.0 CRANE COMMUNICATIONS

Objective

Identify and interpret the OSHA regulations related to crane communications and explain how to communicate with crane operators verbally and nonverbally.

a. Identify and interpret construction-related OSHA regulations associated with crane communications and signaling.
b. Describe the equipment used for verbal communications and how to communicate with and direct a crane operator verbally.
c. Explain how to communicate with and direct a crane operator nonverbally.

Performance Tasks

1. Demonstrate proper crane-communication techniques using a handheld radio or another acceptable verbal-signaling device.
2. Demonstrate each standard hand signal depicted in 29 *CFR* 1926.1400, Subpart CC, Appendix A.
3. Direct an operator to move and place a load using the appropriate hand signals.
4. Direct an operator to move and place a load using voice communication.

Trade Terms

Blind lift: Any lift involving a load that is out of the direct view of the operator. Blind lifts are generally always categorized as critical lifts.

Bridge: In relation to overhead cranes, the part of an overhead crane consisting of one or more girders or beams and the supporting trucks. The bridge is the overhead, weight-bearing structure along which the trolley(s) and load block assembly travels.

Consensus standard: A set of proprietary guidelines published and agreed to by a consensus (representative majority) of members of a given industry. While not legally binding, they are often cited in governmental regulations, such as OSHA standards.

Dedicated spotter: An individual qualified as a signal person who is charged with monitoring the separation between power lines and the equipment, load line, and load, so that the minimum approach distance is not compromised per OSHA standards.

Diver tender: One or more individuals assigned to attend to a diver's needs, including providing assistance in equipment preparation and managing the diver's cables and hoses.

Line of sight: The straight-line path between an observer's eyes and the thing being observed.

Open mike: In electronic communications, the condition where a radio's Transmit button or switch is held continuously without releasing it, even during pauses in speaking.

Trucks: In relation to overhead cranes, a mechanical assembly consisting of a frame, wheels, bearings, and axles that support the bridge of an overhead crane and provide the ability for it to move along a set of parallel tracks.

The methods and modes of communication vary widely in mobile crane operations. The method of communication refers to whether the communication is verbal or nonverbal. The mode is defined by the means of performing the communication. Modes may include bullhorns, radios, hand signals, flags, etc.

2.1.0 OSHA Standards and Requirements

29 *CFR* 1926, Subpart CC, *Cranes and Derricks in Construction* is the primary safety standard related to crane operations in the construction environment. The directives and guidelines it contains are enforceable as federal laws. They are not simply suggestions or examples of best practices. The specific sections that are dedicated to crane communications and the role of signal persons are 29 *CFR* 1926.1419, *Signals—General Requirements* through 1926.1422, *Signals—Hand-Signal Chart*. In addition, 29 *CFR* 1926.1428, *Signal Person Qualifications* provides the information indicated by its title.

There is also one very important communication-related statement found in 29 *CFR* 1926.1417(y), as follows: "The operator must obey a stop (or emergency stop) signal, irrespective of who gives it." This is a very important provision, meant to ensure that any potentially unsafe condition can be recognized and the operation stopped by anyone that recognizes it. All members of a lift team have the authority to display the Stop or Emergency Stop signal, and the crane operator is required to obey it. Even a bystander can display the signal if a hazardous condition becomes apparent, and the crane operator must obey. This is rare, however, as those directly involved with a properly manned lift operation are more likely to recognize a hazard before a casual observer.

The remainder of this section presents detailed information related to crane communications from the relevant OSHA standards. In the case of crane communications, *ASME Standard B30.5, Mobile and Locomotive Cranes*, has not been incorporated by reference into the OSHA standards. As a result, the primary focus of this section is on the enforceable OSHA standards. However, the hand signal set and most of the signaling-related provisions of *ASME Standard B30.5* parallel the OSHA standard.

2.1.1 29 CFR 1926.1419, Signals—General Requirements

Per 29 *CFR* 1926.1419, there are situations in which a signal person must be provided. These situations are outlined as follows:

- When any part of the path of a load being moved, including its origin and destination, is outside of the view of the crane operator
- When the equipment is traveling but the driver's view in the direction of travel is blocked
- When either the crane operator or the personnel handling the load determine that it is necessary

A dedicated spotter is required under certain conditions when a crane is working in the vicinity of power lines. Although they are referred to as *spotters* in 29 *CFR* 1926.1411, *Power Line Safety*, and are assigned to focus their attention on the crane's proximity to the power lines, they must stay in continuous contact with the crane operator. To a certain extent, then, the spotter is serving as an auxiliary signal person, and must meet the signal person qualifications of 29 *CFR* 1926.1428 as stated in 29 *CFR* 1926.1401, *Definitions*. Verbal communication is best for these situations, as the information that a spotter may need to relay to the crane operator may not have any kind of standard hand signal assigned to it.

The standard allows for signals between the signal person(s) and crane operator to be by hand, by voice, or by an audible means other than voice. OSHA simply directs that the chosen method of communication be appropriate for the site conditions. New signals, other than hand, voice, and audible signals, may be used in some conditions if they meet specific OSHA requirements. Note that signal persons are required to provide the signals from the crane operator's perspective of direction. Signal persons must signal in the direction of required crane movement.

Hand signals are designed to be universal and do not require any special equipment. When hand signals are used, they must be those found in 29 *CFR* 1926, Subpart CC, Appendix A. This is referred to as the *Standard Method*. There are two exceptions to the rule of using the OSHA Standard Method:

- When the use of the Standard Method is determined to be infeasible
- When an attachment or required crane movement is not covered by the Standard Method

When an attachment or required crane movement is not covered by the Standard Method, a nonstandard hand signal can be identified and used. OSHA requires that the signal person, crane operator, and lift director discuss any nonstandard hand signals before the operation begins and agree to the signals and their use. Note that there is a difference between the terms *nonstandard signals* and *new signals*. New signals refer to a new method or mode of communicating, while a nonstandard signal refers only to a hand signal that is not part of the Standard Method.

Regardless of the method or mode used, the crane operator must bring the operation to a safe stop if the line of communication is interrupted. For example, if another construction vehicle suddenly blocks the operator's view of the hand signals, the operation must be safely halted until the line of sight is restored. The crane operator can also stop the operation temporarily when any unsafe condition is encountered and discuss the issue with the signal person. The operation resumes only after both parties agree that the issue has been satisfactorily resolved.

29 *CFR* 1926.1419(j) is related to the responsibility of others to display the Stop or Emergency Stop signal. It also refers the reader back to 29 *CFR* 1926.1417(y), which outlines the crane operator's responsibility to obey the signal, regardless of its source. This standard states that "anyone who becomes aware of a safety problem must alert the operator or signal person by giving the Stop or Emergency Stop signal."

A signal person can be in contact with and provide signals to more than one crane or derrick at a time. A system to identify which crane is being signaled must be developed and used. This is generally satisfied by a specific signal chosen and agreed upon by both parties to identify each crane before the functional signal is communicated.

2.1.2 29 CFR 1926.1420, Signals—Radio, Telephone, or Other Signals

OSHA allows a variety of devices to be used to communicate electronically in crane operations. In some cases, hand signals are not practical or appropriate. Any electronic means of communication must be tested at the site to ensure the equipment is fully functional and reliable before the operation begins.

As a general rule, electronic communication must take place on a dedicated channel between the signal person and the operator, with the following exceptions allowed:

- When multiple cranes are using the same signal person, or when multiple signal persons are in use, they may share the channel.
- When a crane is being operated on or near railroad tracks and the crane's movement needs to be coordinated with trains or other equipment moving on the tracks, the channel can be shared.

The final provision of this section is that the crane operator's method of receiving signals electronically must be hands-free. It is acceptable for the operator to use a push-to-talk system, where a button must be pressed to speak, as long as reception is hands-free.

In some cases, the signal person keeps the radio microphone keyed to continuously communicate with the crane operator. An **open mike** is often used when the signal person is speaking progressive information, such as distance to touchdown, during the lift. However, an open mike can prevent receipt of a Stop signal from others on the channel, depending on the equipment involved. This practice may differ from company to company and project to project. Open-mike procedures should be discussed and clarified in the pre-lift meeting. Some radios have an Emergency button on them, which allows Stop signals to be transmitted even when another mike is keyed.

Everyone involved in a lift must exercise some radio discipline. Perhaps you have been using a different radio channel to speak to another craft or your supervisor. Before entering or reentering the crane operations channel, take a few moments to monitor the conversations occurring before speaking. This practice will prevent talking over or interrupting an important communication in progress.

2.1.3 29 CFR 1926.1421, Signals—Voice Signals; Additional Requirements

The OSHA standard in 29 *CFR* 1926.1421 requires crane operators, signal persons, and lift directors to discuss and agree on the verbal signals that will be used. The team will only need to meet and discuss the matter again if a different worker is added or substituted, there seems to be confusion about a signal, or a signal needs to be changed or added.

This standard also outlines the structure of voice signals. Each voice signal must contain these components that are spoken in the following order:

- Function and direction, such as "Hoist Up" or "Hoist Down"
- Distance and/or speed, such as "10 feet and slowly"
- Function, followed by the Stop command, such as "Swing Stop" or "Load Stop"

Providing distance and/or speed information is required. It is typically modified and repeated as the function progresses. A typical voice command from a signal person sounds something like this: "Swing right, 30 feet… 20 feet… 10 feet… 5 feet… swing stop." Another example is "Load down slow… slow… load stop." Note that a verbal instruction such as "Swing left… swing left… swing left… swing stop" does not meet the requirements since no speed or distance information is provided. It is also important to remember to supply the distance as the amount remaining before the load reaches the desired point, rather than as the distance it has already moved. Crane operators typically prefer that the signal person paint a real-time picture of progress and movement. Give the operator as much information as you think the operator needs—if you are providing too much, the operator will tell you.

This section of the OSHA standard ends by requiring that the crane operator, signal person(s), and lift director be able to effectively communicate in the language being used.

2.1.4 29 CFR 1926.1422, Signals—Hand-Signal Chart

Per 29 *CFR* 1926.1422, hand-signal charts must be posted on the equipment in use, typically the crane itself, or in a conspicuous location in the area of the hoisting operation. Most mobile cranes have a hand-signal chart posted on or near the cab of the crane in an easily visible location to satisfy this requirement. Where overhead or tower cranes are in use, the hand-signal chart should be posted in a more accessible location than the equipment itself generally provides.

2.1.5 29 CFR 1926.1428, Signal Person Qualifications

Organizations that employ signal persons have a responsibility to ensure that they are properly qualified as outlined in 29 *CFR* 1926.1428. Employers can choose one of two options to satisfy this OSHA standard:

- The signal person already possesses or obtains documentation from a third-party qualified evaluator (such as NCCER) showing that the individual has demonstrated the necessary skills and meets the qualification requirements.
- The employer provides a qualified evaluator from within the organization that ensures the signal person can demonstrate the necessary skills and then provides the supporting documentation.

This standard also requires employers to maintain the required documentation of signal-persons' skills at the site where they are employed. The documents must indicate which type of signals, such as hand signals or radio communications, that each individual is qualified to perform.

Employers also have a responsibility to ensure that a signal person's performance continues to be sound and accurate. If the performance of a previously-qualified signal person indicates that the individual is not properly qualified, the employer must not allow the worker to continue serving as a signal person until retraining has been completed and the skills are reevaluated through one of the two options outlined above.

The standard provides the following qualification requirements for signal persons:

- Knowledge and understanding of the type of signals being used. For hand signals, the individual must know the Standard Method signals provided in *Appendix A* of 29 *CFR* 1926, *Subpart CC.*
- Competence in the application of the signals used.
- A basic understanding of equipment operation and its limitations. This includes the crane dynamics related to swinging and stopping the movement of loads, and the boom deflection that results from hoisting a load.
- Knowledge and understanding of the requirements found in 29 *CFR* 1926.1419 through 1926.1422, as well as 1926.1428. The requirements of each of these standards have been covered in this section.
- Documentation that these requirements have been met through the successful completion of either an oral or a written test, and a practical test. These tests are administered by the employer's qualified evaluator or a third-party organization such as NCCER.

2.1.6 Miscellaneous Requirements

There are several additional sections of the OSHA standard that mention the role or actions of signal persons. One such section is 29 *CFR* 1926.1431, *Hoisting Personnel.* An occupant of a hoisted personnel platform can serve as the signal person. If the signal person, when needed, is operating from a location other than the personnel platform, the occupants of the platform must remain in direct contact with the signal person at all times. This same standard also requires a pre-lift meeting to be held when personnel are to be hoisted, regardless of the environment. If a signal person will be used during the lift, he or she must attend the pre-lift meeting. If any workers assigned to the operation are later replaced, including the signal person, another meeting is required.

Another requirement is related to cranes that are supporting one or more divers in the water, found in 29 *CFR* 1926.1437(j). Note, however, that this standard clearly applies to floating cranes and derricks, or to land cranes positioned on a floating vessel. When a crane is devoted to diver entry and exit, it cannot be used for any other purpose until the diver(s) is/are safely out of the water. Divers require a **diver tender** who monitors them at all times to ensure safety. Their primary responsibility is to manage the bundle of cables and hoses, known as the diver's umbilical. The diver tender generally serves as the crane signal person when the crane is directly supporting the diver, and must be a qualified signal person to do so. The standard permits hand signals between the diver tender and the crane operator as long as a clear line of sight is maintained. Otherwise, signals must be transmitted electronically. If the diver is not directly connected to the crane and is instead swimming freely, a dive supervisor is likely in direct contact with both the diver and crane operator.

When cranes are working near power lines, a dedicated spotter is often required to ensure that no part of the crane or the load enters the safe zone established around the lines. The dedicated spotter is an individual separate from that of the primary signal person. Per OSHA's definition of a dedicated spotter, the individual must meet the same requirements as a signal person. These requirements are found in 29 *CFR* 1926.1428. In 29 *CFR* 1926.1410(d)(2)(i), dedicated spotters are further required to be in continuous contact with

Know Your Craft

In the late 1990s, a young 24-year-old man was killed on his first day on the job, working at Shoreham Docks in the United Kingdom. He was assigned to assist with unloading bags of aggregate from the hold of a ship. The load block of a crane was descending through the opening in the hold from above when it struck the young man in the head, killing him instantly.

There were a number of errors that lead up to this tragedy. Although he had never done such work before, he received no training before taking his place on the crew. He was not even issued a hard hat by his employer, which could very well have saved his life that day. However, there was already an accident waiting to happen: the crane operator could not see into the hold, and the signal person calling the shots did not speak any English and was not familiar with standard hand signals. The language barrier prevented the signal person and crane operator from even considering a conversation related to signals.

Although many lifts may seem very simple and the idea of a serious accident seems remote, there is always the potential for a tragedy to occur. Being an effective signal person goes beyond just knowing what each hand signal means. It also means having the ability to evaluate and re-evaluate what is happening moment by moment, looking forward into the lift process without losing focus on the here and now. Learning to do that is a process. But the process does begin with knowing how to properly signal a crane without having to dig deep into your memory to find the correct signal. Hand signals should be practiced extensively. Practicing the signals in the mirror can help you determine if the hand and arm positions are appropriate. Practice by looking at the signals and identifying them to yourself, and practice making the signals while someone else calls them out rapidly. Practice in class and practice at home. Whatever you do, don't serve in the role of a signal person until you know the signals. You want to be thinking about what to direct the crane to do next, and not how to make the signal.

the crane operator, rather than communicating through the signal person. The spotter's responsibility is to monitor the separation of the crane, load line, and load from the power lines. No communication is generally necessary unless one of the three components comes too close to, or enters, the safe zone around the power lines. There are other significant requirements related to the use of a dedicated spotter, but they are not related to signaling or communication.

There are occasions when more than one crane is required to manage and position a single load. When more than one crane is involved, clear communication becomes even more critical. According to 29 *CFR* 1926.1432, one designated person who meets the OSHA criteria as both a qualified person and a competent person shall serve as the lift director. Alternatively, a competent person can be assisted by one or more qualified people. In any case, when multiple cranes are used, a pre-lift planning meeting must be held beforehand with all workers participating in the lift. One signal person is generally assigned to control both cranes, but complex situations may lead the lift director to use more than one. A nonstandard signal must be developed and agreed upon to identify which crane is being signaled, since this type of signal is not a part of OSHA's Standard Method.

Whenever multiple signal persons are used, regardless of the reason, it is important for all members of the lift team to know and understand the plan and how it will be implemented. Lifts involving multiple signal persons increase the complexity of the process. A thorough pre-lift meeting must be held to discuss the responsibilities. A blind lift is a good example of when it may be necessary to use multiple signal persons. If one signal person cannot observe both the complete load path and the crane, additional signal person or persons may be required to relay information. Note that relay signaling is not typically preferred and provides an additional opportunity for errors. Lifting operations should therefore move more slowly. When one signal person hands off responsibility to a second, it should be clear that the responsibility for the load has been transferred. The method of hand-off should be clearly discussed and agreed upon during the pre-lift meeting.

> **NOTE**
>
> Relay signaling automatically creates some lag time in signaling that can create problems and must be taken into consideration.

2.2.0 Verbal Crane Communications and Equipment

Verbal modes of communication vary depending on the requirements of the situation. Some of the most common devices used are portable radios, often referred to as *walkie-talkies* (*Figure 3*). Compact, low-power, inexpensive pairs of units can enable a crane operator and signal person to communicate verbally in some environments. They do meet OSHA standards since the operator can hear the signals hands-free, but they usually require a hand to press a button when speaking.

There are some disadvantages to using low-power and inexpensive equipment in an industrial setting. One disadvantage is interference. With basic, low-quality units, the frequency used to carry the signal may have many other users. A crowded channel can cause signal disruptions and lead to accidents. Another disadvantage is the effect of background noise. When attempting to transmit in a noisy area, the person may transmit unintended noise, resulting in a garbled, unintelligible signal for the receiver. On the receiving end, the individual may not be able to hear the transmission clearly due to a high level of background noise.

> Wind and other external factors can create noise, distortion, and feedback in low-fidelity radio communications microphones. You can reduce these effects by cupping your hand around the microphone.

To overcome the shortcomings associated with low-power, handheld units, more expensive units with the ability to use specific, dedicated frequencies and transmit at a higher power level may be needed. An electronic communication standard referred to as DECT (Digital Enhanced Cordless Telecommunications), developed in the 1990s, provides improved range as well as encrypted and secure communications. Only DECT-compatible devices can operate on the specific frequencies allocated to them by the US Federal Communications Commission (FCC), and the frequencies are far enough away from those of other devices to eliminate cross-frequency interference issues. DECT-compatible headsets (*Figure 4*) offer high-quality communications for a large number of users on a single dedicated system. Pairing, or connecting, a group of headsets to a local communications hub, also shown in *Figure 4*, establishes a private audio network. Each headset can be configured for full-duplex operation, meaning that the user can both listen to others and transmit at will, completely hands-free. They can also be configured for listening only (broadcast mode), but returned quickly to full-duplex operation when necessary. Note that the over-ear headsets also provide hearing protection.

Cell phones may also qualify as an electronic device that can be used for crane communications. With a compatible headset of good quality to make them hands-free, preferably with functional noise-cancelling technology, they can provide good service. However, it is important to note that signal strength on some networks may be weak or even non-existent in some work areas. As a result, it is difficult to rely on them exclusively. DECT-compatible wireless communication networks can be established just about anywhere, but even this equipment has limitations related to line of sight, elevation, and distance between hub stations and headsets.

Hardwired communications systems are also still available. These units overcome some of the

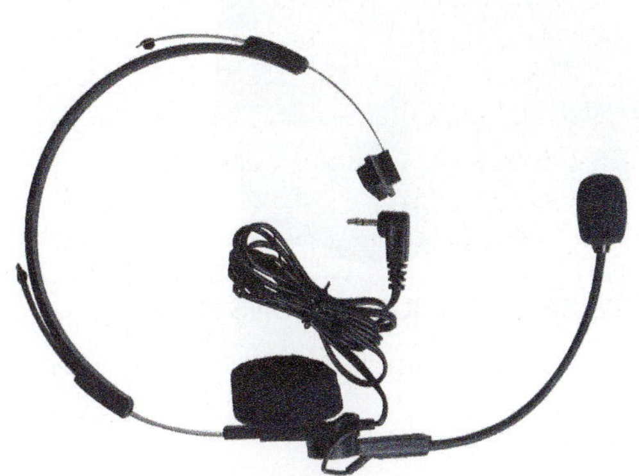

Figure 3 Walkie-talkies with an accessory headset.

(A) HEADSET AND MICROPHONE

(B) HARDHAT-MOUNTED HEADSET

(C) WIRELESS COMMUNICATIONS HUB

Figure 4 Examples of DECT-compatible wireless communications gear.

disadvantages of radio use. When using this type of system, interference from another unit is unlikely because this system does not use a radio frequency to transmit information. Like a telephone system, occasional interference may be encountered if the wiring is not properly shielded from very strong radio transmissions or other electromagnetic interference. Hardwire systems, however, are not very portable or practical, especially when the crane must be moved often. Very long wires are often required and they are easily entangled and/or damaged on an active jobsite. As a general rule, hardwired systems are too clumsy to deploy and operate on most of today's jobsites, and the wires themselves may represent a separate hazard.

Regardless of the type of equipment used, it is important that signal persons remember and use the proper format for all verbal signals transmitted to a crane operator: function and direction, distance and/or speed, and function followed by a Stop command. These skills must be demonstrated during a practical examination. Signal persons should be familiar with the equipment in use, rather than try to figure it out for the first time as a lift progresses.

Remember that all electronic communication devices must be tested before a lift begins. Workers charged with the responsibility of maintaining the communications equipment should ensure that the batteries are kept freshly charged, and that spare batteries are always available on site. Shutting down a complex lift operation temporarily due to a lack of batteries is a very expensive, time-consuming, and often embarrassing way to learn this lesson.

2.3.0 Nonverbal Communications

Although OSHA's Standard Method of hand signaling is the most common type of nonverbal communication used in crane operations, several other nonverbal modes have also been used. One possible mode is the use of a distinct audible signal, such as a siren, buzzer, and/or whistle, in which the number of repetitions and duration of the sounds convey the message. An example of the use of audible signals in crane operations that can often be justified is related to work inside large tanks. Workers must often be inside the tank, receiving components lowered through an opening by a crane. Hand signals are not possible, and the tank itself might interfere with wireless communications. In this case, workers inside the tank might be forced to use a hammer to make a series of rapping sounds on the tank walls to communicate with the outside. However, a hard-wired means of verbal communication is certainly the more practical and safer alternative.

Another nonverbal mode, although rare, is the use of signal flags. This mode might require the use of different colored flags, or a specific positioning of the flags, to communicate the desired message. When there is considerable distance between the signal person and crane operator, this may seem to be a practical solution. However, verbal communication using reliable radio equipment likely provides a better solution, especially since a line of sight evidently does exist if flags are an option. When a line of sight exists, verbal electronic communications function at their greatest range (up to 1,600 feet or 500 meters with some DECT-compatible devices). The disadvantage of a flag-communication mode is that 29 *CFR* 1926.1419(d) requires that any new signals must be shown to be equally effective as the prescribed voice, audible, or Standard Method hand signals, or comply with an equally-effective national *consensus standard*. Since there is no apparent national consensus standard for flags, their use can be difficult to justify in most cases.

The most common mode of nonverbal communication is the use of the Standard Method of hand signals provided by OSHA. Although *ASME Standard B30.5* also provides a standard set of hand signals, it is the OSHA standard that is enforceable by law. The signals of the two sets are nearly identical, although the drawings used to depict the signals are drawn with slight differences. The required OSHA hand signals are shown in a sequence of drawings shown in *Figure 5A* through *Figure 5S*.

Figure 5A Hoist.

HOIST

With arm vertical, forefinger pointing up, move hand in small horizontal circle.

OPERATOR ACTION: Slowly pull the hoist control lever back, controlling the ascent speed of the load (block or ball) with the control lever position. Keep the engine rpm constant until the desired lift is complete, then slowly return the control to the center position.

If the load block or ball is near the boom point, exercise caution to avoid two-blocking.

EXPECTED MACHINE MOVEMENT: The load attached to the block or ball rises vertically, accelerating and decelerating smoothly.

Figure 5B Lower.

LOWER

With arm extended downward, forefinger pointing down, move hand in small horizontal circle.

OPERATOR ACTION: Slowly push the hoist control lever for the desired hoist forward, controlling the descent speed of the load (block or ball) with the control lever position. Keep the engine rpm constant until load lowering is complete, then slowly return the control to the center position.

Do not allow the block or ball to contact the ground or any surface that can cause slack in the load line(s).

EXPECTED MACHINE MOVEMENT: The load block or ball smoothly lowers vertically.

Figure 5C Raise boom.

RAISE BOOM

Arm extended, fingers closed, thumb pointing upward.

OPERATOR ACTION: Slowly pull the boom control lever back, controlling the speed of the boom raising movement with the control lever position. Keep the engine rpm constant until the desired position is reached, then return the control to the center position.

Exercise caution to avoid any obstructions to boom movement in the vertical plane, such as trees or power lines.

If the load or load block is close to the ground in front of the machine, the operator may be required to hoist the load to avoid contacting the crane.

EXPECTED MACHINE MOVEMENT: The boom rises, increasing the hook height and reducing the overall machine height clearance. The operating radius is slowly decreased, thus possibly increasing machine capacity and stability.

Figure 5D Raise boom and lower the load.

RAISE BOOM AND LOWER THE LOAD

Arm extended, fingers closed, thumb pointing up, flex fingers in and out as long as load movement is desired.

OPERATOR ACTION: This requires a two-hand operation. Use your left hand to push the hoist control lever forward, while using your right hand to pull the boom control lever back. Keep the engine rpm constant until the desired position is reached, then slowly return both controls to their center position.

Move both controls independently to maintain the load (block or ball) at an even distance from the ground, with movement horizontal to the level ground plane.

Keep the engine rpm at a high level to ensure sufficient oil flow to sustain smooth load movement. Exercise caution to avoid any obstructions to boom movement in the vertical plane, such as trees or power lines.

EXPECTED MACHINE MOVEMENT: The boom rises, reducing overall machine height clearance, as the load moves horizontally toward the crane. The operating radius is slowly decreased, thus possibly increasing machine capacity and stability.

Figure 5E Lower boom.

LOWER BOOM

Arm extended, fingers closed, thumb pointing downward.

OPERATOR ACTION: Slowly push the boom control lever forward, controlling the speed of the boom lowering movement with the control lever position. Keep the engine rpm constant until the desired position is reached, then return the control to the center position.

Exercise caution to avoid any obstructions to boom movement in the vertical plane, such as trees or power lines.

EXPECTED MACHINE MOVEMENT: The boom will lower, decreasing the hook height and reducing the overall machine horizontal clearance. The operating radius is slowly increased, thus possibly decreasing machine capacity and stability.

Figure 5F Lower boom and raise the load.

LOWER BOOM AND RAISE THE LOAD

Arm extended, fingers closed, thumb pointing down, flex fingers in and out as long as load movement is desired.

OPERATOR ACTION: This requires a two-hand operation. Use your left hand to pull the hoist control lever back, while using your right hand to push the boom control lever forward. Keep the engine rpm constant until the desired position is reached, then slowly return both controls to their center positions.

Move both controls independently to maintain the load (block or ball) at an even distance from the ground, with movement horizontal to the level ground plane.

The engine rpm must be kept at a high level to ensure sufficient oil flow to sustain smooth load movement.

EXPECTED MACHINE MOVEMENT: The boom lowers, increasing overall machine height clearance, as the load moves horizontally away from the crane. The operating radius is slowly increased, thus possibly reducing both machine capacity and stability.

EXTEND TELESCOPING BOOM

Figure 5G Extend telescoping boom.

Both fists in front of body at waist level, with thumbs pointing outward.

OPERATOR ACTION: Using your left hand, push the telescope control lever forward, controlling the boom extension speed with the control position and keeping the engine rpm constant until the desired boom length is reached. Slowly return the controls to the center position. Boom extension may also be accomplished by using the left foot to slowly rock the left foot pedal forward until the desired boom length is reached. Then, slowly return the foot pedal to the center position.

Take care not to bring the hook block or ball too close to the boom head when extending the boom to avoid two-blocking.

EXPECTED MACHINE MOVEMENT: Boom sections telescope out. The load radius is increased, possibly decreasing machine capacity and stability. The load (block or ball) rises vertically.

RETRACT TELESCOPING BOOM

Figure 5H Retract telescoping boom.

Both fists in front of body at waist level, with thumbs pointing toward each other.

OPERATOR ACTION: Using your left hand, pull the telescope control lever back, controlling the boom retraction speed with the control position and keeping the engine rpm constant until the desired boom length is reached. Slowly return the controls to the center position. Boom retraction may also be accomplished by using the left foot to slowly rock the left foot pedal rearward until the desired boom length is reached. Then, slowly return the foot pedal to the center position.

EXPECTED MACHINE MOVEMENT: Boom sections retract. The load radius is decreased, possibly increasing machine capacity and stability. The load (block or ball) lowers vertically.

SWING

Arm extended, point with index finger in direction of boom swing. (Swing left is shown as viewed by the operator.) Use appropriate arm for desired direction.

OPERATOR ACTION: Push the far left swing control lever forward to swing toward the boom, swinging left for right side operator position and right for left side operator position. For a centrally located operator position, control lever movement is the same as for the left side operator position. Pull rearward to reverse the action.

Keep the engine rpm constant. For inexperienced operators, keep the rpm at a lower level than is used for other craning operations.

Acceleration and deceleration should be slow and steady, with swing speed being adjusted near the end of the swing so that the final desired swinging position is not overrun, thus causing the load to swing like a pendulum. Note that when the signal person uses his or her left arm to swing, the swing is to the operator's right.

Exercise caution to avoid obstructions in the path of the swing. The signal person should warn the operator of obstructions, especially when the swing is to the boom side and the operator's vision is limited.

EXPECTED MACHINE MOVEMENT: The boom moves about the center of rotation with the load (block or ball) swinging in an arc, either toward the right or left, while remaining approximately equidistant to a level plane.

Figure 5I Swing.

MOVE SLOWLY
(ANY SIGNALED MOTION)

Use one hand to give any motion signal and place the other hand motionless over the hand giving the motion signal.

OPERATOR ACTION: Perform the action indicated by the hand signal in a slow manner. Pictured is hoist slowly, directing the operator to pull the hoist control lever for the desired hoist toward the operator until the load (block or ball) ascends slowly. Keep the engine rpm constant until the desired lift is complete, then slowly return the hoist control lever to the center position.

Other move slowly signals (not pictured) include hoist down slowly, raise boom slowly, etc.

EXPECTED MACHINE MOVEMENT: Machine movement will vary depending on the signal being given.

Figure 5J Move slowly.

Figure 5K Use main hoist.

USE MAIN HOIST

Tap open hand, palm down, on head and then use regular hand signals to show the desired action.

OPERATOR ACTION: Grasp the hoist up/down control lever for the main hoist and await further signaling from the signal person.

EXPECTED MACHINE MOVEMENT: None. This signal is used only to inform the operator that the signal person has chosen the main hoist for the action to be performed as opposed to the auxiliary hoist.

Figure 5L Use auxiliary hoist (whipline).

USE AUXILIARY HOIST (WHIPLINE)

Tap elbow with open palm of one hand, then use regular hand signal to show desired action.

OPERATOR ACTION: Grasp the hoist up/down control lever for the auxiliary hoist and await further signaling from the signal person.

EXPECTED MACHINE MOVEMENT: None. This signal is used only to inform the operator that the signal person has chosen the auxiliary hoist for the action to be performed, as opposed to the main hoist.

Figure 5M Stop.

STOP

Arm extended, palm down, move arm back and forth horizontally.

OPERATOR ACTION: Return all activated controls to the center or neutral position in a smooth motion at a slow to moderate speed to prevent pendulum action of the load (block or ball).

EXPECTED MACHINE MOVEMENT: None. All movement of the machine ceases.

NOTE: The Stop and Emergency Stop signals are the only signals that may be given by anyone, and the crane operator is required to obey.

NCCER – *Mobile Crane Operations*

Figure 5N Emergency stop.

Figure 5O Dog everything.

Figure 5P Travel / tower travel.

EMERGENCY STOP

Both arms extended, palms down, move arms back and forth horizontally.

OPERATOR ACTION: Immediately return all activated controls to the center or neutral position as quickly as is safe.

EXPECTED MACHINE MOVEMENT: None. All movement of the machine ceases.

NOTE: The Stop and Emergency Stop signals are the only signals that may be given by anyone, and the crane operator is required to obey.

DOG EVERYTHING

Clasp hands in front of body at waist height.

OPERATOR ACTION: Ensure that no controls are activated, then engage all positive locking devices including hoist pawls, swing brakes, and house locks.

EXPECTED MACHINE MOVEMENT: None.

TRAVEL / TOWER TRAVEL

Arms are straight and extended horizontally, moved back and forth in a pushing motion away from the body. All fingers point straight up.

OPERATOR ACTION: Move the crane in the direction indicated.

TRAVEL – BOTH TRACKS
(CRAWLER CRANE)

Position both fists in front of body and rotate them around each other, indicating the direction of travel (forward or backward).

OPERATOR ACTION: Decrease the engine speed to idle. Move the slide pinion to the travel position. Hold down the deadman control button. Move the main drive control lever forward and back slightly to fully engage the slide pinion, depending on the grade of the travel surface (uphill, downhill, or level). Position the travel locks per the manufacturer's directions. Engage the swing lock. Position the boom angle as shown in the manufacturer's travel tables. Move the steering clutch control to the "straight" position, and move the main drive control lever in the desired direction to travel forward or backward.

EXPECTED MACHINE MOVEMENT: Machine travels in the direction chosen.

Figure 5Q Travel — both tracks (crawler crane).

TRAVEL – ONE TRACK
(CRAWLER CRANE)

Lock track on side of raised fist. Travel opposite track in direction indicated by circular motion of other fist, rotated vertically in front of body.

OPERATOR ACTION: Decrease the engine speed to idle. Move the slide pinion to the travel position. Hold down the deadman control button. Move the main drive control lever forward and back slightly to fully engage the slide pinion. Depending on the grade of the travel surface (uphill, downhill, or level), position the travel locks per the manufacturer's directions. Engage the swing lock. Position the boom angle as shown in the manufacturer's travel tables. Move the steering half lock control to either engage for a gradual turn or disengage for a sharp turn. Move the steering clutch control to the desired position to turn right or left. Move the main drive control lever in the desired direction to turn right or left.

EXPECTED MACHINE MOVEMENT: Machine turns in the direction chosen.

Figure 5R Travel — one track (crawler crane).

Figure 5S Trolley travel (tower or overhead crane).

TROLLEY TRAVEL
(TOWER OR OVERHEAD CRANE)

Elbow bent with the palm towards the body and fingers closed; thumb pointing in the direction of motion and moved horizontally back and forth.

OPERATOR ACTION: Use the required controls to move the trolley of a tower or overhead crane in the direction indicated.

EXPECTED MACHINE MOVEMENT: The trolley assembly moves in the direction indicated.

Remember that the hand-signal chart must also be posted conspicuously at the jobsite. These hand signals are recognized by the industry as the standard hand signals to be used on all jobsites. This helps ensure that there is a common core of knowledge and a universal meaning to the signals when lifting operations are being conducted. As discussed previously, this helps to eliminate a significant barrier to effective communication. These same signals apply to tower cranes, including luffing-boom tower cranes (*Figure 6*), as well as mobile cranes.

Additions or modifications may be made for crane functions not covered by the OSHA-illustrated hand signals, such as the deployment of outriggers. The operator and signal person must agree upon any signals and their meaning that are not illustrated in the Standard Method before the lift begins. These signals cannot conflict or be easily confused with any Standard Method signal.

There are two hand signals pictured in *ASME Standard B30.5* that are not included in the OSHA Standard Method. Since they are not pictured in the OSHA Standard Method set of signals, they are technically considered nonstandard. However, they are also a part of a national consensus standard and are commonly used. These two signals (*Figure 7*) are one-handed alternates for the standard telescopic boom retraction and extension signals, typically used when the signal person is also manning a tag line or has one hand otherwise occupied.

ASME Standard B30.2, Overhead and Gantry Cranes, also offers some hand signals (*Figure 8*) that are devoted to the operation of overhead cranes and similar equipment. Again, they are not part of the OSHA Standard Method set of signals, but are endorsed by a national consensus standard. Therefore, they are the best choice when such signals are needed. The signal for Bridge Travel is the same as that for Travel / Trolley Travel used with other cranes. The bridge of an overhead crane is defined as the part of

Figure 6 Luffing-boom tower crane.

(A) EXTEND BOOM

(B) RETRACT BOOM

Figure 7 Alternate one-hand signals for telescopic boom retraction and extension.

a crane consisting of one or more girders and the supporting **trucks** that carry the trolley(s). This basically describes the large, weight-bearing structure above the hook. The trolley assembly moves along the bridge, from side-to-side.

Remember that whenever nonstandard signals are used, OSHA requires the signal person and crane operator to agree on their use and meaning before the operation begins. If it is necessary to switch from hand signals to verbal signals during an operation, all crane motions must be stopped before doing so.

A signal person's position at a lift site is very important, especially when hand signals are used. He or she must be in full view of the lift operation, as well as in the clear view of the crane operator. Signal persons should always wear high-visibility clothing or a vest that contrasts with the surroundings. High-visibility gloves may also be in order, so the crane operator can clearly see the position and/or motion of the hands.

As a general rule, the best possible position for the signal person to be positioned is with the line of sight perpendicular to the boom. In this position the signal person is visible to the operator, as well as able to observe the load and any boom deflection that may occur. Choose the side of the boom that presents the fewest visual distractions or obstructions.

Another common nonverbal signal set is actually one used by the crane operator when moving a mobile crane. These signals are outlined in *ASME Standard B30.5*, Section 5-3.3.7. It is common for the operator to use the following audible travel signals, using the crane's horn:

- *Stop* – One audible signal
- *Forward* – Two audible signals
- *Reverse* – Three audible signals

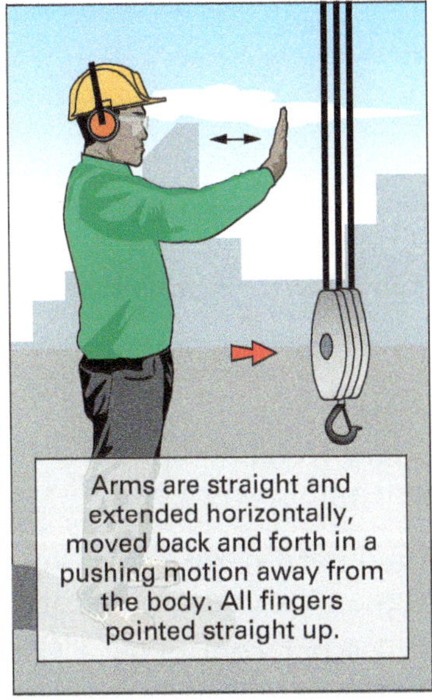

(A) BRIDGE TRAVEL

(B) MULTIPLE TROLLEYS

(C) MAGNET DISCONNECTED

Figure 8 Additional signals for overhead cranes.

Additional Resources

ASME Standard B30.2, Overhead and Gantry Cranes. Current Edition. New York, NY: American Society of Mechanical Engineers.

ASME Standard B30.5, Mobile and Locomotive Cranes. Current Edition. New York, NY: American Society of Mechanical Engineers.

29 *CFR* 1926, Subpart CC, **www.ecfr.gov**

2.0.0 Section Review

1. In regards to a signal person signaling more than one crane at a time, ______.
   a. OSHA standards prohibit it under any circumstances
   b. crane operators must exit their crane cab when they are not the active crane
   c. the Standard Method of hand signaling cannot be used
   d. signals to identify which crane is being signaled must be determined and agreed upon

2. Which of the following is a true statement about verbal communications with a crane?
   a. Cell phones legally qualify as a verbal communication device, but reliable signal strength at every jobsite is difficult to predict.
   b. Hardwired communication equipment is no longer allowed by OSHA standards.
   c. Low-powered, inexpensive walkie-talkie equipment is the best choice for every environment.
   d. DECT-compatible devices are designed to seek out and use any frequency that shows the least amount of signal traffic.

3. OSHA's chart of Standard Method hand signals must be posted ______.
   a. in the lift plan
   b. in a conspicuous location on the jobsite
   c. on each signal person's clothing
   d. on the load being lifted

1. Internal and external barriers to communication affect _____.

   a. only the sender
   b. only the receiver
   c. both the sender and the receiver
   d. only the party to which the message is related

2. Expressing the perceived meaning of something one has read or heard from a sender back to the sender in your own words is referred to as _____.

   a. paraphrasing
   b. passive listening
   c. message filtration
   d. negotiation

3. Verbal communication barriers include language differences, overuse of abstractions, and _____.

   a. body language
   b. feedback
   c. the use of clear language
   d. a lack of confidence

4. The Standard Method of hand signals is found in which standard?

   a. 29 *CFR* 1926, Subpart CC, Appendix A
   b. 29 *CFR* 1926.1428
   c. *ASME Standard B30.5*
   d. *ASME Standard B30.2*

5. The main advantage of a hardwired crane-communication system is _____.

   a. low cost
   b. portability
   c. less radio interference
   d. ease of use

6. A signal person's position at the lift site should be _____.

   a. behind the crane where the operator can see the signal person in the cab's rearview mirrors
   b. in full view of the lifting operation and crane operator
   c. following the load from directly underneath
   d. in full view of the crane operator and within the swing radius of the crane

7. What action is signaled by tapping the palm of your hand on the top of your head, and then following up with signals for other functions?

   a. Lower
   b. Use Main Hoist
   c. Use Auxiliary Hoist (whipline)
   d. Raise Boom and Lower Load

8. When the signal person gives the Dog Everything signal, the crane operator _____.

   a. pulls the telescope control lever toward himself/herself
   b. decreases the engine speed to a fast idle
   c. moves the slide pinion to the travel position and holds down the deadman control button
   d. engages all positive locking devices including hoist pawls, swing brakes, and house locks after ensuring that no controls are activated

9. When preparing to drive a mobile crane in reverse, how many audible travel signals must be given using the crane's horn?

   a. One
   b. Two
   c. Three
   d. Four

10. Alternate one-hand signals to signal telescopic boom retraction and extension are _____.

    a. part of OSHA's Standard Method
    b. found in *ASME Standard B30.5*
    c. found in both the OSHA and ASME crane-related standards
    d. used only if directly approved by an OSHA representative

Fill in the blank with the correct term that you learned from your study of this module.

1. The trolley of a typical overhead crane moves back and forth along the __________.

2. When a signal person continuously holds a radio's Transmit button or switch down, even during pauses in speech, it is referred to as a(n) __________.

3. Repeating the perceived meaning of a received message using different words describes __________.

4. A(n) __________ describes the lifting of a load that is out of sight of the crane operator.

5. Giving someone a thumbs-up signal is a good example of __________.

6. Giving the verbal order "Swing right a hair" is a type of communication __________.

7. A(n) __________ is responsible for managing the umbilical of a submerged diver.

8. Effective nonverbal communications between the signal person and the crane operator depend on a clear __________.

9. The moving, upright portions of an overhead crane that support the bridge are referred to as __________.

10. When working near power lines with a crane, a(n) __________ is often needed to ensure that the minimum approach distance is not compromised by the crane, the load line, or the load.

11. *ASME Standard B30.5, Mobile and Locomotive Cranes* is an example of a(n) __________.

Trade Terms

Abstraction
Blind lift
Bridge
Consensus standard

Dedicated spotter
Diver tender
Line of sight
Nonverbal communication

Open mike
Paraphrasing
Trucks

Robert Capelli

Senior Health, Safety, and Environmental
Manager, Orion Marine Construction

With a wealth of experience, insight, and extensive training from the US Marine Corps, Robert continues to inspire excellence in his role as Senior Health, Safety, and Environmental Manager with a large marine construction company.

Please give a brief synopsis of your construction career and your current position.

My first job after the Marine Corps was as a safety specialist in a roadway maintenance facility operated by the Florida Department of Transportation, which was a great segue into construction. The knowledge and experience I gained there was invaluable. From that foundation, I then worked for a company that had road construction, utility, demolition, and mining divisions. The diversity of work and operations in that one company alone gave me experience that would have taken four times as long to obtain elsewhere and has served me well in dealing with industry business owners and regulators over the years. I now work for a marine construction company as their safety manager.

How did you get started in the construction industry?

After I left active duty in 1991, I planned on going to school to become a firefighter/paramedic, but I ran into problems during school enrollment and was forced to look for work. As it turned out, the safety position I was offered with the Florida Department of Transportation used portions of the risk assessment training program I experienced in the Marines and the fire service.

Who or what inspired you to enter the construction industry?

The need to provide for my family was the motivation and inspiration to accept a position in the construction industry. I had a completely different career path in mind and was not even considering construction as an option, but because of the income and benefits I would lose if I didn't take the job I was offered, the choice was easy to make. That was my inspiration, and it was a good choice.

How has training in construction impacted your life and career? What types of training have you completed?

My training certificate folder is several inches thick, and I have been very fortunate that my careers and volunteer work have overlapped and provided training not available to most safety professionals. The knowledge gained also revealed opportunities to me that were not available to others. After active duty, I continued serving in the Marine Corps Reserve and was the officer in charge of an environmental response team that performed hazardous material storage and remediation activities. Additionally, I was the fire chief of a local volunteer fire department, providing fire and rescue services.

In 2015, I earned a master of public health degree, with a concentration in health, safety and environment. Many courses I have taken applied to more than one field. Hazardous material and environmental classes transcended all three fields. Urban search and rescue technician, confined space, fall protection, rigging, rope rescue, emergency medical technician, pump operator, and fire inspector classes all have applications in both the fire service and construction industries.

One may have twenty years of experience in construction, but is that one year of experience twenty times over, or twenty years of progressive experience with training and growth in the industry? The answer to this question is fairly evident when I perform the rigging practical examinations, where we always screen the candidates to ensure they are not overstating their qualifications. Many of them have struggled even on the basic rigger practical exam because they have not taken any additional training classes and have stayed within their industry segment. This leads to workers that cannot solve problems any more difficult than being confronted with a two-legged bridle sling.

Why do you think credentials are important in the construction industry?

Credentials are important in any profession as a way to validate experience and knowledge in a given field. In many cases, employers seek out credentialed people because they have verifiable knowledge and skills the employer needs.

The construction industry is very transient, with construction workers chasing work from one project to another. A person's reputation and who they know is often the key to getting hired for that next project. That works well if hiring is performed at the local level, but when hiring is centralized or the project is very large, recruiting managers have to sort through hundreds of applications to fill slots. Having an industry-recognized credential, such as the NCCER Certified Plus credential, makes an individual stand out to a hiring manager.

The value of the right credentials presented to acknowledge your skills is huge. Obtaining industry-recognized credentials, such as those provided by NCCER, will help you get ahead.

What do you enjoy most about your career?

I thrive on the variety of work, with every project having its own challenges, and the need to solve problems and develop unique solutions is what keeps the job interesting. I have worked with some really great craft professionals who taught me the business of construction as well as the mechanics of the field, and every one of them had great problem-solving skills.

Would you recommend construction as a career to others? Why?

Absolutely, yes! This industry offers everyone who applies themselves to the effort an opportunity to provide for their family and continue growing as a professional. Academia has perhaps done a generation of Americans a disservice by saying you can only get ahead in life with a college degree. The theory that a four-year college degree is the one true path to success has been debunked over the years, and there are many unskilled workers with college degrees that are not gaining significant value from that education.

Starting out in construction with a broad orientation to the trades and applying yourself over the years will get you ahead. At some point, vocational school training or a bachelor's degree may be necessary to help you progress to the next level, but it is unnecessary at the start of your career. The opportunities to travel, learn new crafts, and move into management positions are unlimited.

What advice would you give to someone who is new to the construction industry?

Apply yourself, learn, seek opportunities, and don't become stagnant in your job. Approach every task by asking yourself, "What could go wrong here?" If you see something wrong or unsafe, fix it or tell a supervisor who can fix it. There is nothing so important that it has to be done right now at the expense of injuring someone, or worse. We always seem to find time to correct things, so why not do it right the first time? In addition, your reputation will follow you forever, so protect it.

How do you define craftsmanship?

Craftsmanship encompasses the physical result of applying your focus, training, and skills to the work effort in the best way possible.

Trade Terms Introduced in This Module

Abstraction: Any form of verbal, graphical, or written communication representing a generalized and nonspecific idea or quality of a thing, action, or event.

Blind lift: Any lift involving a load that is out of the direct view of the operator. Blind lifts are generally always categorized as critical lifts.

Bridge: In relation to overhead cranes, the part of an overhead crane consisting of one or more girders or beams and the supporting trucks. The bridge is the overhead, weight-bearing structure along which the trolley(s) and load block assembly travels.

Consensus standard: A set of proprietary guidelines published and agreed to by a consensus (representative majority) of members of a given industry. While not legally binding, they are often cited in governmental regulations, such as OSHA standards.

Dedicated spotter: An individual qualified as a signal person who is charged with monitoring the separation between power lines and the equipment, load line, and load, so that the minimum approach distance is not compromised per OSHA standards.

Diver tender: One or more individuals assigned to attend to a diver's needs, including providing assistance in equipment preparation and managing the diver's cables and hoses.

Line of sight: The straight-line path between an observer's eyes and the thing being observed.

Nonverbal communication: All communication that does not use words. This includes appearance, personal environment, use of time, and body language.

Open mike: In electronic communications, the condition where a radio's Transmit button or switch is held continuously without releasing it, even during pauses in speaking.

Paraphrasing: Expressing the perceived meaning of something read or heard in one's own words, generally to ensure clarity. Paraphrasing is an important component of active listening.

Trucks: In relation to overhead cranes, a mechanical assembly consisting of a frame, wheels, bearings, and axles that support the bridge of an overhead crane and provide the ability for it to move along a set of parallel tracks.

Additional Resources

This module presents thorough resources for task training. The following reference material is recommended for further study.

ASME Standard B30.2, Overhead and Gantry Cranes. Current edition. New York, NY: American Society of Mechanical Engineers.

ASME Standard B30.5, Mobile and Locomotive Cranes. Current edition. New York, NY: American Society of Mechanical Engineers.

Interplay: The Process of Interpersonal Communication, Ronald Adler, Lawrence Rosenfeld, and Russell Proctor. 13th Edition. New York, NY: Oxford University Press.

NCCER Module 00107, *Basic Communication Skills*.

29 *CFR* 1926, Subpart CC, **www.ecfr.gov**

Figure Credits

© iStock.com/VasilySmirnov, Module opener

Carolina Bridge Co., Figure 2

Motorola Solutions, Inc., Figure 3

Sonetics Corporation, Figure 4

Roy Laney, SME, Figure 6

Section Review Answer Key

Answer	Section Reference	Objective
Section One		
1. b	1.1.2	1a
2. c	1.2.2	1b
Section Two		
1. d	2.1.1	2a
2. a	2.2.0	2b
3. b	2.3.0	2c

User Update

NCCER makes every effort to keep its textbooks up-to-date and free of technical errors. We appreciate your help in this process. If you find an error, a typographical mistake, or an inaccuracy in NCCER's curricula, please submit a User Update form by visiting **https://www.nccer.org/olf**. You can also scan the QR code using the camera on your phone or mobile device to access the form.

Crane Safety and Emergency Procedures

OVERVIEW

Cranes are used to accomplish very important tasks in various construction and industrial settings. When working with or near cranes, safety is always the highest priority. Crane operators and other members of the lift team must embrace their responsibility as the manager of a powerful machine that can both accomplish great things and destroy property and lives. Thousands of successful crane operations occur each day without incident; all of the lifts in the future can end the same way. The goal of this module is to present a wide variety of safety information related to crane operation and prepare lift team members for their role in a safe workplace.

Module 21106

21106 V3.0

From *Mobile Crane Operations, Trainee Guide*. NCCER.
Copyright © 2018 by NCCER. Published by Pearson. All rights reserved.

Crane Safety and Emergency Procedures

Objectives

When you have completed this module, you will be able to do the following:

1. Identify relevant OSHA and ASME standards and general crane safety considerations.
   a. Identify safety standards relevant to mobile cranes and their operation.
   b. Identify general safety considerations for mobile crane operation.
2. Identify mobile crane operation considerations related to specific applications and explain how to respond to various incidents.
   a. Describe the purpose of pre-lift meetings and identify the topics of discussion.
   b. Identify safety considerations related to power lines.
   c. Identify safety considerations related to weather conditions.
   d. Describe safety considerations related to specific crane functions and how to respond to various incidents.

Performance Tasks

This is a knowledge-based module; there are no Performance Tasks.

Trade Terms

Avoidance zone
Competent person
Critical lift
High-voltage proximity warning device
Insulating link
Minimum clearance distance

Prohibited zone
Recloser
Shock loading
Standard lift
Standards

Industry Recognized Credentials

If you are training through an NCCER-accredited sponsor, you may be eligible for credentials from NCCER's Registry. The ID number for this module is 21106. Note that this module may have been used in other NCCER curricula and may apply to other level completions. Contact NCCER's Registry at 1.888.622.3720 or go to **www.nccer.org** for more information.

You can also show off your industry-recognized credentials online with NCCER's digital badges. Transform your knowledge, skills, and achievements into badges that you can share across social media platforms, send to your network, and add to your resume. For more information, visit **www.nccer.org**.

> **NOTE**
>
> This is an elective module and is not required for successful completion of *Millwright Level Four*, nor for the successful completion of the *Millwright* craft credential.

Contents

1.0.0 CRANE SAFETY

Objective

Identify relevant OSHA and ASME standards and general crane safety considerations.

 a. Identify safety standards relevant to mobile cranes and their operation.
 b. Identify general safety considerations for mobile crane operation.

Trade Terms

Competent person: As defined by OSHA, an individual who is capable of identifying existing and predictable hazards in the surroundings or working conditions which are unsanitary, hazardous, or dangerous to employees, and who has the authorization to take prompt corrective measures to eliminate such hazards.

Shock loading: A sudden, dramatically increased load imposed on a crane and rigging, usually as the result of momentum from the load that occurs due to swinging side-to-side, dropping the load and then stopping it suddenly, and similar actions that create momentum.

Standards: As defined by OSHA, statements that require conditions, or the adoption or use of one or more practices, means, methods, operations, or processes, that are reasonably necessary or appropriate to provide safe or healthful employment and places of employment. Standards developed by some organizations are voluntary in nature, while OSHA standards and those they incorporate by reference are enforceable by law.

Equipment can be damaged and people can be severely injured or killed in crane accidents. Lives, careers, and companies can all be lost as the result of a crane accident. This module provides common safety guidelines for the operation of mobile cranes. In addition, it provides an overview of situations that can occur on the jobsite and the steps to take in response to various situations.

Injuries and fatalities related to crane operations happen for a variety of reasons. The vast majority of incidents are preventable. Many incidents fall into the category of struck by / caught between incidents. One of the leading causes of fatalities in crane operations over the years has been electrocution. These are not cases of electrical problems developing in the cranes; they are electrocutions resulting from power line contact. For this reason, there are a number of OSHA directives related to operations around power lines that must be followed without compromise.

Because working on or around mobile cranes can be dangerous (*Figure 1*), members of a lift team must understand that the first responsibility on the job is safety. This responsibility includes personal safety, the safety of others, and the safety of the equipment and materials on the jobsite. One must know the safety requirements for each jobsite and be aware of any unique hazards that may be associated with the work. Accidents can happen anywhere at any time, but they can be prevented when safety is always the first priority.

1.1.0 Safety Standards

The mobile crane industry is very large and complex. The possibility of major damage and loss of life demands that the industry be monitored. There are several groups that monitor and regulate crane operations. The three primary organizations to be introduced here are the following:

- The Occupational Safety and Health Administration (OSHA)
- The American Society of Mechanical Engineers (ASME)
- The American National Standards Institute (ANSI)

ASME and ANSI are nonprofit professional organizations. The principal difference in the two is that ASME does the bulk of the technical research and offers guidance (standards) based on this research and engineering studies. ANSI is more focused on embracing and supporting standards of their choosing through a specific set of procedures to gain consensus; ANSI does not develop standards independently. Both have an international component as well as a domestic function and provide guidance that serves to reduce or eliminate hazards and the resulting accidents. OSHA, on the other hand, is an office of the US Government, established under the Occupational Safety and Health Act of 1970.

There are several terms often used in discussions of publications from these organizations that should be defined, beginning with the term *standard*. A standard, as it applies to the crane industry, outlines specific conditions, or the adoption or use of one or more practices and methods, necessary or appropriate to provide safe, functional products and/or places of employment. Some standards may be referred to as *national consensus standards*. This means several things:

Figure 1 Crane accidents can result in property damage, serious injuries, and fatalities.

- The standard has been adopted by one or more nationally recognized organizations under a specific set of procedures whereby it can be determined that persons affected by it have reached substantial agreement on its adoption.
- The standard was created in a manner that afforded an opportunity for diverse views to be considered.
- The standard has been designated as a national consensus standard by the US Secretary or the Assistant Secretary of Labor, after consultation with other appropriate federal agencies.

OSHA and ASME standards frequently refer to other standards, often informing the reader that those standards are incorporated by reference. This means that the standards referred to must also be considered and recognized as if they were a part of the text. This helps to reduce the duplication of effort to develop a similar piece of work.

ASME develops many standards, some of which apply to cranes and the crane industry. However, ASME and ANSI do not have the power to enforce standards. ANSI selects standards from organizations like ASME and works to gain consensus and acceptance on a national or international scale. However, ANSI standards are considered voluntary and are not written as laws or regulations, since ANSI is also a nonprofit organization.

OSHA, however, is different. OSHA was created under federal law, and employers are required to follow the standards they develop, adopt from others, or incorporate by reference.

OSHA often creates their own enforceable standards, some of which are based on the work of organizations like ASME and ANSI.

In some cases, OSHA may simply adopt or incorporate the standards of other respected organizations by reference. A good example can be found in this statement from 29 *CFR* 1926.1433(b): "Mobile (including crawler and truck) and locomotive cranes manufactured on or after November 8, 2010 must meet the following portions of *ASME B30.5-2004* (incorporated by reference, *see* §1926.6)…" This section of the OSHA standards goes on to list specific passages from the ASME standard that apply. Incorporation by reference into an OSHA standard effectively makes those standards enforceable as well.

It is very important to understand that OSHA standards are not just suggestions; they are enforceable laws. Employers can be punished for failing to comply with OSHA standards. As an employee, you have a responsibility to your employer, as well as to yourself, to follow the OSHA standards. Remember that the standards of other organizations that are incorporated by reference into OSHA standards and are made mandatory by their language also become legally enforceable.

1.1.1 Crane Industry Safety Standards

Mobile crane operations are governed primarily by several standards. It is important to note that all standards related to crane operations typically contain safety information. That is their priority and reason for existence. Even standards such as *ASME Standard B30.10, Hooks* are based on safety. Consider that the standards related to hooks and their design and fabrication are created to ensure that they are safe and reliable when used properly. Of course, this is also true of OSHA standards, all of which exist to support OSHA's mission of safety in the workplace.

29 *CFR* 1926, Subpart CC, *Cranes and Derricks in Construction* is arguably the most important set of standards in the crane industry. This is especially true since OSHA standards are enforceable by law. Subpart CC includes 29 *CFR* 1926.1400 through 1926.1442, plus a listing of other standards that are incorporated by reference. Topics covered in this standard include, but are not limited to, the following:

- Ground conditions for crane support
- Assembly and disassembly of equipment and attachments
- Power line safety
- Equipment inspections
- Wire rope inspection, selection, and installation
- Required safety devices and operational aids
- Crane operation
- Signaling
- Work area control
- Operator, signal person, and crane maintenance personnel qualifications
- Hoisting personnel
- Equipment modifications
- Crane operation and safety when used on floating barges

ASME Standard B30.5, Mobile and Locomotive Cranes is the most important ASME standard relevant to crane operators. Note that some portions of this standard have been incorporated into the OSHA standards by reference. Again, this means they are not simply suggestions, but are legally enforceable. Topics covered in this standard include, but are not limited to, the following:

- *Personnel competence* – "Persons performing the functions identified in this Volume shall meet the applicable qualifying criteria stated in this Volume and shall, through education, training, experience, skill, and physical fitness, as necessary, be competent and capable to perform the functions as determined by the employer or employer's representative."
- *Crane construction and characteristics* – Items covered here include: crane load ratings; boom hoists and telescoping boom mechanisms; crane travel; controls; cabs; and structural performance.
- *Inspection, testing, and maintenance* – This section covers the crane as well as the inspection and replacement of the wire ropes.
- *Operation* – The specific qualifications of crane operators are provided here, including the physical requirements as well as those related to testing. The specific requirements are covered in NCCER Module 21101, "Orientation to the Trade," from *Mobile Crane Operations Level One*. The role and responsibilities of each individual that is part of a typical lift crew, including the operator, are also outlined. Following this information, the standard addresses a wide variety of common crane movements, such as attaching, lifting, and swinging the load, and provides safety guidelines specific to each action. Crane hand signals are also found in the Operation section of the standard.

Another important ASME standard is *ASME Standard P30.1, Planning for Load Handling Activities*. The standard documents lift-planning considerations that extend beyond cranes to other load-handling equipment as well. Guidance is divided into two categories—Standard Lift Plans and Critical Lift Plans— based on the degree of exposure to hazards. Lift planning will be covered in detail in *Mobile Crane Operations Level Three*.

Throughout this module, standards are referenced where appropriate. Note that this text attempts to present the standards as accurately

Glossaries

Some OSHA and ASME standards contain glossaries to clearly define important terms used in the text. Although every trade has its own verbiage that changes over the years, it is helpful to be familiar with the definition of terms as the standard-setting organizations see them. Many of the OSHA and ASME standards that apply to the mobile crane industry have a glossary at the beginning to ensure that the meaning of a given term is not misunderstood or misapplied.

as possible, but does not present all relevant standards or the requirements they contain. It is the responsibility of crane operators, riggers, signal persons, and all other members of a lift team to directly review and follow the appropriate standards. Requests for interpretations and clarifications of the various standards can be addressed directly to OSHA, ASME, or other issuing authority.

1.2.0 Mobile Crane Safety Considerations

Mobile crane operators must be aware of the unavoidable hazards associated with the trade. Lifted loads will be moved above and around other workers, and such loads represent an extreme hazard to workers in the area (*Figure 2*). You may also work during inclement weather conditions where wind, slippery surfaces, and other hazards exist. When working near mobile cranes, look up and be mindful of the hazards above and around you, but do not forget the potential hazards that exist on the ground.

As a result of the industry's efforts and losses experienced by employers, construction-trade contractors have made the development of a safety culture in the organization a priority. However, it isn't just about complying with the laws—most employers truly care about the lives of their employees and their families, and developing a safety culture on the job supports their concerns for employee safety and welfare.

Safety consciousness and helping to build a culture that promotes safety from within is extremely important. The earning ability of injured employees may be reduced or eliminated for the rest of their lives. The number of injured employees can be significantly reduced if each employee is committed to safety awareness and exhibits that attitude in their daily work. Full participation in the employer's safety program is a matter of personal responsibility. Making safety the first priority is the key to reducing accidents, injuries, and fatalities on the job. Most accidents can be avoided, because most result from human error. Show that you are a team player by helping to establish and support a safety culture within your organization and on the jobsite.

1.2.1 Personal Protection

Hard hats, safety shoes, safety glasses, and barricaded cranes to discourage personnel entry into the area are among the personnel-protection requirements for almost every jobsite (*Figure 3*). Gloves are also required in many cases, especially when working with rigging equipment such as wire rope. Other personal protective equipment (PPE) may be required at specific jobsites, such as those that produce hazardous chemicals that could be released to the environment. It is essential that every worker be familiar with the requirements of each individual jobsite, and embrace those requirements consistently.

1.2.2 Basic Rigging Safety

Riggers and other members of lift teams must be capable of selecting suitable rigging and lifting equipment, as well as directing the movement of the crane to assure the safety of all personnel and the load itself. All rigging operations must be planned, supervised, and accomplished by qualified and competent personnel. [OSHA defines competent person in 29 *CFR* 1926.32(f).]

One very important rigging requirement is to determine the weight of all loads before attempting to rig and lift them. Crane operators must

Figure 2 Lifting and positioning large loads is hazardous work.

Figure 3 Wearing the correct PPE is a crucial first step toward a safe working environment.

know the weight of the load to ensure it is within the rated load capacity of the crane under the circumstances of the lift. Riggers, however, must also know the weight of the load to ensure that the rigging equipment and techniques used are suitable for the task.

The following rigging-related safety practices should be followed at all times:

- Determine the weight of the load before rigging. If this is not possible, the load can be lifted slightly while the crane operator monitors the instrumentation and determines the weight. If it does not exceed 75 percent of the crane's rated load capacity at the operating radius required, the lift can be made. If it does exceed that value, the load must be set down and the weight reevaluated per 29 *CFR* 1926.1417(o)(i). Note that rigging components or techniques may need to be changed based on any new weight information that is discovered.
- Ensure that the appropriate rigging equipment and components are available. Using an inappropriate piece of equipment due to an equipment shortage can lead to rigging failures. Know the rated load capacity of the rigging equipment and never exceed the limit.
- Ensure that the rigging equipment has been properly inspected and is in good working condition. Remove any damaged or defective equipment from service.
- Always maintain the manufacturer's information for the rigging equipment in an easily accessible location. The literature provides information on hitch configurations, lift angles, and similar information that may be needed as the rigging process proceeds.
- Recognize factors in the lift that can reduce rigging equipment capacity. Remember that the rated load capacity of all hoisting and rigging equipment is based on ideal conditions; lifts often involve conditions that are less than ideal.
- Use proper padding and protection to protect slings as well as the surface of the load.
- Never place loads on the tip of the hook, where it is weakest and most likely to fail.

Gloves for Everyone

There is a time and place in every construction trade for gloves. Injure your hands, and you have damaged the most versatile and important construction tool you will ever own. Craft professionals are observed every day doing tasks without gloves where it is clear that the protection is needed. There has been a long history of workers rejecting gloves for any number of reasons. Many workers have rejected the use of gloves in years past because they felt too restrictive and awkward.

There are more work gloves on the market today than ever before. Today's gloves are miles ahead of the work gloves of old that fit poorly, were unnecessarily bulky and clumsy, and were constructed only of relatively simple materials such as leather and canvas. Although wearing gloves on the job may seem awkward at first, there is a glove out there that fits you well and offers essential protection for your hands without restricting movement. If you work with the right gloves for a while, you will soon feel naked without them. Look for reasons to wear them instead of reasons to reject them, and find your pair of gloves.

Crane Safety and Emergency Procedures 5

- Observe the area where loads will be placed and ensure that it is clear of obstructions and properly prepared for load placement. Preparing the target area while the load is suspended represents poor planning. The practice of lowering the load just above the landing zone and then placing needed blocking is hazardous since the riggers are forced to work beneath the load. Riggers need to think ahead of the crane.
- When serving as part of the rigging team, do not assume that the crane operator and other members of the lift team see the same potential hazards that you do. They may also see something that you do not see. Discuss the lift prior to beginning and share any concerns about obstructions, power lines, and other hazards with the rest of the team. Also listen to and consider any concerns that other members of the team may share. Every lift offers its own unique hazards and obstructions (*Figure 4*).
- Rig the load and connect it to the crane with the center of gravity directly below the hook.
- Always consider where your fingers, hands, and feet are in relation to pinch points. Wear appropriate gloves when handling rigging equipment.
- Never ride a load or the hook.
- Remain outside the load's fall zone at all times unless it is required to guide or receive a load.
- If there is ever any doubt about the reliability or arrangement of the rigging or you observe something unexpected, stop the lift, lower the load, and report it to lift supervision.

Figure 4 A complex jobsite with multiple cranes.

1.2.3 Pre-Lift Considerations

Careful planning, detailed inspections, and timely maintenance help prevent accidents. Crane operators must demonstrate their attention to detail as they prepare for a lift as well as during the lift. Prior to operating a crane, the operator should accomplish the following:

- Determine if there are any locally established restrictions placed on crane operations, such as traffic considerations or time restrictions for noise abatement.
- Ensure that a complete operating manual is in the crane cab. The manual should remain with the crane at all times.
- Accurately determine the weight of the load. Regardless of the perceived accuracy, begin every lift slowly to ensure there are no surprises in the load weight.
- Confirm that load charts in one form or another are readily available for use and review them. Refer to the load charts for every lift and always remain within the capabilities of the crane.
- Determine the deductions to be made from the rated load capacity due to attachments or other crane-related factors.
- Look for documentation of recent crane inspections, as well as any deficiency-correction statements, and review the results.
- Examine the site and ensure that it is suitable to support the crane. Ask questions and seek information about the presence of underground utilities such as gas, oil, electrical, and telephone lines; sewage and drainage piping; and underground tanks. Also ask if the area has been recently excavated. Determine if the lifting operation is limited in some way by stability or structural concerns.
- Evaluate the weather conditions and be familiar with the wind speed limitations of the crane.
- Determine how close the crane or load path may be to power lines throughout the lift and whether the clearance is sufficient.
- Confirm that the crane boom is assembled correctly or extends as designed.
- Determine the hoist line pull and the maximum permissible line pull.
- Ensure there is a safe path to move the crane around, if point-to-point movement on site is necessary.
- Make sure that the crane can rotate unobstructed in the required quadrants for the planned lift.
- Complete the required daily pre-start inspection.
- Ensure that the crane is level before lifting.

1.2.4 Load-Handling Safety

The safe and effective control of the load involves the strict observance of load-handling safety requirements by the entire lift team, including the crane operator. This includes making sure that the swing path of the crane upperworks remains clear of personnel and obstructions any time the crane is in operation (*Figure 5*). Barricades or other visual barriers are required. Also keep the path of any planned load movement clear. Many people tend to watch the load when it is in motion, which prevents them from watching for hazards on the ground.

Here are a few additional precautions related to crane operation and load handling to consider in every lift:

- Consult and follow all applicable safety standards (29 *CFR* 1926.1402 and *ASME Standard B30.5*) and manufacturer guidelines to properly stabilize mobile cranes. Most modern cranes are equipped with outriggers. To be properly stabilized, the outriggers must be used to relieve the weight from the tires of most truck cranes (*Figure 6*). Crawler cranes can usually operate directly from their tracks, but they may also use outriggers in certain conditions.
- When computing equipment loads, the blocks, hooks, slings, equalizer beams, lifting components, and other equipment below the hook must also be taken into consideration. Crane load ratings only extend to the hook.
- Avoid allowing a suspended load to swing more than necessary. This subjects the equipment to additional side loading that can cause a failure of a component or tip the crane. Keep the load directly below the boom.
- Crane operators must avoid snatching or stopping the descent of a suspended load suddenly. Rapid acceleration and deceleration results in

Figure 5 Crane barricading is required.

Figure 6 Extended and lowered outriggers.

shock loading, greatly increasing the stress on equipment and rigging.
- Physical control of the load beyond the ability of the crane operator may be required. Tag lines are used to limit the unwanted movement of the load as it reacts to the motion of the crane, wind, or other external influences. They are also used to allow the controlled rotation of the load for final positioning in the landing zone (*Figure 7*). Tag lines are attached after the rigger verifies that the load is balanced.

1.2.5 Signaling

Topics of signaling and communication with a crane operator are covered in 29 *CFR* 1926.1419 through 1926.1422. According to these standards, a signal person is required in the following situations:

- When the points of operation, including the load travel path or the area in the vicinity of the load and its landing place, are not in full view of the crane operator
- When the crane will travel and the view in the direction of travel is obstructed
- Any time the crane operator or workers handling the load determine that it is necessary

Voice signals can be used as well as hand signals. When voice signals are used, the crane operator, signal person, and lift director must all agree on the voice signals to be used. 29 *CFR* 1926.1421 requires that voice signals contain three elements, provided in the following order: a function with direction, such as hoist up or boom left; the distance and/or speed of the function; and a command to stop the function. If electronic devices such as radios are to be used, they must be tested at the site before beginning the operation.

Figure 7 Using taglines.

The crane operator's version of any radio or telephone used must allow for hands-free reception.

Using hand signals to communicate with a crane operator is also very common. There are established hand signals used for communicating load navigation directions. The required hand signals are referred to as the Standard Method in 29 *CFR* 1926.1419(c)(1) and they are pictured in the appendix of the publication. In addition, 29 *CFR* 1926.1422 requires that hand signal charts be posted in a conspicuous location near the lift operation.

Standard hand signals, when used correctly and known by both parties, provide the needed information to the crane operator. Nonstandard hand signals may be developed and used by a lift team when standard hand signals are not feasible for some reason or the use and operation of a crane attachment is not provided for in the standard hand-signal set.

Serving in the role of a signal person requires qualification, as outlined in 29 *CFR* 1926.1428. However, it is important to note that any member of a lift team that becomes aware of an issue that affects safety is authorized to display or speak the Stop or the Emergency Stop signals (*Figure 8*). Crane operators are required to obey these two signals regardless of their source. To build flexibility into lift teams, it is not unusual for a crane operator or rigger to also seek certification as a signal person.

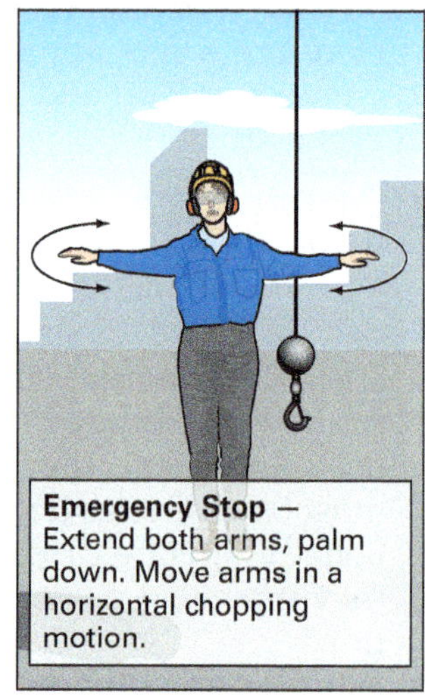

Figure 8 The Stop and Emergency Stop hand signals.

1.0.0 Section Review

1. Which of the following statements is *not* a required characteristic of a national consensus standard?
   a. The standard has been adopted by one or more nationally recognized organizations under a specific set of procedures.
   b. The standard was created in a manner that afforded an opportunity for diverse views to be considered.
   c. The standard has been adopted or incorporated through reference by the American National Standards Institute (ANSI).
   d. The standard has been designated as a national consensus standard by the US Secretary or the Assistant Secretary of Labor.

2. Positioning a load just above a landing zone and then placing any needed blocking or support for the load is _____.
   a. considered the safest way to do it
   b. considered hazardous
   c. required by law
   d. a function of the load owner

2.0.0 SITE SAFETY AND EMERGENCIES

Objective

Identify mobile crane safety considerations related to specific applications and explain how to respond to various incidents.

a. Describe the purpose of pre-lift meetings and identify the topics of discussion.
b. Identify safety considerations related to power lines.
c. Identify safety considerations related to weather conditions.
d. Describe safety considerations related to specific crane functions and how to respond to various incidents.

Trade Terms

Avoidance zone: An area both above and below one or more power lines that is defined by the outer perimeter of the prohibited zone. As the name implies, any part of the crane should avoid this area whenever possible, and may not enter the area except under special circumstances.

Critical lift: As defined in ASME Standard B30.5, a hoisting or lifting operation that has been determined to present an increased level of risk beyond normal lifting activities. For example, increased risk may relate to personnel injury, damage to property, interruption of plant production, delays in schedule, release of hazards to the environment, or other significant factors.

High-voltage proximity warning device: An early-warning device that senses the electric fields created by high-voltage power lines and alerts the crane operator and/or the lift team to the hazard.

Insulating link: An electrical insulating device used on the crane hook to protect workers in contact with the load from the danger of electrocution in the event the crane contacts a power line. The link can also provide some level of protection for the crane if the load alone contacts a power line.

Minimum clearance distance: The OSHA-required distance that cranes, load lines, and loads must maintain from energized power lines. This OSHA term is synonymous with the ASME term prohibited zone.

Prohibited zone: An area of specific dimensions, based on the voltage of a power line(s) that no part of the crane is allowed to enter during normal operations. Special considerations and preparations are required if the crane's task must place any part of it within the prohibited zone. The prohibited zone is a term used by ASME that is synonymous with the term minimum clearance distance used by OSHA.

Recloser: A device that functions much like a circuit breaker, or in conjunction with a circuit breaker, in power distribution and transmission systems that automatically recloses the circuit after a fault has been detected and the circuit has been opened. Reclosers allow the power system to be re-energized quickly after a transient (temporary) condition, such as a tree limb falling across power lines and then falling to the ground, has occurred. If the fault reoccurs upon closure, the circuit will typically remain open until the situation has been addressed by power line workers or operators.

Standard lift: A lift that can be accomplished through standard procedures, allowing load-handling and lift team personnel to execute it using common methods, materials, and equipment.

One of the ways to avoid accidents and incidents in crane operations is to discuss the plan in detail in a pre-lift meeting. However, in spite of such meetings and a consistent focus on safety, accidents and equipment failures can and do happen. This section focuses on some of the common environmental hazards that crane operators encounter and how to respond to a variety of emergency situations.

One of the keys to a successful response to an emergency is the crane operator's intimate knowledge of the equipment and its controls. There is rarely time for research and a great deal of thought when an operator is confronted with an emergency situation. It is far better to consider how you should react to a given problem throughout the process in order to be well prepared for an unexpected event.

2.1.0 Pre-Lift Meetings

One of the best ways to avoid incidents and hazards is to plan fir the lift carefully. *ASME Standard P30.1, Planning for Load Handling Activities* provides guidance in lift planning. The first requirement is to evaluate a load-handling activity and place it in a category based on the following characteristics:

> **NOTE**
>
> Pre-lift planning is discussed in detail in NCCER Module 21304, "Lift Planning," from *Mobile Crane Operations Level Three*.

- The potential hazard to people that the operation represents
- Hazards that exist in close proximity to the operation
- The complexity of the activity
- The potential for problems that may be caused by the weather or other environmental conditions
- The capacity and ability of the load-handling equipment to cope with the stresses involved
- The potential for an adverse commercial impact, such as the loss of a unique or irreplaceable load, or the costly delay of a major project
- Site requirements that are unique, such as the effect on roadways or other infrastructure

The standard does not limit the evaluation process to these areas; other areas of concern can also be factors. Documentation of this evaluation process is not required, but it is certainly a good idea to do so. Once the evaluation is complete, the activity is then placed in one of two major categories—a *standard lift* or a *critical lift*.

A standard lift, per *ASME Standard B30.5*, is one that "can be accomplished through standard procedures, and that the load-handling activity personnel can execute using common methods, materials, and equipment." A critical lift, again per the ASME standard, is one that has been evaluated and it has been determined that the activity "exceeds standard lift plan criteria and requires additional planning, procedures, or methods to mitigate the greater risk." 29 *CFR* 1926.751, *Steel Erection*, defines a critical lift as "a lift that (1) exceeds 75 percent of the rated capacity of the crane or derrick, or (2) requires the use of more than one crane or derrick." Although the term is not defined in 29 *CFR* 1926, Subpart *CC*, both of the above definitions are widely applied in the industry. In fact, both the OSHA and ASME definitions are applied by most organizations. A load that is over 75 percent of the rated capacity becomes a critical lift automatically, based on the OSHA standard, but other conditions can also lead to a lift being labeled as critical. These other conditions represent the influence of the ASME definition.

2.1.1 Standard Lift Planning

A standard lift plan can be written or verbal. There is no OSHA requirement for a standard lift plan to be documented, although its documentation is a good idea. However, many employers require both the evaluation process and the standard lift plan to be documented. A standard lift plan should address the following:

- The load, its center of gravity, and available points of attachment
- Confirmation that the load is within the crane's rated load capacity
- Rigging
- Movement of the crane and/or the load
- The personnel required
- Site conditions such as weather, crane support and ground conditions, and utilities
- Communication method
- Site control of non-essential personnel and pedestrians
- Contingency plans
- Emergency action plans
- Equipment inspection during repetitive processes

Any time the operation is not going according to plan, the operation should stop and the situation evaluated. Any changes should be clearly communicated to all members of the lift team.

2.1.2 Critical Lift Planning

Unlike standard lift plans, critical lift plans are required to be in written form. An example of a critical lift planning worksheet is available in the *Appendix* for review. *ASME Standard P30.1* provides examples and templates for the evaluation process as well as for lift planning.

Essentially, a critical lift plan addresses the same topics as a standard lift plan. However, each topic is considered at a deeper level. Since the lift has been classified as critical, there is at least one element of the lift that requires additional planning and possibly a deviation from normal procedures. This information must be carefully considered and documented in the plan.

The lift director typically schedules a pre-lift meeting to construct, discuss, and review the details of the plan and ensure all personnel involved understand their role. The lift director has overall responsibility for the lift from start to finish. He or she ensures that all the appropriate preparations have been made, the plan is executed as scheduled, and that the lift is stopped if it is not going as planned. Once the activity is stopped for any reason, only the lift director can restart it. Upon completion, a post-lift review is common to assess the process and determine what can be done better in the future. Any recommendations are shared with the lift team and others involved in the process.

2.2.0 Working Around Power Lines

Operating mobile cranes where they can become electrified by power lines is an extremely hazardous practice, although it is sometimes necessary. Work must be performed so that there is no possibility of the crane, load line, or load contacting an energized component and becoming a conductive path. Contact with high-voltage power sources is a major cause of fatalities associated with crane operations. However, these accidents can be prevented.

It is important to note that contact between the crane and power line is not always necessary to initiate an incident. Due to the high voltage carried by some power lines, electricity can jump across an open gap and create a sustainable arc between the energized power line and any path to ground—in this case, a metal crane. Moist air masses allow a larger gap to be crossed. Establishing an arc across a gap is the principle on which automotive spark plugs are based.

Surrounding every energized power line is an area referred to as the prohibited zone (*Figure 9*). The prohibited zone is an area around an energized power line that no part of a crane, boom, load, or load line is allowed to enter. The extent of the prohibited zone is shown in *Table 1* for various line voltages. The table reflects the clearance requirements established by OSHA in 29 *CFR* 1926.1408, Table A, and 1926.1411, Table T. They are identical to the values in tables provided in *ASME Standard B30.5* at the time of this writing (2017). OSHA uses different terminology however, using the term minimum clearance distance in place of prohibited zone. The line voltage determines how much clearance is required. Note that there are different values for cranes in operation versus those that are in transit with no load and the boom lowered.

Figure 9 also shows an avoidance zone. The avoidance zone is the area above and below the prohibited zone, defined by imaginary vertical lines. The distance of the vertical lines from the power lines is determined by the outer edge of the prohibited zone. The avoidance zone exists due to the increased probability of accidental power line contact when working in the area. The prohibited zone, or minimum clearance distance, extends away from the power lines in all directions, so there is a prohibited area above and below the lines as well as to their left and right. The avoidance zone is above and below the prohibited zone.

Note that the term *avoidance zone* is not a term used by ASME or OSHA, but it is commonly used to identify these hazardous areas. OSHA does not address the area above power lines that is beyond the minimum clearance distance. However, 29 *CFR* 1926.1408(d) does address crane operation in the avoidance zone below the power lines. Cranes cannot be used to operate under energized power lines (which is within the avoidance zone) unless any part of the machine or load cannot physically reach the prohibited zone. Although the crane operator may have no intention of fully extending a boom to accomplish the desired task, it could be extended and therefore poses too great a risk.

However, there are times when a task must be done inside the avoidance zone, and sometimes

Did You Know?

Power Transmission and Distribution—What's the Difference?

Power transmission lines carry very high-voltage power from the point of power generation to the numerous general locations served by the system. The power carried by transmission lines is extremely hazardous; physical contact with a common transmission line is not required for serious injury or electrocution. The voltage is sufficient for the power to establish an arc across an air gap to any nearby grounded conductor. The higher the voltage, the larger the gap that the arc can cross. To use this power, it must be transformed to a much lower voltage. This cannot be done with simple pole-mounted transformers and the limited protection features this approach offers. Transmission lines are generally routed to substations for voltage reduction where a great deal more control and safety features are available. The high voltage allows the conductor size to be relatively small.

Power distribution lines carry high-voltage power as well, but not as high as transmission lines. Power distribution lines generally carry power from a substation to our homes and places of business. The voltage applied to a common distribution line is still quite dangerous and deadly, as many squirrels and similar creatures have discovered. The voltage on distribution lines must also be transformed to a usable level, usually using a pole- or ground-mounted transformer. Large industrial users, however, often have a substation of their own that intercepts power from a transmission line or substantial distribution line and transforms the power to the various voltages needed by the facility.

NCCER – *Mobile Crane Operations*

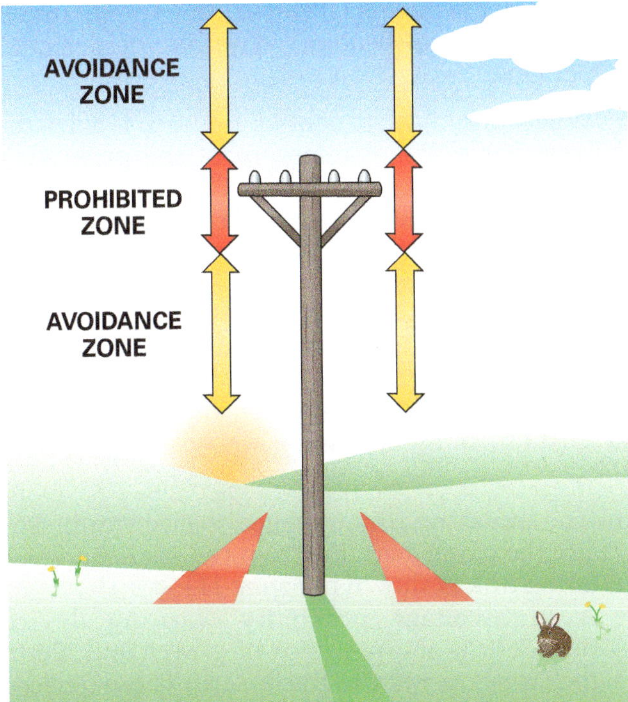

Figure 9 The prohibited zone and the avoidance zone.

CRANE IN OPERATION	
POWER LINE VOLTAGE IN kV	MINIMUM CLEARANCE IN FEET (METERS)
0 to 50	10 (3.05)
50 to 200	15 (4.60)
200 to 350	20 (6.10)
350 to 500	25 (7.62)
500 to 750	35 (10.67)
750 to 1,000	45 (13.72)
Over 1,000	Distance established by the utility owner / operator or registered professional engineer who is a qualified person in power transmission and distribution
CRANE IN TRANSIT (with no load and the boom or mast lowered)[1]	
POWER LINE VOLTAGE IN kV	MINIMUM CLEARANCE IN FEET (METERS)
0 to 0.75	4 (1.22)
0.75 to 50	6 (1.83)
50 to 345	10 (3.05)
345 to 750	16 (4.87)
750 to 1,000	20 (6.10)
Over 1,000	Distance established by the utility owner / operator or registered professional engineer who is a qualified person in power transmission and distribution

(1) Environmental conditions such as fog, smoke, or precipitation may require increased clearances.

within the prohibited zone as well. 29 *CFR* 1926.1410 addresses these situations and outlines the requirements that must be met. Some of these situations are addressed in the sections that follow. However, it is important to read and study the OSHA standards whenever work in the vicinity of power lines is planned, especially when they are energized.

Before operations begin near power lines, the owner of the power lines or an authorized representative must be notified and provided with all relevant information. In addition, the cooperation of the owner must be requested. Any overhead line must be considered to be electrically energized unless and until the owner or utility confirms that it is not energized, per 29 *CFR* 1926.1408(e).

There are four scenarios to consider when operating a mobile crane near power lines:

- Power lines de-energized and grounded
- Power lines energized and the crane operating near the prohibited zone
- Power lines energized and the crane operating within the prohibited zone
- Crane in transit with no load and the boom lowered

Each of these scenarios will be discussed further in the sections that follow.

2.2.1 Near De-Energized, Grounded Power Lines

Working in the vicinity of power lines that have been de-energized and grounded is always the preferred situation, since the vast majority of the hazard has been removed. To ensure power lines have in fact been de-energized, the following steps must be taken:

- The utility or owner of the power lines must be contacted first. When possible, they will de-energize the lines.
- The lines must be visibly grounded to avoid electrical feedback and be appropriately marked at the jobsite location (*Figure 10*).
- A qualified representative of the power line owner or the electrical utility must be on site to verify that the first two steps have been completed and that the lines are not energized.

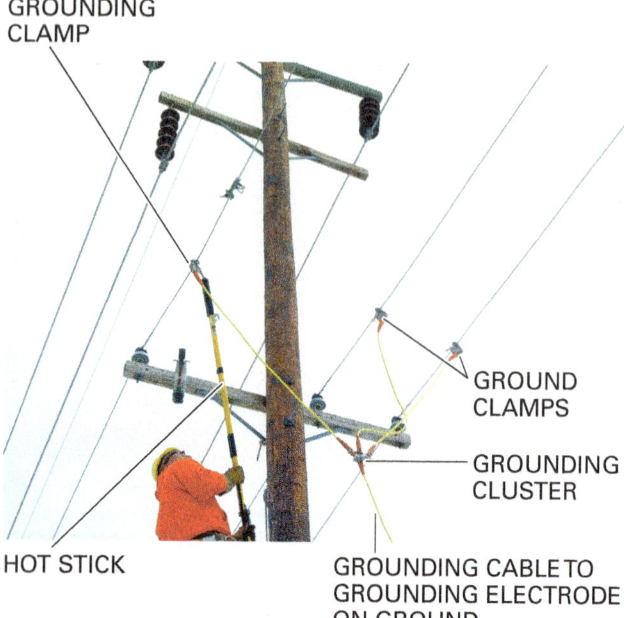

Figure 10 A worker installs temporary grounds on power distribution lines.

Of course, power lines and other lines such as those providing cable and telephone service still represent a significant hazard and an obstruction that can easily become entangled in the boom or hoist lines. Even when they are de-energized, all overhead lines must be treated with great respect.

2.2.2 Near Energized Lines and Near Prohibited Zone

When work must be conducted in the vicinity of the prohibited zone, specific precautions must be taken to ensure that the crane and load do not enter the hazardous areas. Per 29 *CFR* 1926.1408:

- A planning meeting must be held with the lift team and other involved workers to review the plan to avoid encroachment.
- Nonconductive tag lines must be used.
- A visual aid must be erected to aid the crane operator in determining where the prohibited zone boundary begins. For voltages up to 350 kilovolts (kV), or 350,000 volts, the lift team can choose whether to use the minimum clearance distances from the OSHA tables, or to simply use the listed minimum clearance dimension for 350kV lines of 20 feet (6.1 meters). The visual aid must be elevated and can be fabricated several different ways. A suspended warning line with flags attached is one example. If the crane operator cannot clearly see the visual aid, a dedicated spotter must be used to monitor the crane, load line, and load to ensure no part enters the hazardous areas. This individual is in addition to any signal person that may be part of the team. However, the spotter must have the qualifications required of a signal person.

When a dedicated spotter is used, OSHA requires that a visual reference of the prohibited zone be provided to the spotter. This can be done by placing visible lines on the ground, aligned with the edge of the zone; placing a line of small posts or stanchions in a row; or using existing points of reference as a sight line, such as a sign post behind the spotter and a distant object that aligns with the edges of the zones. If the use of a spotter is chosen instead of an operator's aid, at least one of the following devices must also be used:

- An insulating link installed to electrically isolate the crane load line from the load. An insulating link is shown in *Figure 11*.
- A high-voltage proximity warning device that detects the presence of power and alerts the crane operator to the hazard. These devices sense the electric fields around power lines to determine their presence. The alert feature is usually a series of lights—green, yellow, and red—that indicates how close the hazard is to the instrument. The components of the system are shown in *Figure 12*.
- A device that automatically warns an operator to stop movement of the boom or load line.
- A device that automatically limits the movement of the crane.

> **CAUTION**
>
> Many high-voltage proximity warning devices used are unable to sense the presence of direct current (DC) power. Although DC power lines are rare in the United States, they are used in a few power transmission systems, and are more likely to be encountered in Europe, South America, and Asia. DC power is also often associated with power generated through wind and solar systems. When working near energized power lines and related systems, be sure that the equipped proximity alarm system is capable of detecting the power in use.

Keep in mind that power lines tend to move and sway with the wind. Essentially, wind causes the prohibited zone to be in motion. The anticipated horizontal and/or vertical movement of power lines due to the wind must be added to the clearance distances in OSHA's tables. The utility or owner's representative must be consulted to determine the specific distance to be added for a given situation.

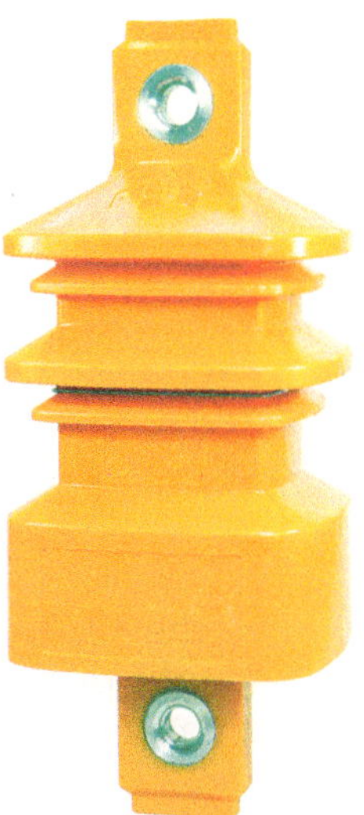

Figure 11 An insulating link.

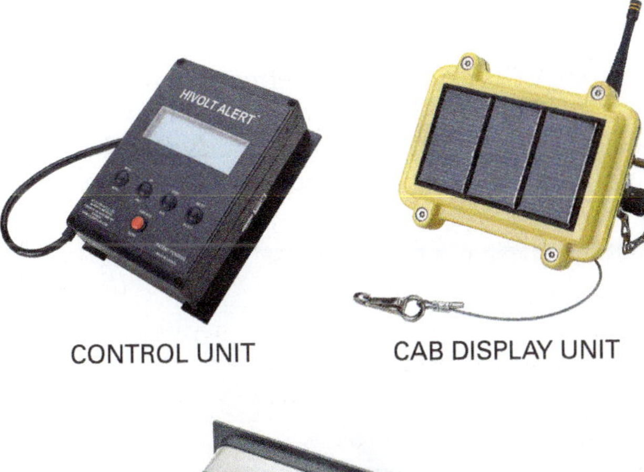

Figure 12 High-voltage proximity warning system.

2.2.3 Within Prohibited Zone and Power Lines Energized

Crane operations can be performed within the prohibited zone if the task is absolutely necessary and the crane employer can show that the task cannot be done in any other practical and safe way. Such work places the crane and lift team in close proximity to a major hazard. 29 *CFR* 1926.1410 provides the majority of the guidance for this situation.

All of the steps associated with operating a crane within reach of the prohibited zone are also required in this case. In this case, the required planning meeting must include the utility operator or owner's representative who is a qualified person in the field of electrical power transmission and distribution. The procedures and techniques that help avoid an incident are determined and documented. The completed documentation must be readily available at the jobsite. Per the OSHA standard, the resulting plans and procedures must include the following:

- Any device such as a **recloser** that can automatically re-energize a power line after a fault occurs must be disabled if possible.
- A dedicated spotter that can communicate with the crane operator directly and is provided with the aforementioned visual references must be in place.
- An elevated warning line to act as a visual aid for the crane operator must be erected.
- An insulating link must be installed to isolate the load from the load line. No worker other than the crane operator can be allowed to contact any part of the crane or load line above the insulating link.
- If any of the rigging devices, such as slings, will be within the prohibited zone, they must be nonconductive. Tag lines must also be nonconductive.
- A perimeter at least 10 feet (3 meters) away from the crane must be established with barricades to prevent workers and others from getting too close to the crane. If there are structures around the crane that prevent placing barricades that far away, they must be placed as far away as possible. All persons must be kept away from the crane and the work area except those that are essential to the task.
- The crane and any other involved equipment must be properly grounded.
- Power line insulating hose and/or blankets (*Figure 13*) must be applied by the utility if such products are available for the voltage of the lines. Note that such products cannot provide effective protection when the voltage is very high.

Figure 13 Installing insulating line hose and blankets on power lines.

In addition to the initial planning meeting, the utility or owner's representative must also meet with the work team(s) at the site to review the procedures. 29 *CFR* 1926.1410(h) directs that involved employers, as well as the utility/owner's representative, together identify an individual that will be responsible for implementing the procedures that have been developed. The individual has the authority to stop work at any time for safety reasons. If the procedures are not working out as planned, the process stops until new procedures can be developed and implemented.

OSHA also requires that all crane operators and crew members involved with lifts in the prohibited zone of power lines must be specifically trained. 29 *CFR* 1926.1408(g) provides a list of the training topics to be covered.

Note that the guidance regarding work around power lines in *ASME Standard B30.5* is slightly different from the OSHA directives. In this case, the related ASME standards have not been incorporated by reference into the OSHA standard, but the ASME standard contains valuable guidance that should be followed regardless.

2.2.4 Crane Transit with No Load and Boom Lowered

While in transit with no load and the boom lowered, the minimum clearance as specified in *Table 1* must be maintained. You will recall that the lower half of the table provides a separate set of clearance requirements for cranes in transit. Consider however, that a crane bouncing along rough terrain or crossing a rise under a power line can become taller than its specified height. The condition can be momentary, but a moment is all it takes to make contact with a power line. When moving around the site, the effect of speed and terrain on the height of the crane must be considered when evaluating the minimum clearance distance. Additional clearance may be in order to accommodate these factors.

2.2.5 Power Line Contact Emergency Procedures

In spite of everyone's best efforts, something has gone wrong and the boom or load has made contact with an energized power line. Now what? First and foremost, the crane operator must not panic.

Power Lines That Re-Energize Automatically

At some point in your life, you have likely experienced a power outage in your home or place of business. Sometimes the power goes off, but returns a moment later. Sometimes it quickly goes off again and stays off for a significant period of time, while on other occasions it may return a second time and stay on. Did you ever wonder what's going on at those moments?

Lots of things can disturb power lines and cause what is known as a fault to occur. For example, a wet tree limb can fall across the lines. This causes a short circuit and the current flow becomes extraordinary. The power line must be de-energized when this happens to prevent serious damage to the system or its many components. In many cases though, the fault is temporary—the limb simply falls to the ground after making initial contact.

Many power distribution systems are protected by a special type of circuit breaker called a recloser (shown here). When a fault is sensed, the recloser opens like a circuit breaker, but is also programmed to close the circuit again after a very short interval. If the fault has cleared itself, power is restored and the event is over. If not, a fault is again detected and the recloser opens the circuit. Reclosers may be programmed for one or more attempts to clear the fault, depending upon the utility's policies and the type of customer being served by the circuit. Leaving a recloser active on a circuit near a crane lift could cause a serious incident such as the boom or other object touching the power line to go from bad to much worse very quickly, as it may try repeatedly to re-energize the line.

If power line contact occurs, first try to gently reverse the action that caused the contact. Snatching or grabbing at the controls in response can cause the load to swing out of control, making matters worse. Side loading or another condition that upsets the balance of the crane can then occur, causing the crane to tip. If the contact between the crane and the power line can be broken, the immediate danger to the operator and lift team has been resolved. However, a power outage may have resulted, and the crane may have sustained damage. The crane must be carefully inspected for damage caused by the electrical contact. Wire rope should be replaced if it touches an energized line since the arc is easily sufficient to melt and/or badly scorch the rope. Arcing can occur in a number of other areas in the crane as well. Assuming all is well because the crane still functions is a dangerous practice.

If there is no immediate sign of fire or explosion, remain inside the cab. The operator is usually safest inside the cab at this moment (often safer than any other team member). The crane operator is at the same electrical potential as the equipment and is not in the path of the power as it seeks a path to ground. Note, however, that this is not true when operating a boom truck with standing controls. In this case, the operator might be standing on the ground while in contact with the controls or the frame of the vehicle. This creates a very dangerous situation for the crane operator. For cranes with cabs, however, unless an extreme emergency such as an explosion or fire involving the crane presents itself, operators should remain in the cab and avoid touching the ground.

If you must exit the crane due to fire or an explosion, try to jump off from the lowest point of the crane. As you jump, make no further contact with the crane in an attempt to stabilize yourself. If contact with the crane is made after your feet contact the ground, you become a path to ground and create a complete circuit. Land on the ground with your feet close together and make no further contact with the crane. Do not exit the crane one foot at a time while holding onto the crane.

While moving away from the crane, do not run or take long strides. Instead, shuffle your feet along in very small steps (about six inches, or 15 cm) or hop away with your feet together until you are a safe distance from the crane. High-voltage current transmitted from the power lines through the crane to the ground energizes the ground around the crane (*Figure 14*). As the distance from the crane increases, the voltage and difference in electrical potential decreases. The rate of the decrease varies depending on the resistance of

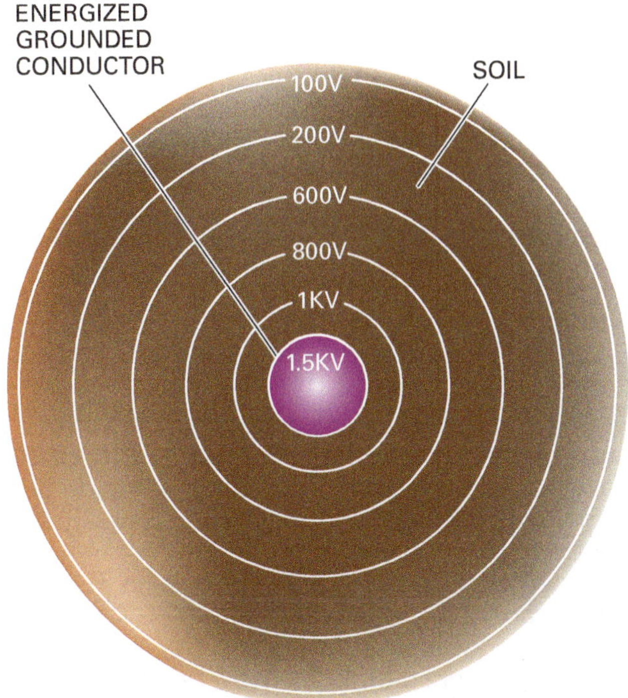

Figure 14 Voltage applied to the ground diminishes with distance.

the surrounding soil. If you take large steps, it is possible for one foot to be in a high-voltage area and the other to be in a lower-voltage area. This increases the difference in electric potential between the two feet, possibly initiating the flow of electricity through the body.

> **WARNING!**
>
> Do not casually step down from an electrically energized crane. Both feet need to touch the ground at the same time to minimize the potential for serious injury or death. Also, if an electrical circuit is created by making contact with the crane and the ground at the same time, the possibility of electrocution is high.

Instruct all other personnel on the site to stay away from the crane and anything connected to it. If they are close to the crane, instruct them to move away in short steps as well.

If you can remain in the crane, wait until the electrical authorities de-energize the circuit and confirm that the crane is no longer energized. It is likely that a substation circuit breaker or a recloser detected the fault and has opened to a point where it must be manually reset. However, this cannot be assumed until qualified personnel provide that information through testing.

Report every incident involving contact with power lines to the electrical authority and safety officer. If there was ever a chance of such an incident occurring due to work within the prohibited zone, utility personnel should have already been on site. As soon as possible, ensure that someone on the site has called for medical assistance or any other help needed on the scene. Lifts are made with cranes in the vicinity of power lines on a daily basis without incident. Take every precaution to ensure your encounters with work in this area are safe and successful as well.

2.3.0 Hazardous Weather

Mobile crane operators work outdoors. Under certain environmental conditions, such as extremely hot or cold weather or in high winds, work can become uncomfortable and maybe dangerously so. For example, snow and rain can have a dramatic effect on the weight of the load and on ground compaction. During the winter, the tires, outriggers, and crawlers can freeze to the ground. This may lead the operator to the false conclusion that the crane is on stable ground. As weight is then added during the lifting operation, an outrigger float, tire, or crawler track may sink into mushy ground below the frozen surface. Heavy rain can also cause the ground under the crane to become unstable. The crane set-up site must be carefully evaluated to ensure that there is sufficient stability, including the condition of the soil below the surface.

High winds and lightning represent significant hazards on the jobsite (*Figure 15*). Both must be taken seriously. Crane operators must be prepared to respond appropriately to weather changes in order to avoid accidents and injuries. Fortunately, it is relatively rare for high winds or lightning to arrive without at least being reported as a possibility in weather reports. As a general rule, the lift team and crane operators have time to react appropriately. The site supervisor or lift director (possibly the same individual, depending on the lift characteristics) is responsible for ensuring that factors such as wind, heavy rain, fog, and the soil conditions that change as a result of weather are properly considered and addressed.

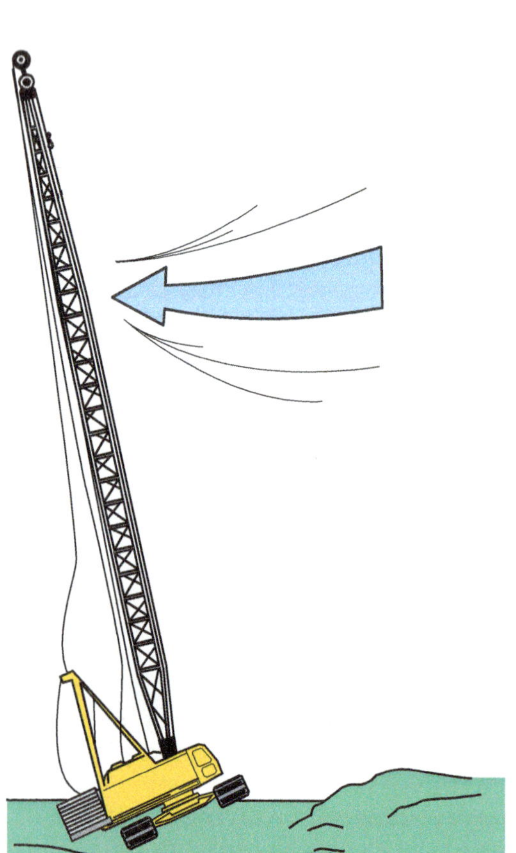

Figure 15 Wind and lightning hazards.

NCCER – *Mobile Crane Operations*

2.3.1 Wind

High winds typically start out as less dramatic gusts. Operators must be keenly aware of changing wind speeds. The crane boom should be down and stowed before the wind becomes too strong, not after the threshold has been passed. Keep in mind that the wind speed can be dramatically higher at the tip of the boom than it is at ground level. The operator must end and secure crane operations as soon as possible when the wind speed is increasing. This involves placing the boom in the lowest possible position and securing the crane. However, since wind speed affects capacity, a lift may have to be postponed due to a loss of crane capacity at wind speeds that are still acceptable for operation in general.

Crane operators should be familiar with and follow the crane manufacturer's guidance related to wind. Their guidelines will differ from model to model. It is important to have the correct information for the specific crane in use. *Table 2* provides an example of a crane manufacturer's wind chart, showing how various wind speeds affect the rated load capacity of the crane. Note that the rated load capacity shown on the load charts is valid through wind speeds of 20 mph (32.2 kph). The chart also shows different capacity deductions for boom lengths less than or greater than 250 feet (76 meters). These reductions are applied to the load chart being used. This particular crane cannot be operated at all when the wind speed is above 45 mph (72.4 kph).

> **CAUTION**
>
> The wind chart shown in *Table 2* is for a specific crane model. The information provided cannot be applied to all cranes. Always check and follow the manufacturer's wind chart speed for the specific crane in use.

It is also important to point out that wind affects the load as much as the crane. It is not unusual for a crane to have the capacity to lift a given load at a wind speed of 30 mph (78.3 kph). But many loads have a very low weight-to-surface area ratio. A sheet pile is a good example. With a great deal of surface area and limited weight, a sheet pile is easily blown around by winds of 30 mph. In some cases, even though the crane is capable of making the lift, the wind's effect on the load has to be a significant factor in the decision. Perhaps additional tagline personnel can be put on the job, but the safer thing to do is wait until the wind speed has dropped to a more acceptable level. In this example, the wind hazard is not about the crane—it is about the load, the workers that must handle it, and other equipment or property in the area that could be damaged by it.

It is important to make this point regarding changing wind speeds. Assume that you are lifting a load with a wind speed of 25 mph. If the wind speed chart in *Table 2* applied, the rated load capacity of the crane must therefore be reduced by 20 percent. Now assume that the load represents 50 percent of the normal rated-load capacity, so the load weight now represents 70 percent of the capacity; still within the parameters of a standard lift plan. However, if the wind speed increases just 6 mph to 31 mph, the operation must be stopped and the crane secured. Although the crane itself can operate at this wind speed, the reduction of capacity is now 40 percent, and the load weight now represents 90 percent of the crane's capacity. Under these conditions, the lift becomes a critical lift that requires a documented lift plan. The alternative is to simply wait until the wind speed is lower. This type of scenario and the related decision-making process is repeated daily in the crane industry.

Table 2 Example of a Wind Speed Chart

Boom and Boom + Jib Lengths Up to 250'	
Description	**Allowable Windspeeds in Miles Per Hour (mph)**
1. Normal Lifting Operation. (See Capacity Charts.)	0–20 mph
2. Reduced Operation. Capacities must be reduced by 20%.	21–30 mph
3. Reduced Operation. Capacities must be reduced by 40%.	31–40 mph
4. Reduced Operation. Capacities must be reduced by 70%.	41–45 mph
5. No Operation. Store attachment on ground.	Over 45 mph
Boom and Boom + Jib Lengths Greater than 250'	
Description	**Allowable Windspeeds in Miles Per Hour (mph)**
1. Normal Lifting Operation. (See Capacity Charts.)	0–20 mph
2. Reduced Operation. Capacities must be reduced by 35%.	21–30 mph
3. Reduced Operation. Capacities must be reduced by 60%.	31–40 mph
4. Reduced Operation. Capacities must be reduced by 70%.	41–45 mph
5. No Operation. Store attachment on ground.	Over 45 mph

2.3.2 Lightning

Because crane booms extend so high and are made of metal, they are easy targets for lightning. Operators must be constantly aware of this threat. Lightning can usually be detected when it is several miles away. As a general rule of thumb, sound travels near the ground about 1 mile in 5 seconds, or about 1 kilometer in 3 seconds. Therefore, if there is a five-second delay between the flash of lightning and the sound of thunder, the lightning strike was roughly one mile away. Be aware, however, that successive lightning strikes can touch down up to 8 miles apart. That means once you hear thunder or see lightning, it is close enough for the next strike to present a hazard.

In some high-risk areas, local proximity sensors provide warnings when lightning strikes occur within a 20-mile radius. Once a warning is given, lightning is spotted, or thunder is heard, the crane operator must secure crane operations as soon as practical.

There have been many cases when the warning signs have not been taken seriously enough. Even if the above common rule of thumb were completely accurate, the process provides no information allowing one to determine when and where the next lightning strike will occur. If lightning is seen or thunder is heard, it is time to secure the crane and ignore the math.

Crane operators and the rest of the lift team must pay attention to the signs of thunderstorms and other weather events developing. It is best not to attempt operations that require a significant amount of time, such as a lengthy concrete pour, when there is a possibility that the operation may have to stop before it is complete. Doing so encourages the team to rush or remain in operation longer than it should once the warning signs are evident, in an attempt to complete the task. Both responses raise the potential for an accident.

Once crane operations have been shut down, all personnel should seek indoor shelter away from the crane. Even with the boom in the lowest position, it may be taller than surrounding structures and could still be a target for lightning strikes. Always wait a minimum of 30 minutes from the last instance of lightning or thunder before resuming work.

If lightning strikes a crane, a thorough inspection of the crane will be required. If lightning strikes the wire rope, for example, it may be damaged beyond safe use. All electrical systems need to be tested before the crane is returned to service, in addition to a thorough visual inspection.

2.4.0 Other Operational Safety Topics and Incidents

There are several other issues that affect the safety of a crane operation, as well as specific incidents to which a crane operator may need to respond. These issues are presented in the sections that follow.

2.4.1 Manufacturer's Requirements and Guidance

To operate a mobile crane safely, the operator must use the manufacturer's data and documentation provided for the specific crane in use. These manuals provide information on required startup checks and periodic inspections, as well as inspection guidelines. These manuals also provide many safety precautions and restrictions of use. Ignorance of any of these requirements or precautions is hazardous to the safe operation of the crane and could make the operator liable if an accident should occur. Operators should always read and follow the manufacturer's instructions. Crane manuals also provide information related to certain types of equipment failures and error messages that may present themselves. The manufacturer has reasons for any specific responses they provide. Follow the manufacturer's recommendations in all such cases.

2.4.2 Moving Cranes Safely

During the course of a job, cranes and other heavy equipment are moved to, around, and away from the site. Many accidents and injuries happen during the movement of heavy equipment. It is important to be especially safety conscious whenever equipment is moving.

Always follow these guidelines when driving equipment on public roads:

- Know and obey all state and local laws.
- Secure all attachments and loose gear.
- Use proper warning signs and flags per state and federal Department of Transportation (DOT) requirements.
- Drive slowly and never speed.
- Allow extra time to enter traffic.
- Stay in the extreme right lane on multi-lane highways.
- Travel with your lights on, day or night.
- Be aware of the crane's turning radius.
- Turn cautiously; allow for extensions or attachments and for structural clearances. Some equipment is top-heavy and will tip over if a turn is made too fast.

- Be aware of the crane's stopping distance. Due to their size and weight, cranes can develop a great deal of momentum. Be especially careful when driving downhill.

When driving on the jobsite, follow these guidelines:

- Never drive a machine on a jobsite, in a congested area, or around people without a spotter or flagger to guide you. The spotter or flagger is responsible for determining and controlling the driver's speed.
- Be sure everyone is in the clear while backing up, hooking up, or moving attachments. When backing, allow a few moments for the back-up alarm to announce your intention before putting the crane in motion.
- If you cannot see your area clearly from the operator's seat and have no spotter, dismount and examine the site for possible hazards before proceeding.
- Wait for an all-clear signal from spotters before moving.
- Signal a forward move with two blasts of the horn; signal a reverse move with three blasts of the horn.
- Yield the right-of-way to moving equipment on haul roads and in pits.
- Maintain a safe distance from all other vehicles.

- When moving, keep the crane in gear at all times; never coast.
- Maintain a speed consistent with ground conditions.
- Pass only when necessary; use caution.
- Watch for overhead electrical power lines and ensure you have sufficient clearance. Refer to the lower portion of *Table 1*.
- Watch for flags indicating buried utilities (*Figure 16*).

2.4.3 Using Cranes to Lift Personnel

Although using a crane to hoist personnel is generally discouraged, it can be done safely with the correct equipment (*Figure 17*) and procedures. There are many personnel-platform styles to choose from, and they can be custom-made by several vendors to suit unique needs. Using a crane to lift personnel is prohibited by 29 *CFR* 1926.1431, unless the employer can demonstrate that the erection and use of a more conventional means to access an area is more hazardous than using the crane. When it is allowed, a personnel platform that meets the requirements of the OSHA standard must be used (with some special exceptions).

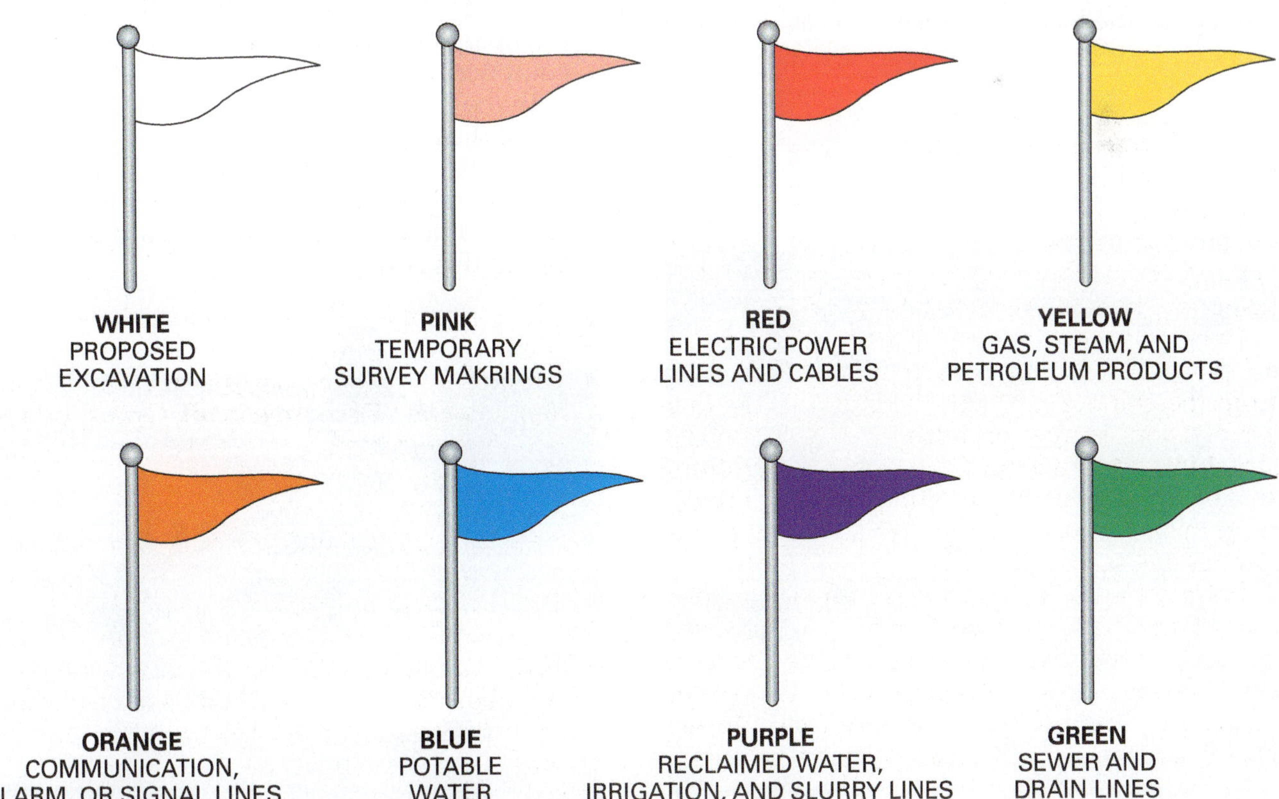

Figure 16 Flag colors used to identify underground utilities and related areas.

ASME Standard B30.23, Personnel Lifting Systems, is devoted exclusively to the topic of hoisting personnel and the equipment requirements, as the name implies. Note, however, that this ASME standard has not been incorporated by reference into the OSHA standards, but the two standards do have a lot of similarities. Some requirements found in the standards include the following:

- The crane must be level within 1 percent, and outriggers must be used if the crane has them.
- The load cannot be more than 50 percent of the rated load capacity of the crane for the configuration and operating radius.
- If the personnel platform is in a stationary working position, the primary and secondary boom and vehicle braking systems and locking features must be engaged.
- The load line hoist drum must be equipped with a system that regulates lowering speed. If the crane has the capability to allow free-fall of the load line, it cannot be used for hoisting personnel.
- A boom angle indicator, a boom hoist limiting device, and anti-two-blocking devices are all required. If a luffing jib is in use, a jib angle indicator and a jib hoist limiting device are also required.
- Trial lifts, using an equal or greater weight than the expected load of the personnel and their equipment, must be made. The crane must lift the load and move it to each location that the personnel will need to access. Trial lifts must continue to be conducted at the beginning of each shift, any time the crane is moved to a new location, and whenever the lift route changes in a way that adds new hazardous factors to the task.
- Proof testing is also required. The platform and rigging must be tested at 125 percent of the platform's rated load capacity and then inspected by a competent person. This testing must be done at each new jobsite and after any repairs or alterations have been performed on the personnel platform. Proof testing can be done in conjunction with the trial lifts. Some manufacturers of personnel platforms have developed a simple system of attaching a weight that equals 125 percent of the capacity to the bottom of the platform for this purpose (*Figure 18*).
- Unless the personnel platform is equipped with crane controls, the operator must remain at the controls in the cab at all times.
- Personnel being lifted must remain in contact with either the crane operator or the signal person (if used) at all times.
- If the wind speed exceeds 20 mph (32.2 kph), a qualified person must determine if it is safe to lift personnel for the required task, or whether the lift should be ended or postponed. Other weather issues may also prompt a qualified person to stop or postpone the lift.
- Occupants of the personnel platform must be equipped with personal fall-arrest equipment, with the lanyard attached to a structural member of the platform.
- Any other lift lines on the crane may not be used for lifting other items while lifting personnel. Pile-driving operations are an exception to this rule.

Figure 17 Enclosed round personnel platform.

Figure 18 Personnel platform with detachable weight for proof testing.

- Unless the task directly involves work on a power line, hoisted personnel cannot be placed within 20 feet (6.1 meters) of lines up to a voltage of 350 kV, or within 50 feet (15.2 meters) of power lines over 350 kV.

Note that there are a number of other requirements, especially for special situations such as pile driving, lifting personnel in and out of drilled shafts, and transferring personnel to the site of a task in a marine environment. The above list does not represent all of the requirements and conditions found in the OSHA or ASME standards. If hoisting personnel is part of your work schedule, it is important to review the requirements that apply to your particular situation.

2.4.4 Incidents During Lifting Operations

Mechanical malfunctions or lapses in judgement during a lift can be very serious. If an equipment failure or operator error causes the operating radius to increase unexpectedly, the crane can tip or the structure could collapse. Loads can also be dropped during a mechanical malfunction. A sudden loss of load on the crane can cause a whiplash effect that causes the crane to tip or the boom to fail. The chance of these types of incidents occurring in modern cranes is greatly reduced because of system redundancies and safety backups. However, failures do happen, so the operator must stay alert at all times.

If a mechanical problem occurs, the operator should attempt to lower the load immediately. Next, the operator should secure the crane, tag the controls indicating the crane is out of service, and report the problem. The crane should not be operated until it is checked and repaired if necessary, by a qualified technician.

Carelessness by the operator can lead to accidents other than those associated with overloading the crane. These incidents include the following:

- *Striking the boom* – The operator must never allow the boom to strike any structure or load. Even what seems to be mild contact can dent, bow, or bend the lower boom chords and compromise the integrity of the boom. A serious incident may result in total boom collapse. If the boom touches or rests on another structure, the boom-loading changes from a compression force to a bending force. The boom is very strong in compression but weak in bending.

If the boom, mast, or jib is struck or damaged, stop the lift and leave the boom where it is, unless it is creating a new significant hazard by remaining in position. The load on the boom increases as the boom is lowered. As a result, a damaged boom or boom suspension could collapse during the lowering process. A second crane may be required to help lower a significantly damaged boom. The site supervisor or lift director will generally make this decision.

- *Backward collapse of a boom* – When operating near the minimum radius, with the boom at its highest angle, boom down as you set the load down. This will compensate for the tendency of the boom to move or jump back against the boom stops when the load is released, especially if the load on the boom is relieved too quickly. This action occurs because of the elasticity in the boom and boom hoist systems (*Figure 19*), and it can result in a backward collapse of the boom.

Another factor that may cause the backward collapse of a boom or upset the balance of the crane is high winds. Consult and follow the wind speed charts for the specific crane in use. Other factors that may contribute to boom collapse include the following:

- Continuing to pull on the hoist line after two-blocking has occurred if the crane is not equipped with a functional anti-two-blocking device
- Starting or stopping a swing suddenly if the boom is at a high angle
- Sudden forward movement of a crane that can send the boom over backward if it is being carried at a high boom angle
- Snubbing the hook block to the boom foot, then pulling it up tight
- Instability in certain positions when the crane is traveling on an incline

- *Two-blocking* – Two-blocking refers to a situation that results in the load block or hook assembly contacting an upper load block (if equipped) or the boom-point sheave assembly. Damage can occur to the sheaves, block, and/or wire ropes. However, if the load block makes contact and the operator continues to wind the drum, the crane is essentially pulling against itself. This can result in serious damage and boom failure. The devices shown in *Figure 20* offer protection against two-blocking. The dangling weight that encircles the hoist rope is attached to a switch. If the load of the weight is removed from the switch due to the load block contacting and raising it up, the switch opens and stops the hoist drum.

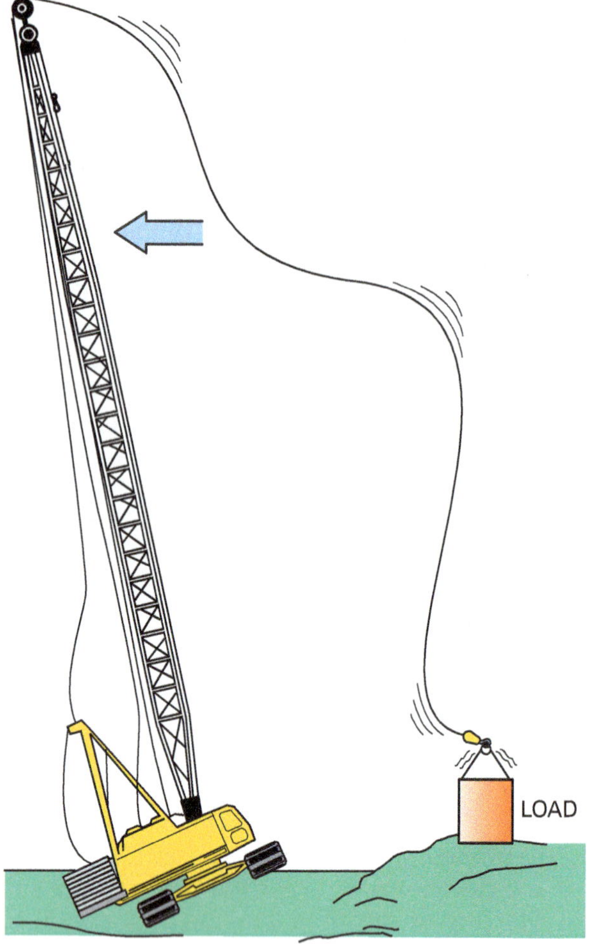

Figure 19 Crane response to the sudden release of a load.

Figure 20 Anti-two-blocking devices.

In *Figure 20*, note the red devices that are inserted into the anti-two-block switches near the sheaves. These devices can be inserted into the switch to disable the anti-two-blocking safety feature. This may be necessary when stowing a mobile crane and preparing it for travel, so that the load block can be drawn up closer to the sheaves. They must not remain in place when the crane begins normal operations.

Crane operators must avoid two-blocking by being attentive to the position of the load block and boom. Do not rely on anti-two-blocking devices as control devices. They are there for safety purposes only.

2.4.5 Fire

The operator's judgment is crucial in determining the correct response to fire. The preferred first response is to cease crane operation, lower the load if practical, and secure the crane. In all cases of fire, evacuate the area even if the load cannot be lowered or the crane secured. After emergency services have been notified, a qualified individual may judge if the fire can be combated with a fire extinguisher. A fire extinguisher can be successful at fighting a small fire in its beginning stage, but a fire can get out of control very quickly. The operator must keep in mind that the highest priority is preventing loss of life or injury. Do not be overconfident in your ability to control a fire. Even trained firefighters using the best equipment can be overwhelmed and injured by fires.

According to 29 *CFR* 1926.1433(d)(6), all mobile cranes are required to have an accessible fire extinguisher on the equipment. *ASME Standard B30.5* indicates that it should be a minimum of a 10BC-rated portable fire extinguisher (*Figure 21*). Note that this has not been incorporated by reference into the OSHA standards. The operator should be trained in its use. This type of extinguisher is designed to combat Class B (flammable liquids) and Class C (electrical) fires. A BC extinguisher is typically charged with dry chemicals. The number 10 is an indicator that the extinguisher should be sufficient to fight a fire that covers 10 square feet (0.9 square meters). The effective range of this type of extinguisher is generally 5 to 20 feet (1.5 to 6 meters).

The extinguisher is constructed so that the extinguishing agent becomes pressurized when the pin is pulled and the handle is compressed. Remember to use the PASS method to fight a fire with a fire extinguisher:

- **P**ull the pin from the handle, breaking the tamper seal.
- **A**im the nozzle at the base of the fire while 8–10 feet (2.5–3 meters) away.
- **S**queeze the discharge handle.
- **S**weep the nozzle back and forth at the base of the flames.

ASME standards require that refueling of the crane be done when the engine is not running and in the absence of smoking, open flames, or any other sources of ignition. If refueling is being done with a portable container, the container must be a safety-type fuel can equipped with an automatic-closing cap and a flame arrester.

The best way to prevent a fire is to make sure the three elements needed for fire—fuel, oxygen, and a source of ignition—are never present in the same place at the same time. Oxygen in the atmosphere is impossible to eliminate, leaving only the fuel source and a source of ignition within human control. Here are some basic safety guidelines for fire prevention:

- Always operate in a well-ventilated area, especially when flammable materials such as shellac, lacquer, paint stripper, or construction adhesives are in use.
- Never smoke, strike a lighter, or light a match when you are working with flammable materials.
- Dispose or store oily rags only in approved, self-closing metal containers. Store other combustible materials only in approved containers.
- Know where to find additional fire extinguishers, what kind of extinguisher to use for different kinds of fires, and how to use the extinguishers when called upon.
- Make sure all extinguishers are fully charged. Never remove the tag from an extinguisher; it shows the date the extinguisher was last serviced and inspected.
- Keep open fuel containers away from any sources of sparks, fire, or extreme heat.
- Do not fill a gasoline or diesel fuel container while it is resting on a truck bed liner or other ungrounded surface. The flow of fuel creates

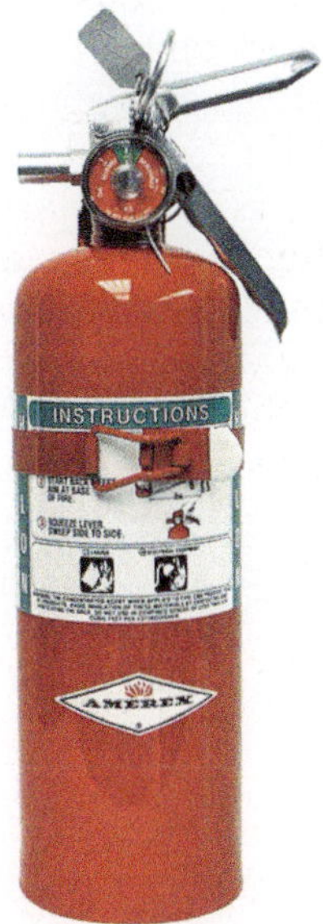

Figure 21 10BC-rated fire extinguisher.

static electricity that can ignite the fuel if the container is not grounded.

- Be prepared at all times to call on professional firefighters, either by using the 911 system or through a direct call to the nearest fire department, even for a small fire. If you are in unfamiliar territory, ask for the location and contact information of the nearest fire department. Time permitting, this call is best made before a personal attempt to fight the fire begins.

2.4.6 Accident Investigations

Lifting operations must always be conducted in the safest manner possible to prevent accidents. However, should an accident occur, the operator should follow the required emergency procedures. Your employer is also likely to have specific procedures to be followed in the event of an accident. The crane operator must have an understanding of the type of information that may be requested on a typical accident investigation checklist. A great deal of information is typically required, including the following:

- Company name and mailing address
- Person receiving the report (name, title, and phone number)
- Investigator's name, title, and company
- Date and time of investigation
- Location and exact time of accident
- Description of the equipment involved, including the manufacturer, model, serial number, age of machine, unit number, and configuration
- Summary of the accident as recalled by witness(es)
- List of people who will make formal statements, including witnesses to the events from one hour before the accident to the end of the accident sequence, all personnel who perform maintenance on the involved equipment, and all personnel involved in determining and planning the lift
- Sketches of the accident scene to scale with as much detail as possible
- Photographs from as many angles as possible
- Weather conditions at the time of the accident
- Ground conditions
- Boom length
- Operating radius
- Actual load weight including load block, sling, and boom attachments
- Background information on the crane operator, riggers, and other members of the lift team—name, age, training, and experience

- Summary of the accident and sequence of events
- Any conclusions based on findings

Normally, a safety officer or inspector from the company responsible for the jobsite and/or crane will conduct the accident investigation and complete the required forms. After the investigation is completed, the report is filed by the responsible company with the proper state and federal authorities.

If the accident results in one or more fatalities that are immediate or occur within 30 days of the incident, the accident must be reported to OSHA within eight hours. If the accident causes inpatient hospitalization, amputation, or the loss of an eye, it must be reported to OSHA within 24 hours. One minor exception relates to the timing of the hospitalization, amputation, or eye loss: If it occurs more than 24 hours after the accident, it is not required to be reported. After a report is submitted, investigators from OSHA and/or the National Institute for Occupational Safety and Health (NIOSH) will also conduct investigations into the accident.

Employers may require the crane operator and others involved in the incident to complete controlled substance and/or alcohol testing immediately following the event.

Additional Resources

ASME Standard B30.5, Mobile and Locomotive Cranes. Current edition. New York, NY: American Society of Mechanical Engineers.

ASME Standard B30.23, Personnel Lifting Systems. Current edition. New York, NY: American Society of Mechanical Engineers.

ASME Standard P30.1, Planning for Load Handling Activities. Current edition. New York, NY: American Society of Mechanical Engineers.

OSHA Standard 1926, Subpart CC, Cranes and Derricks in Construction. **www.ecfr.gov**

Mobile Crane Safety Manual. 2014. Milwaukee, WI: Association of Equipment Manufacturers.

The following websites offer resources for products and training:

American National Standards Institute (ANSI), **www.ansi.org**

The American Society of Mechanical Engineers (ASME), **www.asme.org**

Occupational Safety and Health Administration (OSHA), **www.osha.gov**

North American Crane Bureau, Inc., **www.cranesafe.com**

Electronic Code of Federal Regulations, **www.ecfr.gov**

2.0.0 Section Review

1. Which of the following characteristics would most likely place a lift in the category of a critical lift?
   a. The load weight exceeds 60 percent of the crane's rated load capacity at the required operating radius.
   b. Winds at the time of the lift are forecast to be as high as 15 mph.
   c. A load must be lifted between two occupied buildings that are very close together.
   d. The boom of a hydraulic crane will need to be fully extended.

2. The minimum clearance to be maintained from power lines carrying up to 50 kilovolts (kV) when the crane is operating nearby is ______.
   a. 10 feet (3.05 meters)
   b. 15 feet (4.60 meters)
   c. 20 feet (6.10 meters)
   d. 25 feet (7.62 meters)

3. Which of the following lift factors is most likely to prompt a decision to stop a lift due to wind, even if the load weight is well within the limitations for the situation and the crane in use?
   a. The load has to be lifted over 25 feet up (7.6 meters).
   b. The load is primarily constructed of wood.
   c. The load has a high weight-to-surface area ratio.
   d. The load has a low weight-to-surface area ratio.

4. When driving a mobile crane, the crane operator signals a forward move with ______.
   a. one horn blast
   b. two horn blasts
   c. one forward hand signal
   d. two forward hand signals

5. A crane accident must be reported to OSHA within eight hours if the accident results in ______.
   a. injuries to two or more workers
   b. one or more fatalities
   c. a fire inside the crane cab
   d. property damage exceeding $5,000

1. Which of the following is the most important ASME standard for crane operators?

   a. *ASME Standard B30.20*
   b. *ASME Standard P30.1*
   c. *ASME Standard B30.5*
   d. *ASME Standard B30.23*

2. Information that must be kept in the crane cab at all times includes _____.

   a. the complete operating manual
   b. a copy of *ASME Standard B30.5*
   c. a copy of 29 *CFR* 1910.333
   d. the title to the crane, confirming the owner

3. Pre-lift planning guidance is provided by _____.

   a. *ASME Standard B30.5*
   b. *ASME Standard P30.1*
   c. 29 *CFR* 1926.1431
   d. 29 *CFR* 1910.180

4. The prohibited zone is defined as _____.

   a. any quadrant the crane is not designed to work in according to the manufacturer's guidance
   b. an area around an energized power line that no part of the crane or load should enter
   c. the length and operating radius at which the crane cannot operate if it is making a lift on uneven soil
   d. a circle defined by the outermost point of the crane's outriggers when extended

5. If a visual aid to identify the prohibited zone is not provided for the crane operator when operating near energized power lines, the crane operator must be in constant contact with a _____.

   a. professional engineer qualified in power distribution and transmission
   b. designated representative of the electrical utility or power line owner
   c. dedicated spotter whose sole responsibility is to monitor the required clearance
   d. site supervisor and the local fire department

6. If it becomes necessary to jump off a crane that has contacted a power line, you should keep your feet _____.

   a. as far apart as possible
   b. about one foot apart, side-by-side
   c. about one foot apart, one in front of the other
   d. close together as you land

7. The rate of voltage decrease in the ground surrounding a crane after it has contacted a power line varies depending on the _____.

   a. type of boom
   b. length of the boom
   c. voltage of the power line
   d. resistance of the soil

8. The wind speed at which the operation of a given crane must be limited or halted is determined by _____.

   a. the crane manufacturer
   b. the crane operator
   c. OSHA
   d. crane manufacturer

9. When personnel are being hoisted on a personnel platform, the total weight of the load, basket, and rigging may not exceed _____.

   a. 100 percent of the crane's rated load capacity
   b. 75 percent of the crane's rated load capacity
   c. 50 percent of the crane's rated load capacity
   d. 25 percent of the crane's rated load capacity

10. If the boom, mast, or gantry is struck or damaged, the operator should first _____.

    a. lower the boom
    b. raise the boom
    c. bring the boom to the ground
    d. stop the lift

Trade Terms Quiz

Fill in the blank with the correct term that you learned from your study of this module.

1. A(n) _________ presents an increased level of risk beyond normal lifting activities.

2. Although the ones developed by many organizations are voluntary in nature, the _________ established by OSHA are enforceable by law.

3. An individual that can identify existing and predictable hazards and has the authority to take prompt corrective measures is referred to by OSHA as a(n) _________.

4. As a general rule, cranes are not allowed to handle materials on the ground beneath power lines because this area is part of the _________.

5. The area of specific dimensions that surrounds energized power lines that no part of a crane is allowed to enter is called the _________.

6. A device that senses the electric fields created by power lines and alerts the crane operator to the danger is a(n) _________.

7. A rigger or crane operator can use a(n) _________ to help protect workers in contact with a load from the danger of electrocution in the event the crane contacts a power line.

8. When a lift can be accomplished using common procedures, methods, and equipment, it is referred to as a(n) _________.

9. If a crane operator lowers a load quickly and then brings it to a sudden stop in the air, the crane and rigging will experience _________.

10. OSHA refers to the space around energized power lines that no part of a crane or load can enter as the _________.

11. A brief power outage that is followed by power being quickly restored is probably the result of a(n) _________ doing its job.

Trade Terms

Avoidance zone
Competent person
Critical lift
High-voltage proximity warning device

Insulating link
Minimum clearance distance
Prohibited zone
Recloser
Shock loading

Standard lift
Standards

EXAMPLE — CRITICAL LIFT PLANNING WORKSHEET

POWER CONSTRUCTION

CRITICAL LIFT PLANNING WORKSHEET

PROJECT: _______________________ SUBCONTRACTOR: _______________________

COMPETENT PERSON: _______________________ QUALIFIED RIGGER: _______________________

IS OPERATING ENGINEER CITY OF CHICAGO CERTIFIED? ☐ YES ☐ NO ☐ N/A

IF MULTIPLE CRANES ARE REQUIRED FOR THE LIFT, A SEPARATE WORKSHEET IS REQUIRED FOR EACH CRANE.

CRANE INFORMATION

CRANE OWNER / SUPPLIER: _______________________

BOOM TYPE: ☐ TELESCOPING BOOM ☐ LATTICE BOOM

CRANE BASE: ☐ ON RUBBER TIRE ☐ OUTRIGGERS ☐ CRAWLER ☐ AIRCRAFT

BOOM LENGTH: _______________________

JIB LENGTH: _______________________

COUNTERWEIGHT: _______________________

CAPACITY OF CONFIGURATION: _______________________

ANNUAL CERTIFICATION DATE: _______________________

LOAD DATA & RIGGING

WHAT IS BEING HOISTED?
(TYPE OF MATERIAL / PRODUCT) _______________________

HOW WILL THE LOAD BE HOISTED?
(RIGGING CONFIGURATION) _______________________

WILL ENGINEERED PICK POINTS BE UTILIZED? ☐ YES ☐ NO

WHAT TYPE(S) OF RIGGING IS NEEDED? _______________________

WHO IS PROVIDING THE RIGGING? _______________________

HAS THE RIGGING BEEN INSPECTED? ☐ YES ☐ NO

TAG LINES UTILIZED (IF NOT, WHY) ☐ YES ☐ NO

WEIGHT OF LOAD: _______________________

RIGGING WEIGHT: _______________________

BLOCK & LINE WEIGHT: _______________________

TOTAL LOAD WEIGHT:
(RIGGING + BLOCK & LINE + LOAD WEIGHT) _______________________

IS LOAD GREATER THAN 75% OF CHART? ☐ YES ☐ NO

Critical Lift Planning Worksheet   Revised October 2012

Figure A01A Critical Lift Planning Worksheet (1 of 2).

POWER CONSTRUCTION

CRITICAL LIFT PLANNING WORKSHEET

COMMUNICATIONS & FALL PROTECTION

WHAT TYPE OF COMMUNICATIONS WILL BE USED? ☐ HAND SIGNALS ☐ HARD LINE ☐ 2 WAY RADIO ☐ OTHER: _______

HAND SIGNALS MUST BE POSTED / CELL PHONES ARE NOT APPROVED METHOD

IDENTIFY SIGNAL PERSON: _______________________________

IS FALL PROTECTION REQUIRED FOR SIGNALPERSON? ☐ YES ☐ NO IF YES, WHAT METHODS WILL BE UTILIZED? _______________

SITE CONSTRAINTS & SOIL CONDITIONS

ARE OVERHEAD POWER LINES / OBSTRUCTIONS PRESENT: ☐ YES ☐ NO IF YES, IDENTIFY LOCATIONS: _______

PRECAUTIONS FOR OVERHEAD POWERLINES / OBSTRUCTIONS: _______________

PRECAUTIONS FOR OVERHEAD PROTECTION; PROTECTION OF OCCUPIED SPACES AND PEDESTRIANS: ☐ YES ☐ NO IF YES, WHAT IS PLAN: _______

GROUND CONDITIONS: ☐ ACCEPTABLE ☐ NOT ACCEPTABLE

EXPLAIN REQUIRED ACTION TO CORRECT: _______________

OUTRIGGER PLACEMENT (ATTACH LOAD CHART): ☐ FULL EXTENSION ☐ HALF EXTENSION ☐ OTHER

IS THE CRANE RATED FOR THIS CONFIGURATION? ☐ YES ☐ NO

WILL OUTRIGGERS BE PLACED ON / NEAR SHORING OR OPEN EXCAVATION? ☐ YES ☐ NO

IF YES, IS THE SHORING DESIGNED TO HANDLE THE IMPOSED LOAD: ☐ YES ☐ NO ☐ UNKNOWN (IF NO OR UNKNOWN, CONTACT ENGINEER)

WILL THE OUTRIGGERS BE PLACED ON, OVER, OR NEARLY OVER THE TOP OF UNDERGROUND UTILITIES: ☐ YES ☐ NO

IF YES, WHAT PRECAUTIONS WILL BE TAKEN: _______________

IS LIFT BEING MADE BY AIRCRAFT? ☐ YES ☐ NO (IF YES, REFER TO APPENDIX C OF POWER'S CRANE POLICY)

SUBMITTAL

SUBMITTED BY: _______________________________

REVIEWED BY (POWER REPRESENTATIVE): _______________________________

DATE: _______ *THIS FORM DOES NOT REPLACE POWER'S MOBILE CRANE CHECKLIST*
A SEPARATE MCCL NEEDS TO BE COMPLETED WHEN THE CRANE ARRIVES ON SITE

Critical Lift Planning Worksheet

Revised October 2012

Figure A01B Critical Lift Planning Worksheet (2 of 2).

Avoidance zone: An area both above and below one or more power lines that is defined by the outer perimeter of the prohibited zone. As the name implies, any part of the crane should avoid this area whenever possible, and may not enter the area except under special circumstances.

Competent person: As defined by OSHA, an individual who is capable of identifying existing and predictable hazards in the surroundings or working conditions which are unsanitary, hazardous, or dangerous to employees, and who has the authorization to take prompt corrective measures to eliminate such hazards.

Critical lift: As defined in ASME Standard B30.5, a hoisting or lifting operation that has been determined to present an increased level of risk beyond normal lifting activities. For example, increased risk may relate to personnel injury, damage to property, interruption of plant production, delays in schedule, release of hazards to the environment, or other significant factors.

High-voltage proximity warning device: An early-warning device that senses the electric fields created by high-voltage power lines and alerts the crane operator and/or the lift team to the hazard.

Insulating link: An electrical insulating device used on the crane hook to protect workers in contact with the load from the danger of electrocution in the event the crane contacts a power line. The link can also provide some level of protection for the crane if the load alone contacts a power line.

Minimum clearance distance: The OSHA-required distance that cranes, load lines, and loads must maintain from energized power lines. This OSHA term is synonymous with the ASME term prohibited zone.

Prohibited zone: An area of specific dimensions, based on the voltage of a power line(s) that no part of the crane is allowed to enter during normal operations. Special considerations and preparations are required if the crane's task must place any part of it within the prohibited zone. The prohibited zone is a term used by ASME that is synonymous with the term minimum clearance distance used by OSHA.

Recloser: A device that functions much like a circuit breaker, or in conjunction with a circuit breaker, in power distribution and transmission systems that automatically recloses the circuit after a fault has been detected and the circuit has been opened. Reclosers allow the power system to be re-energized quickly after a transient (temporary) condition, such as a tree limb falling across power lines and then falling to the ground, has occurred. If the fault reoccurs upon closure, the circuit will typically remain open until the situation has been addressed by power line workers or operators.

Shock loading: A sudden, dramatically increased load imposed on a crane and rigging, usually as the result of momentum from the load that occurs due to swinging side-to-side, dropping the load and then stopping it suddenly, and similar actions that create momentum.

Standard lift: A lift that can be accomplished through standard procedures, allowing load-handling and lift team personnel to execute it using common methods, materials, and equipment.

Standards: As defined by OSHA, statements that require conditions, or the adoption or use of one or more practices, means, methods, operations, or processes, that are reasonably necessary or appropriate to provide safe or healthful employment and places of employment. Standards developed by some organizations are voluntary in nature, while OSHA standards and those they incorporate by reference are enforceable by law.

Additional Resources

This module is intended as a thorough resource for task training. The following reference works are suggested for further study.

ASME Standard B30.5, Mobile and Locomotive Cranes. Current edition. New York, NY: American Society of Mechanical Engineers.

ASME Standard B30.20, Below-the-Hook Lifting Devices. Current edition. New York, NY: American Society of Mechanical Engineers.

ASME Standard B30.23, Personnel Lifting Systems. Current edition. New York, NY: American Society of Mechanical Engineers.

ASME Standard P30.1, Planning for Load Handling Activities. Current edition. New York, NY: American Society of Mechanical Engineers.

29 CFR 1926, Subpart C, **www.ecfr.gov**

29 CFR 1926.251, **www.ecfr.gov**

29 CFR 1926.753, **www.ecfr.gov**

Mobile Crane Safety Manual (AEM MC-1407). 2014. Milwaukee, WI: Association of Equipment Manufacturers.

The following websites offer resources for products and training:

American National Standards Institute (ANSI), **www.ansi.org**

The American Society of Mechanical Engineers (ASME), **www.asme.org**

Occupational Safety and Health Administration (OSHA), **www.osha.gov**

North American Crane Bureau, Inc., **www.cranesafe.com**

Electronic Code of Federal Regulations, **www.ecfr.gov**

Figure Credits

Section Review Answer Key

Answer	Section Reference	Objective
Section One		
1. c	1.1.0	1a
2. b	1.2.2	1b
Section Two		
1. c	2.1.0	2a
2. a	2.2.0; Table 1	2b
3. d	2.3.1	2c
4. b	2.4.2	2d
5. b	2.4.6	2d

User Update

NCCER makes every effort to keep its textbooks up-to-date and free of technical errors. We appreciate your help in this process. If you find an error, a typographical mistake, or an inaccuracy in NCCER's curricula, please submit a User Update form by visiting **https://www.nccer.org/olf**. You can also scan the QR code using the camera on your phone or mobile device to access the form.

Glossary

Abstraction: Any form of verbal, graphical, or written communication representing a generalized and nonspecific idea or quality of a thing, action, or event.

Accumulation roller chain: A type of roller chain with rollers that have a larger diameter than the chain side-plate height, allowing the free-spinning rollers to support the conveyed product.

Accumulator: A device that smooths out hydraulic fluid flow by delivering extra pressurized fluid when required.

Actuators: Devices that change electrical, pneumatic, or hydraulic energy into mechanical motion.

Avoidance zone: An area both above and below one or more power lines that is defined by the outer perimeter of the prohibited zone. As the name implies, any part of the crane should avoid this area whenever possible, and may not enter the area except under special circumstances.

Babbitt: A soft metal alloy that typically contains tin, copper, lead, and antimony.

Backlash: Tiny gaps between meshed gear teeth that cause play between the gears as they turn.

Backstop: A device that prevents a shaft from turning in one direction.

Belt whip: A condition where excess slack in a drive belt causes it to begin riding up and out of the sheave grooves, primarily on the slack side. The slack side is the side exiting the drive pulley as it rotates.

Benchmarks: Metal markers that precisely identify specific locations.

Bevel gear: A gear with teeth machined at an angle to its face.

Black starts: Startups conducted on turbine systems while there is no power currently available from the grid.

Blind lift: Any lift involving a load that is out of the direct view of the operator. Blind lifts are generally always categorized as critical lifts.

Bridge: In relation to overhead cranes, the part of an overhead crane consisting of one or more girders or beams and the supporting trucks. The bridge is the overhead, weight-bearing structure along which the trolley(s) and load block assembly travels.

Calibration: Checking and adjusting an instrument so it can be certified as giving results that meet its specifications.

Cam: A rotating component whose shape causes another component to move back and forth as it rests against the cam's surface.

Carbon rings: Self-lubricating packing rings made of carbon that are used to seal the casing and rotor shaft.

Carryback: Conveyed material that fails to unload at the end of a conveyor belt, adhering to or embedding itself in the belt and traveling back to the head of the conveyor on the underside.

Carryover: Any solid, liquid, or vapor contaminant that is entrained in the steam leaving a boiler.

Cavitation: A condition in which bubbles form in a fluid and then collapse violently, creating shock waves that cause vibration and possibly damage.

Churning loss: Energy wasted by gears plowing through lubricating oil as they rotate.

Collinear: Two shafts so well aligned that a single, unbroken line could pass through their centers.

Competent person: As defined by OSHA, an individual who is capable of identifying existing and predictable hazards in the surroundings or working conditions which are unsanitary, hazardous, or dangerous to employees, and who has the authorization to take prompt corrective measures to eliminate such hazards.

Condensing turbine: A steam turbine that has a condenser in place to condense any remaining steam as it exits the turbine. The resulting condensate returns to the boiler or other steam-generating process.

Consensus standard: A set of proprietary guidelines published and agreed to by a consensus (representative majority) of members of a given industry. While not legally binding, they are often cited in governmental regulations, such as OSHA standards.

Coupling stresses: Forces that create misalignment.

Critical lift: As defined in *ASME Standard B30.5*, a hoisting or lifting operation that has been determined to present an increased level of risk beyond normal lifting activities. For example, increased risk may relate to personnel injury, damage to property, interruption of plant production, delays in schedule, release of hazards to the environment, or other significant factors.

Cut-tooth sprockets: Chain sprockets made by machining the teeth for greater precision.

Cylinder: A pneumatic or hydraulic actuator that produces linear motion from a piston sliding inside a hollow tube.

Dedicated spotter: An individual qualified as a signal person who is charged with monitoring the separation between power lines and the equipment, load line, and load, so that the minimum approach distance is not compromised per OSHA standards.

Delamination: The separation or splitting apart of layers.

Directional control valves (DCVs): Devices that route a working fluid down one of several paths based on the device actuator's position.

Diver tender: One or more individuals assigned to attend to a diver's needs, including providing assistance in equipment preparation and managing the diver's cables and hoses.

Eddy current: An induced electrical current that is generated in a conductive material exposed to a moving magnetic field.

Elevation: An object's vertical distance above or below a standard reference, such as sea level.

Emulsion: A mixture formed by two liquids that don't combine, with droplets of one dispersed throughout the other.

Ferrography: A specific type of oil analysis that focuses on lubricant contaminants, their characteristics, and their sources.

Food grade: A lubricant meant to be used in food preparation areas.

Fugitive material: Any material that falls from or escapes a conveyor system, including dust, and doesn't reach the intended destination.

Gear ratio: A single number or a pair of numbers that identifies the rotational relationship between two meshed gears.

Gearbox: A machine that uses meshed gears to transmit power between driver and driven machines.

Gearmotor: A gearbox with an integrated electric motor.

Gears: Wheel-shaped metal or plastic components with teeth machined on their edge or face.

Generator: An electrical apparatus constructed much like an electric motor that converts mechanical energy into electricity.

Height: An object's vertical distance above or below a location.

Helical gear: A gear with angled teeth machined on its outer edge.

High-voltage proximity warning device: An early-warning device that senses the electric fields created by high-voltage power lines and alerts the crane operator and/or the lift team to the hazard.

Hydraulic: Any technology that transfers energy and does mechanical work with a pressurized liquid.

Idler pulley: A pulley or sheave with no attached load, used to help maintain drive belt tension or alignment.

Insulating link: An electrical insulating device used on the crane hook to protect workers in contact with the load from the danger of electrocution in the event the crane contacts a powerline. The link can also provide some level of protection for the crane if the load alone contacts a power line.

Just-in-time (JIT): A strategy that keeps on-site inventory low by ordering required materials just before they're needed for a job.

Kinetic energy: The energy an object contains resulting from being placed in motion.

Laminar flow: Fluid flow in which the fluid travels smoothly in layers that don't interfere with each other.

Laser: A device that emits a single-color light beam that doesn't spread out quickly.

Laser level: An optical instrument that uses a laser beam for measuring heights.

Leveling: Determining an object's elevation by measuring its vertical position relative to a known elevation.

Line of sight: An imaginary horizontal line between an optical instrument and a distant target; the straight-line path between an observer's eyes and the thing being observed.

Line shaft: A shaft driven by a power source that is connected to multiple loads through sheaves or sprockets mounted along its length.

Live-roller conveyor: A roller conveyor that maintains direct contact between the rollers and the conveyed product, with some or all the rollers powered to move the product along.

Lockout/tagout (LOTO): A safety process that secures an activated isolation device and identifies the person responsible for activating it.

Master link: A chain-connecting link that is easily assembled and disassembled for repair or changes in the chain length.

Mechanical energy: The stored (potential) energy plus the moving (kinetic) energy associated with a machine.

Mechatronics: Technology that combines the power of mechanical systems with electronics.

Mineral oil: A lubricant distilled from crude petroleum that has properties like automobile oil.

Minimum clearance distance: The OSHA-required distance that cranes, load lines, and loads must maintain from energized power lines. This OSHA term is synonymous with the ASME term *prohibited zone*.

Motor bell: A flanged cylindrical component that links a flange-equipped motor to another machine. Also called a *motor stand* or *distance piece*.

Noncondensing turbine: A steam turbine that uses any remaining steam exiting the turbine to support other industrial processes.

Nonverbal communication: All communication that does not use words. This includes appearance, personal environment, use of time, and body language.

Offset link: A specific type of connecting link that is used to connect chain with an odd number of links, designed to connect a roller link to a pin link.

Open mike: In electronic communications, the condition where a radio's Transmit button or switch is held continuously without releasing it, even during pauses in speaking.

Optical level: An optical instrument that measures heights, horizontal angles, and distances.

Overhung loads: Sideways forces acting on a shaft.

Oxidation: The process of chemically combining with oxygen.

Paraphrasing: Expressing the perceived meaning of something read or heard in one's own words, generally to ensure clarity. Paraphrasing is an important component of active listening.

Pareto principle: A theory based on the work of Italian economist Vilfredo Pareto that states, for many outcomes, roughly 80 percent of consequences come from 20 percent of the causes or events. Also referred to as the *80/20 rule*, the theory manifests itself in many fields and applications.

Penstock: A channel designed to direct water into a hydroelectric turbine rotor.

Pinion gear: The smaller gear in a meshed pair, usually the driving gear.

Power: The rate at which a machine uses or delivers energy.

Precision alignment: Procedures designed to eliminate nearly all misalignment, often down to 0.002" or better.

Pressure: The force that a fluid develops against a specific area of a container's walls or a surface.

Prohibited zone: An area of specific dimensions, based on the voltage of a power line(s) that no part of the crane is allowed to enter during normal operations. Special considerations and preparations are required if the crane's task must place any part of it within the prohibited zone. The prohibited zone is a term used by ASME that is synonymous with the term *minimum clearance distance* used by OSHA.

Recloser: A device that functions much like a circuit breaker, or in conjunction with a circuit breaker, in power distribution and transmission systems that automatically recloses the circuit after a fault has been detected and the circuit has been opened. Reclosers allow the power system to be re-energized quickly after a transient (temporary) condition, such as a tree limb falling across power lines and then falling to the ground, has occurred. If the fault reoccurs upon closure, the circuit will typically remain open until the situation has been addressed by power line workers or operators.

References: Locations whose positions and/or elevations are precisely documented.

Reticle: A clear disc engraved with lines or a set of fine wires placed inside an optical instrument.

Rotary-lobe blower: A blower that relies on two lobed impellers spinning at high speed to create airflow. Each of the two impellers has either two or three lobes.

Rotational speed: The rate at which a machine or component is turning.

Sensory inspection: A maintenance inspection that incorporates sight, sound, smell, and touch.

Servomotors: Special electric motors that can start and stop very precisely, as well as rotate to a specific position.

Shock loading: A sudden, dramatically increased load imposed on a crane and rigging, usually as the result of momentum from the load that occurs due to swinging side-to-side, dropping the load and then stopping it suddenly, and similar actions that create momentum.

Shock loads: Abrupt, brief, and significant increases in a machine's normal load.

Skiving: The removal of one or more layers of a conveyor belt to accommodate a splice to avoid a significant change in belt thickness.

Soft foot: A coupling stress created by a machine's feet not all resting firmly on the baseplate.

Solenoid: An electrical control device that pushes or pulls when energized.

Sprocket: A toothed wheel or disk designed to engage in the gaps between drive or conveyor chain links, typically for power transmission.

Spur gear: A gear with straight teeth machined on its outer edge.

Standard lift: A lift that can be accomplished through standard procedures, allowing load-handling and lift team personnel to execute it using common methods, materials, and equipment.

Standards: As defined by OSHA, statements that require conditions, or the adoption or use of one or more practices, means, methods, operations, or processes, that are reasonably necessary or appropriate to provide safe or healthful employment and places of employment. Standards developed by some organizations are voluntary in nature, while OSHA standards and those they incorporate by reference are enforceable by law.

Strainer: A filter that removes large particles from a fluid.

Sublimate: To change state directly from a solid to a gas, without passing through a liquid state.

Synchronous belts: Belts with teeth that correspond to grooves in matching sheaves, eliminating slippage, and maintaining synchronized rotation of the shafts; also referred to as *timing belts*.

Synthetic oil: A chemically engineered lubricant with enhanced properties and a long lifespan.

Theodolite: An optical instrument that precisely measures horizontal and vertical angles.

Thermal growth: Changes in a component's dimensions due to temperature change.

Thermoplastics: Describes plastic materials that become more plastic (elastic) when heated and harden again when cooled, allowing them to be reformed. *Thermosets* are plastics that cannot be heated and reformed.

Thrust loads: Forces that push or pull along a shaft's axis.

Torque: A twisting force that produces rotary motion.

Total station: An optical instrument that precisely measures horizontal and vertical angles, as well as distances.

Tribology: The study of lubrication, friction, and the wear of interacting surfaces.

Trucks: In relation to overhead cranes, a mechanical assembly consisting of a frame, wheels, bearings, and axles that support the bridge of an overhead crane and provide the ability for it to move along a set of parallel tracks.

Turbine: A machine that converts the energy contained in a moving stream of fluid to mechanical energy.

Turbulent flow: Fluid flow in which the fluid swirls, changes direction, and interferes with its own motion.

Viscosity: A liquid's thickness, which determines how it flows, pours, and behaves when stirred.

Vulcanizing: Using heat or chemicals along with pressure to create a conveyor belt splice. Hot vulcanization relies on direct heat, while cold vulcanization relies on chemicals to develop the necessary heat and bond.

Water hammer: A hydraulic shock that occurs when rapidly moving slugs of water impact pipe walls, especially when the water must change direction.

Welding procedure specification (WPS): A document specifying all essential procedural details related to project-specific welds.

Working fluid: A liquid or gas used by an industrial system to carry energy and do work.

Worm gear: A cylindrical gear with spiral threads wrapped around its outer surface.